THE IALL INTERNATIONAL HANDBOOK OF LEGAL INFORMATION MANAGEMENT

INTERNATIONAL ASSOCIATION OF LAW LIBRARIES (IALL)

The International Association of Law Libraries (IALL) is a worldwide, cooperative professional body concerned with access to legal information, particularly on a multinational and global scale. It comprises law librarians, law libraries and other persons and institutions active in the acquisition, delivery and use of legal information from sources beyond their own jurisdictions.

The International Association of Law Libraries:

- promotes the work of individuals, libraries, and other organisations concerned with the dissemination of legal information;
- advances the education of law librarians and other legal information professionals by providing substantive educational programmes on foreign and international legal systems in venues all around the world;
- supports educational and professional opportunities for newer legal information professionals, especially those from developing nations, by providing financial support in the form of bursaries and scholarships for annual course attendance and internships;
- shares legal knowledge and scholarship and increases access to legal information on a worldwide basis through the *International Journal of Legal Information* and other publications, and its website at http://iall.org;
- fosters networking and mentoring among legal information professionals on a worldwide basis by creating and maintaining ongoing relationships between IALL and other international, national and regional law library and legal information organisations; and
- supports and encourages the development of national and international legal information policies and promotes free access to legal information on a worldwide basis through policy statements and scholarship.

The IALL is dedicated to international cooperation among law librarians, the promotion of professional knowledge and understanding through international exchange, and the promotion of access to legal information.

The IALL International Handbook of Legal Information Management

Edited by
RICHARD A. DANNER
Duke University, USA
and
JULES WINTERTON
University of London, UK

ASHGATE

Published by
Ashgate Publishing Limited
Wey Court East
Union Road
Farnham
Surrey, GU9 7PT
England

Ashgate Publishing Company
Suite 420
101 Cherry Street
Burlington
VT 05401-4405
USA

www.ashgate.com

British Library Cataloguing in Publication Data
The IALL international handbook of legal information management.
1. Law libraries--Administration. 2. Information storage and retrieval systems--Law.
I. Danner, Richard A. (Richard Allen), 1947- II. Winterton, Jules. III. International Association of Law Libraries.
026.3'4-dc22

Library of Congress Cataloging-in-Publication Data
The IALL international handbook of legal information management / [edited] by Richard A. Danner and Jules Winterton.
p. cm.
Includes bibliographical references and index.
ISBN 978-0-7546-7477-1 (hbk) -- ISBN 978-1-4094-2872-5 (ebk) 1. Law libraries. 2. Legal literature. 3. Legal research. 4. Law libraries--Collection development. 5. Law librarians--Training of. I. Danner, Richard A. (Richard Allen), 1947- II. Winterton, Jules.
Z675.L2I15 2011
026'.34--dc22

2011013241

ISBN 9780754674771 (hbk)
ISBN 9781409428725 (ebk)

MIX
Paper from responsible sources
FSC® C018575

Printed and bound in Great Britain by the MPG Books Group, UK

Contents

List of Figures and Tables

Figures

Tables

List of Contributors

Ruth Bird

Ruth Bird is Bodleian Law Librarian and Head of Social Sciences Libraries, at the University of Oxford, England. In 2010 she was made an Honorary Bencher at Middle Temple. She was the National Convenor of the Australian Law Librarians Association 1994–5, a member of the Council of the British and Irish Association of Law Libraries since 2008, and a Board member of the International Association of Law Libraries since 2007. She managed libraries at two leading Australian law firms and was Head Law Librarian at the University of Melbourne before moving to Oxford. Her research interests are in teaching legal research, information literacy and research training, reflecting her first career as a teacher. She was a Visiting Research Fellow under the Oxford Law Faculty Exchange at the Max Planck Institute for Comparative and International Private Law in Hamburg in 2008, and at the University of Melbourne Law School in 2010.

Michael Crommelin

Michael Crommelin AO is Zelman Cowen Professor of Law and a former Dean of the Melbourne Law School at the University of Melbourne, Australia. His teaching and research interests are in the fields of constitutional law, energy and resources law, and comparative law. He has held visiting academic appointments at the University of British Columbia, l'Université Jean Moulin Lyon III, Georgetown University, University of Virginia and l'Université Panthéon-Assas Paris II. He was a foundation member of AMPLA – The Resources and Energy Law Association and served as its President in 1986. He is a member of the American Law Institute and a fellow of the Australian Academy of Law. In 2009 he was appointed an Officer in the General Division of the Order of Australia for service to the law and legal education.

Sami Cukadar

Sami Cukadar is the Library Director at Istanbul Bilgi University Library and e-Resources in Istanbul, Turkey. He is also a member of the academic staff at Istanbul Bilgi University Faculty of Law and teaches *Research Methods and Accessing Legal Information Resources* to the first-year Law School students. He has been serving as President of the UNAK-Turkish Platform of Law Librarians, on the Statistics Committee of the Anatolian University Libraries Consortium (ANKOS), and as Editor of the University and Research Libraries Association Information World (Bilgi Dunyasi) for law articles. He has written on total quality management in libraries and distance learning and university libraries. His current research focuses on legal information, information literacy and distance education.

Richard A. Danner

Richard A. Danner is Rufty Research Professor of Law and Senior Associate Dean for Information Services at Duke Law School in Durham, North Carolina. He is responsible for the J. Michael Goodson Law Library and the Academic Technologies department at Duke. He has served as President of the American Association of Law Libraries, on the executive committee of the Association of American Law Schools, as First Vice-President of the International Association of Law Libraries. From 1984 to 1994, he served as editor of the American Association of Law Libraries' *Law Library Journal*. He has written on the impacts of information technology on legal education and the effects of electronic publication on scholarly communication in law. His current research focuses on the role of legal information in the development of American law.

Colin Darch

Colin Darch is a Senior Information Specialist at the University Library of the University of Cape Town, South Africa. He has worked in various universities and research institutes in Ethiopia, Tanzania, Mozambique, Zimbabwe and Brazil, and was the Director of Libraries at the University of the Western Cape from 1992 to 1997. He has published in both English and Portuguese. He was a founding member of the Copy South Research Network, and is a member of the Access to Information Committee of the African Network of Constitutional Lawyers. His current research interests include the political economy of intellectual property, and the sociology of freedom of information.

Tanya du Plessis

Tanya du Plessis is a Senior Lecturer, Researcher and Postgraduate supervisor at the Department of Information and Knowledge Management, University of Johannesburg. In 2005, she was awarded the First International Non-US Based SLA Grant (Legal Division). She specialises in Competitive Intelligence (CI) and is involved in projects requiring advanced legal research tools and techniques, strategic environmental focus and planning, organisational virtual learning environment content integration, and CI visual analysis. She holds a D Litt et Phil (Rand Afrikaans University, South Africa, 2004), with the focus on law firm knowledge management. She is a member of the editorial board of the *South African Journal of Information Management* and the *PER Electronic Law Journal*. To witness and encourage students on their route to becoming what they are meant to be, is one of her life's passions.

Lilia F. Echiverri

Lilia F. Echiverri is Assistant Law Librarian and Head of the Reference Section at the University of the Philippines Law Library. She was elected President 2009–10, Council President 2007–8, and member of the Board of Directors of the Philippine Librarians Association, Inc. 2002–4. She was Executive Board member of the Congress of Southeast Asian Librarians 2009–10. She was appointed Member of the Steering Committee of the International Federation of Library Associations and Institutions – Committee on Free Access to Information and Freedom of Expression 2009–13, and Chair of the IFLA-FAIFE Train the Trainers on Internet Manifesto: Philippines Project in 2008–9. She was Vice-President and Member of the Board of Directors of the Philippine Group of Law Librarians 2007, 2008–9 and 2010–11, President of the Special Librarians Association of the Philippines 2000–1, and President of the University of the Philippines Alumni Association 1998–9. She was a recipient of the International Association of Law Libraries Scholarship in 2006. She has received an award for her 'outstanding' performance and dedication to duty over three decades (Model Public Servant) and various other awards for her meaningful participation in professional activities chairing and leading various organisations.

Barbara H. Garavaglia

Barbara H. Garavaglia is Assistant Director of the University of Michigan Law Library where she coordinates reference and faculty services, cataloguing, acquisitions, electronic and systems services and collection development. She received her JD and MLIS degrees from the University of Michigan. She has been on the Board of the International Association of Law Libraries since 2007 and is the IALL Secretary for 2010–13. She is the current Chair of AALL's Indexing of Periodical Literature Committee, having served on the committee for several years, a member of the Board of LLMC Digital, and a long-term member of the State Bar of Michigan Committee on Libraries, Legal Research, and Legal Publications. She taught legal research and writing for LLM students from civil law countries for six years and has served as moderator and panellist on the American Association of Law Libraries annual meeting programmes on developing foreign, comparative and international law collections and the human rights of internally displaced persons.

Claire M. Germain

Claire M. Germain is the Clarence J. TeSelle Professor of Law and Associate Dean for Legal Information at the University of Florida Levin College of Law, Gainesville, Florida, USA. She writes and speaks frequently on comparative law and legal information, from rare books to digital libraries, in the United States, Europe, Canada, Brazil, China, South Korea and Tanzania, and she teaches courses in French law and legal research. She has authored two books, including the award-winning *Germain's Transnational Law Research*, and numerous articles. She is actively advocating for the authentication of digital law, and the introduction of a legal research test on the bar exam in the United States. She has served as President of the American Association of Law Libraries, and as Chair of the American Association of Law Schools Committee on Libraries and Technology. She is currently Secretary of the Law Libraries Section of the International Federation of Library Associations. She was recently honoured with the Chevalier de la Légion d'Honneur (Knight, Legion of Honour) medal, France's highest honour, for her efforts in bridging the American and French legal cultures.

Graham Greenleaf

Graham Greenleaf AM is Professor of Law and Information Systems at the University of New South Wales, Sydney, Australia where he has researched and taught since 1983. He specialises in the relationships between information technology and law. His current areas of research focus are

Asian data protection and privacy laws, public rights in copyright, and the globalisation of free Internet access to legal information. He is a co-founder and Co-Director of the Australasian Legal Information Institute (AustLII), and of AustLII's international projects, WorldLII, CommonLII and AsianLII. He is also the Founding Director (2000–10) of the Cyberspace Law and Policy Centre at UNSW. He is an International Scholar at Kyung-Hee University Law School, Seoul, Korea. In 2010 he was made a member of the Order of Australia (AM) for his contributions to advancing free access to legal information, and to the protection of privacy. He received the 2007 Dieter Meurer Prize for Legal Informatics at the University of Saarbrucken.

Mariana Harjevschi

Mariana Harjevschi is a Director of the Public Law Library, a branch of the Municipal Library 'B.P.Hasdeu', Chisinau, Moldova, a post she has held since 2001. Since September 2001 she has also been an assistant lecturer at the School of Library and Information Assistance at Moldova State University where she teaches Legal Framework for Libraries and Intellectual Freedom courses. In November 2008, she was elected for a four-year term as a vice-president of the National Library Association, with responsibility for coordinating international relations of the association and fundraising activities. She also acts as eIFL IP copyright librarian within eIFL Direct Moldova Consortia, and is a member of eIFL.net and CLM (Committee on Copyright and other Legal Matters) within the International Federation of Library Associations and Institutions (IFLA). She holds a Bachelor Degree in Library Science and Information Assistance (1999) and a Master's in Journalism and Communication Sciences (2001), both from Moldova State University. During 2004–5 she completed the Junior Faculty Development Programme, supported by American Councils for International Education at the School of Library and Information Science, Indiana University in Bloomington, USA.

Penny A. Hazelton

Penny A. Hazelton is Professor of Law and Associate Dean for Library and Computing Services at the University of Washington School of Law in Seattle, Washington. She is responsible for the Marian Gould Gallagher Law Library and the Computing Services department at UW Law. In addition, she has served as an adjunct faculty member and Director of the Law Librarianship Program in the UW Information School. She served as President of the American Association of Law Libraries and as Chair of the ABA Law School Facilities Committee and the Association of American Law Schools Section on Law Libraries. She has written about law school library facilities, law library education and law library administration. Her current research interests are in teaching legal research and the impact of digital library collections on library facilities, services and staff.

Carole Hinchcliff

Carole Hinchcliff is the Law Librarian at Melbourne University's Law School Library in Australia, a position she has held since 2008. From 1984 to 2007 she held various positions at the Ohio State University's Moritz Law Library including Associate Director from 1996 to 2007 and, from 2002, Supervising Attorney and then Associate Professor, Clinical for the Mediation Practicum. In 2004, she received the Ohio State University's Distinguished Staff Award. Carole is the current convenor of the Australian & New Zealand Academic & College Law Librarians Group (ANZACLL) and is a former Chair of the American Association of Law Libraries Continuing Professional Education Committee, Council of Special Interest Sections and Academic Special Interest Section. She has written and presented on a variety of law library topics during her career in law librarianship.

Holger Knudsen

Professor Dr Holger Knudsen is the Director of the Library of the Max Planck Institute for Comparative and International Private Law in Hamburg, Germany. Prior to this appointment he held positions in Cologne, Florence, Boston, Lausanne and Bonn. He has taught law at the Leipzig University of Applied Science since 1993 and served as a member of the Board of Directors, Second Vice President, President, and Immediate Past President of the International Association of Law Libraries from 1995 to 2007. In 2002 he was the founding chair of the Law Libraries Section of the International Federation of Library Associations. He is currently the chair of the permanent nominating committee of the German Librarians' Association and an ex officio member of its Board of Directors. He has worked as a consultant in Armenia, Azerbaijan, Kosovo, Malta and the Netherlands. He has lectured in Argentina, Brazil, Croatia, Latvia and the Philippines.

Ufuoma Lamikanra

Ufuoma Lamikanra is the Readers' Services Librarian at the Nigerian Institute of Advanced Legal Studies (NIALS) at the University of Lagos Campus. While on leave in 2008, she helped to set up the law library of the newly established Babcock University Law School and taught Legal Methods, Environmental Law, Use of the Library, and Evidence to first and fourth year college students. She is also an adjunct lecturer in Business Law for the Distance Learning Institute at the University of Lagos. A Rockefeller-Penn Scholar, from January 2010 to June 2011, and recipient of the 2010 FCIL Schaffer Grant for foreign law librarians, she held a three-month Commonwealth Professional Fellowship at the Institute of Advanced Legal Studies, London, from January 2011. She has authored and edited books and articles on gender law and law librarianship. Her current research focus is on gender equality in the workplace and cities and women's health.

Le Thi Hanh

Le Thi Hanh is Librarian and Vice Director of the Library Information Center of Hanoi Law University, Viet Nam. She has been taking part in the implementation of the project *Strengthen Legal Education in Vietnam* funded by Sida (Swedish International Development Cooperation Agency) since 1998. She received an internship grant from the Swiss Institute of Comparative Law, Lausanne, Switzerland, in 2000 and was sent to the Law Faculty, University of Lund, Sweden, several times for study visits on different subjects related to law libraries. She has written on impacts of information technology on organisation and management of law libraries. Her current research focus is on applying the Library of Congress Classification to Law Libraries and on creating and developing a digital collection for law libraries in Vietnam.

Teresa M. Miguel

Teresa Miguel is Associate Librarian for Foreign and International Law, Latin American Bibliographer, and Lecturer in Law and Legal Research at the Lillian Goldman Law Library at Yale Law School. She received a JD from the University of Richmond, T.C. Williams School of Law, an MA in Information Resources and Library Science from the University of Arizona, a BA in English Literature and Sociology from the University of Wisconsin-Madison, and a Diploma de Español como Lengua Extranjera from the Escuela Oficial de Idiomas, Salamanca, Spain. She has authored several articles, reviews and web guides on foreign and international law and legal research, and has served as moderator or panellist in continuing education programmes at the annual meetings of the American Association of Law Libraries, the American Library Association, and the Seminar on the Acquisition of Latin American Library Materials. She is an active member of the Foreign, International, and Comparative Law Special Interest Section of AALL, and a member of the Arizona and Pennsylvania bars.

Uma Narayan

Uma Narayan is the Chief Librarian of the Honourable Judges' Library of Bombay High Court, Mumbai, India. She has Masters of Arts (History), Master of Library and Information Science and Bachelor of Laws (LLB) degrees. She was invited by the US Department of State to participate in the International Visitor Programme in 2003. She was awarded the IALL Professional Development Bursary of the International Association of Law Libraries in 2004 to their Annual Course in International Law Librarianship held in Finland. She was awarded the Commonwealth Professional Fellowship and the Visiting Fellowship in Law Librarianship at the Institute of Advanced Legal Studies (IALS), University of London, in 2006 and she remains an Associate Research Fellow of IALS. She was also awarded the Research Scholarship by Max Planck Institute of Comparative and International Private Law, Hamburg, Germany in May 2009. She has been elected to the Board of International Association of Law Libraries for the periods of 2007–10 and 2010–13.

Marylin J. Raisch

Marylin Johnson Raisch is the Associate Law Librarian for International and Foreign Law at the John Wolff International and Comparative Law Library of the Georgetown Law Center. She received her JD from Tulane University School of Law. She holds degrees in English literature from Smith College and St. Hugh's College, Oxford. She received her MLS degree from Columbia University School of Library Service. She is the author, co-author, or editor of several articles, reviews and web guides on international and foreign legal research, including the current ASIL European Union Research Guide; the annual book and web surveys for the *Journal of International Economic Law*; and 'Codes and Hypertext: The Intertextuality of International and Comparative Law', for the *Syracuse Journal of International Law and Commerce* (2008). She has served as moderator or panellist in several continuing education programmes at the annual meetings of the American

Association of Law Libraries and is past Chair of its Foreign, International, and Comparative Law Special Interest Section.

Kendall F. Svengalis

Kendall F. Svengalis is President of Rhode Island LawPress, former RI State Law Librarian (1982–2002), and retired Adjunct Professor of Library and Information Studies at the University of Rhode Island. Born in Gary, Indiana, in 1947, he received his BA in English literature (1970) and MA in American history (1973) from Purdue University, and MLS from the University of RI (1975). He is past president of the Law Librarians of New England and the New England Law Library Consortium, and served as editor of the American Association of Law Libraries CRIV Sheet from 1988 to 1994. He was twice the recipient of the Connie Bolden Significant Publications Award from the State, Court & County Law Libraries SIS. In 1998, he received the Joseph L. Andrews Bibliographical Award, the highest honour bestowed by the AALL on works of legal bibliography, for his *Legal Information Buyer's Guide & Reference Manual*, now a standard reference and acquisitions tool in law libraries across the globe. He has spoken widely before law library and legal associations on the cost-effective acquisition of legal information. He makes his home in North Stonington, CT.

Jeroen Vervliet

Jeroen Vervliet is Peace Palace Library Director in The Hague, the Netherlands. The Peace Palace Library serves the International Court of Justice, the Permanent Court of Arbitration, the Hague Conference on Private International Law, and many other international and judicial organisations in The Hague, for example the International Criminal Court, the Iran-US Claims Tribunal, the Dutch Supreme Court. The Peace Palace Library acts as the library for the Hague Academy of International Law during its summer courses and it is the main library for International Law in the Netherlands. He worked at the Dutch Central Bank ('De Nederlandsche Bank') and at the central library and the library of the Faculty of Law of the Leiden University. He was (co-) organiser of the 60 Years Genocide Convention conference in 2008, of the Hugo Grotius-Mare Liberum quadricentenary festival in 2009, and of the 29th Annual Conference of the International Association of Law Libraries (IALL) in 2010. He is currently First Vice-President of IALL.

Jules Winterton

Jules Winterton is Librarian and Associate Director of the Institute of Advanced Legal Studies, School of Advanced Study, University of London and Associate Professor at the Ghana Institute of Advanced Legal Studies. He was President of the International Association of Law Libraries from 2004 until 2010 and received the Wildy-BIALL Librarian of the Year award in June 2010. He is Convenor of the Libraries Sub-Committee of the Society of Legal Scholars, a member of the Board of Trustees of the British and Irish Legal Information Institute, and a former member of the Board of LLMC Digital. He was Chair of the British and Irish Association of Law Librarians in 1994–5 and received its Wallace Breem Memorial Award in 1998 for *Information Sources in Law* (2nd edn). He has been a Visiting Fellow at the Max Planck Institute for Comparative and International

Private Law in Hamburg and at the University of Florence and has given presentations in China, Denmark, England, Ghana, Italy, Nigeria, the Philippines, Scotland, South Africa and the United States, and at IALL and IFLA conferences in various countries.

Foreword

Lawyers are in the information business. They acquire information through education, training, research and practical experience; they retain and share it as part of their stock-in-trade; and they sell information – distilled as knowledge and expertise – to clients who wish it to be applied to their circumstances. The world of lawyers is dominated by information. It is a world packed full of books, papers, emails, word-processed documents and online searches. Indeed, the legal profession is one of the most information-intensive of all sectors.

Lawyers, in other words, are information processors; although these are not perhaps the specific words that most legal practitioners would choose in describing themselves. In contrast, law librarians have for long recognised that lawyering is a type of information processing and indeed much of their work has been built on this very premise. Law librarians have also been some way ahead of most lawyers in embracing the power of IT and recognising the significance of the Internet for legal practice.

With the explosive growth in various information technologies will come great vindication of the past claims and work of law librarians. Calls for better analysis of information needs, more rigorous management of content, greater vigilance in relation to security and privacy, deeper consideration of whether superior information control can offer competitive advantage – all of these and more will now need to be answered by top managers in law firms, legal departments and law faculties.

And it is in this context that I warmly welcome the publication of this book. It will provide law librarians not with a manual of best practice for the administration of law libraries, nor with a science-fictional vision of what the law library might look like many years hence. Instead, a diverse and international group of leading experts has provided professional legal information managers with a definitive guide to the central issues of policy and strategy that are of direct concern to the progressive law librarian (and to the legal profession) of tomorrow. These issues are as wide-ranging as they are fascinating – legal, technical, cultural, ideological, technical, commercial and more.

The book is not only for the traditional law librarian, narrowly construed. What follows will also engage legal information scientists, know-how managers, legal process analysts, legal management consultants, legal knowledge engineers, and many other related specialists.

We live in an era of unprecedented technological change; in an era of exponential increase in processing power; in an era when we generate more information in a few days than we did in the last millennium. In this heady time of astounding flux, we also need – and this book gives us – sober, balanced minds systematically addressing the implications of recent and emerging developments in technology and information management.

I wish the work every success.

Professor Richard Susskind OBE

Preface

Around the world, law librarians and other legal information specialists work in a number of settings: law schools, private law firms and public law libraries of various types. Law librarians are characterised by their expertise in working with legal information its many forms, and by their work supporting legal professionals, scholars or students training to become lawyers. Many law librarians hold degrees in law as well as in library science; some have graduated from library schools with specialised programmes in law librarianship.

Lawyers need ready access to the current texts of authoritative legal materials – statutes, court decisions, and administrative regulations and decisions – issued by a variety of law-making authorities, and often require older materials as well. In legal systems of all kinds, they also require access to expert commentary, scholarship, and other explanatory materials in order to interpret the law and apply it to the situations they face. In the twenty-first century lawyers, scholars and students frequently need materials from jurisdictions beyond their own, often written in languages they do not know. The law librarian's role is to obtain and organise these materials, as well as the indexes and other finding tools needed to use them, and make them accessible and useable.

In many countries most of the materials of legal research are available in full-text electronic formats, sometimes to the exclusion of traditional 'law books'. As a result law librarians are also highly skilled in working with electronic sources and in choosing appropriate information formats to meet the needs of users at specific types of libraries. They work as well to ensure that electronic sources of law are broadly accessible not only to legal professionals but to the citizens whose lives are affected on a daily basis by legislative enactments, court decisions and other sources of authority. They are involved in efforts to ensure that electronically published texts are preserved for future use.

In an ever-shrinking world, often requiring immediate access to information from previously untapped sources, their work is challenging and exciting, calling to the fore their specialised knowledge and skills, regardless of where in the world they practice their profession. Their role within the legal system contributes substantially to the administration of justice and the rule of law.

This *International Handbook* describes the legal environments in which they work and policy issues with which they need to engage. It provides resources, analysis and considered studies both for seasoned international law librarians, those about to enter the field, and others interested in the evolution of legal information in the twenty-first century.

Richard Danner and Jules Winterton

Acknowledgements

The editors, personally and on behalf of the International Association of Law Libraries (IALL), would like to thank the authors for their care, time and patience. Thanks are also due to all the staff at Ashgate Publishing, particularly to Dymphna Evans, for all their assistance and their endurance during a long project and to the Board of IALL and many Association members who provided support and ideas.

We should also like to thank the British and Irish Association of Law Librarians and Loyita Worley in particular, for the original idea for this book, since they published the first edition of the *BIALL Handbook of Legal Information Management* in 2006.

Richard Danner wishes to thank the staff of the J. Michael Goodson Law Library at Duke University for their assistance and support while he was engaged in this project, and is grateful for the support and encouragement of Dean David F. Levi and his other colleagues at the Duke Law School. He also thanks his family for their forbearance and those who inspire his efforts.

Jules Winterton would like to express his thanks to the staff of the Institute of Advanced Legal Studies for their professionalism and forbearance while he was preoccupied with the production of the book and other IALL matters. He is grateful to the Institute and the School of Advanced Study for their encouragement and their support of the profession of law librarianship. He is also extremely grateful to the Max Planck Institute for Comparative and International Private Law for awarding a Research Fellowship to him in June 2010, without which the book could not have been completed, and to his colleague and friend Holger Knudsen, the Director of that Institute's Library, for his support.

Chapter 1
Defining International Law Librarianship in an Age of Multiplicity, Knowledge, and Open Access to Law[1]

Richard A. Danner

Defining International Law Librarianship

Many law librarians are experts in international law and legal research, each knowledgeable regarding the substance of international law, as well as its primary sources, its literature, its finding tools, and approaches to research. They specialise in international law in the same ways that other subject librarians do in other legal disciplines, as well as in the health sciences, business and many other fields. The concept of 'international law librarianship', however, encompasses something more than a field of study in which a group of experts practise their profession. In the broader sense expressed in the title of this book the idea of international law librarianship suggests a common calling, similar interests, and goals shared by librarians with a range of specialties beyond international law, working in all types of law libraries.[2] What things are shared by law librarians who involve themselves internationally and may be active in professional organisations such as the International Association of Law Libraries (IALL) and the Law Libraries Section of the International Federation of Library Associations and Institutions (IFLA)?

The mission statement of the International Association of Law Libraries[3] provides a short list of Association's programmes for 'individuals, libraries, and other organizations concerned with the dissemination of legal information': IALL promotes their work, provides educational programming, offers financial support for new legal information professionals (especially from developing nations), provides forums for sharing professional information and knowledge, fosters networking and mentoring, supports and encourages national and international legal information policies, and promotes free access to legal information worldwide. The IFLA Law Libraries Section mission statement[4] is similar to that of the IALL, but also speaks specifically of its interest in fostering the profession and developing professional standards and practices. While suggestive, neither statement provides a satisfactory definition of international law librarianship.

In writing about foreign, international and comparative law collection building, Holger Knudsen makes a seemingly obvious, but actually rather subtle, point when he writes 'Law is a genuinely national affair and this makes it very different from other fields of knowledge with the exceptions perhaps of some rather limited fields of interest like foreign literature, foreign

---

1 This chapter is based in part on an address offered under the title: 'Taming Multiplicity in the Post-Print Era: Law Librarians, Legal Scholarship, and Access to the Law' at Harvard University, 29 April 2010. Thanks to John Palfrey and Michelle Pearse for the opportunity to speak at Harvard and to Amanda Barratt for her helpful comments on earlier drafts.

2 See Danner et al. (2009) for descriptions of the roles of various types of law libraries.

3 Available at: www.iall.org/about.html, accessed 30 June 2010.

4 Available at: www.ifla.org/en/law-libraries, accessed 1 August 2010.

history and ethnology'.[5] Law of course is not a 'rather limited field of interest', but a subject of vital importance to many. The differences among jurisdictions and legal systems that Knudsen notes create obstacles for those seeking to be knowledgeable about the law either to represent the interests of clients or for purposes of scholarship. Knudsen goes on to point out that the obstacles extend beyond substance to the forms and formats of the published sources of law:

> Lawyers and law librarians dealing with foreign law for the first time are often surprised or even shocked when they notice how much other formats differ from the system they know. While the appearance, layout and handling of legal monographs and periodicals generally do not pose problems of format, official journals, law collections, court decisions, and finding tools do, and to quite an extent. Even experienced reference librarians who have not worked with foreign materials for a while must try to get acquainted with them anew each time they use them. It is simply impossible to memorise all the different formats. (Chapter 12, this volume, 249)

The differences among nations in substantive law, legal systems and the forms, formats and structures of legal information affect not only the work of students, lawyers, legal scholars and law librarians, but also the efforts of anyone seeking to define or apply the concept of international law librarianship.[6] In light of these significant differences it is necessary to identify and consider what things are shared by law librarians worldwide. What commonalities create and sustain the concept of international law librarianship? This chapter suggests that they can be found in: law librarians' common need to respond to the 'multiplicity' of information sources facing twenty-first century legal researchers; the development and nurturing of a shared base of professional knowledge; and a joint commitment to work toward ensuring free and open access to legal information globally.

An American Story

At the International Association of Law Libraries' twenty-first annual course on International Law Librarianship in 2002, I was privileged to share a podium with Morris L. Cohen, who had served as the Law Librarian at Harvard University from 1971 to 1981 before moving to the Yale Law School, where he retired in 1991. Cohen is one of the giants of American law librarianship: one of his major accomplishments is his *Bibliography of Early American Law*, begun in 1984 and published in six volumes in 1998 (Cohen 1998).

Cohen's remit for our presentation to an audience of international law librarians was to provide an historical overview of American law publishing; mine was to discuss 'Contemporary and Future Directions in American Legal Research', a topic I developed around the legal scholar Karl Llewellyn's concept of the 'threat of the available':

> [T]he almost inevitable tendency in any … any study, first to turn to the most available material and to study that--to study it exclusively; [then], having once begun the study of the available, to lose all perspective and come shortly to mistake the merely available, the easily seen, for all there is to see. (Llewellyn 1931, 95–6, quoted in Danner 2003, 182)

5 See Chapter 12, this volume, 248.

6 For an application of the concept, see Chapter 16, this volume, 351 ('Is there a need to develop competencies for international law librarianship on a global scale?').

In his own talk, using an array of slides and images, Cohen guided his listeners through several hundred years of legal publishing in England and the United States, concluding with a description of how:

> in the 1880s, American law publishers produced a series of bibliographic innovations which were to shape legal research for at least the next hundred years ... services designed to serve bibliographic needs that had long existed in the common law system: supplementation and updating of primary sources; subject access to chronologically published material; authority verification of primary sources; and access to descriptive and interpretive secondary sources. (Cohen 2003, 175)

Most importantly, as Cohen put it: 'They also helped to integrate and cross-reference [what he called] the *multiplicity of legal sources* for the convenience of researchers' (Cohen 2003, 175, emphasis added).

He continued for a bit, but for the most part, Cohen had reached the end of his story: the late nineteenth-century innovations in legal publishing he described remained at the core of the US legal information system until the last quarter of the twentieth century, when the first commercial legal research databases Lexis and Westlaw were introduced, followed by the availability of increasing amounts of legal information via the Internet. But, at our programme, that was my story to tell.

Cohen's use of the phrase 'multiplicity of legal sources' to describe the late nineteenth-century legal information environment linked back directly to how American lawyers of the time had described what they saw as the overwhelming number of published sources – mostly cases – with which they needed to deal. Not subject to Llewellyn's 'threat of the available', many were disparagingly referred to as 'case lawyers': lawyers who believed that their job was to find every case possibly on point for the issue with which they were confronted (Davis 1918). The ever-growing number of published opinions swamped them, but their desire to locate every case of possible relevance helped sustain the market for more and more cases to be published.

It was neither new nor unusual for lawyers to complain about 'too much law'. Common law lawyers working in systems relying on the precedents found in judicial opinions had complained about having to deal with too many opinions, too much law, at least as far back as the time of Francis Bacon in the early seventeenth century.[7] Concerns about too many law books are limited neither to common law legal systems nor to the post-Gutenberg age.[8]

In the United States, there were fewer than 20 volumes of American case law in 1810 (Hicks 1923, 111). Still, the authors of the first two major commentaries on American law, Joseph Story and John Kent, each expressed concern over the amount of law with which lawyers had to deal. In a 1921 address, Story warned of 'the fearful calamity, which threatens us, of being buried alive, not in the catacombs, but in the labyrinths of the law' (Story 1829, 31). In the first volume of his *Commentaries on American Law*, Kent noted the 'consequence[s] of the number of books which beset and encumber the path of the student', and '[t]he evils resulting from indigestible heaps of

7 In 'A Proposition to His Majesty ... Touching the Compiling, and Amendment of the Law', Bacon recommended eliminating from the law reports cases that were 'clearly no law', 'cases merely of iteration and repetition', cases 'judged to the contrary' and cases containing 'idle queries'. In addition, 'cases reported with too great prolixity would be drawn into a more compendious report' (Bacon c.1616, 68, 69).

8 Michael Hoeflich has pointed out that the problems of dealing with large amounts of legal sources extend back 2,000 years and not only to common law systems, but he also notes particularly the growth in amount after the mid-fifteenth century prompted not only by the development of printing with moveable type, but the rise of nation-states, which required lawyers to deal with Roman law, canon law and the law of their states (Hoeflich 2002, 92–3).

laws and authorities … [which] destroy the certainty of the law, and promote litigation, delay, and subtility [*sic*]' (Kent 1826–30, I: 441–2). In 1840, a comment in *The American Jurist* feared that 'there are many young lawyers who find themselves in the dilemma of … [Erasmus], called upon to select between law books and clothes' ('Review of Peters's Digest' 1840, 244). At the time there were probably about 600 volumes of American reports for lawyers to contend with (Hicks 1923, 111).

After the American Civil War, the body of US law grew steadily, seemingly exponentially, spurred by geographic expansion, economic growth, increases in the numbers of courts and judges issuing opinions, and the publication of appellate court opinions not only in the official reports issued by the courts but in unofficial commercially-published reporters. Throughout the last quarter of the nineteenth century, the annual meetings of the American Bar Association rang with calls to reduce the 'multiplicity of decisions' being issued by the courts and published in frequently duplicative series of reports. In 1885, it was noted that the decisions of 11 states were available in two or three commercial versions in addition to the official reports published by the states ('The New "Reporters"' 932).

From that period on, American lawyers, law students, scholars, and everyone working with the law have been awash in a constantly rising sea of legal information, staying afloat only because of the tools created by legal publishers to organise and index the law. The West Publishing Company and other US publishers thrived because of the powerful tools they provided to lawyers forced to contend with the ever-growing multiplicity of sources of law. As Morris Cohen put it: '[T]he materials of our law seem to be marked by an accelerating birth rate, an almost non-existent mortality rate, and a serious resistance to contraception on the part of both judges and legislators' (Cohen 1969, 183).

Yet, throughout much of the twentieth century, despite the amount of law being produced, law librarians could feel that they had some control over the literature of the law. Despite its continuing growth – there were an estimated three million reported decisions in the US when the first commercial electronic legal databases were introduced in1975 (Jacobstein and Mersky 1977, 7)[9] – the literature of the law was organised and findable.

The law books were in the law libraries and the systems of legal research were well established. American law librarians knew and understood how the digest system worked, knew how to use loose-leaf services and pocket parts to update volumes, understood the mysteries of the Shepard's citation-checking system and the arcane rules of legal citation, which the *Harvard Law Review* first foisted on legal writers in 1926.[10] They had little reason to question the value of their work or whether there might be other ways to do it. Despite their eventual impacts, the introduction of the Lexis and Westlaw legal research systems in the mid-1970s did not immediately transform the law librarian's work. As Bob Berring has pointed out, these were at first conservative innovations, which 'aped the functions of the old [print] system' (Berring 2000b, 1996). The so-called 'computer-assisted legal research systems' were designed to attract end-user lawyers, so connections to the familiar books of the law were important. Westlaw itself was originally marketed as an index to the cases published in West books.

By the 1980s, legal information in digital formats had become widely accessible to American law students and professors, lawyers, judges and other legal professionals via Lexis, Westlaw and CD-ROMs. After the mid-1990s, when the availability of World-Wide-Web and graphical

9 In 1975, 44,000 new cases were published each year (Jacobstein and Mersky 1977, 17); in 2009, there were over 7,000,000 published reports and 200,000 added each year (Barkan et al. 2009, 32).

10 Available at: www.legalbluebook.com/Public/Introduction.aspx, accessed 17 August 2010.

browsers began to make it possible for anyone to 'travel through the online world along paths of whim and intuition' (Wolfe 1994, 116), not only was legal information increasingly available to wider audiences through the Internet but a new world of non-legal sources became readily accessible and was used by legal professionals. Fred Schauer and Virginia Wise found that, with ready electronic access to materials outside the coverage of Lexis, Westlaw and the law library, US courts were more and more frequently citing authorities other than cases and statutes in their decisions (Schauer and Wise 2000).

Just as 100 years earlier, when lawyers found themselves faced with a 'multiplicity of decisions', in the late twentieth century lawyers, law librarians and others working with legal information were faced with a new 'multiplicity of sources', this time encompassing not only growing amounts of judge-made and statutory law, but also material which fell outside the controlled apparatus of the familiar systems for finding the printed law. Bob Berring had compared the role of West's tools in providing and maintaining a shape to the common law at the end of the nineteenth century, to that played by Blackstone's *Commentaries* in the eighteenth century. At the end of the twentieth century, he was calling for a new Blackstone, 'someone … who can re-conceptualize the structure of legal information' (Berring 2000a, 315).

The Twenty-First Century Legal Information Environment

In his 2008 book, *The End of Lawyers*, Richard Susskind wrote that 'the really exciting developments that will penetrate to the very heart of legal service' are yet to come. Susskind emphasises not only the idea that 'what lawyers have enjoyed so far is little more than improved plumbing', but also that (quoting William Gibson) 'the future has already arrived. It is just not evenly distributed yet' (Susskind 2008, 21–2). This is no doubt true, not only among the world's legal jurisdictions, but within them. However, for law librarians, perhaps more than for other segments of the legal profession, the future has both arrived and is widely distributed. Since the late twentieth century, law librarians in all parts of the world and in all areas of specialisation were forced to consider the impacts of information technologies on their libraries and their profession, and to think harder about what they had in common with other information professionals. Betty Haugen has noted three key characteristics of legal information in the present era:

- Although digitalization has made the flow of information across national borders faster and easier, it has increased the inequality of access …
- The distribution of intellectual content is increasingly in the hands of private industrial corporations … Most of the legal materials are generated in public or academic institutions. As commercial vendors have taken over distribution, access has become restricted for these same public and academic institutions …
- The cost of maintaining access is becoming prohibitive even for relatively affluent law libraries in the Northern Hemisphere, let alone for their poorer Southern counterparts (Haugen 2005, 473)

The US experience of course cannot be taken as representative of other jurisdictions, either in the history of the forms in which is legal information have been published or in the ways that American legal scholars, law students and lawyers access and use legal information in the early twenty-first century. Because of its size, common law heritage, multiple jurisdictions, multi-level appellate court systems, and long reliance on competitive commercial publishers as well as the government to publish and distribute the law, the United States is in many ways unique. In a globalised world, however, changes in the legal information environment, recent and still to come, are likely to impact the work of all lawyers and law librarians no matter where they are, no matter where the changes originate. Increasing amounts of legal information are available (or potentially available since they are created in digital formats) in all jurisdictions; the definition of what is considered to be 'legal information' is expanding; and the Internet is affecting the practice of law, legal education and legal scholarship.

What Librarians Do

In 1996, a report of the American Association of Law Libraries (AALL) Special Committee on the Renaissance of Law Librarianship in the Information Age analysed the churning information environment of the time and defined the mission of law librarianship in terms of 'serving *the information needs of the legal profession and the legal information needs of the public*', noting that the things law librarians do, the things traditionally identified with librarianship: 'acquiring, collecting, organizing, retrieving, and disseminating legal and related information are only *subsets* of that basic mission' ('Toward a Renaissance' 1997, 8–9, emphasis added).

At the time when the report was issued, the notion that providing services to the users of legal information should be the basis for law librarianship's claims to professional status seemed uncontroversial. More recently, however, James Donovan, a librarian at the University of Georgia Law Library, challenged the idea, urging law librarians not to forget the importance of their traditional role in collection development as they face the new challenges of the twenty-first century. From Donovan's perspective, the library's traditional roles: 'acquiring, collecting, organizing, retrieving, and disseminating … information [create] independent obligations toward collection development and the organization and preservation of knowledge and information in all its forms', which 'extend beyond immediate patron services'. For Donovan, 'It is commitment to these higher ends – ends that are not reducible to patron services or satisfactions alone – that elevates librarianship to the status of a profession' (Donovan 2008, 123–4).

Echoing Ranganathan's Laws of Library Science (Ranganathan 1931), Donovan set out 'the librarian's core functions [as] to acquire the right books, to make them accessible, and to assure their continued availability', and stating that collection development is 'perhaps the cardinal function of the library' (Donovan 2008, 124). Harvard University's associate librarian for collection development Don Hazen has noted that librarians have traditionally assembled materials that are not 'not a random bunch of stuff, but can actually support and sustain some kind of *meaningful* inquiry'. Hazen goes on to say, however, that: 'Internet search explodes the notion of a curated collection in which the quality of the sources has been assured … The notion of collection that's implicit in "the universe is at my fingertips" is diametrically opposed, really, to the notion of collection as "consciously curated and controlled artifact"' (quoted in Shaw 2010, 37; emphasis in original). As Nicholas Carr puts it: 'We no longer have the patience to await time's slow and scrupulous winnowing. Inundated at every moment by information of immediate interest, we have little choice but to resort to automated filters, which grant their privilege, instantaneously, to the new and the popular' (Carr 2010, 171).

How much collection development work will there be for librarians in an environment where information of all types is published digitally, sought in digital formats by researchers, needed immediately, and typically accessed through networked sources located beyond the walls of the libraries? For librarians, as Hazen notes, 'Internet search engines fundamentally challenge our understanding of where we add value to this process' (quoted in Shaw 2010, 37).

Harvard Law Librarian John Palfrey has written that 'Libraries must perceive our primary function as serving communities rather than building collections' (Palfrey 2010, 185). In his 2010 keynote address to the American Association of Law Libraries, library educator R. David Lankes followed suit, stating that 'The mission of librarians is to improve society through facilitating knowledge creation in their communities' (Lankes 2010). How best do we do this? In law, certainly, the reason for librarians' efforts to select, organise and preserve legal information has been to enable those who need that information both to find it and to use it effectively; it has not been to create collections for their own sake. Still, to argue that service to communities is the basis for the profession of law librarianship in the digital environment, it is necessary to determine what services users of legal information will require and whether librarians are likely to be positioned to provide them.[11]

Libraries and Librarians in the Twenty-First Century

Most prognosticators on the future of libraries and librarians see little reason for librarians to be complacent regarding their future roles in a changing information environment over which they have little control. Many criticise the profession not only for realising too late that the Internet has dramatically diminished the value of local collections and services (see for instance Ross and Sennyey 2008, 146), but for failing to recognise that digital information is not the same as print – despite the attraction of pretending that it is (Joint 2006, 15).

In the United States, there is plenty of evidence that direct electronic access to information – to the stuff of scholarship – has affected researchers' use of the library and perceptions of its role. A series of reports from Ithaka S + R[12] documents a continuing and growing disconnection between faculty and librarian perceptions regarding the importance of the several roles played by the library and librarians in support of research and scholarship (see Schonfeld and Housewright 2010). Based on surveys conducted in 2000, 2003, 2006 and 2009, the Ithaka studies suggest that, although faculty respondents continue to value highly the library's roles, particularly as purchaser of shared resources and archive, they (with some variations by discipline) view the library as playing an increasingly less important role in providing gateways to information they need for their research. The results indicate that faculty perceptions of the library's importance are based less on their need for librarians to help them locate and evaluate information than on the library's purchase and preservation of collections, which in print formats are becoming less important for research in many fields. Humanities scholars continue to place more importance on the library's gateway role than researchers in the hard sciences, with social scientists (including legal scholars) between the two, but the decline 'has been steady and consistent over the last ten years, holding across disciplinary groupings' (Schonfeld and Housewright 2010, 8–14, 12).

The most recent Ithaka report did not present information about librarians' attitudes, but the report from 2008 suggested that faculty perceptions of the decreasing importance of the library's role as a gateway to information stood 'in stark contrast' to librarians' own sense of the importance of that role. Over 90 per cent of librarians surveyed in 2006 saw the gateway role as 'very important' and almost as many expected it to remain so (Housewright and Schonfeld 2008, 6). Other research, however, indicates that 'classroom faculty often rate librarians as one of the least likely sources to which they would turn when seeking information' (Kotter 1999, 296).

---

11 See Windsor and Friedman (2010) for a suggestion that in the law firm environment, the idea of 'library as service' may be best effected through outsourcing.

12 Available at: www.ithaka.org/ithaka-s-r, accessed 21 August 2010.

In a 2010 article in *Educause Review* Richard Katz explains this in terms of the new 'information and scholarly communication environments that are emerging in the Digital Age [which] are empowering scholars and are enriching scholarship in palpable ways' by providing:

- rapid and low-cost connection with other scholars
- tools that promote the capacity for multi-tasking, multi-processing, and otherwise dividing our attention, and
- access to an abundance of easily discovered recorded knowledge (Katz, R. 2010, 48)

For Katz, the Internet's greatest boon to scholarship is direct access to research information, because it frees scholars from what he calls the 'busy-ness' of scholarship:

> the tyranny and expense of finding, acquiring, sorting, verifying, annotating, collating, validating, and classifying information. Before the Internet … tasks of looking endlessly through search aids, waiting for the machinery of interlibrary exchanges of materials to issue forth … [earning] the right to delight in finally gaining access to rolls of nearly unreadable microfilm. (Katz, R. 2010, 48)

Now, says Katz: 'The discovery of rich content is mediated and simplified by search engines … The results … can be a personal scholarly library that is richly annotated and fully searchable using computer-based text or data analysis'; this for Katz is 'the liberating impact of digital technologies on the scholarship of discovery' (Katz, R. 2010, 49).[13] For librarians, of course, the suggestion scholars might consider library-centred research to be a matter of 'busy-ness' could be read more starkly as 'perhaps … they really don't need us'.

Law Librarians and Law Libraries in the Twenty-First Century

In much of the world, law professors and practising attorneys are well-accustomed to the rich full-text resources of legal information databases, and to desktop delivery of new scholarship through electronic working papers services like the Social Science Research Network (SSRN) or the vast journal repositories provided by HeinOnline, other aggregators, and journal publishers. As in other fields of study, the Internet has transformed the research process in law by bringing a wealth of published and unpublished information to the desktop, and by allowing scholars and attorneys to move easily and seamlessly from source to source, paper to paper, article to article, conversation to conversation (see Susskind 2008, 276). As Nicholas Carr says: 'the Internet is a machine designed for the efficient, automated collection, transmission, and manipulation of information' (Carr 2010, 150).

No doubt, this 'important lesson' from the 2008 Ithaka report applies to law, as it does to other fields:

> [T]he library is in many ways falling off the radar screens of faculty. Although scholars report general respect for libraries and librarians … [r]esearchers no longer use the library as a gateway to information, and no longer feel a significant dependence on the library in their research process

13 Some research suggests, however, that ready electronic access to the scholarly journal literature has led researchers to find and read fewer articles than before, and to cite more recent articles, leading online researchers both to more easily find 'prevailing opinion' and to follow it. 'This research intimates that one of the chief values of print library research is poor indexing' (Evans 2008, 398).

> … In short, although librarians may still be providing significant value to their constituency, the value of their brand is decreasing. (Housewright and Schonfeld 2008, 30)

At a 2008 colloquium on 'The Law Librarian's Role in the Scholarly Enterprise', noted scholar Stanley Katz said that: 'digital scholarship is almost by definition collaborative … Digital scholars are … co-makers and end-makers rather than end-users of technology and information in this new environment. This is a challenge to the humanities tradition of lonely scholarship, and this has also been the tradition that has been dominant in law schools' (Katz, S. 2010, 364). Where do librarians fit into this new collaborative scholarly environment?

In universities, scholars know little about what *librarians* do; they know about the *library* and its collections of resources, and the services it offers in support of their teaching and research. Their views of librarians are strongly coloured by what they observe librarians doing: usually reference librarians practising their profession, offering assistance to those seeking information. They do not see librarians doing the things that they and other faculty do; they do not see them doing research to advance knowledge in their field or teaching what they know to others. As Barbara Kellogg puts it: 'the very "practice" of librarianship makes it the application of knowledge and not the advancement of knowledge' (Kellogg 1987, 605). One study suggests that '[F]aculty see librarians as a resource (in some cases, a last resort) for gaining access to materials, not as experts who may play a central role in the preparation and execution of a research project' (Christiansen et al. 2004, 119).

In part, of course, the disconnection is based in the faculty's view that librarians' work is service-oriented, while their own work 'focus[es] on the production and dissemination of knowledge'. Because they usually encounter librarians providing reference services, they have little sense of other things that librarians do: 'research projects and publishing, creating new systems and techniques for searches, the development of collections, the development of courses, and so forth' (Christiansen et al. 2004, 119, 148–9). Based on what they see, they have little reason to think of librarians in roles beyond providing services in support of their own research and teaching. Is emphasising service then no better for librarians' professional status than emphasising collection development?

Law librarians and other librarians often argue that greater collaboration with faculty – becoming partners in their research – is essential to the future of the profession. However, collaboration has proven to be something much easier for librarians to discuss among themselves, to propose, than to put into practice (Christiansen et al. 2004, 117). It is rarely something scholars raise among themselves or discuss with librarians. (Most studies on the subject are conducted by librarians; how better to collaborate with librarians is not a topic to generate much interest in other disciplines).[14] Research on faculty/librarian relations consistently shows that the barriers to collaboration are significant.

To work effectively with faculty, law librarians must do more than become familiar with a professor's current research interests. To be creative in finding new ways to support faculty research, they need also to be knowledgeable about *how* scholars work,[15] to understand the cultural differences between librarians and the creators of scholarship, and how the Internet has impacted

14 One review of the literature on librarian–faculty relations notes that most studies on the subject are in the literature of librarianship; there has been little interest in the social sciences (see for instance Christiansen et al. 2004). For a comprehensive review of the literature on librarian–faculty relations, see Kotter (1999).

15 For perspectives on the cultures of today's law faculties, see Lewis (2002, 90–2); Schilt (2007, 195–7); Boon and Webb (2010, 79–88); Davidson (2010). See also the discussion 'On Disciplinary Cultures' in Lamont (2009, 53–106).

relationships between the two groups. The studies indicate that, despite the potential for interaction and collaboration that librarians see in the academic workplace, 'there is an asymmetrical disconnection … between librarians and faculty'. While the culture of libraries encourages 'sharing, cooperation, and collaboration', faculty are more likely 'to value solitary work highly and to maintain exclusive control over teaching and research projects' (Christiansen et al. 2004 117, 118).

Clearly, however, increased interest in collaborative and interdisciplinary scholarship is altering the traditional image of the solitary scholar in law just as in other fields of study. When they think of collaboration, however, law professors and others think in terms of working with scholars in fields beyond their own (Christiansen et al. 2004, 118). They are not disposed to think of librarians as fellow faculty members, nor to consider librarianship a field of study or discipline like their own or those of faculty in other academic departments. Librarians are not seen as having the kinds of expertise needed to be thought of as likely collaborators. Collaborators become co-authors of published research papers; librarians are acknowledged for their contributions in footnotes.

It is well established that the concept of academic discipline is crucial to the way that faculty members think about matters of status and relationships within the university (see for instance Kellogg 1987, 602). When they think about research, faculty members have in mind a fundamental process aimed at advancing the body of knowledge within their discipline. Law professors understand the research process in their own field and know that something similar takes place in other disciplines. Because they understand that interdisciplinary research may provide powerful new insights into their own research interests, they increasingly seek collaborative relationships with scholars from other disciplines, their peers in the scholarly enterprise. What potential for scholarly collaboration does the law librarian bring to the table from an interdisciplinary perspective?

Professional Knowledge: The Study of Legal Information

From its origins in trade and practice, in many countries law has become a recognised discipline in the academy, a field of study like many others. In addition, the standard subjects taught in law school courses, as well as areas of specialised legal practice or of scholarly research are themselves often referred to as 'legal disciplines'.[16] Under this rubric, constitutional law is a discipline, as are intellectual property, contracts, evidence and other areas of specialised study, research and practice. Do law librarians have a field of study, an area in which there is a body of knowledge to be learned, developed, nourished and taught?[17]

Law librarians have argued that legal research provides the substantive discipline for their field. Yet, not only law librarians, but law professors, attorneys, paralegals and other legal professionals engage in legal research, write about it and teach it.[18] Moreover legal research is not a field generally

16 For lists of legal disciplines, see the subject headings for University of Washington Marian Gould Gallagher Law Library Current Index to Legal Periodicals (http://lib.law.washington.edu/cilp/revsub.html, accessed 30 September 2009) or the 'Browse by Discipline' page for the NELLCO Legal Repository (http://law.bepress.com/repository/subject_areas.html, accessed 29 September 2009).

17 In 1992, library educator Sydney Pierce questioned whether librarianship itself is a field characterized either by seminal thinkers or by 'a common body of knowledge shaping the intellectual traditions of the field' (Pierce 1992, 641).

18 In the United States, legal writing teachers, whose status in the academy is similar to that of law librarians, are probably unlikely to cede a legal research discipline to law librarians (especially if it were recognized as a legitimate field of study).

thought to be on a par with other legal specialties. In 1975, at about the time that Lexis and Westlaw were being introduced to US lawyers, Peter Nycum began a paper titled: 'Legal Research – The Unrecognized Legal Discipline' with the observation that 'legal research is not unrecognized as existing … rather [it] is unrecognized as being of any consequence to the profession' (Nycum 1975, 82).

Though dated in many respects, Nycum's paper remains a valuable review of reasons why the importance of legal research is not recognised either by legal scholars or by practising lawyers. Nycum found hope, however, in the newly established field of information science, referencing an article by noted library scholar Jesse Shera, who had recently argued that information science would provide a 'theoretical base for the practice of librarianship' (Shera 1968, 64). Nycum called for the blending of 'the two disciplines, law and information [to] creat[e] a unified specialized discipline of legal information science'. Sketching out what would be needed to develop the new discipline, Nycum stated that 'leadership for the [new field] will have to come from either the law schools, the practising bar or zealous individuals'. Noticeably absent from his list were law librarians, who Nycum believed would not take leadership in the effort in part because the number of law librarians 'who can contribute to the intellectual and theoretical base of legal information science is very small' (Nycum 1975, 98).

A new discipline of legal information science did not develop along the lines suggested by Nycum. By the mid-1980s, however, growing academic interest in the impacts of information technologies on the law began to foster a new literature on the role of legal information. In the United States, M. Ethan Katsh introduced to legal scholarship the idea that the forms through which information is communicated can be as influential on values and institutions as its content (Katsh 1984). In the same year, Jon Bing of the Norwegian Research Center for Computers and Law published his edited work: *Handbook of Legal Information Retrieval*. Bing's *Handbook* was a major contribution which updated an earlier volume (Bing and Harvold 1977) and included an international survey of legal information retrieval systems (Bing 1984, 247–497).

The publication of these works and other scholarship in the mid-1980s signalled an evolution in the literature of law and information technology away from its original focus on the technical aspects of legal information systems to consideration of the ways in which the formats of both print and digital legal information and the systems that deliver the information affect the practice of law and legal scholarship. In the United States, Bob Berring and other law librarians, law professors and scholars in the information sciences, developed a rich literature on the impacts of legal information (Danner 2008). A conference in 2006 celebrating the contributions of Berring and other writers demonstrated that this literature remains vital and wide-ranging, and is recognised by legal scholars in other specialties (Danner and Houdek 2008).

The scholarly literature on the role of legal information is both interdisciplinary[19] and international in scope. In Europe, Jon Bing has continued to make significant contributions. In the United Kingdom, Colin Tapper's work on online information systems has been noted for its international impact (Treitel 2003, viii) and for bringing academic approaches to the field (Bing 2003, 148). Richard Susskind's several books on the impacts of information technologies on the law and the legal profession include thoughtful and provocative commentary on topics of legal information and access to the law (see for instance Susskind 2008). Peter Wahlgren's book, *The*

19 It is important that the subject of research interest to law librarians also be of interest to scholars in law and other disciplines. When Sydney Pierce's article questioning the knowledge base of librarianship was published in 1992, a sidebar presented prominent librarians' lists of those whose scholarship had influenced the field. The lists included librarians but also a range of scholars from other disciplines. The short article noted that 'all professions are derivative' (T.G. 1992, 643).

Quest for Law: Law Libraries and Legal Information Management of the Future, appeared in 1999. The *BIALL Handbook of Legal Information Management* was published in 2006 (Worley 2006); Abdul Paliwala's *A History of Legal Informatics* in 2010. In Australia, the works of Graham Greenleaf and colleagues have shaped the international development of open access to the law (see for instance Greenleaf 2004; Greenleaf 2010).

Throughout its history, the *International Journal of Legal Information* (*IJLI*) has published notable contributions on topics of legal information and the broader impacts of online legal information on legal research and the law by librarians and law professors from throughout the world. Papers presented at the annual courses of the International Association of Law Libraries have been regularly published in the *IJLI* and occasionally in separate volumes of proceedings. Works on legal information frequently appear in other journals of law and librarianship as well.

Today, an SSRN e-journal makes available new scholarship and working papers on the topic of Legal Information & Technology alongside the other legal disciplines listed by SSRN.[20] Many of those papers are written by law librarians, belying Nycum's doubts that the profession would make meaningful contributions to the development of its own knowledge base.[21] New scholarship by law librarians is presented, just as for other legal disciplines, at conferences of national law library associations, associations of legal educators,[22] at the annual courses of the International Association of Law Libraries, at programmes of the IFLA Law Libraries Section, and elsewhere. In addition to the *International Journal of Legal Information* there are a number of established national journals publishing scholarship on topics of legal information.[23] Law library associations also offer research agendas listing topics of importance for research.[24]

Perhaps the discipline Peter Nycum called for in the 1970s is emerging. Whether it will be recognised by scholars in other legal disciplines and become of interest for collaborative projects remains to be seen. However, the scholarship produced throughout the world by law librarians and others on the subject of legal information has certainly created a knowledge base for law librarianship that answers Sydney Pierce's concerns regarding the existence of a 'common body of knowledge', and creates one of the commonalities of international law librarianship.

Access to the Law

Library historians point out that in the early twentieth century, librarians not only acted as guardians of information resources, but were also the primary creators of the indexes and other finding tools that researchers used to locate the resources needed for their work. Stuart Sutton suggests that this role ended after the First World War, when 'the profession went … to sleep and its practitioners became mere tool-users … [losing] much of the power to enable the profession' (Sutton 1995, 9). Kenneth Carpenter has argued that, as universities came increasingly to focus on the *creation* of

20 Available at: www.ssrn.com/lsn/index.html, accessed 2 August 2010.

21 In the United States one reason for this is presumably the growth since 1975 in the number of law librarians with advanced degrees in both law and library or information science. Data compiled by the American Association of Law Libraries indicate that 30.1 per cent of academic law librarians in the United States hold both law and library science degrees (*AALL Biennial Salary Survey* 2009, 11).

22 See, for example, 'Law Librarian as Scholar: Legal Authority and Research in an Age of Accessibility', in *Association of American Law Schools 2010 Annual Meeting Program: Transformative Law* 43 (2009).

23 See list in Chapter 16, this volume, 355–6.

24 See Chapter 16, this volume, 343; *AALL Research Agenda* (2000). Available at: www.aallnet.org/committee/research/agenda.asp, accessed 20 July 2010.

knowledge rather than its *dissemination*, academic occupations focusing on dissemination have been devalued. Within this environment librarians have been passive disseminators of information, rather than 'pursu[ing] an active, intellectual role in providing access to the contents of material' (Carpenter 1996, 87–8).

Faced with a new multiplicity of sources in the twenty-first century, librarians might consider how they responded to the information environment of 100 years ago. Perhaps it is time to become tool-builders again: to develop the technical expertise to add value to information for researchers and create knowledge as well as to facilitate access to it. As Jerry Campbell wrote at the beginning of the Internet era: 'Increasingly, librarians need deep technical proficiency. Without it, we are a step removed from being able to conceptualize, design, and re-engineer the information and knowledge delivery systems of the near future' (Campbell 1993, 562). In this environment, can law librarians become the new Blackstones Bob Berring calls upon to use their knowledge and tool-building skills to re-conceptualise the structure of legal information now as William Blackstone did for the common law in the eighteenth century, and as John B. West and his associates did for American lawyers facing the multiplicity of sources of the late 1800s? (Berring 2000a, 315, 317–18).

As noted earlier, Betty Haugen has identified three major characteristics of legal information in the early twenty-first century: increased inequality of access, increased private control over the distribution of intellectual content, and prohibitive costs of maintaining access to legal information even for law libraries in affluent parts of the world (Haugen 2005, 473). To influence the resolution of these global issues, law librarians with international concerns must think harder about what they can do to facilitate free and open access to legal information.

The mission statements of both the IALL and the Law Libraries Section of IFLA proclaim support for free and open access to legal information. The IALL 'promotes free access to legal information on a worldwide basis through policy statements and scholarship';[25] the IFLA section 'recogniz[es] that equitable and permanent public access to authentic legal information is a necessary requirement for a just and democratic society worldwide'.[26] To accomplish these goals, law librarians worldwide need to become more knowledgeable about the Free Access to Law Movement and other efforts to improve access to the law, and to be more active participants in efforts to assist those outside the legal profession to make use of the growing amounts of legal information available electronically.[27] There are at least three areas in which law librarians can make significant contributions to these efforts: improving access to legal scholarship and commentary about the law; leading the way in ensuring that legal information published in digital formats is authenticated and preserved; and working with others to provide guidance to non-professional users of online legal information.

Improving Access to Scholarship and Commentary

It is understandable, given the nature of their mission and commitment, that the legal information institutes and others involved in the Free Access to Law Movement have so far provided only limited access to legal scholarship and other forms of commentary on the law (Danner 2008, 362–3). Yet, as Michael Carroll has written, if '[a]ccess to law matters … access to legal

25 Available at: http://iall.org/about.html, accessed 9 August 2010.

26 Available at: www.ifla.org/en/about-the-law-libraries-section, accessed 9 August 2010.

27 See Chapter 10, this volume, 201. The World Legal Information Institute (WorldLII) website provides access to the resources made available by the LIIs, as well as background on the Free Access to Law Movement. Available at: www.worldlii.org, accessed 17 August 2010.

scholarship matters too' (Carroll 2006, 743). What also matters is how the two literatures are linked together and how web tools can be used to develop and better connect commentary on the law to the texts of the law. Surely there is a role here for librarians in service to the broader communities created though open access to law and legal scholarship. John Willinsky's Access Principle promotes the idea that open access to scholarship is not merely a good thing to do, but an obligation. For Willinsky, the transformation from print to online means that not only researchers and scholars, but also 'scholarly societies, publishers, and research libraries have now to ask themselves whether ... they are using this new technology to do as much as they can to advance and improve access to research and scholarship' and recognising that a 'commitment to the value and quality of scholarly research carries with it a responsibility to extend the circulation of such work as far as possible and ideally to all who are in interested in it and all who might profit by it' (Willinsky 2006, vii). This is an obligation that includes all participants in the scholarly communications system, particularly librarians.[28]

Preservation and Authentication of Legal Information

Law librarians can also bring to the open access movement their special concerns with preservation of digitally published legal materials. In the long term, open access to legal materials must encompass more than merely providing access to documents: because they can be easily manipulated in electronic formats, legal texts must be authenticated; they must be preserved in electronic formats; and they must be both easily and permanently accessible.[29] Yet, authentication and preservation are not likely to be primary concerns either for lawyers or for public users of legal information.[30]

One question is whether, in their own rush to make digital texts available, librarians themselves will remember the importance of authentication and proper preservation of authoritative legal information. But, if not law librarians, then who? A positive development in the United States has been the support and involvement of law librarians in the Law.Gov project, an effort to ensure that governmental institutions make the primary legal materials of the United States readily available to all as distributed, authenticated, well-formatted data.[31] John Palfrey has posited a similar goal for other countries (Palfrey 2010, 181–2).

Access to Legal Guidance and Justice

In his book: *The End of Lawyers?*, Richard Susskind argues that 'access to justice is as much about *dispute avoidance* as it is about dispute resolution' and that 'readier, cheaper, and more widespread

28 Obvious means for librarians to promote open access to legal scholarship include collaborating to establish institutional repositories of their faculty's scholarship (see for instance the Nellco Legal Scholarship Repository. Available at: http://lsr.nellco.org, accessed 18 August 2010) and working to encourage freely accessible web publication of law journals (see Durham Statement on Open Access to Legal Scholarship. Available at: http://cyber.law.harvard.edu/publications/durhamstatement, accessed 18 August 2010) (Danner et al. 2010).

29 Specific issues and concerns for preservation of legal materials have been well articulated in a report of the Legal Information Preservation Alliance (Cobb and Allen-Hart 2005).

30 As put by Jason Wilson in an aptly named blog posting: 'I don't know that many lawyers who have given the problem of authentication much thought. In most conversations about case law access, the issues I have discussed are scope of coverage and whether the site's UI and search tools are both easy to use and robust enough to keep you from wasting too much time looking for authority' (Wilson 2009).

31 Law.Gov: A Proposed Distributed Repository of All Primary Legal Materials of the United States. Available at: http://resource.org/law.gov/index.html, accessed 12 August 2010.

access to legal guidance should give rise to a more just society in the same way that immunization leads to a healthier community' (Susskind 2008, 231, emphasis in original). A major factor in improving access to justice (a 'building block' in Susskind's parlance) should be improved access to the law via the Internet. *Making the Law Work for Everyone*, a 2008 report of the United Nations Commission on Legal Empowerment of the Poor, applies the idea specifically to poorer nations, groups and individuals:

> Empowering the poor through improved dissemination of legal information and formation of peer groups (self-help) are first-step strategies towards justice … Modern information and communication technologies are particularly well suited to support interventions geared towards strengthening information-sharing groups, teaching the poor about their rights, and encouraging non-formal legal education. (*Making the Law Work* 2008, vol. I, 64)

Writing at the end of the twentieth century, Bob Berring envisioned a complex legal information environment where 'researchers will yearn for guidance and the reliability of individual expertise. More personal, more interactive, and more specialized, such information systems can hold things together' (Berring 2000a, 315). As more and more legal materials become available for free on the web, law librarians will need to engage in meaningful collaboration with others who are committed to making the law not only available, but meaningfully accessible and understandable. To make their open access initiatives truly valuable, to provide this guidance, librarians will need 'to write more code … and [to] dig deeper into the culture of information access that our users are increasingly a part of – for good and for ill' (Palfrey 2010, 187). Richard Susskind's vision for improving access to justice and law through accessible legal information systems calls for more than increased free postings of legal texts by government agencies or the LIIs.[32] For the United Kingdom, he looks forward to 'a Wikipedia-like service' that:

> would evolve a corpus of UK law like no other: a resource readily available to lawyers and lay people; a free web of inter-linked materials; packed with scholarly analysis and commentary, supplemented by useful guidance and procedure; rendered intensely practical by the addition of action points and standard documents; and underpinned by direct access to legislation and case law. (Susskind 2008, 260)

For Susskind, accessible legal information systems will be in place only 'when citizens can go online and … secure digestible and actionable guidance that helps them in their own precise circumstances' (Susskind 2008, 261). Philip Leith uses a biblical analogy to place citizen access to the law within the broader movement for e-government:

> The central notion is that there is – like the Protestant and God's word in the Bible – a direct link between the citizen and the law, without the requirement for a priestly intermediary to explain either the Bible or planning/property legislation. This is the ideal for eGov – the citizen enabled to understand the law of his or her land. (Leith 2010)

---

32 As Philip Leith and Karen McCullagh said at a BILETA conference in 2003: 'It is well known that law is difficult to access – even systems such as BAILII, which are free and available, do not really enable "understanding" of the law since they do not apply any coherent conceptual overview onto the materials. That, of course, is not their aim' (Leith and McCullagh 2003). For a comparative perspective, see Barendrecht (2010).

Who will put these systems together? Leith says that re-engineering access to the law 'must mean the coming together of lawyers and these technologists to describe and test tools which might make citizen access to law better' (Leith 2010). To Susskind: 'This online resource could be established and maintained collectively by the legal profession; by practitioners, judges, academics, and voluntary workers' (Susskind 2008, 260). In the United States, Ian Gallacher has called upon American law schools to create a comprehensive open access archive of US law (Gallacher 2008). Is there not room in these visions for the skills of law librarians committed to working in collaboration with others using open access tools to expand access to justice for everyone?

At the 2009 Law via the Internet Conference Olivier Charbonneau, a librarian and doctoral candidate in law at Concordia University in Montreal, presented a paper inspired by the UN report: *Making the Law Work for Everyone*. In his paper: 'Collaboration and Open Access to Law: How Can Web 2.0 Technologies Help Us Understand the Law?', Charbonneau develops an intriguing model to describe the interactions between legal information users and content (or, as he terms them, 'agents and documents'). He proposes applying Web 2.0 applications to facilitate collaboration and sharing of information about legal texts by creating links between primary sources and formal or informal commentary on the texts or point of law under study.

And there are efforts underway to build such systems. In the United States, the Cornell Legal Information Institute's WEX is a collaboratively-edited legal dictionary and encyclopaedia, intended for broad use by 'practically everyone, even law students and lawyers entering new areas of law'.[33] Spindle Law, another US initiative, aims to guide lawyers (and presumably others using the site) 'to the legal information they need and [help] them write their legal documents as they research. It supports the creation of reliable content by designated experts and other Spindle users, activating a dynamic online legal community and opening a new kind of discussion about the law'.[34] JurisPedia: the Shared Law[35] is a wiki-based encyclopaedia of 'worldwide law, legal and political sciences' in multiple languages with the stated 'modest' ambition 'to offer simple information on countries law systems and particularly on those least represented on the legal Internet'. Staffan Malmgren has described his project to create a site providing free commentary on Swedish statutory law,[36] using collaborative writing tools and law student volunteers (Malmgren 2010).

I noted earlier John Palfrey's statement that 'Libraries must [now] perceive our primary function as serving communities rather than building collections' (Palfrey 2010, 185). The open access repositories and journals created at law schools and universities expose legal scholarship to broader, indeed to worldwide, audiences, both within and outside the academy. Of course, law school scholarship repositories and open access law journals add to the 'multiplicity of sources' with which legal researchers and others must deal, but coupled with thoughtful application of new communications technologies they may also provide an opportunity for librarians to facilitate the creation of new knowledge of value to others beyond their local constituencies. Open access expands the communities served by individual law schools and universities not only to other academic institutions, but to anyone seeking knowledge about the law.

By definition, open access initiatives expand the communities served by libraries, creating opportunities not only for new services, but for librarians to develop and use new tools to enable not only the dissemination but the creation of new knowledge. There is no reason for librarians not to embrace efforts to link primary sources of law to expert and public commentary about the law.

33 Available at: http://topics.law.cornell.edu/wex/FAQ, accessed 8 August 2010.

34 Available at: http://spindlelaw.com/about, accessed 8 August 2010.

35 Available at: http://en.jurispedia.org/index.php/Main_Page, accessed 18 August 2010.

36 Available at: https://lagen.nu, accessed 18 August 2010.

This is a time in which users of legal information are faced with a new 'multiplicity of sources', a problem that is unlikely to be tamed by focusing on development of local collections, but by serving communities broadly defined.

Conclusion: Defining International Law Librarianship

A definition of international law librarianship can only be constructed on the basis of the commonalities shared by law librarians throughout the world. In the early twenty-first century, all law librarians face an information environment that is moving rapidly from print towards an all-electronic future: a future characterised by a new multiplicity of sources for legal research which will provide excitement and challenges, not only in the new formats in which legal information is accessed and retained, but in the changed roles that libraries and librarians will play working with those who use that information professionally, for scholarship, or in their daily lives.

As they face these challenges, law librarians can call upon a vibrant shared professional literature which developed over 25 years as librarians and others grappled with the impacts of electronic publishing and the Internet on the relatively stable and predictable print-based legal research environment of the twentieth century. In the twenty-first century law librarians with global interests can readily share and develop their professional knowledge and expertise in ways not possible before.

Although in many countries the print environment failed to provide equitable means of access to the law for those unable to pay the costs for commercial publications or without access to public law libraries, it did allow law librarians to develop and preserve collections and provide help for those who made use of their services. Now, one area in which the knowledge and skills of international law librarians will be most needed and best applied is in providing ready and meaningful access to law for both legal professionals and citizens alike. In the legal information environment of the twenty-first century, the communities served by law libraries and law librarians have expanded to encompass all those with needs for accurate legal information and the ability to understand how it affects them. Here perhaps is where we will find the future of international law librarianship.

References

AALL Biennial Salary Survey & Organizational Characteristics (2009), (Chicago: American Association of Law Libraries).

Bacon, F. (*c*.1616), 'A Proposition to His Majesty … Touching the Compiling, and Amendment of the Law', in Spedding, J., Ellis, R. and Heath, D. (eds) (1861–79), *The Works of Francis Bacon*, vol. 13 (London: Longman).

Barendrecht, M. (2010), 'Legal Aid, Accessible Courts or Legal Information? Three Access to Justice Strategies Compared', Tilburg University Legal Studies Working Paper No. 24/2010. Available at: http://ssrn.com/abstract=1706825, accessed 8 March 2011.

Barkan, S., Mersky, R. and Dunn, D. (2009), *Fundamentals of Legal Research* (9th edn) (New York: Thomson Reuters/Foundation).

Berring, R. (2000a), 'Legal Research and the World of Thinkable Thoughts', *Journal of Appellate Practice and Process* 2:2, 305–18.

Berring, R. (2000b), 'Legal Information and the Search for Cognitive Authority', *California Law Review* 88:6, 1673–708.
Bing, J. (ed.) (1984), *Handbook of Legal Information Retrieval* (Amsterdam: Elsevier).
Bing, J. (2003), 'The Policies of Legal Information Services: A Perspective of Three Decades', in Mirfield, P. and Smith, R. (eds), *Essays for Colin Tapper* (London: LexisNexis).
Bing, J. (2010), 'Let There be LITE: A Brief History of Legal Information Retrieval', *European Journal of Law and Technology* 1:1. Available at: http://ejlt.org//article/view/15, accessed 20 August 2010.
Bing, J. and Harvold, T. (1977), *Legal Decisions and Information Systems* (Oslo: Universitets Forlaget).
Boon, A. and Webb, J. (2010), 'The Legal Professions as Stakeholders in the Academy in England and Wales', in Cownie, F. (ed.), *Stakeholders in the Law School* (Oxford and Portland: Hart).
Campbell, J. (1993), 'Choosing to Have a Future', *American Libraries* 24:6, 560–4.
Carpenter, K. (1996), 'A Library Historian Looks at Librarianship', *Daedalus* 96:1, 77–102.
Carr, N. (2010), *The Shallows: What the Internet is Doing to Our Brains* (New York: Norton).
Carroll, M. (2006), 'The Movement for Open Access Law', *Lewis and Clark Law Review*, 10:4, 741–60.
Christiansen, L., Stombler, M. and Thaxton, L. (2004), 'A Report on Librarian-Faculty Relations from a Sociological Perspective', *Journal of Academic Librarianship* 30:2, 116–21.
Cobb, J. and Allen-Hart, J. (2005), *Preserving Legal Materials in Digital Formats* (Legal Information Preservation Alliance). Available at: www.aallnet.org/committee/lipa/LIPA_White_Paper_Final.pdf, accessed 12 August 2010.
Cohen, M. (1969), 'Research Habits of Lawyers', *Jurimetrics Journal* 9:4, 183–94.
Cohen, M. (1998; supp. 2003), *A Bibliography of Early American Law* (Buffalo: Hein).
Cohen, M. (2003), 'An Historical Overview of American Legal Publishing', *International Journal of Legal Information* 31:2, 168–78.
Danner, R. (2003), 'Contemporary and Future Directions in American Legal Research: Responding to the Threat of the Available', *International Journal of Legal Information* 31:2, 179–204.
Danner, R. (2007), 'Applying the Access Principle in Law: The Responsibilities of the Legal Scholar', *International Journal of Legal Information* 35:3, 355–95.
Danner, R. (2008), 'Legal Information and the Development of American Law: Writings on the Form and Structure of the Published Law', in Danner and Houdek.
Danner R., Estes, M. and Meadows, J. (2009), 'Law Librarianship', in *Encyclopedia of Library and Information Sciences* (3rd edn), 1:1, 3212–34.
Danner, R. and Houdek, F. (eds) (2008), *Legal Information and the Development of American Law* (St. Paul: Thomson/West).
Danner, R., Leong, K. and Miller, W. (2010), 'The Durham Statement Two Years Later: Open Access in the Law School Journal Environment', *Law Library Journal* 103:1, 39–54.
Davidson, S. (2010), 'Way Beyond Legal Research: Understanding the Research Habits of Legal Scholars', *Law Library Journal* 102:4, 561–79.
Davis, J. (1918), 'The Case for the Case Lawyer', *Massachusetts Law Quarterly* 3:3, 99–110.
Donovan, J. (2008), 'Skating on Thin Intermediation: Can Libraries Survive?', *Legal Reference Services Quarterly* 27:2/3, 95–116.
Evans, J. (2008), 'Electronic Publication and the Narrowing of Science and Scholarship', *Science* 321:5887, 395–9.
Gallacher, I. (2008), '"Aux Armes, Citoyens!:" Time for Law Schools to Lead the Movement for Free and Open Access to the Law', *University of Toledo Law Review* 40:1, 1–52.

Greenleaf, G. (2004), 'Jon Bing and the History of Computerised Legal Research – Some Missing Links', in Torvund, O. and Bygrave, L. (eds), *Et tilbakeblikk på fremtiden* [*Looking Back at the Future*] 61–75 (Oslo: Unipub).

Greenleaf, G. (2010), 'The Global Development of Free Access to Legal Information', in Paliwala, A. (ed.), *A History of Legal Informatics* (Zaragoza: University of Zaragoza Press).

Haugen, B. (2005), 'The Impact of Globalisation on Law Libraries', *International Journal of Legal Information* 33:3, 471–8.

Hicks, F. (1923), *Materials and Methods of Legal Research with Bibliographic Manual* (Rochester: Lawyers Co-operative).

Hoeflich, M. (2002), 'The Lawyer as Pragmatic Reader: The History of Legal Common-Placing', *Arkansas Law Review* 55:1, 87–122.

Housewright, R. and Schonfeld, R. (2008), *Ithaka's 2006 Studies of Key Stakeholders in the Digital Transformation in Higher Education*. Available at: www.ithaka.org/ithaka-s-r/research/Ithakas%202006%20Studies%20of%20Key%20Stakeholders%20in%20the%20Digital%20Transformation%20in%20Higher%20Education.pdf, accessed 18 August 2010.

Jacobstein, J. and Mersky, R. (1977), *Fundamentals of Legal Research* (Mineola: Foundation).

Joint, N. (2006), 'Digital Libraries and the Future of the Library Profession', *Library Review* 56:1, 12–23.

Katsh, M. (1984), 'Communications Revolutions and Legal Revolutions: The New Media and the Future of Law', *Nova Law Journal* 8:3, 631–70.

Katz, R. (2010), 'Scholars, Scholarship, and the Scholarly Enterprise in the Digital Age', *Educause Review* 45:2, 44–56.

Katz, S. (2010), 'The Law Librarian's Role in the Scholarly Enterprise Colloquium', *Journal of Law & Education* 39:3, 355–64.

Kellogg, R. (1987), 'Faculty Members and Academic Librarians: Distinctive Differences', *College & Research Libraries News* 48:10, 602–6.

Kent, J. (1826–30), *Commentaries on American Law* (New York: O. Halstead).

Kotter, W. (1999), 'Bridging the Great Divide: Improving Relations between Librarians and Classroom Faculty', *Journal of Academic Librarianship* 25:4, 294–303.

Lamont, M. (2009), *How Professors Think: Inside the Curious World of Academic Judgment* (Cambridge, MA: Harvard University Press).

Lankes, R. (11 July 2010), Keynote Address, 103rd Annual Meeting of the American Association of Law Libraries. Available at: www.softconference.com/aall/sessionDetail.asp?SID=208430, accessed 21 July 2010.

Leith, P. (2010), 'Re-engineering Sources of Law for Unaided Litigants', *European Journal of Law and Technology* 1:1. Available at: http://ejlt.org//article/view/20/36, accessed 19 August 2010.

Leith, P. and McCullagh, K. (2003), 'Developing European Legal Information Markets based on Government Information: First Findings from the Add-Wijzer Project', 18th BILETA Conference: Controlling Information in the Online Environment, April, 2003, QMW, London. Available at: www.bileta.ac.uk/Document%20Library/1/Developing%20European%20Legal%20Information%20Markets%20Based%20on%20Government%20Information%20-%20First%20Findings%20from%20The%20Add-Wijzer%20Project.pdf, accessed 19 August 2010.

Lewis, S. (2002), 'A Three-Tiered Approach to Faculty Services Librarianship in the Law School Environment', *Law Library Journal* 94:1, 89–100.

Llewellyn, K. (1931), 'Legal Tradition and Social Science Method – A Realist's Critique', in *Essays on Research in the Social Sciences* (Washington, DC: Brookings Institution).

Making the Law Work for Everyone (2008) (New York: United Nations Commission on Legal Empowerment of the Poor).

Malmgren, P. (2010), 'Crowdsourcing Legal Commentary', *VoxPopulii*. Available at: http://blog.law.cornell.edu/voxpop/2010/03/31/crowdsourcing-legal-commentary/, accessed 18 August 2010.

'The New "Reporters"' (1885), *American Law Review* 19:6, 930–2.

Nycum, P. (1975), 'Legal Research – The Unrecognized Legal Discipline', in May, R. (ed.), *Sense & Systems in Automated Law Research* (Chicago: American Bar Association), 81–108.

Palfrey, J. (2010), 'Cornerstones of Law Libraries for an Era of Digital-Plus', *Law Library Journal* 102:2, 171–90.

Paliwala, A. (ed.) (2010), *A History of Legal Informatics* (Zaragoza: Prensas Universitarias de Zaragoza).

Pierce, S. (1992), 'Dead Germans and the Theory of Librarianship', *American Libraries* 23:8, 641–3.

Ranganathan, S. (1931), *The Five Laws of Library Science* (Madras: Madras Library Association; London: E. Goldston).

'Review of Peters's Digest of Cases' (1840), *American Jurist* 23:45, 243–5.

Ross, L. and Sennyey, P. (2008), 'The Library is Dead, Long Live the Library! The Practice of Academic Librarianship and the Digital Revolution', *Journal of Academic Librarianship* 34:2, 45–152.

Schauer, F. and Wise, V. (2000), 'NonLegal Information and the Delegalization of Law', *Journal of Legal Studies* 29:1, 495–515.

Schilt, M. (2007), 'Faculty Services in the 21st Century: Evolution and Innovation', *Legal References Services Quarterly* 26:1/2, 187–207.

Schonfeld, R. and Housewright, R. (2010), *Faculty Survey 2009: Key Strategic Insights for Libraries, Publishers, and Societies*. Available at: www.ithaka.org/ithaka-s-r/research/faculty-surveys-2000-2009/Faculty%20Study%202009.pdf, accessed 18 August 2010.

Shaw, J. (2010), 'Gutenberg 2.0: Harvard's Libraries Deal with Disruptive Change', *Harvard Magazine* May–June 2010, 36–41, 82–3.

Shera, J. (1968), 'Of Librarianship, Documentation and Information Science', *Unesco Bulletin for Libraries* 22:2, 58–65.

Story, J. (1829), 'An Address Delivered before the Members of the Suffolk Bar, at their Anniversary, on the Fourth of September, 1821, at Boston', *American Jurist* 1:1, 31.

Susskind, R. (2008), *The End of Lawyers? Rethinking the Nature of Legal Services* (Oxford: Oxford University Press).

Sutton, S. (1995), 'Core Competencies for the Information Professions and the Evolution of Skill Sets', *Education Libraries* 18:3, 6–11.

T.G. (1992), 'Some of These "Dead Germans" are Neither Dead nor Germans', *American Libraries* 23:8, 643.

'Toward a Renaissance in Law Librarianship: Report of the Special Committee on the Renaissance of Law Librarianship in the Information Age', in Danner, R. (ed.) (1997) *Toward a Renaissance in Law Librarianship* (Chicago: American Association of Law Libraries).

Treitel, G. (2003), 'Foreword', in Mirfield, P. and Smith, R. (eds), *Essays for Colin Tapper* (London: LexisNexis).

Wahlgren, P. (1999), *The Quest for Law: Law Libraries and Legal Information Management of the Future* (Stockholm: Jure AB).

Willinsky, J. (2006), *The Access Principle: The Case for Open Access to Research and Scholarship* (Cambridge, MA: MIT Press).

Wilson, J. (2009), 'Screw Authenticity. I Just Want it for Free', *rethinc.k: Thoughts on the Business of Legal Publishing*. Available at: www.jasnwilsn.com/2009/07/10/screw-authenticity-i-just-want-it-for-free, accessed 18 August 2010.

Windsor, E. and Friedman, R. (2010), 'Law Libraries Transformed', *LLRX*. Available at: www.llrx.com/features/lawlibrariestransformed.htm, accessed 18 August 2010.

Wolfe, G. (1994), 'The (Second Phase of the) Revolution Has Begun: Don't Look Now, but Prodigy, AOL, and CompuServe are all Suddenly Obsolete – and Mosaic is Well on its Way to Becoming the World's Standard Interface', *Wired Magazine* 2:10, 116–21, 150–4. Available at: www.wired.com/wired/archive/2.10/mosaic.html, accessed 4 July 2010.

Worley, L. (ed.) (2006), *BIALL Handbook of Legal Information Management* (Aldershot: Ashgate).

Chapter 2
Globalisation and Legal Information Management

Jules Winterton

Introduction

Any work which deals with legal information management, whether explicitly in an international context or not, must consider the impacts of globalisation. Globalisation in all its various manifestations and ramifications is a complex series of processes which has affected all our lives. It has had a profound impact on law, the legal profession and legal education and so it has also had at least an equal impact on legal information management, on law libraries, and on the profession of law librarianship. The consideration of globalisation and legal information implies an examination of trends and challenges affecting the future of legal information, law libraries and of law librarians, as well as their recent past.

This chapter is a relatively brief survey of what globalisation means in the field of legal information management and what effect it has had and will have on a range of activities and policy areas relevant to the practice of legal information management. There are firstly some comments towards a definition of globalisation for the purposes of this chapter and then a survey of the following in the light of that definition: legal systems, information consumers, legal information needs, information and management, legal publishing, digitisation, intellectual property rights, lobbying and advocacy on policy issues (the politics of law librarianship), international networking, and legal information managers and law librarians of the future.

The reason for describing this chapter as a relatively brief survey is that the subject of globalisation, even in the context of legal information management or more narrowly law libraries, is big, very big, and affects almost everything. In fact it might be difficult to mention changes which have not been affected by globalisation. Although the survey is broad in scope and necessarily superficial in its treatment of each of the areas which are mentioned, the other chapters in this book each concentrate on an aspect or policy area affecting legal information management and deal with the subject in more depth. In this way I hope this chapter may form an introduction to the other chapters in the book.

It is particularly appropriate that a discussion of globalisation should appear in a book on international legal information management sponsored by and published in association with the International Association of Law Libraries (IALL). The IALL is itself a product of globalisation and, in earlier perceptions, internationalisation and the increasing interdependence of our world. It was founded in 1959 in recognition that the roles of law libraries and law librarians were already affected by the growing importance of international legal relationships and systems and the documentation which emanated from them. Any member of the IALL could write this chapter, each from a different perspective and each with a different emphasis.[1] It is hoped that by assembling a

1 A talk on 'The Impact of Globalization on Law Libraries' was given by Betty Haugen at a session organised by IALL at the 2005 IFLA World Congress in Oslo (Haugen 2005).

diverse group of authors, each associated with the IALL, a broad range of approaches and opinions will be captured within this book.

All the developments and changes imply trends for the future of law libraries and new challenges and opportunities for law librarians in their vital role in the service of the administration of justice and the rule of law in a national or international context.

Globalisation

Internationalisation is not new; human interaction across borders has existed since national borders were invented, particularly within empires and their trading areas. As a term, however, globalisation has become widely used only since the 1980s. Is globalisation just a buzzword, a fashionable way to refer to a complex series of unrelated developments, or a useful shorthand way of describing complex groups of related changes with a discernable trend? Since the term refers to changes in many aspects of our lives and implies relationships between those aspects of our lives, it can be approached, described and explained in a variety of contexts, for example economic, business management, sociological and political (Muchlinski 2003). The term is also intimately bound up with the transformation of processes of communication and the impact of information and communications technology (Susskind 2006). Each of these different approaches, and many others, merit full analysis which is not possible in the scope of this chapter. However, one can discern the impact of globalisation on legal researchers and the law librarians who serve them in areas of interest as diverse as crime, AIDS, the music industry, and general principles of human rights.

Globalisation is not just a high rate of internationalisation, an increased rate of transactions between nation-states; it is also a qualitative change to global structures. If globalisation is difficult to define in all its various aspects, can we discover the direction of travel of the multitude of changes which it encompasses? One thing is certain, that no adequate definition can be found on the Internet. There are a large number of sites which can be retrieved by a simple search for globalisation (or 'globalization') but each seems to promote a particular point of view. This only emphasises the role of the librarian in attempting to provide impartial or balanced information.

Does globalisation imply free trade, a way to lift poorer countries out of poverty, to promote interdependence and therefore avoid conflicts, to promote democracy and demonstrate its material rewards, to enable diverse lifestyles, and create wealth? All are benefits claimed for globalisation, but they beg the question of why there are such vociferous critics and such active demonstrations against some organs of globalisation, for example world trade. Some critics have a very different understanding of globalisation and identify within it changes which engender a transfer of power from nation-states to supranational corporate institutions not accountable to democratic processes, the pursuit of cheap labour and unregulated production around the world, and the commoditisation of information and knowledge.[2]

So globalisation encompasses what are perceived as contradictory trends (Fischer 2009). It is not just a process or group of processes heading in one direction but contains vigorous opposing reactions. Some of the icons of globalisation in the commercial arena are fast food chains which dream of outlets for every 30,000 people around the globe. The book jacket of *Fast Food Nation* carries the message 'To a degree both engrossing and alarming, the story of fast food is the story of post-war America' (Schlosser 2001). To a degree, it is also a history of various aspects of globalisation. One of the critical reactions to this phenomenon is the Slow Food movement, a

2 See Rikowski (2005) on globalisation, information and libraries.

non-profit organisation which promotes diversity and cultural identity and originated in Italy in response to the expansion of the fast food corporate enterprise.[3] A more recent academic work treats 'slow living' which develops concepts of post-materialism and the new traditionalism (Parkins and Craig 2006). Globalisation, internationalisation and commoditisation may be inevitable processes and may bring significant benefits but the counter-trends and reactions to them are also significant and will also have significant impacts on our lives. These counter-trends are significant in areas of policy affecting legal information management and law libraries even where globalisation appears to be the overwhelming influence.

Legal Systems

The internationalisation of law has a long history. Since nation-states formalised their relationships, their citizens have entered into various transactions, and international legal orders were created. The globalisation of law has become a familiar concept not just with the growth of trans-border economic activity; every aspect of law has been affected by the interconnectedness of our world.[4] The movement of people, goods and information creates problems and disputes which national law struggles to deal with and brings more complex problems of public and private international law. To some degree, whole areas of law are subject to supranational regimes such as international treaties or regional trading and political legal environments such as the European Union. Norms are increasingly created by non-state institutions, which have proliferated, and there is a growing acceptance of the emergence of international norms, such as fundamental principles of human rights.

If international aspects of law and legal information management were important before, they are far more important now. It is now necessary, even for local law practices and local judiciary at district level, to be aware of the international aspects of litigation (Dejarnatt and Rahdert 2010).[5] Disputes which are litigated even in the lower courts increasingly require the consideration of legal systems other than local domestic law. In some legal systems, comparative legal research has been built into the fabric of the legal system itself. For example in South Africa the contemplation of constitutional rights includes the comparative study of legal norms in other legal systems, not just during the framing of its progressive constitution, but also to an extent in its later interpretation by the courts.[6]

There has been significant convergence of national legal systems in recent years. As more nations subscribe to more international treaties and international legal orders, their national legal systems include more similar provisions. Further, there has been a gradual but nonetheless dramatic recognition and adoption of fundamental legal norms and universal rights, which is one of the most valuable and important phenomena linked to globalisation.

The process of rebuilding and reconstructing the legal order of many countries continues around the world. Huge strides have been taken in the introduction of new constitutions and new legal frameworks for economic activity. The wholesale rewriting of legal systems in Central and

---

3 The Slow Food movement. Available at: www.slowfood.com, accessed 25 June 2010.

4 A keyword search of the *Index to Foreign Legal Periodicals* in September 2010 covering articles from 1985 to date shows 236 using the word globalisation (or globalization) of which 88 were published before 2000. In HeinOnline's Law Journal Library a full text search retrieved 23 articles between 1970 and 1979; 316 between 1980 and 1989; 6,431 between 1990 and 1999; and 25,154 between 2000 and 2009.

5 This paper includes the results of a survey of the approximately 10,000 members of the Philadelphia Bar Association regarding the extent to which they encounter foreign and international law issues in practice.

6 Constitution of the Republic of South Africa 1996, Chapter 2, s. 39 Interpretation of Bill of Rights. Available at: www.info.gov.za/documents/constitution/index.htm, accessed 25 June 2010.

Eastern Europe in the post-communist era has involved large scale borrowing from existing legal systems. Armies of legal advisers have been made available to advise on the best models on which to base new legislation. This may be a process of imparting knowledge, although at times it may seem to display a new aspect of cultural imperialism. In order for it to be a success, it is necessary for the local legal systems and their history to be understood, a reciprocal imparting of knowledge. The reception of law is of course not new and one needs only to point to the spread of the English common law or the adoption of well-developed codes of laws from some European countries which have been adopted by countries around the world.

One could also point to examples of the coming together of the civil and common law systems in Europe (Markesinis 2000) including the controversial but significant project for a European Civil Code (Hartkamp et al. 2004) or at least, for example, a European Contract Law.[7] These projects seem to be good examples of both the movement towards global or at least regional law and also the counter-trends.

As with many aspects of globalisation, how far can the process go? How far is law an expression of culture and identity and how far will that culture become globalised? Will there be a global moral community? The expressions of cultural identity within the laws of a nation-state are deep-rooted and opinions differ as to whether changes in the law driven by globalisation can lead to changes in society and how far the reverse will take place.

Discussing comparative law methodology and the importance of comparative legal studies and legal information, Muchlinski suggests that:

> one is left with the feeling that comparative law method is at a politically significant cross-roads: either it takes a more academically credible route, along the lines suggested by Legrand and others, towards the study of difference, with all the problems of political diversity that that entails for the ideal of a global world order, or a cosmopolitan law – if you like. Or, it continues to be based on a search for crude a-historical, and culturally suspect, similarities of meaning and purpose in legal phenomena, which will deliver the illusion of an emergent global law serving as the legal expression of globalisation. (Muchlinski 2003, 239–40)

As a methodology to address these questions and to understand the global legal environment with all its convergence and diversity, comparative legal study is an important element in its own right both for research and as part of the legal training of lawyers and forms a part of the environment in which legal information managers operate.[8] Moreover, globalisation challenges not only national legal orders and comparative legal studies but 'seemingly offers fundamental challenges to contemporary legal theory' (Twining 2000, 10).

Information Consumers

In university law schools in the United Kingdom there are more law students than ever before. In 1996/7 there were 54,767 law students[9] (45,539 from the United Kingdom, 3,168 from the rest of

7 The Commission on European Contract Law, the Lando Commission, whose website at http://frontpage.cbs.dk/law/commission_on_european_contract_law/index.html, accessed 25 June 2010, contains a bibliography, many of whose materials are available freely for download.

8 Comparative legal studies are treated in depth in Chapter 15, this volume.

9 According to the Higher Education Statistical Agency, www.hesa.ac.uk, accessed 25 June 2010, including part-time and full-time students at undergraduate and postgraduate levels.

the European Union, and 6,060 from other countries). This number had grown to 92,110 in 2008/9 (74,105 students from the United Kingdom, 5,480 from the rest of the European Union, and 12,525 from other countries), a 68.2 per cent increase overall in 12 years (a 74 per cent increase in students from the rest of the European Union and a 106.7 per cent increase from other countries). In addition there are many more programmes of study which involve some time, perhaps a semester or perhaps a year, overseas and may lead to a dual degree and count towards professional qualification in two jurisdictions. Students at most institutions are also likely to be drawn from more diverse ethnic, cultural and educational backgrounds and possess a wider range of knowledge and ability than ever before. These differences expose built-in assumptions in teaching and assessment, and in the provision of services including library services.[10]

This aspect of globalisation of legal education leads to an increasing need for intercultural skills among law librarians and all those who come into contact with the increasingly diverse student constituency.[11] There is an increasing need for many students to undertake language skills training. About 30 per cent of those undertaking Master's degrees in law at the University of London in 2008/9 took language classes before starting the degree.

Concentrating on the term 'globalisation' alone, there is an increasing number of Master's degree courses offered around the world which will bring together students from many countries and exemplify likely areas of development of the law: 'Public international law and globalisation' (University of Aberdeen), 'International business law and globalisation' (University of Utrecht), 'International mobility, globalisation, and law' (University of Kent), 'Globalisation and international law' (Dublin City University), 'Globalisation and law' (Maastricht University), 'Globalisation, justice and law' (Ottawa University) and many others around the world. Although not in a course title, the word globalisation appears in the materials advertising many of the LLM programmes available from law schools wherever they are based. It is also clear that the market for the LLM degree, as well as the scope of the curricula, is global.

There are more distance learning and part-time students in study than ever before. These students require a different pace of delivery of teaching and training with an emphasis on self-directed and self-paced learning (which of course also delivers a cost saving for mass higher education). Both in the delivery of research skills training and in the general requirement to have an ever closer relationship between delivery of library and information services and delivery of teaching, librarians are increasingly required to take roles as trainers and teachers, and many are now encouraged to take qualifications in teaching in higher education. There are implications in all this for the availability of library and information services, access to these services and all aspects of their delivery. These go further than the delivery of services on a 24-hour basis including extensive remote access to information; they also impinge on the library's role in constructing virtual learning environments and virtual research environments. The customisation or indeed commoditisation of the delivery of teaching and learning materials and all supporting information resources requires a growing collaboration between librarian and teacher. The same need for collaboration exists in the support of research, albeit the opportunities for commoditisation and the predictability of demand, one hopes, are much less. The library is less and less a separate service and increasingly must be one sufficiently aligned with and in real collaboration with the activities of the law school. *A Statement of Standards for University Law Library Provision in the UK* covers services and collections and is supported by annual surveys (Society of Legal Scholars 2009).

---

10 See Chapter 4, this volume.

11 See the cross-cultural training resources at www.ukcisa.org.uk/about/material_media/pubs_crosscultural.php, accessed 28 September 2010.

Practising lawyers and academic lawyers are also much more mobile in the new environment and both law firms and the faculties of law schools are more likely than ever before to contain more lawyers who originally qualified in another jurisdiction under a different legal system. This enriches their institutions and allows a much wider scope for legal business or the offer of courses of comparative and international scope, and places additional demands on the legal information resources and services provided for them. The formation of global law firms by collaboration, merger and takeover has had the same effects in terms of scope, and has enhanced the firms' access to expertise, authoritative legal information and advice (Bierman and Hitt 2007; Sokol 2007).[12] Law schools have more recently formed multinational consortia to enhance the ability to offer global law courses, such as the Center for Transnational Legal Studies established in 2008 as a joint venture between 10 leading law schools from around the world.[13]

Information literacy is an essential to study and research.[14] Providing training in the evaluation and organisation of information is an increasingly important role for law librarians and some universities now have fully realised information literacy plans in place. As more students undertake more extended writing projects, research skills training becomes even more important. Although training in legal research has become fully embedded as an assessed component of legal study in some countries, in many others there is still much to be achieved to obtain recognition of the importance of legal research skills training and to afford it the time and importance which it deserves within the framework of a law degree. The inclusion of training in international and foreign legal research in legal research skills programmes is still something that needs to be advocated even among the most developed programmes (Rumsey 2009; Dejarnatt and Rahdert 2010). The development from legal research training into an education in information literacy is a further and major step and one which the globalisation of information consumers and resources demands.

The nature of study and of research and scholarly communication is changing in law as in other disciplines. The globalisation of communications may liberate and speed the processes of collaborating in research and distributing its results, but it may also diffuse concentration and may even lead to the most popular result being accepted as the right result. 'In this electronic age we see ourselves being translated more and more into the form of information, moving toward the technological extension of consciousness' (McLuhan 1964, 57). The new online technologies and channels of communication offer great opportunities for teaching, reaching the distance learners and more diverse student community described above, but not all are equally successful or suited to teaching legal research (Herrick and Burriesci 2009).

Legal Information Needs[15]

In terms of the development and delivery of collections of legal information, there is obviously more material which is changing in content more quickly. This has been made possible by electronic publishing and delivery. There is also a need to make access to legal materials available from a wider range of jurisdictions including regional and international

12 See Chapter 5, this volume.

13 See the website hosted at Georgetown Law School. Available at: http://ctls.georgetown.edu, accessed 25 June 2010.

14 For more information see Chapter 7, this volume.

15 See Chapter 4, this volume.

organisations.[16] The law itself has engulfed more and more areas of human activity with the growth of areas of study such as human rights, environmental law, information technology law, and other more recent and more niche-based areas of law. More than that, legal education and the practice of law have become broader, more inclusive and more diverse. The study of law has developed and grown to value other disciplines and has begun to incorporate the interdisciplinary patterns of study associated in the United Kingdom with socio-legal studies and empirical research in law.[17] In the practice of law, there is more need for business and financial information alongside legal information.

Therefore there is a necessity for legal researchers to have more frequent access to more publications in other disciplines. In larger general institutions there is a greater argument for combining collections and not maintaining a separate law library; gone are the days when law faculties and libraries operated in isolation from the rest of the university. However, there is still a role for specialist legal research libraries as centres of excellence and expertise to supplement the legal resources of libraries which may largely be occupied with supporting law teaching and unable also to support research in changing areas of law in sufficient depth.

Of course in the virtual law library where delivery of legal information is primarily in electronic form, it might be argued that the physical place of a law library may be less significant. It is now the norm in some countries to expect 24-hour remote delivery of materials and of services from libraries. However, this has yet to be achieved even in relatively wealthy countries. It will require more sophisticated access management systems established at a national level with interaction to nationally purchased resources and a solution to the present model of licensing in order to be fully successful.

There is an expectation that services are customisable, for example 'My Space Library' services to create a personal information environment including relevant course materials, teaching materials, submission of course work, and all forms of administrative interaction with the university. The question remains what role librarians will play in creating these online services and whether, in relation to a variety of legal information resources, librarians within the institutions or commercial legal publishers will play the most significant role. At present the major legal publishers are working extremely hard to enable their products, which encompass the widest range of legal information content, to be integrated into the work flow of practising lawyers such that their product might saturate the market and become as indivisible from the work of their customers as Microsoft's products.

If we consider the counter-trends to the scenario developed in the paragraphs above, one should note that students generally express a need for physical library space in order to carry out their work in comfort and in a social and scholarly environment. Commoditisation of the delivery of some levels of legal education and its supporting materials may simplify and reduce costs. However, it is also clear that, as law schools become more diverse in their approaches and syllabuses and teaching methods, the need to customise local information environments for their own students and staff becomes more imperative both to achieve their own academic aims and to preserve their unique selling points and competitive advantage. There is also considerable evidence that, although online access to learning materials is very popular, many students would also like more contact time with teaching staff.

16 See a survey of the needs of researchers in the UK who require access to foreign legal materials (Clinch 2000), which led to the development of the 'FLAG' database of collections of foreign law in the UK. Available at: http://ials.sas.ac.uk/library/flag/flag.htm, accessed 25 June 2010.

17 The Socio-Legal Studies Association in the UK, 'where law meets the social sciences and the humanities'. Available at: www.kent.ac.uk/slsa, accessed 25 June 2010; see also the Nuffield Inquiry on Empirical Legal Research in Law. Available at: www.ucl.ac.uk/laws/socio-legal/empirical, accessed 25 June 2010 and its report (Genn et al. 2006).

Information and Management

Librarians have always been managers but the scope of their operations has grown. Particularly in law firms, but also generally, libraries are no longer only repositories of published information but dynamic environments for the management of information. Librarians are proactive managers of external and internal information and the intellectual output of the firm or other institution. All that is wrapped up in the term knowledge management, which is concerned with a much wider definition of information than the purchased output of publishers.[18]

In a global legal environment the efficient and strategic use of all information resources, whether brought in or generated within the institution, is an absolute necessity. During these changes, which might threaten the existence of libraries in the traditional sense, new opportunities have arisen for law librarians. The paradigm shift in the role of law librarians has been exemplified in law firm libraries for some years (Mansfield 1999; McTavish and Duggan 1999).

The emerging opportunities for new roles in information and knowledge management are accompanied by needs for re-skilling and by potential threats as the boundaries between roles of law librarians and practitioners become less well defined. Some aspects of the role of the professional support lawyer may suggest the emergence of a true hybrid post combining legal and information skills.

Other institutions including universities have been slow to adopt this approach and slow to identify and make use of the skills of information managers and librarians. Librarians have filled the senior management posts of the combined library and computing services in many universities in the United Kingdom, thanks to their greater direct exposure to the needs of their primary constituencies of students and staff. However, although back in 1993 an official report recommended that all UK universities draw up an information strategy in the broadest terms (Joint Funding Councils' Libraries Review Group 1993), it has taken a considerable time for information management to be drawn into the heart of senior institutional management.

Legal Publishing

The efforts of commercial legal publishers and of the free-to-Internet publishers have gone a long way towards providing an electronic legal research library of up to date materials.[19] However there is still a need for a large amount of printed legal materials of various types which are either not available in electronic form or there are good reasons why one should still purchase them in print.[20]

There is an ongoing process of globalisation in commercial legal publishing through merger and acquisition. The largest companies have acquired huge portfolios of traditional national legal publishers.[21] This has enabled them to offer, in an increasingly electronic format, real progress towards a library of international legal materials although the process of integrating the various national libraries of legal materials into a seamless product has proved to be a long-term project.

The companies are no doubt reacting to market needs and have made a huge investment in content and delivery systems. This has made it easier for customers to acquire foreign content offered via a familiar interface. In turn this promotes more dependence on fewer products and more

18 See Chapter 5, this volume.

19 See Chapter 13, this volume.

20 See Chapter 12, this volume.

21 See Chapter 11, this volume.

inertia in the market, especially as products become more customisable and integrated into the workflow of the information consumer, making it more difficult to change suppliers. This has been exemplified by the launch of new 'platforms' or versions of the product which require consultants placed in each law firm retraining and merging the new product into each individual firm's intranet. The products become more akin to new versions of major software suites or operating systems and achieve almost as much penetration into organisations.

All this availability of legal information from around the world contained within sophisticated retrieval systems, which are updated frequently and supported extensively, comes at a cost. The cost, although shared by large numbers of customers around the world, must support all this plus the very high profit margins which are regularly reported by the largest of these publishing conglomerates. In 2007, after the introduction of a new version of a product in the United Kingdom, an informal survey by the British and Irish Association of Law Libraries showed that 45 per cent of academic institutions had a price increase of between 60 and 100 per cent in one year and increases ranged up to 533 per cent with the initial lowest buy-in price for the product having trebled. As institutions move from print to electronic products, the inevitable increases in price (and in some cases the imposition of sales tax not levied on print materials), creates an inevitable temptation to reduce the amount of space devoted to libraries by relinquishing ownership of sets of printed materials. The danger is that database owners may believe they can increase the price to whatever level they choose since the institution no longer has any ownership over the information, only access to what the latest annual subscription can buy.

The counter-trends to this are growing in number and strength. There is a welcome return of small and niche publishers as well as alternative publishing initiatives. There is now again a market for individual research monographs in a way that had almost disappeared some years ago as major publishers bought up smaller publishers and concentrated on in-house production.

Marshal McLuhan declared that 'Xerox made everyone a publisher'.[22] Now the Internet has made everyone a *global* publisher (and perhaps everyone an author). In the old model an author could create content but was not good at quality control, distribution and preservation. Publishers controlled quality and the distribution but were not good at preservation. Libraries were good at long-term preservation, bibliographic control, and sharing the content. Under the new model of communication the author or their institution has gained the ability to distribute but must also assume the responsibility of preservation. There has been a dramatic vertical integration of processes of communication which might threaten the traditional role of libraries through direct desktop delivery, but also the role of publishers (and their revenue streams) since content creators may be able to undertake quality control and distribution without the traditional costs of publication. Globalisation offers the advantages of technical standardisation such that worldwide distribution can take place without either control or support of individual means of access to the material.

Free-to-Internet publishing, whether by institutions such as universities or governments, international organisations, or non-profit organisations, is now a major trend. It has the potential to replace a wide range of commercial products, particularly those which exist through the repackaging of free information without substantially adding to the value of that information.

There has been a continuing crisis in scholarly publishing as authors sign away copyright and universities buy back the content. As the market shrinks and prices go up in a strange distorted economic model, the situation becomes unsustainable and has engendered government and European Union enquiries into academic journal publishing. One response has been the creation of

22 Marshall McLuhan, interview with the *Washington Post* quoted in the *Guardian Weekly*, 12 June 1977.

institutional and disciplinary repositories of scholarly work which enhance institutional visibility while operating within a network of global interoperability and federated searching.[23]

Public institutions, government and courts are generally now accepting responsibility for publishing their primary legal materials and providing court assigned citations rather than relying on commercial publishers to repackage the information and sell it to information consumers. These developments have implications for various vital policy issues such as the need to verify authentic versions of information, to reproduce it in a comprehensive and trustworthy fashion, to ensure access by the citizen, and to offer guarantees of long-term preservation.[24] In some countries non-profit organisations have led the way in opening up free access to primary legal materials and have constructed large multi-jurisdictional databases. The Commonwealth Legal Information Institute,[25] for example, has enabled smaller jurisdictions to take advantage of its technical infrastructure to publish their own legal materials free to the Internet. Elsewhere in this book Graham Greenleaf describes the successes and struggles of the legal information institutes and others comprising the Free Access to Law Movement in releasing primary legal materials from restrictive practices and commercial agreements to make them available to the citizen.[26]

Digitisation

There is also, of course, a huge accumulated corpus of legal materials of all types which have been published in the past and have yet to appear in electronic form. Although a proportion of the materials may be rendered into digital form by commercial publishers despite their age when there is significant demand, the majority of the materials may not offer a commercial opportunity for publishers. However, there is a growing number of projects to digitise existing resources to form shared national and international resources and there may be national infrastructures to encourage and support such projects. Collaboration is vital if best use is to be made of the available finance: there is no such thing as an institutional or even a national project.

Of course these projects, often based in libraries, tend to look small compared to the efforts of major projects which are worldwide in their scale. Those are generally based on a combination of image based delivery and full text searching based on an optical character recognition file of the text. One is from a non-profit consortium of law libraries; another two are commercial, but in different senses.

LLMC Digital,[27] whose mission is both preservation of legal titles and government documents, and making the content accessible and searchable, is developing a very large global database of law, based on its highly valued microform collections and on further ongoing digitisation of large collections. The Common Law Abroad project (Dupont 2001), for example, is characterised as a high quality project overseen by people with law library expertise concerned with bibliographical control, intended to recoup costs from subscribers but operated overall on a non-profit basis.

HeinOnline[28] is an enormous commercial project that has a large range of US content and a quickly growing amount of foreign and international material, and has established itself as an essential service to many legal research libraries. The company, with generations of experience in the provision of legal materials, has shown considerable sensitivity to the concerns of library

23 Available at: www.arl.org/sparc and www.openarchives.org, accessed 29 June 2010.

24 These issues are discussed in Chapter 9, this volume.

25 Available at: www.commonlii.org, accessed 25 June 2010.

26 See Chapter 10, this volume.

27 Available at: www.llmc.com, accessed 29 June 2010.

28 Available at: http://heinonline.org, accessed 29 June 2010.

managers about the dominance of the commercial duopoly and about guarantees of long-term preservation.

The other project is of course the Google digitisation project which makes materials freely available on the Internet without cost to the information consumer. There is no space here to chronicle the long saga of discussions, negotiations, litigation and compromises which have characterised the life of the project nor the different cultural significances attributed to the project by different regions and countries. The sheer scale of the project dwarfs all other digitisation projects but it is well known that the project also suffers from large quantity but low quality with the drawbacks of bad images, missed pages, censorship, and poor bibliographic control. Major university libraries with large digitisation projects (such as that at the University of Michigan) were each digitising only about 5,000 volumes each year whereas the Google project has already accomplished the digitisation of millions of volumes. However, even though they are made available free on Internet, the page images are not in the public domain. In this connection one should be aware of the reservations voiced by Greenleaf about the usefulness of the Google project for legal research.[29]

The Google project example highlights all the questions arising when libraries are no longer unique repositories of material. Interestingly universities which have benefited from collaboration in the Google project and obtained copies of the page images are now looking to a role where they add value to the images and a new task of organising content, and are looking for more input from specialist librarians with knowledge of the material as well as of the research community which might make use of it. This mirrors the challenges for every library moving from collection based librarianship towards more proactive service based librarianship. The medium may have changed, but the message remains the same; libraries were always more than collections of books on shelves, just as databases of electronic information do not in themselves make for research resources. Their value in both instances comes from the expertise of library staff and their ability to work both with the materials and with the researchers.

Intellectual Property Rights

The global intellectual property rights regime is constantly under pressure to extend duration, reduce fair dealing, protect databases containing facts and public domain information, and generally subsume published knowledge under the same regime as entertainment media. Copyright is often 'seen more as an instrument of … trade policy rather than a means to protect authors and stimulate creativity' (Oakley 2003, 1). The commoditisation of information and knowledge and its effect on libraries and other cultural and educational services are regulated under the World Trade Organization[30] (in particular under the General Agreement on Trade in Services and the Agreement on Trade Related Aspects of Intellectual Property Rights (TRIPS)) and is discussed in Rikowski (2005). Colin Darch described the situation and its impact on some countries around the world at the conference of the International Association of Libraries in Cape Town in 2003 (Darch 2004); he builds on that paper in his contribution to this book.[31]

The counter-trend has been the introduction of the development agenda at the World Intellectual Property Organization (WIPO).[32] The Preamble to the WIPO Copyright Treaty of 1996[33] expresses

29 See Chapter 10, this volume, at 220.

30 Available at: www.wto.org, accessed 27 September 2010.

31 Chapter 6, this volume.

32 Available at: www.wipo.int/portal/index.html.en, accessed 27 September 2010.

33 Available at: www.wipo.int/treaties/en/ip/wct/trtdocs_wo033.html, accessed 29 June 2010.

the need to maintain a balance between rights of authors and the larger public interest. The Geneva Declaration on the Future of WIPO,[34] signed by many individuals and organisations including the American Association of Law Libraries, the International Association of Law Libraries and the International Federation of Library Associations, asserts that the balance has been distorted by restrictive intellectual property rules which negatively affect education, research and development, especially in developing countries.

The public law governing intellectual property rights may not be satisfactory for information consumers or their representatives – librarians and information managers – but information use is increasingly governed by private law since most electronic resources are licensed by the copyright owner rather than sold. The control of licences and permissions is a major challenge to librarians since the conditions and extent of use of electronic materials vary widely for each publisher and possibly for each package of materials or each individual deal negotiated. There is a significant need for international efforts to standardise and simplify such licences and reduce the amount of effort expended on behalf of both licensors and licensees in understanding, managing and implementing the terms of licences. Publishers themselves often seem to have little experience or expertise in drawing up licences and neglect to obtain proper advice in framing them. Their licences would often not meet the tests of plain language (admittedly much legislation falls into the same category). There is also a crying need for a solution for licensing little used research material where institutional licences which assume large-scale use are not appropriate.

The Politics of Law Librarianship

Decisions on legal issues affecting libraries are often taken at regional or international levels as well at the national level without the implications for libraries being fully recognised and consultation taking place. The library world has an organisation, the International Federation of Library Associations and Institutions (IFLA), to represent its interests at an international level although as a body it shares the same challenges as other international bodies in coming to a consensus on any policy issue. However, lobbying and formal responses to consultation increasingly need to be carried out on an international basis (Oakley 2003). The International Association of Law Libraries has collaborated with the IFLA for many years and recently, with the American Association of Law Libraries, sponsored the formation of a Section of Law Libraries within the IFLA.[35] It is to be hoped that the IALL together with the Section of Law Libraries in the IFLA can play an increasingly important role in international policy.[36]

A model for the successful involvement of the profession of law librarianship in guiding and putting relevant information before legislators in the context of a government relations and lobbying programme is the Washington Office of the American Association of Law Libraries (AALL). The AALL has a strong agenda in the public policy arena and overseas members can admire its participation in advocacy, lobbying and policy-making at regional and national level. This demonstrates how important leadership of professional associations can be in channelling and directing informed opinion when issues of regulation and compliance are being framed.

34 Available at: www.futureofwipo.org and the IFLA statement at www.ifla.org/III/clm/CLM-GenevaDeclaration2004.html, accessed 29 June 2010.

35 Available at: http://archive.ifla.org/VII/s48/index.htm, accessed 29 June 2010.

36 The sections on 'Law Librarianship around the World' in Chapter 8 identify policy issues affecting law librarianship and it is intended that they will form the first part of an extensive survey. Chapter 16 identifies various issues which require research to provide evidence supporting policy initiatives.

The Washington Government Relations Office of the AALL has been involved in a range of information policy issues with their root in access to legal information, which ultimately relates to access to justice and civil liberties. Issues and policy areas include intellectual property rights and fair use in the digital environment, data protection, privacy and freedom of information, freedom of expression, funding of libraries (especially the Law Library of Congress which is effectively the national law library in the United States), provision by government of information and official publication programmes, and the nature and strategy of electronic information provision by government and the courts. The AALL has been particularly effective in setting the agenda for government publications in the digital age, drawing up statements of best practices and criteria for evaluating the authenticity, reliability, integrity, accessibility and persistence of government digital publications, and management of the life cycle of online government information.[37]

The AALL Government Relations Office[38] not only works on information policy issues, and mounts and coordinates advocacy efforts for the AALL, but it keeps the AALL's over 5,000 members informed and briefed about current and upcoming policy issues through blogs, briefs and other communications on issues, government procedures, and members of government. The Office also educates the AALL members in advocacy techniques and provides toolkits and other resources, encouraging them to act as change agents in influencing public policy. Although few, if any, other organisations representing law librarians or even general library associations can provide such resources, and some information is very specific to the United States, there is much that may be of use to law librarians in other countries.

International Networking[39]

Professionals form communities of practice to share knowledge and skills through personal contacts and through the formation of professional bodies

> We shall not cease from exploration
> And the end of all our exploration
> Will be to arrive where we started
> And know the place for the first time.[40]

The lines above from one of Eliot's *Four Quartets* provide one of the best explanations and justifications for international networking. Networking and conference attendance in particular often give an insight into other approaches to law librarianship, perhaps the philosophical underpinnings of our profession, perhaps a good solution to a particular problem, a new way of expressing one's aspirations or a simple new procedure. Beyond the specifics, you get the opportunity to look at your own library services with new eyes, a new sense of perspective that helps to clarify priorities and perhaps unsettles your sense of satisfaction with the status quo. Networking is an essential and enjoyable part of a professional job, and the opportunities and

---

37 See the work of the Electronic Legal Information Access and Citation Committee of AALL at www.aallnet.org/committee/eliac and its predecessor committee, the Access to Legal Information Committee at www.aallnet.org/committee/aelic, both accessed 29 June 2010 and the discussion in Chapter 9, this volume.

38 Available at: www.aallnet.org/aallwash, accessed 29 June 2010.

39 This section is based on Winterton (2004) whose title is from another line by T.S. Eliot: 'In order to arrive at what you do not know you must go by a way which is the way of ignorance', *East Coker* III, 40.

40 T.S. Eliot, *Little Gidding* V, 26–9.

benefits of international networking have increased with globalisation and the larger environments of legal information in which we work.

The process of learning each other's roles and realities which takes place in an international dimension may take a greater intellectual leap than at regional and national conferences because you may have less in common with other delegates, but there is more to learn for the same reason. The process of international networking can also often offer an opportunity to contribute. There may be a chance to set up a publications exchange programme or internship, to volunteer some time or effort. However, anyone who has been involved in programmes of assistance, consultancy or voluntary work knows that the teacher rapidly becomes the student. The two-way nature of the process of learning is extremely important; the benefits are reciprocal.

One of the interests and challenges of law librarianship has always been that each country has a different legal system and a different system of legal publications, indeed each country may well have multiple jurisdictions. The legal systems may belong to larger families of legal systems and they may have influenced each other, but they remain an expression of the culture and identity of a jurisdiction. Globalisation has changed but not reduced the complexity. The demand for access to legal information from these jurisdictions has increased.

As law librarians, we increasingly need to be aware of foreign and international legal systems, to understand the sources of law, and to have recourse to expertise beyond our local resources. International contacts not only broaden our horizons and make us aware of other legal systems and responsive to enquiries about them; they also provide back-up for materials, language skills and expertise. Many of us are thankful for our international contacts at the end of a phone or an email. Discussion lists provide much needed expertise, although the cost-effectiveness of numerous people helpfully going off to do the same thing may be questioned. The right contact for the right problem is often a much better answer.

The Directors of the Library of the Institute of Advanced Legal Studies (IALS) in London were all internationalists. Muriel Anderson was given leave of absence for an extended period to assist in setting up the Library of the Nigerian Institute of Advanced Legal Studies in Lagos. In the process she forged an enduring link between the two institutions which is mirrored in the growing relationship between the IALS and the new Ghana Institute of Advanced Legal Studies. The late Willi Steiner, who was for many years editor of the *Index to Foreign Legal Periodicals*, was one of a generation of émigrés from continental Europe who enriched legal scholarship and law librarianship in the common law world. As we lose that generation, it becomes increasingly important to cultivate a new cadre of foreign, comparative and international law librarians with an understanding of foreign legal systems, a need expressed in the strategic plans of the AALL. K Howard Drake, the first Librarian of the Institute, was a figure of international standing in law librarianship and was one of the moving forces behind the creation of the International Association of Law Libraries of which he was President at the time of his early death.

One of the watchwords of modern librarianship is collaboration. We know we need each other. Take the example of digitisation of materials discussed above. We need to collaborate by utilising international standards for data formats, for electronic manipulation of metadata, and metadata content. We need to collaborate in order to make the most efficient use of available funds for digitisation projects and ensure that no material is digitised twice, that no project unnecessarily duplicates the efforts of another. Such collaboration is important not just locally and nationally but internationally.

There are aspects of globalisation that can give us cause for optimism. As standards become global rather than regional, there are more opportunities to learn from each other and share experience. It is always reassuring to discover that we face similar challenges, serve researchers with similar motivations and needs, and encounter similar problems. It is also extremely helpful to know we are using increasingly similar data formats, are able to employ similar strategies and utilise similar bibliographic utilities, communicate with each other's systems, and indeed often use the same automated systems.

International networking can start at home and, of course, it can be virtual. You can participate through lists and discussion groups, membership in other associations, reading their publications, and building up contacts by email. There are associations of law librarians and law libraries around the world from South Africa to the Nordic countries, from Britain and Ireland to New Zealand. There is also a wide range of discussion lists with a focus on foreign and international law and legal information. The organisations[41] and the discussion lists can be found on the Internet.

Meeting people in person is important. Many initiatives and collaborative projects rely on coordination of efforts, which ultimately relies on contacts between a relatively few people and meetings between individuals. If you find that you are increasingly dealing with foreign law enquiries, consider a trip to meet your international colleagues. There are various professional events dedicated to law librarianship and there is an international calendar of such events on the IALL website,[42] which also appears in the *International Journal of Legal Information*.

Perhaps the quintessential example of international networking for law librarians is the International Association of Law Libraries (IALL). The IALL is a worldwide organisation of librarians, libraries, and others concerned with the acquisition and use of legal information emanating from sources other than their own jurisdictions. The IALL has been dedicated since its foundation in 1959 to bringing together and facilitating the work of law librarians who use foreign and international legal resources. It publishes the *International Journal of Legal Information*, holds an annual course in international legal information and law, and maintains a scholarship programme of conference and internship grants which is not limited to association members.[43]

The IALL conference in 2003 was at the University of Cape Town, South Africa, and attracted law librarians from about 25 countries. It dealt with the transformation of the legal system in South Africa and we heard from speakers including judges from the Constitutional Court and the Cape High Court, members of the Truth and Reconciliation Commission, the Gender Commission, and the Treatment Action Campaign, from people who helped to write the new Constitution and people responsible for interpreting it. We also stood within the former Maximum Security Prison on Robben Island, now a museum, and listened to Dr Ahmed Kathrada, the Chairperson of the Museum Council and a former member of the government who spent 18 years as a political prisoner within those walls. Perhaps you can never really know about those experiences which are so fundamental to the understanding of law but you can get a little closer by being there and listening. International networking can take you to places where you would not otherwise go.

Each of the national and regional associations also has a meeting. The AALL annual meeting provides opportunities to attend sessions on foreign, comparative and international themes, often sponsored by the Foreign, Comparative & International Law (FCIL) Special Interest Section (SIS). The FCIL SIS administers the Schaffer Grant for Foreign Law Librarians to provide financial assistance to ensure the presence and participation of a foreign law librarian at the

41 IALL list of law library associations and related organizations. Available at: http://iall.org/partners-other.html, accessed 29 June 2010.

42 Available at: http://iall.org/calendar/newcal/show.asp, accessed 29 June 2010.

43 See http://iall.org/scholarship.html and http://iall.org/internship.html, accessed 16 September 2010, and Chapter 17 of this book for further details.

AALL annual meeting and to enrich the event by sharing their own perspective.[44] The American, Australian, British and Irish, and Canadian associations have each hosted joint study institutes to cultivate interchange and give an opportunity to learn about the legal system, heritage and traditions of the host countries.

The World Congress of the International Federation of Library Associations and Institutions (IFLA) is a massive meeting and not one which concentrates on law librarianship. There are one or two sessions each year to bring law library matters to the attention of a wider audience of librarians in different sectors, traditionally arranged by the IALL and more recently by the Section of Law Libraries originally formed through the sponsorship of the IALL and AALL. The IFLA also plays a role in international policy issues, such as intellectual property and international trade, which now impinge on all libraries. This is international networking at a strategic level and may offer us all a stronger voice in advocacy at an international level.

An extended visit to a library in another country provides a potentially much more valuable and immersive experience than a conference. The FCIL SIS has an Internships and International Exchanges Committee which channels information to law librarians interested in opportunities to visit libraries abroad.[45]

Several years ago the Institute of Advanced Legal Studies, University of London, created a Visiting Fellowship in Law Librarianship as part of its academic research programme.[46] Although the fellowship provides no funding, it provides a powerful argument to a librarian's employer for paid leave. It is designed to place an experienced law librarian in a research and research library environment and encourage research of mutual benefit to the Visiting Fellow and the Institute Library. Visiting Fellows have come from the Squire Law Library of the University of Cambridge, the Law Courts Library in Sydney, the Diana M Priestly Law Library at the University of Victoria in British Columbia, Harvard Law School Library, the Nigerian Institute of Advanced Legal Studies Library, Yale Law School Library, Los Angeles County Law Library, the Law Library of the University of Bergen in Norway, the Honourable Judges' Library of the Bombay High Court, Wichita State University Libraries and the Alaska State Court Law Library. This has proved a flexible and exceptionally rewarding programme and might be combined for example with an IALL internship grant.

All the new roles for law librarians and legal information managers mentioned in this chapter require new skills and real budgets for staff development. But, despite the costs, law librarians need to understand foreign and international legal systems and their sources of law, and to have recourse to expertise beyond their local resources. International contacts broaden horizons and provide valuable contacts for materials, language, expertise, and partners for projects. Our motto should be: travel safely but not too wisely, we do not know all the answers!

Future of Law Libraries and Law Librarianship

The opportunities for new roles for law librarians: as managers, teachers, publishers or lobbyists while remaining librarians have been explored in various articles over the past decade (Danner 1998; American Association of Law Libraries 2000; Winterton 2006, 36–9).[47] Possibly the best

44 The terms of the Schaffer Grant and applications forms are available at: www.aallnet.org/sis/fcilsis/grants.html, accessed 16 September 2010.

45 Available at: www.aallnet.org/sis/fcilsis/internships.html, accessed 16 September 2010.

46 Available at: www.ials.sas.ac.uk/fellows/fellapp.htm, accessed 16 September 2010.

47 See also Chapters 1 and 3, this volume.

source for a community view of the future of law libraries and law librarians is a work which is dated but was drawn up after wide consultation among the profession in the United States, *Beyond the Boundaries* (American Association of Law Libraries 2002).

It is interesting to compare the view of the future expressed in this report with the descriptions of law libraries and law librarianship which have been drawn up by law librarians from various countries around the world who have received grants to attend the conference of the International Association of Law Libraries over the past decade.[48] Their description of the state of the profession and the law libraries in its care in their countries shows how much work we all have to do to achieve our vision and how much research and development there is still to do in support of the vision and its achievement around the world.

If the impact of digital technology is mutating traditional models of communication, it is also mutating models of information management. This goes far beyond questions of collection development and format of material to be acquired, or what particular nature of hybrid library to adopt at a particular time. It involves a redefinition of the role of law librarian (Danner 1998; Susskind 1999).

The new model of communication offers librarians various roles in capturing, organising, describing, indexing (implying a rediscovery of the importance of metadata and selection), and preserving information, as well as in sharing intellectual content and opportunities in the sophisticated management of resources, aspects of publishing information, retrieving and packaging information for research, and education and training, using traditional skills of information management and the flair for collaboration which has been their trademark.

In general the management of an increasingly broad range of information at more times in its life and more points in the chain of communication is likely to reinforce the role of law librarians as intermediaries. The impacts of technology and globalisation in its broadest sense are changing the roles of librarians as surely as they are changing the role of lawyers (see Susskind 2010a, 2010b; Cannan 2007). The physical role of law libraries and the human role of law librarians are likely to remain important elements in the process of legal education and legal research:

> The virtual law library offers many opportunities and challenges and we will each see our world changing to take advantage of these. Librarians can cement their roles in the virtual library by ensuring that the clients never forget that the human component is integral to any library, virtual or physical. (Whelan 2001, 22)

References

American Association of Law Libraries (2000), *Leadership for the 21st Century: New Realities, New Roles* (Chicago: AALL).

American Association of Law Libraries. Special Committee on the Future of Law Libraries in the Digital Age (2002), *Beyond the Boundaries: Report of the Special Committee...* (Chicago: AALL).

Bierman, L. and Hitt, M. (2007), 'The Globalization of Legal Practice in the Internet Age', *Indiana Journal of Global Legal Studies* 14:1, 29–34.

48 See Chapter 8, this volume.

Cannan, J. (2007), 'Legal Reference from Mumbai: Will Law Librarian Jobs be the Next Outsourced Overseas?', *AALL Spectrum* 11:5, 12–15 and 25, also available at: www.aallnet.org/products/pub_sp0703/pub_sp0703_Mumbai.pdf, accessed 29 June 2010.

Clinch, P. (2000), 'FLAG Project: Survey Results', *Legal Information Management* 1:2, 45–58, Summer 2001. Also available as *Foreign Law Guide (FLAG) Project: Report of a survey conducted during Summer 2000, into the needs of researchers who require access to foreign legal materials* at: http://ials.sas.ac.uk/library/flag/docs/SRVYREP.DOC, accessed 29 June 2010.

Commission on European Contract Law (the Lando Commission). Available at: http://frontpage.cbs.dk/law/commission_on_european_contract_law/index.html, accessed 25 June 2010.

Commonwealth Legal Information Institute. Available at: www.commonlii.org, accessed 29 June 2010.

Danner, R. (1998), 'Redefining a Profession', *Law Library Journal* 90:3, 315–56.

Darch, C. (2004), 'Digital Divide or Unequal Exchange: How the Northern Intellectual Property Rights Regime Threatens the South', *International Journal of Legal Information* 32:2, 488–501.

Dejarnatt, S. and Rahdert, M. (2010), 'Preparing for the Global Law Practice: The Need to Include International and Comparative Law in the Legal Writing Curriculum', *Temple University Legal Studies Research Paper No. 2010–10*. Available at: http://ssrn.com/abstract=1586005, accessed 16 September 2010.

Dupont, J. (2001), *The Common Law Abroad: Constitutional Legal Legacy of the British Empire: An Annotated Bibliography of Titles Relating to the Colonial Dependencies of Great Britain Held by Twelve Great Law Libraries* (Littleton: Rothman).

Fischer, T. (2009), *What's Wrong with 'Globalization'!?* (Durham, NC: Carolina Academic Press).

Genn, H., Partington, M. and Wheeler, S. (2006), *Law in the Real World: Improving Our Understanding of How Law Works; Final Report and Recommendations* (London: Nuffield Foundation). Also available online at: www.ucl.ac.uk/laws/socio-legal/empirical/docs/inquiry_report.pdf, accessed 25 June 2010.

Hartkamp, A.S., Hesselink, M., Hondius, E., Joustra, C., du Perron, E. and Veldman, M. (eds) (2004), *Towards a European Civil Code*, 3rd edition (Nijmegen: Ars Aequi).

Haugen, B. (2005), 'The Impact of Globalization on Law Libraries', *International Journal of Legal Information* 33:3, 471–8.

Herrick, S. and Burriesci, S. (2009), 'Teaching Legal Research Online', *Legal Reference Services Quarterly* 28:3/4, 239–70.

Joint Funding Councils' Libraries Review Group (1993), *Report* [*The Follett Report*]. Available at: www.ukoln.ac.uk/services/papers/follett/report, accessed 25 June 2010.

McLuhan, M. (1964), *Understanding Media: The Extensions of Man* (New York: McGraw-Hill).

McTavish, S. and Duggan, F. (1999), 'Law Firm Libraries in Britain and Ireland', *Law Librarian* 30, 56–63.

Mansfield, S. (1999), 'Role of Legal Information Professionals in Law Firms', in Kinahan, A. (ed.), *Now and Then* (London: Sweet & Maxwell), 127–38.

Markesinis, B. (ed.) (2000), *The Coming Together of the Common Law and the Civil Law* (Oxford: Hart).

Muchlinski, P. (2003), 'Globalisation and Legal Research', *International Lawyer* 37:1, 221–40.

Oakley, R. (2003), 'International Public Policy and Libraries', *AALL Spectrum* 8:3, December, centre insert 1–4.

Parkins, W. and Craig, G. (2006), *Slow Living* (Oxford and New York: Berg).

Rikowski, R. (2005), *Globalisation, Information and Libraries: The Implications of the World Trade Organisation's GATS and TRIPS Agreements* (Oxford: Chandos).

Rumsey, M. (2009), 'The Skills They Need: International and Foreign Legal Research', *Legal Reference Services Quarterly* 28:1&2, 133–49. Available at: http://ssrn.com/abstract=1437233, accessed 29 June 2010.

Schlosser, E. (2001), *Fast Food Nation: The Dark Side of the All-American Meal* (Boston: Houghton Mifflin). Published as (2002), *Fast Food Nation: What the All-American Meal is Doing to the World* (London: Allen Lane/Penguin Press).

Society of Legal Scholars (2009), *A Library for the Modern Law School: A Statement of Standards for University Law Library Provision in the United Kingdom 2009 Revision.* Available at: http://www.legalscholars.ac.uk/documents/SLS-Library-for-a-Modern-Law-School-Statement-2009.pdf.

Sokol, D. (2007), 'Globalization of Law Firms: A Survey of the Literature and a Research Agenda for Further Study', *Indiana Journal of Global Legal Studies* 14:1, 5–28.

Susskind, R. (1999), 'The Future of the Law Librarian: An Interview with Richard Susskind', *Law Librarian* 30, 147–54.

Susskind, R. (2006), 'The Next Ten Years', *Computers and Law* 17, 5–13.

Susskind, R. (2010a), 'Legal Informatics: A Personal Appraisal of Context and Progress', *European Journal of Law and Technology* 1:1. Available at: http://ejlt.org//article/view/18, accessed 29 June 2010. This article is an edited extract from chapter one of Susskind (2010b).

Susskind, R. (2010b), *The End of Lawyers: Rethinking the Nature of Legal Services*, Revised Edition (Oxford: Oxford University Press).

Twining, W. (2000), *Globalisation and Legal Theory* (London: Butterworths).

Whelan, D. (2001), 'Virtual Law Librarian: Adding Value in a Virtual World', *Chicago Association of Law Librarians Bulletin* 180, Spring 2001, 16 and 22. Available at: www.aallnet.org/chapter/call/publications/callbull180.pdf, accessed 29 June 2010.

Winterton, J. (2004), 'The Way of Ignorance. Members' Briefing on International Networks', *AALL Spectrum* 8:6, April 2004, centre insert 1–4. Available at: http://hdl.handle.net/10065/376, accessed 29 June 2010.

Winterton, J. (2006), 'Law Libraries and their Users', in Worley, L. (ed.), *BIALL Handbook of Legal Information Management* (Aldershot: Ashgate). Available at: http://hdl.handle.net/10065/382, accessed 29 June 2010.

Chapter 3
The Education and Training of Law Librarians

Penny A. Hazelton

Introduction

This chapter describes the history, present, and future state of education and training of law librarians around the world. While it does not explicitly address the status of the profession of law librarianship, the study of law librarians' education and training will have a lot to say about the health and vigour of the profession.

To provide context, the first section considers the competencies of law librarianship. Because the tradition of law librarianship education is more strongly developed and has a longer history in the United States than in other countries, the second section describes law librarianship education and training in the United States. The third section covers the education and training of law librarians who specialise in foreign, comparative and international law, a specialisation that provides wonderful opportunities for improving the status and role of law libraries throughout the world. The final section covers training and education for law librarianship in other countries. In each, the history, current state, and future of education and training of law librarians is described.

Competencies for Law Librarianship

It is necessary to know the purpose for education in order to design programmes and opportunities for learning and to assess their success. What skills, knowledge, abilities and personal characteristics will distinguish superior performance in law librarianship? What kinds of educational experiences can best develop these competencies?

The most recent statement of competencies for law librarianship was adopted in 2001 by the American Association of Law Libraries (AALL) (American Association of Law Libraries 2001). The statement includes a list of 16 core competencies for all law librarians that should be developed early in a career and 46 competencies falling into five areas which relate to the specialised work done by law librarians:

- library management
- reference, research and client services
- information technology
- collection care and management
- teaching

The competencies provide a checklist of knowledge and skills for the aspiring law librarian, a way of defining the profession itself.

A law librarian can develop these competencies through *formal education*, *informal training and education*, and *experience*. For the purposes of this chapter, *formal education* includes coursework and programmes that lead to a graduate or undergraduate degree. These include legal education, degrees in library and information science, and degrees in related fields (e.g. business administration, social sciences). An internship or externship for which a student receives credit is considered formal education.

Training and education obtained outside degree-granting programmes will be referred to as *informal training and education*. This includes programming at professional meetings, institutes, workshops, seminars, webinars, continuing education, and training by information vendors or other professionals. *Experience-based education and training* includes skills and knowledge learned from the performance of actual work, whether paid or voluntary. Learning from colleagues, reading relevant literature, keeping up with new developments in law librarianship are all encompassed in learning from experience. The distinctions tend to blur but the continuum from formal educational experiences to on the job training does capture the models of education for law librarianship.

The core competencies listed by the AALL involve: commitment to service; recognition of diversity; understanding of parent institution; knowledge of the legal system and legal profession; understanding the context of the legal system; knowledge of librarianship; understanding the ethics and values of librarianship; leadership; collaboration; information management; multidisciplinary issues; shared knowledge; promotional abilities; communication skills; participation in the profession and networking; and pursuit of continuing education.

Most of the AALL competencies are not unique to law librarianship and can be gained outside a specialised law librarianship programme. Only 11 of the 62 competencies specifically include either ‘law’ or ‘legal’. However, law librarianship has always been defined by its close ties to the law, to legal information resources, and to the legal profession. To improve law librarianship education around the world, close ties to the legal profession are essential. Recognition of these ties is a primary reason why law librarians in the United States play significant roles in legal organisations and institutions.

The AALL also included a statement of competencies for law librarians in its 1988 Guidelines for Graduate Programs (American Association of Law Libraries 1988). These guidelines provided a roadmap for formal library and information science programmes and courses in law librarianship and were an ambitious statement of the skills and knowledge needed for work in the profession. Only two or three graduate programmes in library and information science could claim to include most of these guidelines in their curriculum. The guidelines included four general competencies:

- reference and research
- library management
- collection management
- organisation and classification

and four subject competencies:

- the legal system
- legal profession and its terminology
- literature of the law
- law and ethics

Because they were designed for formal instruction programmes, the Guidelines for Graduate Programs listed the core courses taught in most library and information science schools as general competencies. The subject competencies would provide a law librarian with the knowledge base in law to succeed in the profession. Though out of date in many ways, these guidelines rightly emphasise the skills of information science and librarianship within the context of the subject of law.

Education and Training of Law Librarians in the United States

History

In her 'revisionist history', Christine A. Brock, then law library director at DePaul University Law Library, makes it clear that the beginning of law librarianship was deeply entwined with the collections of law books that made up the early law libraries in the United States. It is impossible to understand the history of the education of law librarians without knowing something about the history of law libraries themselves:

> The first law libraries in America were the private collections of law books owned by the men who administered justice and practiced law in the early colonies. Practitioners of law are dependent on books of law … [L]aw books accompanied civilization. (Brock 1974, 326)

As lawyers selected books for their personal practice collections, they organised them and made sure they were always at hand for consultation. The original law librarians, then, were the lawyers who created their own private working legal collections. In the eighteenth century, personal law libraries were the norm.

In the late nineteenth century, when the number of law books published began to be more than even a wealthy lawyer could collect, bar associations began to develop law libraries as one of the services offered to their members. These law libraries were 'organized by some segment of the bar, supported by funds from their members or other private sources, and controlled and run accordingly' (Brock 1974, 329). Because these libraries were privately funded by their members, their services were highly personalised. In a very real sense the early bar libraries were extensions of the private legal collections of the previous century.

Executive committees of the bar libraries made policy and the administrative and intellectual decisions: what to buy, how to organise it, and how to use it. Many of the physical details of the collection were handled by a custodian who was sometimes given the title of librarian and did clerical work such as locating material for members, re-shelving books, and the like. Over time the early custodian librarians came to know the collection and their users' needs and many were probably as well versed in the law as the lawyers themselves, some even obtaining a legal education. Gradually some of these early law librarians were given responsibilities regarding policies, selection of books and their organisation. The profession of librarianship was virtually non-existent during the nineteenth century but the first law librarians created printed catalogues of their collections and organised the books by form or type or jurisdiction just as lawyers had been organising their collections for years.

This close tie between the lawyer and his books persists today. In many public, bar and law firm law libraries, law librarians do not have complete control over the selection of materials for the library. A library committee or board of trustees, often composed of lawyers and judges, may still play a large role in the decision-making process.

When librarianship began to develop as a distinct profession in the early twentieth century, the specialised structure and purposes of law libraries seemed to discourage a partnership with librarianship, rather emphasising relationships with the law and the legal profession. In addition the need to organise legal collections as they became larger and more complex was hindered by those who thought the old organisational methods were good enough. Was law librarianship more closely tied to the legal profession than to librarianship? What kind of training was most relevant to the practice of law librarianship? Debate has raged for decades in the United States about whether law librarians could properly perform their duties without law degrees. The establishment of the American Association of Law Libraries in 1906 as a professional association separate from the practising bar and from librarianship provided concrete evidence of this dilemma. Frank Houdek's history of the AALL is essential reading for this period in the development of the profession of law librarianship in the United States (Houdek 2008).

A full discussion of how best to educate law librarians took place during the early years of the twentieth century. Education for law librarianship had begun with on-the-job training – the custodian librarians – and the law degree. Even as late as 1957 some questioned whether there was any reason to encourage future law librarians to have a library science education (Hazelton 1993, 322; Oakley 1990, 147).

Over time basic library science competencies were recognised as essential to the successful management and operation of the modern law library. But, how would law librarians learn about the law and legal materials if they earned only degrees in librarianship? One choice was to earn a law degree as well; another was to bring specialised law librarianship courses into the library school curriculum; a third was to learn about legal materials and legal methods on the job or through professional training.

Each model was in place as early as 1913 when the first formal independent course in law librarianship was offered at the New York State Library School in Albany. In 1937 a law library administration course was offered through the Columbia University School of Library Service. The first graduate Bachelor of Arts in Law Librarianship was started in 1939 by Arthur Beardsley, Professor and Law Librarian at the University of Washington in Seattle. This programme required a law degree for admission and offered four courses in law librarianship as well as librarianship courses (Hazelton 1993, 322–3).

Over the years librarianship became a post-baccalaureate programme of study in the United States and graduate programmes in library and information science added law librarianship courses or specialisations to their curriculum. In 1986 the Conference of Law Library Educators was founded. Law librarians who regularly teach in master's degree in library and information science (MLIS) programmes meet annually to discuss common issues including: teaching legal research and other law librarianship topics to library science students, development of specialisations in law librarianship, access to Westlaw, LexisNexis and other electronic databases for all MLIS students in special law librarianship courses and recruitment to the profession.

The AALL provided informal opportunities for education in law librarianship from its very beginnings. Annual meetings offered educational programming and law librarians who could not attend the meeting could read about the programmes in the *Law Library Journal*. In the 1980s the AALL began offering audio recordings of annual meeting programmes which were purchased by many individual law librarians and law libraries.

The AALL Publications Series began issuing monographs (there are over 75 now) on topics of interest to law librarians in the late 1950s. *Pimsleur's Checklists of Basic American Legal Publications*, first published in 1962, remains a standard reference work (Pimsleur 1962–). Frank Houdek's *AALL Annual Meetings: An Annotated Index of the Recordings* makes the rich content of AALL programming more easily accessible (Houdek and Goldner 1989–). A two-volume work covering all aspects of law librarianship in law libraries of all types was published in 1983 (Mueller and Kehoe 1983). For many years these volumes were used as textbooks for law librarianship courses in library science programmes.

The formation of regional and local AALL chapters provided more opportunities for informal education. Regional and city-wide groups of law librarians met closer to home, sometimes monthly, and focused on various issues of the law and librarianship. Most chapters issued newsletters that sometimes included summaries of programming offered at the meetings. Chapters also provided scholarships to support travel to AALL annual meetings and attendance at their own programmes. In the 1990s, the AALL encouraged its chapters to become involved with local library and information science schools. These partnerships encouraged students to consider law librarianship and facilitated internship opportunities for potential law librarians.

There were still few opportunities, however, for law librarians to explore professional topics in depth after their formal library science education. In the 1970s the AALL began to co-sponsor three- to five-day educational institutes just before the AALL annual meeting. The topics were diverse, ranging from financial issues in academic law libraries to micrographics to the civil law and teaching legal research. However, adding several more days to the annual meeting was exhausting for participants. After nearly 10 years, the AALL found that the institute model was no longer financially viable and stopped its sponsorship of this wonderful educational format. A small revival of the institutes in the mid-1990s helped begin the structured education of foreign, comparative and international law librarian specialists new to the field.

The first AALL Special Interest Section (SIS) was approved in 1975. The SISs were based in types of law libraries (private, academic, court), functions (technical services, micrographics) or subject interests (legal history and rare books, social problems). Education was a high priority and SIS-sponsored courses and publications added to the rich array of informal educational opportunities for law librarians. In addition the SISs provided great networking forums for experienced and inexperienced law librarians.

Throughout the twentieth century, on-the-job training continued to be an important way to gain experience to succeed in law librarianship. Many experienced law librarians have been happy to mentor and work with newer members of the profession. During the last 100 years in the United States, formal, informal and on-the-job learning provided a wide array of opportunities for prospective law librarians to learn their craft.

Current

By the end of the twentieth century, the MLIS had become the most important credential for aspiring law librarians. Eighty-five per cent of all US law librarians hold the MLIS, a postgraduate degree in the United States since the mid-1940s, while only about 30–40 per cent have both the MLIS and the Juris Doctor (JD).[1] Today the profession continues to offer many job opportunities for librarians without formal legal education. However, some positions do require both degrees.

There are several specialised law librarianship programmes active in the United States. Some, such as the University of Washington and the University of Texas, require a law degree for admission; some, such as the Catholic University of America and the University of North Texas, do not. The programmes normally offer from two to five specialised courses in law librarianship along with core required courses in librarianship. Opportunities to work in law libraries as part of this formal education are often available.

---

1 The Juris Doctor degree is the first degree in law in the United States and is taken as a postgraduate degree after completion of an undergraduate degree in another subject.

Collaboration with law schools has increased opportunities to study jointly for the JD and MLIS degrees, and this can reduce the time needed to earn both degrees. A difficulty is that prospective law librarians need to know before starting their combined studies that they want to go into law librarianship. Few future law librarians know about the profession before they attend library or law school. An additional hurdle is that students must be admitted into both professional schools to earn the joint degree. Thus, the joint degree is not the most common educational path taken, even though 14 library and information science programmes offer it. Awareness of law librarianship as a career improved in 2006 when *US News and World Report* began ranking library and information science graduate programmes and included rankings for the best law librarianship programme. (The University of Washington, for example, has received more applications for its specialised programme since these rankings began to be published.) In recent years Emporia State School of Library and Information Management collaborated with the University of Kansas Law School to create a new degree that combined courses in law, law librarianship, and librarianship. Lack of recognition of the degree together with a low enrolment and corresponding lack of funding brought this creative idea to a halt.

In part because of concerted efforts by AALL members in the late 1980s and 1990s, most US library and information schools now offer at least one law librarianship course. These courses enable MLIS students to get at least an introduction to legal materials and the profession. Even if a formal law librarianship course is not available, interested students can often work in a nearby law library to gain some experience with the materials.

Law librarianship offers many informal education opportunities. In the United States, the AALL now offers over 75 programmes at its three-day annual meeting. There, law librarians can learn about every area of law librarianship. The content is now available in streaming audio, MP3 files and CD-ROM.

Occasional multi-day educational conferences have been offered by law schools, the Practising Law Institute, the Association of American Law Schools, the American Bar Association and other sponsors. Topics have included: legal research, recruiting the next generation of academic law library directors, the teaching of legal research, law for the non-JD, the scholarship of Robert C. Berring Jr., law school facilities, the legal dictionary. All have enriched the educational landscape for law librarians.

In 2009, the AALL launched a new platform for educational outreach to its members, AALL2Go (www.softconference.com/aall), based on the principle that education needs to be available to all members in multiple formats. Some programming is available at no cost; some has a small cost. Often the content is delivered online through webinars and other technology-driven alternatives.

On-the-job learning is no less important today than in the time of the custodian law librarian of the nineteenth century. The world we live in changes every day and lifelong learning is as essential for a successful career in law librarianship as in other fields. Keeping up with changes in legal information systems and understanding the habits and information needs of library users are key ingredients in professional development.

Many future law librarians had their first work experiences volunteering or working as students in a law library. Some law libraries host student interns to provide practical experience within a degree programme. Over the years hundreds of law librarians have given their time and expertise to mentor and train law librarians entering the profession. On-the-job training is everyone's business, whether the person is a staff member, a student, or a new law librarian being hosted for specialised training.

Law libraries generally do not have extensive volunteer programmes. The need to understand legal materials is such an important part of working in most law library jobs that they require at least basic legal bibliography skills learned through classes in an MLIS programme or in law school. There may be opportunities, however, to work in law libraries for those studying to be a law librarian.

Future

What will be the future of law librarianship education in the United States? Will law libraries require the MLIS, the JD, the MBA or entirely new qualifications? Has formal law librarianship education in the United States stabilised with programmes that continue to meet the needs of the profession and are economically viable? What informal educational opportunities will be available? Is more on-the-job training likely? Will budget cuts reduce the impact of this historically important source of training?

The number of specialised law librarianship graduate programmes in library and information schools has grown slightly in the past five years with the University of Arizona, the University of Denver and SUNY Buffalo developing a range of courses and fellowship programmes to attract potential students. Joint degrees in law and information science are also on the increase. Will there be more double-degree professionals in American law libraries? The answer depends on several factors.

First, will there be a continuing supply of lawyers who decide in law school or after that they wish to pursue another career path? In other words, will the practice of law change in ways that keep outstanding lawyers in the profession or encourage some to find careers in law librarianship?

Second, the qualifications sought by employers will dictate the future of the MLIS/JD law librarian. If employers stop requiring the law degree for their vacant positions, the demand for the JD as a qualification will certainly decline. At this time, the demand for JD/MLIS law librarians is being met. It is hard to predict whether a large increase in the pool of entry-level law librarians with both degrees will increase the number of JD/MLIS librarians in the profession.

A third factor is economics: earning an MLIS is an expensive proposition. If graduate school comes after incurring the expenses of a JD degree, a lawyer who wants to be a law librarian may be discouraged because of the cost of additional education. As of 2007/8 the median debt of law school graduates in the United States is $59,324 (public law school graduates) and $91,506 (graduates of private law schools) (ABA Section of Legal Education and Admissions to the Bar 2008). Will law school graduates wish to add to this debt to qualify for a job with relatively low status and salary? The AALL and other library associations offer some scholarships but the best way to make the MLIS degree affordable may be to provide fellowships or resident programmes that pay students to work in a law library and waive the cost of tuition for the MLIS degree. Excellent programmes at the Universities of Arizona, Denver, Illinois, Texas, North Carolina and Washington provide significant financial support to people interested in law librarianship as a career. One other option is for people who already have the MLIS to earn a JD with reduced law school tuition in exchange for working in their law school's library.

Fourth is the fact that only 57 schools in the United States and Canada offer the MLIS in contrast to the 200 law schools approved by the American Bar Association (Hartman 2009). Until the recent creation of online MLIS degrees, a student interested in librarianship had to move to the location of one of these 57 schools, creating more expense and an additional barrier to access. As of 2008, 50 graduate schools offer online alternatives while 14 of them conduct an entirely online or distance degree programme. Only a few graduate programmes in the United States include any law librarianship courses in their online offerings.

A fifth factor regards the technology skills needed to practice law librarianship in a world of electronic-only resources. Lawyers typically do not choose law school because they love technology. In general, applicants for MLIS programmes with JD degrees are average users of technology. Should the technology skills needed for success in law librarianship begin to outstrip the interests and skills of law-trained applicants to MLIS programmes, the number of law librarians with both the JD and MLIS may actually decline.

There is no question that the MLIS will continue to be the most important degree for entry into law librarianship. The law degree will be required for many reference, faculty services, and management positions in academic law libraries, but may be more optional for jobs in other sectors, like government, public law libraries, and law firms.

If the expense of attaining a graduate degree in library science or law becomes prohibitive, informal educational opportunities will become more relevant. More opportunities will be made available to wider audiences through technology but these distance/online programmes will not replace the formal degree requirements for entry into law librarianship. Most people in the profession recognise the relationship between formal and informal education, and understand that each enhances the other, especially in a fast-changing environment.

What will be emphasised in the future? Programmes about the application of new technologies in libraries will be extremely important, and programming that revisits assumptions about law libraries, our users and our collections will be increasingly relevant for the experienced law librarian, as will programming geared to librarians in specific types of law libraries. Examples of this type of programming include the University of Colorado-Boulder's programme to encourage law librarian scholarship and other programmes created for future academic law library directors, law librarians who teach, or law firm librarians who work with knowledge management systems. Many of these educational opportunities are offered outside the AALL, a trend that is likely to continue as institutions try to find their niche in a competitive marketplace.

Even when budgets are tight, libraries are likely to recognise the importance of keeping current in professional issues and skills but there is a risk that face-to-face informal education will be cut back or lost due to its cost. Newer Web 2.0 technologies and future technological advances may be used to promote education and training at lower costs to wider audiences. Those interested in creating continuing education know that law librarians can do their jobs only if they are continually learning new skills and applying them to meet the sophisticated services demanded by our users.

Law libraries will continue to recognise their obligation to provide on-the-job training for their employees but few law librarians have the time to train them in the basics of librarianship or legal information. The formal educational requirements of the MLIS help organisations limit training only to what can be delivered locally: introduction to the institution, its users, policies and information resources.

Using the AALL's core competencies as a guide, potential law librarians can develop personal checklists of skills, knowledge and personal attributes to help decide what education they need. The balance between legal and information science education is a matter of personal preference, economics and career aspiration. A rich array of formal, informal and on-the-job opportunities is available to law librarians in the United States.

Access to Education and Training of Foreign Nationals as Law Librarians in the United States

Foreign nationals who wish to enrol in an MLIS programme in the United States should be aware of at least three barriers to such an education. First, moving to the United States since the terrorist attacks in 2001, even for educational purposes, is much more difficult. Finding your way through the federal and local institutional bureaucracy is essential. Large universities often have offices which have some expertise in this area. Second, most foreign nationals will need full funding for non-resident tuition and other expenses in hand. Financial assistance for foreign nationals is hard to find. Third, most graduate programmes require a combination of education and national tests for admission. Foreign nationals may also need to score well on the Test of English as a Foreign Language (TOEFL) which measures English language proficiency.

Most library and information schools in the United States welcome foreign nationals in order to promote diversity of thought and ideas. In addition, many graduate programmes permit individuals with library degrees to be admitted as non-matriculated students, enabling them to take only specific courses and to meet different admission requirements. In law librarianship, education of professionals who work competently within the legal profession in other countries helps everyone in this global economy.

Education and Training of Foreign, Comparative and International Law Librarians in the United States

Doing business around the world necessitates understanding the legal systems and the laws of other countries. The international legal regime is important worldwide and the global economy has spurred the development of new information systems around the world. These factors have driven the creation of a specialisation in US law librarianship: the law librarian who works exclusively or mostly in foreign, comparative and international law (FCIL). FCIL librarians handle a wide array of library tasks requiring language skills, including selection, acquisition, cataloguing and reference.

There are significant differences between the concepts *foreign*, *comparative* and *international law*. Simplified, *foreign law* includes the national and sub-national (for example state or provincial) laws of other jurisdictions; *comparative law* is the study of the differences and similarities between the legal systems and laws of countries or jurisdictions; and *international law* covers the laws governing relations between nations or international organisations (public international law) as well as the laws governing the interactions between citizens or entities of different nations (private international law) (Rumsey 2006, 73–5). In discussing education and training of law librarians, I will refer without distinction to foreign, comparative and international law (or FCIL), although each area raises slightly different issues in the law library context.

History of FCIL Law Librarianship

Early in the twentieth century, a few US law libraries collected foreign and international legal materials to meet the demands of their users. The Law Library of Congress assumed responsibility for foreign and comparative legal research in 1917. Encouraged by the leadership of John T. Vance, the thirteenth Law Librarian of Congress, the first Foreign Law Division (Latin American Law Section) was created in the 1940s (The Law Library of Congress at 175 2007). Larger academic law libraries such as Harvard and Michigan, as well as county law libraries like the Los Angeles County Law Library, bar law libraries such as the Association of the Bar of the City of New York, and such law firms as the New York firm of Curtis, Mallet-Prevost, Colt and Mosle built significant FCIL collections (AALL Annual Meeting Proceedings 1945, 135–40; 1946, 196–205; see also Wade 1991, 1–5).

Some law libraries had specialists who worked primarily with the foreign, international and comparative collections and the users of those collections. Many were lawyers from Europe who, unable to practice law when they emigrated to the United States, sought employment as law librarians. The first FCIL law librarian was Florence Ferner Zagayko, the International Law Librarian at Columbia Law School, who was appointed in 1930, the same year the Parker School of Foreign and International Law was established at Columbia (Wade 1991, 4).

The seeds of FCIL librarianship were sown in the fertile years before and after the Second World War. Early in the 1940s, the AALL established a Committee on Cooperation with Latin American Law Libraries in order to supply legal materials from the United States to these countries. Discussions about this committee's activities developed into a broader interest in the collection of foreign legal materials by law libraries in the United States. In 1945–7 a serious debate took place among members of the AALL about this question. At the centre of the discussion was William B. Stern, then Foreign Law Librarian at Los Angeles County Law Library, who argued forcefully that foreign law books have a place in all types of law library collections (American Association of Law Libraries Annual Meeting Proceedings 1945, 138–40; 1946, 200–5; 1947, 158–68). His 1947 brief argued that foreign legal materials are an essential part of any American law library for these reasons:

- Law schools teach foreign and comparative law courses
- Approximately 100 articles on foreign law subjects are indexed annually in the Index to Legal Periodicals
- Comparative law aids research and preparation of domestic legislation
- Unification of international law projects would be furthered by access to collections of foreign law materials
- Expansion of international trade makes access to foreign laws a part of daily legal life in the United States

A list of the most important foreign law reference books in English was appended to his report.

Stern argued that foreign law collections of various dimensions belong in all American law libraries. Stern was representative of many lawyers who fled Europe in the 1930s and 1940s. With the discipline of a legally-trained mind, foreign language skills, and the practice of law prohibited without an American legal education, Stern, like his colleagues, took to law librarianship with seriousness and discipline. They built large collections of foreign law materials, created classification systems to organise these collections, produced important scholarship in FCIL, and participated with energy and imagination in the AALL.

In 1950 the AALL Committee on Cooperation with Latin American Law Libraries became more globally focused and was renamed the Committee on Foreign Law (later the Committee on Foreign, Comparative, and International Law). Throughout the next three decades, the Committee prepared bibliographies of foreign law materials, corresponded with foreign law libraries, created exchange agreements for both people and books, and worked with lawyer organisations interested in closer ties with foreign jurisdictions. Over these years the *Law Library Journal* is replete with articles about foreign and international law research topics.

The number of foreign law specialists in American law libraries during and after the war years is unknown, but it is clear that they worked in a variety of roles in different types of law libraries. Acquisition, cataloguing, organisation and providing reference services required library staff with appropriate language skills. Our profession was fortunate to have such creative and hard-working foreign-trained law librarians at such a pivotal juncture (Kulpa 1996, 203–13).

In 1959 the International Association of Law Libraries (IALL) was founded to connect law librarians and law libraries around the world to each other and to broaden the understanding of legal systems and legal materials in other countries. Former AALL president William B. Roalfe, Librarian at Northwestern University Law School Library, was its first president. William Stern was an active leader in IALL work.

Increasing interest in access to FCIL materials and the changing information needs of scholars and practitioners led to the creation in 1960 of the *Index to Foreign Legal Periodicals* (*IFLP*), which was a joint venture between the AALL and the Institute of Advanced Legal Studies at the University of London. William Stern was a strong advocate for this new publication. Willi Steiner of the Squire Law Library at the University of Cambridge, and later Librarian of the Institute of Advanced Legal Studies, was the first editor. The *IFLP* remains the pre-eminent multilingual index to legal articles and book reviews, as well as to legal essays published in collections, festschriften, mélanges and congress reports. Since 1984, the *IFLP* has been edited by Tom Reynolds, formerly FCIL Librarian at University of California, Berkeley Law Library.

Since there were no formal educational programmes aimed at law librarians wishing to specialise in FCIL work (and no standard set of educational requirements), most education was either of the informal type or gained on the job. Many FCIL law librarians learned their craft through self-study (Wade 2006, 59).

The AALL Committee on Foreign, Comparative, and International Law became the Foreign, Comparative, and International Law Special Interest Section (FCIL-SIS) (www.aallnet.org/sis/fcilsis) in 1985 (American Association of Law Libraries 1985). The FCIL-SIS became a regular sponsor of educational programming for law librarians interested in foreign, comparative and international law at AALL annual meetings. In addition, articles about FCIL topics were published in the *Law Library Journal* and the Section offered workshops as part of annual meetings in 1987, 1988 and 1989.

By the mid-1980s it was clear that many of the first foreign-born and foreign-educated FCIL specialists would be retiring and that the profession had done little to train their successors. In 1989, the AALL Committee on National Legal Resources (NLR) declared that 'the most severe personnel need of the legal information community is for foreign law specialists to replace the post-war émigré lawyer-librarians reaching retirement' (Price 1989, 366). This gave great impetus to the creation of more comprehensive educational programming to teach the basic skills needed for FCIL work to newer law librarians. Under the leadership of Claire Germain, the NLR completed a plan in 1991–2. *Training the Future Generation of International and Foreign Law Librarians* called for 'a continuing education program that systematically coordinates discrete activities such as sequenced courses, internships and self-instruction' (Wright 1992, 5).

The cornerstone of this continuing education was a sequence of five institutes 'presenting a set of topics designed to be comprehensive and to provide a panoramic perspective of all areas of foreign and international law' (Wright 1992, 7):

1993	Foreign Legal Systems
1993	International Organizations
1994	Transnational Legal Transactions
1995	Tax and Business
1996	Public International Law

The institutes and a series of accompanying books published by Oceana did much to educate law librarians during those years.

In the mid-1990s the AALL joined with the British & Irish Association of Law Librarians (BIALL) (www.biall.org.uk) and the Canadian Association of Law Libraries/Association Canadienne des Bibliothèques de Droit (CALL/ACBD) (www.callacbd.ca) to create a rotating series of Joint Study Institutes, at which the host country's legal heritage and traditions would be featured. The Institutes have been held biennially since 1998, hosted in turn by one of the sponsoring countries. The Australian Law Librarians' Association (ALLA) (www.alla.asn.au) joined the group in 1998. The New Zealand Law Librarians Association (NZLLA) (www.nzlla.org.nz) requested membership in 2006.

Current

Today there are still no formal programmes aimed specifically at the educational needs of law librarians doing work in foreign, comparative and international law. Most specialised FCIL jobs today require an MLIS degree and perhaps a JD, LLB or LLM degree. Lyonette Louis-Jacques has written about courses that an aspiring FCIL law librarian should take when earning the MLIS (Louis-Jacques 1991, 7–17). An eager student working towards an MLIS degree could also take substantive law courses in international and comparative law or one of the FCIL legal research courses which are taught in many law schools. In addition, the MLIS student who wants to specialise in FCIL work can develop relevant projects within the scope of course assignments. JD and LLM students may find it harder to take library classes while earning their law degrees but could work in the school's law library on FCIL-oriented projects.

In addition, most law schools and many library schools have fieldwork or externship requirements. Many law librarians welcome opportunities to mentor and work with aspiring FCIL librarians in internships. There are exchange schemes to facilitate the arrangements (American Association of Law Libraries. Foreign Comparative and International Law Special Interest Section 2009; International Association of Law Libraries 2009).

Practising law librarians also have many opportunities to participate in informal education and training. If they are employed in a law school, the opportunity to take substantive courses or a legal research course in FCIL should not be ignored. Likewise, virtually any law librarian can take language courses or invest in self-study opportunities to improve or learn new languages. The ability to read languages is an important skill in FCIL law librarianship even if complete fluency is not always a realistic goal.

Workshops and programming continue to be offered by professional organisations such as the International Association of Law Libraries. The IALL website (www.iall.org) and journal, the *International Journal of Legal Information*, are essential reading. In the United States the AALL annual meeting always includes educational programmes developed by the FCIL-SIS, and regional and local AALL chapters often feature FCIL programmes. The Canadian Association of Law Libraries (CALL) and the British Irish Association of Law Libraries (BIALL) also offer programmes and publications of interest to emerging FCIL law librarians. The CALL's *Canadian Law Library Review* and the BIALL's *Legal Information Management* are excellent means for staying informed. Library, legal and subject-oriented organisations with interests in particular areas of the world may also provide opportunities for informal education. For example the Association for Asian Studies has a Council on East Asian Libraries (www.eastasianlib.org). In recent years the American Society for International Law (www.asil.org) has become important for FCIL research assistance and educational programming.

On-the-job learning and self-study are the third form of education for FCIL-minded law librarians. Learning on the job suggests learning from one's own projects, while self-study suggests proactively seeking new learning systematically outside the day-to-day activities of a job. For law librarians lucky enough to work where there are FCIL specialists, there is no substitute for learning from the experts.

Future

What will become of FCIL law librarianship? What will the continuing shortage of knowledgeable and experienced FCIL librarians mean for legal education, the legal profession and law librarianship? Will the specialty and its practitioners be absorbed into the mainstream of reference librarians or will the demand for FCIL specialists grow?

From 2005 to 2009 several new graduates of the University of Washington's law librarianship programme were interested in FCIL jobs. In prior years I had actively discouraged students from thinking about this speciality since it seriously limited their job prospects. By 2005 several FCIL jobs were posted by law schools obviously seeking an entry-level librarian. Of the 37 graduates of the University of Washington law librarianship programme from 2005 to 2009, five began their first jobs focusing on FCIL librarianship, four were full-time FCIL jobs and one was a reference job with a segment of FCIL responsibility.

My own thoughts about the future of FCIL law librarianship in the United States are based on the UW placement experience and the excellent works represented in the research for this chapter. An environmental scan of legal education and the practice of law would note these factors:

- The global recession has tightened budgets for many organisations including law libraries
- Many countries are skipping printed legal materials and moving quickly to the development of electronic legal resources for their own laws and regulations; however this movement is hampered in many developing countries by inadequate infrastructure and training
- The globalisation of legal practice is undiminished
- The growth of FCIL curriculum in law schools continues
- The surge in LLM programmes in US law schools that attract foreign-trained lawyers is unabated

It is unlikely that the degree requirements for FCIL law library jobs will change; the MLIS is sure to be a requirement and either the JD, LLB or LLM a probable qualification. While there is a large potential group of language- and law-qualified students in international LLM programmes in the United States, these lawyers will need to earn the MLIS before they begin to solve the shortage of FCIL librarian specialists. There are many barriers to obtaining the MLIS degree in the United States for the international student with an American LLM degree, including financing the education, visa issues, the lack of an American JD, and English language proficiency.

Take as an example the specialised law librarianship programme at the University of Washington's Information School. The academic programme is only one year (compared to most graduate MLIS programmes which extend to two years) and is premised on the fact that students understand the US legal system, are very familiar with US legal materials, are fluent in English, and understand libraries in the US culture. The JD is required of all applicants. Requiring an international student to take a longer general librarianship MLIS programme exacerbates the financial and visa issues of the students. In MLIS programmes where there are limited law librarianship courses, the international student may get the important introduction to library culture and services in the United States but will miss out on the important law librarianship courses. Unless American law libraries decide to subsidise an MLIS education for international LLM students, another wave of immigrants working in FCIL specialist jobs in the United States does not seem likely. Therefore we have been growing our own, so to speak.

How are employers filling vacant FCIL positions? When experienced FCIL law librarians are not available to fill vacancies, employers choose one of three options.

Some law library directors realise they will have to train their own FCIL specialists and look for entry-level librarians who are smart, trainable and motivated. No doubt, many employers keep in mind Wade's 'necessary aptitude' as they screen candidates (Wade 2006, 56–8). As part of a self-assessment, Wade suggests these factors should be considered:

- value of lifelong learning
- attitude of thriftiness and frugality
- advancement in FCIL law librarianship likely requires relocation
- facility with new technologies to improve learning and access to information
- aptitude and proficiency for foreign language study
- sincere interest in library patrons to understand their needs
- desire to help students learn through teaching

A more extensive list can be found in the Planning Session notes from the 1991 National Legal Resources meeting (Wright 1991, 2).

A second group of employers have integrated FCIL services with regular library services in reference, collection development, digitisation and acquisition. As probably the most interesting example, Harvard Law School Library announced its reorganisation in August 2009 to do just that (Palfrey 2009). Even though the FCIL librarians still have titles indicating their specialisation, they are working more broadly in reference outside of the standard FCIL subject areas.

A third group of employers are trying to provide FCIL services with current and available staff trained to do new, additional work. This may mean training staff to do work they have not done before in order to take advantage of the language skills of the library's staff.

Whether a library employs dedicated FCIL specialists or librarians who work on FCIL projects as part of their broader portfolios, there is still a need for baseline knowledge.

Some argue that the availability of so much foreign and international law on the Internet has changed the playing field, that there is no baseline of knowledge needed for FCIL librarianship, and that, even if minimum knowledge is required, it can easily be acquired through currently available resources. It is hard to believe, however, that basic understanding of the materials and structure of foreign and international law is not needed. Informal education is most likely to continue in the future to provide this needed content. Certainly, most libraries will prefer to employ law librarians with such background.

Excellent articles by Wade and Rumsey offer ideas for self-education (Wade 2006; Rumsey 2006), and could be used to create a handbook or checklist to educate and train new FCIL specialists and librarians who will have FCIL responsibilities. A new law librarian seeking to become a self-taught FCIL specialist may be overwhelmed by the amount of literature and the number of legal research guides available. Even to be self-taught would be an exhausting enterprise. The FCIL-SIS would perform a great service if it provided very specific advice to gain the education and training needed to be an FCIL law librarian.

The AALL FCIL-SIS provides directories of country specialists who can help with FCIL problems and encourages mentoring, exchanges of personnel, externships and foreign placements. The SIS also offers programmes at AALL annual meetings and identifies other conferences that might appeal to FCIL-inspired law librarians. Missing, however, is the systematic exposure to the basics of foreign, comparative and international law research that was provided by the Institutes of the mid-1990s. This suggests a need to reform the programming process in the AALL or look to other organisations for collaboration opportunities, or both.

Library graduate trainee programmes such as the one at the Institute of Advanced Legal Studies in London (http://ials.sas.ac.uk) are a wonderful way to enhance FCIL education either before or after earning the MLIS.

Partnering with other interested organisations like the IALL and ASIL has been successful and educational programming and professional development opportunities abound. However, the basic and systematic education that specialists in FCIL need is not likely to be provided by these organisations, whose programmes are aimed primarily at practising professionals.

Using newer technology to make educational programming accessible at the desktop certainly helps but those efforts will miss the mark without knowing the educational objectives to be achieved. More programming itself is not the answer; programming focused on providing a basic level of knowledge seems to be what is needed. It may be necessary to recreate the AALL Institutes in content, if not in the same format.

It is possible that law libraries will move away from hiring FCIL specialists. This will actually increase the number of law librarians who need informal education and on-the-job learning to become competent in foreign, comparative and international law research. Concentration on all types of educational programming for law librarians who do FCIL work and gathering basic materials for self-education will be critical for law librarians to provide the services needed in the global economy. The same rationale that William Stern provided in 1947 for the collection of foreign legal materials in American law libraries applies today for educating law librarians who work with foreign, comparative and international legal materials.

Education and Training of Law Librarians – Worldwide

History

The wide range of educational opportunities for law librarians in the United States includes specialised law librarianship programmes and courses in graduate library and information schools, a robust professional association with education of its members a priority, and a myriad of internships, externships and directed fieldwork opportunities. Elsewhere, law librarianship includes fewer formal educational opportunities but is blessed with creative informal and self-study opportunities.

Professional organisations around the world have had very positive effects on education of law librarians but none has had a more profound impact worldwide than the International Association of Law Libraries. Founded in 1959, the IALL is today a worldwide, cooperative, non-profit organisation, which (in pertinent part):

- promotes the dissemination of legal information
- advances the education of law librarians and other legal information professionals
- supports educational and professional opportunities for newer legal information professionals, especially those from developing nations
- shares legal knowledge and scholarship through the *International Journal of Legal Information* and other publications, and its website
- fosters networking and mentoring among legal information professionals

- supports and encourages the development of national and international legal information policies and promotes free access to legal information

The IALL's first educational programme was held in conjunction with the AALL Annual Meeting in Boston, Massachusetts in 1961. By 1966, the IALL was hosting multi-day conferences at prestigious institutions around the globe under the title 'Courses on International Law Librarianship'. The first course was offered in Luxembourg on 'Librarianship and Legal Bibliography with Special Reference to European Law'. IALL courses have been held annually since 1993. Being held in locations around the world had prompted greater visibility for law librarianship and motivated countries to improve education, networking and recognition for law librarianship and law libraries.

The IALL also promotes its educational mission through a journal which began in September 1960 as the *IALL Bulletin*, then became the *International Journal of Law Libraries*, and finally the *International Journal of Legal Information* in 1982. From the beginning the *IJLI* has published articles of substance about the law, legal information and law librarianship worldwide, as well as the proceedings of the annual courses (Schwerin 1984, 5). Many other publications have been written and published by IALL member librarians over the years.

Regional and country-wide professional organisations for law librarians have been fostered by the IALL, and the educational programming offered by these organisations has certainly helped develop better-educated law librarian professionals in many countries. A list of the websites for these organisations is on the IALL website (International Association of Law Libraries 2010).

The IALL joined the International Federal of Library Associations (IFLA) in 1961 and has regularly sponsored educational programmes in conjunction with IFLA annual meetings. In 2005 a Section of Law Libraries (www.ifla.org/en/law-libraries) was formed within the IFLA at the prompting of the IALL and AALL. The Section's mission differs from the IALL in that the IFLA is recognised by international organisations like UNESCO, WIPO and others as the information policy voice for all library associations worldwide. The IFLA Section of Law Libraries has over 40 members and holds programmes as part of the IFLA's on-site educational mission.

One of the most active professional law library organisations is the British and Irish Association of Law Librarians (BIALL) founded in 1969. BIALL has several affiliate groups, specialised by function or geography, a robust publications programme, an annual course on the law for librarians, partnerships with related law librarianship groups to sponsor the Joint Study Institutes, and outstanding substantive programmes at its annual conference. The original impetus for the BIALL was to provide an organisation that could bring legal information specialists (law librarians) together to solve common problems and provide educational opportunities for its members. Institutional memberships in the BIALL are encouraged, but the focus of this group remains primarily on the professional development of the people who are its members.

Current

Over the past 50 years the profession of law librarianship has gathered momentum within and outside the United States. While there are no formal specialised educational programmes in law librarianship outside the United States, informal education and self-study provide significant opportunities for law librarians throughout the world.

There has been experimentation with law librarianship courses in formal postgraduate degrees in librarianship, for example at the University of Sheffield library school and the partnership between the Department of Law and the College of Librarianship at the University of Wales College, Aberystwyth (Jeffries 1989, 684). As of 1997 the University of Northumbria at Newcastle offered a Legal Information Unit as part of their programme in the Department of Information and Library Management (Day 1997, 192–3). To be successful, such courses require significant enrolment. Information schools in the United States sometimes keep costs low by having librarians from their institution's law school teach the law librarianship course for no additional compensation. Considering the obstacles, it is not surprising that these formal options are no longer offered.

The law library at the Institute of Advanced Legal Studies (IALS) at the University of London is one of the most important trainers of legal information specialists outside the United States. Created as a work opportunity for one year, this graduate internship normally precedes postgraduate work in library and information science. An intensive in-house training programme accompanies the intern work in the IALS law library. Each intern gets a strong introduction to foreign, comparative, and international legal materials as a graduate library trainee. There is a post-library school approved in-post training course and a range of short-term internships for overseas law librarians, as well as a non-stipendiary Visiting Fellowship in Law Librarianship.

Informal educational opportunities through the programmes and publications sponsored by professional law librarian associations like the IALL, BIALL, CALL and others provide one important source of law librarianship education. Finding creative ways to provide informal education and training for law librarianship offers some hope of improving the educational situation worldwide.

Twinning (partnering with a similar type of law library in another country) is an innovative way to improve the education of law librarians. The Australian Law Librarians' Association started a twinning programme in 1991 with law libraries in the South Pacific. Today, that programme, administered by the Lionel Murphy Library at the Australian Attorney-General's Department, involves 14 Australian and New Zealand law libraries twinned with 22 law libraries in the Cook Islands, Fiji, the Solomon Islands, and others. South Pacific law librarians have received advice, legal materials for their libraries, and training from their twins. Twinning with the law library at Middlesex University has been important for an Albanian University, the University of Tirana (Lynnwood 2003, 204).

The IALL gives grants for law librarians to visit or work in other countries' law libraries (IALL 2009). In addition, in the United States the FCIL-SIS keeps a registry of foreign placements and internship opportunities (American Association of Law Libraries. FCIL-SIS 2009). Both groups also have scholarships to host foreign law librarians at their professional annual conferences.

Other law librarians have worked with their institution or government to take advantage of opportunities to help educate law librarians in other countries. One law librarian became a US Information Service/American Library Association Library Fellow and taught legal research and trained law library staff in Ghana (Elliot 1998, 7). A request for training on legal research databases at the University of Jos in Nigeria attracted a volunteer law librarian from the IALS in the UK (Power 2007, 18). A law librarian in the United States working with her law school's clinic became interested in the Extraordinary Chambers in the Courts of Cambodia (ECCC) and volunteered to help centralise the courts' library materials and services (Thai-Parker 2009, 1 and 3).

A fascinating opportunity to create a comprehensive collection of Afghan and international laws available to the Afghan people was funded by USAID and the Afghanistan American Bar Association Rule of Law Initiative (ABA-ROLI). The Independent National Legal Training Center in Kabul was administered by an Afghan national law librarian. Most unfortunately funding for this important law library has been on hold since early 2009 and at the time of writing the law library is closed (Olejnikova 2009, 5).

The BIALL has aimed to improve understanding of the law and legal literature among its members by offering a Legal Foundations Course in cooperation with the University of Westminster (Fogg 2005, 160–61). A very popular one-day seminar on Legal Reference Materials is also offered in London through the BIALL. Given the cost of sponsoring such regular informal educational offerings, such programming is usually limited to the largest and most developed countries.

The current landscape of education and training for law librarians worldwide is evolving with most emphasis on informal education and self-study. Strong leadership will be needed worldwide to improve the depth and availability of educational opportunities.

Future

What is the future for law librarianship education worldwide? Can robust programmes such as those in the United States be created in other countries?

In advocating for the creation of the International Association of Law Libraries in 1972, Dahlmanns stated:

> Widely, law libraries are still but marginal enterprises with their stewards lacking the bare necessities. These circumstances alone would already call for a worldwide professional organization. But there is more to this alliance. For it operates into three directions. For one it provides, in self-helping fashion, the individual member with basic information and material to master his daily intricate chores and through personal contact aids in solving questions before they turn into real problems. For another it tries to achieve a universal appreciation of the basic functions of law libraries and their staff in order to improve their training, their facilities and status. Finally its aims and purposes immediately serve society as a whole which in every respect eventually depends upon the complete, reliable and speedy availability of the law. Seldom has a concern of one group been identical to such an extent with that of society in general. (Dahlmanns 1972, 11)

But even with the IALL's successes, the profession of law librarianship remains marginalised in many countries. It is important to note some of the conditions which have slowed the progress of the profession.

First, because in most countries legal education is not a postgraduate programme, law libraries are often part of larger academic libraries where specialisation as law librarians may be discouraged. Supporting undergraduates earning their LLB is very different from the support required in a professional, postgraduate programme such as in the United States. This contributes to a lack of visibility for the academic law library and the law librarian. Faculty scholarship, which receives heavy support in the United States by law librarians, is also much more limited in undergraduate programmes. The availability of more JD, LLM and PhD programmes could change this dramatically. At the IALS, for example, the law library is a robust service organisation which does support graduate librarianship education.

Second, the lack of resources hampers efforts in many countries to train law librarians and to provide user services and develop collections. Often this results from lack of recognition of the role that law librarians can play in access to legal information. This refrain is repeated consistently in the literature. It is a vicious circle: law librarians are not professionally trained, which leads to low status and inability to increase resource levels; the lack of resources then contributes to lack of respect.

Third, in developing countries with many competing priorities, law librarianship will necessarily take a backseat to development of the rule of law and legal systems. However, useful and accessible legal information systems should be created as part of the establishment of the rule of law. Law librarians can play, and in some cases have played, major roles in such efforts.

Fourth, legal information in many countries is only available to the few or only to those who have the resources to pay. The culture of access to the law as a driver of democracy is not an aspiration or value in all countries. The development of free legal information systems may be challenged by established commercial vendors, unstable electrical sources, unreliable access to the Internet, and poor equipment and training.

Fifth, most countries lack standards for law libraries, including the education and training of the law library staff. The standards of the American Bar Association, the body that accredits law schools in the United States, are quite specific regarding the role of the law library within the law school. No other type of US law library has the same kind of standards, although guidelines have been drafted for court, state and county law libraries. However, concerns about lack of standards may beg the more fundamental question: is the role of the law library deemed to be central to the mission of the institution of which it is a part?

Sixth, most countries lack a formal association of professionals through which law librarians can cooperate and work together to improve the legal information environment. In countries with strong professional associations, collaboration and networking can improve the status and education of law librarians (Philippine Group of Law Librarians 2010).

It is clear that in countries where some law librarians hold law degrees, their status and the status of their profession is more highly regarded at all levels of government and in society.

How can law librarianship acquire the respect and professionalism needed to provide effective leadership in the information age? Certainly, the efforts already being made in individual countries to plan educational programmes, to offer assistance and exchanges, and to help create legal information systems that can be accessed by everyone must continue.

I would urge two other efforts. First, bring law librarianship education to lawyers in other countries who have an interest in access to legal information. Such programmes might facilitate foreign lawyers coming to the United States for an educational programme of several weeks or programmes could be developed that can be taught to lawyers and law librarians in their home countries. Perhaps an LLM in Law Librarianship degree could be created in the United States. Since the LLM is highly prized in the rest of the world, as demonstrated by the large number of foreign lawyers in LLM programmes in the United States, this could be a way to enhance the profession of law librarianship elsewhere. Such a programme would have to be carefully crafted to include significant library science courses as these will be the most needed by foreign nationals who already have a legal education.

The second effort is no more than a continuation of the good work that is being done already. Partnerships and collaboration must be extended in many different directions, all with the aim of improving the profession of law librarianship around the world.

Within any one country, partnerships might pair law schools with library schools to improve education for law librarianship and recruit lawyers into the field. Collaboration between law libraries to provide better service and improve the profession's visibility through professional organisations is another option. Pairing the country's professional organisation with a law school to bring needed education to law librarians has also met with success. Encouraging the best law libraries to provide internships or exchanges or temporary work opportunities for law librarians in other parts of the country is another possibility.

What can be done country-to-country? Twinning to match law library to law library and encouraging sister arrangements between law schools in different countries can have beneficial consequences. Working with government agencies and non-profit foundations to spread the influence of law librarianship through conferences and other professional activities in other countries is also an option, as is including education for law librarianship as a topic at international conferences about legal information, such as the 2009 US–China Conference on Legal Information and Law Libraries held in Beijing.

Law librarians in the United States can help improve the state of law librarianship in developing countries by seeking partnerships with the various projects sponsored by the American Bar Association Rule of Law Initiative (ABA-ROLI). To date few law librarians have been involved in these efforts but they provide excellent opportunities to work on the ground floor in building a country's legal information infrastructure, while improving law libraries and the skills of those who work in them.

Conclusion

This chapter has explored the history, current practices, and future of the education and training of law librarians by looking at the models in the United States, the model for training specialised US law librarians in foreign, comparative and international law work, and the many models of law librarianship education throughout the world. A set of competencies, such as those approved by the AALL, can help define the profession of law librarianship in any country and offer a framework for the educational needs of the profession. Every type of education from the formal to the informal to on-the-job learning must be present in a robust educational environment.

The law librarian's connection to the practice of law and legal education must be strengthened in many parts of the world. This closer connection to a profession of status and respect may help give law librarianship the stature to play an important role in the expansion of the rule of law throughout the world. Thus, an emphasis on training and educational programmes aimed at lawyers with a passion for the dissemination of legal information should be a priority.

Dahlmanns said it best as he gave his assessment of the achievements of the first 10 years of the IALL:

> Law is an indispensable key to the progress of mankind and to a peaceful, worthy life on this planet. But law cannot be used unless it is available. As it is getting more and more complicated and mammoth in scope, it can increasingly be made available only by a specially trained and well equipped group of experts. These, the law librarians, are no more just keepers of their house and holdings. They must provide, no matter how intricate the task will be, full access to the law, and in addition supply the materials, reference and research services necessary to aid its future development. (Dahlmanns 1972, 11)

In an increasingly globalised world, the role of the law librarian is especially crucial. The need for education and training is equally compelling. All law librarians must be involved in making the law available and accessible to everyone. The success or failure of the rule of law may depend on our contributions as professional law librarians.

References

ABA Section of Legal Education and Admissions to the Bar (2008), *Average Amount Borrowed for Law School, 2001–2008*. Available at: www.abanet.org/legaled/statistics/charts/stats%20-%20 20.pdf, accessed 28 June 2010.

American Association of Law Libraries (1942–51), Annual Meeting Proceedings, Report of the Committee on Cooperation with Latin American Law Libraries, *Law Library Journal* vols. 35–44, various pages.

American Association of Law Libraries (1985), AALL Committees, *Law Library Journal* 77:4, 771.

American Association of Law Libraries (1988), *AALL Guidelines for Graduate Programs*. Available at: www.aallnet.org/about/graduate_guidelines.asp, accessed 3 February 2010.

American Association of Law Libraries (2001), *Competencies of Law Librarians*. Available at: www.aallnet.org/prodev/competencies.asp, accessed 3 February 2010.

American Association of Law Libraries (2009), *Directory and Handbook 2009/10* (Chicago: AALL).

American Association of Law Libraries. Foreign, Comparative and International Law Special Interest Section (2009), *Internships and International Exchanges*. Available at: www.aallnet.org/sis/fcilsis/internships.html, accessed 3 January 2010.

Brock, A. (1974), 'Law Libraries and Librarians: A Revisionist History; or More that You Ever Wanted to Know', *Law Library Journal* 67:3, 325–61.

Conference of Law Library Educators. Available at: http://lib.law.washington.edu/colle, accessed 3 February 2010.

Dahlmanns, G. (1972), 'The International Association of Law Libraries: An Interim Account', *International Association of Law Libraries Bulletin* 28, 7–12.

Day, J. (1997), 'Bridging the Gap: Education for the Profession', *Law Librarian* 28:4, 191–6.

Elliot, C. (1998), 'A Library Fellow in Equatorial West Africa', *Information Outlook* 2:7, 8.

Fogg, H. (2005), 'A Change of Name at Twenty – BIALL's Legal Foundations Course', *Legal Information Management* 5:3, 160–1.

Gasaway, L. and Chiorazzi, M. (eds) (1996), *Law Librarianship: Historical Perspectives*. AALL Publications Series, no. 52 (Littleton: Rothman).

Hartman, K. (2009), 'From a Distance', *American Libraries* 40:10, 48–51. Available at: http://americanlibrariesmagazine.org/archives/issue/october-2009, accessed 14 March 2011.

Hazelton, P. (1993), 'Law Libraries as Special Libraries: An Educational Model', *Library Trends* 42:2, 319–41.

Houdek, F. (2008), *The First Century: One Hundred Years of AALL History, 1906–2005* (Buffalo: William S. Hein & Co.).

Houdek, F. and Goldner, S. (1989–), *AALL Annual Meetings: An Annotated Index of the Recordings*, 3 vols. AALL Publications Series, no. 32 (Littleton: Rothman for AALL) [Looseleaf].

IMLS Study on the Future of the Library Workforce, Panel on Law Libraries. Available at: www.aallnet.org/services/future_of_library_workforce.pdf, accessed 4 February 2010.

International Association of Law Libraries (2009), *IALL Placement and Internship Grants*. Available at: http://iall.org/internship.html, accessed 3 January 2010.

International Association of Law Libraries (2010). Available at: www.iall.org, accessed 3 January 2010.

Jeffries, J. (1989), 'Law Librarianship in the United Kingdom: Preparation, the Profession, and the British and Irish Association of Law Librarians', *Law Library Journal* 81:4, 679–90.

Kulpa, L. (1996), 'The Contributions and Unique Role of Foreign-Born, Foreign-Educated Law Librarians', in Gasaway and Chiorazzi (1996).

The Law Library of Congress at 175: A Timeline (published online February 2007). Available at: www.loc.gov/law/about/history/law-timeline.pdf, accessed 2 January 2010.

Louis-Jacques, L. (1991), 'Training the Next Generation of Foreign and International Law Librarians: Challenges of the Nineties and Beyond – An Issue Brief', in Wright (1992).

Lynnwood, W. (2003), 'Legal Education in Albania Programme (LEAP)', *Legal Information Management* 3:3/4, 204.

Mueller, H. and Kehoe, P. (1983), *Law Librarianship: A Handbook*, 2 vols. AALL Publications Series, no. 19 (Littleton: Rothman for AALL).

Oakley, R. (1990), 'Education for Law Librarianship: Avoiding the Trade School Mentality', *Journal of Library Administration* 11:3, 147–64.

Olejnikova, L. (2009), 'FCIL Schaffer Grant Recipient Masoud Speaks at AALL', *FCIL-SIS Newsletter* 24:1, 5.

Palfrey, J. (2009), Reorganizing the Harvard Law School Library. *Et Seq.; the Harvard Law School Library Blog* (posted 10 August 2009). Available at: http://etseq.law.harvard.edu/index.php/site/reorganizing_the_harvard_law_school_library, accessed 18 January 2010.

Philippine Group of Law Librarian. Available at: http://pgll.org, accessed 18 January 2010.

Pimsleur, M. (1962–), *Pimsleur's Checklists of Basic American Legal Publications*. AALL Publications Series, no. 4 (Littleton: Rothman for AALL) [Looseleaf].

Power, G. (2007), 'Visit to the Faculty of Law in the University of Jos, Nigeria', *Legal Information Management* 7:1, 17–19.

Price, M. (1989), 'Setting the Legal Information Agenda for the Year 2000: Preliminary Report of the National Legal Resources Committee', *Law Library Journal* 81:2, 349–75.

Rumsey, M. (2006), 'Foreign and International Law Librarianship', *Legal Reference Services Quarterly* 25:2/3, 73–88.

Schwerin, K. (1984), 'The International Association of Law Libraries: Its Beginnings', *International Journal of Legal Information* 12:1/2, 1–6.

Thai-Parker, T. (2009), 'ECCC Library in Cambodia', *FCIL-SIS Newsletter* 23:3, 1 and 3–4.

US News and World Report, *Best Graduate Schools*. Available at: http://grad-schools.usnews.rankingsandreviews.com, accessed 28 January 2010.

Wade, D. (1991), 'The Education, Training and Experience of Foreign and International Law Librarians Now Working in United States Law Libraries', in Wright (1992).

Wade, D. (2006), 'Wisdom from Mount Nebo (Hiei): Advice to a Young Person Aspiring to Become a Foreign and International Law Librarian', *Legal Reference Services Quarterly* 25:2/3, 51–71.

Wright, J. (1991), 'Training the Next Generation of Foreign and International Law Librarians: Planning Session', in Wright (1992).

Wright, J. (1992), *Training the Future Generation of International and Foreign Law Librarians: Issues Papers, Summary Plan* (Chicago: AALL).

Chapter 4
Global Legal Education and its Implications for Legal Information Management

Michael Crommelin and Carole Hinchcliff

Introduction

Global legal education presents a multi-faceted challenge. First, there is curriculum. While familiar, this matter now has a new dimension. In recent years, globalisation has moved from the periphery to the centre of curriculum design. Closely related to curriculum is the matter of pedagogy. Globalisation has accelerated the trend away from learning the rules towards resolving the problems. Then there is the matter of participation in legal education. Globalisation has promoted geographical, social and cultural diversity among faculty and students involved in legal education. This is an exciting development. Lastly, there is the matter of programme structure, reflecting myriad arrangements for institutional collaboration and increasing mobility of faculty and students. All of these aspects of global legal education have significant implications for the management of legal information.

Curriculum

Public international law, private international law, comparative law and foreign law have all been included in the curriculum of many, perhaps most, law schools for many years. These subjects were regarded as exotic extras when law schools were driven by parochial concerns, providing legal education to prepare their graduates for practice in their local jurisdictions. Globalisation now requires a fundamental reconsideration of the place of these subjects in the curriculum.

The explosive growth in public international law in the second half of the twentieth century has been a significant factor in this inexorable process. In terms of subject matter, public international law now extends to conflict avoidance and resolution, employment and labour relations, trade, health, human rights, refugees, indigenous peoples, natural resources, the environment, the sea, space, banking and finance, intellectual property, poverty and crime, with a correspondingly broad array of organisations and institutions such as the United Nations,[1] International Court of Justice,[2] International Labour Organization,[3] World Trade Organization,[4] World Health Organization,[5]

1 Available at: www.un.org, accessed 28 September 2010.

2 Available at: www.icj-cij.org/homepage/index.php, accessed 28 September 2010.

3 Available at: www.ilo.org/global/lang--en/index.htm, accessed 28 September 2010.

4 Available at: www.wto.org, accessed 28 September 2010.

5 Available at: www.who.int/en, accessed 28 September 2010.

World Bank,[6] International Monetary Fund,[7] G20,[8] World Intellectual Property Organization[9] and International Criminal Court.[10]

In addition, there has been the emergence of regional, supranational organisations, perhaps best exemplified by the Council of Europe,[11] the European Union[12] and the Asia-Pacific Economic Cooperation forum.[13] The judicial branches of the first two of these, the European Court of Human Rights[14] and the European Court of Justice,[15] have exerted significant influence on the development of the law not only within their jurisdictional boundaries (extensive in themselves) but also far beyond. The result has been a proliferation of legal doctrine from sources outside national jurisdictions, on an unprecedented scale.

During the same period, aspects of globalisation such as mobility of people, goods, services and capital across national boundaries, aided if not driven by the revolution in information technology, have added a new dimension to private international law which is now relevant to activities which are commonplace rather than exceptional. Again there has been extraordinary growth in legal organisations and legal doctrine in response to these commercial and human demands.

Comparative law and foreign law have also acquired a relevance which they previously lacked, derived from practical application. No longer are they the preserve of legal theorists. Like domestic law, they too respond to the needs of people, corporations and states enmeshed in a global community which increasingly recognises interdependence before isolation. Their significance in legal education has strengthened accordingly.

Initially, it was not difficult to find a place for international law, comparative law and foreign law in the law curriculum. That place was on the edge. In most common law jurisdictions, at least, there was a clear demarcation between compulsory and elective components of the curriculum, firmly established several decades ago. The compulsory component typically represented between 50 and 60 per cent of the total curriculum. It was devoted almost exclusively to domestic law. International law, comparative law and foreign law belonged in the elective component, which was sufficiently elastic to accommodate their remarkable growth without intruding upon the core elements of the curriculum.

Only in recent times has this comfortable arrangement come under threat, in belated recognition of the significance of international law, comparative law and foreign law in the modern era of globalisation. That significance is, in part, quantitative. The sheer weight of international law, comparative law and foreign law can no longer be ignored. However, the significance is also qualitative, because international law, comparative law and foreign law increasingly impinge directly and indirectly upon domestic legal systems, regardless of the doctrinal basis for reception of international law into domestic law. Legal barriers have seldom, if ever, held back the tides of economic and social change. Confronted with globalisation, these barriers are demonstrating unsurprising permeability.

The principal task of curriculum design has therefore become the relocation of international law, comparative law and foreign law from the elective periphery to the compulsory core. That

6 Available at: www.worldbank.org, accessed 28 September 2010.

7 Available at: www.imf.org/external/index.htm, accessed 28 September 2010.

8 Available at: www.g20.org, accessed 28 September 2010.

9 Available at: www.wipo.int/portal/index.html.en, accessed 28 September 2010.

10 Available at: www.icc-cpi.int, accessed 28 September 2010.

11 Available at: www.coe.int, accessed 28 September 2010.

12 Available at: http://europa.eu, accessed 28 September 2010.

13 Available at: www.apec.org, accessed 28 September 2010.Available at:

14 Available at: www.echr.coe.int/echr, accessed 28 September 2010.

15 Available at: http://europa.eu/institutions/inst/justice/index_en.htm, accessed 28 September 2010.

is indeed a formidable task, if only for the reason that the centrality of domestic law must not be destroyed in the process. Success requires the integration of domestic law into the emerging global legal system, and redefinition of the relationships between domestic, international, comparative and foreign law. Many law schools have embraced this challenge with enthusiasm in recent years.

In Australia, this development has occurred at the initiative of law schools rather than professional admitting bodies. The prescribed areas of knowledge recommended by the Law Admissions Consultative Committee[16] for adoption by professional admitting bodies in Australian states and territories in the accreditation of law degrees for admission to legal practice do not include international law, comparative law and foreign law.[17] In contrast, the CALD Standards for Australian Law Schools adopted by the Council for Australian Law Deans on 17 November 2009 urge law schools to develop, through the curriculum, knowledge and understanding of 'international and comparative perspectives on Australian law and of international developments in the law' (Council of Australian Law Deans 2009, 2.3.3).

The current Melbourne JD curriculum, introduced in 2008, includes two compulsory courses taught in the first semester, providing frameworks in public law and private law for understanding the place of Australian law in the global legal system. Principles of Public Law establishes the foundation for public international law, constitutional law and administrative law, while Obligations performs a similar role for contracts, property, equity, unjust enrichment and remedies. The Melbourne JD curriculum also has an integrated structure together with a relatively high proportion of compulsory courses (17 out of 24) permitting sequential, coherent development of legal understanding and skills. One of the notable features of this structure is the opportunity which it provides to establish links between the subject matter of courses taught concurrently, and to explore the artificial boundaries between such courses, through joint teaching and assessment. This opportunity promotes understanding of the place of a domestic legal system in the global legal order.

It may be that legal scholars in federal systems can draw upon some previous experience in the performance of this important task of curriculum design. More than a century ago, in the United States and Australia, for example, it became necessary to reshape legal education in response to the emergence of national legal systems from state and colonial origins. Meeting this need took time, and was far from easy. But it was successfully accomplished, just as legal education is being transformed today in many parts of the European Union. The task of global legal integration is much more difficult, even though the outcome seems inevitable.

One thing is certain. The proliferation of legal sources, doctrine and material in a global information market requires innovation and imaginative approaches to the management of legal information and mastery of the various technologies which themselves drive globalisation. These requirements have themselves shaped the law curriculum.

Those who learned about legal systems, legal information and legal research in the era of print had to visit a law library. Primary legal materials, largely cases, statutes and subordinate legislation, were arranged by jurisdiction. It was essential to know which of these titles were authorised or official, and to understand the hierarchy of secondary legal materials and commentary that would assist in the identification and application of the law in resolving legal problems.

---

16 LACC (commonly known as the 'Priestley Committee') consists of representatives of the Law Admitting Authority in each Australian jurisdiction, the Council of Australian Law Deans, the Australasian Professional Legal Education Council and the Law Council of Australia. It is responsible to the Australian and New Zealand Council of Chief Justices. See http://www.lawcouncil.asn.au/lacc.cfm, accessed 26 April 2011.

17 Available at: http://www.lawcouncil.asn.au/shadomx/apps/fms/fmsdownload.cfm?file_uuid=30440CF8-1C23-CACD-222E-59CF362D9B5A&siteName=lca, accessed 26 April, 2011.

Print resources still support a law school's teaching and learning activities, albeit through smaller collections that have been weeded of multiple copies, especially of case reports and sets of legislation. Nowadays, however, using a computer or mobile device and the Internet, students can readily gain access to a vast body of legal information from anywhere at any time. It is not necessary for them to visit a law library to consult discrete sets of books. They no longer routinely use traditional print tools such as legal encyclopaedias and digests to become familiar with the structure and context of law. Instead, they must achieve mastery of the online versions of these tools and other electronic databases and the new search technologies, along with an understanding of the significance of information within legal systems and hierarchies. The law curriculum must provide them with this capacity.

Pedagogy

As Jeffrey Lehman has said, 'American legal education … deemphasizes the mastery of any particular body of rules and instead stresses the development of intellectual skills' (Lehman 2008). This pedagogical development occurred, probably as a matter of necessity, when American legal education redirected its emphasis away from state law towards the national legal system. The shift did not exclude state law from the ambit of legal education. Instead, it placed state law firmly in the broader context of the national legal system.

Today, national law itself must be understood in the context of the global legal system. This understanding requires the development of intellectual skills commensurate with the complexity of the global legal order. International law, comparative law and foreign law, along with domestic law, make invaluable contributions to lawyers' development of these skills by providing the essential ingredients of context and complexity.

Australian law deals with common social problems in particular ways. An Australian legal education must provide the capacity to identify both the problems and the rules devised by legal institutions for resolving them. But nowadays that capacity is merely the first step in a much longer journey. Legal education should also include an appreciation that other societies may well adopt other rules for dealing with such problems and that the social consequences of rules differ depending on context. This is where comparative law and foreign law come into their own, by demonstrating not only the diversity of legal rules but also the rationale for and consequences of selection of particular rules. International law, in the meantime, provides a large body of international rules, some destined for incorporation into domestic legal systems, others providing benchmarks for critical evaluation of domestic laws against international norms.

This approach to legal education depends upon access to a broad and ever increasing range of sources of primary and secondary law and, given the current interdisciplinary approaches to legal education, often sources of information relating to other disciplines. The capacity to locate information efficiently, determine its significance, and apply that information in resolving legal problems is one of the critical skills to be developed in legal education. Professional law librarians have the expertise required to teach these skills.

Mobility

A notable consequence of globalisation has been a marked change in the composition of the student body in many law schools. Overseas students, drawn from a wide range of countries, now constitute

20 per cent of the student body at Melbourne Law School. They bring very different social, cultural, educational and legal backgrounds. Student exchange programmes, which have proliferated during the last decade or so, have also contributed significantly to changes in the composition of the student body.

The increasingly heterogeneous student body has three important consequences. First, it reinforces the rationale for the relocation of international law, comparative law and foreign law from the periphery to the core of the law curriculum. Second, it provides further justification for the pedagogical shift from mastery of rules to development of intellectual skills. Finally, and most importantly, it provides a valuable opportunity during student learning to exploit the differences in student backgrounds, through class discussions and activities, joint student work in syndicates and other groups, and informal student interaction. Legal education has long recognised the importance of students' learning from their peers. That learning is strengthened immeasurably by the rich diversity of student cohorts in the global era.

The mobility which is part and parcel of the modern era of globalisation allows engagement of 'global faculty' on a far more flexible and extensive basis than the long established arrangements for appointment of visiting scholars. Each year about 50 international faculty teach courses in the Melbourne Law Masters programme. The courses are taught in a highly intensive format, based on models developed in graduate business schools. These international faculty usually make regular visits to Melbourne, every year or two. They add a significant global dimension to the Masters programme, with their international expertise and experience. They also make a broader contribution to the intellectual life and outlook of the law school. This contribution, while difficult to quantify, is undoubtedly important. It provides a platform for the continuous exchange of ideas at a personal level, an understanding of the history and philosophy of legal education at the institutional level, and the development of enduring institutional links based on shared values.

Programme Structure

The Australian regulatory framework provides considerable scope for experimentation in programme structure and delivery. In general, such matters have traditionally been left to particular universities to determine, subject to the overall scrutiny of the Australian Universities Quality Agency (AUQA).[18] Legislation has been recently introduced into the Australian Parliament to establish a new regulatory body, the Tertiary Education Quality and Standards Agency (TEQSA). The Council of Australian Law Deans (CALD) Standards for Australian Law Schools are non-prescriptive regarding programme structure; with regard to delivery, they require '[a]ppropriate tuition, either face to face or electronically' (Council of Australian Law Deans 2009, 2.2.3). There is a long-standing practice of 'external' delivery of legal education in Australia, previously by correspondence, nowadays electronically. Professional admitting bodies have also left matters of programme structure and delivery largely to law schools, which have established a wide variety of arrangements for international delivery of part of their programmes, often in conjunction with overseas institutions.

Simon Chesterman has suggested that 'the first mark of globalization as distinct from transnationalization was the move from exchange programmes to double-degree programmes across national jurisdictions' (Chesterman 2009, 884). There are now many examples of dual degree programmes. For example, Melbourne students may combine their JD with the BCL at Oxford, the JD or the LLM at New York University, or the LLM in Chinese Business Law at the Chinese University of Hong Kong.

---

18 Available at: www.auqa.edu.au [and] http://www.auqa.edu.au/aboutauqa/teqsa/, accessed 26 April 2011.

Most dual degree programmes involve little if any joint responsibility for curriculum design and teaching. Instead, each law school assumes responsibility for the design and teaching of its degree component. One notable exception is NYU@NUS, the dual degree programme offering master of laws degrees from each of the participating institutions, New York University and National University of Singapore, taught in Singapore by NYU, NUS and visiting faculty (Chesterman 2009, 884). Other exceptions are now emerging in Europe in the form of LLM programmes designed and taught jointly by law schools in different countries.

The next stage involves collaboration between law schools in different jurisdictions, preferably jurisdictions with different legal systems, in the design and delivery of 'first' law degrees such as the JD and the LLB. These degrees usually provide a large part of the legal education required for admission to practise law in a particular jurisdiction, unlike the LLM which provides advanced, often specialised education in selected fields of law unrelated to admission requirements. This stage promotes understanding of domestic law in a global context, but requires imagination and ingenuity to accommodate competing demands between professional competence and international perspective.

A step in this direction was taken in 2008 with the establishment of the Center for Transnational Legal Studies[19] in London by a consortium of 10 law schools led by Georgetown Law Center. Melbourne Law School was a founding member. The CTLS programme of international, transnational and comparative law is designed to educate students for practice in the global legal environment. It is taught by faculty drawn from participating law schools for a semester or an academic year. Joint course design and teaching are strongly encouraged, as too is research collaboration. Students come from law schools which are members of the consortium or affiliated with the Center. They obtain credit for courses completed at the Center from their home institutions towards their JD or LLB programmes.

The Association of Transnational Law Schools (ATLAS) is a consortium of 10 law schools established to pursue the general themes of transnational law and governance and comparative law and globalisation, especially at the doctoral level. Its membership comprises London School of Economics and Political Science; New York University; Osgoode Hall Law School of York University (Toronto); University of Cape Town; Universidad de Deusto (Bilbao); Melbourne Law School; Université de Montréal; Bucerius Law School (Hamburg); Bar-Ilan University (Tel Aviv); and National University of Singapore. The signature activity of ATLAS is the annual Agora, an intensive residential programme for doctoral candidates in law drawn from its member institutions (Bevans and McKay 2009).

Implications for Legal Information Management

The modern world of legal information is a hybrid of print and digital primary and secondary sources, a world revolutionised by the Internet. In addition to the commercial legal publishing arena, dominated by a few multinational corporations which publish both print and online legal materials, there are courts, other government bodies, universities and private entities that now provide free access to legal information. Only 20 years ago, commercial publishers were the major providers of both print and online legal information, a situation which restricted access to subscribers and their authorised users. Since then, the Internet has broadened access immeasurably.

---

19 Available at: http://ctls.georgetown.edu, accessed 24 August 2010.

The volume of available online material can present the legal researcher with an overwhelming number of choices of where to find legal information. It also means that law librarians spend more time than ever comparing and evaluating sources of information to determine when paid subscription services better meet the needs of their users than free Internet services.[20] Instead of purchasing online legal material, law libraries subscribe to online legal information because this is the business model adopted by most online legal publishers. In the academic law library environment, this shift from ownership to access entails annual reviews of subscriptions and negotiation of the pricing and terms of complex licence agreements. Cancellation of an online subscription for a journal can result in loss of access to back issues of that journal.

The move to provide e-books in academic law libraries has begun, now that larger numbers of scholarly law e-book titles are available, although e-textbooks are yet to be widely available for law subjects. E-books offer the capability to search text, some annotating and note-taking features, and limited printing. These features vary depending on the platform. A computer or an e-reading device is required to read the book; at this stage, portable e-readers are far from ubiquitous. E-books can be available any time anywhere, which suits mobile law students and faculty. However, print books are still favoured by many because they provide an immersive reading experience that facilitates reflection. Given the realities of current budgets, academic law libraries cannot currently afford routinely to provide law monographs in both electronic and print formats. Difficult choices lie ahead.

Standards for academic law library collections now acknowledge that law libraries can provide print or online formats in the combination that best meets the needs of the law school's user community. In Australia, section 5 of the CALD Standards for Australian Law Schools prescribes standards for law libraries, including minimum standards for the law collection. Where a law school provides teaching in the law of any overseas legal system, the collection must include sufficient primary legal materials and official publications from that legal system. The collection may be accessible in printed form or electronically, or both. No minimum requirements are prescribed for the print component of the collection (Council of Australian Law Deans 2009, 5.4).

Surveys for comparing and measuring academic law libraries were developed in the print world, based on the assumptions that everyone paid the same price for the material and that ownership of more titles and volumes translated into a bigger, better law library. The shift in emphasis from ownership of information to access to information has required a shift in mindset for law librarians. Determining the amount of money spent on online information for use of law school communities is fraught with difficulties. Law schools often pay different amounts for subscriptions, depending on factors such as the size of the user community, whether a law school subscribes as part of a larger university, or whether a law school participates in a consortium. Such arrangements cast doubt upon the practice of comparing law libraries by measuring inputs such as expenditure on monographs and texts, serials, staffing and other library services. In response, there has been a call to define, measure and compare the outputs and impacts of services provided by academic law libraries. The debates on how to do this have now begun, but the answers remain elusive.

For most law faculty and students, online sources of cases, legislation and law journals are used first, and print materials are consulted (often begrudgingly) only when online versions are not available. While law librarians have welcomed free Internet access to primary legal materials, especially online information from courts and legislatures, they have also expressed concern that it is not usually apparent whether an online primary source is authentic and will be permanently available into the future. In the print world of legal materials, the trustworthiness

20 See Chapter 13, this volume, at 263.

of official or authorised versions of cases or legislation is indisputable because the text is fixed at the point of publication. The status of official or authorised sources is also clearly established. In the online world, there are no comparable assurances. In 2006, the American Association of Law Libraries conducted a survey of US primary legal resources in 50 states to ascertain the trustworthiness of state high and intermediate appellate cases, statutes and session laws, administrative codes and registers. The report concluded that these primary sources of state law could not be deemed trustworthy. While a number of these state online resources are 'official', none was 'authenticated' or afforded ready authentication by standard methods (Matthews and Baish 2007).

Law librarians have been enthusiastic supporters of the Free Access to Law Movement[21] that has made freely available a wide variety of legal information. In 1992, Cornell University Law School capitalised on the advent of the World Wide Web by establishing the Legal Information Institute,[22] which began providing free access to United States federal statutes and United States Supreme Court decisions. In 1993, LexUM[23] began as the precursor to the Canadian Legal Information Institute.[24] AustLII[25] was launched in 1995 to disseminate primary law from Australian jurisdictions. The LIIs have increased in number and are continuing to provide easy access to a variety of legal materials (Greenleaf 2010). In a vision for 'a legal information ecosystem that is global in scope', John Palfrey has called for a commitment by bodies creating law throughout the world to making available online versions of primary law as the official versions. These stable, open versions of laws in standardised formats would be mirrored or backed up by libraries in other jurisdictions. Palfrey claims that such an open, greener ecosystem will promote the rule of law and facilitate more effective teaching and learning about the law, better research by scholars, and improved cross-cultural understanding (Palfrey 2010, 181).

Some academic law libraries have collection development policies that now state a preference for online over print for specified categories of legal materials such as law journals. Space is at a premium in most law schools and many academic libraries have moved print volumes off-site or weeded them to expand student study space or to provide for other faculty and student uses. Nevertheless, in a world where not all legal materials are available online in suitable, stable formats, legal researchers are still reliant on historical collections of print material. Academic law librarians must ensure that a minimal number of print copies of primary legal materials is retained and that archives of born-digital legal information are created and preserved for the benefit of future legal researchers. Examples of such initiatives are the Legal Information Preservation Alliance's print retention programme for United States legal materials and its Chesapeake Project to create a model regional digital archive of United States legal materials.[26] In the United Kingdom, a group of law libraries that collects foreign law has prepared an inventory of their holdings and is working cooperatively to ensure that current foreign law collections for different jurisdictions continue to be available and that legal researchers know where this information resides.[27]

21 Available at: http://www.worldlii.org/worldlii/declaration/, accessed 26 April 2011.

22 Available at: www.law.cornell.edu, accessed 28 September 2010.

23 Available at: www.lexum.com/en/index.html, accessed 28 September 2010.

24 Available at: www.canlii.org, accessed 28 September 2010.

25 Available at: www.austlii.edu.au, accessed 28 September 2010.

26 Available at: www.aallnet.org/committee/lipa/history.asp, accessed 24 August 2010.

27 FLARE, Foreign Law Research Group. Available at: http://ials.sas.ac.uk/flare/flare.htm, accessed 24 August 2010.

Law libraries now support legal scholarship by providing services extending beyond traditional reference and research assistance to the editors of their law reviews and journals. These services extend to finding documents to verify citations and to identifying online versions of documents that differ from print versions. Law librarians have also worked closely with the law review authors engaged in the preparation of new editions of legal citation guides such as the Harvard Uniform System of Citation and the Australian Guide to Legal Citation.

In 2009, a group of academic law library directors from some of the most prestigious United States law schools announced the Durham Statement on Open Access to Legal Scholarship.[28] The Durham Statement calls for the cessation of the publishing of law journals in print format and reliance instead on 'electronic publication coupled with a commitment to keep the electronic versions in stable, open digital formats'. The Statement proposes that law schools take responsibility for the publication of their law reviews, journals and other new forms of legal scholarship, and for making legal scholarship available free to all around the globe now and into the future (Danner 2010).

In recent years the literature of law librarianship has embarked upon a lively discussion of the concept of information literacy and how this needs to be incorporated in the teaching and learning of legal research skills. The Law Student Research Competency Standards Task Force of the American Association of Law Libraries has produced a set of Law Student Research Competency and Information Literacy Principles that students should acquire during their law school education (American Association of Law Libraries [2011]). Another US-based initiative is the Boulder Statement on Legal Research Education which outlines the relationship between legal educational theories and legal research instruction and forms the foundation upon which a signature pedagogy for legal research education is being developed.[29] This statement builds upon the influential report by the Carnegie Foundation on legal education in the United States (Sullivan et al. 2007). In Australia, the CALD Standards for Australian Law Schools encourage law schools to develop 'the intellectual and practical skills needed to research and analyse the law from primary sources, and to apply the findings of such work to the solution of legal problems' (Council of Australian Law Deans 2009, 2.3.3). Information literacy is implicit in this exhortation; however, law schools are left to determine the content and method of legal research instruction. Law librarians who teach legal research may, as needed, look to general information literacy frameworks developed by academic libraries and organisations such as the American Association of College & Research Libraries (ACRL).[30] No distinction is drawn between print and electronic forms of information.

Conclusion

Law operates within and between societies, responding to needs for governance, order, justice and economic prosperity. Globalisation has altered the social landscape dramatically by subjecting existing societies to powerful external influences and by drawing those societies into complex supranational organisations, regional and global, which are themselves evolving rapidly into societies in their own right. This process has required the rapid development of international law

28 Available at: http://cyber.law.harvard.edu/publications/durhamstatement, accessed 24 August 2010.

29 Available at: www.colorado.edu/law/events/legalResearchEducation.pdf, accessed 24 August 2010.

30 Available at: http://www.ala.org/ala/mgrps/divs/acrl/issues/infolit/overview/intro/index.cfm, accessed 26 April 2011.

and legal institutions leading inevitably to a fundamental reappraisal of the relationship between the various components, national and international, of the global legal order.

The impact of globalisation on legal education is indelible. The challenges presented by global legal education are widely acknowledged. While there is no lack of enthusiasm for meeting those challenges, the required transformation of legal education is still in its infancy. Student mobility has underlined the urgency of the situation, and information technology has ensured access to the necessary materials. Curriculum and pedagogy, however, need much more imagination and work. While steps have been taken in the right direction, they have so far been understandably tentative. There are signs that law schools may rely increasingly on collaboration rather than individual effort in meeting the demands of curriculum and pedagogy. To the extent that this collaboration crosses jurisdictional boundaries, it will reflect the true spirit of globalisation.

The changes already under way in curriculum and pedagogy have enormous implications for the management of legal information. The incorporation of international law, comparative law and foreign law in the compulsory core of the law curriculum depends heavily on faculty and student access to and understanding of information sources that were previously in the domain of library specialists. The pedagogical shift in emphasis from learning rules to development of intellectual skills provides the opportunity for faculty and students to acquire the capacity to work effectively beyond their domestic jurisdiction. Law librarians must be drawn further into the task of designing the core curriculum and must participate directly in the learning process devised for acquisition of mastery over a broad range of complex sources of legal information. The demarcation line between faculty and librarians, already blurred, seems destined to become even less clear, and perhaps disappear.

References

American Association of Law Libraries (2011), *Law Student Research Competencies and Information Literacy Principles*. Available at: http://www.aallnet.org/about/LawStudentResearchCompetenciesInformationLiteracyPrinciples.pdf, accessed 28 April 2011.

Bevans, P. and McKay, J. (2009), 'The Association of Transnational Law Schools' Agora: An Experiment in Graduate Legal Pedagogy', *German Law Journal* 10, 929–57. Available at: www.germanlawjournal.com/pdfs/Vol10No07/PDF_Vol_10_No_07_SI_929-958_Bevans_McKay.pdf, accessed 24 August 2010.

Chesterman, S. (2009), 'The Evolution of Legal Education: Internationalization, Transnationalization, Globalization', *German Law Journal* 10, 877–88. Available at: www.germanlawjournal.com/pdfs/Vol10No07/PDF_Vol_10_No_07_SI_877-888_Chesterman.pdf, accessed 24 August 2010.

Council of Australian Law Deans (2009), *The CALD Standards for Australian Law Schools*. Available at: www.cald.asn.au/resources.htm, accessed 12 September 2010.

Danner, R. (2010), 'The Durham Statement on Open Access One Year Later: Preservation and Access to Legal Scholarship' published online on 15 June 2010. Available at: http://ssrn.com/abstract=1628622, accessed 24 August 2010.

Greenleaf, G. (2010), 'The Global Development of Free Access to Legal Information', *European Journal of Law and Technology* 1:1. Available at: http://ejlt.org//article/view/17, accessed 24 August 2010.

Lehman, J. (2008), *China's First US-Style Law School: Five Narratives in Search of an Author*, Woodrow Wilson International Center for Scholars, 21 May 2008. Available at: http://jeffreylehman.com/wilson_center_five_narrativ.html, accessed 18 August 2010.

Matthews, R. and Baish, M. (2007), *State-by-State Report on Authentication of Online Legal Resources* (Chicago: American Association of Law Libraries. Access to Electronic Legal Information Committee and Washington Affairs Office). Available at: www.aallnet.org/aallwash/authenreport.asp, accessed 24 August 2010.

Palfrey, J. (2010), 'Cornerstones of Law Libraries for an Era of Digital-Plus', *Law Library Journal* 102, 171–90. Available at: http://www.aallnet.org/products/pub_llj_v102n02.asp, accessed April 26 2011.

Sullivan, W., Colby, A., Welch Wegner, J., Bond, L. and Shulman, L. (2007), *Educating Lawyers: Preparation for the Profession of Law* (San Francisco: Jossey-Bass).

Chapter 5
Global Legal Practice and Information Management

Tanya du Plessis

The Sophistication is Under the Hood

In business and social conversation 'wheels' are often the topic. Many young graduates strive to own the coupé they've been dreaming of since their first year of studies, candidate attorneys envy directors' seats (behind the wheels of the sleekest autos imaginable) and many law firm directors are sweating hard and billing long hours in pursuit of the newest 4x4 to drive into the sunset, if they ever take the time off, particularly in a global workplace.

Somehow a lawyer's work never stops, not in South Africa and it seems also not in the rest of the world. Are the sunsets the same in New York, New Delhi, London and Melbourne? No, for obvious reasons, skylines differ, but it's the same sun. Like a wheel in motion the same earth provides us with a location. Some things we know, we even know the 'location' of that knowledge (hopefully in our own head); many things we don't know. Who are we to think we 'know' things, how do we get to know things, what is it you know and how can I know what you know, especially if I don't know you and you don't know what I need to know? Should we get to know each other (better) and manage to put what we know together to apply what we know to best effect? How can we continue that effect?

If the Basic Design has Good Effect then Keep it

The basic design of automobiles hasn't changed that much over the years but there are some recent features that enhance the driving experience, improve safety and attempt to reduce the environmental impact. The same goes for information management technology. The basics will probably remain largely unchanged but systems, tools and techniques to manage data, information and knowledge are continuously improved. The analogy of a car to information management may seem absurd, but think about it: technology to manage information has been with us for a very, very long time. We need to keep in mind one rule: wheels are round for a reason.

Wheels are Round for a Reason

Time is not to be wasted on reinventing the wheel. Practising law, whether small firm or global legal practice, is an information- and knowledge-intensive business and a variety of functions, including information and knowledge management, play a fundamental role in the efficiency of legal practitioners. Lawyers rely on information, be it print or electronic resources. Except for internal information sources and systems, law firms invest in value-added external sources, systems, applications, toolkits, software-as-a-service solutions, cloud computing, etc. from commercial vendors and IT service providers. Law firms use different tools to build and maintain a strategic set of knowledge assets and foster client relationships. Global legal practice especially depends on technologies such as intranets, portals, extranets and other applications for communicating, organising and accessing their valuable work product. Lawyers' work product mostly falls into the category of 'knowledge work', although not all work is 'knowledge' and not all knowledge can be managed.

Defining Knowledge

Years of discussion and attempts to define data, information and knowledge 'management' signify its complexity (or obscurity). Managing data and information, it seems, is less complex but adds the tacit knowledge of humans and the intangible collective memory of an organisation to the equation and many would conclude that knowledge cannot be managed, it can only be shared. To share knowledge is not to manage knowledge. Can all knowledge be shared? Can shared knowledge be managed? Can all knowledge be managed?

Unlike information, the nature of knowledge is about the beliefs and commitment of individuals. People organise, select, learn and judge according to their 'internal knowledge' as much as, or even more than, from information and logic. The power of knowledge comes from the values and commitment of individuals and has a great impact on the knowledge of an organisation (Davenport and Prusak 2000; Nonaka and Takeuchi 1995). Understanding the nature of knowledge is simplified by exploring aspects such as the creation, location, levels and conversion of different types of knowledge.

Knowledge Types

Generally knowledge can be categorised as either tacit or explicit. Tacit knowledge is the 'contextual' type of knowledge which Takeuchi (1998) describes as an individual's intuition, perspectives, beliefs, values, insights, hunches, inspirations and so forth. Tacit knowledge has a technical dimension which encompasses the kind of skills or 'know-how' called 'expertise' gained after years of practice. Tacit knowledge also has a cognitive dimension which refers to the mental models stirred by beliefs, perceptions, ideals, values and emotions so ingrained in an individual that they are taken for granted and very difficult to articulate and share with others. Explicit knowledge, on the other hand, can be transmitted more readily between individuals both formally and systematically by way of words, numbers and symbols.

Considering the possibility of managing knowledge requires an outline of what constitutes knowledge. Nielsen and Michailova (2007, 316) describe three of the most widely recognised views on knowledge. First, knowledge may be viewed as an object. Managing such 'objects' will involve gathering, storing and transferring. In large organisations a department dedicated to these processes will have the centralised responsibility of information customisation. Secondly, knowledge may be seen as a process. Here the focus is on the process of knowledge flow, the sharing of primarily explicit knowledge found throughout the organisation. Third is the view of knowledge as a capability. Capability combines tacit and explicit knowledge and suggests the creation of new knowledge.

Knowledge Creation and Conversion

It can be assumed that new knowledge is sometimes created through the interaction between tacit and explicit knowledge and how it is transferred. Research by Faulconbridge (2007) shows that the relational networks between individuals in multinational law firms are vital to the creation of knowledge and knowledge conversion is vital to efficient legal practice. Knowledge conversion is mainly achieved through human interaction but can also take place by means of a technical system. Criticised or commended, the SECI model by Nonaka and Takeuchi (1995) is well-known and includes four modes of knowledge conversion: socialisation (tacit to tacit); externalisation (tacit to explicit); combination (explicit to explicit); and internalisation (explicit to tacit). Attempting to manage knowledge is essentially about encouraging these four knowledge conversion modes with the focus on the location of knowledge.

Knowledge Location

With knowledge created or residing in the minds of people, a major problem is how to make it locatable. Locating knowledge is a precondition for its effective and efficient use. This comprises finding out who has knowledge about what and where it is stored. This is especially a problem in organisations that act globally and where various knowledge levels are evident.

Knowledge Levels

Knowledge creation, conversion and location occur at various levels (Gottschalk 2007; Rusanow 2001; Kucza 2001).

Internal and External Knowledge Level At this level the distinction is made between internal knowledge, which is already adapted to the specific needs of the law firm, and external knowledge, which still needs to be adapted before it can be utilised.

Knowledge Holder's Level Here the distinction is made according to the holder of knowledge. A 'holder' is a person, a group, or the law firm as an entity. Group knowledge is the combined knowledge of individuals who collaborate on a shared interest (collaborative intelligence created within communities of practice). Knowledge at entity level is that embedded into the overall business processes: collective intelligence that layers the organisational memory.

Knowledge Scope Level This level of knowledge is concerned with the scope of knowledge, which has horizontal and vertical differences. The vertical difference is seen as varying from more abstract to less abstract knowledge. The horizontal difference includes knowledge from the more operational level to the more executive level.

Knowledge Depth Level This level of knowledge ranges from an initial awareness of facts and the ability to apply data to certain situations, resulting in appropriate actions to the level of specialisation, which entails a detailed understanding and ability to apply knowledge not only leading to appropriate actions but to innovation, advancement, expansion and higher levels of knowledge.

Fundamental Knowledge Level This level forms the base for the next two levels and includes the core knowledge required for daily operations. It involves general information, data and knowledge applications, such as knowledge of the law, knowledge of the courts, knowledge of clients and knowledge of procedures, and so forth.

Highly Relevant Knowledge Level This knowledge – applied knowledge – differentiates the law firm and its services from other firms (summating in business intelligence). Examples are: knowledge of successful procedural case handling, expert knowledge of important court rulings in specialist areas and highly specialised law applications.

Highest Value Knowledge Level

In the competitive business environment this knowledge – lentoid knowledge – combines and exceeds other knowledge levels. Lentoid knowledge (competitive intelligence) is what not only differentiates but accentuates 'the best' law firms. For example, this would be the firm that constantly reaches successful settlements through innovative applications of technology by experienced lawyers, not only highly skilled in law, but having a mix of individual, collaborative and collective thinking skills. Spengler (1928, 464), who echoed Nietzsche, claimed that the newspaper killed the book and with it individual thought and purpose. One wonders what Spengler would have made of the Internet, the World Wide Web, online resources, social media technology and the semantic web and whether he would perhaps revise his view on 'killing individual thought'. None of the abovementioned knowledge levels exist without individual input.

Knowledge and Value

Each of the knowledge levels should be directly aimed at effectively reaching the law firm's objectives. Leading law firms focus their knowledge on intensifying their business objectives. Business objectives are set according to client needs. What clients need is to experience value creation to their benefit. Value is created when knowledge is deployed strategically and in different ways. Value is created through the application of existing knowledge available for application when needed (actionable information). Value is furthermore created in new knowledge when new knowledge is required (innovative information). New knowledge is created as a result of knowledge conversion and knowledge linkage (connected intelligence). New knowledge is of value when it is made available to all the parties involved in offering a service to a client (distributed intelligence).

The real value of information (explicit knowledge) lies in the way it is applied. It is the knowledge embedded in the business processes of a firm and in the skills and expertise of individuals within the firm (tacit knowledge) that provide the firm with unique capabilities to deliver a product or service of high value to its clients. Instead of attempting to mechanise knowledge relationships, the nature and characteristics of knowledge should be taken into account when sharing and managing this resource (Khandelwal and Gottschalk 2003, 15). Examples of explicit and tacit legal information and knowledge are listed in Table 5.1.

Legal knowledge of all types, whether explicit or tacit, should be shared and managed effectively so that it is easily accessible whenever and wherever needed. At a fundamental level, information and knowledge in the practice of law are the intellectual capital of individual lawyers and law firms as corporate bodies. Managing this asset enhances its value and closes the gap between knowledge and action.

Knowledge and Action

The discussion above covered some of the more observable characteristics of knowledge, but knowledge is a complex result of intricate cognitive system processes influenced by many different internal and external factors. Firestone argues that if knowledge is information

Table 5.1 Examples of Explicit and Tacit Legal Information and Knowledge

Explicit legal information and knowledge	Tacit legal information and knowledge
• Case law • Legislation • Precedents • Best practice and model documents • Business and industry information • Checklists, methodologies, policies and procedures • Third party information, such as outside counsel, experts, judges and witnesses • Financial information relating to cases or matters	• Skills and expertise of lawyers • Skills and expertise of law firm staff • Client information • Lessons learned from past matters and projects • Tips at drafting pleadings or documents • Leads from experts on a research topic • Hints at arguing motions and applications • Casual conversations during law firm social events – informally sharing knowledge that has been acquired over time

transformed into capabilities for effective action then, in effect, knowledge is action (Firestone 2003, 170). This is not necessarily true. There exists a gap between knowledge and the capability for taking action. Rather, knowledge is a necessary condition for effective action, and not sufficient by itself.

Knowledge Management

The global economy suffers from modern organisations who find that organisational knowledge is often less an asset than a burden. Regardless of their already realised knowledge management (KM) activities, many global companies are yet to find effective ways of managing knowledge, a somewhat elusive multi-faceted concept (Hsieh et al. 2009, 4087).

Managing knowledge entails the processes that address the gap between knowledge and action. Knowledge per se cannot be managed, thus the concept of 'knowledge management' (KM) is hard to define, although many researchers have ventured in this direction:

- KM is the art of creating value by leveraging the intangible assets of an organisation, which involves the processes of capturing, distributing and effectively using knowledge (Davenport and Prusak 1998)
- KM is the organisation-wide focus on gaining knowledge from its own experience and the experience of others, and the judicious application of that knowledge (Wenig 1998)
- KM is accessing, evaluating, managing, organising, filtering and distributing information in an end-user friendly manner, blending an organisation's internal and external information and turning it into actionable knowledge via a technology platform (DiMattia and Oder 1997)
- KM is the creation of systems or processes in a learning environment that allow all employees to have access to the information resources they need to develop the knowledge necessary to do their jobs (Srikantaiah and Koenig 2008)
- KM is a framework and toolset for improving the organisation's knowledge infrastructure, aimed at getting the right knowledge to the right people in the right form at the right time (Schreiber 2000)

- KM is a discipline focused on systematic and innovative methods, practices and tools to simplify and improve the processes of acquiring, capturing, protecting, exchanging, using, sharing, distributing, understanding and creating knowledge. Generally speaking, this has to include the identification of the current state, the determination of needs, and the improvement of affected processes in order to address these needs. It is not only about managing knowledge-intensive activities within an organisation but also between organisations operating in the global workplace (Kucza 2001)

Embedded Spaces of Social Practice

Adding to these explanations of knowledge management, Faulconbridge (2007) highlights the link between KM and learning, and specifically global learning relevant to law firms where the 'production and management of knowledge across transnational organizational networks is essential'. He argues that diverse corporate networks need to be viewed as 'embedded spaces of social practice'. Note the word 'social': within these embedded spaces, learning often results due to knowledge conversion.

Whether 'collective intelligence', 'connected intelligence' and 'distributed intelligence' are only hypothetical murmurings of lecturers trying to find new angles to KM in coursework or whether the hype should be duly noticed in global legal practice is yet to be determined. As noticed by Lykourentzou et al. (2010, 18) one of the main challenges facing large organisations is the way in which 'machine-facilitated understanding of the collected corporate knowledge' is used by intelligent individuals performing knowledge intense tasks to develop their shared intelligence. The Lykourentzou research team investigated a novel expert peer matching algorithm, applied in a corporate wiki that searches the human network of the organisation to select the most appropriate peer employee who will best add value to a specific task at hand. The algorithm is based on feed-forward neural networks and operates within a space created by what is generally known as Web 2.0 technology. Socially established examples of Web 2.0 applications include wikis, online social networks, blogs and RSS feeds.

Also in this context the application of social media technologies in the form of Enterprise 2.0 applications is gaining popularity. There are many case studies[1] on the relevance of corporate wikis, blogs and RSS feeds in legal information, but social media technology in the workplace is not readily accepted. The most likely reason for lack of employer enthusiasm for technology similar to Facebook, YouTube and Twitter is the social nature of such networking sites, which are assumed to have a negative impact on employee productivity and not bear organisational benefit. Despite the negative hype, social media technology can be used to increase collaboration between individuals who share a common interest or goal (Ferreira and Du Plessis 2009). Concurring, Lykourentzou et al. (2010, 18) emphasise the need to develop Web 2.0 utilisation in the work environment to 'create new inferences regarding corporate issues, thus promoting the collective organizational intelligence' and to 'sustain competitive advantage in the global economy'.

The Virtual Workplace

The saying goes: 'if it is not broken, don't fix it', but 'it' must really work. For example, if the document management system has been proven to be effective then continue its use. However,

---

1 See, for example, the International Legal Technology Association (ILTA) case studies and law firm technology surveys available at www.iltanet.org and www.insidelegal.com, and various Melcrum strategic business information reports on how to transform your intranet, structure internal communication, measure internal communication, communicate business strategy to employees, and enhance communication with clients, www.melcrum.com, accessed 22 June 2010.

keep in mind that the definition of a document a century, decade, year, week and a second ago may differ significantly from now. Today a document may also include an avatar self-recording in Second Life, active online community competitive intelligence alerts, expert deposition testimonies, e-briefs and cases, and counsel emails, to list some examples. The virtual workplace features a variety of document types.[2]

The absence of time and space in virtual workplaces affects knowledge location and knowledge conversion. Communication differs in global virtual activities and shifts the foundations and applications of intelligent knowledge transfer. In virtual space 'human moments' happen and require attention to be given to the cultural implications of collaborative information technologies in international teams. Lawyers must deal with expectations of ubiquitous availability and suffer from stress related to connectivity, lack of privacy and steep virtual learning curves. Lawyers often have to adopt new media developments and operate in an augmented and delicate business reality which relies on networking and trust and involves virtual leadership, distance work relationships, virtual clients and less face-to-face mentoring opportunities. In the virtual workplace skills such as legal research and writing are evolving with progressively more sophisticated features being added to boilerplate systems[3] and the application of user-friendly twenty-first century Ontology-based Web Mark-up Languages (OWLs).[4]

Although a variety of technologies assist lawyers in virtual workplace collaboration, lawyers still have to build and negotiate virtual identity, become accustomed to virtual politics, learn virtual genderedness, address the divide effected by the lay-expert audience and adjust to rapid virtual enterprising to manage complex and high-risk assets. This description of a global virtual workplace leads to the question: do we perhaps need more than wheels?

Global Legal Practice: A Knowledge-Intensive Service Industry

The legal profession, in essence, provides knowledge-intensive services. Law firms sell legal and law-related expertise which relies mostly on internal 'human capital', that is the knowledge and experience of lawyers, paralegal staff and other staff. Segal-Horn and Dean (2006) and Jennings et al. (2009, 341) divide the law firm workforce into two human capital categories, namely partners and associates. Law firm partners (also referred to as directors) share ownership, they engage in providing services to clients, and strategically manage the firm. This category constitutes the highest-value knowledge levels. The second category typically constitutes the bulk of the professional workforce which engages primarily in practising law and they mainly represent the fundamental knowledge and highly relevant knowledge levels. The partnership governance model emphasises peer monitoring rather than supervision; it embraces mentoring and allows for collegiality in decision-making. This model is highly suitable for knowledge conversion, although the transfer of knowledge is all but a matter of course. Not all modern law firms follow this model;

2 Zemliansky and St. Amant (2008) provide a comprehensive overview of the virtual workplace and the new nature of business practices. Also see the many aspects of Internet law and regulation (which is not the focus of this chapter) to observe the many new types of legal resources resulting from work in virtual space (Smith et al. 2007).

3 Comprehensive knowledge repositories with templates to avoid misappropriation of knowledge in the virtual workplace, for example the application of forms and precedents.

4 OWLs form part of current semantic technologies and include ontology, taxonomies, folksonomies and clustering intended to provide context to content by formally describing concepts, terms and relationships within a given knowledge domain.

some firms have shifted the emphasis from values of professionalism to commercialism without compromising professional values, thereby not detracting from attempts to transfer knowledge. In this model of global law firms a shift is being made from professional autonomy to a 'managed commercial firm'. Notwithstanding the business model followed, global legal practice is often characterised by its merged nature.

Merged law firms participating in global legal practice may suffer from post-merger processes and integration issues. Many law firms face operational challenges related to common technology platforms, common systems practices, common human resources management practices, and common knowledge management systems. Global legal practice is continually challenged by its multinational and multicultural nature, especially in terms of knowledge management. Agourram (2009, 129) and Long (2009) identify the three most prominent current IT and KM challenges: to succeed firstly in implementing systems, then in measuring the outcome of the systems and finally in evaluating continuously the cost-efficiency of legal services delivery through the most effective use of constrained IT and KM budgets. Determining the efficiency of KM systems is complex and multilayered. Hsieh et al. (2009, 4098) suggest continuous improvement that must be governed by a strong maturity framework. This KM maturity measurement approach is aimed at assessing and benchmarking various aspects of law firm culture, KM processes and IT integration in a holistic manner.

Knowledge Management in Global Legal Practice

Knowledge management in a law firm is about providing the firm's lawyers and staff with cost-effective tools to support the daily processes through which an understanding of 'the law', 'the world' and 'the client' is created and shared in order to solve problems and address client needs. Many KM tools are computer-based and involve a variety of IT applications, such as word processing programmes combined with document assembly and document management systems, enterprise content management systems, expert identification, relational and object databases, groupware and workflow systems, data warehousing systems and data mining systems, and so forth. Law firms also apply financial management systems for the purpose of time billing and accounting, while information on client matters is kept in case management systems or client relationship management systems. These systems are often integrated with other business management information systems and marketing management systems that together make up only part of the law firm's KM infrastructure. The practice of KM – knowledge sharing – is a human and not a systems function (Rusanow 2001).

Many law firms have implemented intranets or more sophisticated technologies such as enterprise information portals and context-based searching tools. However, KM is not only technology-based: it centres on individual participation making it important to develop a KM culture that encourages and invests in the sharing of both explicit and tacit knowledge. Managing tacit knowledge is difficult, costly and considered by some to be impossible (Tseng 2008, 158–9). Because KM systems can be expensive, it is recommended that law firms consider the value of the knowledge in light of the cost of making it available. Some practical examples of law firm KM are listed in Table 5.2. These examples include both simple KM activities and fairly sophisticated KM applications.

From these examples it may be noted that not all KM activities require expensive KM applications. One example of an inexpensive KM system is Gurteen's Knowledge Cafés which entails people moving from one coffee hotspot to another, stirring what they know with what other people know into a rich aroma. A whiff or a burst – it is what differentiates successful law firms and this valuable resource needs to be managed.

Table 5.2 Examples of Knowledge Management in a Law Firm

KM activity or application	Result
Word processing and document management	Sample letters and notices for estate administrations can be saved, copied and modified for similar future transactions.
Ten-pinning	Ten 'hot' questions pertaining to a particular topic are asked to ten experts (internal and external) and their brief answers are documented, presented in an easy to read format and shared with others currently involved in the same practice area, case or transaction.
Annotation	Record-keeping of, for example, the dates of information changes, or why particular clauses were written the way they were written, or why and when they should or should not be used in particular situations.
Creating a computerised document drafting system	Automatically prepares legal documents, e.g. wills, trusts, and powers of attorney when information about the client's estate plan is entered.
Indexing for information searching and retrieval	Documents containing the results of legal research or analysis can be retrieved by subject, author, keywords, etc.
Creating spreadsheet templates	Performs financial analysis that may be reused for multiple clients, e.g. tax analysis on entering client specific data.
Intranet content management	All of the statutes, regulations, rulings, court rules, forms and other information that might be relevant to a particular law practice area are put together, organized with applicable metadata and made available via the law firm intranet in HTML or PDF format. This information can be accessed, shared and easily referred to by one or more lawyers without it being necessary that the lawyer visit the offices or law firm library.
Information management through loose-leaf updating	All forms needed for a particular type of transaction are put into a notebook, which is manually updated as new forms arrive.
Podcasting, RSS collection feeds and tagging	Library systems allowing librarians to build collections of feeds and podcasts and assign them to groups according to lawyer profiles. At the same time, lawyers and other staff involved in legal research should be able to submit and tag feeds and podcasts for distribution by the library system.
Individual blogging and ferreting individual blogs	Individuals may take the time to blog on something they know or what they have learned or what they remember that had been tried in the past and who did it. When others again seek someone who might know of a solution to a particular legal or regulatory hurdle it may take only a moment to scan the law firm's intranet blogosphere for valuable information.
Creating a law firm intranet wiki and twittering	To aggregate highly relevant material organised by industry or speciality and 'advertising' its availability.
Applying taxonomies in enterprise content management systems	To create and maintain classification structures within the law firm's information and knowledge systems to cluster related documents, to extract and generate key concepts, and to analyze content based on its context regardless of its format.
Creating of expert systems	Through artificial intelligence particular legal problems can be analysed and a set of complex standardised rules applied, e.g. application of grantor trust rules in selecting a trustee for a trust.

Value of Managing Legal Information and Knowledge

Culture and processes, particularly in global law firms, must adapt wholly to the digital economy to realise the potential of knowledge management. It is necessary to determine the value of managing law firm information and knowledge resources before initiating a costly firm-wide KM programme.

Prior to initiating KM in a law firm, it is important that key decision-makers discuss and define the precise outcome or benefits they expect to see in their own law firm. This could include augmenting efficiency and productivity through the reuse and sharing of experience and know-how to uphold quality of work product and to continue practitioner training, which could increase the value of service to the client. The value of KM can be measured in terms of its benefits, such as:

- Law firm information is captured, stored, organised, indexed, contextualised and can be retrieved
- Knowledge sharing
- Information security is ensured
- Workflow processes are established
- Information is distributed within the firm
- Quicker problem solving
- Better decision-making
- Enhanced customer relations
- Improved client service
- Productivity and efficiency
- Market visibility
- Increased lawyer work independence
- Competitive advantage
- Developing lawyer's research skills
- Fewer mistakes
- Less work redundancy
- Reduced research development costs
- Ability to direct work to skilled specialists
- Consistency of work product across offices or practice areas
- Faster delivery times
- Quality control
- Reduced frustration in searching for documents
- Interactivity and client collaboration

Knowledge Management Systems

Most of the benefits of KM stem from effective knowledge leveraging processes. These processes are aimed at improved efficiency in client service. Competitive law firms do not wish to waste valuable time and therefore pursue the benefits of KM. This involves making the information and knowledge that lawyers actually require accessible in systems that will both increase productivity and reduce stress. Such systems should give lawyers the ability to reduce time spent on, for example, research – with the emphasis on having high-value information readily accessible. For this, global law firms utilise intranet technologies or portal applications with secure access to internal and external information and knowledge and other necessary applications (for example email, calendaring and electronic conferencing) through a single user interface. If properly designed the portal can enhance a firm's workflow processes and improve processing of routine tasks and transactions, as well as responsiveness.

The main benefit of a portal or intranet designed with the specific law firm's needs in mind lies in the added value from the integration of its resources and the impetus towards collaboration and knowledge sharing. In this secure environment integration of information and knowledge from multiple locations is made possible. Lawyers apply document, content and case management systems for faster document retrieval and information processing, storage compaction, avoidance and easy recovery of human error, control over document security and access, provision of audit trails, business flow management and paperwork reduction. These robust systems are effectively applied to maintain large work product collections, ensuring the easy access, sharing and reusing of the law firm's intellectual capital as well as enabling easy utilisation of external resources. This promotes productivity, service quality and consistency.

Other benefits of case, practice and matter management systems include: a better understanding of client needs by investigating client profiles and their industries; establishing client trust, for example when a new contact lawyer has access to all relevant client or matter history; leveraging of client–lawyer relationships and network extension; better tracking of new business efforts; faster orientation in terms of possible conflicts of interest with new clients or matters; recording referrals in order to reward lucrative sources of business, ultimately increasing possible future work; and attractively positioning the law firm in the eyes of clients who could use the firm's services in other practice areas. These systems also facilitate collection of information, for example, industry trends and competitive threats the client might be facing and making new business proposals of relevance to the client; lawyer mobility; integration with other programmes, which saves time at typical practice management procedures, for example automated billing, document assembly, automatic reminders of due-dates and deadlines.

These benefits are obvious to most lawyers. Law librarians apply many other legal information management systems and KM applications typical to electronic libraries to provide access to primary and secondary sources of law. This is done without taking up much physical storage space and provides lawyers with the benefits of portability.

Law firm knowledge managers apply and maintain expertise systems, expert systems with artificial intelligence applications, heuristics, ontology, taxonomies, folksonomies and other semantic technologies in attempts to capture expert knowledge and to retain expertise even after an expert retires or leaves the firm. Although it has been argued that capturing human expertise is impossible, Shah (2003) discusses the feasibility of describing individual behaviour in a particular circumstance, then putting that description into a system that others can access, enabling them to learn from expert behaviour. This saves time and facilitates more productive client service. Litigation lawyers can also use these applications better to manage their work and the litigation itself through enhanced knowledge acquisition, organisation, retrieval, analysis and disclosure. In law firms where lawyers share a common language captured in legal ontology, they can better relate concepts across departments or practice areas, or across generations or cultural or racial areas, thus saving time and augmenting teamwork where necessary.

Knowledge Management and Communication Systems

A vital part of a law firm's information infrastructure is its communication system. Typical tools used for communication and collaboration in law firms include email, calendaring, group scheduling and shared task lists, time management and discussions programmes. Email has become a routine means to send memoranda, discuss strategy with clients, and mark up drafts of briefs with co-counsel and it has become a means to help improve the law firm's organisational memory. Most law firms have opted to move away from uncontrolled email systems and shared network drives as a repository for managing law firm knowledge. Used in association with an enterprise content management system, emails sent or received on a particular case or matter can now be gathered together and filed with every other client or case document or related information. This makes it easier for lawyers to find older messages and keep all records of the same matter together. Many systems also allow scanning of incoming letters, notices and documents to be stored as electronic images, making them more easily accessible. Also in a lawyer's research activities email is an easy method to canvass others who may provide insight or who has encountered a particular issue before. Email is a convenient, cost-effective and faster alternative for delivering legal correspondence, receiving information and transferring briefs and opinion letters, especially if the lawyer travels often. With the newest security mechanisms, sending confidential information can be done safely and securely. Using email and transferring all electronic correspondence to client files in a document or case management system makes discussion with clients and related other parties more accessible. Most systems will also allow researchers to perform full-text searches within past lawyer–client correspondence.

Lawyers may also apply social media technology such as online social networking and instant messaging to exchange information and discuss common problems, saving time and delivering a valuable service to the client. Social media technology is beneficial in fostering knowledge exchange among communities of practice members; converting lawyers from information consumers to knowledge contributors; enabling lawyers as knowledge workers to become collective innovators; stimulating strategic thinking; and identifying appropriate actions in collaboration with others. This expands the firm's knowledge base, leads to significant improvements in efficiency and effectiveness, and leads to organisational growth. Another way of communication in law firms is utilising slide shows, keynotes and other presentation programmes, which capture the results of lawyers' research activities in podcasts, interactive charts, diagrams, figures and tables, videotaped documents with rolling transcripts, scanned images and voice recordings, annotation and tagging. Combined with other IT applications presentation tools can help the lawyer organise and explore case information, for example by entering facts, issues, witnesses, allegations, documents and other critical data.

Although electronic communication and presentation programmes are not KM tools per se, if applied with KM objectives in mind, they become applications to manage information and knowledge for personal as well as firm-wide benefit.

Knowledge Management and Professional Development

The same principles hold true with regard to applications for learning and professional development in legal practice. In legal practice it is crucial to develop the skills of newcomer lawyers, paralegals, non-legal assistants, non-practising lawyers assigned to other duties, or any lawyer to perform more higher-level work. This is done through professional development programmes, informal and formal mentoring and training programmes. Recent developments in learning technologies provide a variety of e-learning applications to supplement traditional mentoring and learning programmes. Global law firms in particular are addressing the need for secure virtual learning environments (VLE) by implementing learning management systems in order quickly to link learners to subject matter experts and content. The VLE provides learning-tolerant individuals with access to relevant content and the subject knowledge of others residing in a centralised knowledge repository. Legal information in the VLE provides lawyers with just-in-time learning and on-demand learning opportunities. Thus, with integrated learning content management systems in place, lawyers can choose which training to undergo when it suits them best without physically attending a training session.

In legal research, activities such as problem solving and brainstorming often include the processes of associative thought and relational learning. To some extent, applying KM taxonomy principles such as the ordering, structuring and highlighting of information relationships in the VLE, may help the legal researcher to reason more clearly. Also, the managing of information and knowledge into more structured form may help the researcher to place ideas in context. This might lead, for example, to more focused questioning of the facts and issues at hand.

More speculative but worth mentioning is the benefit of legal risk management. KM aims to create a learning environment for the effective transfer of knowledge that is necessary to avoid a professional negligence suit against a lawyer who might otherwise be ignorant of a particular legal development. As Kabene et al. (2006) and Kay (2003) point out, though knowledge systems can and should incorporate training of lawyers, they are not substitutes for legal training, but at best tools for acquiring knowledge, enabling lawyers to become more effective and efficient; developing expertise; and training lawyers to be acutely sensitive in risk avoidance.

Challenges to Knowledge Management in Law Firms

The discussion above featured tools and technologies used in knowledge management aimed at enhanced global legal practice. There are many other approaches to knowledge management in law firms, large and small. However, many benefits of KM have proved elusive to law firms faced with typical KM challenges.

The complex goals of KM, for example knowledge sharing and capturing expertise, cannot be solved by technology and information systems alone. This is made clear by the experiences of law firms facing the challenges of successfully implementing KM systems. For example, in the past it was hoped that document management systems could be applied to manage reusable work product. This required, amongst other things, the participation of fee earning lawyers to profile their documents, which was generally not successful because of lack of time and incentives and other cultural barriers (Khandelwal and Gottschalk 2003, 17). Except for the cultural barriers and KM issues that law firms need to address, global law firms are increasingly confronted with challenges in developing and maintaining portals, intranets and extranets with integrated systems for document and case management, legal information and expert systems, and secure communication and collaboration facilities.

In order to save the time of busy fee-earners, some law firms employ other staff or hire content managers to attend to KM activities. With large expenditure this approach can be successful, but limited budgets hamper maintaining KM benefits.

Large and small law firms are faced with challenges such as the inability to collect documents from the document management system, lack of reliability and functionality in some in-house developed precedent databases, and most often lack of coordination between systems. Law firms with portals and enterprise content management systems, installed to systematise the firm's workflow processes, are challenged by high costs, lengthy payback periods, software development risks, scalability and extensibility. Often law firms encounter obstacles to the dispersal of information and knowledge across departments and offices by systems that 'hide' these resources rather than make them retrievable. Then there is the challenge of digitising legal information when large amounts are not yet in electronic format. Sometimes the challenge is to structure vast amounts of electronic legal information stored in unstructured systems. Amidst the available customisation tools, some law firms are still faced with the challenge of providing personalised web access to their many internal and external users. Then, regardless of the many proactive measures taken, law firms remain to a lesser or larger extent challenged by viruses, systems failure, electricity failures and misuse by staff. These are only some of the challenges that law firms face in pursuing KM for competitive advantage.

Possible Solutions to Knowledge Management Challenges

Srikantaiah and Koenig (2008) advise perseverance in the face of KM challenges. KM in a law firm is never complete and new projects often bear new challenges that need to be remedied innovatively. Tseng (2008, 158–9) and Stearns and Roberts (2003) hold that the solution is to be found firstly not in something – and especially not in more technology, but in someone. There are no technology-only solutions to fill the knowledge management gap. People with specialised knowledge of information management are required to apply relevant technology as well as technology-free measures to meet the firm's KM challenges. However, these specialists alone cannot provide solutions customised to the KM needs of lawyers, because in general non-lawyers and non-practising lawyers cannot fully perceive the needs of lawyers. Therefore lawyers should be the main force behind developing a KM strategy and commit to its implementation, face its challenges and provide for sustained consistency in the quality of its information and knowledge infrastructures.

There are many technology solutions available in the marketplace today, offering a wide variety of web applications, intranet developments, portal packages (too many to list here). Obviously it will be sensible for law firms to investigate a variety of solutions and be intelligent in determining whether a solution is open and scalable to support future growth. Depending on the situation, for example, if the law firm has current business-specific third-party knowledge applications, it should be able to integrate them seamlessly in all its practice areas, especially the corporate and litigation departments. Hsieh et al. (2009, 4098) suggest approaching some of the challenges of KM in a law firm by guiding and managing change and continuously monitoring gaps in the current KM system. For example, if it is necessary to maintain or increase participation from some or all law firm knowledge workers, then it is necessary to lead the change that needs to take place for KM initiatives to be successful.

Identifying and Eliminating Gaps in the KM System

A global law firm's entire information infrastructure is not necessarily developed with knowledge management as its sole purpose in mind but the KM advantages are visible in the infrastructure's reach, depth, richness and aggregation capabilities. According to Hsieh et al.:

- *Reach* pertains to information access and connection, and the efficiency of such access
- *Richness* presumes that the information-carrying capacity of a medium is inherent because of its feedback capability, language type, and available communication cues
- *Depth* focuses on the detail and amount of information that can be effectively communicated over a medium
- *Aggregation* concerns the ability to store and quickly process information of large volumes of information drawn from multiple sources (Hsieh et al. 2009, 4087)

An effective knowledge management system should perform at least the following functions:

- capture information and knowledge
- store information
- organise and index information
- ensure information security
- facilitate access to information
- link people with information and knowledge sources
- deliver precision and relevance information retrieval
- establish a workflow process
- disseminate information

Every law firm has its own way of dealing with data, information and knowledge, and creates its own systems, structures and positions responsible for executing knowledge management; there is no standard KM method. But if the law firm's information infrastructure and other attempts to manage its knowledge do not provide the four capabilities (reach, richness, depth and aggregation) nor the basic functions mentioned above, then the firm's directors should reconsider the value of knowledge management.

The first problem is usually not with KM in itself but with how it is or was introduced to the firm. Secondly, due to the practical impossibility of truly sharing and capturing tacit knowledge, KM is doomed to fail in its attempts to convey the richness of the context in which it was originally applied. There are no easy solutions to resolve these issues. Because managing information and knowledge is key to the success of global legal practice it is necessary to be able to identify and address gaps in the law firm's KM system.

Knowledge Management System Typology

Firstly, obviously, one should know what type of system or systems are used by your firm. This can be quite confusing as there are countless systems, of which many are impracticable. The practical typology of KM systems by Nielsen and Michailova (2007) is useful.

In the KM system typology the first category is that of fragmented KM systems in which knowledge is mostly viewed as an object. The 'object' is predominantly explicit information, independent knowledge commonly available. The KM processes entail fragmented, unstructured efforts to store law firm information. Knowledge flows spontaneously and KM processes are not managed by designated KM units or positions; some individuals initiate ad hoc, informal KM activities; employees are not introduced to KM and are not aware of the benefits. This category of system does not reward individuals for knowledge sharing.

A second category is content-based KM systems. Here, too, knowledge is viewed as an object but structured efforts are aimed at storing and codifying information and knowledge. Knowledge flow is characterised by a top-down nature and specific individuals, for example project managers, engage in maintaining formal systems for managing knowledge content. The firm provides some training in content management and the issue of rewarding individuals for knowledge sharing emerges from time to time.

Thirdly, in process-based KM systems, knowledge is viewed as a process. Systems are developed and managed by KM units at the head office and KM subsidiaries play an important role in KM programmes. These programmes are mainly aimed at managing complex and explicit knowledge, both independent and systemic. Concerted systematic efforts are aimed at identifying, sharing and utilising existing knowledge. Law firm knowledge brokers are identified and their direct lateral knowledge flows are leveraged. Top management is involved and support formal systems to transfer knowledge between (mostly internal) knowledge sources. These firms are characterised by specific KM related training (either outsourced or offered by the firm's KM unit). Systems to recognise and reward individuals' knowledge sharing activities are mostly established, though not always fully implemented firm-wide.

The fourth category classifies knowledge as a capability. In capability-based KM systems, simple and complex, tacit and explicit, independent and systemic knowledge have the potential to lead to appropriate and timely action and to spark new knowledge creation. To do this, systematic efforts are aimed at creating, sharing and utilising not only existing knowledge but also new knowledge. This involves facilitating and leveraging the multilateral knowledge flows between internal as well as external knowledge brokers. Activities are managed throughout the entire firm and all management levels are involved, not only in KM activities but also in establishing a learning organisation. Multinational firms with these types of systems provide specific and elaborated KM training and functional reward systems related to learning and problem-solving are implemented.

Knowledge Management Gap Analysis

The above typology sets the scene for identifying gaps in a firm's KM approach. Further tools such as the gap analysis models suggested by Tseng (2008) and Fleisher and Bensoussan (2003) assist in identifying and addressing gaps with regard to global legal practice and information management. Gap analysis first pertains to asking questions then to identifying gaps between expectations and outcomes, possible reasons and solutions to the problem.

Some questions in the gap analysis process:

1. What are the absolute core software applications being used in the law firm?
2. When a server goes down, do you have to load up a new one with an operating system and application software?
3. What applications are used by one or two users only?
4. How dependent is day-to-day work on PC hardware and operating systems?
5. How are upgrades or new applications installed to desktops?
6. How proactive and responsive is the vendor to the needs of lawyers and the firm?
7. How stable is the vendor organisation's management structure?
8. Does the vendor have sufficient global representation?
9. How extensively does the vendor organisation invest annually in research and development?
10. How flexible is the vendor organisation's maintenance and yearly enhancement plans?
11. What does the vendor organisation's development plan cover?
12. How many third-party interfaces are supported by the vendor organisation?
13. What email management and information integration tools are provided?
14. What e-discovery, business intelligence[5] and competitive intelligence tools are delivered, specifically according to the law firm's needs?
15. What options are offered by the vendor in terms of software-as-a-service?
16. What are the advantages/risks to storing work-product 'outside' the firm?
17. Do lawyers travel with confidential documents on external memory devices?
18. Why would lawyers apply KM in their daily practice?
19. How easy is it to locate relevant documents or information in a timely fashion?
20. Do lawyers in the law firm suffer from too much or too little information?
21. How up-to-date are all law firm employees (not only lawyers) with relevant information?
22. When a lawyer leaves the firm, is that expertise then lost?
23. How do lawyers exchange key knowledge, learn and capture what they need for their work?
24. How can others in the firm tap into individual lawyers' skills and competencies that may be useful to the rest of the firm and to the client?
25. How do individual lawyers share the knowledge they generate, mediate or synthesise?
26. What internal and external contacts do individual lawyers use for referral purposes?
27. What approaches do lawyers follow to get the inside track on a problem?

---

5 Business intelligence technologies help a business to understand its information more quickly so that the company can make faster, more informed decisions.

28. What reward or incentive would induce a lawyer to share or exchange expertise?
29. How fast can the people who have the required knowledge be identified and consulted?
30. How effectively is cycle time reduced from receipt of client instructions to delivery or reporting on the completed task?
31. What cost-effective technology not currently used by the firm can be used to deliver high quality services called for by a generation of connected clients?
32. Are the approaches to using technology by different generations, for example entry-level attorneys, duly considered to improve client service and satisfaction?
33. Are all law firm staff (not only lawyers) eager to learn and continuously improve services?

Two examples of gaps in knowledge management systems:

> Gap A: the gap between the availability of information and knowledge required for a known purpose (single use) and the ready access to similar information and knowledge for future reference (multiple use).
> Gap B: limited by economic constraints, the gap between the support offered in terms of access to information and the level of information relevance to an individual's interests and needs.

Reasons for these gaps and possible solutions:

> Gap A: depending on the case or situation at hand a lawyer may need either to surface-read an information source quickly or read it in great depth. Time may be wasted and valuable information may be 'lost' for presentational reasons. Effective information management determines the ideal presentation of information to enable information end-users to extract the gist of information quickly. The KM system should help the user recollect, aggregate again when required and reuse the information. This may seem very basic but some systems somehow seem not really to fill this gap, especially when time is of the essence and intermediaries are not available. Solutions involve high-level knowledge management incorporating metadata, ontology, taxonomy, content management, email management, VLE content integration, flexible browsing and searching tools in conjunction with various collaboration tools.
> Gap B: the reason is often the focus on managing *all* information and not on assessing *specific* information needs. One solution may be in the form of automated recommendation systems 'on the premise that situational relevance is reflected in day-to-day decisions that people make within the network' (Attfield et al. 2010). The aim of KM should always be to reduce information overload. If the gap is identified as linking the right people with the right information and if you are working on a limited budget, then consider social media for bulletins, newsletters, tweets, profiling users and sending single items of high relevance to individuals.

Just Look For it Under the Hood

Keep in mind that the sophistication is probably under the hood, just look for it but don't look too far. Without the Internet and existing law firm information management technologies global legal practice and information management could probably not be described as either 'global' or 'managed'. Today the Internet is a rich source of information and competitive intelligence (CI). Law firms have access to a variety of specific search engines for searching the Web, business information websites, news providers, commercial and public databases, blogs, video, podcasts and scholarly sites. Many tracking sources are available to find people online; television and radio news transcripts are available; legislative monitoring and tracking services; RSS feeds from practice specific newsletters, business related newspapers, journals and news sources; tools for monitoring trends, companies and products; identification of company legal representation; online tools for competitor monitoring; Westlaw watch and Lexis trackers; benchmarking and country profiles; CI pathfinders and link collections; web directories and portals; legal information professional's listservs, too many to mention. The challenge, however, remains as in the words of Germain (2007):

> Information reliability, authenticity, precision, relevance, accuracy, version control. The challenges posed by digital libraries are many. The long term consequences of the digital world are unknown. There is so much information available, but without any context; this raises educational issues. In the field of law, it is not only a matter of digital competence, but also of legal consequence.

Lawyers as professionals are used to unpredictable situations and skilled in confronting complexity and anticipating potential problems or negatives and viewing matters from as many angles as possible in dispute resolution or in arranging agreements. They already have skills that are essential in global legal practice. This is a world of digital communications, transactions and transferring of electronic information, a world of digital relationships and interaction in virtual societies with virtual rules. In this type of world, lawyers may be required partly to shift their mindset to an environment where, in general, time is accelerated and distance is compressed, where change is rapid and continuous, and relationships are quickly formed but of uncertain duration, where information verification is uncertain, where anonymity rules and hacking prevails. It is in such a world where lawyers are increasingly expected to internalise information and knowledge management values to succeed as knowledge workers.

Sunset

When the sun sets in South Africa our lawyers are mostly still working. If you are in offices in New York, it's good morning; in Sydney, sleep tight. We may have access to the same resources, share knowledge and know our reasons for working long hours. We will also know that in global legal practice information and knowledge management is about not reinventing wheels but owning them, and not any set of wheels, only the best wheels will do.

Lawyers are generally rewarded for how highly effective they are in applying their knowledge. Lawyers have to excel in the speed and efficiency of creating and transferring legal knowledge. They can do this by skilfully utilising the most appropriate tools to streamline communication and reduce costs for their clients. For several years the significance of the information era has been growing on legal practitioners and reality has proven that, to a large extent, legal practice today depends on information and communication technologies. This tendency stresses the need for sound legal information and knowledge management practices. IT is a significant force that has made KM more achievable but it remains important to recognise that technology is an enabler of KM and that KM is not always technologically based. Through information management it is possible for people to access, retrieve, gather and share information, unconstrained by the boundaries of space and time. The key to building and maintaining strategic sets of knowledge assets in global legal practice is information and knowledge management.

References

Agourram, H. (2009), 'Defining information system success in Germany', *International Journal of Information Management* 29, 129–37.

Attfield, S., Blandford, A. and Makri, S. (2010), 'Social and interactional practices for disseminating current awareness information in an organizational setting', *Information Processing and Management* 46:6, 632–45.

Davenport, T. and Prusak, L. (2000), *Working Knowledge: How Organizations Manage What They Know* (Boston: Harvard Business School Press).

DiMattia, S. and Oder, N. (1997), 'Knowledge management: Hope, hype, or harbinger?', *Library Journal* 15, 33–5.

Faulconbridge, J. (2007), 'Relational networks of knowledge production in transnational law firms', *Geoforum* 38, 925–40.

Ferreira, A. and Du Plessis, T. (2009), 'The effect of online social networking on employee productivity', *South African Journal of Information Management* 11:1. Available at: www.sajim.co.za/index.php/SAJIM/issue/view/39, accessed 9 June 2010.

Firestone, J. (2003), *Enterprise Information Portals and Knowledge Management* (London: Butterworth-Heinemann).

Fleisher, C. and Bensoussan, B. (2003), *Strategic and Competitive Analysis: Methods and Techniques for Analyzing Business Competition* (Upper Saddle River: Pearson Education).

Germain, C. (2007), 'Legal information management in a global and digital age: Revolution and tradition', *International Journal of Legal Information* 35:1, Summer, 134–63. Available at: http://scholarship.law.cornell.edu/ijli/vol35/iss1/10, accessed 9 June 2010.

Gottschalk, P. (2007), 'Sharing knowledge in law firms', *International Journal of Innovation and Learning* 4:3, 255–73.

Hsieh, P., Lin, B. and Lin, C. (2009), 'The construction and application of knowledge navigator model (KNM™): An evaluation of knowledge management maturity', *Expert Systems with Applications* 36, 4087–100.

Jennings, J., Jennings, P. and Greenwood, R. (2009), 'Novelty and new firm performance: The case of employment systems in knowledge-intensive service organizations', *Journal of Business Venturing* 24, 338–59.

Kabene, S., King, P. and Skaini, N. (2006), 'Knowledge management in law firms', *Journal of Information Law and Technology* 1, 26 February 2007. Available at: http://go.warwick.ac.uk/jilt/2006_1/kabene, accessed 22 June 2010.

Kay, S. (2003), 'Cost, value and ROI for knowledge management in law firms'. Available at: www.llrx.com/features/kmcost.htm, accessed 4 September 2003.

Khandelwal, V. and Gottschalk, P. (2003), 'Information technology support for interorganizational knowledge transfer: An empirical study of law firms in Norway and Australia', *Information Resources Management Journal* 16:1, 14–23.

Kucza, T. (2001), *Knowledge Management Process Model VTT Publications 455:101* (Espoo: Technical Research Centre of Finland).

Long, W. (2009), 'Benchmarking survey: Law firm partnering 2009', *Practical Law*, 10 March 2009. Available at: http://ld.practicallaw.com/5-385-2396, accessed 9 June 2010.

Lykourentzou, I., Papadaki, K., Vergados, D., Polemi, D. and Loumos, V. (2010), 'CorpWiki: A self-regulating wiki to promote corporate collective intelligence through expert peer matching', *Information Sciences* 180, 18–38.

Nielsen, B. and Michailova, S. (2007), 'Knowledge management systems in multinational corporations: Typology and transitional dynamics', *Long Range Planning* 40, 314–40.

Nonaka, I. and Takeuchi, H. (1995), *The Knowledge-creating Company* (New York: Oxford University Press).

Rusanow, G. (2001), 'Culturing lawyers in knowledge management', *Knowledge Management* 1:1, 1, 5, 7, 9–11.

Schreiber, G. (2000), *Knowledge Engineering and Management: The CommonKADS Methodology* (Cambridge, MA: MIT Press).

Segal-Horn, S. and Dean, A. (2006), 'The globalization of law firms: Managerial issues', *International Journal of Service Industry Management* 18:2, 206–19.

Shah, B. (2003), 'Capturing tacit knowledge: Do you know more than you think? An examination of the challenges involved in capturing tacit knowledge', *Practical Law Company*, 14 October 2003. Available at: http://uk.practicallaw.com/5-102-4700?q=shah+tacit&qp=&qo=&qe=#null, accessed 9 June 2010.

Smith, G. and Bird & Bird (2007), *Internet Law and Regulation* (4th edn) (London: Sweet & Maxwell).

Spengler, O. (1928), *The Decline of the West, Vol. II: Perspectives of World-history*. Translated (with authorisation) from the German and edited by C.F. Atkinson (New York: Alfred A. Knopf), original edition (Munich: Beck, 1922).

Srikantaiah, T. and Koenig, M. (2008), *Knowledge Management in Practice: Connections and Context* (Medford: Information Today).

Stearns, S and Roberts, L. 2003. Successful knowledge management at a law firm: A case study. (Online Web Conference: July 2003).

Takeuchi, H. (1998), 'Beyond knowledge management: Lessons from Japan'. Available at: www.sveiby.com/articles/lessonsjapan.htm, accessed 9 June 2010.

Tseng, S.-M. (2008), 'The effects of information technology on knowledge management systems', *Expert Systems with Applications* 35, 150–60.

Wenig, R. (1998), 'Malhotra's compilation of definitions of knowledge management'. Available at: www.brint.com, accessed 9 June 2010.

Zemliansky, P. and St. Amant, K. (eds) (2008), *Handbook of Research on Virtual Workplaces and the New Nature of Business Practices* (New York: Information Science Research).

Chapter 6
Ideology, Illusion and the Global Copyright Regime

Colin Darch[1]

Introduction

The US Chamber of Commerce takes intellectual property (IP) seriously. It believes that copyright, patents and trademarks underpin 'economic prosperity and human progress' (Global Intellectual Property Center 2008, 1). It has set up the Global Intellectual Property Center (GIPC) to champion intellectual property rights (IPRs) because they are 'vital to creating jobs, saving lives, advancing global economic growth, and generating breakthrough solutions to global challenges' (Global Intellectual Property Center 2008, 1). These are strong words and large claims about desirable objectives – who could possibly be opposed to saving lives or solving global challenges?

As it turns out, there *are* people who don't care much for IP. The GIPC says there are two 'serious threats' to the current IP regime in the world – and hence, presumably, to prosperity, progress and 'breakthrough solutions'. The first comes from organised crime and terrorist groups, 'criminals who have built a $600 billion global criminal enterprise of counterfeiting and piracy that destroys jobs, undermines innovation, and endangers consumers' (Global Intellectual Property Center 2008, 1). The second comes from a group of people driven by 'ideology'. These are the critics of the copyright and IP system, and they constitute:

> a growing movement of anti-IP activists drawn from universities, foundations, non-governmental organizations (NGOs), ideologically driven interest groups, and even governments. These activists promote the idea that IP rights should not be recognized and that the protection of IP impedes progress and hurts the poor. They are spending tens of millions of dollars annually to transform this ideology into governmental and multinational policy. (Global Intellectual Property Center 2008, 1)

Authors of critical texts on the copyright system may find it chilling to be identified as a serious threat – and by the largest lobbying organisation in Washington, no less – alongside the owners of a '$600 billion global criminal enterprise'. It would be uncharitable, nevertheless, to suppose that any such effect was intended, and it is encouraging to know that the world's biggest business federation keeps up with the academic literature, even if, on the basis of the summary quoted, it has not grasped all the nuances of the debate.[2]

By contrast, if the global scale of routine copying and downloading is anything to go by, ordinary people do not share the Chamber of Commerce's concerns. They treat IPRs with scant respect. They ignore the law whenever they want to make a photocopy of a text, or to download a popular

1 This chapter extends arguments about the political economy of IP first put forward in Darch 2004, 488–501. An earlier version was presented to the III CopySouth Workshop in Brazil in June 2010.

2 At the risk of stating the obvious, few critics would seriously argue in such crude terms that 'IP rights should not be recognized' or that 'the protection of IP impedes progress'. The critique is rather that there are too many protections and they last too long, that the main beneficiaries are corporations rather than creators, and that developed countries derive significant advantage at the expense of poor countries.

song or movie, not caring whether such behaviours are legal or illegal. The boundary between original, copy and counterfeit is blurred. People buy cheap 'pirate' CDs and DVDs, football shirts and sports shoes, and even – recklessly – medicines from street vendors and discount stores. In this environment, IPRs become 'as fleeting as the scent of jasmine':

> BEIJING – Settling not on the industrious sons of China, nor on their ware-covered blankets, ownership rights of intellectual property fluttered silently by, unseen, on Monday, as does the gentle mayfly on a warm harvest-time breeze. 'Is this a pirated DVD of Transformers 2 dreaming it is an original? Or is it an original Transformers 2 dreaming of an adventurous life as a pirate?' a sidewalk merchant in Tiananmen Square whispered to a moment already gone, as his hands clutched some worldly illusion of the Michael Bay film. 'Eight dollars. Plays anywhere in the world'. In their great wisdom, the merchants also carried forth the ancient teachings of Zhuangzi – who spoke of how time is a riddle answered by eternity – to the equally fleeting earthly conceits of trademarked wristwatches, electronics, clothing items, Starbucks, and automobiles. ('Intellectual property rights' 2009)

We can guess from the references to Zhuangzi and the butterfly's dream that *The Onion* is onto something serious here.[3] When digital objects – films, recorded music, software programs and written texts – can be reproduced at negligible cost, 'authentic' and 'inauthentic' copies may be indistinguishable, and IPRs can indeed become as fragile and fleeting as a 'mayfly's wing in autumn'.[4]

These then are two contrasting views of the socio-economic importance of the copyright and IP system. One sees the system as beneficial in terms of wealth creation and innovation. If some IP protection is a good thing, more IP protection is even better. The other sees copyright as an irrelevant legal technicality that is largely unenforceable. It can be made fun of. The point that both sides agree on is that breaking the rules has never been easier. How can these contradictory viewpoints be reconciled and explained?

This chapter first presents an examination of the matrix of discourses that characterise the literature on copyright and IP, showing the role played by ideology, illusion and deceit. Second, starting from the premise that the modern, generalised expansion of protection (propertisation) is a system failure, the text argues that the change from metaphorical to literal in reading the expression 'intellectual property' is both cause and effect of the shift towards privatising knowledge. Third, appropriating aspects of Lowi's 'abdication theory' to describe how copyright policy is made and diffused, evidence is presented to show how industry bodies such as the Recording Industry Association of America (RIAA) or the Motion Picture Association of America (MPAA) help constitute a form of sub-government or 'iron triangle' (McCubbins 1999, 32). Bureaucrats, politicians and the self-selected members of industrial interest groups collude to make policy, pass legislation and protect big capital from risk – especially in the entertainment industries – at public expense. This is an unacknowledged core function of IP in the age of the knowledge economy. The conclusion to the chapter turns to the claim that piracy and counterfeiting are sources of funding for terrorist groups and organised crime, citing research that argues for a less alarmist and more nuanced assessment of this 'fear and threat leavened topic' (van Duyne and Vander Beken 2009, 262).

3 In an extensive literature, see especially Chong 2006, 370–91.

4 The *counterfeiting* of tangible goods such as medicines constitutes a distinct category of offence against IP protection mainly because in the absence of quality control the consumer is exposed to risk. But this is an argument for regulation rather than patent protection, since generics are safe.

IP and Competing Discourses

The first response to the problem of reconciling the assertion that vigorous IP protection is fundamental to human well-being with an almost universal lack of respect for copyright law, is to point to a *disjuncture* in the discourses around the issue. The system is seen by many to be 'broken', and the means of ignoring the law – photocopiers, video machines, computers – are readily available to almost everybody in the global north and to many in the global south, with little risk of consequences. As a result, copyright and IP are the subjects of parallel and sometimes competing discourses. There are legal, political, economic and information-science analyses that are frequently compartmentalised from each other. There are multiple debates and propaganda wars. There are technical apologetics and political critiques. Within this cross-disciplinary and methodological matrix it is possible to discern four broad categories of intervention, characterised below as 'conventionalist', 'deconstructionist', the 'champions' and the 'conjurers'.

This situation derives from technological developments that gathered momentum in the 1970s, and destroyed the implicit social contract at the heart of IP. Before this, copyright violations were typically committed only in the sphere of commercial competition; subsequently, consumers themselves became the main offenders, and in vast numbers. The first change came in the area of photocopying. In the mid-1970s, the Xerox Corporation, which had enjoyed a near monopoly in dry photocopying from the 1950s, became involved in a series of anti-trust lawsuits that led to the freeing of its patents and its abandonment of the small-copier end of its market (Owen 2004, 279; Jacobson and Hillkirk 1986, 70–75; Kearns and Nadler 1993, 62–8). Cheap, adaptable machines from Japanese manufacturers made it possible for individual consumers to accumulate personal libraries of journal articles and chapters from books at a lower cost than buying the original works. Soon afterwards, in the 1980s, improvements in the quality of audio cassettes allowed listeners to put together their own extensive recorded music collections, more flexibly and cheaply than by buying vinyl records. The introduction of the video cassette created a similar environment for recording television programmes and broadcast films. The last step was to move from analogue appliances to digital devices. The distinction between text, music, video and image disappeared. All became digital objects, and 'entertainment devices [... became] copying machines with easy distributive capacity' linked globally by the Internet and the World Wide Web (van Duyne and Vander Beken 2009, 262).

This process in several previously distinct fields – printed text, recorded music, film – created a new popular perception about legitimate practice with regard to protected material. Behaviour changed significantly. For the first time, instead of reading a scholarly article in the library while making notes, students could take a photocopy home at negligible financial cost. Music fans could make cassette anthologies of their favourite pieces, organised in any way they pleased.[5] The battles that have raged in recent years over the protection of 'content' from this kind of consumer freedom – and the threat to the profits of the international entertainment industry – have been fought with a sharp awareness of the fragility of IP in public consciousness.

One outcome has been a panicky tendency on the part of the big entertainment conglomerates to go after their own customers, with mixed results. In a report published in late 2007, for example, the *Washington Post* wrote that 'despite more than 20,000 lawsuits filed against music fans … the recording industry has utterly failed to halt the decline of the record album or the rise of digital

5 Ironically, the Hollywood film *High Fidelity*, starring John Cusack (2000, dir. Stephen Frears) includes scenes in which the main protagonist ruminates on the aesthetic principles of making such tapes for his girlfriends.

music sharing' (Fisher 2007). A year later, in 2008, the industry federation, the RIAA, switched tactics and decided to start suing Internet service providers instead (Albanesius 2008). Consumers, distributors and analysts seemed as far apart as ever, talking different languages and deploying different discourses.[6]

Conventionalists or Conceptual Technicians

In terms of legal philosophy, 'conventionalists' – often academics – operate within a framework of legal formalism. This position treats law as a self-contained and coherent thought system that need take little account of social reality. Thus the fairness, effectiveness and character of the IP system are taken for granted; the questions asked are about its administration. Surprisingly, perhaps, there is even a body of literature in this category produced by African scholars (see, for example, Uvieghara 1992; Mazonde and Thomas 2007; Seuna 2008), uncritical apologists of the copyright regime *as a regime*, concerned primarily to explain its workings in their own national circumstances and to implement it locally as fully as possible, starting from the assumption that:

> the developing world lags behind in taking advantage of the move towards the commercialising [of] intellectual property. (Mazonde and Thomas 2007, 1)

IP is assumed to play a developmental role, and to function in the same way in both industrialised and pre-industrial economies.

Deconstructionists or Critics of the System

Unlike conventionalists, the deconstructionists are philosophically more inclined to legal realism. They are interested in how concrete knowledge of local social conditions might lead to better IP policies. They share the belief that the system is 'broken' and needs to be either fixed or abandoned. They dispute whether IP still serves the purpose of encouraging creativity; whether it has ever served such a purpose, or was always a mechanism to restrain trade and benefit particular entrepreneurs; whether it now acts internationally, by design or accident, to keep control of knowledge production in the global north.

The argument about original purpose takes the title of the Statute of Anne and the wording of the copyright clause in the US Constitution at face value. These expressions of an Enlightenment sensibility identify the primary beneficiaries of protection as authors and creators. Unfortunately, the idea that this group benefits significantly:

> is no longer true … Proposals … to extend the term of copyright … present us with a striking snapshot of how far adrift current copyright thinking is … Instead of protecting authors, these proposals are heavily weighted in favor of distributors such as publishers … term extensions are being pushed by the estates of long deceased authors. (Patry 1997, 908)

---

6 For a detailed analysis of this particular tactic, pursued mainly by the RIAA and MPAA federations rather than the companies themselves, see Hughes 2005, 725–66. Hughes criticises the quality of statistical data on downloading, and describes the argument that 'every music download corresponds to a lost sale' as 'obviously wrong' (Hughes 2005, 736).

But another view of the copyright system says it was designed from the beginning to benefit *distributors* (printers, booksellers and publishers). The rest is merely smoke and mirrors:

> the publishers … created this right for themselves as a necessary protection for their business … the interest protected was still essentially, in its practical effect, the publisher's exclusive right to copy. (Phillips et al. 1997, 12)[7]

Either way, contemporary copyright is far from being 'a vehicle for the promotion of learning' and has become rather a 'form of business protectionism divorced from the creation of new works … little more than a set of industry-drafted technical requirements prohibiting all access except as approved by the corporate rights holder' (Patry 1997, 909–10).

The third argument takes this insight a step further. Copyright has a negative effect on information flows between industrialised or developed countries and the global south. This issue has only recently begun to attract widespread analytical attention, mainly by scholars from Asia, the Americas and Africa (see, for example, Navarrete 2006). The argument rests on a particular approach to the political economy of the information society (Story et al. 2006). Indeed, by following 'the usually reliable idea that one looks for the largest source of revenue to discern motive' it is easy to see that the international IP regime may well not be entirely 'consistent with the public interest', at least in poor countries (Patry 1997, 925, fn. 82 contd). A key moment in the development of the southern critique of IP occurred in the mid-1990s, when international trade rules were redefined during the demise of the GATT system. The new regulations imposed:

> a definition of intellectual property rights directly disadvantageous to Third World countries which [… had] been brought within the scope of a regime where they will be held strictly accountable for their state of exponentially increasing indebtedness. (Frow 1996, 89)

Deconstructionists may be academics but can also be artists, writers and activists. Although they are critical of the way in which the IP regime works, they do not necessarily agree on the remedy: some want to abolish or abandon protection altogether, in favour of other ways of rewarding creators, while others believe that the system can be reformed. The group includes such figures as John Perry Barlow, Lawrence Lessig, Jessica Litman, Siva Vaidhyanathan, Peter Drahos, James Boyle and others. Their critique of copyright derives mainly from a northern perspective – in other words, they have no special interest in the impact that IPRs have in the global south in terms of culture, language or access to education.

The Champions or Organisational Defenders

The institutional weight of government agencies and international organisations such as WIPO, Unesco and others, is usually placed behind the rapidly expanding global regime of IP protection. Thus the World Trade Organization (WTO) pushes for TRIPS agreements, while the Office of the US Trade Representative (USTR) has a special section (the Office of Intellectual Property and Innovation) which 'uses a wide range of bilateral and multilateral trade tools to promote strong intellectual property laws and effective enforcement worldwide' (Office of the US Trade

7 For a more detailed account of this argument, see Darch 2004, 493–5.

Representative 2011). This includes negotiating, implementing and monitoring trade agreements, especially bilateral ones, which are designed to protect US economic interests. The USTR also publishes an annual report card that takes a patronising tone towards sovereign governments that it places on a 'priority watch list' for IP violations. Thus, Thailand could try harder, and its government:

> made little progress over the past year in addressing the widespread problems of piracy and counterfeiting. The United States is encouraged, however, by the positive statements made by senior Thai officials … on the new Government's intentions to make IPR protection and enforcement a higher priority and to address the longstanding deficiencies. (Office of the US Trade Representative 2009, 21)

This discourse is characterised not only by its tone of unquestioning self-righteousness, but by an assumption that IPRs are both neutral and absolute, socially and economically beneficial and have only to do with trade.

The Conjurors or Vested Interests

Large commercial vested interests are often organised into industry federations or think-tanks, producing ostensibly objective research and statistics. Two of the most influential of these have already been mentioned, the Recording Industry Association of America (RIAA) and the Motion Picture Association of America (MPAA). Other examples taken more or less at random might include the Alliance Against Counterfeiting and Piracy (AACP); the Alliance Against IP Theft; Business Action to Stop Counterfeiting and Piracy (BASCAP); the International Federation of the Phonographic Industry (IFPI); and the International Intellectual Property Alliance (IIPA). There are many others, sometimes nested into each other like Russian dolls.

These organisations are 'conjurors' because they produce and perpetuate 'facts' – assertions unsupported by evidence – out of thin air. To take a specific example, it has often been stated that 750,000 jobs have been lost in the United States because of IP infringement, and that the annual cost of such infringements is somewhere between $200 and $250 billion – that is, about 28 percent of the total value added to the US gross domestic product by the 'core copyright industries' in 2007.[8] These 'authoritative' figures were being quoted as early as 2002, and continue to be cited up to the present in both industry and government publications, with reference to fields as diverse as earth-moving equipment and high fashion (US Customs and Border Protection 2002; US Chamber of Commerce 2007; 'From fake handbags to fake cars' 2009; Miller and Taylor 2010). They appear in documents issued by US government agencies such as the Department of Commerce, the Customs and Border Patrol, and the Patent and Trademark Office. However, the real source of these numbers is untraceable:

> Try to follow the thread of citations to their source, and you encounter a fractal tangle of recursive reference … Usually, the most respectable-sounding authority to cite for the numbers (the FBI for the dollar amount, Customs for the jobs figure) is also the most prevalent – but in each case, that authoritative 'source' proves to be a mere waystation on a long and tortuous journey. (Sanchez 2008)

8 Total value added taken from Siwek 2009, 3.

The earliest occurrence of the number of job losses attributable to IP infringement appears to have been nearly a quarter of a century ago, in 1986, when US Secretary of Commerce Malcolm Baldridge was quoted as estimating the figure as falling in the range 'anywhere from 130,000 to 750,000' (Sanchez 2008). Similarly, the $250 billion figure can be tracked back to an article on counterfeit products in *Forbes Magazine* for 25 October 1993 (Sanchez 2008). But what the magazine article actually says is that counterfeiting is a global industry worth '$200 billion'. It is obvious that the value of a worldwide industry, however illegal, is unlikely to be the same as the losses incurred by the national economy of the United States as a result of its existence.

The seemingly endless chain of references to these numbers creates the powerful impression that despite the best efforts of the valiant defenders of creativity and innovation, the whole mighty edifice of IP is about to come crashing down about our ears:

> both numbers are seemingly decades old, gaining a patina of currency and credibility by virtue of having been laundered through a relay race of respectable sources … these numbers are always invoked as proof that the piracy problem is still dire – that everything we've done to step up international enforcement of intellectual property laws has been in vain [… the International Anti-Counterfeiting Coalition]'s 2005 publications still cite … 1995 congressional testimony, from which it seems safe to infer that they have no more recent source. (Sanchez 2008)

It seems likely that other numbers like the GIPC's '$600 billion global criminal enterprise' – are of similarly doubtful provenance. The clear lesson is that in the field of IP analysis, perhaps more than in any similar sub-discipline, an attitude of Cartesian scepticism, especially towards statistical data, is absolutely essential.

Metaphorical and Literal Readings of the IP Concept

The 'propertisation' of the scientific record and literary production is the logical consequence of a process of labelling.[9] If we call something 'property', even metaphorically, then we should not be surprised if it ends up being treated as property, as something that can be stolen (Turner 2010). What metaphors do is to take two points of reference and map them conceptually onto one another. 'All the world's a stage', Shakespeare famously said; life is similar to a theatre because we make an entrance when we are born, we play a part or parts throughout our lives, and we make an exit when we die. It is clear, however, that while the world may be *like* a theatre in some respects, this is not the same as saying that it actually *is* a theatre. In the sphere of law, to take another example, improperly obtained evidence is *like* the 'fruit of a poisoned tree' because the impropriety at the root of the process 'poisons' everything that depends on it. Again, we understand that this is not the same thing as saying that improperly obtained evidence is *literally* toxic. By analogy, although IP may be *like* real property in significant respects, this is not the same thing as saying that *it is* real property. The metaphorical character of many phrases has weakened over time until they can be described as 'dead metaphors'. An idea may be easy to 'grasp', for instance, even though a moment's thought tells us that we cannot actually take hold of it with our hands.

Colourful and metaphorical expressions are commonplace *within* IP discourse, although some of them may not even be noticeable as such. The most obvious examples include 'pirates' and

9 'The duration and scope of IP rights expand without limit. Courts … describe IP as a type of absolute property, bereft of any restraints' (Carrier 2004, 4).

'piracy', but even 'theft' in this context is a metaphor.[10] Nevertheless, hardly any researchers have systematically explored the idea that the choice of the word 'property' to describe IP itself has had a determinant effect on the way we conceptualise it, and thus on the 'propertisation' outcome.[11] By calling ideas property, we 'choose sides' and align ourselves with those who argue that:

> intangible creations deserve to be treated the same as material – corporeal – holdings, with many of the same attributes and the same rights of ownership in perpetuity. The use of the word 'property' in this sense serves as a metaphor intended to underline the identity … between corporeal things and intangible matter. (Baron 2007, 7)

Such a formal 'property' relation in ideas is technologically determined. It cannot exist before the invention of printing, although very early texts do recognise problems around what might be termed moral proto-rights. The Bible contains a stern warning on respecting textual integrity,[12] and the Romans seem to have recognised 'plagiarism' as a moral offence, as an often-cited quotation from Martial demonstrates.[13] But even Martial was using the word *plagiari* (kidnappers of children for sale as slaves) *metaphorically* to describe those who 'stole' his poetry. Although it is widely believed that 'intellectual property' is a comparatively recent coinage, dating from the middle of the nineteenth century, recent research has traced usages of the word 'property' attaching to authors' and publishers' rights in such expressions as 'literary property' back to the beginning of the modern copyright period. Its use in other European traditions is widespread and venerable. In Spain, for example, the term 'propiedad intelectual' was conterminous with copyright throughout much of the nineteenth century (Hughes 2009, 15). Early drafts of the Statute of Anne mention 'the Property of Copies of Books', although this usage may have been referring to the physical objects themselves rather than intangible 'works' in the modern sense (Hughes 2006, 1012).

The two key cases of eighteenth-century British copyright law (*Millar* v. *Taylor* [1769] and *Donaldson* v. *Beckett* [1774]) can be read as marking the end of this early literalism about the 'property' character of copyright,[14] although copyrights continued to be 'unequivocally viewed as property' well into the nineteenth century (Hughes 2009, 1018). It is hard, therefore, to argue that any shift from a metaphorical to a literal understanding of the term 'intellectual property' was linear or chronological. Nonetheless, there are still significant differences, even today, between property and intellectual property.

By mapping the relationship between property and 'intellectual property' graphically, it is possible to see how such a change in understanding has occurred, and what the implications are. In Figure 6.1, the expression 'intellectual property' is mapped as metaphor, explicitly as 'ideas ≈ property' or 'ideas are similar to property'.[15] The overlapping area marked 'some shared similarities' is the area of congruency, where the shared characteristics of property and IP exist. The remaining areas, which do not overlap, are where the non-congruent qualities of property and IP lie. Thus, for example, while economic IPRs can be alienated or sold, moral rights are inalienable; IP is non-rivalrous; and it is intangible.

10 For an analysis of *internal* metaphor in the field, see Loughlan 2006, 211–26.

11 'relatively little work has been done to isolate and analyse the use of metaphor in the discourse of intellectual property' (Loughlan 2006, 216).

12 Revelation 22:18–19 threatens extremely severe consequences for either adding to or taking away from 'the words of the book of this prophecy'.

13 Martial, *Epigrams*, 1:52.

14 'The lesson of these two cases [is] one in which the property construct failed' (Hughes 2009, 1018).

15 Note that the mathematical symbol is ≈, not =, i.e. 'is similar to' not 'is equal to'.

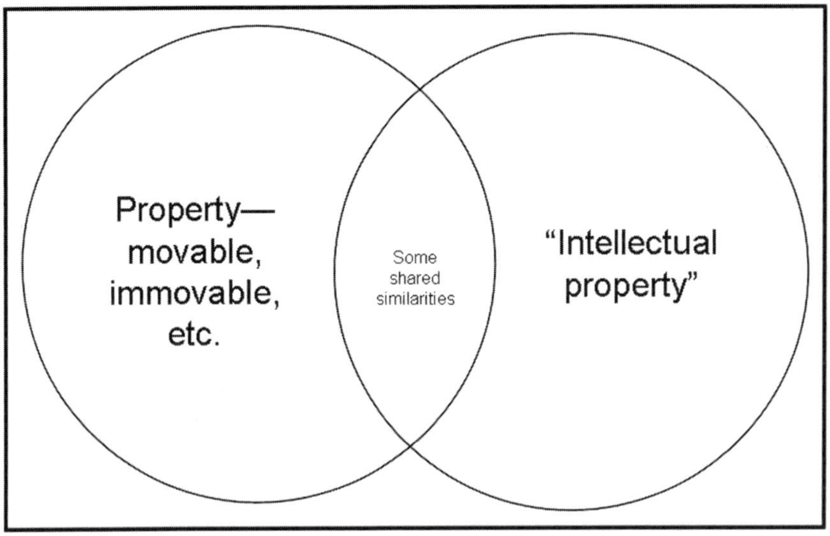

Figure 6.1 Intellectual Property as Metaphor

The second stage in the propertisation process is the transformation of IP into a conceptual category that is neither similar to nor subordinate to property – i.e. is not a *sub-category* or *kind* of property – but is rather *coordinate* with it, a parallel concept. Thus we may map the two concepts as 'ideas ≠ property', or 'IP and property are not the same', but are logically coordinate with each other. The force of metaphor is partly lost, as 'intellectual-property' becomes a special legal relation with its own sub-categories (see Figure 6.2).

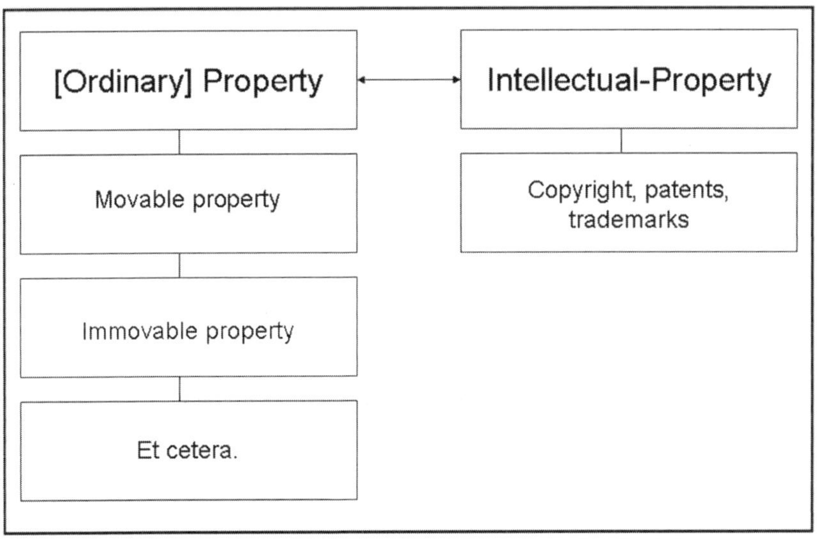

Figure 6.2 Intellectual Property as a Parallel (Coordinate Category)

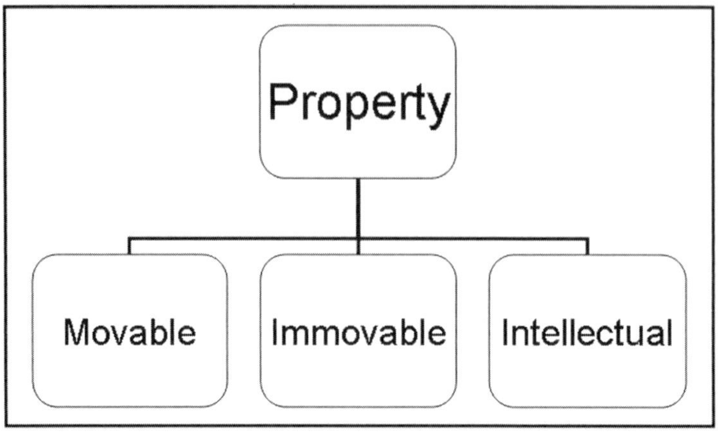

Figure 6.3 Intellectual Property as a Sub-Type of Property

The final stage in the process occurs when 'propertisation' is complete, and intellectual property becomes simply another kind of property, alongside the tangible sub-categories. The metaphorical character of the expression is completely embedded, and we can map the relation between the two terms as 'ideas $\leq$ property' or 'ideas are a subgroup of property' (see Figure 6.3).

But if IP is a metaphorical conceptualisation that has got out of hand, what are the alternatives? An easy thought experiment has been proposed to rethink non-exclusive ways of expressing a creator's legitimate interest in literary, cultural or scientific works. We might, for example:

> think of intellectual property … as an agricultural marketing board, with intellectual property law functioning as the market intermediary. Intellectual property law provides a guaranteed return on investment (an incentive) for creators, and determines a fair price for consumers … we might think of intellectual property as a state corporation, such as a public utility. Intellectual property law makes decisions about the amount and distribution of knowledge assets based on governmental policy … We might even characterize intellectual property as a form of state subsidy … a response to a systemic private sector funding gap in a particular industry or geographical location. Intellectual property law fulfills a similar function, providing the necessary supplemental financing to the private sector to fund the production of knowledge assets. (Adams 2009)

By recognising that there is an 'unacknowledged process of associative thinking that accompanies linear legal reasoning' we can thus begin to imagine other ways in which the benefits of cultural and scientific behaviours might be shared in society (Adams 2009). Metaphors can and do assist in 'constructing legal meaning' and the property metaphor is not the only possible way of constructing meaning around authorship and the diffusion of ideas.[16] At the present time, however, it remains the determinant one.

16 For an exercise in exactly this kind of re-imagining, see Smiers and van Schijndel 2009.

Political Economy, 'Financier's Copyright' and Abdication Theory

The GIPC, already mentioned, has no doubt about the overriding importance of IP and IPRs. They are, says the GIPC, 'the defining economic currency of the 21st century [… they drive] innovation, job creation, and [US] global competitiveness' (Global Intellectual Property Center 2008). The first part of the statement may be partially true, but the second part is by no means the whole story. To fully grasp what is actually going on, it is necessary to understand the importance of the so-called 'copyright industries' to the US economy; the 'distinct conception of copyright' that the film and recorded music industries have been instrumental in developing (Drahos with Braithwaite 2002, 176); the role of the state in socialising large-scale economic risk in the United States, and the consequent capture of the legislative process by organised special interests; the imposition by the United States of its own IP system on the rest of the world; and the distortion of IP discourse by the 'conjurors' in the service of this process.

First, the economic importance of IP, especially in the United States; there is compelling evidence that the 'copyright industries' do indeed make a significant ongoing contribution to US economic well-being. The *core* copyright industries, as defined by the World Intellectual Property Organization (WIPO) for statistical purposes, consist of nine broad categories, namely the press and literature; music, theatrical productions and operas; motion pictures and video; radio and television; photography; software and databases; the visual and graphic arts; advertising services; and copyright collective management societies (*Guide* 2003, 28). Between 2003 and 2007 these 'core copyright industries' consistently accounted for over 6 per cent of the total US gross domestic product, amounting in dollar terms to $700 billion at the beginning of the period and just under $890 billion by the end (Siwek 2009, 3). By a broader definition, which includes the core industries listed above and three other more marginal WIPO-approved categories, the sector was worth $1.52 trillion or 11 per cent of US GDP by 2007 (Siwek 2009, 3). These percentages held steady up to the end of 2007 – it is still unclear what impact the global recession that started in December 2007 has had. Moreover, in 2007, according to a presumably authoritative survey by the International Intellectual Property Alliance:

> the 'core' and 'total' copyright industries' contribution to real economic growth was 22.74% and 43.06%, respectively, having increased from 13.40% and 31.19% in 2006, more than double the current dollar shares of US GDP achieved by the copyright industries in those same years. (Siwek 2009, 3)

These industries did not become important through the unmediated operation of market forces, however, but through a venerable tradition of 'cartelism and protectionism' initiated by the Hollywood motion picture industry, and supported by the major media and entertainment multinationals, including the recorded music industry (Drahos with Braithwaite 2002, 174). The concept of 'financier's copyright', as Drahos and Braithwaite have termed it:

> rests on the view that copyright must serve the financier of copyright works by guaranteeing rights of exploitation in whichever markets the financier chooses to operate. If new technologies … come along … then the financier is entitled to new rights that allow him or her to manage the contingencies of the technology … all other interests … are subordinated to the producer's interest in maintaining a global system of production and distribution … private informational assets must never enter the public domain where they can be the subject of market competition … Ideally in

> this world corporations would be globally recognized as the actual authors of copyright works. (Drahos with Braithwaite 2002, 174)

What are the mechanisms through which an industrial sector – Hollywood, recorded music, publishing, entertainment – manages to manipulate the legislative process to produce in law a concept of IP that includes not only a literalist reading of the 'property' metaphor, but also a complete abandonment of Enlightenment purpose? How can a sector manipulate political processes to produce simultaneous but contradictory public perceptions that IP is an immensely powerful instrument in the service of social well-being, and so fragile that it is under threat from organised crime, terrorism and even academic criticism?

To answer these questions, which have a direct bearing on an increasingly globalised IP regime, it is necessary to look to a debate about the emergence of the 'administrative state' in the United States. The US Congress, it is argued, has historically delegated more and more of its policy-making power to Federal agencies governing such sectors as trade and commerce, agriculture, transport and securities. In the 1930s these sectoral bureaucracies freed themselves from effective political oversight by elected politicians, and grew significantly in size and number, first under the New Deal, and then in conditions of wartime:

> parceling out policy-making power to the most interested parties tends strongly to destroy political responsibility. A program split off with a special imperium to govern itself is not merely an administrative unit. It is a structure of power with impressive capacities to resist political control … The public is shut out. (Lowi 1979, 59)

By the 1960s, bureaucrats themselves were making policy, under the influence of organised interest groups lobbying for particular outcomes. The Congress had become a 'consensual body', and had 'abdicated' its responsibilities (Lowi 1979, xii). Indeed, after the Roosevelt administration, argued Lowi, 'the historic continuity of [US] national politics [had] been broken' (Lowi 1979, xiii).

Lowi's 'abdication thesis' is mainly of interest here for the extraordinary accuracy with which it characterises the processes by which copyright legislation is currently drafted and adopted in the United States – and hence, eventually, enforced in the rest of the world through such devices as 'harmonisation' or bilateral Free Trade Agreements. Policies, says Lowi, do not come:

> from voter preferences or congressional enactments but from a process of tripartite bargaining between the specialized administrators, relevant members of Congress, and *the representatives of self-selected organized interests*. (Lowi 1979, xii)

There is evidence that the process of developing copyright legislation fits the abdication thesis closely, with only formal gestures towards what Lowi called the 'process of tripartite bargaining' between industry representatives, agencies and elected representatives. In a short memoir written in 1996, Patry describes how copyright interest groups 'draft legislation [that] they expect Congress to pass *without any changes*' (Patry 1996, 141, emphasis added):

> they [i.e. the interest groups] are drafting the committee reports and haggling among themselves about what needs to be in the report … some copyright lawyers and lobbyists actually resent members of Congress and staff interfering with what they view as *their* legislation and *their* committee report … we have, I believe, reached a point where legislative history *must* be ignored

> because not even the hands of congressional staff have touched committee reports. (Patry 1996, 141, emphasis in original)

Patry describes how in May 1994 an 'industry consensus' bill was submitted to Congress, and although it was initially rejected, 'a revised bill *drafted entirely by the industry*' was eventually passed in June 1995 (Patry 1996, 142, emphasis added). He comments that processes like this are 'not legislating. It is letting those who had a seat at the private sector table divvy up the spoils among themselves' (Patry 1996, 143).

The last stage in this process is spreading these industry-defined IP practices from the United States to other countries around the world. This is increasingly done through the imposition of bilateral trade agreements:

> Promoting the enforcement of IPR is an important component of US international trade policy. Since … 1995 … trade policy has been used to enforce IPR abroad … The United States … pursues international IPR support through regional and bilateral free trade agreements (FTAs), which often include IPR commitments by US partners exceeding their TRIPS Agreement obligations … Other trade policy tools also are available for US efforts to advance international IPR … the Office of the US Trade Representative (USTR) identifies countries providing inadequate IPR protection in its annual 'Special 301' report … the United States may consider a developing country's IPR policies and practices as a basis for offering preferential duty-free entry to certain products from the country, and can suspend GSP benefits if IPR protection is lacking. (Ilias and Ferguson 2009, unpag. summary)

When financier's copyright meets congressional abdication and trade policy in this way, global taxpayers shoulder the burden of insuring national copyright industries. Lowi calls this the 'state of permanent receivership' (Lowi 1979, 279–89). In such a situation, the state socialises business risk by underwriting in various ways 'any institution large enough to be a significant factor in the community', guaranteeing social and economic stability 'regardless of inequities, inefficiencies, or costs of maintenance'.[17] We have seen this system in operation in the series of bailouts that followed the financial crisis of late 2007. But any company or sector that is regarded as too big or important to be allowed to fail itself represents a regulatory failure, because ordinary market forces are inoperative. Whatever else one thinks of it, capitalism *cannot* mean insuring commercial enterprises from mistakes, environmental changes or competition. It is necessary to realise that the copyright system itself is also a vital part of this 'general floor under risk'. Its function is *precisely* to guarantee the stability of US core copyright industries and to protect them *against* both market forces and technological change. The rest is illusion.

IP, Organised Crime and Terrorism

It is common for industry associations to declare that counterfeiting and other IPR violations generate funds for 'organised crime' and terrorist organisations. Such claims have been made by, amongst others, the Alliance against Counterfeiting and Piracy (AACP), by the International Federation of the Phonographic Industry (IFPI), and by Rand Corporation researchers on behalf of the Motion Picture Association (*Proving the Connection* 2003; *Music Piracy* 2004; Treverton

17 Lowi 1979, 279–80.

et al. 2009). The idea that such a link might exist derives from police intelligence information. In the United Kingdom the National Criminal Intelligence Service, which was merged into the Serious Organized Crime Agency in 2006, started the ball rolling in its National Threat Assessment for 2000, where 'IP theft' was listed for the first time as a 'threat':

> Although anecdotal, we knew that these links existed because of the evidence which our members' anti-piracy units were turning up … none of it was being systematically documented. Then, for the first time, the National Criminal Intelligence Service (NCIS) listed intellectual property theft in its 2000 National Threat Assessment and accorded it a high impact assessment … The connection was reinforced in the following year's National Threat Assessment, but there were issues … which caused a real lack of coordination of any hard facts. (*Proving the Connection* 2003, 1, emphasis added)

The European Organized Crime Threat Assessment (OCTA) for 2006 also identified intellectual property theft as requiring 'focused attention on the common EU level' (van Duyne and Vander Beken 2009, 276). But in the opinion of some researchers, this is all a 'ritual dance with lots of smoke and shady procedures to decide on the "truth" about organized crime' (van Duyne and Vander Beken 2009, 275). There are indeed difficulties, above all in the fuzziness of the concepts deployed. The term 'threat', as in threat assessment, does not mean exactly the same as 'risk', or the likelihood and consequences of something happening:

> agencies tasked with the responsibility of public and national security … generally rely on the negative aspect of impact, and thus the likelihood of events or actions (which they then define in terms of threat) is often the defining variable. The main focus of threat assessments is on the intent and capability of the criminal actors involved … not on the consequences … this might cause … It is also possible … to study … to what extent capable and willing offenders (threat) have the opportunity to commit their acts and cause harm to society (impact) … there is a fundamental flaw: none of the terms being used has an operationalised, unambiguous content. (van Duyne and Vander Beken 2009, 273)

Similarly, 'organised crime' is a contested concept, with varying definitions: 'it is like an elephant – it is difficult to describe but you know it when you see it' (quoted in van Duyne and Vander Beken 2009, 267). In fact, the whole process is deeply flawed:

> are these manifestations of 'knowledge based' policy making sincere or just displays of ritual dancing accompanied by socially and politically acceptable incantations? Our description and analysis point at a predominance of ritualism. This … can be observed from the onset of organised crime policy making, in which 'belief statements' exceed fact/observation based statements … organised crime political decision making is actually not knowledge based at all. Decisions are made and budgets spent because this is what decision makers want to do, not what evidence shows them to do. Further, the secrecy and rituals hamper discussions … and cover up substantial data collection problems and important flaws in the conceptual framework. (van Duyne and Vander Beken 2009, 278–9)

So, although the conjurors would like us all to believe that by taking a critical view of copyright and IP we are crossing over to the dark side and aligning ourselves with *Mafiosi* and terrorists, there are sufficient doubts around methodology, data collection and definitions for Cartesian scepticism to hold sway here too. Of course street vendors are likely to be hustlers too. Of course counterfeit medicine or counterfeit spare parts for aircraft represent a danger to consumers. Of course authors and musicians should be able to earn a decent wage. All this goes without saying. What does need to be said is that the copyright and IP system as it operates at present has been corrupted and co-opted by cynical vested interests who manipulate it against the best interests of the citizenry. We have a duty to examine their claims about its true nature with a very beady eye indeed.

References

Adams, W.A. (2009), 'Meaning and metaphor: Associative thinking and the unacknowledged images of "use" in intellectual property', McGill University, Faculty of Law. Available at: http://m-m.mcgill.ca/sem1_WAA.html, accessed 12 March 2010.

Albanesius, C. (19 December 2008), 'RIAA confirms it will take piracy fight to ISPs', *Extreme Tech.* Available at: www.extremetech.com/article2/0,2845,2337337,00.asp, accessed 9 March 2010.

Alliance Against Counterfeiting and Piracy (AACP) (2003), *Proving the Connection: Links between Intellectual Property Theft and Organised Crime* (London: AACP).

Baron, R.A. (2007), 'Metaphor and polemic in the wars over the public domain', *Art and Museum Law Journal* 2:1, 1–29.

Carrier, M.A. (2004), 'Cabining intellectual property through a property paradigm', *Duke Law Journal* 54:1, 1–145.

Chong, K. (2006), 'Zhuangzi and the nature of metaphor', *Philosophy East and West* 56:3, 370–91.

Darch, C. (2004), 'Digital divide or unequal exchange? How the Northern intellectual property rights regime threatens the South', *International Journal of Legal Information* 32:2, 488–501.

Drahos, P. with Braithwaite, J. (2002), *Information Feudalism: Who Owns the Knowledge Economy?* (London: Earthscan).

Fisher, M. (30 December 2007), 'Download uproar: Record industry goes after personal use', *Washington Post.* Available at: www.washingtonpost.com/wp-dyn/content/article/2007/12/28/AR2007122800693.html, accessed 9 March 2010.

'From fake handbags to fake cars, the problem is real: At *Harper's Bazaar*, fakes are never in fashion' (22 April 2009). Available at: www.fakesareneverinfashion.com/fakes_summit_09.asp, accessed 8 March 2011.

Frow, J. (1996), 'Information as gift and commodity', *New Left Review* 219, 89–108.

Global Intellectual Property Center (GIPC) (2008), *Intellectual Property: Creating Jobs, Saving Lives, Improving the World* (Washington, DC: US Chamber of Commerce). Available at: http://gipcdev.blackbarn.net/sites/default/files/reports/documents/gipc_ipbook.pdf, accessed 1 March 2010.

Hughes, J. (2005), 'On the logic of suing one's customers and the dilemma of infringement-based business models', *Cardozo Arts and Entertainment Law Journal* 22:3, 725–66.

Hughes, J. (2006), 'Copyright and incomplete historiographies: Of piracy, propertization, and Thomas Jefferson', *Southern California Law Review* 79:5, 993–1084.

Hughes, J. (July 2009), 'Notes on the origin of "intellectual property": Revised conclusions and new sources', Benjamin N. Cardozo School of Law Jacob Burns Institute for Advanced Legal Studies, Working Paper No. 265, cited by permission of the author.

International Federation of the Photographic Industry (IFPI) (2004), *Music Piracy – Serious, Violent and Organised Crime* (London: IFPI).

Ilias, S. and Ferguson, I.F. (2009), *Intellectual Property Rights and International Trade* (Washington, DC: Congressional Research Service).
'Intellectual property rights as fleeting as the scent of jasmine, mayfly's wing in autumn' (22 July 2009), *The Onion.* Available at: www.theonion.com/content/news_briefs/intellectual_property, accessed 2 March 2010.
Jacobson, G. and Hillkirk, J. (1986), *Xerox: American samurai* (New York: Collier Books).
Kearns, D.T. and Nadler, D.A. (1993), *Prophets in the Dark: How Xerox Reinvented Itself and Beat Back the Japanese* (New York: HarperBusiness).
Loughlan, P. (2006), 'Pirates, parasites, reapers, sowers, fruits, foxes … the metaphors of intellectual property', *Sydney Law Review* 28:2, 211–26.
Lowi, T.J. (1979), *The End of Liberalism: The Second Republic of the United States* (2nd edn) (New York: Norton).
McCubbins, M.D. (1999), 'Abdication or delegation? Congress, the bureaucracy and the delegation dilemma', *Regulation* 22:2, 30–7.
Mazonde, I.N. and Thomas, P. (2007), *Indigenous Knowledge Systems and Intellectual Property in the Twenty-first Century* (Dakar: CODESRIA).
Miller, C.M. and Taylor, J.A. (3 February 2010), 'Combating counterfeiting in an electronic era'. Available at: www.cafezine.com/depts/article.asp?id=24034&deptid=3#_ftn1, accessed 12 March 2010.
Navarrete, L.Á. (2006), *Derecho de ¿autor? El debate de hoy* (Havana, Cuba: Editorial de Ciencias Sociales).
Office of the US Trade Representative (30 April 2009), *2009 Special 301 Report* (Washington, DC: USTR).
Office of the US Trade Representative (2 March 2011), 'Intellectual property'. Available at: www.ustr.gov/trade-topics/intellectual-property, accessed 29 April 2011.
Owen, D. (2004), *Copies in Seconds* (New York: Simon & Schuster).
Patry, W. (1996), 'Copyright and the legislative process: A personal perspective', *Cardozo Arts and Entertainment Law Journal* 14:1, 139–52.
Patry, W. (1997), 'The failure of the American copyright system: Protecting the idle rich', *Notre Dame Law Review* 72:4, 907–34.
Phillips, J.J., Durie, R. and Karet, I. (1997), *Whale on Copyright* (5th edn) (London: Sweet and Maxwell).
Sanchez, J. (8 October 2008), '750,000 lost jobs? The dodgy digits behind the war on piracy', *Ars Technica.* Available at: http://arstechnica.com/tech-policy/news/2008/10/dodgy-digits-behind-the-war-on-piracy.ars, accessed 12 March 2010.
Seuna, C. (2008), *Droit d'auteur et droits voisins au Cameroun* (Yaoundé: SOGESIC).
Siwek, S.E. (2009), *Copyright Industries in the US Economy: The 2003–2007 Report* (Washington, DC: International Intellectual Property Alliance).
Smiers, J. and van Schijndel, M. (2009), *Imagine There is No Copyright and No Cultural Conglomerates Too: An Essay* (Amsterdam: Institute of Network Cultures).
Story, A., Darch, C. and Halbert, D. (eds) (May 2006), *The Copy/South Dossier: Issues in the Economics, Politics, and Ideology of Copyright in the Global South* (Canterbury: Copy/South Research Group). Available at: www.copysouth.org/en/documents/csdossier.pdf, accessed 10 March 2010.
Treverton, G.F., Matthies, C., Cunningham, K., Gouka, J. and Ridgeway, G. (2009), *Film Piracy, Organized Crime, and Terrorism* (Santa Monica: Rand Corporation).

Turner, M. (11 March 2010), 'James Murdoch: Illegal downloading is theft', *Hollywood Reporter.* Available at: www.hollywoodreporter.com/hr/content_display/technology/news/e3if3d775aa9c43698e9c3e0250a20eb6fe, accessed 15 March 2010.

Uvieghara, E.E. (ed.) (1992), *Essays on Copyright Law and Administration in Nigeria* (Ibadan: Y-Books).

US Chamber of Commerce (June 13, 2007), 'US Chamber and US Patent and Trademark Office partner to educate businesses on threats of counterfeiting and piracy'. Available at: www.uschamber.com/press/releases/2007/june/07-102.htm, accessed 8 March 2011.

US Customs and Border Protection (2002), *US Customs Announces International Counterfeit Case Involving Caterpillar Heavy Equipment.* News release, published 29 May 2002. Available at: www.cbp.gov/xp/cgov/newsroom/news_releases/archives/legacy/2002/52002/05292002.xml, accessed 15 March 2010.

van Duyne, P.C. and Vander Beken, T. (March 2009), 'The incantations of the EU organised crime policy making', *Crime, Law and Social Change* 51:2, 261–81.

World Intellectual Property Organization (WIPO) (2003) *Guide on Surveying the Economic Contribution of the Copyright-based Industries* (Geneva: WIPO).

Chapter 7
Legal Information Literacy

Ruth Bird

Introduction

The legal profession has been affected by the information revolution of the past 20 years more than most professions. After many centuries of dependence on books and paper, there has been a shift towards an important, or possibly predominant, role for electronic information in legal practice and scholarship. By its very nature, electronic information is subject to continuous change; even more than paper it requires guarantees of authenticity and authoritativeness.

During library instruction librarians have defined research paths which clearly showed which sources to use and which paths to follow to locate relevant information, be it in law reports, legislation or other sources. Now that there is an amorphous mass of electronic information and the associated information overload, librarians are anxiously looking for precision, in particular because the field of law, as all scientific disciplines, tends to specialise more and more.

Information-seeking behaviour follows a familiar pattern. Starting with a lack of knowledge, researchers select relevant materials, become more optimistic, continue their exploration, then often feel overwhelmed by how many useful documents they find, and eventually achieve a clear focus, regain confidence, repackage the collected materials and present the results. As with the traditional reference interview, these stages need to be transferred to the new circumstances of the digital world. Librarians may have been inclined to make use of IT staff to improve information literacy but it is the law librarian who is knowledgeable about the legal resources that a scholar or practitioner needs to consult in order to be well informed on the subject matter at hand.

The Legal Landscape

The recognition of the role of information literacy skills in developing improved approaches to research training in the law is a relatively recent development. There was a time not so long ago in common law countries when legal research training concentrated on mastery of a clearly defined body of information organised by type of material: namely law reports, legislation, digests and journals. Understanding the individual characteristics of such material was regarded as core knowledge for those wanting to be lawyers, legal academics, or in other ways associated with the legal world. The appropriate application of legal research tools was vital for successful legal researchers; knowing how to navigate these resources to locate an important point of law was a crucial building block in becoming a well-rounded lawyer.

For librarians working alongside lawyers it was generally accepted that knowing the function and idiosyncrasies of a library catalogue and general reference sources were of lesser relevance to a lawyer. In non-specialist librarianship, early information literacy training was based on the functions of certain tools in reference services, the context in which they would be of relevance, and the benefits they would deliver to the savvy researcher or general user of library materials.

Lawyers with good legal research skills knew when to refer to a legal digest in preference to a legal encyclopaedia; they understood the process of law report publishing from the handing down of a judgment to its appearance in a paper law report series, and relied on the capability of the legal publishers to identify and annotate the most relevant case law. With regard to legislation they knew how to track amendments, be aware of commencement dates, and how to locate relevant parliamentary materials.

Being able to trust in the expertise of law book editors was vital for lawyers intent on researching points of law when using relevant keywords and subject indexes to cases. The cross-referencing needed for tracing the legal history or development of a point of law relies on the total thoroughness of the filtering and editing work done by the lawyers employed as editors by legal publishers.

This reliance is relevant to the recent changes in the information landscape for lawyers. When the literature of the law was easily identified, when jurisdictional boundaries of research were clearly defined, and when the resources to be consulted were limited in number, a legal researcher could usually say with confidence that the end point of research had been reached. However, at the end of the first decade of the twenty-first century, it is more problematic for lawyers to reach such a confident conclusion than it was for their predecessors.

The legal resources landscape has changed beyond recognition. The impact of the change on legal information and its users requires us all to have an understanding of the growing role that good information literacy skills can play in ensuring students are equipped for the information-rich world in which they live and work. By themselves, legal research skills are no longer enough to meet the information needs of lawyers.

What is Information Literacy?

The term information literacy gained currency in the 1990s as new terminology appeared to describe the impact of computer technology on people, work and society.

A review of the literature shows that there are many definitions, but all have a common thread. In 2003 Johnston and Webber synthesised existing definitions and produced the following:

> Information literacy is the adoption of appropriate information behaviour to identify, through whatever channel or medium, information well fitted to information needs, leading to wise and ethical use of information in society. (Webber and Johnston 2003, 113)

Definitions of information literacy and accompanying standards, together with indicators of competency, have been adopted and adapted by library organisations in many countries, with a range of variations in terminology (Beljaars 2009). The common threads through all the statements and definitions are a recognition of the increasing abundance and complexity of information and the aspiration by librarians to guide individuals to make informed choices in finding and using it.

Table 7.1 outlines several definitions of information literacy adopted by leading library associations, and then lists the key literacy skills needed by the information-literate person under each definition. It is recognised that information is no longer limited to traditional resources, and that an understanding of the importance of selection, evaluation, location, use and effective application of information will equip a person for life well beyond their formal education.

The 2009 Horizon Report, an annual report on emerging technologies, lists the critical challenges facing learning organisations over the coming five years, and the first item on its list states: 'There is a growing need for formal instruction in key new skills, including information literacy, visual literacy and technological literacy' (Johnson et al. 2009, 6).

Table 7.1 Information Literacy Definitions and Core Skills from Selected Organisations

	Definitions of information literacy	Skills and competencies of the information literate person
UNESCO	Information literacy empowers people in all walks of life to seek, evaluate, use and create information effectively to achieve their personal, social, occupational and educational goals. It is a basic human right in a digital world and promotes social inclusion in all nations.	• Recognise the information needs • Locate and evaluate the quality of the information • Store and retrieve information • Make effective and ethical use of information • Apply information to create and communicate knowledge
ACRL	Information literacy is a set of abilities requiring individuals to 'recognize when information is needed and have the ability to locate, evaluate, and use effectively the needed information'.	• Determine the extent of information needed • Access the needed information effectively and efficiently • Evaluate information and its sources critically • Incorporate selected information into one's knowledge base • Use information effectively to accomplish a specific purpose • Understand the economic, legal and social issues surrounding the use of information, and access and use information ethically and legally
IFLA (and ALA)	To be information literate, a person must be able to recognise when information is needed and have the ability to locate, evaluate and use effectively the needed information. The information literate individuals are those who have learned how to learn.	• Access – The user accesses information effectively and efficiently • Evaluation – The user evaluates information critically and competently • Use – The user applies/uses information accurately and creatively
SCONUL	For the development of the information literate person a model is proposed based on seven sets of skills developing from a basic competence in library and IT skills.	• Recognise information need • Distinguish ways of addressing the gap • Construct strategies for locating • Locate and access • Compare and • evaluate • Organise, apply and communicate, synthesise and create

Table 7.1 Continued

	Definitions of information literacy	Skills and competencies of the information literate person
CILIP	Information literacy is knowing when and why you need information, where to find it, and how to evaluate, use and communicate it in an ethical manner.	• A need for information • The resources available • How to find information • The need to evaluate results • How to work with or exploit results • Ethics and responsibility of use • How to communicate or share your findings • How to manage your findings
CAUL	Information literacy is an understanding and set of abilities enabling individuals to recognise when information is needed and have the capacity to locate, evaluate and use effectively the needed information.	Information literate people: • Engage in independent learning through constructing new meaning, understanding and knowledge • Derive satisfaction and personal fulfilment from using information wisely • Individually and collectively search for and use information for decision-making and problem solving in order to address personal, professional and societal issues • Demonstrate social responsibility through a commitment to lifelong learning and community participation

Note: UNESCO – United Nations Educational, Scientific and Cultural Organisation; ACRL – Association of College & Research Libraries, US; IFLA – International Federation of Library Associations and Institutions; ALA – American Library Association; SCONUL – Society of College, National and University Libraries, UK; CILIP – Chartered Institute of Library and Information Professionals, UK; CAUL – Council of Australian University Librarians.

Legal Information Literacy

Law librarians have been at the forefront of librarianship in seeing training of library users as an integral part of their role, and providing targeted instruction and guidance for all aspects of legal research methods and skills. The complexity of printed legal resources, particularly in common law jurisdictions, has encouraged law librarians to offer training sessions and courses, generally aimed at demystifying the nature of printed legal resources. In most instances this was done by concentrating on the structure, organisation and usage of formats that were core to the legal profession: law reports, legislation and codes (in various guises), digests, legal journals and loose-leaf publications.

The success of these efforts and the acceptance of this approach to legal research instruction by the law firms, courts and law faculties served by law libraries often resulted in the refinement of legal research skills training in isolation from the substantive law courses taken concurrently by law students.

Growth in the use of legal databases and related e-resources broadened the instruction to include the use of these resources, often focusing on access and retrieval within a unique resource, rather than an all-encompassing approach dealing with generic concepts of search and retrieval applicable to all e-resources. The providers of these e-resources did not make it easy for librarians or for the end users, utilising complex and idiosyncratic search syntax and less than friendly interfaces. The complexities of print had, in effect, been transferred to the electronic.

Initially many legal e-resources were provided in CD-ROM format, or on networks via modems and phone lines. In some countries, adoption of new digital resources took place sooner than in others. Until the emergence of the Internet in the mid-1990s as a general and increasingly popular means of accessing e-resources, approaches to legal research skills training continued to move in parallel with, but separate from, the development of information literacy standards in the broader library and information world, often missing the widespread adoption of information literacy concepts in other areas.

Card catalogues had been superseded by online catalogues but this change had not had a great impact on most lawyers, who relied more on digests and indexes to law reports and legislation than on library catalogues. It was the early adoption of digitised cases and legislation by legal publishers, Lexis in particular, that led those involved in managing legal information resources to be at the forefront of selecting and providing alternate electronic formats of information for the users.

The complexities arising from the diversity of access, presentation, indexing and searchability of these new formats presented early dilemmas for librarians. On the one hand the whole concept of searching for information by free-text word searching, rather than structured taxonomies in indexes created by legal publishers, was new and somewhat alien. Did one approach training by dealing with the features of each resource separately, or emphasize the concepts of electronic searching, explaining the abstruse use of Boolean operators to users who just wanted to get the answer and were neither interested in the route that needed to be travelled, nor the rationale for travelling that route? In a discipline where precise interpretation of the meaning of words is paramount, variations in search results based on algorithms and mathematical constructs needed to be understood, or at least recognised, by the legal researcher.

There are numerous examples of law librarians who adapted information literacy competencies to make them applicable to legal research skills. However, many continued to concentration on the particular skills required for successful legal research techniques. In many instances, technology training was the domain of the computing section of the organisation and librarians were either discouraged from, or did not have the confidence for, training across the broader spectrum of information technology skills when they were applied to the use of legal e-resources.

This was not helped either by legal academics or by practitioners of law, both groups frequently taking the view that students come to university, or work, already equipped with these skills and are there to 'learn the law'. This assumption will be explored later in this chapter but it is worth noting here that this attitude has been a stumbling block for those librarians and academics who wish to integrate information literacy into the legal curriculum or workplace in a comprehensive and holistic manner.

An early discussion of the relationship between legal research and information literacy outlined the range of literacies that were being pursued as isolated strands which had a common core that needed to be drawn together (Cuffe 2002). These were information technology literacy, computer literacy, library literacy and information skills. As recently as 2005, the perception was reported that 'the legal information community has largely ignored information literacy for too long' (Peoples 2005, 679).

Defining Legal Information Literacy

Definitions of legal information literacy are based upon the broader definitions of information literacy outlined earlier, adapted to reflect the nature of legal information and research. An early study defines legal information literacy as searching skills, evaluative skills and ICT skills (Andretta 2001).

The following definition goes further, in saying that 'applied to law, information literacy means the ability to':

- Locate legal materials (primary and secondary). Implicit in this is the knowledge of retrieval tools and techniques
- Evaluate the relevance, applicability and value of the materials to the task at hand
- Manage the information (to sort, categorise, rank the information)
- Use the information for the task at hand (for example advising on the law or formulating a policy argument) (Carroll et al. 2001)

In 2009 a group of concerned United States law librarians began working on a set of 'Law Student Information Literacy (LSIL) Standards', reinforced by practical applications of what a law student needs to do to achieve successful outcomes. The following year the group submitted its draft standards to the American Association of Law Libraries Executive Board, which in turn established the Law Students Research Competency Task Force to develop the proposed standards for eventual approval by AALL (see Kim-Prieto 2010, 7–8).

In March 2011, the task force presented to the board its report which included a set of Law Student Research Competencies and Information Literacy Principles (see Table 7.2) as a first step toward developing more specific, detailed standards. The AALL Board approved the report and its recommendations, and authorised the appointment of a new task force to draft standards in line with the principles and to determine any further action necessary on behalf of AALL.

The practical application of these standards synthesises many of the concerns held by law librarians which may appear pedantic to academics or lawyers and are often addressed by the profession only when poor research results in an adverse outcome such as losing a case. The following are examples of applied information literacy skills in a legal setting:

- Knowing about the need for authentication of sources on the Internet
- Some awareness of the great differences in search engines and the importance of asking the right question in the right way
- Understanding what is being searched, which in law could mean distinguishing between digests, encyclopaedias, cases, opinions

Legal information literacy broadens the scope of legal research teaching so that the librarian can become a more active partner in the training process in whatever work environment the library is located. Differing legal workplaces have different clients and varying requirements but information literacy is a core lifelong skill that is necessary in all legal environments, from academia (both

Table 7.2 Law Student Research Competency and Information Literacy Principles

Principle I: A successful researcher should possess fundamental research skills

- Law students should have an understanding of the complexities of the legal system.
- Law students should know how to effectively use secondary sources.
- Law students should have an awareness of the cost of research.

Principle II: A successful researcher should implement effective, efficient research strategies

- Law students should select appropriate sources for obtaining required information.
- Law students should construct and implement efficient, cost-effective search strategies.
- Law students should confirm and validate research results, incorporating existing work product and expertise.
- Law students should document research strategies.

Principle III: A successful researcher should critically evaluate legal and non-legal information and information sources

- Law students should critically evaluate the validity and credibility of information sources.
- Law students should critically evaluate retrieved information.
- Law students should synthesize the results of their research to construct new concepts applicable to resolving the problem at hand.

Principle IV: A successful researcher should apply information effectively to resolve a specific issue or need

- Law students should understand the context for the legal issue under analysis.
- Law students should modify the initial research strategy as suggested by preliminary results.
- Law students. should determine when research has provided sufficient background to explain or support a conclusion.
- Law students should use the results of their research to formulate their legal analysis and to prepare their work product.

Principle V: A successful researcher should be able to distinguish between ethical and unethical uses of information and understand the legal issues arising from discovery, use, and application of information

- Law students should have a mastery of information ethics and should be able to articulate the factors that determine whether an information use is ethical.
- Law students should apply laws, rules, and other legal authority that govern a lawyer's use of information in the course of practice.

Source: American Association of Law Libraries (2011).

students and academics) to law firms (from graduate trainees to experienced practitioners). It also has its place in training at the Bar among pupils, juniors and experienced barristers, with the judiciary for both associates and judges, and with lawyers working within large corporations and in law commissions, government and legal aid.

Traditional legal research training emphasised the specific skills needed to use a set of tools, usually books or legal databases, and often presented in isolation from subjects being taught in other courses or the practical work done in a legal practice. In legal information literacy training, however, the emphasis is less on developing specific skills with a particular database, than on mastery of a set of broader competencies applicable not only to the substantive legal issue at hand, but with broader applicability for solving future problems as well. Ideally for law students the training would be incorporated into substantive legal subjects as part of a research process for the work product, such as an essay. The importance of this integrated approach to legal information literacy has become more urgent as the gap between academic legal education and practical legal education for graduates in practice narrows, just as the amount of information available to the student or lawyer has exploded. Knowing how not only to locate, but to identify, evaluate and synthesise information effectively will be the hallmark of the successful law student or lawyer of the twenty-first century.

The Changing Nature of Legal Information

The amount of information, legal and otherwise, confronting everyone on a daily basis is so extensive that reference is often made to *oceans* of information, being *inundated* by information, or *drowning in a sea* of information. These nautical allusions illustrate the enormity of the problem, and the lack of control that people often feel in the face of it.

The challenge for law students and for practising lawyers is to develop the ability to navigate information, to identify what is relevant or important, to evaluate it critically for authenticity and scope, and then to use it effectively.

The Past

The paper foundations of the law are clear-cut. Cases can be found in law reports; legislation can be located in loose parts published during the parliamentary year and then in bound volumes and annotators in subsequent years. For many jurisdictions, codes bring the legislation together in clearly defined topics. Subject-based approaches can be simplified through the use of case digests, and citators help track the judicial history of cases. Complexity was added in the 1970s with the expansion of loose-leaf services for specialised legal topics; these often provided current commentary on legislation and case law, and formed a major new approach to legal publishing, successful because of the currency that was provided.

These books and serials formed the basic tools needed for legal research. As publishers developed electronic versions of these resources, they were, in most cases, books online, with little innovation shown in the way publishers presented them. Graduating from books to these early e-resources did not mean moving to an alien landscape; the delivery was online, the content was still structured the same way as with the paper. A comfort zone was provided to the users of the first wave of e-resources by this familiar structure and approach. Knowing the relevant print resources meant that the online versions were familiar to the user, who knew the scope and structure of what was being searched and retrieved.

Existing law publishers were leaders in online provision for the traditional legal resources, and worked within structures with which they were familiar to transpose the paper versions to online, searchable imitations of the books.

The Present

Not only has the amount of available legal information expanded greatly with the growth of the Internet, with both free and subscription-based resources, the nature of the information needed for legal research has altered. Legal information is no longer limited to electronic versions of digests, encyclopaedias, law reports and legislative sources, and other information that was expertly selected by legal editors. Now it incorporates the vast range of what would have previously been unreported cases, in addition to subject and opinion based blogs, social networking sites of people intimately or peripherally involved in the law, YouTube videos or webcasts, and netletters.

A recent article cites several cases in which Wikipedia or Google were used as information sources by judges or one of the parties to a case. In the same article the authors claim the difference between generations of users of electronic legal research is that for the older ones, the 'mental concepts remain rooted in the print format' (Michels and Lewis 2009, 67). To know the scope of what is being searched is a great advantage in legal research as it helps to delineate the extent to which one needs to pursue a query:

> [O]f paramount importance is to help students understand differences between retrieval and search using one search engine or another, and real legal research. Retrieval is not research, and finding something is no substitute for finding everything, or finding the right thing. Law students should be taught how indispensable context is to their work, and that legal information systems already in place are structured specifically to give that context. (Knott 2009, 103)

In contrast to selective, expert-driven print resources, such as law reports, which are still produced in print by law publishers, many electronic resources do not have expert filtering. Instead they provide a wealth of added value with hyperlinks to commentary or case histories or further citations. The responsibility for quality achieved through selection and evaluation of information has moved from the legal publishers, experts and editors to the researcher. In this situation an understanding and awareness of the skills of information literacy can work in the researcher's favour.

In addition to digital versions of traditional sources, much new material is born digital, from blogs to presentations to websites. New forms of scholarly information are not easily corralled into the traditional formats familiar to users of libraries. These materials can sometimes be identified through aggregated legal sites or search engines but they are not indexed in traditional ways. Sometimes they have metadata associated with them, but they are rarely catalogued in conventional library management systems.

Increasingly, universities are housing their own researchers' scholarly publications in open access institutional repositories, creating new bodies of information that can also be difficult to identify or locate without excellent search techniques. These resources rely on researchers knowing what they are searching for, rather than browsing tables of content or indexes. Preprints of articles can often be located in depositories such as SSRN, the Social Science Research

Network.[1] Law is well served by this repository with its own section, the Legal Scholarship Network, which houses papers from authors in approximately 590 law schools around the world. Some contents are only retrievable with institutional membership via the popular search engines which are commonly used by students, and this can be a frustration for those who expect full text results from every search.

Complications can arise with some new forms of scholarly communication because they are not always fully retrievable on the 'free' Internet. Researchers who assume that all information is discoverable when using a search engine may be limiting the range of information they can actually retrieve. Retrieval is equally limited if researchers only use free online resources and ignore the databases provided commercially, usually via their libraries. Just as the landscape appears fully occupied with blogs, wikis, tweets and social networking, further complexity arises with the application of 'mash-ups' (selecting from and combining existing sources of information) to create new bodies/sites/entities of information.

The Future

There are many predictions for the future of technology, mobile applications, cloud computing, the semantic web, research paths and information dissemination which are outside the scope of this chapter. For those dealing with information literacy, the issue of the algorithms behind the search engine and its ability to 'interpret' a query will impact on the skills related to searching. In the United States, Westlaw has released WestlawNext, a tool that uses the semantic web concept to base results on prior learning by the search engine, bringing together related documents previous searchers have found useful. This is similar to the tool already popular on Amazon: 'others who bought this item also liked these items'. Work on the semantic web will be further developed across a range of services and products, not least legal applications. A prototype project at the Institute of Law and Technology of the Autonomous University of Barcelona,[2] assists judicial officials in resolving complex legal questions based on information built up from prior cases. (In the days before web search engines, librarians called this process of refinement of the query 'the reference interview'.)

Within the confines of legal information literacy, the outcomes of some developments could be alarming. If current trends are allowed to run unchecked, the change from reliance on *best* information to *good enough* information will accelerate, and precision, rigour and, above all, accuracy, will be lost over time. The challenge for law librarians is to ensure the more positive scenario of well prepared, information literate researchers, students and lawyers who make intelligent and informed decisions in their research ventures. It may appear difficult to plan for a structured approach that anticipates change on many fronts, but by understanding that the necessary skills themselves do not change, only the mode of delivery and discovery, we can future-proof students by equipping them for future developments in online research.

The Changing Nature of the Study of Law

The study and the practice of law have been greatly influenced by globalisation. Transactions are routinely cross-jurisdictional; international law, via treaties and conventions, impacts on civilian,

1 Available at: www.ssrn.com, accessed 24 June 2010.

2 Available at: http://idt.uab.es, accessed 24 June 2010.

family and military situations. Lawyers are often expected to know about other legal systems and laws as well as their own. Understanding foreign and international legal systems places new demands on research methods, and an ability to transfer skills learned in a home jurisdiction can facilitate undertaking new areas of research.

In addition, interdisciplinary studies have emerged across a range of legal subjects, such as socio-legal studies, law and economics, law and politics, and legal philosophy. These require broader skills such as an understanding of data management, survey methodology, and other information gathering skills that are outside the familiar parameters of legal research.

Adaptability to change and the ability to use information literacy skills to expand beyond known boundaries will prepare researchers to deal with the changing nature of the law. It will be important to understand the pressures brought about by a wealth of globalised information resources on the Internet and whether easier access to foreign law equates to better research capability or whether it merely adds unwanted complexity for the legal researcher.

The Changing Nature of Users of Legal Information

Eighteen-year-olds of 2010 exhibit one or all of the following behaviours. They are constantly sending text messages on their cell phone; concurrently, they are accessing their Facebook pages on their laptop, or on their iPhone. If there is a television in the room, it is turned on. On the move, the iPhone plays music through earphones, perhaps from a video clip. Just as easily, it could be showing a film on the small screen. There is no down time; members of this generation are always connected from morning rise to the end of the day. A gathering with friends could see them clustered around with their laptops/iPhones/etc., linked to social networking sites; chat will centre on who is writing what and why. This is the reality for many tertiary students outside the classroom.

The wired generation, digital natives or Google generation are commonly used terms for the demographic group covering those born from the mid-1980s onwards. These labels can be applied to the majority of students, graduates and younger lawyers with whom librarians engage. Whilst law librarians also have to deal with the issues of information literacy for mature students or older lawyers set in their research strategies, in most instances the focus for training and teaching is necessarily on this younger cohort.

There is a belief that this generation undertakes little evaluation of search engines and their search capabilities, or of available e-resources, and seeks instant gratification in its information seeking behaviours. 'Left to their own devices, most students will develop restrictive, inadequate and often quite misleading methods of conducting legal research' (Seguin 2005, 82).

It is common in the literature to reflect on the extensive level of information illiteracy among incoming tertiary level students. In a report on the information behaviour of future researchers, new forms of information seeking behaviour were characterised as being 'horizontal, bouncing, checking and viewing in nature. Users are promiscuous, diverse and volatile' (Rowlands et al. 2008, 294). The problem lies in a generation who think they know how to search and do not know what they don't know. In a law specific context, there is additional anecdotal evidence of students and young lawyers not being prepared to read and analyse the full text of cases, preferring synopses or abstracts. Once a database has been identified as user-friendly and adequate in coverage, users tend to forget about other potential sources; they don't experiment with sophisticated features provided in databases and rarely seek a more effective or thorough way of finding what they need.

The concern is that 'students appear to equate the ability to access the material with the mastery of the material. They view downloaded information as learned information' (Lien 1998, 118). Taking the information that has been retrieved and knowing how to go about turning it into a reflective essay, assignment or argument, is a skill that is often lacking.

Two surveys of law students produced similar responses. One sought to assess research capabilities of incoming law students and found that 'many do not have even a foundational understanding of how to conduct research' (Hensiak et al. 2004, 867). Of concern were the lack of awareness of any resources not online, inability to distinguish between index and full text searching, and the view held by students that they were, nonetheless, good researchers. Those surveyed were students based in US law schools who had already completed an undergraduate degree.

Data in the second survey suggests that 'incoming law students have a strong belief in their reading, writing and research skills [but] it appears that this belief is founded on the perception that previously successful strategies for performing well in an academic setting will continue to prove effective in law school'. The conclusions reached, based on student performance and surveys of legal employers, 'suggest that this perception is flawed, and that not enough students will develop strong legal information literacy skills in law school' (Gallacher 2007, 155).

Writing about the current generation of students, Vie cautions that students lack critical technological literacy skills, inhibiting their ability to 'define, access, evaluate, manage, integrate and communicate information through real-time, scenario-based tasks'. 'This "Generation M" are media-savvy and multitasking'; they are 'equally at ease handling multiple instant messaging conversations as they are downloading ringtones to their cell phones and forwarding viral videos, these students possess technological know-how and access to computers but lack critical technological literacy skills'. Teachers need to incorporate into the teaching the 'online social networking sites, podcasts, audio mash-ups, blogs, and wikis' with which students are familiar, but about which they do not think critically (Vie 2008, 10).

In 2009 an extensive survey of over 2,000 college students in the United States found that the information seeking behaviour was based on a consistent strategy whether related to study or everyday research. Unsurprisingly the results confirmed earlier surveys that the key sources accessed for both purposes were Google and Wikipedia. The conclusion reached was that 'students conceptualize research, especially tasks associated with seeking information, as a competency learned by rote, rather than as an opportunity to learn, develop, or expand upon an information-gathering strategy which leverages the wide range of resources available to them in the digital age' (Head and Eisenberg 2009, 1).

It is incumbent on law librarians not only to create an awareness of the relatively poor research abilities of many students but also to convert academic staff, who lack faith in their own technological know-how. They need to understand that their students do not necessarily have better search and retrieval skills than they themselves do, but have greater confidence in their use of the technology itself.

The challenge for librarians and educators is to develop successful strategies to re-educate the large number of students whose search practices and online research habits have been good enough to meet the expectations of them at school and even at college. Their ability to recognise that there is a next step, and then taking it, will determine the level of future success. 'Many students are not experienced in gathering information, and absorbing, assimilating, breaking down, analysing and reorganising the information gathered' (Roach 2008, 312). As a result, their skills of legal analysis are suffering. Concerns are not limited to those studying law. Librarians in law firms are finding an increasing reluctance by young graduates to read the full text of cases or legislation. There is limited understanding of the importance of asking the right question, both of the database and also of the instructing lawyer. Too often little understanding is displayed of the issue being searched on a database, and of the importance of the process of working through a legal issue thoroughly. Although anecdotal, this observation has been made by librarians in various countries, informally on lists and in blogs.

Students who can learn to assimilate the standards of information literacy into their routine of research will find the process and the outcomes more effective and rewarding, and will have suitable transferable skills to equip them for the workplace or for research.

Role of Librarians in Teaching Legal Information Literacy

For the past 20 or 30 years, law librarians have been central to teaching legal research skills in law schools and law firms. Not only was this teaching often separate from the mainstream curriculum being taught, it was also frequently taught in the first year of study, in a well intentioned effort to ensure the students were exposed to the information necessary to smooth their path in tackling legal resources.

However, in most instances the first year of a law course is one of packaged materials, specific and limited reading from reading lists, and little opportunity for self-guided and original research. 'We are spoon-fed facts and ratios with a dose of public policy on the side' (Seguin 2005, 80). In addition, for many students there seems to be little relevance in legal research courses if they are not part of the assessable curriculum. The model has been varied and altered and in some cases integrated into the mainstream courses, or else made an assessable component in its own right. There is much anecdotal evidence from later year law students lamenting their inability to recall the lessons learnt in first year legal research courses. 'It is not until the upper years that students have the necessary legal foundation to learn and retain adequate researching skills' (Seguin 2005, 82).

Specific legal research skills have had to be adapted by law librarians over the years as the sources changed and e-resources gained dominance. Courses incorporating information literacy skills are now frequently included either in compulsory legal research and writing courses, research and mooting courses or in the core subjects taught in the law degree. Examples include:

- Integration of skills with course instruction, and using a student research manual (Carroll et al. 2001)
- Integration of skills into a module on English Legal System (Davies and Jackson 2005)
- Course based on self-paced online learning, quizzes and self-assessment ('LIST') (McLaurin-Smith and Presser 2005)
- Compulsory first year core skills programme (Meredith 2005; Carritt 2007)
- Compulsory SKILLS module – a timely, integrated approach (Pope 2009)
- Social networking tools for tailored online topic guides, wiki, and a blog (Albon 2009)

Information literacy comprises a transferable skill set with lifelong application and relevance. As mentioned earlier, the difficulty we face is how we ensure our students acquire this skill set, given that many students come to tertiary education believing they know how to research information effectively. Efforts by librarians to teach these skills separately, similar to the approach to teaching legal research skills, may not succeed. Teaching any form of information literacy in isolation from the substantive subjects in a degree may relegate these skills to irrelevancy for the Google generation.

The teaching of information literacy skills must be undertaken with a great deal of planned collaboration with the academic staff, or practising lawyers, to ensure examples, exercises and themes are as closely aligned to the subject matter as possible. In this way the core literacy and research skills that we believe to be part of the education of a lawyer can be incorporated into the substance of the content relevant to the student.

This approach is not new, and is one that has long been advocated in other subject areas: 'The successful implementation of literacy skills is regarded as dependent on collaboration between library and academic staff to ensure full integration of information literacy into the curriculum' (Wilson 1994). The importance of a working relationship of mutual trust between librarians and law teachers cannot be overstated.

The challenge in establishing an information literacy curriculum arises firstly in convincing the faculty that these skills need to be taught by integration into the real curriculum. Some of the programmes listed above serve as examples of successful implementations. The bibliography at the end of this chapter provides further detailed examples of successful programmes; from these it is obvious that there is no one correct solution. Librarians must evaluate the environment in which they work and the resources they have available, and work closely with like-minded faculty members, or lawyers, not only to develop programmes but also to manage the preparation, teaching and evaluation involved. Course-based research assignments or essays would be structured:

> to allow for the collection, analysis, synthesis of multiple viewpoints from many sources, so that the transfer of information literacy and critical thinking competencies may be more actively called upon, practiced and learned by students. (Head and Eisenberg 2009, 34)

Because it will not always be possible to work within the curriculum, it is important for librarians to incorporate information literacy skills into their everyday work with students. An interesting and useful approach developed at the Institute of Advanced Legal Studies Library has been the creation of a table demonstrating how law library staff can address the identified information literacy skills in all aspects of their work (Power 2009). It shows that information literacy skills can be reinforced in many library interactions with students and provides a checklist of examples. The table is based on the skills in the 'seven pillars' model (Society of College, National and University Libraries 2007) which explains what each skill means for students and relates questions students may ask to work in teaching, training and enquiry roles in the library.

Collaborating with users to improve information literacy via new technologies will also engage them in the process, either in groups or on an individual basis according to their specific needs. Social networking and Web 2.0 solutions can be used creatively to support the courses, ensuring an alternative approach which has the added benefit of being available 24 hours a day online.

There are students who will require additional individual, tailored guidance and support to do excellent legal research, such as postgraduates coming to law from other disciplines, with different research experiences. No matter what experience law students bring with them, they need to be equipped with a range of suitable transferable legal information literacy skills in order to be successful users of information in law school and in their profession.

The Skills of Law Librarians

The role of the librarian is as much pedagogical as it is managerial, organisational or technical. In the past law librarians were not expected to be teachers and for some this role does not come easily. However, it is a role that enhances the information management responsibility of librarians. Curating collections, managing them and cataloguing them are no longer the valued core function of libraries that they once were. To support the objectives of the parent organisation, librarians must ensure the users of the library know how to access, select, evaluate and get best use from the resources. Additional training of law librarians in teaching, presentation and related skills can help develop their ability to devise successful teaching strategies to support the objectives of the parent organisation.

The training and support librarians offer to students extends beyond classes to support materials offered as guides, as information on websites, or as appropriate utilisation of Web 2.0 technologies. This is a core library service that adds value and relevance to the work of libraries within their parent organisations.

In addition to teaching skills, law librarians need to keep up to date with technological developments on the web, so that they can understand what students are using, or exposed to. Social networking is already deeply embedded in the daily life of many students, colleagues and other library users. Knowing about evolving apps, the use of mash-ups to blend and re-work sources – in fact the whole rapid ongoing evolution of Web 2.0 or 3.0 applications – gives the librarian the opportunity to anticipate a new trend, or an application, that can be incorporated into the ways information literacy skills training is delivered.

Another challenge for law librarians is to make sure that the academics or lawyers are aware of the issues in information-seeking behaviours of students. In many instances, once initial library instruction has been undertaken by librarians, the lecturers become the gatekeepers to whom the students turn for advice, in preference to the librarians. Librarians need to seize the initiative and use their skills to develop varied programmes to update the faculty in information seeking methodologies to ensure that they pass on best practice to their students.

Conclusion

Law librarians were leaders among librarians in the provision of research training for their users. The commitment to developing courses and materials was extensive, as well as collaborative. But this commitment also meant that opportunities to incorporate new information literacy standards, broader in scope than the skills of legal research, were missed along the way. It is now time that information literacy skills are recognised as being of even greater importance and relevance to our students, and for this to be addressed much more widely by law librarians.

The new *Law Student Research Competencies and Information Literacy Principles* (American Association of Law Libraries [2011]) have universal applicability. Law librarians can use these standards as a common framework from which to create, revise and enhance courses, classes and materials. There is an urgent need to broaden what we teach to incorporate information literacy skills and to advise and instruct students through the process. We need to work with our faculties or law firms to ensure that the methodology we adopt is part of every student's course experience, whether it takes place early in the degree, or at a later stage.

This is an evolutionary process in which we recognise the changing nature of our users, their knowledge and expectations, at the same time taking into account fast moving technological developments. Working together with our academic colleagues we have the opportunity to embed information literacy standards into law courses and law firm training, enhancing the solid foundations we have established in legal research skills training. Our reward will be information literate legal researchers, academics and lawyers who are better prepared for the ever changing information challenges of the future.

Further Reading

Association of College and Research Libraries (2000), *Information Literacy Competency Standards for Higher Education*. Available at: www.ala.org/ala/mgrps/divs/acrl/standards/information literacycompetency.cfm, accessed 21 June 2010.

Australian Library and Information Association (2006), *Information Literacy for all Australians*. Available at: www.alia.org.au/policies/information.literacy.html, accessed 21 June 2010.

Berkowitz, R. and Eisenberg, M. (2007), *What is the Big6?*. Available at: www.big6.com/what-is-the-big6, accessed January 2010.

Bundy, A. (2004), *Australian and New Zealand Information Literacy Framework: Principles, Standards and Practice*, 2nd edition. Available at: www.caul.edu.au/info-literacy/InfoLiteracyFramework.pdf, accessed March 2010.

Catts, R. and Lau, J. (2008), *Towards Information Literacy Indicators* (Paris, UNESCO). Available at: www.lilacconference.com/dw/speakers/cattsandlau.pdf, accessed 10 June 2010.

Chartered Institute of Library and Information Professionals (2004), *Policy and Advocacy – Information Literacy: Definition* (published online December 2004). Available at: www.cilip.org.uk/get-involved/advocacy/learning/information-literacy/Pages/definition.aspx, accessed 10 June 2010.

Clinch, P., Barber, M., Jackson, C. and Wakefield, N. (2006), *Teaching Legal Research*, 2nd edition (Warwick: UK Centre for Legal Education). . Available at: www.ukcle.ac.uk/resources/tlr/index.html, accessed 10 June 2010.

Davidson, S. (2010), *Way Beyond Legal Research: Understanding the Research Process of Legal Scholars* (published online 15 January 2010). Available at: http://ssrn.com/abstract=1537336, accessed 10 June 2010.

Gallacher, I. (2006), 'Forty-Two: The Hitchhiker's Guide to Teaching Legal Research to the Google Generation', *Akron Law Review* 39, 151.

Garvey, J. (2009), 'Making Law Students Client-ready: A New Model in Legal Education', *Duke Forum for Law and Social Change* 1, 101–29.

Harris, C. (2009), 'Excuse Me. Do You Speak Digital? Harvard's John Palfrey Explores what it is Like to be a Digital Native', *School Library Journal* September 2009. Available at: www.schoollibraryjournal.com/slj/printissue/currentissue/857834-427/excuse_me._do_you_speak.csp, accessed 25 June 2010.

Information Literacy (UK national website of information and resources). Available at: www.informationliteracy.org.uk, accessed 10 June 2010.

International Federation of Library Associations and Institutions. Information Literacy website. Available at: www.ifla.org/information-literacy, accessed 10 June 2010.

International Federation of Library Associations and Institutions, UNESCO and the National Forum on Information Literacy (2005), *Beacons of the Information Society: The Alexandria Proclamation on Information Literacy and Lifelong Learning*. Available at: http://archive.ifla.org/III/wsis/BeaconInfSoc.html, accessed 10 June 2010.

International Federation of Library Associations and Institutions. Information Literacy Section (2006), *Guidelines on Information Literacy for Lifelong Learning, Final Draft by Jesús Lau*. Available at: http://archive.ifla.org/VII/s42/pub/IL-Guidelines2006.pdf, accessed 10 June 2010.

Jayasuriya, K. and Brillantine, F.M. (2008), *Student Services in the 21st Century: Evolution and Innovation in Discovering Student Needs, Teaching Information Literacy, and Designing Library 2.0-Based Services*. Available at: http://ssrn.com/abstract=1103090, accessed 10 June 2010.

Murray, L. et al. (2005), 'Netskills and the Current State of Beliefs and Practices in Student Learning: An Assessment and Recommendations', *British Journal of Educational Technology* 36:3, 425–38.

National Forum on Information Literacy (US national site of information and resources). Available at: www.infolit.org, accessed 10 June 2010. Especially bibliography. Available at: www.infolit.org/resources.html.

Palfrey, J. (2010), 'Cornerstones of Law Libraries for an Era of Digital-Plus', *Law Library Journal* 102:2, 171–90. Available at: www.aallnet.org/products/pub_llj_v102n02/2010-11.pdf, accessed 10 June 2010.

Rumsey, M. (2009), 'The Skills They Need: International and Foreign Research', *Legal Reference Services Quarterly* 28:1–2, 133–49. Available at: http://ssrn.com/abstract=1437233, accessed 10 June 2010.

Valentine, S. (2010), 'Legal Research as a Fundamental Skill: A Lifeboat for Students and Law Schools', *University of Baltimore Law Review* 39:2, 175–227. Available at: http://ssrn.com/abstract=1537871, accessed 21 June 2010.

Webber, S. (2007), *Information Literacy: Marketing and Educational Views ... and Some Research*. Available at: www.slideshare.net/sheilawebber/information-literacy-marketing-and-educational-views-and-some-research, accessed 10 June 2010.

Weiner, S. (2010), 'Information Literacy: A Neglected Core Competency', *Educause Quarterly* 33:1. Availableat:www.educause.edu/EDUCAUSE+Quarterly/EDUCAUSEQuarterlyMagazineVolum/InformationLiteracyANeglectedC/199382, accessed 10 June 2010.

Blogs

Michael Lorenzen: www.information-literacy.net.
Sheila Webber: http://information-literacy.blogspot.com.

References

American Association of Law Libraries (2011), *Law Student Research Competencies and Information Literacy Principles*. Available at: http://www.aallnet.org/about/LawStudentResearchCompetenciesInformationLiteracyPrinciples.pdf, accessed 28 April 2011.

Albon, E. (2009), 'Innovative Involvement not Embarrassing Intervention: Using Technology to Connect with Students Without Treading on Virtual Toes', *Legal Information Management* 9:4, 240–5.

Andretta, S. (2001), 'Legal Information Literacy: A Pilot Study', *New Library World* 102:7/8, 255–64.

Beljaars, B. (2009), 'Implementing Legal Information Literacy: A Challenge for the Curriculum', *International Journal of Legal Information* 37:3, 320–32. Original published online in 2007 in Dutch, 'Juridische informatievaardigheden implementeren: een curriculumuitdaging'. Available at: http://hdl.handle.net/1765/10676, accessed 10 June 2010.

Carritt, A. (2007), 'Teaching Research Skills Outside the Curriculum: Lessons Learnt at Oxford University', *Legal Information Management* 7:4, 239–43.

Carroll, R., Johnston, S. and Thompson, E. (2001), 'Information Literacy and Legal Research Skills Education in the UWA Bachelor of Laws Degree', *Teaching and Learning Forum 2001 Proceedings* 2001. Available at: http://lsn.curtin.edu.au/tlf/tlf2001/carroll.html, accessed 21 June 2010.

Cuffe, N. (2002), *Law Student Experiences of Information and Information Technology – Implications for Legal Information Literacy Curriculum Development*. Available at: www.aare.edu.au/02pap/cuf02169.htm, accessed 10 June 2010.

Davies, J. and Jackson, C. (2005), 'Information Literacy in the Law Curriculum: Experiences from Cardiff', *Law Teacher* 39:2, 150–60.

Gallacher, I. (2007), *Who are Those Guys? The Results of a Survey Studying the Information Literacy of Incoming Law Students* (published online 31 July 2007). Available at: http://ssrn.com/abstract=1004088, accessed 10 June 2010.

Head, A. and Eisenberg, M. (2009), 'Lessons Learned: How College Students Seek Information in the Digital Age', *Project Information Literacy Progress Report 1 December 2009* (Seattle, WA: Information School, University of Washington). Available at: http://projectinfolit.org/pdfs/PIL_Fall2009_Year1Report_12_2009.pdf, accessed 10 June 2010.

Hensiak, K., Burke, S. and Nixon, D. (2004), 'Abstract, Assessing Information Literacy among First-Year Law Students: A Survey to Measure Research Experiences and Perceptions', *Law Library Journal* 96:4, 867–8.

Johnson, L., Levine, A. and Smith, R. (2009), *The Horizon Report* (Austin: The New Media Consortium).

Johnston, B. and Webber, S. (2005), 'As We May Think: Information Literacy as a Discipline for the Information Age', *Research Strategies* 20:33, 108–21.

Kim-Prieto, D. (2010), *How Law Student Information Literacy (LSIL) Standards Address Deficits Identified by the MacCrate Report and the Carnegie Report, and What They Mean for Legal Research Education and Training* 17–22. Available at: http://ssrn.com/abstract=1678146, accessed 8 March 2011.

Knott, C. (2009), 'On Teaching Advanced Legal Research', *Legal Reference Services Quarterly* 28:1, 101. Available at: http://ssrn.com/abstract=1448084, accessed 10 June 2010.

Lien, M. (1998), 'Technocentrism and the Soul of the Common Law Lawyer', *American University Law Review* 48:1, 85–134.

McLaurin-Smith, N. and Presser, P. (2005), 'Embed with the Faculty: Legal Information Skills Online', *Journal of Academic Librarianship* 31:3, 247–62.

Meredith, S. (2005), 'Lessons Learnt from the Legal Research Skills Programme', *UKCLE Seminar on Teaching and Learning for Legal Skills Trainers*, February 2005. Available at: www.ukcle.ac.uk/resources/biall/meredith.html, accessed 10 June 2010.

Michels, D. and Lewis, M. (2009), 'The Changing Shape of Legal Information', *Canadian Law Library Review* [*Revue canadienne des bibliotheques de droit*] 34:2, 67–71.

O'Sullivan, C. (2006), 'Is Information Literacy a Basis for Life-long Learning? Observations from the Workplace', *ANZIIL Symposium Series Six, Transitions*. Available at: www.anziil.org/events_meetings/2006/events/symposium-series-six/overview.htm, accessed October 2009.

Peoples, L. (2005), 'The Death of the Digest and Pitfalls of Electronic Research: What is the Modern Legal Researcher to Do?', *Law Library Journal* 97:4, 661–79.

Pope, A. (2009), 'Integrating Legal Research Skills into the Curriculum and into Life', *Legal Information Management* 9, 246–49.

Power, G. (2009), *Some Information Literacy Skills for Law Students* (London: Institute of Advanced Legal Studies). Unpublished, copy with author.

Roach, C. (2005), 'Is the Sky Falling? Ruminations on Incoming Law Student Preparedness …', *The Journal of the Legal Writing Institute* 11, 295–327.

Rowlands, I., Nicholas, D., Williams, P., Huntington, P., Fieldhouse, M., Gunter, B., Withey, R., Jamali, H., Dobrowolski, T. and Tenopir, C. (2008), 'The Google Generation: The Information Behaviour of the Researcher of the Future', *Aslib Proceedings* 60:4, 290–310.

Seguin, P. (2005), 'Ignorance of the Law is No Excuse: A Student's Perspective on Developing Legal Information Literacy', *Canadian Law Library Review* 30:2, 80–4. Available at: http://ssrn.com/abstract=1158597, accessed 20 October 2010 [listed by later name: Pengelley, P.].

Society of College, National and University Libraries (2007), *Seven Pillars Model for Information Literacy*. Available at: www.sconul.ac.uk/groups/information_literacy/sp/model.html, accessed 10 June 2010.

Vie, S. (2008), 'Digital Divide 2.0: "Generation M" and Online Social Networking Sites in the Composition Classroom', *Computers and Composition* 25, 9–23. Available at: https://shop.elsevier.com/authored_subject_sections/S06/S06_345/misc/computers_omposition1.pdf, accessed 10 June 2010.

Webber, S. and Johnston, B. (2003), 'Assessment for Information Literacy: Vision and Reality', in Martin, A. and Rader, H. (eds), *Information and IT Literacy: Enabling Learning in the 21st Century* (London: Facet).

Wilson, V. (1994), 'Developing the Adult Independent Learner: Information Literacy and the Remote External Student', *Distance Education* 15:2, 254–78.

Chapter 8
Law Librarianship Around the World
Introduction

Jules Winterton

This chapter contains profiles of law librarianship each written by experienced law librarians from various countries around the world: India, Moldova, Nigeria, the Philippines, Turkey and Vietnam.[1]

Each country profile addresses topics which describe and explain the overall environment in which law librarians operate in their country. The profiles give the number of practising law librarians in the profession, if that number can be quantified and if indeed there is an identifiable cadre of professionals who can be termed law librarians. The education and training of law librarians is explained, including the general qualifications needed to practise as a librarian, any particular qualifications which are available to law librarians, and the usual qualifications held by law librarians including the prevalence of law degrees. Reference is made to any association or organisation for law libraries or law librarians which engages in some or all of the following activities: networking, continuing professional development, oversight of professional qualifications, collaboration in services, and lobbying about policy issues affecting librarianship in general and law librarianship in particular. The libraries in various sectors which hold major law collections, including separate law libraries and libraries with a more general role but with substantial holdings of law, are identified and described. Legal publishing in the country is briefly described, noting major legal publications in print and electronic form, and freely available and reliable sources of legal information are mentioned. Authors were also requested to identify major policy issues affecting law librarianship in their country. It is hoped that the assessments from these and further country profiles of law librarianship, which will be collected by the International Association of Law Libraries, will over time provide evidence and direction for the formation of international legal information policy. Reference is made throughout to other materials for further study.

The International Association of Law Libraries (IALL) makes available financial assistance each year to enable practising law librarians who are normally unable to benefit from Association activities to attend its Annual Course in International Law Librarianship that forms the annual conference of the Association.[2] The IALL offers three bursaries each year to attend its Conference comprising the following benefits: the conference registration fee is waived, a grant to assist with accommodation and travel costs of up to US$1,500 in 2010, and membership of the IALL for one year including the *International Journal of Legal Information*. These grants are not limited to members of the Association.

---

1 Several other sections were commissioned from law librarians in countries in Africa, the Caribbean and South America but, for reasons beyond the authors' control, it was not possible to complete them. However, it is hoped that further country profiles will be written and included on the website of the International Association of Law Libraries at: http://iall.org.

2 Information about this programme of grants to attend the IALL conferences is available at: http://iall.org/scholarship.html.

Each contributor to this chapter has been a awarded a grant or scholarship in the past by the International Association of Law Libraries either to attend its Annual Course in International Law Librarianship or to undertake an internship at an overseas institution and each plays a significant role in the profession in their country. There have been 23 recipients of these grants since 2001 when the programme was first introduced with two grants each year (subsequently extended to three grants each year in 2005). These recipients (listed at: http://iall.org/scholarship-previous.html) have been drawn from 18 countries: Bosnia and Herzegovina, Brazil, Egypt, England, Estonia, Haiti, India, Kenya, Korea, Malaysia, Moldova, Nigeria, Philippines, Puerto Rico, South Africa, Turkey, United States and Zimbabwe. A further three grants were awarded in 2010 and the successful applicants were from Canada, China and Malawi. Each grant has been awarded to applicants who have demonstrated promise and are likely to make a significant contribution to the profession of law librarianship.

The IALL also offers a grant to assist law librarians who are financially unable to undertake a placement, internship, non-stipendiary fellowship, or an extended visit to a law library outside their own country. The programme is intended to support not only professional development but also research projects in law librarianship and legal information management. The programme, which was introduced in 2008, provides a grant each year to assist with the cost of travel and accommodation of up to US$3,000 in 2010 and the provision of advice to assist in identifying possible host institutions (although this is not a placement service and applicants need to make arrangements with a host institution prior to application).[3] A grant was awarded in 2008, although the successful applicant has not yet undertaken the internship. No award was made in 2009 but two awards were made in 2010 to applicants from Korea and Turkey.

Since the awards in both categories, each of the recipients has continued to work with legal information and in law librarianship and has made substantial contributions to the profession. Four of the countries mentioned above have hosted the IALL conference and a fifth, Malaysia, will host the conference in 2011 and eight of the recipients have been or are actively involved in planning those conferences. The IALL conferences, apart from their main educational and networking purposes, have a significant impact on law librarianship in the host country and help to improve the status of law librarians and recognition of their role in society. The various senior judges, chief justices, government ministers, deans of law schools, and other eminent figures in the legal systems of the host country have participated in exceptional events organised by and for an association of professionals drawn from around the world who represent an important element in legal systems, the administration of justice and the rule of law.

The IALL has played an important part in the formation of national and regional associations of law librarians and law libraries over the past 50 years. The IALL conferences have encouraged efforts to create such associations in some of the host countries, most recently and successfully in Turkey as described in the country profile in this chapter, as well as in the countries of grant recipients and of delegates.

It is intended that a coherent picture of law librarianship around the world will emerge from these and further country profiles of law librarianship and that this will help to generate interest and recognition of the value of law librarianship, and will encourage action to address the policy issues which are identified.

3 Details of the IALL internship grants programme are available at: http://iall.org/internship.html.

Law Librarianship in India

Uma Narayan

> Librarians are almost always very helpful and often almost absurdly knowledgeable. Their skills are probably very underestimated and largely underemployed.
>
> (Medawar 1978, 41)

Introduction

India has a rich cultural heritage and has always been a great seat of learning and written literature. There were well known universities with vast libraries in ancient India. However, despite the influx of literature in many fields, the growth and development of law libraries and legal information centres has been rather slow. Law librarianship did not develop as a recognised profession until recently, having gone through a plethora of changes before slowly emerging as a steadfast, engaging and challenging profession.

Law librarianship, especially in judicial institutions, is different from librarianship in other disciplines. A law librarian caters to the particular and specialised needs of lawyers. Solicitors and judges need the constant inflow of the right information and research citations at the appropriate time. A law librarian has to be well-versed in law, alert and quick-witted.

Law and Librarianship

A law librarian in India today is a skilled professional with a specialised degree in library science and law. The profession requires knowledge of law, technology and library science combined with an ability to assimilate the correct information within a short period of time. This is a huge challenge, considering the vastness of the Indian law and the Constitution.

Indian law and the Indian Constitution are largely modelled on the British legal system. This is a legacy of the long British Raj in India. Indian law is based on the common law of England, although there are distinctions to accommodate the wide cultural and religious diversity in India. Family law in India, for example, differs according to the religion followed by the person.

One can therefore appreciate the challenge faced by law librarians who are expected to be well versed in the differing family laws and keep the required references ready for the legal counsel.

Education and Training of Law Librarians

Even though law librarians need special skills to serve library users, there are no specialised training courses in law librarianship in India. The general qualifications required for law librarians in India are the Master's degree in Library and Information Science together with a law degree and computer skills. There is a recent initiative to start a Certificate in Law Librarianship course for training librarians in law librarianship and legal research. SNDT Women's University, Mumbai, has expressed interest in starting such a course.

The 26th Annual Conference of the International Association of Law Libraries (IALL) was held in India in December 2007 in Mumbai and generated considerable interest (Deshpande 2007a and 2007b).

A Seminar on 'Perspectives on Law Librarianship in India' organised in collaboration with SNDT Women's University in Mumbai and held at the university was attended by many law librarians. Some efforts are being made to start CPD (Continuous Professional Development) Sessions for Court Librarians. There are some informal collaborative groups like Lawnet, a Yahoo group for law librarians. An effort is again being made in 2010 to establish an Association of Law Libraries.

Law Libraries

In order to understand the challenges faced by law librarians it is imperative to understand the structure and types of law libraries in India. There are three types of law libraries: academic, judicial and research.

Academic law libraries predominate. There are about 950 law schools spread all over India imparting legal education as approved by the Bar Council of India.[4] There are also National Law Schools which are autonomous and were started to enhance professionalism in the legal field. These law schools have modern sophisticated libraries with the latest technologies due to good financial grants. The academic law libraries include university libraries. Delhi University Law Library is regarded as one of the best law libraries in India; it was established in 1924 and has a collection of about 100,000 volumes.

Judicial court libraries consist of the Supreme Court Library, High Court Libraries, Subordinate Court Libraries and Judicial Academy Libraries. In addition there are Advocate Libraries run by the Bar Associations attached to the Supreme Court and the High Courts. The Supreme Court Library located in New Delhi is one of the largest libraries with 300,000 volumes. There are 21 High Courts for 28 states in India and there are in all about 400 District Courts.[5]

The Parliament of India Library[6] serves the ministers and legislators. There are also law libraries at the Departments of Law and Justice at the Central and State Governments.

Organisations involved in legal research have their own legal libraries. The major such organisation is the Indian Law Institute in Delhi (see below) which has a rich collection and compiles the useful *Index to Indian Legal Periodicals*.

Major Law Libraries of India

Supreme Court Judges' Library

The Supreme Court Judges' Library[7] was established in New Delhi in 1937, when it was known as the Federal Court Library. It contains significant legal literature to support the need of Honourable

4 Available at: www.barcouncilofindia.org, accessed 22 October 2010.

5 Details of various courts are available at: www.indiancourts.nic.in, accessed 22 October 2010.

6 Available at: http://164.100.47.132/LssNew/Library/parliament_library.html, accessed 22 October 2010.

7 Available at: www.supremecourtofindia.nic.in, accessed 22 October 2010.

Courts and Judges and has a collection of about 250,000 legal documents, which include books, monographs, commission/committee reports, government publications, central and state legislation, other legislative materials, and e-resources in the form of online and CD-ROM legal databases. It subscribes to about 200 Indian and foreign journals and law reports. The Supreme Court Judges' Library is a grid of libraries. In addition to the Central Library, it also maintains working collections in 12 Bench libraries and 26 residential libraries of Honourable Judges. The Supreme Court Judges' Library is essentially a reference and research wing of the Court.

High Court Judges' Libraries

There are 22 High Courts with their benches in India each having their own Judges' libraries and Advocates' libraries. The subordinate courts also have small libraries with important legal collections. Access to electronic databases is provided to all court libraries.

Bombay High Court Law Libraries

The Bombay High Court Library[8] was established in 1862 with the establishment of the High Court. It is a well-equipped library for the Honourable Judges, located on the ground floor and third floor of the main building in Mumbai. The library caters to the requirements of Honourable Judges by providing latest case laws, legal news, articles, commentaries and law reports to enable them to discharge their responsibility effectively. The main library is located in Mumbai and there are libraries at the benches of Nagpur, Aurangabad and Goa.

The library collections comprise law commentaries, law reports, Government Gazettes, Bare Acts (Central Acts and State of Maharashtra Acts), Law Commission reports, manuals and general law books. The total book collection is approximately 130,000. The Bombay High Court Judges' Library has viewed technology as a means to offer efficient and effective library services and to add new services to help carry out the mission of the library. Two major initiatives are to develop law library management software using LAMP[9] technology for maintaining all library records and to develop e-law library web pages. The initiatives have led to the use of technology in administrative, technical and public services departments.

The Library uses Supreme Court Cases Online, Bombay Cases Reporter Online, LJSoft, Manupatra, Westlaw and LexisNexis extensively to provide quick information.

The Bombay High Court has its principal bench at Mumbai and three other benches at Nagpur, Aurangabad and Goa. The Libraries at the Benches of the Bombay High Court are managed by librarians. The Library at Nagpur Bench has approximately 97,000 books which include law commentaries, Bare Acts, Gazettes and rare books. The Nagpur Bench also has an exclusive Criminal Law Library. The Library at Aurangabad Bench has approximately 50,000 books including law commentaries, Bare Acts and Gazettes. The Library at Goa Bench has approximately 35,000 books which include law commentaries, Bare Acts, Gazettes and rare books.

---

8 Available at: http://bombayhighcourt.nic.in/libweb/judlibwebindex.html, accessed 22 October 2010.

9 LAMP is an acronym for an open source web development framework, originally derived from Linux-Apache-MySQL-PHP.

Indian Law Institute Library

The Library of the Institute[10] in New Delhi, established in 1956, is one of the leading law libraries in Asia and attracts scholars from all over the world for legal research. The Judiciary, Central and State Government officers, various Embassies and High Commissions in Delhi also use the referral services of the Library.

The Indian Law Institute Library collection development policy emphasises acquisition of the complete primary resources of India. The legal resources of the United Kingdom, United States of America, Canada, Australia and New Zealand are also extensively acquired. Over the years, the library has developed collections on jurisprudence, judicial process, constitutional law, intellectual property, public international law, environmental law, human rights, criminal law, international business transactions, laws of the European Community, and laws of the ASEAN nations. The library currently houses a unique collection of 70,000 books and periodicals, and 25 CD-ROM titles.

National Law School of India University, Bangalore

There are six major National Law Schools, the earliest being the National Law School of India University at Bangalore.[11] The Library is an integral part of academic endeavour in the Law School and is being constantly enriched by acquisition of the latest books and journals to further the advancement of the university's academic activities. It has a collection of over 40,000 volumes covering a wide range of general and special subjects and has introduced computerised facilities for housekeeping as well as information retrieval.

Legal Publishing and Law Reporting In India

Legal publishing in India is growing very rapidly, at about 10–15 per cent annually, and is worth approximately US$60 million annually. There are many legal publishers in India. Some are well established and publish authentic literature by well known authors. Recently legal publishers in parallel with their print products also provide CD-ROMs and Internet-based access. The electronic information includes court judgments, amendments of legislation, and notifications of the government departments. Publishers have started to provide electronic versions of their law reports with good search facilities. Still, the progress is slow.

In India law reporting began as early as 1774 when the Supreme Court of British India was established. In 1862 the British Government established High Courts. A need was felt to report the judgments of the High Courts but there was no standard system of reporting. The Indian Law Reports Act was passed in 1875 to improve the quality and to authorise the publication of High Court cases. As a result, the *Indian Law Reports* series started publication.

Now the trend is changing in law libraries. Although some libraries are committed to purchase print titles there is a steady increase in the use of electronic formats. The attitude of law librarians is changing slowly as they find it easy to use the electronic versions with their search facilities compared with the print version.

10 Available at: www.ilidelhi.org/library.htm, accessed 22 October 2010.

11 Available at: www.nls.ac.in/library.html, accessed 22 October 2010.

The Indian Central Legislation is available for free in the India Code website[12] which is official website of the Legislative Department. The legislation is published officially by the Central and the State Governments in print in the form of Gazettes. There are also commercial publishers who have both Central and State Legislation in electronic format as well as print format. The other major sources apart from Gazettes for Central Legislation are *A.I.R. Manuals* published by All India Reporter, Nagpur having all the Central legislation, *Malik & Manchanda's Encyclopedia of Statutory Rules (under Central Acts)* published by Law Publishers(India) Pvt. Ltd. of Allahabad. Similarly publishers in each Indian state publish the local legislation.

Court judgments are officially published by the courts; the *Supreme Court Reports* are published by the Supreme Court of India and the *Indian Law Reports* series are published by some High Courts. The Judgment Information System[13] provides free access to the full text of all the court judgments officially available. Many commercial publishers publish court judgments in print and electronic format. The oldest and best-known commercial law reporters are *All India Reporter* and *Supreme Court Cases*, both of which are available on CD-ROM as well as via the Internet. There are annual digests of cases such as the *Supreme Court Yearly Digest* published in print by Eastern Book Company of Lucknow, and digests arranged by subject published in print by various publishers.

The Law Commission recommends legislative reforms from time to time, which are published officially as Reports by the Law Commission of India, Ministry of Law & Justice. There have been 234 reports at the time of writing and all are available for free on the Internet.[14]

The debates of both houses of Parliament, namely the Lok Sabha (House of the People) and the Rajya Sabha (Council of States), and much other documentation, are available on Indian Parliament website.[15]

Major publishers of secondary legal sources include Eastern Book Company of Lucknow, Eastern Book House of Kolkata, Universal Book Publishing of New Delhi, Law Publishers (India) Pvt. Ltd. of Allahabad; Wadhwa & Co of Nagpur has merged with LexisNexis Butterworths, New Delhi.

Major Policy Issues in Law Libraries in India

Lack of finance and trained staff are the main problems faced by law libraries.

There is a need for specialised training for law library work. It is now realised that the Master's degree in Library Science has to be more specific in relation to the nature of the library. There is also a lack of proper law librarianship courses to train librarians to work in a law library. Universities should take a lead to do the same.

Limited finance restricts acquisition of books. There are many electronic legal databases coming onto the market but their cost is an issue for smaller academic libraries. The other major challenge for governmental libraries wishing to subscribe to electronic databases, is to convince the governmental accounts departments that electronic databases are same as the printed legal sources since they are not yet ready to accept change and still follow age-old systems.

12 Available at: www.indiacode.nic.in, accessed 22 October 2010.

13 Available at: www.judis.nic.in, accessed 22 October 2010.

14 Available at: lawcommissionofindia.nic.in, accessed 22 October 2010.

15 Available at: http://parliamentofindia.nic.in, accessed 22 October 2010.

There is a lack of proper networking and collaboration among Indian law libraries although the libraries do assist each other with important materials available to them. There is a need for an association of Indian law libraries which could bring together all law librarians, organise regular training and continuous professional development sessions, and provide a common platform for law librarians to share their experiences. Two attempts have been made to start an association, the first by H.C. Jain, then Librarian of the Indian Law Institute, who tried in the late 1960s and 1970s, and the second was a recent attempt initiated by C.U. Navalgund, Librarian of the National Law School of India University in Bangalore in 2007. Unfortunately, neither of the attempts succeeded in formally establishing an association.

The autonomous law school libraries have good infrastructure and modern technology but governmental libraries and some law college libraries lack proper infrastructure and modern systems. Realisation of the importance of libraries is as yet limited in India.

References

Deshpande, S. (2007a), 'Five-day law librarians' meet set to begin today', *Times of India*, 1 December 2007.

Deshpande, S. (2007b), 'Law librarians treated to chapter of Asiatic history', *Times of India*, 5 December 2007.

Index to Indian Legal Periodicals (1963–), Semi annual (New Delhi: Indian Law Institute).

Medawar, C. (1978), *The Social Audit Consumer Handbook* (London: Macmillan).

Further Reading

Alexandrowicz, C. (ed.) (1958), *A Bibliography of Indian Law* (Madras: Oxford University Press).

Jain, H. (1970), *Indian Legal Materials: A Bibliographical Guide* (Bombay: N.M. Tripathi Private Ltd.).

Chander, S. and Jain, H. (1984–5), 'Law libraries in India', in Gupta, B., Jain, V., Nathan, S., Kumar, P. and Ramaiah, L. (eds) *Handbook of Libraries, Archives and Information Centres in India* (New Delhi: Information Industry Publications), vol. 1, 188–208.

Mahr, T. (1990), 'An introduction to law and law libraries in India', *Law Library Journal* 82, 91–128.

Narayan, U. (2007), 'Sources of Indian legal information', *Legal Information Management* 7, 133–9.

Srivastava, R. (2008), 'Law librarianship in India with special reference to the judicial library system', *International Journal of Legal Information* 37:2, 275–99. Available at: http://scholarship.law.cornell.edu/ijli/vol36/iss2/12, accessed September 2010.

Law Librarianship in Moldova

Mariana Harjevschi

There is still enormous work to be undertaken in the law library system in Moldova. Despite the recognition that law libraries or legal information centres are essential for active citizenship, effective legal education and progress in building the rule of law, they rarely receive the attention they deserve in terms of professional organisation, adequate funding and trained staffing enabling them to perform their important roles. Chaotic publishing activity, scarce publications with legal content, obstacles to access to legal information, and deficiencies in access to legal information on the web are the predominant problems that encompass the legal information system in Moldova. The absence of vital law libraries, along with a shortage of law librarians and trained legal information specialists has a negative impact on the conduct of efficient and effective legal research both by members of the legal profession and the ordinary citizen.

Law Librarianship

An exact number of law librarians, as well as of law libraries, is hard to identify. The library system in Moldova is a complex, diverse and interactive national network, comprising over 2,911 libraries spread throughout the country. The National Bureau of Statistics in 2010 showed a total of 4,661 librarians including 2,504 public librarians and 2,017 academic librarians. Regarding special librarians, the Bureau collects figures only about medical, agrarian and technical librarians, currently numbering 223 librarians. The deficiency of information on law librarians demonstrates an undeveloped law library system and a lack of advocacy that needs to be voiced by the Library Association.

Law libraries within legal institutions or organisations, such as ministries, courts or law firms, are merged with legal information centres, legal departments or archives. In this situation, archivists, legal specialists and communication officers perform librarians' duties and responsibilities. In addition, university libraries with general collections do not consider it necessary to have law librarians. Recently, a significant development took place at the University Library of the International Free University. In order to facilitate legal research, a 'legal and business reference librarian' was appointed. This approach is considered a relatively new concept in Moldovan librarianship.

Usually library staff, especially those employed in universities, hold a university degree in library science from the Library and Information Assistance Department within the Journalism and Sciences of Communication Faculty at the Moldova State University, the only university where a degree in library science can be obtained. Some librarians hold a second degree in law, public administration or related fields. In the last three years, annually between 30 and 40 (full- and part-time programmes) librarians graduated with a Licentiate degree (equivalent to a Bachelor's degree) in Communication Sciences with the minor in the field of professional training, entitled *Library Science, Informational Assistance and Archives* (three years of studies with 180 credits) and 10 students with a Master's degree in Communication Sciences with specialisation in *Info-documentary Institution Management* (two years of studies with 120 credits). Staff in courts and law firms hold a degree in law or a similar degree but very rarely a library science degree. The Library and Information Assistance Department, besides core courses, offers only one optional course, 'Legal Information Resources', to prepare legal information specialists. In order to apply for a librarian position, usually a diploma in library science is a requirement but there are no requisite qualifications for someone to be employed and/or designated as a law librarian. Usually a law librarian has academic training and qualifications in both library or information science and law but in some libraries a university degree will suffice.

In spite of appeals to the national Library Association of Moldova, neither a separate association of law librarians nor a section of law librarians within the national association has yet been formed. The Library Association of Moldova was formed in 1992 and currently has 1,800 individual members. Among the membership are law librarians but the exact number cannot be traced. The reason is that usually law librarians are considered academic, public or special librarians, so they are considered members of these sections within the Library Association.

Between 2001 and 2006 a training centre, the Librarianship School of Moldova, was founded and supported by the Soros Foundation of Moldova and the Open Society Institute from Hungary for the purpose of updating the professional knowledge and skills of Moldovan librarians and information specialists. The centre, run as a project, was supposed to be supported further by the Ministry of Culture but closed due to limited financial assistance. Since then many efforts have been undertaken to achieve a strategic approach to continuous education for librarians. The National Library of Moldova is currently advocating an 'Agreement on Organizing Training Courses for Librarians from Public Libraries' between the Institute of Education Sciences and the Ministry of Culture. The Library Association has submitted a 'Regulation on the Continuous Training of Librarians in Public Libraries' to the Ministry of Culture for approval. The regulation was developed in accordance with Article 18(2) of the Legea cu privire la biblioteci [Law on Libraries] (1994) and a Government Decision 'On the Organization of Continuing Training'. In addition the Library Association has approved an 'Action Plan on Continuing Training for Librarians'. The target groups for the first call are directors of municipal and regional public libraries, deputy directors and librarians responsible for methodological work. The two-week programme is ambitious and includes all aspects of current library activity. Neither the initial programme of the Librarianship School of Moldova, nor the others planned, focus on law librarians.

As there is no association of law librarians, or other professional entities or collaborative groups for law librarians, no seminars, workshops or conferences have been organised in recent years. However, on a voluntary basis, the Public Law Library branch of the Chisinau Municipal Library annually organises various workshops on legal research for public librarians from the city library network.

Law Libraries

According to the Legea cu privire la biblioteci [Law on Libraries] (1994) the National Library System of Moldova is composed of the following networks of libraries: public, academic and specialised. Law libraries can be found in a few major institutions, for example the Library of the National Institute of Justice, the Parliament Library, the Public Law Library and the Law Library of the Moldova State University. So the law library system can be structured as follows:

Specialised Libraries

These libraries offer special information and documentation in the area of law and related areas. Usually they are established within courts, ministries, departments, enterprises, institutions, associations or professional organisations.

Law libraries for the judiciary These include the libraries of the Supreme Court of Justice, Court of Appeal, Military Court and other courts. They are fairly small libraries and mainly contain legislation (printed collections of the official gazette), law reports, legal periodicals and small collection of treatises and monographs. In practice these libraries are merged with archives and keep all the decisions and other official documents of the institution. The Supreme Court Library is mainly a reference library containing legal literature in Romanian and Russian and only some foreign literature. It was restructured on 24 October 2003 and currently its collection encompasses more than 13,000 legal items. The library allows access to a limited number of readers, usually officials of the court. As a matter of principle, they do not lend books outside their building and do not participate in interlibrary loans. Among court libraries, the Constitutional Court Library and those that belong to the appeal courts are organised similarly.

Administrative law libraries In Moldova there are administrative libraries at various government and state public institutions, for example Parliament, Government, Ministry of Justice, Ministry of Foreign Affairs and European Integration. The Parliament Library is a reference library for Members of the Moldovan Parliament but lawyers may be allowed to use the reading room and by special permission to borrow books. The collection consists of about 62,000 items and concentrates on law, politics and social policy. It contains parliamentary debates, codes and all reports of Moldovan Commissions. It has strong holdings of official publications. The library is supervised by one librarian. The library within the Ministry of Justice is administered by two librarians and has quite a good collection of treaties and works on public international law and is relatively better stocked with law reports. These libraries are designed primarily to serve public officials, especially ministry employees, and therefore have a limited clientele. Another library considered important for law is the Information and Documentation Centre of the State Agency for Intellectual Property which contains 24 million items on copyright including books, reviews, patents and designs.

Private law libraries In general, these libraries, for example libraries of law firms and commercial enterprises, are comparatively small and not of importance to the public. Access to these libraries is strictly limited to employees. Law firms are focused more on access to legislation and court decisions, which is usually is offered either by means of printed collections of the official gazette or local databases. Sporadic acquisitions are made but essentially directed by lawyers.

Law libraries of NGOs These libraries in particular are focused on collecting the publications of non-governmental organisations (NGOs) which are usually received as donations from similar organisations. They operate as public information centres specialised in a particular law areas. The major NGOs active in developing individual libraries are the Centre of Law, IDIS Viitorul, Helsinki Committee for Human Rights, Lawyers for Human Rights, 'EX LEGE' Agency for the Support of Legal Education and Law and other organisations.

The Information Office of the Council of Europe in Moldova can also be included in this category. Its library comprises around 14,000 copies of the most important Council of Europe publications about the organisation's structure and activities. The collection also includes the complete case law of the European Court of Human Rights and conventions adopted by the Council of Europe. The documents are available in English and French and are accessible by the public.

In January 2001 the National Library of Moldova established a United Nations Information and Documentation Centre, as part of the UN Depository System, having the status of a full deposit library and the library now owns valuable collections of UN documents.

Academic Libraries

University law libraries These libraries support faculty research and teaching in law schools. In most Moldovan universities there is a central library, often referred to as the main library, and there also may be faculty and/or departmental libraries which are treated as branches of the central library. As a result, faculty or departmental librarians, including law librarians, are under the supervision of the Library Director who administers funds for the entire library system. Similarly, acquisition, indexing and cataloguing are centralised in nearly all Moldovan universities. The major law libraries are those from the Moldova State University[16] (1946) and the Free International University[17] (1992), Academy of Police (1992), Academy of Public Administration Office of the President of the Republic of Moldova (1993) and College of Management, Economics and Law (1996). Only law students and faculty have access to academic law libraries.

Law libraries at research institutes One of the most important libraries in this category is the Library of the National Institute of Justice, opened on 9 November 2007. The National Institute of Justice[18] is a modern facility for training candidates for the position of judge and prosecutor, continuing training of judges, prosecutors and others who contribute to the administration of justice. The library is under development and currently the collection consists of more than 2,000 books and law reviews. Two librarians with legal qualifications are employed.

Public Law Libraries

The Public Law Library[19] was opened on 24 May 2001 with financial support from the Soros-Moldova Foundation and the 'B.P.Hasdeu' Municipal Library. It was primarily designed to benefit the legal community (prosecutors, judges, lawyers, law faculty and students), as well as ordinary people. Since its opening the Public Law Library has proved to be a strong and useful institution through updated, accurate and comprehensive legal resources. Currently the Public Law Library provides free access to a unique collection of more than 14,396 books and 75 legal periodicals that are continually being extended. Legal information services are also delivered through two national leading legal databases: Jurist (National Legislation) and Practica Judiciară (National Jurisprudence); there is also access to HeinOnline and to the legislation of neighbouring countries. Along with reference services to the general public, the Public Law Library annually assists around 4,700 registered users. Daily between 300 and 350 users benefit from library services: book loan, reference services, searching databases, access to national legislation. The Public Law Library provides domestic, foreign and comparative legal and legislative information

16 Available at: www.usm.md, accessed 28 June 2010.
17 Available at: www.ulim.md, accessed 28 June 2010.
18 Available at: www.inj.md, accessed 28 June 2010.
19 Available at: www.pll.md/ro, accessed 28 June 2010.

to researchers and individual ordinary citizens. Moreover the library constantly develops and diversifies library services to the community. The library operates an online reference service, 'Ask a Librarian', that offers assistance to library users in finding information and answering questions.

The National Library, along with public libraries from all regions of Moldova, holds also law books, legal periodicals and offers access to legal periodicals.

Legal Publishing

Traditionally, the legal publications in Moldova can be divided into primary materials, which include the *Official Gazette* along with court decisions, and *secondary materials*, for example legal books, usually published by commercial publishers, universities and NGOs. A guide to Moldovan legal materials and legal research is available online (Harjevschi and Andrițchi 2010).

The primary print resources are published by a state agency named Moldpresa.[20] The official gazette is the *Monitorul Oficial* which is printed in Romanian and Russian. All codes are published separately by various publishing houses. There are two major fee-based databases, Jurist (National Legislation) and Practica Judiciară (National Jurisprudence).[21]

Statistically, a minimal amount of doctrinal legal publications appears annually. In recent years legal publishing has increased significantly but still could be characterised by an inherent unpredictability in publication activity, lack of uniform strategy and particularly a lack of specialised legal publishing houses. Ordinary publishing houses occasionally publish law books but the lack of specialised publishing houses reduces the research resources available to legal communities.

The major institutions for the publication of legal materials are still the universities that run small printing centres, where the law school faculties publish textbooks and monographs as a part of their academic responsibilities. This characteristically only occurs, however, in certain universities where financial assistance supports the scientific research, for example the Moldova State University, Free International University and the Police Academy.

Few publishing houses are focused on legal publications. Cartier Publishing House publishes a collection called Cartier juridic, including legal textbooks, studies and separate codes. In 2008 a special legal publishing house, Cartea juridică, was launched. The following major publishing houses also publish legal books: Cartdidact, Arc, Pontos and Museum.

Compared to textbook and monograph publications, periodical publishing has been more successful. During the 1990s several professional publications appeared: in Romanian *Revista Națională de Drept*, *Avocatul poporului*, *Dreptul Muncii* and *Justiția Constituțională* and in Russian *Business i pravo* and *Zakon i jizni*. Additionally major law schools have their own law reviews, the most common title is *Analele Științifice*, published annually.

Legal electronic publishing is currently evolving to meet user needs. Only the Practica Judiciara database offers access to several legal journals from Moldova, Romania and Russia. Separate electronic legal reviews can be accessed on the websites of the following institutions: the Institutul de Istorie, Stat si Drept (Institute of History, State and Law),[22] Universitatea de Stat din Moldova (Moldova State University).[23]

20 Available at: www.moldpresa.md, accessed 28 June 2010.

21 Available at: www.lex.md, accessed 28 June 2010.

22 Available at: http://iisd.md, accessed 28 June 2010.

23 Available at: www.usm.md, accessed 28 June 2010.

Legal practitioner-oriented literature is much more developed and this is explained by the nature of the market. This type of literature is written under different projects, carried out by various NGOs and published randomly by various publishers, but heavily used by the law community.

Sporadic financial assistance is available occasionally for legal publications from international organisations, such as the SOROS-Moldova Foundation,[24] United Nations Development Programme,[25] American Bar Association,[26] Central European and Eurasian Law Initiative,[27] and others.

Major Policy Issues

There are two major problems affecting law librarianship in Moldova.

The first is the lack of adequate professionally trained staff. One aspect of this problem is that there is currently no institution primarily concerned with specialised training of law librarians at any level. There is a need to develop the law librarianship profession in the country through formal training and appropriate curriculum for basic and continuing education. A degree of specialisation of law librarians, or special courses for students integrated in the curriculum and delivered at the Library School and Information Assistance within Moldova State University,[28] could be an incentive for teaching fundamentals in law librarianship for future law librarians.

The second is a need for the establishment of an association of law librarians in Moldova or a section or committee of law librarians within the national Library Association,[29] which would be committed to the development of law librarianship.

References

(Previously no studies on law libraries or law librarianship have been undertaken.)

Biblioteca Naţională a Republicii Moldova (Moldova National Library). Available at: www.bnrm.md [Contains annual statistical data].

Ghidul bibliotecilor din Chişinău (2007) (Chişinău: Epigraf).

Harjevschi, M. and Andriţchi, S. (2010), *Performing Legal Research: The Moldovan Experience. Update by Mariana Harjevschi.* March 2010. Available at: www.nyulawglobal.org/globalex/moldova1.htm, accessed 28 June 2010.

Legea cu privire la biblioteci [Law on Libraries] (1994), no. 286 of 16 November 1994. *Monitorul Oficial* [*Official Gazette*], 12 January 1995.

24 Available at: www.soros.md, accessed 28 June 2010.
25 Available at: www.undp.org, accessed 28 June 2010.
26 Available at: www.abanet.org/rol, accessed 28 June 2010.
27 Available at: www.ceeliinstitute.org, accessed 28 June 2010.
28 Available at: www.usm.md, accessed 28 June 2010.
29 Available at: www.abrm.md, accessed 28 June 2010.

Law Librarianship in Nigeria

Ufuoma Lamikanra

Introduction

The growth and development of Nigerian law libraries have not been matched by commensurate increases in law library collections and in the quality of staff. This profile of law librarianship in Nigeria discusses the history and challenges facing Nigerian law libraries and proffers solutions in the light of a rapidly changing information world.

Historical Development

The history of law libraries and law librarianship is closely associated with the history of the legal profession in Nigeria. The legal profession in Nigeria began with the introduction of English law into the then Lagos settlement or colony, with effect from 4 March 1863.[30] Shortly afterwards, in April 1863, the Supreme Court of Her Majesty's settlement of Lagos was established to provide for the better administration of justice within the settlement.[31]

English-type courts were later established in the Niger basin and in the Northern Nigeria Protectorate, while the jurisdiction of the Lagos Supreme Court was extended to cover most of the Yoruba states (Adewoye 1977, 15). Law libraries were established to serve lawyers, magistrates and judges who made use of these courts. The earliest recorded law library was a one-room library located in the Court House at Tinubu Square, Lagos, manned by a third class clerk (Jegede 1985, 230). Other government departments, including the Federal Ministry of Justice, whose library dates back to 1900 or earlier (Jegede 1985, 229) maintained libraries with limited stocks (Adewoye 1977, 15). A few successful private legal practitioners also had fairly large law libraries (Adewoye 1977, 15). Not unexpectedly, since then, there has been an increase in the number and types of law libraries of various sizes in the country.

Law Libraries

Today, law libraries can be classified into six broad groups, as follows:

- Academic Law Libraries: the 36 universities offering law degrees all have Faculty Libraries in addition to the University Law Libraries and Nigerian Law School libraries (4)
- Ministries of Justice Libraries, one Federal and 36 states

30 Ordinance no. 3 of 1863.

31 Supreme Court Ordinance no. 11 of 9 April 1863.

- Court Libraries including the Supreme Court Library (1), Court of Appeal Libraries (12), Federal High Court Libraries (36), State High Courts Libraries (37), and the National Industrial Court Library
- Legislative Libraries: one Federal and 36 States Houses of Assembly
- Law Firms' Libraries
- Research Law Libraries, including the Nigerian Institute of Advanced Legal Studies Library, National Judicial Institute Library, Human Rights Commission Library, and the Law Reform Commission Library

The *Directory of Law Libraries in Nigeria* published in 1970 listed 33 law libraries (Jegede 1985, 230). In 2010, in the absence of a current directory, it is difficult to ascertain the exact number of law libraries in Nigeria but an estimate based on the above classification is about 600.

The Nigerian Institute of Advanced Legal Studies (NIALS) Library is the largest law library in Nigeria, with a collection of 49,234 volumes. NIALS, established on 17 March 1979, is the apex institution for research and advanced studies on law in Nigeria. The idea of establishing the Institute was first discussed at the 1963 annual meeting of the Association of Law Teachers. The four universities then teaching law had difficulties in organising postgraduate studies because of inadequate library facilities and the absence of specialised supervision; this informed the sending of Nigerian Law graduates abroad for research work. To avoid duplication of effort and resources a centre for legal research and supervision for postgraduate research work was set up by the four universities at the University of Lagos.[32] The University of Lagos was chosen because Lagos was then the Federal Capital and because the Nigerian Law School and Libraries of the High Court of Lagos State (the oldest in the country), the Court of Appeal and the Supreme Court 'could provide an invaluable adjunct to the Institute's Library' (Nigerian Institute 1980). NIALS has a library in Lagos, with an office in Abuja and proposed offices in the other five Geo-Political Zones of Nigeria. The system of accreditation of Faculties of Law by the Council of Legal Education and the Nigerian Universities Commission has contributed immensely to the growth and development of university law libraries. Accreditation may be withheld or cancelled if the recommended minimum holdings are not met (National Universities Commission 1989, 21–2).

Several law libraries in the five other types of law libraries listed above also have, over time, developed sizeable collections. They include some Superior Courts, the Federal and some States Ministries of Justice, but some have had their stocks depleted by the increase in the number of states.[33]

The 55,000 Barristers and Solicitors registered to practice by the Supreme Court of Nigeria[34] are not all practising lawyers with law libraries. However, the possession of a good library, a mandatory requirement for the conferment of the rank of Senior Advocate of Nigeria (SAN), the equivalent of the rank of Queen's Counsel in the United Kingdom and Canada, by the Legal Practitioners Privileges Committee, ensures that the over 300 Senior Advocates of Nigeria and many other aspiring lawyers maintain standard law libraries. Legal practitioners' libraries that have fairly large law collections include those of the late Gani Fawehinmi, the late FRA

32 At present, the Institute is no longer under the control of the Universities but is now managed by a Council. See s. 2, Nigerian Institute of Advanced Legal Studies Act Cap. N112, Laws of the Federation of Nigeria 2004.

33 The increase from three regions in 1960 to 36 states in 1996 left judicial and State Ministries of Justice libraries of split states with the daunting task of how best to share their holdings. Such law libraries are yet to recover fully from the forced depletion of their stocks.

34 See the Nigerian Bar Association website. Available at: www.nba.org, accessed 14 June 2010.

Williams, Aelex Legal Practitioners and Arbitrators, Afe Babalola & Co, Aluko and Oyebode, and Wale Babalakin Chambers.

Law Librarians

The contradictory responses to a questionnaire administered at a recent Law Library Workshop, on the number of law librarians in Nigeria, show the difficulty in establishing an accurate number of law librarians, in the absence of a current directory. However, there should be about 500 law librarians in active practice in 2010, with about 300 being members of the Nigerian Association of Law Libraries (NALL).[35] Since Lagos has the largest concentration of law firms,[36] one can assert that law librarians are located mainly in Lagos. Although many Lagos law firms have branch offices in Abuja, the federal capital, these tend to be outposts, usually without standard libraries or librarians.

Qualifications

Professionals with librarianship training have for long taken the place of the clerks who staffed the early law libraries. Although there has been a general improvement in the number and quality of librarians, there is still a need for enhanced qualifications for law librarians. Reacting to the lack of qualified personnel in law libraries, Jegede bemoaned the 'mixed grill with all sorts of training and varied disciplines' who staffed law libraries (Jegede 2001, 216).

Today the number of qualified law librarians is still far from adequate, mainly because no specialist qualification is needed for appointment as a law librarian, except for university law libraries. In this case, the Council of Legal Education and the National Universities Commission, the two accreditation bodies for Nigerian universities, require that in addition to a library qualification, the University Law Librarian must hold a Bachelor's Degree in Law (National Universities Commission 1989, 20). In other law libraries, a degree in librarianship and experience of working in a law library is all that is needed to become a law librarian. There are however a few law libraries, in both the public and private sectors, staffed by persons with lower academic qualifications and a general training in librarianship (Utor 2004, 17).

This anomaly cannot fully be addressed by the Nigerian Association of Law Libraries alone. The Librarians (Registration, etc.) Council of Nigeria set up 'for the registration of Librarians and to make provisions for the practice of the profession and other matters connected therewith',[37] which would have taken care of this irregularity, has remained dormant and moribund since its inauguration in 2002.

It is trite that law librarians in Nigeria are also affected by the low status of librarians all over the world. Dada argues rightly that the necessity for law librarians to be lawyers or at least to receive good legal training 'may be one of the ways of improving their image' (Dada 1993).

Training for Law Librarians

In 1962 the Institute of Librarianship of the University of Ibadan awarded certificates to the first professionals trained in Nigeria. Three years later the Institute introduced the postgraduate Diploma in Library Studies (Awaritefe 1983, 21). There are at present over 20 universities and other tertiary

35 According to the Assistant Secretary of NALL, Mrs Kemi Olowu.

36 See The Nigerian Bar Association website. Available at: www.nba.org, accessed 14 June 2010.

37 Librarians (Registration, etc.) Council of Nigeria Act, Cap. L13, Laws of the Federation of Nigeria 2004.

institutions offering various courses in library science (*Joint Admission and Matriculation Board Brochure 2010/11*) but none has included legal studies in its curriculum.

The vacuum created by the absence of law librarianship courses in curricula of library schools and the lack of formal continuing education for law librarians is being filled by the Nigerian Institute of Advanced Legal Studies Library. Since its inception over 5,000 librarians and information practitioners have attended national workshops, courses, seminars and lectures organised by the Institute Library. In addition the Institute Library also offers short training courses to individual law librarians, at the request of their libraries. This is not sufficient. The inclusion of legal studies in Nigerian library schools' curricula should help produce suitable staff for law libraries.[38]

The Nigerian Library Association organises annual general meetings and conferences while specialist groups of the NLA like the Cataloguing, Classification and Indexing, Reference Services and the Information Technology Sections hold annual workshops for their members. The National Library of Nigeria also organises regular national workshops on topical issues for librarians in general.

Nigerian Association of Law Libraries

The Nigerian Association of Law Libraries, inaugurated on 7 March 1975, serves as a forum to advance the cause of Law Librarianship in the country. Its annual workshops and conferences create good continuing education and networking opportunities for law librarians.

Legal Publishing

The Federal and State governments and their agencies, academic institutions and commercial firms (including law firms) are the major actors in the Nigerian legal publishing industry today. While the Federal and State governments publish laws enacted by their legislatures, commercial publishers usually concentrate on student and practitioner books.

Legislation

The earliest forms of legal publications in Nigeria were official Gazettes and Statutory Enactments dating back to the late nineteenth century, produced by the Government Printers or Crown Agents and distributed by the colonial administration itself as the publishers (Bankole 1991, 167). The Federal and State governments have continued to publish such official documents through their Press Departments. The output of Government publications has been slow and irregular. Private participation, under licence, has resulted in faster and more effective production and marketing of some Federal and State statutory publications. Odade Publishers, a commercial publisher, publishes and sells the current laws of the federation and some states laws.

Law Reports

Reports published in Nigeria may be classified as Official Reports and Private or Commercial Reports.

38 These courses, etc. organised by the Institute, cannot adequately meet the need for training in law librarianship which can only be properly done in a library school setting.

Official reports These comprise government and court-sponsored reports. The first of such reports was the *Nigeria Law Reports* series started in 1910 by the Judicial Department (Bodunde 1991, 159). Official reports are either federal in coverage or restricted to individual states. Virtually all jurisdictions in Nigeria have official law reporting bodies which either alone, or in conjunction with private enterprises, publish cases decided in each jurisdiction. Official reports are usually in accordance with court hierarchy and are not subject-based except where the jurisdiction coincides with legal specialisation.

Private or commercial law reports The first Nigerian law reports, *The Law Report (Colonial) Nigerian*, was a one-volume work authored and edited by Mr Justice John S. Smith covering selected judgments by him between 1884 and 1892, published in 1911 (Bodunde 1991, 159–60). Until 1967 both official and private law reports were produced regularly and contemporaneously (Olaitan 1997, 44). After 1967, there was an extinction of some series while others took their place but many have had a chequered life, some with very irregular or short life spans. Since 2000 the situation has improved remarkably with law reports of the superior courts having increased from just one regular title in 1985 to about 30 titles in 2010.

However, most of these law reports are not specialised and concentrate on the judgments of superior courts, carrying the same cases, especially of the Supreme Court. Suggestions have been rightly made for the reporting of decisions of inferior courts, especially Customary and Area Courts, since most cases are heard and end in these courts (Olaitan 1997, 165).

In addition to private individuals, a few corporate and academic bodies such as the Nigerian Bar Association, the Faculties of Law and some daily newspapers include a 'Case Review' section in their publications.

Law Journals

The first Nigerian legal journal, the *Nigerian Law Quarterly Review*, started publication on 11 August 1949 and is no longer in print. Most legal periodicals are published by academic institutions and corporate bodies but, like law reports, law journals 'have had a fitful existence in Nigeria' (Bankole 1991, 169). Inadequate funding and lack of commitment have led to a large number of periodicals having very short life spans or not being published regularly.

Law Books and Monographs

Multinational publishers and more recently universities and a number of private indigenous publishers have been involved in the publication of law books and monographs.

A study of Indigenous Law Textbook Publishing (ILTP) in Nigeria between 1960 and 1999 (Edem and Okwilagwe 2008) showed that the Nigerian legal publishing industry is not keeping pace with the increasing book demands of law students. Only 215 titles of Nigerian legal textbooks were published in the 40 years covered by the study. The study identified the factors that have contributed to the slow output of legal textbook as including:

- relative complacency of Nigerian scholars as a result of the oil boom
- publishing abroad by Nigerian scholars due to underdevelopment in the Nigerian publishing sector
- decline in the Naira (Nigerian currency) and the lure of earning hard currency
- sharp rise in bank loan interest rates

- unstable political situation
- poor purchasing power of law libraries
- law teachers are not as productive as expected in spite of the promotion requirement to 'publish or perish'

Another major problem faced by the publishing industry in Nigeria today is piracy. The Nigerian Copyright Commission[39] has not been able to curb the activities of book pirates that have almost crippled the book trade (Ojiji 1992, 188). In spite of these problems active law publishers include: MIJ Professional Publishers, Nigerian Institute of Advanced Legal Studies, Nigerian Law Publications, Odade Publishers and Spectrum Books Ltd.

Online Publishing

Globalisation has led to an increased emphasis on comparative and international law in legal education, research and practice and, as a result, more reliance on electronic resources especially the Internet. There is a dearth of Nigerian legal materials on the Internet. The few websites with fair coverage of Nigerian law in general include:

- Guide to Nigerian Legal Information (Dina et al. 2010)[40]
- International Centre for Nigerian Law[41]
- Intute Law – Nigeria[42]

Websites on specific Nigerian law topics include:

- Nigerian Environmental Law[43]
- Nigerian Telecommunications Laws[44]
- Nigerian Legislation[45]

Major Policy Issues for Law Libraries

Gaps in the runs of legal periodicals, outdated editions of textbooks, absence of new titles, print-based services[46] are common features in many Nigerian law libraries today. The reasons for the deplorable state of law libraries include:

- Inadequacy of collections; some factors affecting acquisition from the Nigerian book market include lack of bibliographic control, lack of promotional activities for published

39 Set up by the Copyright Act Cap. C28 LFN 2004, to combat all forms of piracy of music, films, software, books and all other protected works.

40 Available at: www.nyulawglobal.org/globalex/Nigeria1.htm, accessed 14 June 2010.

41 Available at: www.nigeria-law.org, accessed 14 June 2010.

42 Available at: www.intute.ac.uk/cgi-bin/browse.pl?id=120498, accessed 14 June 2010.

43 Available at: http://ncseonline.org/PopPlanet/issue.cfm?countryid=2&iid=17, accessed 14 June 2010.

44 Available at: www.ncc.gov.ng, accessed 14 June 2010.

45 Available at: www.nassnig.org, accessed 14 June 2010.

46 The fully automated law libraries in Nigeria today are a few law firm libraries. The other types of libraries are either not automated or still in various stages of automation.

titles, insufficient distribution outlets and difficult payment terms on the part of publishers and book sellers (Bankole 1991, 172)[47]

- Limited budgets
- Paucity of Nigerian legal literature and common standards for their treatment in knowledge classification (Lawal 2010)
- Poor or lack of infrastructure such as unreliable power supply and slow Internet access
- Shortage of law librarians with law degrees and/or information technology knowledge
- High prices and poor maintenance of software and hardware

Conclusion

The increase in the number and types of law libraries in Nigeria has not been matched by a comparable boost in collection development. The complexity of the Nigerian legal system, which makes attempts at complete bibliographic coverage difficult, the absence of a viable law publishing industry coupled with the dearth of indigenous legal literature authorship have resulted in poorly-stocked law libraries. The advent of information and communication technology which has revolutionised information delivery services in other countries has had little impact on Nigerian law libraries due mainly to poor infrastructure and inadequate funding. The shortage of qualified law librarians needed to staff the rapidly increasing number of law libraries needs urgent attention. Legal and IT training and retraining of law librarians must be addressed for effective and efficient provision of legal information services to meet the expanding needs of clientele in an increasingly globalised world.

Further Reading

Dada, T. (1989), 'The Legal and Professional Responsibilities of the Law Librarian', in Ajomo, M. Ayo (ed.), *New Dimensions in Nigerian Law* (Lagos: NIALS).

Deru, A. (2003), *Researching the Law on the Internet* (Lagos: Kdlaw Pub.).

Jegede, O. (1992), *Law Libraries without Legal Books – A Way Out* (Nigerian Institute of Advanced Legal Studies Occasional Paper) (Lagos: NIALS).

Jegede, O., Malomo, J. and Solaja, E. (eds) (2006), *Readings in Law Librarianship, 1994–1999* (Lagos: Nigerian Association of Law Libraries).

Ogbeide, N. (1976), 'Law Librarianship in Nigeria, History, Development, and Problems', *International Journal of Law Libraries* 4:1, March 1976, 19–26.

Omekwu, C. (ed.) (2007), *Law Libraries in Nigeria* (Abuja: Nigerian Association of Law Libraries).

References

Adewoye, O. (1977), *The Legal Profession in Nigeria, 1856–1962* (Ikeja: Longman).

Awaritefe, M. (1983), 'Attitude Towards Librarianship: A Test Case', *Nigerian Libraries: Journal of the Nigerian Library Association* 19:1–3, 21–33.

47 Although the paper was written in 1991, the problems remain the same.

Bankole, S. (1991), 'Law Publishing in Nigeria', in *Proceedings of the 3rd Course in Law Library Services, May 21–June 7, 1991* (Lagos: NIALS).

Bodunde, S. (1991), 'Law Reporting in Nigeria', in *Proceedings of the 3rd Course in Law Library Services, May 21–June 7, 1991* (Lagos: NIALS).

Dada, T. (1993), *Mission without an Audience: The Dilemma of the Nigerian Law Librarian.* Seminar pages presented at the Staff Seminar Series of NIALS on Tuesday 13 April 1993. [Unpublished].

Dina, Y., Akintayo, J. and Ekundayo, F. (2010), *Guide to Nigerian Legal Information. Update, January/February 2010.* Available at: www.nyulawglobal.org/globalex/Nigeria1.htm.

Edem, M. and Okwilagwe, A. (2008), 'An Assessment of Indigenous Law Textbook Publishing in Nigeria, 1960–1999', *Gateway Library Journal* 11:1, 1–15.

Jegede, O. (1985), 'Development in Law Libraries and their Services', in Akinola Aguda, T. (ed.), *The Challenge of the Nigerian Nation: An Examination of its Legal Development, 1960–85* (Lagos: NIALS).

Jegede, O. (2001), 'Law Libraries and Law Librarianship in Nigeria', in Olanlokun, S. and Salisu, T. (eds), *Libraries and Librarianship in Nigeria: A Festschrift for Ezekial Bejide Bankole* (Lagos: Ikofa Press).

Joint Admission and Matriculation Board Brochure 2010/11 (2010) (Lagos: JAMB).

Lawal, O. (2010), *Technical Services in Law Libraries. A Keynote Address presented at the National Workshop on Technical Services in Law Libraries, 27th–29th April 2010* at the Nigerian Institute of Advanced Legal Studies, Lagos. [Unpublished].

National Universities Commission (1989), *Approved Minimum Standards in Law for All Nigerian Universities* (Lagos: NUC).

Nigerian Institute of Advanced Legal Studies, University of Lagos (1980), *Information Brochure*, 2nd edition (Lagos: NIALS).

Ojiji, C. (1992), 'The Development of Intellectual Property and Book Piracy', in Uvieghara, E. (ed.), *Essays in Copyright Law and Administration in Nigeria* (Ibadan: Y-Books), 179–95.

Olaitan, M. (1997), 'Law Reports/Publications: the State of the Art in Nigeria', *Lagos Librarian* 18:1 & 2, 44–8.

Utor, J. (2004), 'Types and Characteristics of Law Libraries in Nigeria', in Utor, J.K. (ed.), *The Principles and Practice of Law and Legislative Libraries in Nigeria* (Lagos: [n.p.]).

Law Librarianship in the Philippines

Lilia F. Echiverri

The practice of law librarianship in the Philippines includes the management of the law libraries, the conduct of training for the competencies of its members, and the provision of altruistic services. Law librarianship has been recognised in the country as a vocation of specialised training.

This contribution presents brief information on professional preparation of law librarians, library associations in the Philippines, law libraries, the role of the national library and congressional and senate libraries in society, and the laws affecting library service and policy issues.

Professional Preparation of Law Librarians

The Philippines 'recognizes the essential role of librarianship as a profession in developing the intellectual capacity of the citizenry thus making library service a regular component for national development' (Philippines 2004, Art. I, Sec. 2). Librarians or law librarians, therefore, are mandated to contribute to the development of the intellectual capacity of the Filipino people. This is the most important reason for the grant of professional status for librarianship.

Education and Training of Law Librarians

Preparatory education for librarianship ranges from the general college degree to a baccalaureate or master's degree in library science, or library and information science, and even bachelor of laws.

There are few articles about Philippine law librarianship. 'Formal Education in Law Librarianship' by Professor Myrna Feliciano (1990), the first formally educated law librarian in the country and a full-fledged librarian and a lawyer, describes the legal system and the information environment in which the law librarian operates. A survey of law librarianship followed, tracing the development of formal courses and identifying foreign universities where it is offered. Feliciano underscored the need for such a course in the Philippines and proposed that graduates of a Bachelor's degree be eligible for the law librarianship programme or for the Master of Library Science with specialisation in law librarianship. Feliciano submitted a draft curriculum to support the proposed programme, entailing 37 units of graduate work of which 12 would involve specialised courses in a law or a library science school.

The Diploma in Law Librarianship was established and approved by the University of the Philippines Board of Regents in 1989 and included in the Graduate Programme curriculum on 16 April 2002. The University of the Philippines School of Library and Information Studies is the only library school in the country that offers the programme, which includes courses in legal bibliography, legal reference work and law library administration that are taught through a mixture of lectures, practicum, personal contacts and library field work.

At present training in law librarianship is mainly in the form of in-service training, seminars and conferences, workshops, fora and dialogues. Some law librarians become successful without law training, but this takes time, with plenty of hits and misses. Many have been sent on short but advanced training abroad and as many have benefited from training programmes sponsored by the Philippine Group of Law Librarians and other library associations.

Philippine Librarianship Act

The success of librarianship as a profession in the Philippines was not achieved until 1990 due to controversies and political struggles that marred the country in 1972 and 1986. It was a long wait but it was worth it. Librarianship was recognised by the State through the enactment of Republic Act (R.A.) no. 6966, known as the *Philippine Librarianship Act of 1990* (Philippines 1990). After 14 years, R.A. 6966 was repealed by R.A. no. 9246, known as *The Philippine Librarianship Act of 2003*. The law covers:

1. title, statement of policy, definition of term, scope of the practice
2. creation of the Professional Regulatory Board for Librarians to regulate the practice of the librarian profession and prescribe the necessary qualifications
3. licensure examination and registration
4. practice of librarianship
5. penal and final provisions

The licensing of a librarian in general, and law librarians in particular, involves the issuance of a Certificate of Registration after passing the licensure examination and taking the Oath of Librarian Profession. Licensure examinations for librarians have been conducted by the Professional Regulation Commission every first week of December starting in 1992. Certificates of registration were also issued to those who, at the time of approval of the law, possessed the necessary qualifications *sans* examination. Foreign librarians may practice the librarian profession in the Philippines subject to the provision on reciprocity of R.A. 9246: a foreign librarian may qualify, be licensed and practice if their country allows Filipinos to do the same.

Continuing Professional Education

The Professional Regulation Commission pursues an intensive continuing professional education programme to upgrade knowledge, competence and awareness on progressive development in the professions including librarianship. Pursuant to Executive Order no. 266 dated 25 July 1995, the Commission directed the professional regulatory board of each profession to create a Continuing Professional Education Council to promote the development, accreditation and implementation of CPE programmes for each profession. The Certificate of Registration or licence to practice librarianship is renewable every three years subject to completion of appropriate training as prescribed by the Continuing Professional Education Council of the Board for Librarians.

The Philippine Group of Law Librarians

The Philippine Group of Law Librarians (PGLL) was established on 20 August 1980 during the 46th General Congress of the International Federation of Library Associations and Institutions held in Manila. As part of the Congress, the International Association of Law Librarians (IALL) held a Round Table Discussion on the theme 'Collection Development and Documentation of Human Rights' sponsored by the University of the Philippines Law Center. There were 35 participants:

17 Filipinos and 18 librarians from Australia, Canada, Japan, Malaysia, Nigeria, Thailand and the United States. The events evidently 'gave a good stimulus to further development of law librarianship in the region' (Sprudzs 1980). It was on this occasion that former Dean Froilan M. Bacuñgan of the University of the Philippines College of Law brought out the idea of organising a local chapter that should affiliate with the International Association of Law Libraries.

The PGLL was established in 1981 to foster and stimulate greater cooperation among its members; promote knowledge, awareness and appreciation of the role a member plays in their organisation; unite its members to advance the cause of their profession in Philippine society; further research in the field of law; and provide a forum for consideration and analysis of problems and issues affecting law librarianship.

The number of law librarians in the Philippines today is approximately 450, both licensed and unlicensed, working in law school libraries, court libraries, government agency libraries, law firm libraries, bar libraries, private corporate libraries and educational foundations which operate a law library or maintain a substantial collection of legal materials. The Association has few members compared with other associations but it has the determination to unite as one solid force to attain a high degree of professionalism and upgrade the status of law librarianship in the country. PGLL members have played important roles and shared their expertise in the various activities and programmes of other library organisations like the Philippine Librarians Association, Inc. (PLAI) and Association of Special Libraries of the Philippines (ASLP).

The PGLL organises regular residential seminars and other educational programmes (Winterton 2009). The PGLL publishes the *PGLL Newsletter* and *Philippine Journal of Law Librarians* (*PJLL*). Other publications include *A Union List of Legal Periodicals of Metro Manila Law Libraries* (April 1986) and *Union List of Human Rights Resources in the Philippines* (1989).

The PGLL contributed significantly to the crafting, passage and dissemination of the legislation described above, R.A. no. 6966 and R.A. no. 9246. However, a discussion of Philippine librarianship will not be complete without mentioning the role of the Philippine Librarians Association Inc. (PLAI), the Accredited Professional Organization (APO) by the Professional Regulation Commission, in the promotion of librarianship. The PLAI has more than 2,000 members from among 6,191 licensed librarians. The PLAI is tasked to undertake major activities for which other library associations may not be legally authorised, for example to propose a librarian on whom may be conferred the prestigious Outstanding Professional of the Year Award by the Professional Regulatory Commission of the Government. It is designated as Member in the Secretariat of the Continuing Professional Education Council of the Board for Librarians. The task to recommend the Chairman and Members of the PRC Board for Librarians is also the responsibility of the PLAI. While the PLAI is the PRC APO-Accredited Association for librarianship, there is a range of specialist associations in law of which the Philippine Group of Law Librarians is only one.

Law Libraries

In the Philippines there are 50,787 (as of January 2010) practising lawyers, produced by 120 law schools in 16 regions of the country, who make use of law libraries in one form or another.

Most of the law libraries in the Philippines are small. The few large law school and academic law libraries are located in Metro Manila: the University of the Philippines College of Law, Ateneo de Manila University Law School Library, San Beda College of Law Library and University of Santo Tomas Faculty of Civil Law Library. These law libraries are relatively large based on student enrolment, members of faculty, size of collections, and their consistent top ranking in the bar examinations.

The University of the Philippines College of Law was established in 1911 and offers a four-year undergraduate Bachelor of Laws (LLB) degree; a five-year undergraduate programme for working students leading to Bachelor of Laws (LLB) degree; and a graduate Master of Laws (LLM) degree, primarily for prospective law teachers and professional specialists. However, admission to the graduate programme has been suspended indefinitely.

The Ateneo de Manila University Law School was established in 1956 and offers a four-year degree of Bachelor of Laws and the Juris Doctor degree.

After the Second World War the San Beda College expanded its role in the higher education of Filipino Youth and the San Beda College of Law opened in 1948, progressively opening a full four-year programme for the degree of Bachelor of Laws. A Master of Laws programme is also offered.

The University of Santo Tomas Faculty of Civil Law is the oldest lay college in the Philippines, established in 1734, the same year that the Faculty of Canon Law was founded, with a curriculum identical to that adopted in leading universities of Europe. It offers a Bachelor of Laws (LLB), Master of Laws (LLM), and Doctor of Civil Law (DCL) degrees.

Role of the National Library of the Philippines

The National Library of the Philippines is an attached agency of the National Commission for Culture and the Arts of the Office of the President by virtue of Executive Order no. 80 dated 5 March 1999. It is the repository of the printed and recorded cultural heritage of the country and other intellectual, literary and information sources and serves as the national bibliographic agency in the country. It acts as the central node of the public library system throughout the country and provides guidance and technical assistance to local government units in the establishment, development and maintenance of public libraries and plans and conducts training programmes, meetings, seminars and conferences for public librarians.

The National Library of the Philippines provides updated information to the public through its website,[48] which includes a description of the agency, news, links to various information sources, past and upcoming events of the library. Additional features of the website include a bulletin board for sharing knowledge, issues and concerns.

At present there are 1,271 affiliated public libraries in different provinces, cities, municipalities and *barangays* (villages) in the country. In 2009, newly affiliated public libraries were noted as follows: 101 city libraries, five congressional libraries, 579 municipal libraries, 49 provincial and 537 *barangays* (villages).

Role of the Congressional and Senate Libraries in Society

The Congressional Library and Senate Library serve the House of Representatives and House of the Senate and their resources are geared towards responsiveness to economic, social and political information needed as inputs for legislation. Indirectly, it contributes to the nation's development through the collection and dissemination of laws that affect the lives of the people. It acts as a principal source for legal information and for copies of laws, resolutions and executive issuances.

48 Available at: http://web.nlp.gov.ph, accessed 17 June 2010.

It readily provides by fax, airmail or courier service copies of laws, and committee and plenary deliberations which may have been requested.

Legal Publishing

Legal publishing is changing and has grown through the years and there is a shift from print to electronic. In the Philippines legal publishing is regulated by the Book Publishing Industry Development Act (R.A. no. 8047, 1995) which is the first comprehensive piece of legislation on book publishing and includes a broad declaration of policy, provisions for the formulation of a National Book Policy, a national book development plan, and the creation of the National Book Development Board.

A detailed guide to legal research in the Philippines by Milagros Santos-Ong, Director of Libraries for the Supreme Court (2009a), is freely available online and covers various aspects of the legal system and sources of law, as well as information resources and citations; there is further detail in a printed research guide and bibliography (Santos-Ong 2009b).

The National Printing Office[49] publishes the weekly *Official Gazette* which serves as a primary source for legislative materials and selected Supreme Court decisions. It is one of the most sought after government publications by lawyers and other professionals. The NPO also publishes the *Philippine Reports* containing all Supreme Court decisions but the *Supreme Court Reports Annotated* published by Central Book Supply Inc. is often used in preference.

Among the well-known law book commercial publishers are the Rex Book Store,[50] Central Book Supply Inc.,[51] and Anvil Publishing Inc.[52] Electronic materials are available from local commercial publishers: Lex Libris databases for laws, jurisprudence and other legal information of CD Asia Technologies[53] in two formats: on CD-ROM and online. The publisher has embarked on a joint project, 'Electronic SCRA', to digitise the *Supreme Court Reports Annotated.*

Philippine websites that provide free legal information play an important role in legal research. The Supreme Court e-Library[54] is an extensive primary research tool in the speedy delivery of justice. Jurisprudence of the Supreme Court is posted for free together with decisions of other courts and tribunals, legislative, constitutional and other legal materials and this makes legal research very quick and easy. The Philippine Supreme Court's own site[55] also contains the 1987 Constitution, the Rules of Court, a complete listing with full text of circulars and orders, decisions as well as the Court's minute resolutions.

Other useful websites are the Arellano Law Foundation's Lawphil Project,[56] the Virtual Library maintained by the Chan Robles Law Firm,[57] a utopia to any Filipino legal researcher with comprehensive listings of law-related materials arranged by topic featuring the full text of laws and jurisprudence. The Jaromay, Laurente, Pamaos law office online library offers similar

49 Available at: www.ops.gov.ph/npo, accessed 17 June 2010.
50 Available at: http://rexroac.tripod.com/rbook.htm, accessed 17 June 2010.
51 Available at: http://central.com.ph, accessed 17 June 2010.
52 Available at: www.anvilpublishing.com, accessed 17 June 2010.
53 Available at: www.cdasiaonline.com, accessed 17 June 2010.
54 Available at: http://elibrary.judiciary.gov.ph, accessed 17 June 2010.
55 Available at: http://sc.judiciary.gov.ph, accessed 17 June 2010.
56 Available at: www.lawphil.net, accessed 17 June 2010.
57 Available at: www.chanrobles.com, accessed 17 June 2010.

facilities.[58] There is an archive of selected cases from 1901 to 2004 and legal briefs.[59] Government websites of use in legal research include the Office of the President,[60] the Senate,[61] the House of Representatives,[62] the National Economic and Development Authority,[63] and the Securities and Exchange Commission.[64]

Major Policy Issues

In the Philippines, the Integrated Bar of the Philippines (IBP), unlike the American Bar Association, has no policy guidelines, direct or indirect, relating to library and information resources. Only the Department of Education, Culture and Sports, DECS Order no. 27, s. 1989, which mandates the Policies and Standards on Legal Education as proposed by the Philippine Association of Law Schools, pertains to law libraries.

Librarians face problems with copyright law and other provisions impinging on their work such as the Electronic Commerce Act of 2000, R.A. no. 8792, and the Optical Media Act of 2003, R.A. no. 9239, Sec. 19, par. a. Copyright owners have the exclusive right of reproduction but this is not absolute. Under Philippine law fair use of a copyrighted work for criticism, comment, news reporting, teaching including multiple copies for classroom use, scholarship, research, and similar purposes is not an infringement of copyright (R.A. no. 8293, Sec. 185.1, 1997). Philippine libraries are allowed to make only a single copy as fair use and, in the case of replacement volumes, only when the book is no longer available from the publisher (Sec. 188.1). Librarians are often questioned and troubled by the possibility of being accused of abetting violations and finding themselves as co-defendant in copyright infringement cases. Librarians in the Philippines are bound by the ethical rules of profession which is the Philippine Code of Ethics for Registered Librarians (1992).

Further Reading

Feliciano, M. (2009), 'The Law Library: Revisiting Traditional Legal Research Methods', *Integrated Bar of the Philippines Journal* 34:2, March 2009, 172.

References

Feliciano, M. (1990), 'Formal Education in Law Librarianship', *Philippine Journal of Law Librarians* 1, 1–13.

Philippine Group of Law Librarians (2005), *PGLL@25: Working Towards Global Information Sharing*, Silver Anniversary Souvenir Programme (Manila: PGLL).

58 Available at: www.jlp-law.com/library, accessed 17 June 2010.

59 Available at: www.abogadomo.com, accessed 17 June 2010.

60 Available at: www.news.ops.gov.ph, accessed 17 June 2010.

61 Available at: www.senate.gov.ph, accessed 17 June 2010.

62 Available at: www.congress.gov.ph, accessed 17 June 2010.

63 Available at: www.neda.gov.ph, accessed 17 June 2010.

64 Available at: www.sec.gov.ph, accessed 17 June 2010.

Philippines (1990), *An Act Regulating the Practice of Librarianship and Prescribing the Qualifications of Librarians*, Republic Act no. 6966, *Official Gazette* 86:47, 8783.

Philippines (2004), *An Act Modernizing the Practice of Librarianship in the Philippines thereby Repealing Republic Act No. 6966 …*, Republic Act no. 9246, *Official Gazette* 100:15, 2105.

Santos-Ong, M. (2009a), *Philippine Legal Research: Update published June 2009*. Available at: www.nyulawglobal.org/globalex/Philippines1.htm, accessed 17 June 2010.

Santos-Ong, M. (2009b), *Philippine Legal Research and Bibliography*, 2nd edition (Manila: Central Book Supply).

Sprudzs, A. (1980), 'IALL Week in Manila', *International Journal of Law Libraries* 8, 193.

Winterton, J. (2009), 'On Starfish Island: The Philippine Group of Law Librarians Seminar of April 2008', *Legal Information Management* 9:1, 57–61. Also available at http://hdl.handle.net/10065/1792, accessed 17 June 2010.

Law Librarianship in Turkey

Sami Cukadar

In this contribution Turkish librarianship education, professional associations, law librarianship and law libraries, legal publications and bibliographies in Turkey are briefly introduced and the library services are explained.

Librarianship Education in Turkey

There are five universities that have an Information and Document Management department which offers undergraduate and graduate programmes. As their main goal, these departments strive to be the first choice of students who wish to work as information professionals; to contribute to science at national and international levels by carrying out research; to create their own resources; and have a respected status in the society.

The first programme on librarianship was opened in 1954/1955 at the Faculty of Letters of Ankara University. Other programmes were established: Istanbul University in 1964, Hacettepe University in 1972, Ataturk University in 1994 and Baskent University in 2002 (Gurdal and Subasioglu 2006). The Department of Archives of Marmara University was opened in 1987 and was renamed Department of Information and Document Management in 2002.

Following a decision of the Higher Education Council in 2002, the sections of librarianship, archiving, and documentation and information at all departments of librarianship were merged and the departments of librarianship were renamed Department of Information and Document Management with a new curriculum (Hacettepe University Department of Information and Document Management 2009).

Associations and Other Organisations for Librarians

Turkish Librarians' Association

The Turkish Librarians' Association was the first vocational organisation in Turkey for librarians, established in 1949. It has been actively serving as an NGO of the world of books and libraries and as the voice of the librarians. Today it has 25 branches and 1,931 members. From 1952 onwards it has been publishing *Turkish Librarianship* and has published 154 books (Celik and Bayir 2008).

University and Research Librarians' Association

The University and Research Librarians' Association (UNAK) was established in 1991, aiming to examine issues arising from the rapid change and advance of technology for university and research libraries, documentation and information centres and private libraries, and compare these to similar issues and solutions in other countries; investigate and resolve issues concerning the personnel working in these information centres; and implement new technology (Celik and Bayir 2008).

Anatolian University Libraries Consortium

The Anatolian University Libraries Consortium (ANKOS) was established in 2000 with 12 member libraries and three database subscriptions. In 2010 ANKOS has 119 member libraries and 83 database subscriptions. The essential aim of ANKOS is to provide a common policy among its members on issues related to the subscription or purchase of e-resources, considering the collection's rational growth and allowing access to more sources for the educational and research needs of participating users (Anatolian University Libraries Consortium).

The Innovative Library Initiatives Promotion Group (ILIPG)

ILIPG is a group of librarians in Istanbul who run and support activities to improve the standards of public libraries in Turkey, activate and expand librarians' networking (both within Turkey and internationally), and stimulate lobbying efforts for libraries (Innovative Library Initiatives Promotion Group).

UNAK-Turkish Platform of Law Librarians (UNAK-TPLL)

UNAK-TPLL was established by librarians in 2007 to increase cooperation and information sharing between the libraries, and documentation and information centres which serve in the area of law (Cukadar 2008). Its objectives (Turkish Platform of Law Librarians 2007) are:

- To increase cooperation and sharing of information between libraries in Turkey which serve in the area of law
- To broadcast the activities of law libraries
- To give announcements and arrange panels and workshops in the annual meetings of the University and Research Librarians Association
- To share studies about law in Turkey with international law platforms and associations
- To pioneer to create a legal materials database in Turkey in accordance with international standards
- To support the actions on the institutional archive and open access

Legal Education in Turkey

There are 96 state universities, 51 non-profit private universities and six military colleges in Turkey (Council of Higher Education): 49 of them have law faculties and give undergraduate and graduate programmes. Traditionally Turkish law schools have a four-year curriculum leading to a Bachelor's degree (LLB). The main objective of legal training in Turkey is to transfer knowledge of systematic information about legal concepts and institutions, a broad knowledge of general and universal principles of law, the content of legislation, and jurisprudence and teachings of legal scholars. A Bar Examination, which is a competency exam administered by the General Assembly of Bar Associations, has been in effect since 2006 (Yenisey 2004).

Law Libraries, Law Librarians and their Education

Although there have been some studies in law librarianship and legal information management since the establishment of the Turkish Platform of Law Libraries, law libraries are not yet a separate type of library in the universities. Especially in university libraries, legal information resources are located in the general collection or as a separate faculty collection named by the faculty library in a different building. Most courts, law firms and bar associations have their own special legal information libraries.

In general professionals who work in library institutions have a bachelor, master or PhD degree from a university Department of Information and Document Management. Some librarians graduate in other disciplines and get a graduate degree from a Department of Information and Document Management. Paraprofessionals also assist the library services.

The total number of law librarians in Turkey is not known due to unclear job descriptions. In a university library with a legal collection, for example, books are catalogued by the cataloguer who is not specialised in law, but reference services, public relations and user education programmes may be given by a subject specialist. For an overview of law librarians and libraries, some data was collected in 2009 via email and telephone:

- 49 out of 146 universities have a faculty of law and their libraries have legal collections
- The Constitutional Court library has three qualified librarians
- The Court of Accounts library has two qualified librarians and three paraprofessionals
- The Council of State library has one qualified librarian and one paraprofessional
- The Supreme Court library has one qualified librarian and three paraprofessionals
- The Library of the Grand National Assembly of Turkey has 23 qualified librarians and 40 persons from other disciplines
- There are 76 Bar Associations in various cities and 23 of them have libraries (Turkiye Barolar Birligi 2009). Two qualified librarians and 21 other staff work in these libraries
- Numbers of law firms with libraries are increasing in recent years. There are 75 law firms in Turkey (Martindale.com 2009), 51 of these have their own libraries. Four qualified librarians and 21 other staff work in these libraries

There is no specific course related to law librarianship or legal information management at any of the Departments of Information and Document Management. There are two courses which allow students to specialise at Hacettepe University Department of Information and Document Management. The first is 'Information Needs and User Groups' and the second course is 'Information Retrieval in Medicine' (Hacettepe University Department of Information Management 2009).

Major Libraries with Legal Information Resources

Ankara University Faculty of Law Library

Ankara University Faculty of Law Library[65] was established in the same year as the Faculty in 1925. The Library, in the earliest higher education institution of the Republic of Turkey, has expanded throughout the years and is in service of its readers in a three-storey building. In 2009 the library

65 Available at: www.law.ankara.edu.tr/en, accessed 23 June 2010.

had nearly 90,000 textbooks, 1,100 graduate theses and 24,000 bound volumes of journals; it subscribes to 103 periodicals in the Turkish Language and 87 periodicals in other languages. Many publications in the library are law books which are out of print; 135 of these are displayed in the museum within the library and accessible in digitised form.[66] The library has access to electronic resources such as HukukTürk, Kazancı Bilişim, Resmi Gazete, Westlaw International, LexisNexis, SwissLex, Legios, BeckOnline and HeinOnline databases.[67]

Istanbul University Faculty of Law Library

Construction of the Istanbul University Faculty of Law Library started in 1947 and the library opened in 1950. The building is a two-storey building with a reading hall, OPAC, computer room, information desk, photocopy and study rooms on the top floor. On the ground floor, there is an area for lecturers and their assistants and a depot for books and periodicals. Internet access is available on all computers as well as a computer for visually impaired students.

The library uses the Library of Congress classification system and there has been an online catalogue for acquisitions since 1986. There are over 80,000 printed books and 20,000 bound volumes of journals accommodated in an open shelf system. The library collection also has subscriptions to 27 periodicals in Turkish and 89 periodicals in other languages.

Users of the library are the students of the university and of other universities, lecturers and administrative staff, lecturers within the country and from abroad, as well as users from the business world (Istanbul Universitesi Hukuk Fakültesi 2003).

Istanbul Bilgi University Faculty of Law Library

Bilgi Law Library[68] offers an extensive system to support university degree programmes, research and teaching. An impressive collection of books, periodicals, e-books, e-journals, academic Internet resources and other printed materials are available in the library. Online access to digital resources required for all courses is available on the intranet. Electronic reserves are available online to students for 24 hours a day.

Information managers provide assistance in using the library's printed and electronic resources, formulating research strategies and answering general and in-depth questions. Classes and workshops are available at all levels, and focus on general orientation, research tools, electronic resources and academic uses of the Internet. Individual student instruction is also available.

Bilgi University has three libraries. Library resources which are available on a campus other than where the law library is located can be requested via the In-Transit system. Istanbul Bilgi University faculty members and graduate students can borrow and return any library resource at their own campus library. There is an interlibrary loan and document delivery service available to registered faculty members to obtain loans or photocopies of material not owned by Bilgi Library.

Bilgi e-Library as a whole contains 50,000 electronic books, 29,400 electronic journals, 79 electronic databases and encyclopaedias. Access to these resources is via Internet, on-campus or off-campus and free Wi-Fi access is provided in all Bilgi Library locations. Some of the Bilgi e-Library databases are: ALPSP Law Collection, Beck Online, HukukTürk: Mevzuat ve İçtihat

66 Available at: http://auhf.ankara.edu.tr/muze, accessed 23 June 2010.

67 Correspondence with F. Türker of Ankara University Faculty of Law Library on 29 July 2009.

68 Available at: http://library.bilgi.edu.tr, accessed 23 June 2010.

Bilgi Bankası (Turkish Law Database), Kazancı Mevzuat ve İçtihat Bilgi Bankası (Turkish Law Database), Lebib Yalkın Yayımları (Turkish Law Database), LexisNexis Academic, Resmi Gazete (Turkish Official Gazette), Swisslex-Westlaw, United Nations Treaty Collection, Westlaw International and Yargıtay Hukuk Bilgi Bankası (Republic of Turkey Supreme Court Decisions).

The library is open to scientists, students, researchers, and everyone who is interested in benefiting from the university's resources. They may use all printing and electronic resources in the library (Istanbul Bilgi University Library 2009).

User Education Programmes

There are user education programmes and courses in the universities; classes and workshops are available at all levels and focus on general orientation, research tools, electronic resources, library collections and academic Internet resources. They are offered several times each semester by faculty, subject and reference librarians for undergraduate and graduate students, and staff, as well as for external users and special visitors. Faculty and subject specialist librarians help students and staff learn how to access and use legal information resources in the libraries.

Istanbul Bilgi University Faculty of Law, for the first time in Turkey, has added a compulsory course 'LAW 105 – Research Methods and Accessing Legal Information Resources' to its curriculum for the first-year students. The course provides students with a working knowledge of academic research processes and research methods, covering printed and electronic legal information resources with recent academic research on the subject. The goals of the course are to develop students' academic writing skills, increase their exposure to the various applications used in academic research, and to help them become proficient in using traditional and online library systems (İstanbul Bilgi University).

Similar user education programmes have been given to users at law firms, courts and other related libraries. It can be stated that there will be more courses and programmes for legal information users in future years.

Legal Publishing in Turkey

Books

According to 'Turkish Books In-print' (*Türkiye Yayın Kataloğu* 2010), there are 2,266 publishers, 131,337 books in Turkish and 3,144 books in English on the Turkish book market. Of 2,266 publishers, 170 have published books on some area of law. Legal Yayıncılık (Legal Publishing) is one of the important publishers of legal information in Turkey and according to this publisher:

- 10,616 books on legal information are actively on the market
- In 2009: by July 602 new law books had been published
- In 2008: 1,194 new law books were published
- In 2007: 1,350 new law books were published

The publication of legal information resources is increasing recently in Turkey (Legal Yayıncılık 2006).

Periodicals

More than 5,000 serials have been published in Turkey, of which 244 are related to law. Some of these journals have completed their publication life-cycle and some have a long publishing history, for instance *İstanbul Universitesi Hukuk Fakültesi Mecmuası* has been published since 1923 and *Annales de la Faculté de Droit d'Istanbul* since 1951.

Government and Court Online Databases

Resmi Gazete, the official gazette, is published by the Prime Minister's Office General Directorate of Regulatory Development and Publication and is accessible online free of charge since 7 February 2011.[69]

E-Mevzuat Bilgi Sistemi (e-Legislations Information System) was created by the Prime Minister's Office General Directorate of Regulatory Development and Publication. Laws, decree-laws, by-laws, regulations, communiqués, and some important international agreements are accessible online free of charge.[70]

Yargıtay Hukuk Bilgi Bankası (Supreme Court Information Database) contains leading cases, European Court of Human Rights decisions, and all the Supreme Court decisions. It is accessible free of charge.[71]

Anayasa Mahkemesi Kararlar Bilgi Bankası (Decisions of Constitutional Court Information Database) contains decisions of the Constitutional Court including English summaries, the full text of the Constitution of the Republic of Turkey with an English translation, a law journal titled *Kararlar Dergisi* and more and is accessible free of charge.[72]

Ministry of Foreign Affairs Database of Multilateral Conventions covers all the international agreements to which Turkey is a party, such as Lausanne Peace Treaty, Charter of the United Nations, Universal Declaration of Human Rights, The European Convention on Human Rights, Vienna Convention on Diplomatic Relations and Optional Protocols, and so on.[73]

Commercial Online Law Databases

There are more than 10 companies working on Turkish legal information; the most well known are HukukTurk, Legal, and LebibYalkin. The companies focus on some part of the legal information system and concentrate their resources in that field so there are many database companies.

These databases on Turkish law include laws, regulations, by-laws, Council of Ministers decrees, international law treaties, directives, translations of judgments of the European Court of Human Rights, the *Official Journal of the Republic of Turkey* as well as an extensive collection of the case-law of the Court of Appeals, Council of State and the Constitutional Court. Researchers may access this information over the Internet and most of the databases are updated daily.

Recently a Turkish e-books database has been created by a commercial company with some law books.[74]

69 Available at: http://rega.basbakanlik.gov.tr, accessed 23 June 2010.

70 Available at: www.mevzuat.gov.tr/Default.aspx, accessed 23 June 2010.

71 Available at: www.yargitay.gov.tr, accessed 23 June 2010.

72 Available at: www.anayasa.gov.tr, accessed 23 June 2010.

73 Available at: http://ua.mfa.gov.tr, accessed 23 June 2010.

74 Available at: www.hiperkitap.com, accessed 23 June 2010.

Open Access Legal Scholarship

Universities especially offer open access on the Internet to some of their books and journals in Turkey. Ankara University is one of the important universities that allows open access; 350 books, 34 journals and four bulletins, including many books and journals on law, are available. For instance all issues since the first of *Ankara Üniversitesi Hukuk Fakültesi Dergisi* (Ankara University Law Faculty Review) are available online.[75]

Bibliographies

The *Makaleler Bibliyografyası/Bibliography of Articles in Turkish Periodicals* has been published since 1952, appears quarterly and is also available online with English search facilities since 1995.[76] A bibliography specific to law, *Hukuk Bibliografyası* (Turkish Law Bibliography), is prepared by various persons and publishers such as Istanbul University Law Faculty, Ankara University Law Faculty and Ankara Bar Association. The periods covered by the bibliography are 1727 to 1957 and 1960 to 2001.

Major Issues for Law Librarians

Professional law librarianship in Turkey is quite young and, paradoxically, has a long established history. There have been law library services for a long time but professional law librarianship activities have been increasing since the establishment of UNAK-Turkish Platform of Law Librarians in 2007:

- Since that time law librarians have a discussion list at unak-hukuk@yahoogroups.com to communicate and share information on legal information
- A web page[77] was created to announce news, legal information resources, law libraries and other topics related to legal information
- Law librarians arrange panels, workshops and seminars at the Annual Conference of the University and Research Librarians Association
- Law librarians in several cities meet and discuss the current issues each year
- The literature on legal information management and law librarianship is rapidly growing
- The International Association of Law Libraries (IALL) 28th Annual Course on International Law Librarianship[78] was held on 11–15 October 2009 in Istanbul. This conference was a great opportunity to establish networks and exchange information among legal information professionals worldwide. In addition to this, it was a great impetus for developing Turkish law librarianship

Although there are some developments and implementations in the field, there also are some basic problems for law libraries in Turkey. These are briefly as follows:

75 Available at: http://onlineyayinevi.ankara.edu.tr, accessed 23 June 2010.

76 Available at: http://makale.mkutup.gov.tr, accessed 23 June 2010.

77 Available at: http://thk.bilgi.edu.tr/default_en.asp, accessed 23 June 2010.

78 Available at: http://iall.org/iall2009, accessed 23 June 2010.

- law libraries do not usually have a separate entity
- lack of education on the resources of law and librarianship in the departments of information and document management
- unqualified staff
- insufficient number of personnel

Conclusion

Turkish librarianship has been rapidly changing and developing in recent years, as explained in this contribution. All departments of librarianship were restructured and renamed as Departments of Information and Document Management with a new curriculum. New courses on user groups, medical and economic librarianship were introduced with the new curriculum and content. It is reasonable to assume that there will be a course on law librarianship in the future.

After establishing the UNAK-Turkish Platform of Law Librarians (TPLL), librarians created a listserv covering the current situation of law librarianship, problems, solutions and future plans. So an electronic network has been created among universities that have faculties of law, bar associations, court and firm libraries. The TPLL continues to work extensively in this field.

Print and e-legal information resources are rapidly increasing all over the world as well as in Turkey. The e-government projects, especially allowing free access to legal information sources for everyone, increase interest in legal information management. Publishers and aggregators are also creating databases covering law journals, cases, codes, legislation, regulations and so on. More online legal resources available from government and companies allow legal information users to find and access relevant information resources in the shortest time.

Finally, it can be concluded that with the establishment of the TPLL, there have been several developments in education and training for librarians who specialise in legal information management in terms of an updated curriculum and additional opportunities, with the TPLL organising and attending panels, workshops, seminars and conferences at the national and international level. Law librarianship will be progressively developed in the coming years in Turkey.

Further Reading

Turkish Platform of Law Librarians (2007). Available at: http://thk.bilgi.edu.tr/hakkimizda_en.asp, accessed 13 July 2009.

Yazici, S. (2009), *A Guide to Turkish Public Law and Legal Research*, update published January 2009. Available at: www.nyulawglobal.org/Globalex/Turkey1.htm, accessed 18 June 2010.

References

Anatolian University Libraries Consortium (2009). Available at: www.ankos.gen.tr/index.php?option=com_content&task=view&id=12&Itemid=223, accessed 17 July 2009.

Celik, H. and Bayir, D. (2008). 'A General Outlook on Turkish Librarianship and Libraries', in *Turkish Libraries in Transition: New Opportunities and Challenges* (İstanbul: Turkish Librarians' Association). Also available: *Liber Quarterly* 18:3–4, December 2008, 470–9. Available at: http://research.sabanciuniv.edu/11465/1/article.pdf, accessed 18 June 2010.

Council of Higher Education. Available at: www.yok.gov.tr/en/content/view/527/222, accessed 3 August 2009.

Cukadar, S. (2008), 'Turk Hukuk Kutuphanecileri Platformu'nun Olusum Sureci'/'The Establishment Process of Turkish Platform of Law Librarians', *Bilgi Dünyasi/Information World* 9:2, October, 541–53 [in Turkish with English abstract].

Gurdal, O. and Subasioglu, F. (2006), 'The Plane Tree Turns Fifty: A History of the Department of Librarianship at Ankara University', *Library Philosophy and Practice* 8:2, Spring, 7. . Available at: http://unllib.unl.edu/LPP/gurdal.htm, accessed 18 June 2010.

Hacettepe University Department of Information and Document Management (2009). Available at: www.bby.hacettepe.edu.tr/eng/index.asp, accessed 24 July 2009,

Innovative Library Initiatives Promotion Group. Available at: www.library.itu.edu.tr/ilipg/pe01_about_us.html, accessed 12 June 2009.

Istanbul Bilgi University, from Course Catalog. Available at: www.register.bilgi.edu.tr/coursecatalog/yeni/detay.asp?lang=en&cid=LAW%20105, accessed 4 August 2009.

Istanbul Bilgi University Library (2009), from Library and e-Resources. Available at: http://library.bilgi.edu.tr, accessed 12 June 2009.

Istanbul Universitesi Hukuk Fakültesi (2003). Available at: www.istanbul.edu.tr/hukuk/kutuphane_hakkinda.htm, accessed 12 June 2009.

Legal Yayıncılık (2006), from Legal Banks. Available at: www.legal.com.tr/urunler.asp, accessed 12 June 2009.

Martindale.com (2009), from Search Results, country=Turkey. Available at: www.martindale.com/Results.aspx, accessed 10 August 2009.

Turkish Platform of Law Librarians (2007). Available at: http://thk.bilgi.edu.tr/hakkimizda_en.asp, accessed 13 July 2009.

Turkiye Barolar Birligi (2009). Available at: www.barobirlik.org.tr/barolar, accessed 12 June 2009.

Türkiye Yayın Kataloğu – Turkish Books in Print (2010) (Istanbul: Turdav A.S Yayın Grubu).

Yenisey, F. (2004), *Legal Education in Turkey*, paper to the American Association of Law Schools Conference 'Educating Lawyers for Transnational Challenges', May 2004. Available at: www.aals.org/international2004/Papers/yenisey.pdf, accessed 21 June 2009.

Law Librarianship in Vietnam

Le Thi Hanh

Law Librarians in Vietnam

There are about 90 law librarians in Vietnam in 2010. They are mainly located in the capital, Hanoi, and in the major cities such as Ho Chi Minh City, Hue, Da Lat and Can Tho.

In terms of professional associations for librarians in Vietnam, there is the Vietnam Library Association (VLA) which was founded in Hanoi on 22 October 2006 (Le Thuy 2006) and is hosted at the Vietnam National Library, itself originally founded in 1917. The VLA's declared objectives are to:

- Advance and strengthen the Vietnamese librarianship; enhance the roles and positions of librarians and library institutions in the Vietnamese people's social and cultural life; make positive contributions to the economic, social and cultural development of the country
- Establish, maintain and strengthen networks, partnerships and linkages among Vietnamese and foreign librarians, libraries, library schools and library associations and related organisations in the areas of experience sharing and improved professional knowledge; foster the development and international integration of Vietnamese librarians and library institutions
- Serve as a national forum for library professionals, library related people and library friends to share experience, to promote mutual understanding and to unite their intellectual power to solve major issues of the Vietnamese library profession

Vinh-The Lam (2001) had pointed out that 'Vietnam has a fairly large body of dedicated library professionals working in a well structured library system. It is an anomaly that Vietnam does not have a national library association' and this is now remedied. Before the formation of the VLA there were several library associations for different types of library: the Library Club, the Northern Academic Library Association and the Southern Academic Library Association for university libraries, seven regional public library associations, and the Vietnam Association for Scientific and Technical Information and Documentation. However, there is no organisation or association of law librarians at all.

Education and Training

No specialist qualification is required to become a law librarian. Essentially you need to hold a bachelor degree of library science or a bachelor degree of information management. You should then be encouraged to study further to get a degree in law as a second degree and continue to be trained and develop various professional skills depending on your position and your daily tasks at the library.

Commonly the law library's workforce includes not only people who have knowledge of library science but also knowledge of law and other fields. According to the author's survey, 65 per cent of librarians in law libraries have a degree in library science, 24 per cent of librarians graduated from a law university, 11 per cent of librarians have a degree in other fields and 20 per cent of librarians have degrees in both library science and law.

Although law librarians have made much progress, they do not yet meet the demands of the job in the context of the digital age. They need more skills and techniques for interacting with people, skills of identifying and utilising information resources, web management skills, and especially skills of working professionally. So, various kinds of training such as seminars, workshops, short courses on specific topics and in-house training are necessary.

Law Libraries in Vietnam

There are about 15 law libraries in Vietnam. They include libraries of the state and government, libraries of legal research institutions, court libraries, procuracy[79] libraries and law university libraries.

State and government libraries include the Vietnam National Assembly Library, the Library of the Ministry of Justice and the Institute of State and Law Library. The main users of these libraries are the members of the National Assembly, researchers and scholars. The collections are not very large but they hold specialised legal information resources such as: legislation and related documents, research papers and other legal documents. 'The National Library has a collection of diverse materials including legal materials. Notably, it has certain resources on the old legal texts and legal system before the establishment of the current government of Vietnam' (Luu 2010).

The Supreme People's Court has two libraries: the Institute of Judicial Science Library and School of Court Staff Training Library. However, these libraries are quite small and each library has only one librarian.

At the local level there are no independent libraries at the provincial courts and the district courts. There is a storage department which serves lawyers and judges at each court with the main function of keeping all the files of case law. Similarly, the library is a part of the Storage Division belonging to the Office of Supreme People's Procuracy. Provincial procuracy and district procuracy offices have a 'legal bookcase' with a tiny number of law books.

The major law libraries, in contrast, are the law university libraries which have large collections as well as a good number of librarians. They included the Hanoi Law University Library, Ho Chi Minh City University of Law Library, the Judicial Institute Library, libraries of the law faculties of others multi-faculty universities such as Hanoi National University, Open University (in Hanoi), Hue University (in central Vietnam), Da Lat University (central highland) and Can Tho University (Cuu Long Delta area).

The two biggest law libraries in Vietnam are the Hanoi Law University Library and the Ho Chi Minh City University of Law. A modern library opened at the Hanoi Law University in 2007 and at the Law University in Ho Chi Minh City in 2009 as part of the a project which started in 1998, 'Strengthen Legal Education in Vietnam', funded by the Swedish International Development Agency (Le Thuy Duong 2009).

Hanoi Law University Library[80] has a collection of more than 10,000 titles with 200,000 volumes, thousands of undergraduate theses, master's degree theses, doctoral dissertations, and

79 The Supreme People's Procuracy of Vietnam is responsible for initiating public prosecutions and acts to ensure legal compliance by government, government agencies and citizens.

80 Available at: http://lib.hlu.edu.vn, accessed 26 June 2010.

reference and bibliographical works, and 85 current law journal titles. It serves about 6,000 full-time students, 400 master's degree students and 20 PhD candidates, and 423 university staff. The library has a staff of 24 librarians.

Ho Chi Minh City University Library[81] has a collection of more than 8,000 titles with 80,000 volumes, more than 1,000 undergraduate theses, master theses, doctoral dissertations, reference and bibliographical works, and 75 current titles of law journals. The number of users includes 4,000 full-time students, 200 postgraduate students and more than 200 university staff. The library staff includes eight librarians and 10 part-time assistant librarians.

Besides their extensive collections in print, these two libraries also have some international legal databases including databases such as Westlaw, HeinOnline and Elin@Vietnam[82] that are freely accessible on campus. The information infrastructure and facilities of these libraries are quite modern. There is a high-speed Internet connection via leased line 2MB connection and a wireless network covering the entire university; all computers are connected to the Internet. Hanoi Law University Library and Ho Chi Minh City University Library have established an inter-library loan service between the two libraries and opened a Z39.50 connection for exchanging information with other libraries.

In contrast, the libraries of law faculties of other universities are quite small and belong to the main library of the universities. Each faculty law library has only one or two librarians.

Legal Publishing

Legal publishing in Vietnam is undertaken by commercial legal publishers and government publishers.

Commercial publishers include Judicial Publishing House, National Political Publishing House, Socio-Labour Publishing House, People's Security Publishing House and Social Sciences Publishing House. Among these publishers only Judicial Publishing House has law books as its main product and the other publishers publish various kinds of books of which law books is only one category. Most of the publications are in print.

Legal documents are published by the state and governmental agencies. The National Assembly[83] publishes a database of legislation 'Vietnam Law'. The government publishes a database of legal documents that is posted on the portal of government.[84] The portals of 63 provinces and cities throughout the whole country are connected to the government portal. On the portal of each province and city there is a menu item, *Cong Bao*, which includes all documents that are approved by the provincial government. In addition, the Office of the Vietnam Government also publishes legal documents in print under the title *Cong Bao* that is a daily publication. The *Official Gazette* is the translation of *Cong Bao*.[85] The Ministry of Justice[86] also has a national legal database that integrates legal documents approved by state, government and ministries.

81 Available at: http://lib.hcmulaw.edu.vn/opac, accessed 26 June 2010.

82 ELIN@Vietnam is an implementation of the ELIN@ service developed by Lund University Libraries, Sweden. It provides a single entry point to federated searching across multiple digital resources and offers librarians an excellent content management tool. Available at: www.lub.lu.se/en/about-lub/organisation/lund-university-libraries-head-office/information-about-elin.html, accessed 26 June 2010.

83 Available at: www.na.gov.vn, accessed 26 June 2010.

84 Available at: www.chinhphu.vn, accessed 26 June 2010.

85 Available at: www.na.gov.vn/htx/English, accessed 26 June 2010.

86 Available at: www.moj.gov.vn, accessed 26 June 2010.

Legal journals resources are published by various institutions: the Office of National Assembly, the Supreme People's Court, the Supreme People's Procuracy, the Institute of State and Law, the Ministry of Justice and law schools; almost all of them are in the Vietnamese language. There is only the *Vietnam Law and Legal Forum*, a periodical in English, which has annual summary in English of the contents of the *Official Gazette*.[87]

Generally, legal publishing is adequate to meet the demands of education, training and researching. However, the number of commercial publishers is limited and most of them focus on publishing books in print only; there are no publishers or providers who supply e-books or e-journals. That is the main disadvantage of legal publishing in Vietnam.

Major Policy Issues

There are three main points which should be made on policy in regard to law librarianship.

Firstly, most law libraries work independently. There is not any collaboration except between Hanoi Law University Library and Ho Chi Minh City University of Law Library. For example, there are 10 law libraries in Hanoi. Three of them use the same library system, Libol (Hanoi Law University Library, Ministry of Justice Library, National Assembly Library), which can help libraries to exchange bibliographic records, share online catalogues as well as provide inter-library loan services. In fact, despite some discussions about collaboration, no substantial progress has yet been made.

Secondly, in Vietnam there is no organisation or association for law librarians. This means that there is no forum for exchanging ideas, sharing information resources and library services. The suggested resolution to this situation is that a Vietnamese Law Libraries Association should be established as soon as possible and the first step would be to join the International Association of Law Libraries.

Lastly, in the digital age, libraries cannot survive and develop if they lack electronic resources. So building up the electronic collections is one of the main goals of most law libraries' strategies. Commercial publishers in Vietnam should be interested in publishing both e-books and e-journals as well as books and journals in print. Publishers should have a policy to encourage libraries to buy and disseminate e-materials to community. This is the best way to develop our law libraries and make the library services more effective and users will benefit from this advancement.

Further Reading

Dang Van Thong (2007), *Promoting Activities of Legal Information at Law Libraries in Vietnam*. Master's thesis (Ho Chi Minh: Ho Chi Minh City Law University).

Le Thi Hanh (2005), *Activities of Organizing, Managing Hanoi Law University Library in the Context of Applying Information Technology*. Master's thesis (Hanoi: Hanoi Law University).

Stueart, R. (2010), 'Vietnam: Libraries, archives and museums', in Bates, M. and Maack, M. (2009–10), *Encyclopedia of Library and Information Services*, 3rd edition (London: Taylor & Francis).

87 Available at: http://vietnamlaw.vnanet.vn, accessed 26 June 2010.

References

Le Thuy Duong (2006), *Vietnamese Library Association Founded*, 30 October 2006, Congress of Southeast Asian Librarians website. Available at: www.consal.org/index.php?option=com_content&view=article&id=102:vietnamese-library-association-founded&catid=47:vietnam&Itemid=146, accessed 19 June 2006.

Le Thuy Duong (2009), *New Law Library Opens in Ho Chi Minh City*, Congress of Southeast Asian Librarians website. Available at: www.consal.org/index.php?option=com_content&view=article&id=240:new-law-library-opens-in-ho-chi-minh-city&catid=47:vietnam&Itemid=146, accessed 20 June 2010.

Luu, Anh (2010), *Vietnam Legal Research*, update published July 2010. Available at: www.nyulawglobal.org/Globalex/Vietnam1.htm, accessed 30 September 2010.

Vinh-The Lam (2001), 'A national library association for Vietnam', *New Library World* 102:1166/1167, 278–82.

Chapter 9
Digitizing the World's Laws

Claire M. Germain

Introduction

Where does one find the foreign investment laws of Botswana? What about the copyright law of the Netherlands, the corporation laws of Japan, or an English translation of the Egyptian Civil Code? In 1991, Wallace Baker, the founder of the Paris office of the law firm Baker & McKenzie, remarked that 'foreign law has become the daily bread of lawyers everywhere who formerly had totally domestic practices' (Germain 1991, xii). Since then, the need to access foreign law has increased exponentially. The importance of improving global access to foreign law via the Internet was highlighted at a 2008 international Meeting of Experts on Global Co-operation on the Provision of Online Legal Information on National Laws, organized by the Hague Conference on Private International Law.[1] (I attended this meeting at the invitation of its Secretary-General Hans van Loon.) This chapter evaluates the current state of progress in online access to the content of foreign law, provides a world snapshot, and discusses such digital law issues as authentication and preservation for long-term access.

The Context

The Need for Access

Lawyers, judges, notaries and other legal professionals need ready access to the law to perform their duties, but access to domestic legal information is also necessary for citizens to know the law that applies to them and what their rights are, for the conduct of business and to ensure the rule of law. The principle 'no one is deemed to be ignorant of the law' goes back to the Latin: *nemo legem ignorare censetur*,[2] expressed in common law countries as 'ignorance of law is no excuse', *ignorantia legis non excusat*. Both expressions can be traced back to Roman times.[3]

1 Available at: www.hcch.net, accessed 21 June 2010.

2 The Roman *Digest* devoted the entire Title 6 of Book 22, distinguishing 'ignorance of the law', from 'ignorance of fact', which was by nature excusable (Cartier 2008, 58). As François Terré, an eminent French law professor remarked, 'the maxim is considered in Antiquity and even now as translating a principle of reason without which life in society would be impossible. It is not written anywhere in the corpus of legal rules, but it dominates the entire body of law' [author's English translation] (Cartier 2008, 58; see also Wagner and Cacciaguidi-Fahy 2008).

3 In tracing the origin of these two expressions, it seems that the former is used in civil law countries and the latter in common law countries, even though they both refer the origin of the concept to Roman law and the explanations are similar. The standard English work only mentions the latter, but cites the same source in the *Digest* and the identical explanation, the difference between ignorance of fact and ignorance of law (Broom 1900, 205).

In civil law countries, where the legal system is based primarily on written law, the need to publicize new laws has an old origin (Cartier 2008, 57; Saint-Prix 1809; Gaudemet 1993; Laferrière 1949). New laws can only become effective if they are published and made known to citizens. Traditionally, the law typically entered into force some days after its publication in the country's official gazette, allowing for enough time to distribute copies. In France, the period was one full day after publication in the French *Journal officiel* (Szladits and Germain 1985). In Brazil, it was 45 days after official publication in *Diaro oficial da uniao* (Passos 2008). This changed with the possibility of notification via the Internet, which provided both savings (no more paper and mailing costs) and immediate distribution. Countries increasingly share the philosophy that governments have a duty to make their laws freely available to the public. In France, unless otherwise provided, a law now takes effect one day after publication in the electronic *Journal officiel*, which is the official and authentic text. This *droit au droit* reached the level of a principle of constitutional value in a 1999 French Constitutional Council decision.[4] By contrast, legislation in common law countries, such as the UK, is judicially noticed whether it has been published or not.[5] Publication is therefore not a formal legal requirement for a law to come into force as is the case in Continental law systems.

The globalisation of national economies and legal cultures increases the need to consult legislation from countries other than one's own. Because of the regional integration of the economies, access to European and foreign legislation has become a regular, practical need in the 35 countries of the European Union and the European Economic Area (Berger 2009). Across the world, many issues involve more than one legal system, requiring parties and their advisers to determine what law applies to their relationships and transactions. International instruments at the regional level, such as the EU Regulations Rome I and II on the law applicable to contractual obligations and to torts, and at the global level, such as the Hague Convention on Choice of Court Agreements, enhance the need for access to the content of foreign law (Hague Conference on Private International Law 2009).

Before digitization, accessing legal information was particularly challenging. The online availability of laws improved access to foreign law considerably starting in the 1960s for pre-Internet adopters, and dramatically since the early 1990s. The main reason for the progress is, of course, the revolutionary impacts of technology and the Internet on legal information. A second reason is the e-government information policies now expressly stated by a number of countries, which pay particular attention to the dissemination of the legal sources in order to ensure the effective implementation of the rule of law, and for legal security. A major consequence of this

4 The decision was about a challenge to a law allowing the government to use the procedure of art. 38 of the Constitution to legislate via ordinance, rather than parliamentary legislation, because of the urgency of enacting nine codes into law. The Constitutional Council approved the law, mentioning that the goal of the law met the 'goal with constitutional value of accessibility and intelligibility of the law; that the equality before the law mentioned in art. 6 of the Declaration of the Rights of Man and the Citizen and the "guarantee of rights" required by its article 16 may not be effective if citizens do not have enough knowledge of the norms that are applicable to them'. Décision 99-421 DC du 16 décembre 1999, Loi portant habilitation du Gouvernement à procéder, par ordonnance, à l'adoption de la partie législative de certains codes, JORF, 22 décembre 1999 (Cartier 2008).

5 UK Interpretation Act 1978, c. 30, s. 3, 'Every Act is a public Act to be judicially noticed as such, unless the contrary is expressly provided by the Act'. Further, s. 4, 'An Act or provision of an Act comes into force … (b) where no provision is made for its coming into force, at the beginning of the day on which the Act receives the Royal Assent'.

revolutionary change has been the evolution from fee-based databases to free online information systems.

Definitions and Scope of the World Laws

Access to the world laws is needed in various contexts. Researchers may be legal professionals well-versed in the legal system of a country, citizens worried about their rights, or businesspersons looking for commercial laws: different needs in different contexts. The focus in this chapter is on access to the official word of the law, specifically to statutes, codes, regulations, court decisions and international agreements ('primary sources' in common law countries) that are binding on the courts, in contrast to 'secondary sources' such as commentaries on the law, treatises and law reviews. In civil law countries, the primary source of law is legislation, normally published in a country's official gazette.[6] Court decisions and scholarly writings (*la doctrine*) play an essential role in these legal systems, but are not usually at the top of the formal hierarchy of binding norms. A typical example of the law to be found is described in a guide to legal research in Costa Rica:

> The laws passed by the Costa Rican legislature are the primary source of law. Once a law has been approved by the Legislature it must be published in the official gazette known as *La Gaceta*. The record of all laws published by the Gazette may be searched via the Internet at the site of the National Printing Office. In addition to the laws passed by the legislature the Costa Rican government may issue regulations (*Reglamento*) to a specific law. Furthermore, the President and other government Ministries may issue Decrees (*Decreto*) regarding specific topics. Whether it is a law, a regulation or a decree all must be published in the official gazette before they become binding. A record of all laws, executive decrees and regulations in existence in Costa Rica is available from the National Legislation System database (*SINALEVI*) where the user can search the database based upon different types of search criteria. (Petersen 2010)

Of course, there are other families of legal systems beyond those belonging to the common law and civil law traditions, for example mixed systems, religious and customary law, and one cannot separate access to these sources from access to legal information in general.[7]

Access to Law and Understanding of the Law

Finding a particular law is often not good enough, more comprehensive access may be sought, or the need to make sure that legislation is current, has not been repealed, and is still in force. For court decisions, one needs to ascertain that they are still good law. Often, one needs not only the current law, and all the laws currently in force, but also the law as it was at an earlier point in time, for instance at the time of the litigation. This calls for access to amended and repealed versions of the laws, the ability to go back and forth between the various versions, as well as access to an accurate, up to date and final version of a particular text. Some websites do well in that regard: in

---

6 Legal systems have many variants, even within the same families. The world map offered by the University of Ottawa gives a good pictorial representation of the countries covered. Available at: www.juriglobe.ca/eng/index.php, accessed 21 June 2010.

7 How to formulate classifications of different families of legal systems is a classic question for comparative law scholars. The classifications proposed here are mainly to help show what constitutes the law in a particular country and to find a common denominator.

Canada and Estonia, the government websites specify that they provide 'current legislation as at any date'.[8] A caveat is that they may not go back to the beginning of publication.

Of course, in dealing with different legal systems, knowledge of the role of the sources of law and the hierarchy of norms is important to appreciating the value of a particular law or case. One may sometimes want to know the state of the law in a particular subject area. In such instances, it is useful to consult a treatise first, to get an introduction and references to specific codes and specific articles within that code.

How much can one understand about a law by looking at a text? If no context is provided, it may be harder to understand procedures and other matters. The greatest danger is that non-professionals may have the letter of the law, but not the context. The Internet makes legal information much more accessible to the public, but greater accessibility does not necessarily make the law more understandable. Some countries have taken steps to make the law understandable to citizens.

E-Government Policy Agendas

National governments in established democracies, as well as countries moving in that direction, increasingly use technology to help citizens and researchers understand the law they need to know. Some emerging countries are spurred by technological advances, sometimes as part of a rule of law project. Some countries make their e-government policies explicit on their websites. The Bangladesh website, produced by the Ministry of Law, Justice and Parliamentary Affairs, endeavours to make available all existing laws, and keep them updated and user-friendly to 'ensure access to law and justice and make an effective e-governance'.[9] Estonia's electronic official gazette has an express statement of user assistance via email and helpline, and justifies free access to new laws because 'one of the preconditions of understanding legislation is the legislation's availability, which is why the eRT Internet database can be used free of charge'. Further it states that 'librarians and local government officials have completed a training course on using the eRT and are obligated by law to provide persons with instructions and help them in finding the necessary acts'.[10]

Technology helps foster the rule of law. The Global Legal Information Network (GLIN), operated by the Law Library of Congress in the United States, is a public database of laws and other documents, contributed on a decentralized basis by government agencies in countries of the world.[11] Gabon, one of the most recent member countries, states its reasons for joining GLIN as 'part of the implementation of the policy of transparency and good governance as well as natural resource management and sustainable development' (Olouna et al. 2009). Kuwait's Ministry of Justice website mentions GLIN prominently on its front page, as well as its own e-justice project.[12]

The Hague Interest

The Hague meeting of experts in November 2008 produced several useful ideas and a draft declaration of principles, centred on a platform to facilitate access to the content of foreign law and work on standard-setting. The draft report proposed an agenda of work to be done through a new Hague Convention in three parts:

---

8 Available at: http://canada.justice.gc.ca/eng/notices-avis.html [and] www.riigiteataja.ee/ert/intr/en.htm, accessed 21 June 2010.

9 Available at: www.bangladesh.gov.bd, accessed 21 June 2010.

10 Available at: www.riigiteataja.ee/ert/intr/en.htm, accessed 21 June 2010.

11 GLIN is examined below at page 192–2.

12 Available at: www.moj.gov.kw/index_en.asp arabic, accessed 21 June 2010.

> Part I: Facilitating access to online legal information on foreign law. This part would focus on assuring the free accessibility of a country's or regional economic integration organisation's main legal materials, particularly legislation, case law and international agreements (and potentially *doctrine* that would be important in civil law jurisdictions) for online publication and re-publication / re-use; it could possibly provide some guidance on realistic quality standards or best practices for such free access and online publishing, and perhaps the provision of a permanent body of experts to monitor the development of practical standards and/or best practices in these areas, also with a view to the compatibility or 'interoperability' of global online publishing standards.
>
> Part II: Cross-border administrative and/or judicial co-operation. This part would provide for the handling of requests for information in response to concrete questions on the application of foreign law in relation to a specific matter that arises in court proceedings (and possibly also in other contexts), and for which information available online is not sufficient.
>
> Part III: A global network of institutions and experts for more complex questions. This part would address situations where there may be a need for accessing more in-depth information on complex legal questions in specific areas (e.g., insolvency or inheritance), or in the course of complex litigation that involves the interface of multiple areas of foreign and / or local law(s). Here, one might think of a series of networks of qualified organisations (bar associations, comparative law institutes, organisations of notaries and other specialists, whose services would not be free) facilitated via the Permanent Bureau. (Hague Conference on Private International Law 2009)

Fee-Based or Free Access

Some countries have either copyrighted their legal materials or entered into exclusive publication or distribution agreements with quasi-governmental or private publishers. These agreements can present obstacles to free access to legal information, but the increasing trend is towards free access. These changes are best illustrated by briefly recalling the history of the online editions of the official gazettes in civil law countries in Europe and Latin America. The official gazette of a particular country is the main source for publication of legislation, that is laws, regulations and decrees, legal notices, sometimes treaties, and in some countries even texts of court decisions (Belize, Costa Rica, Estonia are a few).[13] Official gazettes were among the first legal websites created, starting in the late 1990s. Most were initially fee-based, but the situation has changed. In Europe, most official databases (29 out of 35 – some countries have several official databases) can now be accessed free of charge (Berger 2009, Table 3, Annex 1). The overall trend is towards free access.[14] In some, free access is provided to both current and retrospective issues. In other countries, the current edition and a few recent months are freely accessible, but one needs to pay to access the archives. In some countries the gazettes are still subscription-based. In Chile a private company has the legal duty to publish the state official bulletin, the *Diario Oficial* (Endress Gómez 2008), but free abstracts going back to 1950 are available through GLIN. Some countries,

13 For definitions of legal gazette, official journal, official gazette see Berger (2009).

14 A current list of some 60 official gazettes, which is not exhaustive, is kept by the Swiss Institute of Comparative Law. Available at: www.isdc.ch/en/bibliotheque.asp/4-0-10552-5-4-1/5-0-1630-11-4-2, accessed 21 June 2010.

for example France, have switched from fee-based access with the government contracting with a private publisher to free open access.

In several countries, notably Australia, Canada and the United States, pioneering efforts to exploit new technologies to provide legal information came from universities, along with a strong philosophy of free access to law. The first was the Legal Information Institute[15] under the leadership of Peter Martin and Thomas Bruce at Cornell Law School in the United States, which created the first websites for the decisions of the US Supreme Court and the New York Court of Appeals, the highest court in New York State, in 1992. Other universities created websites for federal circuit courts of appeals. The LII philosophy spread and inspired the creation of legal information institutes in other parts of the world and the establishment of the Free Access to Law Movement.[16] In the United States most federal and state legal publications are in the public domain and not subject to copyright. Today all federal and state governmental entities have developed websites to distribute bills, statutes, court decisions and regulations over the Internet (Germain 1998b). Cooperation between government entities, universities and other non-profit organisations continues to improve access to the law, by providing useful search engines and linking to other sources. Cornell's Legal Information Institute collaborates with the US Supreme Court for the delivery of US Supreme Court decisions, and has improved the indexing and delivery of the official US Code version provided by the US government.

Germany and Argentina provide examples of robust systems developed using other business models through a combination of government and commercial partnerships. Juris, the major legal information system for laws and cases in Germany, was established in the 1970s by the Federal Ministry of Justice and privatized in the 1980s. The majority share is still held by the German federal government, the other shares were bought by Netherlands-based publisher SDU (Exter and Kammer 2008). Now, *Gesetze im Internet* (Federal Laws on the Internet) is a free service to the public provided by the Federal Ministry of Justice in cooperation with Juris, and features the current consolidated versions of nearly all federal laws. *Makrolog – Recht für Deutschland* is a part free, part fee-based online service offering the *Federal Law Gazette* and other official compilations/law gazettes. Argentina offers a combination of free and fee-based services.

Cost recovery systems also differ by country. In Norway, legal information is produced and distributed through a private foundation. Some is free but most is fee-based. The databases are offered for a modest sum and a cost recovery mechanism takes into account the needs of the public and the market offered by the legal profession.[17] Kenya has entrusted the National Council for Law Reporting with the exclusive mandate to publish the official *Kenya Law Reports*. It also publishes the laws of Kenya with a search engine, the official gazette, and other legal information.[18] Access is free and permission is granted to copy and print but no portion can be commercially reproduced unless a subscription fee is paid to offset the costs of production. In Bermuda, access to laws and statutory instruments is free but access to case law is fee-based, provided by Justis Publishing, a commercial company.[19] Botswana recently opened up the previously restricted Laws of Botswana website to the public.[20]

---

15 Available at: www.law.cornell.edu, accessed 21 June 2010.

16 Available at: www.worldlii.org/worldlii/declaration, accessed 21 June 2010.

17 Available at: www.lovdata.no/info/lawdata/html, accessed 21 June 2010.

18 Available at: www.kenyalaw.org/update/index.php, accessed 21 June 2010.

19 Available at: www.bermudalaws.bm; www.gov.bm, accessed 21 June 2010.

20 Available at: www.laws.gov.bw, accessed 21 June 2010.

A World Snapshot

General Themes and Comments

To assess progress, in early 2010 I conducted an empirical survey of as many as possible of the 192 countries listed by the United Nations, mostly by going directly to the government websites of each country. Two online guides were particularly useful: the free New York University Globalex research guide series[21] and the fee-based Reynolds and Flores' *Foreign Law Guide*[22] are both thorough and thoughtful, well researched, and provide context for the primary and secondary sources (in common law terminology), as well as a standard table of contents for each country, which is useful for comparisons. Neither is always quite up to date for Internet resources, because it is impossible to keep up with the fast-evolving landscape. This first world snapshot shows much progress and the overall picture that emerges is very positive, showing worldwide evolution towards the availability of more information.

This chapter reviews mostly governmental and free websites, while recognising that in some countries commercial, fee-based sources play an important and even a predominant role in providing information to the legal profession, particularly for case law and legal literature but sometimes also for legislation. In the past decade more and more government websites have appeared, leading to a great increase in the online accessibility of world laws. Looking at the world coverage, one notes that most, if not all, countries have some presence on the Internet. The coverage of legal information is uneven, however. Some countries have robust and sophisticated digital law websites; some have few resources available.

Countries are at different stages of e-government, depending on their political structure, commitment to the rule of law, size, level of government intervention, and available funding. They use a variety of avenues, depending on which department or branch of government initiated and developed the technology. Sometimes a special technology branch of government is created for Internet activities; sometimes private initiative creates a legal site.

Several countries have developed an integrated legal information system on a single central site that provides comprehensive access to laws and codes, regulations and decrees, court decisions, treaties, bills, and documents from other government entities. Argentina,[23] Austria,[24] Belarus,[25] Belgium,[26] Costa Rica,[27] Finland,[28] Honduras,[29] Jersey,[30] Kenya,[31] Mongolia,[32] Peru[33] and Sri Lanka[34] are a few examples. These sites are exemplary in using the Internet to disseminate legal information to their citizens and by extension to the world.

21 Available at: www.nyulawglobal.org/globalex, accessed 21 June 2010.
22 Available at: www.foreignlawguide.com, accessed 21 June 2010.
23 Available at: www.saij.jus.gov.ar, accessed 21 June 2010.
24 Available at: http://ris.bka.gv.at, accessed 21 June 2010.
25 Available at: http://law.by, accessed 21 June 2010.
26 Available at: www.belgiumlex.be, accessed 21 June 2010.
27 Available at: www.pgr.go.cr/scij, accessed 21 June 2010.
28 Available at: www.finlex.fi, accessed 21 June 2010.
29 Available at: www.poderjudicial.gob.hn/juris/principal.aspx, accessed 21 June 2010.
30 Available at: www.jerseylaw.je/Home/WhatsNew/default.aspx, accessed 21 June 2010.
31 Available at: www.kenyalaw.org/update/index.php, accessed 21 June 2010.
32 Available at: www.legalinfo.mn, accessed 21 June 2010.
33 Available at: http://spij.minjus.gob.pe/spij_quienessomos.asp, accessed 21 June 2010.
34 Available at: www.lawnet.lk, accessed 8 March, 2010.

The Belarus Legislation Databank ETALON 'is a full-text search system containing legal texts issued by the President, Parliament, Government, National Bank, ministries, Constitutional Court, Supreme Court, Supreme Economic Court, and international treaties'.[35]

The Mongolia website, created with the assistance of the World Bank's 'Legal and Judicial Reform Project', and implemented by the Mongolian Ministry of Justice and Home Affairs, explains: 'Our objective is to create a single official source for Mongolian law and legal information by providing free and public access to all valid and enforceable laws and related documents. This service is crucial to ensure the protection of human rights and to improve respect for the rule of law'.[36] The European Union, as a regional system, is particularly well-developed.[37]

Some countries started the process with individual websites but have moved to create overall portals for legal information offered through central government websites which produce and host some of the information, then point to other separately-maintained websites. France, Germany and the United States offer such examples.[38]

Australia and Canada have strong government websites, but access to their laws has been greatly facilitated by the umbrella of the Australasian and Canadian Legal Information Institutes (AustLII and CanLII),[39] created to provide free access to law, which serve as overall portals, sometimes in a quasi-official capacity. GLIN[40] also serves as a portal site to the laws of a number of countries.

Most countries now offer websites containing legislative information. Most countries from the civil law tradition now have sites for their official gazettes (often from the country's national printing office) and a legislation portal. Often there are separate sites, which may originate from the country's parliament, ministry of justice, or even a presidential website, for example in Colombia, which provides full texts of laws in PDF.

Common law countries have historically put more emphasis on access to court decisions but also provide access to official gazettes, statutes and regulations, consolidated legislation, and treaties.

The organisation and sophistication of government websites vary depending on a country's current stage of development. Some provide online access to the official gazette, together with access to laws in force, and consolidated texts. Some publish new laws in chronological order, sometimes in PDF format without search capabilities. Others provide a search engine. Some provide consolidated texts and legislative texts from any point in time, for example Canada for consolidated legislation[41] and Estonia. Estonia's site provides 'official, current legislation as on any given date, and user-friendly and free of charge'.[42] The consolidated texts can be viewed for any date. One can locate former or current drafts of legislative acts and access potential revisions of the acts in bill form. Each draft of a consolidated text is linked to its preceding and subsequent drafts, allowing users to 'move in time' from the previous draft of the consolidated text to the next

35 Available at: http://law.by, accessed 21 June 2010.

36 Available at: www.legalinfo.mn, accessed 21 June 2010.

37 Available at: http://eur-lex.europa.eu, accessed 21 June 2010. The European Union official portal (www.europa.eu, accessed 8 March 2010) comprehensively covers news and information about its activities, institutions, policies and programmes, including full texts of official documents.

38 Available at: www.legifrance.gouv.fr, www.justiz.de, www.usa.gov, accessed 21 June 2010.

39 Available at: www.austlii.org, www.canlii.org, accessed 21 June 2010.

40 Available at: www.glin.org, accessed 21 June 2010.

41 Available at: http://laws-lois.justice.gc.ca/eng/MainPage, accessed 21 June 2010.

42 Electronic Riigi Teataja-ERT, www.riigiteataja.ee/ert/intr/en.htm, accessed 21 June 2010.

and back. As a result, a user does not have to ascertain the validity of a legislative act or locate its current draft by searching for amendments.

Often the process starts with individual government entities creating their own sites. Some countries have court portals, or portals for individual courts, usually the constitutional court will be the first online. For some countries, for example Portugal, one needs to search separate portals for legislation and court decisions.

In some countries more than one ministry posts laws and other information, for example in Morocco, the websites of the Ministry of Economic and General Affairs.[43] Some countries are on their way to developing good legal information systems. Egypt's information portal is not specifically on legal information but provides data and information to Egyptian citizens and states that 'Information access is a right for each citizen'.[44]

Most if not all countries now have a web presence, some kind of a central government portal or an embassy website. For instance, Liberia has a presidential website and a Ministry of Foreign Affairs website.[45] Sometimes, laws can be found through other organisations. Haiti has only a government website[46] but its legislation can be found through GLIN and constitutional court decisions through the Association of Supreme Courts (*Cassation*) of Countries Sharing the Use of French.[47] The laws of the Cooperative Republic of Guyana can be found through the regional organisation CARICOM, which provides access to the laws of several other Caribbean countries.[48] Countries without legal databases may have official government websites, which provide legislation, as in Angola.[49] The Republic of Congo Brazzaville website is general in scope and somewhat dated but provides some information on the Constitutional Court.[50]

Several emerging countries have received money from other governments or organisations to modernize their legal systems, create a better technological infrastructure, and develop websites. Technology has helped some countries as an instrument of law reform and democracy, to facilitate the rule of law. Some now explicitly acknowledge a duty to make their laws and court decisions more accessible to the public and to uphold the rule of law. Bhutan, which has built a democracy and an independent judiciary within the past few decades and has used technology with the help of the Danish government, provides an example. The government Royal Court of Justice website states as its mission:

> to improve accessibility to Justice by making Courts user friendly; uphold and protect Due Process of Law, Fair Trial, Rule of Law and Review system; build public confidence and respect through continuing professionalism; improve legal language and retain Bhutanese terminology that reflect and command Bhutanese values; harness technology for efficiency and cost effectiveness; improve infrastructures and capacity building; make judicial process responsive, effective, faster, better, and easier; and impart legal Education.[51]

---

43 Available at: www.affaires-generales.gov.ma/bibliotheque.asp?LIB3, accessed 21 June 2010.

44 Available at: www.eip.gov.eg, accessed 21 June 2010.

45 Available at: www.mofa.gov.lr/index.php, accessed 21 June 2010.

46 Available at: www.haiti.org, accessed 21 June 2010.

47 Available at: www.ahjucaf.org, accessed 6 July 2010.

48 Available at: www.caricomlaw.org, accessed 21 June 2010.

49 Available at: www.governo.gov.ao/LegislacaoTodos.aspx, accessed 21 June 2010.

50 Available at: www.presidence.cg/accueil, accessed 21 June 2010.

51 Available at: www.judiciary.gov.bt/index.htm, accessed 21 June 2010.

The legal information institutes and GLIN have been influential in partnering with countries to put laws online. Burkina Faso has good technological infrastructure with several government websites for various courts, thanks to technological help from LexUm and funding from several international organisations. It is now embarking on a project with GLIN.[52]

Australia has benefited greatly from the work of the Australasian Legal Information Institute, a non-profit organisation created expressly for the purpose of facilitating free access to Australian primary legal materials. AustLII has been most successful in obtaining free public access to data from government and court sources, providing user-friendly comprehensive access through a central server.

France as a Case Study

The history of the digital law movement in France is enlightening in understanding how a pioneer country in the use of digital technologies and technological innovation moved from a fee-based structure to free open access databases. France launched the Minitel, considered one of the world's most successful pre-web online services in 1982, allowing users to make online purchases, search the phone directory, and chat. One of its first applications was access to the official gazette. The first official French electronic databases for legal information (statutes, regulations, case law), possibly the first in the world, were created in the 1960s by university laboratories in collaboration with the Ministry of Justice, the offices of the Prime Minister and the supreme courts (Cottin 2002). The government started an official 'public service of dissemination of law' for citizens, legal professionals and law vendors in 1984 (France 1984), which was made available on the Internet in 2002 (France 2002). One of the major components was the digitization of the official gazette (Cottin 2005). For a number of years, the government contracted with a commercial vendor, ORT. The past five days of the official gazette were available free but the archives were fee-based. In 1997 French Prime Minister Lionel Jospin declared that public legal data should be available to the public free of charge. This led to the creation of Legifrance (Germain 1998a). From 1997 until 2002 there were two services: Legifrance was free, and Jurifrance was fee-based. The philosophical underpinnings and foundation of 'public service for the dissemination of law' are threefold: intelligibility of the law; accessibility of the legal rule; anonymisation of court decisions. As noted earlier, in a 1999 decision the *Conseil constitutionnel* gave constitutional value to this right to information.

Today, the French government offers strong access to laws, and official portal websites that aim to make the law not only accessible but understandable to the public. The philosophy is that it is not enough to have access to the law, citizens must be able to understand their rights. France offers an impressive range of websites directed towards legal professionals and the public. Service-public.fr[53] provides a single front office for administrative information. For each topic, it collects all relevant information and helps citizens find answers to such questions as: the price of a passport; formalities on getting married; buying a house; and many other procedures. According to the standards of the website, the information must be clear, efficient and precise enough to inform or direct the user, complete in the relevant field, and up to date and accessible to all regardless of the channel used. Parts are available in English. Vie-Publique.fr[54] is a governmental portal site for public policies and official information on political, social and economic life in France. It provides 'dossiers' on news, current events and studies to citizens and professionals.

52 Available at: www.legiburkina.bf, accessed 21 June 2010.

53 Available at: www.service-public.fr/langue/english, accessed 21 June 2010.

54 Available at: www.vie-publique.fr, accessed 21 June 2010.

Official, Intergovernmental Multi-Jurisdictional Portals

Several systems offer cross-border searching of cases or legislation, a single access point with a common search interface, sometimes with a thesaurus, sometimes in several languages.

For Europe, the Common Portal of National Case Law, created by the Network of the Presidents of the Supreme Judicial Courts of the European Union and released in 2007, provides a meta-search engine to query simultaneously various search engines and allow for comparisons of judicial solutions.[55] The Portal was conceived not only as an online database but to change work habits and, by providing supreme court justices with an opportunity to inform themselves about the law of other countries, to help create, develop and strengthen a common judicial culture in Europe. It includes automatic translation facilities (Network of the Presidents 2009).

Worldwide, the Association of Supreme Courts (*Cassation*) of Countries Sharing the Use of French was created in 2001, bringing together 48 supreme and cassation courts.[56] It has created a database of full text decisions for these courts that allows searching by country and provides access to courts which do not have their own websites, for example Haiti. Another association, the Association des Cours Constitutionnelles ayant en Partage l'Usage du Français (Association of Constitutional Courts sharing the Use of French) points to websites maintained by each country.[57]

The European Union's N-Lex website,[58] launched in 2006, provides a single access point with a common search interface to national legislation implementing EU measures. Produced by the EU and the participating national governments, it offers an interesting experiment, since one can query official databases for national law of 23 EU countries via a standard search screen in 22 of the EU's official languages. A multilingual dictionary (EUROVOC) facilitates searches across multiple languages. It requires considerable ongoing collaboration on all sides to create a stable standardized system.

Most, if not all, international organisations, for example the United Nations,[59] World Intellectual Property Organization (WIPO),[60] International Labour Organization (ILO)[61] and International Court of Justice (ICJ),[62] publish their information, including treaties and other international agreements, online.[63] These official portals contain an amazing, and ever growing amount of authoritative information

Overall Portals

The GLIN model The Global Legal Information Network (GLIN)[64] operated by the Law Library of Congress, is a public database of laws, regulations, judicial decisions and complementary legal sources contributed by governmental agencies in countries in the Americas, Europe, Africa and Asia, and from international organisations. GLIN members contribute the official

---

55 Available at: www.reseau-presidents.eu/rpcsjue/?lang=en, accessed 21 June 2010.

56 Available at: www.ahjucaf.org, accessed 21 June 2010.

57 Available at: www.accpuf.org, accessed 21 June 2010.

58 Available at: http://eur-lex.europa.eu/n-lex/pays.html?lang=en, accessed 21 June 2010.

59 Available at: www.un.org, accessed 21 June 2010.

60 Available at: www.wipo.org, accessed 21 June 2010.

61 Available at: www.ilo.org, accessed 21 June 2010.

62 Available at: www.icj-cij.org, accessed 21 June 2010.

63 The Cornell Law Library helped create the first website of the International Court of Justice and mirror sites for the ICJ and the ILO websites.

64 Available at: www.loc.gov/glin, accessed 21 June 2010.

full texts of published documents to the database in the original languages. Each document is accompanied by a summary in English and subject terms selected from a multilingual index. All summaries are available to the public and public access to full texts is also available if the country allows it.

GLIN is an interesting model because it works as a decentralized intergovernmental organisation; it is a cooperative non-profit federation of government agencies, usually legislative agencies or ministries of justice that contribute national legal information to the GLIN database. The data are stored centrally at the Library of Congress in Washington, DC and access is equally shared by all participating national GLIN stations.[65]

Gabon provides an example of how the system works. The GLIN Gabon station is located at the Directorate of Official Publications (DPO), the body responsible for the publication of the *Official Journal of the Gabonese Republic* (Olouna et al. 2009, 2–3). The GLIN Gabon Station includes a director responsible for coordinating the activities and the daily management of the station; three legal analysts responsible for literature review, indexing of legal texts for implementation of abstracts and submitting them to the Network; and a scientist responsible for the administration of accounts and the digitization process.

GLIN's strength is that it works government to government; it encourages governments to provide authoritative information in a digital format that is usable in the GLIN system and helps emerging countries put their laws online and access free legal information. GLIN originated as a card index to Latin American legislation created to meet the needs of the US Congress, and was developed with the support of the Congress, the World Bank interest and the Inter-American Development Bank (IABD). It is currently under review towards the goal of establishing an overall portal.

The WorldLII Model Legal information institutes around the world have played an essential role in fostering the online availability of laws worldwide and they have rendered an invaluable service to the citizens of the world, legal professionals and the rule of law. The WorldLII portal is invaluable, and very clearly organized; it brings together data from the various legal information institutes around the world and also provides a search engine customized to retrieve legal information elsewhere on the Internet. For discussion of the formation of the legal information institutes and their future development see Chapter 10, this volume.

English Language Information and Translations

The websites for many countries offer English versions of texts and sometimes versions in other languages. The information in the English 'libraries' is usually limited and sometimes only in summary form. When seeking the full text of legal documents, one must be prepared to deal with sites in vernacular languages. The quality of translations varies widely. Some countries make serious efforts to provide translations of their laws and decisions. Brazil's Infolegis compiles texts of Brazilian legal rules translated into English, French and Spanish.[66] The Estonian Legal Language Centre offers a database providing translation of Estonian legislation into English and translation of EC legislation into Estonian.[67] These sites usually state that the translations are for information

65 Building the Global Legal Information Network (GLIN) retraces the history of GLIN. Available at: www.glinfoundation.org, accessed 21 June 2010.

66 Available at: www.infolegis.com.br, accessed 4 August 2010.

67 Available at: www.legaltext.ee/indexen.htm, accessed 4 August 2010.

purposes only and that the official text is that in the original language. To the extent that English is the new *lingua franca*, there is a strong demand for English language translations. Some countries provide an English language 'window' into their website with introductions and explanations, but not the full texts of the documents.

The use of translation devices and software is hazardous to say the least but may be useful as a first approach if followed by human intermediation.

Digital Law Issues

Official and Authentic Digital Legal Sources

The terms 'official' and 'authentic' are sometimes used interchangeably but mean different things. An online official legal resource is one that possesses the same status as a print official legal resource. In the United States, for instance, the definition of an official version of court opinions, statutes, session laws or regulatory materials is one 'that has been governmentally mandated or approved by statute or rule. It might be produced by the government, but does not have to be' (American Association of Law Libraries 2007). This definition is firmly rooted in the print world. Courts and public officials turn to official legal resources for authoritative and reliable statements of the law and require citation to such sources in the documents that come before them. By itself, an online official legal resource offers no such automatic assurance.

Authenticity refers to the quality and credibility of the document. It means that the text is provided by competent authority and that it has not undergone any alteration in the chain of custody.[68] An online authentic legal resource is one for which a government entity has verified the content by to be complete and unaltered from the version approved or published by the content originator. Typically an authentic text will bear a certificate or mark certifying that the text is authenticated. The standard methods of authentication include encryption, especially digital signatures and public key infrastructure (PKI), or similar technologies.[69] Authentication of digital law varies by country; some provide authentication through a digital signature or PKI infrastructure, others through secure servers and certificates (Hietanen 2007).

Some countries do not recognize the official status of their electronic publications. Bermuda, for instance, states on its website that '[T]he laws on this website are provided for informational purposes only and do not yet have official sanction'.[70] The European Union Eur-Lex website states that 'Only European Union legislation published in paper editions of the Official Journal of the European Union is deemed authentic'.[71] Other countries declare their digital law documents

68 The International Organization for Standardization (ISO) has published standard ISO 15489-1 Information and Documentation – Records Management. Clause 7.2.2. defines authenticity: 'An authentic record is one that can be proven a) to be what it purports to be, b) to have been created or sent by the person purported to have created or sent it, and c) to have been created or sent at the time purported' (Hietanen 2007, 9).

69 A Public Key Infrastructure (PKI) is 'an asymmetric cryptography security environment that supports the transmission, delivery, and receipt of digital communications over a non-secure communications channel. PKI uses a pair of cryptographically related keys known as public and private keys which verify the identity of the sender (signing) and/or ensure privacy (encryption)'. Information provided by Mike Wash, Chief Technical Officer, US Government Printing Office.

70 Available at: www.bermudalaws.bm/disclaimer.html, accessed 21 June 2010.

71 Available at: http://eur-lex.europa.eu/en/editorial/legal_notice.htm, accessed 21 June 2010.

to be official and authentic. In France, the *Journal officiel* electronic version has been declared authentic (authenticated) since 2004.[72] In Brazil, until December 2002, the texts of legal rules available on the Internet had only an informative nature. With the advent of Decree No. 4,520, all official documents are published by the *Official Gazette of the Federal Government* and the *Official Gazette of the Justice*, are available at the official website of the National Press, and are certified by the Brazilian Public Key Infrastructure (ICP-Brazil), thus giving them the same authenticity and validity as the printed ones.[73] Canada states that its consolidated legislative texts have official status and are admissible in court.[74]

Authenticity matters because in an environment where online sources are replacing official print versions of legal information, citizens need to be able to trust digital versions of the law, in the same way that they have trusted print. Because the digital medium is vulnerable to errors in management and control, corruption and tampering, it is of utmost importance to make digital legal information not only official but authentic. What is at stake is the transmission of official documents, 'the word of the law', to future generations (Germain 1999).

In the United States, the American Association of Law Libraries (AALL) has been active and successful in encouraging federal and state government entities to take the necessary steps to ensure authentic digital law. As AALL President in 2006, I commissioned a 50-state survey, which revealed that a significant number of the state online legal resources were deemed official, but none were authenticated by standard methods (American Association of Law Libraries 2007).[75] A subsequent National Summit on Authentic Legal Information in the Digital Age in 2007[76] prompted the US National Conference of Commissioners on Uniform State Laws (NCCUSL) to investigate online authentication of legal materials. In January 2010, the NCCUSL issued a draft Authentication and Preservation of State Electronic Legal Materials Act to assist states in preparing legislation on authenticating and preserving electronic legal materials.

At the federal level, the US Government Printing Office (GPO) Federal Digital System (FDsys) provides information from all three branches of government (executive, legislative and judicial) and keeps it permanently available in electronic format, authenticated, with version control, and accessible via the web for searching, viewing, downloading and printing.[77]

European countries use a variety of measures to ensure authenticity, but some countries do not take special measures. Estonia uses secure servers.[78] The Canadian province of Ontario does not specify any special authentication of their documents:

> A copy of an official law that is printed by the Queen's Printer or accessed from the e-Laws website in a prescribed form or format is an official copy of the law, unless there is a disclaimer indicating that it is not official. Unless the contrary is proved, official copies of the law are accurate statements of the law. (Ontario 2006)

72 Available at: www.journal-officiel.gouv.fr, accessed 21 June 2010.

73 Available at: www.iti.gov.br, accessed 4 August 2010.

74 Available at: http://laws-lois.justice.gc.ca/eng/FAQ, accessed 21 June 2010.

75 The survey investigated six sources of law: state statutes and session laws, state high and intermediate appellate court opinions, and state administrative codes and registers. For each, the question asked was: is the digital version considered official? Is it considered authentic?

76 Available at: www.aallnet.org/summit, accessed 21 June 2010.

77 Available at: www.gpo.gov/fdsys, accessed 21 June 2010.

78 Available at: www.riigiteataja.ee/ert/intr/en.htm, accessed 21 June 2010.

GLIN's security policy assures users that the full text is a true representation of the source material, has not been modified, and is a certified document from GLIN. For new texts the Certification of Authenticity is issued by an authenticated user and carries a signature.[79]

The importance of authentication of digital law is perceived differently in different countries. Some are still exploring the challenges of putting laws online; their first priority is the quality of texts and their accessibility (Petitcollot 2008). Overall, it is a goal towards which all countries should strive.

Digital Preservation and Long-Term Access

A major problem with digital information is its vulnerability. Under good conditions, official court reports, session laws and codes printed on acid-free paper will last for centuries. The same information published in digital form may become obsolete within a few years if it is not migrated to a new platform. The technical problems related to the fragility of the digital medium are numerous, as are the legal and policy issues such as who is responsible for preserving the content (Rieger 2008). There are special concerns for the preservation and long-term access to born digital content with no paper equivalent. As of 2010, no permanent solutions exist. The best technological systems can only guarantee a fixed number of years, no more than 50 years,[80] and information needs to be regularly migrated to new software, or to a new platform, so it is not lost.

With legal materials an issue of particular importance is the need to make sure that in a paperless world there will be a permanent record of the law in its many forms, and that the record will be authentic. This is an area where there is a great role for libraries to preserve the digital heritage of mankind (Germain 2006). It is important for libraries to work as partners with governments, the legal information publishing industry, the information technology industry, computer scientists, and other interested stakeholders. Although the field of digital preservation is in a constant state of flux, much progress has occurred over the past decade. A number of interesting projects and organisations have emerged, together with new tools, services and best practices for the preservation of digital content (Rhodes 2010). The issues relate to what intellectual content to preserve, in what systems and formats, and what standards to use. The Open Archival Information System (OAIS) reference model addresses a full range of preservation functions, including ingest, archival storage, data management, access and dissemination. Specifically applicable to organisations with long-term preservation responsibilities, it has provided a framework and a common language for digital preservation discussions and planning activities, especially for their technical and architectural aspects (Consultative Committee 2002). An Online Computer Library Center (OCLC)/Research Libraries Group (RLG) and National Archives and Records Administration (NARA) task force has developed an Audit Checklist for Certifying Digital Repositories to assess reliability, commitment and readiness to assume long-term preservation responsibilities (Center for Research Libraries 2007). Another issue is whether to maintain both an open access online repository and a separate dark digital preservation system (Rhodes 2010).

79 Available at: www.glin.gov/helpTopic.action?topic=9010, accessed 21 June 2010.

80 Conversation with Ladislav Borhy, SUN Microsystems Czech Republic, at 2009 CASLIN meeting in Tepla, Czech Republic, June 2009.

The most prominent archival systems today are HathiTrust,[81] LOCKSS[82] and Portico.[83] There is no single solution. The following guidelines from Portico, an archiving service, help explain the principles of digital preservation. Although Portico is mainly meant to preserve the content of scholarly journals, the principles can be extended to the preservation of legal information.

1. The integrity of the scholarly record must be preserved. The archive must accept the content as it was published and should not correct or alter the record.

2. The archive must preserve the intellectual content of the electronic journal as completely as possible, although we recognize that some electronic content may have already been lost. [...]

4. Portico's primary preservation methodology is migration, which involves transitioning content from one file format to another as technology changes and as file formats become obsolete. An initial migration is performed when the source files are received and normalized to the archival format.

5. Portico's archival format is based on the open standard Journal Archiving and Interchange DTD and it uses the Metadata Encoding and Transmission Standards (METS) and the Open Archival Information System (OAIS) Reference Model.

Among recent noteworthy efforts, the Library of Congress's National Digital Information Infrastructure and Preservation Program (NDIIPP) has funded several projects to preserve state government digital information and implement a trustworthy information management system, to capture, preserve and provide access to 'at-risk' digital content from state legislatures.[84] The Chesapeake Project, originally involving three partner libraries in the District of Columbia, Maryland and Virginia, preserves online government, policy and legal information from the region (Dockendorf 2009). Harvard Law Library joined the Project in 2010. The Legal Information and Preservation Alliance (LIPA),[85] founded in 2003, has the mission to preserve vital legal information by defining objectives, endorsing and promoting the use of appropriate standards and models, creating networks, and fostering financial and political support for long-term stability. LIPA is working with the Chesapeake Project in the formation of the Legal Information Archive, a collaborative digital preservation programme for the law library community modelled after the Chesapeake Project.[86]

Several organisations can host digital content at a secure off-site location and manage system updates and migration. Non-profit organisations such as Portico and LOCKSS (Lots of Copies Keep Stuff Safe) function as preservation systems. The Internet Archive offers an 'Archive-It' service for the preservation of websites.[87] The US Department of Labor contracted with the Internet Archive to take a digital 'snapshot' and archive the content of all departmental websites (United States Department of Labor 2009).

81 Available at: www.hathitrust.org, accessed 21 June 2010.

82 Available at: http://lockss.stanford.edu/lockss/Home, accessed 21 June 2010.

83 Available at: www.portico.org, accessed 21 June 2010.

84 Available at: www.digitalpreservation.gov, accessed 21 June 2010.

85 Available at: www.aallnet.org/committee/lipa, accessed 21 June 2010.

86 Available at: http://listproc.ucdavis.edu/archives/law-lib/law-lib.log1003/att-0117/01-LegalInfo Archive.pdf, accessed 7 July 2010.

87 Available at: http://archive-it.org, accessed 21 June 2010.

The US Library of Congress National Digital Information Infrastructure and Preservation is collaborating with DuraSpace on a pilot programme, to test the use of cloud technologies to enable perpetual access to digital content.[88]

LOCKSS, based at Stanford University Libraries, provides libraries with digital preservation tools and support so that they can easily and inexpensively collect and preserve their own copies of authorized e-content. The technology provides an open source, peer-to-peer, decentralized digital preservation infrastructure, for all formats and genres of web-published content. The intellectual content, which includes the historical context (the look and feel of the texts), is preserved. LOCKSS is OAIS-compliant; the software migrates content forward in time; and the bits and bytes are continually audited and repaired. CLOCKSS (*Controlled* LOCKSS)[89] is a non-profit joint venture between the world's leading scholarly publishers and research libraries. Its mission is to build a sustainable, geographically distributed dark archive to ensure the long-term survival of Web-based scholarly publications for the benefit of the global research community.

Conclusion

The future looks promising and it will be interesting what further systems develop as the legal information systems mature. There are various issues still to be resolved that will affect the future of large-scale free Internet legal information systems.

One fundamental issue is whether there is a need for a global legal information service which everyone could search for all the world's laws. Another important question is whether the funding and sustainability of free open access systems will continue into the future. Many of the Legal Information Institutes (LIIs) developed since 1992, which have been so influential, are funded not by usage charges or advertisements but by contributors interested in facilitating access to legal information.

Another challenge is language. In our global environment, English is the major language but it will be important to respect all languages and some languages may become more important.

The future is bright and exciting and there is a great role for librarians as the research experts in providing access to legal information and as custodians of information for the long term, in any format, print or digital. The successful advocacy efforts of the American Association of Law Libraries in the United States show that librarians can influence information policy decisions for the benefit of all citizens. There is a great interest in bringing this advocacy to the international level to develop international standards, possibly within the International Federation of Library Associations, a major stakeholder for information policy.

References

American Association of Law Libraries (2007), *State-by-State Report on Authentication of Online Legal Resources* (Chicago: AALL). Available at: www.aallnet.org/aallwash/authenreport.asp, accessed 21 June 2010.

Berger, A. (ed.) (2009), *Access to Legislation in Europe, Guide to the Legal Gazettes and Other Official Information Sources in the European Union and European Free Trade Association* (Luxembourg: Publications Office of the European Union).

88 Available at: www.digitalpreservation.gov/partners/duracloud/duracloud.html, accessed 21 June 2010.

89 Available at: www.clockss.org/clockss/Home, accessed 21 June 2010.

Broom, H. (1900), *A Selection of Legal Maxims: Classified and Illustrated*, 7th edition by Manisty, H. and Chitty, H. (London: Sweet & Maxwell).

Cartier, E. (2008), 'Accessibilité et communicabilité du droit', *Jurisdoctoria: Revue Doctorale de Droit Publique Comparé et de Théorie Juridique* 1, 51–76. Available at: www.jurisdoctoria.net/pdf/numero/aut1_CARTIER.pdf, accessed 4 August 2010.

Center for Research Libraries and OCLC Online Computer Library Center (2007), Trustworthy Repositories Audit & Certification: Criteria and Checklist, Version 1, February 2007 (Chicago and Dublin, OH: CRL and OCLC). Available at: www.crl.edu/sites/default/files/attachments/pages/trac_0.pdf, accessed 4 August 2010.

Chiorazzi, M. and Russell, G. (eds) (2002), *Law Library Collection Development in the Digital Age* (Binghamton, NY: Haworth Information Press).

Consultative Committee for Space Data Systems (2002), Reference Model for an Open Archival Information System (OAIS), January 2002. Available at: http://public.ccsds.org/publications/archive/650x0b1.pdf, accessed 4 August 2010.

Cottin, S. (2002), *Historique de la Documentation Juridique Electronique*. Available at: www.servicedoc.info/article.php3?id_article=88&lang=fr, accessed 4 August 2010.

Cottin, S. (2005), 'Le Service Public de Diffusion du Droit Français sur l'Internet', *Revue Acta Universitatis Sibiu (Romania)* 2005 Supplement, 115–40.

Dockendorf, D. (2009), 'The Chesapeake Project: Preserving "Born Digital" Documents', *Virginia Lawyer* 58, 53.

Endress Gómez, S. (2008), *Update: Essential Issues of the Chilean Legal System*, March 2008. Update by Fernández-Acevedo, F. and Depolo, R. Available at: www.nyulawglobal.org/globalex/Chile1.htm, accessed 4 August 2010.

Exter, R. and Kammer, M. (2008), *Legal Research in Germany Between Print and Electronic Media: An Overview*, February. Available at: www.nyulawglobal.org/globalex/Germany.htm, accessed 4 August 2010.

France (1984), 'Décret n° 84-940 du 24 octobre 1984 relatif au service public des bases et banques de données juridiques', *Journal official* 25 October 1984, 3336. Available at: www.dsi.cnrs.fr/RMLR/textesintegraux/volume4/4143-d84-940.htm, accessed 21 June 2010.

France (2002), 'Décret n°2002-1064 du 7 août 2002 relatif au service public de la diffusion du droit par l'internet'. Available at: www.legifrance.gouv.fr/affichTexte.do;jsessionid=B913959487EF7849E4D8162DF50911F6.tpdjo05v_2?cidTexte=LEGITEXT000005633251&dateTexte=20091229, accessed 21 June 2010.

Gaudemet, Y. (1993), 'Promulgation et Publication des Lois', *Jurisclasseur Civil* 11.

Germain, C. (1991), *Transnational Law Research: A Guide for Attorneys*. Looseleaf (Ardsley-on-Hudson, NY: Transnational Juris Publications).

Germain, C. (1998a), *L'Accès Electronique aux Droits de Langue Française Vu d'un Pays Anglo-Saxon* [*Electronic Access to Law of French Language Countries: Seen from an Anglo-Saxon Country*] (Paris: Centre Français du Commerce Extérieur).

Germain, C. (1998b), 'Digital Legal Information: Here Today, Gone Tomorrow', *Syllabus (ABA)* 17.

Germain, C. (1999), 'Digital Legal Information: Ensuring Access to the "Official" Word of the Law', 26 *Cornell Law Forum* 11–14.

Germain, C. (2006), 'Introduction to "Permanent Public Access to Legal Information"', *AALL Spectrum* 10:3, Members Briefing insert, 1. Available at: www.aallnet.org/products/pub_sp0512/pub_sp0512_MB.pdf, accessed 4 August 2010.

Hague Conference on Private International Law, Permanent Bureau (2009), *Prel. Doc. No. 11A, March 2009 – Accessing the Content of Foreign Law and the Need for the Development of a Global Instrument in this Area – A Possible Way Ahead.*

Hietanen, A. (2007), *Electronic Publishing of Legislation – Towards Authenticity*. Final working group report (Helsinki/Tallin).

Laferrière, J. (1949), 'De l'Authenticité du Texte des Lois, Publiées au Journal Officiel', *Revue du Droit Public* 65, 113–52.

Network of the Presidents of the Supreme Judicial Courts of the European Union (2009), 'Information Meeting on the Common Portal of Case Law', *Newsletter* no. 11, November, 4. Available at: www.network-presidents.eu/IMG/pdf/NewsletterNov09B.pdf, accessed 21 June 2010.

Olouna, D., Ondo Meltchard, E. and Gladys-Obame, P. (2009), 'Field Focus: GLIN Station Gabon', *GLIN Global Journal* 7, 2–3. Available at: www.loc.gov/law/news/glin/pdf/GGJ_May09.pdf.

Ontario (2006), *Ontario Legislation Act 2006* (S.O. 2006, c. 21, Sched. F). Available at: www.e-laws.gov.on.ca, accessed 21 June 2010.

Passos, E. (2008), *Update: Doing Legal Research in Brazil*. Available at: www.nyulawglobal.org/Globalex/Brazil1.htm, accessed 4 August 2010.

Petersen, R. (2010), *Update: A Guide to Legal Research in Costa Rica*. Available at: www.nyulawglobal.org/globalex/Costa_Rica1.htm, accessed 4 August 2010.

Petitcollot, P. (2008), *L'édition electronique authentifiée de la legislation en Europe* [*Authentication of Digital Legal Information in Europe*]. 2nd Version, 9 August 2008. Available at: http://archive.ifla.org/IV/ifla74/papers/157-Petitcollot-fr.pdf, accessed 4 August 2010.

Reynolds, T. and Flores, A., *Foreign Laws of the World: Current Sources of Codes and Basic Legislation in Jurisdictions of the World*. Available at: www.foreignlawguide.com, accessed 4 August 2010. Subscription-based, first print, now online.

Rhodes, S. (2010), *Preserving Born-Digital Legal Materials ... Where to Start?*. Available at: http://blog.law.cornell.edu/voxpop/2010/01/10/preserving-born-digital-legal-materials, accessed 4 August 2010.

Rieger, O. (2008), *Preservation in the Age of Large-Scale Digitization: A White Paper.* CLIR Publication 141 (Washington, DC: Council on Library and Information Resources). Available at: www.clir.org/pubs/abstract/pub141abst.html, accessed 4 August 2010.

Saint-Prix, B. (1809), *Recherches sur les différentes formes de publication des lois depuis les Romains jusqu'à nos jours* (Paris).

Szladits, C. and Germain, C. (1985), *Guide to Foreign Legal Materials: France* (New York: Oceana).

United States Department of Labor (2009), 'Department of Labor Announces Digital "Snapshot" Project to Archive Content of all Departmental Web Sites', *OASAM News* Release 8 January 2009. Available at: www.dol.gov/opa/media/press/oasam/archive/oasam20091865.htm, accessed 4 August 2010.

Wagner, A. and Cacciaguidi-Fahy, S. (eds) (2008), *Obscurity and Clarity in the Law: Prospects and Challenges* (Aldershot: Ashgate).

Chapter 10
Free Access to Legal Information, LIIs, and the Free Access to Law Movement[1]

Graham Greenleaf

Before Free Access or LIIs

Prior to the Internet's World Wide Web there were many online legal information systems and numerous legal information products distributed on CD-ROM, but there was no significant provision of free access to legal information anywhere in the world. Both government and private sector online legal publishers charged for access. This pre-Internet history from the late 1950s is summarised by Bing (2010) who points out that 'though lawyers are not known for being technological *avant gardists*, text retrieval was actually developed by lawyers and for lawyers, due to the need to consult the authentic text for legal interpretation'. The pre-web years, at least up to the rise of CD-ROMs and the PC in the late 1980s, are seen by Bing as the pursuit of a vision of 'one, integrated, national [legal] information service' (at least in Europe). It is a vision which he now sees as having since receded in some respects, but perhaps being revived in other respects by the growth of free access to legal information (Bing 2010, 44).

From the mid-1990s the web has provided the necessary technical platform to enable free public access to computerised legal information – a low-cost distribution mechanism. For publishers it was close to a 'no cost' distribution mechanism if they were not required to pay for outgoing bandwidth. The ease of use of graphical browsers from around 1994 and the web's use of hypertext as its principal access mechanism (at that time) meant that the web provided a simple and relatively consistent means by which legal information could be both provided and accessed. This was an attractive alternative to the proprietary, expensive and training-intensive search engines on which commercial online services largely relied. The development of free access Internet law services was based on these factors (Greenleaf 2004).

Legal Information Institutes

In many countries the first attempts to exploit the advantages of the web for providing legal information came from the academic sector rather than government, and did so with an explicit

1 An earlier version of this chapter (to April 2009) was published as 'The Global Development of Free Access to Legal Information' in *Paliwala* (2010). Some parts were previously published on the GlobaLex website in Greenleaf (2008). Helpful comments have been received from Abdul Paliwala, Andrew Mowbray, Philip Chung, Pierre-Paul Lemyre, Joe Ury, Kerry Anderson, Kevin Pun, Martin Backes and Jill Matthews (who also assisted with editing), but responsibility for content remains with the author. The chapter states situations existing as at March 2010.

ideology of free access provision.[2] Within a few years of the formation of the first legal information institute in 1992 the first group of such organisations became known collectively as 'legal information institutes' or 'LIIs'. Those expressions became synonymous with free access to legal information, though in fact they have a narrower meaning.

Two distinguishing characteristic of the 'LIIs' (in my usage) are that (1) they publish legal information from more than one source (not just 'their own' information), for free access via the Internet, and (2) they collaborate with each other through membership of the 'Free Access to Law Movement'. Most but not all share three other characteristics. They collaborate through data sharing networks or portals, and also technical networks for back-up security purposes. Most are independent of government, though this is diminishing as a distinguishing feature. The majority use one of two open source search engines (Poulin et al. 2007): the Sino search engine[3] developed by AustLII (previously shared with other LIIs, and open source since 2006), and the Lucene search engine[4] utilised by LexUM in the development of various LIIs.

'Legal information institute' (or 'LII'), as used here, therefore refers to a sub-set of the providers of free access to law, namely those from across the world who have decided to collaborate both politically and technically. Taken together, the LIIs are the most coordinated, and among the largest, providers of free access to legal information, but they are far from alone in providing free access to legal information. This chapter is not about 'free access to law' in its entirety, but focuses on a particular grouping of providers of free access to legal information, while discussing the more general context of 'free access to law' in which they operate.

As at March 2010 there are 33 members of the Free Access to Law Movement, listed in Appendix 1. Many are discussed at least briefly in this chapter, but more detailed descriptions are available elsewhere.[5]

The Earliest LIIs

Three LIIs played key roles in early developments: the Legal Information Institute (Cornell), AustLII, and LexUM. They each developed from research projects on various aspects of legal automation going back to the 1980s, and were ready to capitalise on the World Wide Web's sudden emergence into public prominence around 1994.

The Legal Information Institute[6] was started at Cornell University Law School in 1992, and had by 1994 developed a number of databases primarily of US federal law (particularly the US Code and US Supreme Court decisions). 'The LII', as it became known, was the first significant source of free access to law on the Internet, and demonstrated that a free access service could provide both high quality document presentation, and very high rates of access. It also assisted the development of one of the first other LIIs, the Zambian Legal Information Institute (ZamLII)[7] in 1996. US federal law is still the main focus of the LII (Cornell), with its State coverage being limited to New York State. It has instead concentrated on various innovative projects: 'Libraries' of commentary

2 For a summation of these ideals, see Poulin (2004); an early statement is in Greenleaf, Mowbray, King and van Dijk (1995).

3 AustLII, *Sino Free Text Search Engine* AustLII Web Page. Available at: www.austlii.edu.au/techlib/software/sino, accessed 1 March 2010.

4 'Apache Lucene – Overview'. Available at: http://lucene.apache.org/java/docs, accessed 1 March 2010.

5 'Part II: A-Z of legal information institutes', in Greenleaf (2008).

6 Available at: http://topics.law.cornell.edu/wex, accessed 1 March 2010.

7 Available at: www.zamlii.ac.zm, not available 1 March 2010 – appears to be defunct.

on legal ethics and social security; Wex,[8] a collaboratively built, free access legal dictionary and encyclopaedia[9] (perhaps the first attempts by a LII to use wiki technology to develop and present content); and a research project concerning electronic rulemaking.[10]

The Australasian Legal Information Institute (AustLII) was started by two Law Schools in Sydney, Australia, in 1995,[11] based on work as the 'DataLex Project' going back a further decade.[12] It borrowed the 'LII' suffix from Cornell, as others have done since. By 1999 it had developed databases from all nine Australian jurisdictions covering key providers of case law, legislation, treaties and some other content. AustLII's initial significance was that it was the first attempt worldwide to build a comprehensive national free access legal information system in some respects rivalling that of commercial publishers. Now AustLII provides nearly 400 databases of Australian law[13] including: consolidated legislation from all nine jurisdictions; annual legislation and bills from some; point-in-time legislation from three States;[14] decisions from over 120 Courts and Tribunals (a third of which are not otherwise available online); all Australian Treaties since 1900;[15] law reform reports from all jurisdictions;[16] and over 60 databases of law journals and other legal scholarship in full text.[17] It is starting to develop subject-oriented 'libraries'[18] which automate the aggregation of all legal materials on AustLII into a searchable collection (Greenleaf 2009).

LexUM[19] at the University of Montreal commenced in 1993, with a Law Gopher server (then via the Public Law Research Center), and created the first Canadian legal site and the first legal site available in French, while carrying out many research and consultancy projects.[20] During the 1990s it built various Canadian law sites including the Judgments of the Supreme Court of Canada.[21] In 2000 LexUM built the Canadian Legal Information Institute[22] (CanLII), which quickly became a very large national LII comprehensively covering Canada's federal system, matching AustLII in size and usage (Poulin et al. 2000). LexUM initially used the Sino search engine, then adopted the open-source Lucene search engine and other development tools. CanLII's databases now include decisions of Canadian superior courts and a broad range of

8 Available at: http://topics.law.cornell.edu/wex, accessed 1 March 2010.

9 Available at: www.law.cornell.edu/wex, accessed 1 March 2010; Wex is developed in part from the LII (Cornell)'s previous 'Law About …' series.

10 Available at: http://ceri.law.cornell.edu, accessed 1 March 2010.

11 Available at: www.austlii.edu.au, accessed 1 March 2010; University of Technology, Sydney (UTS) and University of New South Wales (UNSW).

12 Summarised in Greenleaf, Mowbray and van Dijk (1995); and see AustLII Publications (1995–), www.austlii.edu.au/austlii/publications.html, accessed 29 July 2010, with links to over 50 publications since 1992 including DataLex Project publications.

13 Available at: www.austlii.edu.au/databases.html, accessed 1 March 2010.

14 Available at: http://portsea.austlii.edu.au/pit, accessed 1 March 2010; New South Wales, Queensland and South Australia.

15 Available at: www.austlii.edu.au/au/other/dfat, accessed 1 March 2010.

16 Available at: www.austlii.edu.au/au/special/lawreform, accessed 1 March 2010.

17 Available at: www.austlii.edu.au/au/journals, accessed 1 March 2010.

18 For example, the Taxation Law Library. Available at: www.austlii.edu.au/au/special/tax.

19 Available at: www.lexum.umontreal.ca/index_fr.php?lang=en, accessed 1 March 2010.

20 See www.lexum.umontreal.ca/publication.epl?lang=en, accessed 29 July 2010, for extensive LexUM publications.

21 Available at: http://scc.lexum.umontreal.ca/en/index.html, accessed 29 July 2010; for others see www.lexum.umontreal.ca/partners.epl?lang=en, accessed 29 July 2010.

22 Available at: www.canlii.org, accessed 1 March 2010.

administrative tribunals (over 150 databases), with historical scope[23] typically back to around 2000 but sometimes considerably earlier (to 1985 for Supreme Court decisions). It also publishes historical and up-to-date versions of legislation from all 14 Canadian jurisdictions, doing so using CanLII's point-in-time legislation system for all jurisdictions.[24] It has a bilingual (English-French) user interface. CanLII innovations include the Reflex[25] citator which provides for each decision on CanLII a 'RefLex record' listing related decisions, 'noteups' (decisions citing the decision), and legislation and decisions cited.

The LII Movement Expands

From 2000 AustLII started to use its search engine (Sino[26]) and other software to assist organisations in other countries, initially limited to those with academic roots, to establish LIIs with similar functionality. Between 2000 and 2004 AustLII helped to establish servers and databases for six LIIs (BAILII,[27] PacLII,[28] HKLII,[29] SAFLII,[30] CyLaw[31] and NZLII[32]). It operated the servers from Sydney for a period on behalf of its local partners, with progressive local takeover of operations. All use AustLII's Sino search engine. Responsibility for obtaining and developing legal data was usually undertaken by the local partner from the outset.

The British and Irish Legal Information Institute[33] (BAILII), formed in 2000, is based at the Institute of Advanced Legal Studies, London and operated by the BAILII Trust. BAILII includes 80 databases[34] covering six jurisdictions (United Kingdom, England and Wales, Scotland, Northern Ireland, Ireland and some European court decisions), including case law, legislation and law reform reports from all the jurisdictions it covers. Back capture of cases and law reform documents through its Open Law Project[35] gives it considerable historical depth.

The Pacific Islands Legal Information Institute[36] (PacLII) is operated by the University of the South Pacific (USP) School of Law, located in Vanuatu. PacLII was re-developed with AustLII in 2001, from substantial content provided by the School of Law's site from 1997. PacLII provides 180 databases of the laws of 20 island countries and territories of the Pacific. It is the principal source of case law and legislation for many of these countries, is the most substantial free access to law facility in developing countries, and was the earliest regional system (Hamilton 2007; Blake 2002).

23 Available at: www.canlii.org/en/databases.html, accessed 1 March 2010.

24 Available at: www.canlii.org/en/blog/index.php?/archives/44-Legislation-From-the-Northern-Territories.html, accessed 1 March 2010.

25 Available at: www.canlii.org/en/info/reflex.html, accessed 1 March 2010.

26 Available at: www.austlii.edu.au/techlib/software/sino, accessed 1 March 2010.

27 Available at: www.bailii.org, accessed 1 March 2010.

28 Available at: www.paclii.org, accessed 1 March 2010.

29 Available at: www.hklii.org, accessed 1 March 2010.

30 Available at: www.saflii.org, accessed 1 March 2010.

31 Available at: www.cylaw.org, accessed 1 March 2010.

32 Available at: www.nzlii.org, accessed 1 March 2010.

33 Available at: www.bailii.org, accessed 1 March 2010.

34 Available at: www.bailii.org/databases.html, accessed 1 March 2010.

35 Available at: www.bailii.org/openlaw/introduction.html, accessed 1 March 2010.

36 Available at: www.paclii.org, accessed 1 March 2010.

The Hong Kong Legal Information Institute[37] (HKLII) has been operated since 2002 by the University of Hong Kong with 13 databases of the law of the Hong Kong Special Administrative Region (SAR) (Greenleaf et al. 2002). It is a bilingual system and has developed its own search engine for the Chinese content (Pun et al. 2004, 2004a). An innovation is its joint operation of the Community Legal Information Centre[38] (CLIC), a bilingual community legal information website with extensive links to HKLII. HKLII was the second LII in Asia, founded slightly after LawPhil in the Philippines.

The Southern African Legal Information Institute[39] (SAFLII) publishes over 60 databases of superior court judgments from 16 English-speaking and Portuguese-speaking counties in Southern and Eastern Africa, and four regional tribunals, and is moving beyond case law to legislation and law reform. It is endorsed by the Southern African Judges Commission. It was established in 2003 by the University of the Witwatersrand (Wits) Faculty of Law (which had pioneered the Internet provision of South African law during the 1990s) (Montgomery 2004) and AustLII, but only covered South African law. In 2006 its operations were transferred to the South African Constitutional Court Trust, which gave it a regional orientation and significant resources, while AustLII continued to provide technical support. Since then it has rapidly become a landmark in the transparency of Africa's legal systems, playing a major role in the whole continent (Anderson 2007). It is very deliberately fostering the development of new LIIs in countries for which it initially operated the databases, namely Uganda (ULII[40]) and Malawi (MalawiLII[41]), a process which it refers to as 'devolution'. As of early 2010 its long-term operational structure was under review.

The New Zealand Legal Information Institute[42] (NZLII), based at University of Otago's Faculty of Law since 2004, now has 40 databases covering almost all significant New Zealand Courts and Tribunals, legislation in all forms, bilateral treaties, law reform reports, and four law journals, and is expanding rapidly. It required many years of effort to obtain content for free access (Buckingham 2005). NZLII and AustLII have agreed to long-term collaborative development of NZLII's databases (also searchable through AustLII) and joint systems resources.

CyLaw[43] in Cyprus was established in 2002 by a local lawyer using AustLII's Sino search engine and contains all judgments issued by the Supreme Court of Cyprus since 1997 (in Greek) and other databases. Independently operated from inception, it is now merging with a local university to provide a more comprehensive system, and continues close technical cooperation with AustLII.

All of the systems AustLII has assisted are now operated with independent local control and resources. This is the major reason for their success. AustLII's aim of assisting partners to achieve full or partial local takeover as quickly as possible has been effective, but has also shown that ongoing collaboration is often necessary. AustLII aims to achieve much more extensive 'devolution' of the databases on the AsianLII system (discussed below) to local control than has been achieved so far.

Having established CanLII, LexUM used the tools it had developed to create, with local partners, Droit Francophone (2003), JuriBurkina (2003) and JuriNiger (2007). Droit Francophone is discussed later. JuriBurkina[44] is the judicial information centre of Burkina Faso, launched in

37 Available at: www.hklii.org, accessed 1 March 2010.

38 Available at: www.hkclic.org/en, accessed 1 March 2010.

39 Available at: www.saflii.org, accessed 1 March 2010.

40 Available at: www.ulii.org, accessed 1 March 2010.

41 Available at: www.malawilii.org, accessed 1 March 2010.

42 Available at: www.nzlii.org, accessed 1 March 2010.

43 Available at: www.cylaw.org, accessed 1 March 2010.

44 Available at: www.juriburkina.org/juriburkina, accessed 1 March 2010.

2004 and operated by the Burkina Faso Bar Association with LexUM's assistance, providing over 1,000 decisions to 2007 from eight of the country's courts and tribunals (Apikul 2006). JuriNiger[45] provides nearly 2,000 decisions of five courts, but has not been updated since 2007. It was developed by LexUM in conjunction with the Ordre des Avocats du Niger, and operated from the LexUM servers.

Cooperation and the Free Access to Law Movement

The Free Access to Law Movement (FALM), established in 2002, is a loose affiliation of 33 legal information institutes (as of March 2010). The group of LIIs associated with the LII (Cornell), LexUM and AustLII made the initial attempts to establish collaboration and organisation to further free access to law globally,[46] but FALM has become a broader grouping since then.

The 'Law via Internet' Conferences[47] have been the principal means by which this cooperation was established. The first was hosted by AustLII in 1997, as were the 2nd (1999), 3rd (2001) and 5th (2003). LexUM/CanLII hosted the 4th (2002), French organisations (as FrLII[48]) hosted the 6th (2004), PacLII the 7th in Vanuatu (2006), LexUM/CanLII the 8th (2007), the Istituto di Teoria e Tecniche dell'Informazione Giuridica (ITTIG) in Florence the 9th (2008), and SAFLII the 10th Conference in Durban, 2009. In 2009 AustLII hosted the first regional LII Conference, the AsianLII Conference in Sydney. Many of the conference papers are available online[49] and comprise a considerable resource on the topic of legal information systems.

The Free Access to Law Movement (FALM) meets annually during the Conference (if one is held) and operates by an email list between Conferences. The first sustained attempt to build some form of international network took place at Cornell in July 2000,[50] involving participants from the United States, Canada, Australia, the UK and South Africa. The expression 'WorldLII' was first used there to describe a collaborative LII portal. A prototype of WorldLII was demonstrated at the Law via Internet Conference in Sydney in 2001. The FALM was formed at the 2002 Conference in Montreal, and adopted the *Declaration on Free Access to Law*[51] (see Appendix 2 for text). The Declaration has had some amendments since then. Membership is by invitation, with members nominating new candidates, and consensus required. The membership criteria are not fixed but involve adherence to, and support of, the Declaration and activities similar to (but not necessarily identical with) those of a LII. At the 2007 meeting initial steps were taken to turn the 'Movement' into a more formally constituted 'Association' (FALA), but these have not yet proceeded further.

The membership of FALM has expanded beyond the initial members discussed above, and the four portals discussed below, to include other national LIIs from France, Ireland, Kenya, Germany and the Philippines (in 2006 and 2007), and then Juridicas[52] (UNAM, Autonomous University of Mexico), the Thai Law Reform Commission, Droit.org (France), Jersey Legal Information Board,

45 Available at: http://juriniger.lexum.umontreal.ca/juriniger, accessed 1 March 2010.

46 For details of the initial steps, see Greenleaf, Chung and Mowbray (2007).

47 Available at: www.austlii.edu.au/austlii/conference, accessed 1 March 2010.

48 Available at: www.frlii.org, accessed 1 March 2010.

49 They are variously in an AustLII database (1997, 1999, 2001, 2003, 2005), www.austlii.edu.au/au/other/CompLRes, on the FrLII website (2004) www.frlii.org, or on LexUM (2002, 2008).

50 LII Workshop on Emerging Global Public Legal Information Standards hosted by the LII (Cornell).

51 Available at: www.worldlii.org/worldlii/declaration, accessed 29 July 2010, also called the 'Montreal Declaration'.

52 Available at: www.juridicas.unam.mx/infjur/leg, accessed 1 March 2010.

and Ugandan Legal Information Institute (ULII) (in 2008), and AltLaw (USA), the Kathmandu School of Law (Nepal), and MalawiLII (in 2009). In addition there is now a class of members which we could loosely describe as 'those who facilitate the technical development of free access to law, rather than primarily publishing their own databases for free access', including ITTIG (Italy), the Institute of Law and Technology (Autonomous University of Barcelona, Spain), IIjusticia (Argentina) and the Cardiff Index to Legal Abbreviations. The 33 current members are listed in Appendix 1.

The Declaration on Free Access to Law and FALM's Aims

The principal aim of the FALM, re-affirmed at its 2007 meeting, is the provision of assistance by its members to organisations wishing to provide free access to law in countries in which that has not yet occurred. It has been reasonably successful in this, as outlined above. It also provides mutual support to organisations already providing free access to law. The Declaration recognises 'the primary role of local initiatives in free access publishing of their own national legal information'. A second aim stated in the Declaration (as discussed below) is that 'All legal information institutes are encouraged to participate in regional or global free access to law networks'. As the Declaration puts it, the aim is 'To cooperate in order to achieve these goals and, in particular, to assist organisations in developing countries to achieve these goals, recognising the reciprocal advantages that all obtain from access to each other's law'. The main activities of the FALM, in light of these aims, have been sharing of software, technical expertise and experience on policy questions such as privacy issues.

Development of LII Networks and Portals from 2002

The Declaration encourages LIIs to 'participate in regional or global free access to law networks'. Before 2002 there were some national and regional LIIs, but no multi-LII networks. BAILII and PacLII were multi-country regional systems from inception (and SAFLII became one), but did not involve material from other LIIs.

The World Legal Information Institute[53] (WorldLII), launched in 2002, was the first multi-LII site, initially providing search accesses to the databases from AustLII, BAILII, PacLII, HKLII and CanLII, and from South Africa (before SAFLII was formed). The Free Access to Law Movement adopted it as their joint portal in 2002 (Poulin 2004). It has four main aspects: as a portal making multiple LIIs simultaneously searchable; its own databases; its catalogue and web search; and the LawCite citator involving collaboration from all the LIIs involved in WorldLII (except CanLII). WorldLII is organised primarily by country, providing from its page for each country in the world as many complementary legal research facilities (databases, catalogue and web-search facilities) as possible.

WorldLII's networking of multiple LIIs makes it the largest free access legal research facility on the Internet because it makes simultaneously searchable the databases provided by the collaborating LIIs. By the time of the tenth Free Access to the Law Conference in November 2009 this comprised 1,190 databases from 165 countries in all continents. Databases from the 11 LIIs that cooperate most closely with AustLII (plus the databases it maintains) are the principal source of the databases searchable via WorldLII, mainly because their use of a common search engine

53 Available at: www.worldlii.org, accessed 1 March 2010.

(AustLII's Sino) makes technical cooperation easier to achieve. The databases from 50 countries of the Global Legal Information Network (GLIN) (discussed below) are another significant searchable component. WorldLII also includes over 700,000 US Circuit Court of Appeals cases republished from public US sources, and access to the US Code provided by the LII (Cornell). Databases from Droit Francophone are not at present available (see below), and updates of CanLII's databases are not available. WorldLII's own databases are primarily 22 databases of decisions of international Courts and Tribunals in the International Courts and Tribunal Library[54] (the largest such searchable collection available via the Internet), about 35 constitutions, and some databases in the Privacy Law Library.[55] A new element of WorldLII (from 2009) is the creation of 'virtual databases' for each country in the world, drawing on the law journal articles, treaties, international court decisions and other globally-relevant content available through WorldLII to create country-specific databases. This means there is now some searchable database content for every country.[56]

The WorldLII Catalog[57] is the largest law-specific catalogue on the Internet, with links to over 15,000 law-related websites concerning every country, most international institutions, and a subject index. It is one of the few global law catalogues still being maintained (though only minimally at present) in the face of the popularity of search engines. It is biased towards English-language content. The web search facility uses AustLII's web spider to make searchable the full texts of as many sites as possible in the Catalog (Greenleaf, Chung and Mowbray 2007), but its scope and interface is at present far inferior to commercial search engines, and it may be discontinued. WorldLII (and CommonLII and AsianLII discussed below) also provide a 'Law on Google' facility for each country, which translates a search in WorldLII's Sino syntax into an effective search over Google, limited to material from the country concerned and limited to legal content. This facility is far more effective, and may be generalised to allow use of search engines other than Google in future.

WorldLII is not yet a global legal information service. It provides a primarily English language interface, and its databases are primarily in English, with some searchable content in other languages, primarily Chinese, Bahasa Indonesian and Portuguese. AustLII's Sino search engine is being developed gradually to make it capable of searching double-byte Asian language encodings.

The collaborating LIIs that provide the databases searchable via WorldLII draw those databases mainly from the Pacific, Asia, Australasia, Africa, the United States and South America. Apart from the UK and Ireland, its European coverage is as yet slight.

LawCite, a free access global citator for cases and other legal materials,[58] is the most recent development related to WorldLII (Mowbray et al. 2009). It is based largely on collaboration between the same group of LIIs. It uses citator software developed by AustLII which employs heuristics to recognise and extract references to cases from over 15,000 law report and journal series from the content provided by those LIIs and other sources. It was released for public access in December 2008, and now provides citation records for just over three million cases and journal articles. The records are usually updated daily.

The *Global Legal Information Network* (GLIN),[59] operated by the US Library of Congress since at least 2001 (Prescott 2005), is a database primarily of official texts of legislation, but also

54 Available at: www.worldlii.org/int/cases, accessed 1 March 2010. See discussion Greenleaf, Chung and Mowbray (2005).

55 Available at: www.worldlii.org/int/special/privacy, accessed 1 March 2010.

56 These virtual databases are ignored in any database counts in this chapter.

57 Available at: www.worldlii.org/catalog/270.html, accessed 1 March 2010.

58 Available at: www.worldlii.org/LawCite, accessed 1 March 2010.

59 Available at: www.glin.gov/search.action, accessed 1 March 2010.

includes treaties and judicial decisions and other complementary legal sources for some countries. They are contributed by governmental agencies and international organisations, which provide to GLIN the full texts of their published documents in their original languages. GLIN's member countries are predominantly from Latin America but include quite a few other countries (for example Romania, South Korea and Spain). Each document is accompanied by a summary in English and in additional languages in many cases, plus subject terms selected from the multilingual index to GLIN, prepared by Library of Congress Staff. Over 150,000 items have been contributed. All summaries are available to the public, and public access to full texts is also available for 25 of the 40 jurisdictions covered by GLIN. Searching is the only access mechanism, but allows results to be sorted by relevance, by date or by jurisdiction. The translations of summaries of legislation in English and other languages are probably the main value of GLIN, at least to an English-speaking audience. In 2007 the GLIN databases of abstracts were added to WorldLII's search scope (and a facility to browse by country or year was added), and GLIN became a FALM member. This gives WorldLII a South and Central American dimension previously lacking, as well as additional legislative databases from other countries in Asia, the Middle East, Europe and West Africa. It is very useful (at least to English-speakers) when full text translations of legislation are not available.

A linguistic focus to the creation of a multi-country LII was taken in 2003 by LexUM's development of Droit Francophone,[60] the French language legal portal of the Organisation internationale de la Francophonie[61] (OIF). It is described as 'multi-LII' because it included JuriBurkina content. Its databases of over 4,000 texts included legislation from 21 countries from across the whole Francophonie, and case law from 10. A web-based interface allows for remote decentralised management of content by representatives from each of the national structures in charge of access to law, who meet annually sponsored by OIF (Lemyre 2004; Lemyre et al. 2004). Droit Francophone also provided a catalogue of more than 4,000 legal websites concerning law of the Francophonie, evaluated and commented, and a web search engine indexing those websites. It is now being reorganised by OIF,[62] and at the time of this writing has been unavailable since 15 April 2009. If it is revived, it will be valuable.

In 2005 AustLII developed the Commonwealth Legal Information Institute (CommonLII)[63] covering Commonwealth and Common Law countries. It was in some respects an English-language response to LexUM ('droit Anglophone' is its nickname). CommonLII relies principally upon the content of existing LIIs (AustLII, BAILII, CyLaw, PacLII, HKLII, NZLII, SAFLII and ZamLII), but also added over 50 databases from 20 additional countries which do not yet have their own LIIs (mainly in South Asia and the Caribbean). The South Asian databases provide over 250,000 cases. There are major legislation collections from Asia and the Caribbean. CanLII declined to allow its content to be included for searching purposes. Part of CommonLII's purpose is to encourage new LII development in these countries and regions, and development has started with four leading Indian law schools on a LII for India (with AusAID and other Australian funding).

A major addition to CommonLII in 2008 was 125,000 cases from the English Reports 1220–1873,[64] the basis of the common law worldwide. CommonLII is supported by a range

60 Available at: http://droit.francophonie.org, accessed 1 March 2010.

61 Available at: www.francophonie.org, accessed 1 March 2010.

62 A notice on the site states 'Dear Internet, The International Organization of la Francophonie is doing maintenance work on its portal Droit Francophone. For this reason, the site will be unavailable during this period of work, but our teams are working for a rapid return to normal operation. We thank in advance for your understanding and your loyalty' (translation from French by Google).

63 Available at: www.commonlii.org, accessed 1 March 2010.

64 Available at: www.commonlii.org/int/cases/EngR, accessed 29 July 2010.

of Commonwealth institutions,[65] including the Commonwealth Law Ministers Meeting, the Commonwealth Secretariat Legal and Constitutional Division, the Institute of Advanced Legal Studies (Greenleaf et al. 2004; Greenleaf et al. 2010). Financial support for CommonLII has been primarily from Australian sources to date, but the Commonwealth Secretariat is now funding a Commonwealth-wide Criminal Law Library on CommonLII, using virtual database techniques, and a Caribbean law project.

The Asian Legal Information Institute (AsianLII)[66] developed by AustLII in 2006, drew on CommonLII's content (for eight Asian Commonwealth countries), PacLII (for Papua New Guinea), LawPhil (for the Philippines) and HKLII (for Hong Kong), and is therefore a multi-LII network. However, most of its content comprises databases from 17 additional Asian countries which do not yet have local LIIs. AsianLII provides over 200 databases[67] from 27 of these 28 countries in ASEAN, Myanmar excepted (Afghanistan to Japan; Mongolia to Timor-Leste). It also includes databases from regional organisations such as APEC, the Asian Development Bank (ADB) and the International Development Law Organisation (IDLO). A principal aim of AsianLII (and the reason it has AusAID funding in relation to 10 developing countries) is to assist development of new local LIIs, some of which are likely to emerge from AsianLII's 'Country Supporting Institutions'[68] in these countries. AsianLII is supported by many regional law organisations[69] (including LAWASIA, the Inter-Pacific Bar Association, APEC, ADB and IDLO) (Greenleaf 2007; Greenleaf, Chung and Mowbray 2007a), with funding from Australian sources including AusAID.

Extent of Coverage of LII Portals

The development of CommonLII and AsianLII also significantly expanded the content searchable via WorldLII. Cooperation between the 15 LIIs and FALM members that collaborate in the provision of WorldLII (see Table 10.1) has resulted in their joint provision of nearly 1,200 databases from 165 countries (as at November 2009), searchable from one location. WorldLII is best seen as the largest portal to this collaborative network, but is only one of a number of such portals – regional, linguistic/political, translation-based, and potentially from other perspectives.

The number of databases provided by all of the LIIs of the Free Access to Law Movement has been growing rapidly ever since 2002. WorldLII and the other 15 LIIs that collaborate in its provision held 1,190 databases at the time of the 2009 LII Conference in Durban (see Table 10.1). While the databases from many of the countries covered by WorldLII are quite small, from others they are very substantial. From Canada, Australia, Hong Kong, India, Papua New Guinea, the Philippines, Indonesia, South Africa, Ireland, the UK, New Zealand and many Pacific Island countries, what the LIIs offer is very substantial, including content not available from commercial legal publishers. Furthermore, WorldLII, as the global portal of the LIIs, compares well with its two commercial counterparts (the international portals of LexisNexis and Westlaw) in terms of scope of countries covered, though not in depth of coverage for some countries.

---

65 Available at: www.commonlii.org/commonlii/sponsors, accessed 1 March 2010.

66 Available at: www.asianlii.org, accessed 1 March 2010.

67 Available at: www.asianlii.org/databases.html, accessed 1 March 2010.

68 Available at: www.asianlii.org/asianlii/sponsors/#country_supporting_institutions, accessed 1 March 2010.

69 Available at: www.asianlii.org/asianlii/sponsors/#rsi, accessed 1 March 2010.

Table 10.1 Searchable Databases in Multi-LII Systems (as of 19 November 2009)

Systems	AsianLII	CommonLII	WorldLII	Countries
AltLaw	–	–	14	–
AsianLII	98*	–	98*	24
AustLII	–	335	335	1
BAILII	–	78	78	4
CanLII	–	–	165***	1
CommonLII	49*	69*	69*	22
CyLaw	–	6	6	1
GLIN	4	–	42	34**
HKLII	13	13	13	1
LawPhil	16	–	16	1
LII (Cornell)	–	–	3	1
NZLII	–	35	35	1
PacLII	25	156	180	19
SAFLII	–	56	63	18
ULII	–	7	7	1
WorldLII	–	–	66*	35
TOTAL	*205*	*755*	*1,190*	*164*

Note: * non-Australian databases; ** updates subsequently expanded this to 50; *** CanLII content is not being updated.

In Table 10.1, the 'Countries' column indicates the number of additional countries that a particular LII adds to the total number of countries whose databases are searchable via WorldLII. Of the total of 165 countries, the only databases from about 40 are the Constitution of the country, but even if those are deducted, the LIIs collaborating in WorldLII provide databases from 125 countries. AustLII maintains 233 of the non-Australian databases (marked * in the table), on AsianLII, CommonLII and WorldLII, in addition to the 335 on AustLII (at that time).

Since September 2009, the total number of databases on the LIIs collaborating in relation to WorldLII has increased by at least 100.

Models for Networking Free Access to Law

If a user wants to search legal information from more than one jurisdiction, the following models can be used:

- Provide links between each of the sources, leaving the user to search each site (a catalogue).
- Send a search to each site, collect multiple sets of search results and merge them ('federated search')
- Send a web spider/robot to each site, create a central index of all content (periodically updated) which users can search to obtain a consolidated set of results, but take users back to the original sites to view results (all Internet-wide search engines from Alta Vista onwards, including Google)
- Obtain replication of the content of all sites on a periodic basis, as an Internet-wide search engine

- Republish all the content of the sources on a centralised site, so that users need only search and go to pages on that site

The LII networks provided through WorldLII, CommonLII and AsianLII utilise a replication/synchronisation model (Mowbray et al. 2007; or more briefly Greenleaf, Mowbray and Chung 2007). A copy of all LII data is held in Sydney by AustLII, replicated daily using rsync.[70] Searches over the locally stored concordances at AustLII produce rapid search results, and users are then returned to the databases on the originating LII when they choose to access a particular search result. The PacLII mirror at AustLII is seen by users outside the Pacific, due to slow access speeds to the Vanuatu server. Some LII content is also mirrored at other LIIs in the network. Because WorldLII, CommonLII and AsianLII all republish and maintain some databases of their own, they are a mixture of the fourth and fifth models above.

An issue currently under discussion in FALM and between LIIs concerns the advantages and disadvantages of a federated search model (with searches sent to cooperating systems) in contrast to a replication/synchronisation model. On the one hand it is argued that a federated search cannot be operated with fast enough access speeds or useful relevance ranking and many LIIs are comfortable with making their data available for replication. On the other hand it is argued that the replication/synchronisation model implies a hierarchical, centralised approach, is ultimately less scalable, and places copies of the data outside the direct control of the LIIs to which the data were entrusted. LexUM/CanLII's preference for a federated search approach is one reason that CanLII has not participated in CommonLII, and its databases are not able to be updated in WorldLII. It is proposing to develop an API to allow federated searching.

As yet, there are no known successful examples of federated search systems for providing free access to legal information, at least not of any serious size. The European Commission's N-Lex,[71] developed jointly by the EU publications office and EU governments, is subtitled 'a common gateway to national law'. Launched in 2006, it now covers 24 official EU *national legislation sites*, and aims to include all EU countries. It is still labelled 'experimental' and 'a pilot project'. It aims to provide a similar search interface to each of 24 different systems, and assists with the translation of search terms from one language into another. However, it does not allow simultaneous searches of even two systems, let alone 24, so it is not a 'federated search' system, and therefore does not provide any capacity for merger of search results. If you want to search European national legislation, 24 searches are required, with 24 sets of results that cannot readily be compared. The European Forum of Official Gazettes covers more countries but has fewer functions.[72] A federated search engine of *national case law*[73] has been operated by the Network of the Presidents of the European Supreme Courts since April 2007. Although it allows selection of searching over 19 databases from 15 countries[74] it warns that searches may fail if over more than five, and tests verify this. European-wide searching would therefore take at least four repetitions. It is also quite slow. It provides a federated search facility, and therefore cannot provide relevance ranking of merged search results. This facility is not likely to satisfy the needs of many legal researchers. However, it

70 Available at: http://samba.anu.edu.au/rsync, accessed 1 March 2010.

71 Available at: http://eur-lex.europa.eu/n-lex/pays.html?lang=en&info_lang=en, accessed 29 July 2010.

72 Available at: http://circa.europa.eu/irc/opoce/ojf/info/data/prod/html/index.htm, accessed 29 July 2010, links to legislative databases in 29 European states but no common search interface, translations or merged search results.

73 Available at: www.reseau-presidents.eu, accessed 29 July 2010.

74 Austria, Belgium, Cyprus, Germany, Estonia, Finland, France, Croatia, Lithuania, Malta, Netherlands, Portugal, Slovakia, Slovenia and United Kingdom. Liechtenstein, unlisted, is also covered.

provides simultaneous translations of search queries into multiple languages, which is impressive. There are therefore no sufficiently effective and efficient comprehensive portals for European national law, whether one is looking for all sources of law, or only legislation or case law.

The efforts so far by European governments and institutions, such as the three portals discussed above, do not demonstrate what could be possible from more effective networking of national free access legal information in Europe. In other parts of the world, direct cooperation between States and their institutions has not made any better progress.[75] The non-government sector and methods other than federated searching have a better track record.

How Global is the Free Access to Law Movement?

The membership of the Free Access to Law Movement has to date been drawn primarily from LIIs based in academic institutions. However, recent members have included GLIN (US Library of Congress), SAFLII (now based at the South African Constitutional Court and operated by its Trust), the Kenya Law Reports (a semi-government body) and the Thai Law Reform Commission. The key condition for government-based members in the Declaration (as amended in 2007) is that they 'Do not impede others from obtaining public legal information from its sources and publishing it'. In other words, a government body cannot be a member if it provides free access to law in a way that monopolises the publication of that information or supports such monopoly publication. The key test is whether republication of government information is allowed. Freedom to republish official sources is at the heart of the Free Access to Law Movement, and essential for the operation of LIIs.

The other criterion for FALM membership is that government services provide something equivalent to data from different sources. Providing the annual Acts of a single jurisdiction via the web, or the decisions of a single court, is not regarded as sufficient, even though the republication of such content is valuable free access to law and its republication the essential building blocks of any LII. There needs to be something more, whether it be the aggregation of the decisions of multiple courts (or legislative sources), or publication of legislation beyond the normal output of the legislative process such as point-in-time legislation, or translations into other languages. This is a pragmatic barrier, designed to make FALM membership something of value because of the 'something more' that it recognises and encourages.

There are many European, Asian, South American and other significant government providers of free access to legal information that are not yet members of the FALM, nor have they been invited to join. It is not certain that all could do so, as their positions on the question of not impeding republication of government information may vary, and some may also have difficulty in becoming members of a non-government organisation. Some might not want to. In any event, FALM's members have only made intermittent efforts to recruit new members from existing free access providers.

Nevertheless, it is clear that there is far more free access to law than is provided by the current members of the Free Access to Law Movement. As yet the Free Access to Law Movement only includes a minority of the organisations who are potentially its members, and whose involvement could make it more significant both politically and technically. The most obvious field for expansion of membership is those government providers of free access to law from multiple sources who also meet the republication criteria.

75 GLIN, discussed earlier, is a partial exception but it does not provide full text searching.

Other possible non-government members, not yet invited to join, may come from university-based free access providers of primary materials, from some repositories of legal scholarship (for example, BePress Legal Repository[76] or the SSRN Legal Scholarship Network),[77] and from developers of new collaborative forms of legal scholarship such as Wikipedia (which has extensive law content)[78] or JurisPedia[79] if it continues to develop.

The geographical scope of FALM membership is therefore as yet far more limited than the spread of free access to law as an idea and a reality, being concentrated on the Anglophone and Commonwealth countries, some parts of the Francophonie, and parts of Asia. While Africa is well-covered (among both the Anglophone and Francophone countries), Latin America, the Middle East, most of Europe and the States of the United States are not yet involved (except indirectly via GLIN). This is a challenge for a movement which is potentially global, but also indicates that the Free Access to Law Movement and the development of LIIs may yet be far from reaching its maximum impact.

One future direction for the LII networks, and the Free Access to Law Movement, is to provide a global alternative to the expanding global reach of the current legal publishing duopoly. AustLII has adopted a policy of 'making WorldLII global' and is trying to obtain databases from as many countries as possible, and to sustain them until their operation can be taken over by local LIIs. In helping to provide and sustain better access to law in many countries, the FALM can encourage organisations in those countries to join in a global project that supports economic progress, the rule of law and democracy.

Free Access Outside the FALM and LIIs

Government Providers

The number of courts, tribunals and legislatures providing free access to their own outputs is now legion. Free Internet access to primary legal materials has become the default policy in most countries across the world. This is the reverse of the situation 15 years ago when Cornell Law School started its LII. It is beyond the scope of this chapter to examine why this has occurred or to provide details of its features or exceptions.

However, what is of more interest, and still far less common, is the prevalence of multi-sourced free access government-provided national legal information systems of the type that FALM aims to have as its members. They may publish decisions from many courts and tribunals, or from many different types of legislation databases (including translations), or they may combine all of these and more into national portals.

Outside the existing FALM membership there are many examples. In Europe they include Legifrance[80] (France), FINLEX[81] (Finland), Jersey Legal Information Board[82] (Jersey), Albanian Official Publications Centre[83] (Albania) and BelgiumLex.[84] The many differences in free

76 Available at: http://law.bepress.com/repository, accessed 1 March 2010.

77 Available at: www.ssrn.com/lsn/index.html, accessed 28 July 2010.

78 Available at: http://en.wikipedia.org/wiki/Law, accessed 1 March 2010.

79 Available at: www.jurispedia.org, accessed 1 March 2010.

80 Available at: www.legifrance.gouv.fr, accessed 1 March 2010.

81 Available at: www.finlex.fi/en, accessed 1 March 2010.

82 Available at: www.jerseylaw.je/Home/WhatsNew/default.aspx, accessed 1 March 2010.

83 Available at: www.legjislacionishqiptar.gov.al, not available 1 March 2010.

84 Available at: www.belgiumlex.be/V2/belgiumlex/website/en, accessed 1 March 2010.

access national European systems are documented in relation to France (Cottin 2009), Finland (Hietanen 2009), Denmark (Koch 2009), Italy (Lupo 2009), Switzerland (Moret 2009) and Austria (Schefbeck 2009).

Perhaps the most outstanding example of free access to European law, EUR-Lex,[85] comes from a regional organisation, the European Union. The history of the first 25 years leading to EUR-Lex has been documented comprehensively (European Commission 2006; Berger 2009).

In South America, InfoLeg[86] (Argentina) is one of many examples. Those in Brazil, Mexico and Uruguay are documented by Galindo (2009) and in other countries by Gregario (2009). In Africa the outstanding example of a successful comprehensive semi-government national free access system is *Kenya Law Reports*.[87] Some of the issues in Africa are discussed in Paliwala (2009) and Badeva-Bright (2009).

Examples in Asia include Vietnam's multi-lingual legislation system,[88] the Korean Legislation Research Institute[89] (legal translations) and Mongolia's Legal Unified Information System.[90] All countries in Asia publish legislation via the Internet for free access, with the exceptions of Myanmar and North Vietnam, at least in the national language, and very often with significant bodies of legislative translations into English (Greenleaf 2009).

LawNet Sri Lanka[91] is a cautionary tale: in 2009 it was the most impressive comprehensive government LII in Asia (with World Bank funding), but it was off the Internet when the outsourcing company hosting the databases went under in the Global Financial Crisis and has only recently reappeared. For a time, the databases on CommonLII extracted from LawNet – but unfortunately not up to date – were the only free access means of accessing that data.

Impediments to Full Free Access to Law are Decreasing

Most countries do not claim copyright in any form of primary legal materials (or other government-produced materials), sometimes including translations. They have generally adopted the option in the Berne Convention that allows no copyright in such materials. For example, the most common copyright position in European states,[92] shared by 32 of 37 States and territories surveyed,[93] is that there is no copyright in any texts of a legislative, judicial or administrative nature. In at least 21 of those States the position for free access is even better as it is explicitly stated that there is no copyright in any official translations of those exempted materials, so any official English language version may also be republished.[94] In the other 11, official translations may come within the exempt materials, but this is a question of statutory

85 Available at: http://eur-lex.europa.eu, accessed 1 March 2010.

86 Available at: http://infoleg.mecon.gov.ar, accessed 1 March 2010.

87 Available at: www.kenyalaw.org/update/index.php, accessed 1 March 2010.

88 Available at: http://vbqppl.moj.gov.vn/vbpq/en/pages/vbpq.aspx, accessed 29 July 2010.

89 Available at: http://elaw.klri.re.kr, accessed 29 July 2010.

90 Available at: www.legalinfo.mn/pages/1/page72.php?vmenuclick=72, accessed 1 March 2010.

91 Available at: www.lawnet.lk, accessed 28 June 2010.

92 Survey of the copyright laws of 37 European states (including all major states) for the purpose of this chapter, April 2010. The copyright position in the other European states has not yet been determined.

93 The 21 states in the next footnote, plus Austria, Belgium, Denmark, Finland, Germany, Greece, Hungary, Italy, Netherlands, Poland and Turkey.

94 Albania, Belarus, Bulgaria, Croatia, Czech Republic, Estonia, Latvia, Lithuania, Liechtenstein, Luxembourg, Norway, Portugal, Romania, Russian Federation, Serbia, Slovak Republic, Slovenia, Spain, Sweden, Switzerland and Ukraine.

interpretation. Also, only five of the 37 jurisdictions surveyed (the UK, Ireland, Gibraltar, France and Malta) assert some form of government copyright in such official materials, but the first four do allow their legislation and case law to be reproduced in free access LIIs, so the copyright situation is no impediment in fact. The situation is little different in Asia (Greenleaf, Chung and Mowbray 2007a), with assertions of state copyright in only a couple of the 28 jurisdictions surveyed.

There are few other practical impediments to free access to the major sources of legislation and case law data from most countries in the sense of the right and ability to reproduce national laws. Almost all countries now publish their legislation on the Internet for free access, so there are good prospects of obtaining access to that data. There are free access legislation databases for all EU countries[95] with the exceptions of Bulgaria and Cyprus (being remedied), and for most other European countries. Where courts and tribunals publish case law, it is usually anonymised in countries influenced by European privacy laws, but often available in identified form in common law countries, due to a different tradition in relation to open justice. But in both cases the data are increasingly likely to be available via the Internet from official sources, and there are likely to be few impediments to publication. These official websites rarely use the Robot Exclusion Protocol to exclude others from copying data from their sites, except in non-US common law countries where case data is identified but data protection regimes along European lines apply. In these countries, legal publishers (commercial or free access) can usually get permission for republication even if others cannot.

Free Access to Translations

Even collections of translations of legislation into other languages, an expensive business, are increasingly becoming freely accessible from government sources. In Europe there are government-provided (though not necessarily 'official') databases of English translations of collections of significant legislation from at least 12 countries:[96] Austria, Armenia, Belarus, Bosnia-Herzegovina, Estonia, Finland, France, Lithuania, Malta, Montenegro, Sweden and Switzerland. In most other countries if there is no official database of English translations, there will be numerous English translations of sets of legislation, or individual Acts, on the websites of many government agencies. In Asia the position is much the same, with large government-supported free-access collections of English legislation translations from Japan, Korea, China, Vietnam and Laos.[97] The hegemony

95 European Forum of Official Gazettes 'Comparative Table 3: Online Access to Legislation'. Available at: http://circa.europa.eu/irc/opoce/ojf/info/data/prod/html/Annex1_Online_access_to_legislation.html?keepThis=true&TB_iframe=true&height=520&width=990, accessed 29 July 2010.

96 Websites are respectively: RIS – Austrian Laws in English, www.ris.bka.gv.at/Englische-Rv; Armenian National Assembly, www.parliament.am/legislation.php?sel=alpha&ltype=3&lang=eng; Belarus National Legal Internet Portal, www.law.by/work/EnglPortal.nsf/Razdely/033; Laws of Bosnia/Herzegovina, www.fbihvlada.gov.ba/english/zakoni/index.php; Estonia Law in Estonian and English, www.legaltext.ee/en/andmebaas/ava.asp?m=022; Translation of Finnish Acts and Decrees, www.finlex.fi/en/laki/kaannokset; Legifrance Codes and Texts (in English), http://195.83.177.9/code/index.phtml?lang=uk; Siemas of the Republic of Lithuania, www3.lrs.lt/dokpaieska/forma_e.htm#; Maltese Legislation, www.doi.gov.mt/EN/parliamentacts/malta%20legislation.asp; Selected Laws of Montenegro, www.gov.me/en/Library/zakoni; Swedish Statutes in Translation, www.sweden.gov.se/sb/d/3288; Swiss Classified Compilation of Federal Legislation, www.admin.ch/ch/e/rs/rs.html, all accessed 29 July 2010.

97 All of these can be found on AsianLII. Available at: www.asianlii.org, accessed 29 July 2010.

of English is such that there are few if any large-scale examples of free-access translations of legislation into languages other than English for primarily foreign consumption.[98]

Policy Tensions in Free Access to Law

There are some disagreements among those who advocate free access to law about the best strategy for long-term success. Different preferences in models of LII networking, between a replication/synchronisation model and a federated search model, have already been discussed.

Most FALM members would be likely to reject Jon Bing's argument in favour of state-run legal information services that only provide a limited amount of free access (Bing 2003). I have described it as a 'statist model' and likely to fail because it is based around monopolies over legal information (Greenleaf 2004). However, Bing has now moved away from this vision, and has 'upgraded' it by accepting that there need to be multiple systems (competition) within a country (Bing 2010, 51). LIIs have not abandoned Bing's vision of comprehensive national legal information services, only the idea that they should be either commercial or state monopolies. Bing also sees a need for free access international services like WorldLII (or commercial services like CaseLex) to provide comparative international law services. Most thoughtful commentators would probably now accept that what can be provided by commercial publishers, non-monopolistic government providers, independent LIIs and Internet-wide search engines like Google, can be complementary, but also that this is likely to play out differently in every country. The differences will be the subject of long and complex stories.

Tom Bruce of the LII (Cornell) also has been pessimistic about the long-term role of LIIs in providing free access to law, arguing for a radically decentralised model where the courts and legislatures will publish everything themselves, for free, and according to standards (Bruce 2000, 2000a). This argument, however, fails to show that third-party republication is doomed, or unnecessary, only that publication at source is good (Greenleaf 2004a). As yet, the future of LIIs may not be certain, but that they have a future has not been disproved.

Another difference of opinion, although not as well articulated, is over the value to the diffusion of free access to law of creating regional or linguistic multi-country LIIs where there may not be direct local participation from all of the countries covered, at least not initially. Must all initiatives be 'bottom up' to be valuable, or can 'top down' initiatives sometimes result in engaging local participation, eventually resulting in decentralisation and new LIIs? Or might this stultify local initiatives? AustLII's approach, particularly with AsianLII, has been explicitly 'top down' (it included databases from 27 of 28 countries and territories from inception), but with an equally explicit goal of engaging 'bottom up' local LII development. Both approaches are agreed on the value of maximum decentralisation to local LIIs: it is a question of how many ways you can get there.

Citations, Standards and 'Reliability'

Although it has not been formally developed as a standard, there is widespread common usage of the same type of 'LII citation' of the format: '[<year of publication>] <designator> <sequential number>'. The 'designator' is an abbreviation for name of the court or tribunal (either designated

98 This excludes bilingual legislative jurisdictions, such as in Hong Kong, Macau or Canada, where translations are made primarily for domestic reasons.

by it, or applied by the LII with its agreement),[99] and the sequential number is that of the decisions available for publication from the court for that year. So '[1998] HCA 1' was the first decision of the High Court of Australia for 1998 released for publication (and in fact the first decision published using this system). This method of neutral citations for decisions published on LIIs is used by AustLII, BAILII, PacLII, SAFLII and NZLII, and for the case databases originating on CommonLII, AsianLII and WorldLII. In all Australian, English and Singaporean Courts, and New Zealand's Supreme Court, this method of citation has been adopted officially by the courts, and the expression 'Court-designated citations' is probably best used to describe these citations (see also references to 'neutral citation' in Wikipedia 'case citations').[100] These LIIs have also unilaterally applied the citations to the decisions they publish, as publishers usually do, and in some cases have retrofitted them to collections of old cases (in which case the 'year' is the year in which a court made a decision). CanLII has developed its own slightly different system of neutral citations.[101]

There has been some pooling of parallel citation tables to facilitate development of automated hypertext linking between LIIs, but this has not advanced far. For many LIIs it has now been overtaken by AustLII's development of LawCite and their use of it to enhance their own data. CanLII has also made considerable progress in enhancing its own data through development of its RefLex system to recognise and utilise parallel citations,[102] though it is unlike LawCite in that it involves considerable editorial input.

The Draft Hague Principles – Upgrading the Declaration?

The Declaration on Free Access to Law has remained largely unchanged for almost a decade. The most concerted discussion of some of its principles, and further development of them, took place at an expert meeting called by the Hague Conference on Private Law in 2008, which resulted in 18 Draft Principles on desirable conduct of State Parties in relation to free access to legal information[103] (see Appendix 3).

The Draft Principles are still being considered by the Hague Conference and as yet have no official status. They generally encourage State Parties to act to make their legal materials available for free access, but of the highest quality. The one obligation proposed is in Principle 1, which states that:

> State Parties shall ensure that their primary legal materials, in particular legislation, court and administrative tribunal decisions and international agreements, are available for free access in an electronic form by any persons, including those in foreign jurisdictions.

Fourteen non-mandatory principles follow, covering topics as diverse as republication; integrity and authoritativeness; 'downstream authoritativeness' in republication; removal of obstacles to court recognition; preservation; access to historical materials; neutral citations; free access translations; multi-lingual capacities; open standards; knowledge-based systems; inclusion of metadata; and privacy protection.

99 For an AustLII example, see www.austlii.edu.au/techlib/standards/designators.html, accessed 1 March 2010.

100 Available at: http://en.wikipedia.org/wiki/Case_citation, accessed 1 March 2010.

101 Available at: www.canlii.org/en/info/canliicite.html, accessed 1 March 2010.

102 Available at: www.canlii.org/en/info/reflex.html, accessed 1 March 2010.

103 The original draft omitted stating that the right to republish needs to respect local privacy laws, but this was addressed in subsequent amendments.

The FALM needs to reconsider its Declaration in light of these draft principles, since many FALM members were involved in their formulation. It is beyond the scope of this chapter to give them the consideration they deserve.

Funding Free Access to Law

The main constraining factor of the non-government LIIs is funding: they are free to use, but not free to build. Every LII looks after the funding of its own system, and the models on which LIIs are funded vary greatly. AustLII has the most complex 'multi-contributor' model, with over 270 institutional contributors, plus individual contributors (mainly lawyers) (Greenleaf 2009). AustLII sees this diversity of funding sources as one of its principal assets, despite the cost of maintaining it, because it provides something close to a guarantee against a 'single point of failure' in sustainability of funding. No single type of funding source can affect more than about 10 per cent of AustLII's funding stream.

BAILII is similar in having multiple contributors, though fewer than AustLII. The LII (Cornell) annually solicits funds from the public. Most LIIs have had a considerable amount of academic funding and academic institutional support (including HKLII, PacLII, AustLII, LawPhil and BAILII). CanLII is funded primarily by the Canadian legal profession: every Canadian lawyer provides over C$20 per year via their professional associations. Other LIIs have not been able to replicate this, and most would like to. But it does have disadvantages, for example CanLII does not include treaties, law reform reports or law journals, in part at least because these types of legal information are not valued as much by the legal profession as cases and legislation.

International aid and development agencies have made significant contributions to the development costs of PacLII, SAFLII, Droit Francophone, AsianLII and WorldLII. Strategic alliances with some legal publishers have helped AustLII. A small LII like CyLaw is a personal project. NZLII still lives on 'the smell of an oily rag' and help from other LIIs, while it searches for longer-term funds, as does CommonLII. Kenya Law Reports is trying to move from a model combining government funding with subscription income to one which does without subscriptions for its online resources.

There is no single source likely to fund global free access to law long-term, but that doesn't mean it can't be done. Fund-raising has been done with ever-widening scope for over a decade. There is not one formula, but as with many other aspects of open content, there are many non-business models by which numerous stakeholders can be engaged.

There are as yet few government-based FALM members, but government-based 'LIIs' face different funding challenges. GLIN is unusual in having obtained sustained government funding. While there are many individual courts and legislatures who publish their own output for free access (often from their own budgets), there are relatively few governments who fund multi-sourced free access national legal information systems (the usage of 'LII' in this chapter), and they are mainly from Europe and some in Latin America (examples are given above).

In many developing countries, there are no funds available for development of online legislation or case law unless it is provided by international aid agencies such as the World Bank, Asian Development Bank, CIDA or AusAID. In recent years the World Bank has funded major free access systems in Sri Lanka (mentioned above) and Mongolia. The sustainability of these free access facilities, particularly in terms of updating data, often becomes problematic once the initial aid funding ceases. Where this happens, engagement with the FALM members, and the assistance they can provide, may be valuable. In the past, aid and development agencies have often invested considerable funds into national legal information systems, without requiring that free-access systems be developed, and sometimes requiring to the contrary that they adopt 'pay for use' models in the hope they will become self-funding. Such strategies sometimes fail, such as when PacLII was called in to 'bail out' a failed project given to the commercial sector in Papua New Guinea. In a few other instances (for example CariLaw) a service may succeed in attracting enough users to keep going. In both cases the result is that relatively few users get to use services that public funds have helped to build. The FALM and its members need to help convince aid and development agencies that free access models can be more sustainable and socially beneficial in developing countries than closed 'pay for use' models.

The models on which sustainable free access to law can be based are as yet little studied, though there are some initial essays (Lemyre 2009; Greenleaf 2009). A study conducted by LexUM with a focus on Western African countries aims to develop a methodology to assess some aspects of the impact of free access to law developments (Mokanov 2009). More work is needed, including in comparing the different models adopted to date.

Internet Search Engines, 'Open Content' and LIIs

The policy of LIIs concerning republication of government information stated in the FALM Declaration does not mean that a LII must declare its content to be 'open content' (available for re-use by anyone), but only that it must not hinder others from obtaining the data from official sources and republishing it. In some countries where doctrines of Crown Copyright still apply (for example, Australia) a LII is not at liberty to permit users to reproduce its data for all purposes. LawPhil is the only LII to provide all its data via a Creative Commons licence at this point. CanLII has quite liberal Terms of Use[104] for re-use of data on the CanLII site, possible because of Canada's Reproduction of Federal Law Order.[105] For some LIIs, the question of re-use is further complicated by privacy and strategic issues. Each LII has different views about the need to protect its own databases, often for privacy reasons with case law (Pelletier 2007) (this varies between jurisdictions), but more generally to avoid losing the benefit of its investment of public monies in collecting data from disparate sources and adding value to it.

The search engines, and networks, of the LIIs still matter in a post-Google world. General Internet search engines such as Google do not provide what the LII networks (or individual LIIs) provide. One reason is that many LIIs use the Robots Exclusion Standard[106] (see also The Web Robots Pages)[107] to exclude spiders/robots from at least their case law (variously on privacy policy grounds, as required by data sources, and as required by privacy laws). They include CanLII, BAILII, AustLII, NZLII, HKLII and the networked LIIs. SAFLII allows web spider access to some cases, because of a policy choice valuing dissemination above privacy in the African context, and LawPhil provides 'open content' under a Creative Commons licence. Some LIIs exclude robots from all data (on strategic and technical grounds).[108] Networking LIIs can also add many forms of organisation of the data shared between LIIs, such as restricting the scope of searches to legislation

104 Available at: www.canlii.org/en/info/faq.html#5.2, accessed 1 March 2010.

105 Available at: www.canlii.org/en/ca/laws/regu/si-97-5/latest/si-97-5.html, accessed 1 March 2010.

106 Available at: http://en.wikipedia.org/wiki/Robots.txt, accessed 1 March 2010.

107 Available at: www.robotstxt.org, accessed 1 March 2010.

108 See the robots.txt file at the root of any LII plus its privacy policy, for individual details, for example, www.austlii.edu.au/robots.txt, accessed 1 March 2010.

from many jurisdictions, that general search engines do not yet provide. The long-term relationship between search engines and LIIs is still developing, with unresolved questions such as the effect of search engines on the sustainability of the value the LIIs add to raw legal data, from which search engines profit. At this point, 'free access' does not necessarily mean 'free to be found through any search engine'.

References

Anderson, K. (2007), 'The Southern African Legal Information Institute (SAFLII) – Achievements & Challenges' [PPT] 8th Law via Internet Conference, Montreal, 2007. Available at: www.lexum.com/conf2007/index_en.html, not accessible 29 July 2010.

Apikul, C. (2006), 'Making Legal Information Freely Available – JuriBurkina, Burkina Faso' (International Open Source Network Case Study). Available at: www.iosn.net/foss/case-studies/juriburkina, accessed 29 July 2010.

Badeva-Bright, M. (2009), 'Re-thinking "Open" in Free and Open Access to Law', in Peruginelli and Ragona.

Berger, A. (ed.) (2009), *Access to Legislation in Europe, Guide to the Legal Gazettes and Other Official Information Sources in the European Union and European Free Trade Association* (Luxembourg: Publications Office of the European Union).

Bing, J. (2003), 'The Policies of Legal Information Services: A Perspective of Three Decades', in Bygrave, L. (ed.), *Yulex 2003* (Oslo: Institutt for rettsinformatik/Norwegian Research Centre for Computers and Law).

Bing, J. (2010), 'Let There be LITE: A Brief History of Legal Information Retrieval', in Paliwala.

Blake, R. (2002), 'Islands in Time: The Pacific Islands Legal Information Institute (PACLII)', 4th Law via Internet Conference, Montreal, 2002. Available at: www.lexum.com/conf/conf2002/actes/blake.pdf, accessed 29 July 2010.

Bruce, T. (2000), 'Tears Shed over Peer Gynt's Onion: Some Thoughts on the Constitution of Public Legal Information Providers', *Journal of Information, Law and Technology* (*JILT*) 2. Available at: www2.warwick.ac.uk/fac/soc/law/elj/jilt/2000_2/bruce, accessed 29 July 2010.

Bruce, T. (2000a), 'Public Legal Information: Focus and Future', *Journal of Information, Law and Technology* (*JILT*) 1. Available at: www2.warwick.ac.uk/fac/soc/law/elj/jilt/2000_1/bruce, accessed 29 July 2010.

Buckingham, D. (2005), 'What's in a Name? New Zealand and the Growth of Free On-line Legal Information', 7th Law via Internet Conference, Vila, Vanuatu. Available at: www.worldlii.org/au/other/CompLRes/2005/2.html, accessed 29 July 2010.

Cottin, S. (2009), 'Free access to Legal and Legislative Information: The French Approach Through the Enlightenment of the Strategic Reviews of Better Regulation in the European Union', in Peruginelli and Ragona.

European Commission (2006), *25 Years of European Law Online* (Luxembourg: Office of Official Publications of the European Communities).

Galindo, F. (2009), 'Free Access to the Law in Latin America: Brasil, Argentina, Mexico and Uruguay as Examples', in Peruginelli and Ragona.

Greenleaf, G. (2004), 'Jon Bing and the History of Computerised Legal Research – Some Missing Links', in Torvund, O. and Bygrave, L. (eds), *Et tilbakeblikk på fremtiden* [*Looking Back at the Future*] (Oslo: Institutt for Rettsinformatikk).

Greenleaf, G. (2004a), 'Full Free Access to Law: Global Policy Aspects' [PPT] 6th Law via Internet Conference, Paris, November 2004. Available at: www2.austlii.edu.au/~graham/publications/2004/Policies_Paris.ppt, accessed 29 July 2010.

Greenleaf, G. (2007), 'Free Access to Japanese and Asian Law – The Launch of AsianLII in Japan', *UNSWLRS* 60. Available at: http://law.bepress.com/unswwps/flrps/art60/, accessed 1 March 2010; presentation at the Launch of the Asian Legal Information Institute in Japan, 4 August 2007, Meiji University, Kanda, Tokyo.

Greenleaf, G. (2008), 'Legal Information Institutes and the Free Access to Law Movement'. Available at: www.nyulawglobal.org/globalex, accessed 1 March 2010.

Greenleaf, G. (2009), 'Subject Libraries in Free Access Law Services', in Rüßmann, H. (ed.), *Festschrift für Gerhard Käfer* (Saarbrücken: Juris GmbH).

Greenleaf G., Chung, P. and Mowbray, A. (2004), 'A New Home Online for Commonwealth Law: A Proposal for a CommonLII', *Journal of Information, Law and Technology* (*JILT*) 2. Available at: www2.warwick.ac.uk/fac/soc/law/elj/jilt/2004_2/greenleafmowbrayandchung, accessed 29 July 2010.

Greenleaf, G., Chung, P. and Mowbray, A. (2005), 'Responding to the Fragmentation of International Law – WorldLII's International Courts & Tribunals Project', *Canadian Law Library Review* 30:1, 13–21.

Greenleaf, G., Chung, P. and Mowbray, A. (2007), 'Emerging Global Networks for Free Access to Law: WorldLII's Strategies 2002–2005', *SCRIPT-ed* 4:4, 319. Available at: www2.warwick.ac.uk/fac/soc/law/elj/jilt/2004_2/greenleafmowbrayandchung, accessed 1 March 2010.

Greenleaf, G., Chung, P. and Mowbray, A. (2007a), 'Challenges in Improving Access to Asian Laws: The Asian Legal Information Institute (Asian LII)', *University of New South Wales Faculty of Law Research Series (UNSWLRS)* 42. Available at: http://law.bepress.com/unswwps/flrps/art42, accessed 1 March 2010; *Proceedings of the 4th Asian Law Institute Conference*, Jakarta, May 2007.

Greenleaf, G., Chung, P. and Mowbray, A. (2010), 'Building a Commons for the Common Law – The Commonwealth Legal Information Institute (CommonLII) after Four Years Progress', *Commonwealth Law Bulletin* 36:1, 127–34.

Greenleaf, G., Mowbray, A. and Chung, P. (2007), 'Networking LIIs: How Free Access to Law Fits Together', *Internet Newsletter for Lawyers*, March/April.

Greenleaf, G., Mowbray, A. and van Dijk, P. (1995), 'Representing and Using Legal Knowledge in Integrated Decision Support Systems – DataLex WorkStations', *Artificial Intelligence and Law* 3:1–2, 97–124.

Greenleaf, G., Mowbray, A., King, G. and van Dijk, P. (1995), 'Public Access to Law via Internet: The Australasian Legal Information Institute', *Journal of Law & Information Science* 6:1. Available at: www.austlii.edu.au/austlii/articles/libs_paper.html, accessed 29 July 2010.

Greenleaf, G., Chung, P., Mowbray, A., Chow, K. and Pun, K. (2002), 'The Hong Kong Legal Information Institute (HKLII): Its Role in Free Access to Global Law via the Internet', *Hong Kong Law Journal* 32:2, 401–27.

Gregario, C. (2009), 'Access to Judicial Information via the Internet in Latin America: A Discussion of the Experiences, Trends and Difficulties', in Peruginelli and Ragona.

Hamilton, L. (2007), 'A Presentation on PacLII' [PPT] 8th Law via Internet Conference, Montreal, 2007. Available at: http://conf.lexum.umontreal.ca/proceedings_documents/1-Lenore_Hamilton.ppt, not accessible 29 July 2010.

Hietanen, A. (2009), 'Free Access to Legislation in Finland: Principles, Practices and Prospects', in Peruginelli and Ragona.

Koch, N. (2009), 'Free Access to Legislation in Denmark: Advantages in Inter-institutional Cooperation', in Peruginelli and Ragona.

Lemyre, P (2004), 'Droit francophone: de catalogue à portail', www.frlii.org/article.php3?id_article=168, not accessible 30 July 2010; 6th Law via Internet Conference, Paris, 2004.

Lemyre, P. (2009), 'The Evolving Ecology of the Legal Information Market', in Peruginelli and Ragona.

Lemyre, P., Coulibaly, B. and Viens, F. (2004), 'Access to Law in the French-Speaking World: A Renewed Strategy', *UTS Law Review* 6, www.austlii.edu.au/au/journals/UTSLRev/2004/5.html, accessed 29 July 2010.

Lupo, C. (2009), 'Free Access to Legislation in Italy: The Role of Standards for the Integration of Information Systems', in Peruginelli and Ragona.

Mokanov, I. (2009), 'After 15 Years, Is Free Access to Law Here to Stay?', in Peruginelli and Ragona.

Montgomery, J. (2004) 'Free Access to Primary Legal Documents in Southern Africa', *OSALL Organisation of SA Law Libraries Newsletter* 15:1, 1–2.

Moret, M. (2009), 'Free Access to Legal Information in Switzerland', in Peruginelli and Ragona.

Mowbray, A., Chung, P. and Greenleaf, G. (2009), 'Free-Access Case Law Enhancements for Australian law', in Peruginelli and Ragono.Mowbray, A., Greenleaf, G., Chung, P. and Autin, D. (2007), 'Improving Stability and Performance of an International Network of Free Access Legal Information Systems', *Journal of Information Law & Technology* (*JILT*), 2. Available at: www2.warwick.ac.uk/fac/soc/law/elj/jilt/2007_2/mowbary_etal, accessed 29 July 2010.

Paliwala, A. (2009), 'Free Access to Law in Africa: Issues for Network Society', in Peruginelli and Ragona.

Paliwala, A. (ed.) (2010), *A History of Legal Informatics* (Zaragoza: Presnsas Universitarias de Zaragoza).

Pelletier, F. (2007), 'L'accès aux jugements / Access to Judgments', [PPT] 8th Law via Internet Conference, Montreal, 2007. Available at: http://conf.lexum.umontreal.ca/proceedings_documents/5-Frederic_Pelletier.ppt, not accessible 29 July 2010.

Peruginelli, G. and Ragona, M. (eds) (2009), *Law via the Internet: Free Access, Quality of Information, Effectiveness of Rights* (Proceedings of the IX International Conference 'Law via the Internet') (Florence: European Press Academic Publishing).

Poulin, D. (2004), 'Open Access to Law in Developing Countries', *First Monday* 9:12, 6. Available at: http://firstmonday.org/htbin/cgiwrap/bin/ojs/index.php/fm/article/view/1193/1113, accessed 29 July 2010.

Poulin, D., Mowbray, A. and Lemyre, P. (2007), 'Free Access to Law and Open Source Software', in *Handbook of Research on Open Source Software* (Hershey and New York: Information Science Reference).

Poulin, D., Salvas, B. and Pelletier, F. (2000), 'La diffusion du droit canadien sur Internet', *Revue du Notariat* 102:189.

Prescott, D. (2005), 'The UN and the Global Legal Information Network', 4 *UN Chronicle Online Edition*. Available at: www.un.org/Pubs/chronicle/2005/issue4/0405p57.html, accessed 1 March 2010.

Pun, K., Ip, G., Chong, C., Chan, V., Chow, K., Hui, L., Tsang, W. and Chan, H. (2004), 'Processing Legal Documents in the Chinese-Speaking World: The Experience of HKLII', 3rd Law via Internet Conference, AustLII 2003.

Pun, K., Chan, E., Chow, K., Chong, C., Hui, L., Ma, J., Tsang, W. and Chan, H. (2004a), 'Cross-Referencing for Bilingual Electronic Legal Documents in HKLII', 6th Law via

Internet Conference, Paris, 2004. Available at: www.austlii.edu.au/cgi-bin/sinodisp/au/other/CompLRes/2003/4.html, accessed 29 July 2010.
Schefbeck, G. (2009), 'Free Access to Legal and Legislative Information: The Austrian Approach', in Peruginelli and Ragona.

Appendix 1

Members of the Free Access to Law Movement

AltLaw – Columbia Law School, USA
AsianLII – Asian Legal Information Institute, AustLII, UTS/UNSW, Australia
AustLII – Australasian Legal Information Institute, UTS/UNSW, Australia
BAILII – British and Irish Legal Information Institute, BAILII Trust, Institute of Advanced Legal Studies, UK
CanLII – Canadian Legal Information Institute, Canadian Law Societies/LexUM, Canada
Cardiff Index to Legal Abbreviations, UK
CommonLII – Commonwealth Legal Information Institute, AustLII, UTS/UNSW, Australia
CyLaw, Cyprus
Droit francophone
Droit.org – Institut Francais d'information Juridique, France
GLIN – Global Legal Information Network, Law Library of Congress, USA
HKLII – Hong Kong Legal Information Institute, University of Hong Kong, Hong Kong SAR
IIjusticia, Argentina
Instituto de Investigaciones Jurídicas UNAM (IIJ-UNAM), Mexico
Institute of Law and Technology, Autonomous University of Barcelona, Spain
IRLII – Irish Legal Information Initiative, University College Cork, Ireland
ITTIG – Institute of Legal Information Theory and Techniques, Italy
Jersey Legal Information Board, Jersey
JuriBurkina, Burkina Faso
JuriNiger, Niger
Juristisches Internetprojekt Saarbrücken, University of Saarbrucken, Germany
Kathmandu School of Law, Nepal
KenyaLaw – Kenya Law Reports, Kenya
LawPhil, Arellano School of Law, Philippine
LexUM – Law Faculty, University of Montreal, Canada
LII (Cornell) – Legal Information Institute, Cornell Law School, USA
MalawiLII – Malawi Legal Information Institute, Malawi
NZLII – New Zealand Legal Information Institute, University of Otago, New Zealand
PacLII – Pacific Islands Legal Information Institute, School of Law, University of the South Pacific, Vanuatu
SAFLII – Southern African Legal Information Institute, Constitutional Court Trust, South Africa
TLRC – Thai Law Reform Commission, Office of the Council of State, Thailand
ULII – Ugandan Legal Information Institute, Uganda
WorldLII – World Legal Information Institute, AustLII, UTS/UNSW, Australia

Appendix 2

Declaration on Free Access to Law

This declaration was made by legal information institutes meeting in Montreal in 2002, as amended at meetings in Sydney (2003), Paris (2004) and Montreal (2007).

Legal information institutes of the world, meeting in Montreal, declare that:

- Public legal information from all countries and international institutions is part of the common heritage of humanity. Maximising access to this information promotes justice and the rule of law
- Public legal information is digital common property and should be accessible to all on a non-profit basis and free of charge
- Organisations such as legal information institutes have the right to publish public legal information and the government bodies that create or control that information should provide access to it so that it can be published by other parties

Public legal information means legal information produced by public bodies that have a duty to produce law and make it public. It includes primary sources of law, such as legislation, case law and treaties, as well as various secondary (interpretative) public sources, such as reports on preparatory work and law reform, and resulting from boards of inquiry. It also includes legal documents created as a result of public funding.

Publicly funded secondary (interpretative) legal materials should be accessible for free but permission to republish is not always appropriate or possible. In particular free access to legal scholarship may be provided by legal scholarship repositories, legal information institutes or other means.

Legal information institutes:

- Publish via the Internet public legal information originating from more than one public body
- Provide free and anonymous public access to that information
- Do not impede others from obtaining public legal information from its sources and publishing it, and
- Support the objectives set out in this Declaration

All legal information institutes are encouraged to participate in regional or global free access to law networks.

Therefore, the legal information institutes agree:

- To promote and support free access to public legal information throughout the world, principally via the Internet
- To recognise the primary role of local initiatives in free access publishing of their own national legal information
- To cooperate in order to achieve these goals and, in particular, to assist organisations in developing countries to achieve these goals, recognising the reciprocal advantages that all obtain from access to each other's law

- To help each other and to support, within their means, other organisations that share these goals with respect to:
  - Promotion, to governments and other organisations, of public policy conducive to the accessibility of public legal information
  - Technical assistance, advice and training
  - Development of open technical standards
  - Academic exchange of research results
  - To meet at least annually, and to invite other organisations who are legal information institutes to subscribe to this declaration and join those meetings, according to procedures to be established by the parties to this Declaration
  - To provide to the end users of public legal information clear information concerning any conditions of re-use of that information, where this is feasible

Appendix 3

The 'Hague Conference' Draft Principles on Desirable Conduct of States in Relation to Free Access to Legal Information (2008)

[These 18 principles were developed by a group of experts on legal information systems, and on conflict of laws, who met on 19–21 October 2008 at the invitation of the Permanent Bureau of the Hague Conference on Private International Law as part of its feasibility study on a Future Instrument concerning 'access to foreign law'. A main purpose of the discussion was to assess how free access to law websites could be used by courts in obtaining reliable versions of foreign laws. These draft principles have no official status as yet.]

Free access

1. State Parties shall ensure that their primary legal materials, in particular legislation, court and administrative tribunal decisions and international agreements, are available for free access in an electronic form by any persons, including those in foreign jurisdictions.

Reproducing and re-use

2. State Parties are encouraged to permit and facilitate the reproduction and re-use of those legal materials by other bodies, in particular for the purpose of securing free public access to the materials, and to remove any impediments to such reproduction and re-use.

Open formats, metadata and knowledge-based systems

3. State Parties are encouraged to make their legal materials available in open and re-usable formats and with such metadata as available.

4. States Parties are encouraged to cooperate in the development of common standards for metadata applicable to legal materials, particularly those intended to enable and encourage interchange.
5. Where State Parties provide knowledge-based systems assisting in the application or interpretation of their legal materials, they are encouraged to make such systems available for free public access, reproducing and re-use.

Integrity and authoritativeness

6. State Parties are encouraged to make available authoritative versions of their legal materials provided in electronic form.
7. State Parties are encouraged to ensure that, when authoritative legal materials are reproduced or re-used by other bodies, they are of the highest integrity and carry clear indications of their origins and integrity (authoritativeness).
8. State Parties are encouraged to remove obstacles to the admissibility of these materials in their courts.

Protection of personal data

9. Online publication of court and administrative tribunal decisions and related material should be in accordance with protection of personal data laws of the State of origin. Where applicable, anonymization of the text of such decisions and related material should be undertaken by the competent authority making the decision, unless provided otherwise by the law of its State.

Historical materials

10. State Parties are encouraged to provide historical legal materials.

Preservation

11. State Parties are encouraged to ensure long time preservation and accessibility of their legal materials as made available under paragraphs 1 and 10 above.

Citations

12. State Parties are encouraged to adopt neutral methods of citation of their legal materials, including methods that are medium-neutral, provider-neutral and internationally consistent.

Translations

13. State Parties are encouraged, where possible, to provide translations of their legislation and other materials, in other languages.

14. Where State Parties do provide such translations, they are encouraged to allow them to be reproduced or re-used by other parties, particularly for free public access.

15. State Parties are encouraged to develop multi-lingual access capacities and to co-operate in the development of such capacities.

Support and co-operation

16. State Parties and re-publishers of their legal materials are encouraged to make those legal materials more accessible through various means of interoperability and networking.
17. State Parties are encouraged to assist in sustaining those organisations that fulfil the above objectives and to assist other State Parties in fulfilling their obligations.
18. State Parties are encouraged to co-operate in fulfilling these obligations.

Chapter 11
Globalisation and Commercial Legal Publishing

Kendall F. Svengalis

The radical transformation of the legal publishing industry since 1979 is largely the consequence of the confluence of two twentieth-century developments: (1) the dramatic relaxation of the antitrust standards governing mergers and acquisitions; and (2) the realisation by international investors of the profit potential presented by professional publishing, of which legal publishing emerged as a significant specialty at the end of the twentieth century. This chapter discusses the transformation of the legal publishing industry after describing how United States antitrust law evolved over the course of the century to create an environment conducive to the emergence of a globalised and highly concentrated commercial legal publishing industry.[1]

Legal Publishing and the Emerging Oligopoly

For most of its history the legal publishing industry did not attract scrutiny from antitrust enforcers or regulators. The reasons for this are not difficult to discern: (1) legal publishing served a limited, professional market; (2) the industry was sufficiently fragmented to preclude the negative attributes of market concentration; (3) there was sufficient ease of entry into the market for new participants. By 1980, however, these conditions had begun to change.

Over the past 30 years the legal publishing industry in the United States has been transformed from one comprising more than two dozen competitors of some size and professional reputation into an oligarchy dominated by three international conglomerates: Thomson Reuters, Reed Elsevier and Wolters Kluwer.

An oligopoly has been defined as:

> [a] highly concentrated market containing only a few firms. The firms may be able to arrive at a consensus about price and output without implicitly agreeing with each other about anything. For example, if a market contains one very large firm and two or three smaller ones, the smaller ones may have to watch the larger firm's pricing decisions very closely. If the larger firm sets a high, relatively profitable price, the smaller firms will be invited to follow and participate in the monopoly profits. But if they refuse to follow, the dominant firm will lose market share and may have ways of retaliating. Under such circumstances, the firms may reach an understanding about price even though they may not formally communicate with each other. (Hovenkamp 2005, 98).

Although American legal publishing had its origins in the nineteenth century, led chiefly by the emergence of the West Publishing Company in 1876 and the Lawyers Cooperative Publishing

---

1 For a perspective from Europe on the development of national and global electronic legal publishing including commercial systems and also state funded national systems and free access systems, see Bing (2010).

Company in 1882, it did not attract the attention of outside investors until a century later. Following its initial acquisition of Callaghan & Company in 1979, the Thomson Corporation of Canada, until then a newspaper and media business, came to appreciate the strategic investment potential of professional publishing and, specifically, legal publishing. Among the characteristics which attracted investors to legal publishing were:

1. high profitability
2. reliable cash flow from subscription sales
3. a relatively affluent customer base
4. lower risks in product development, and
5. customer inattention to publisher practices, all of which contributed to the desirability of acquiring legal publishing entities

What distinguished the late twentieth century wave of mergers and acquisitions in the legal publishing field from those which preceded them was that practically all the existing legal publishing entities were in play and that they were acquired by non-US corporations primarily interested in their profit potential (Svengalis 2009, 3–4). It is necessary to understand the development of US antitrust law in order to understand how these legal publishing giants, which control increasing amounts of world legal publishing, were created.

Origins of Antitrust Law

Antitrust law in the United States consists of a body of statutes, federal regulations, court decisions, and enforcement guidelines and activities designed to control business activities that pose a threat to free market competition. It is predicated upon a fundamental belief that economic issues are best left to private, independent and competitive decision-making enterprises that seek to attract customers who are motivated to achieve maximum advantage by selecting from among market alternatives. The aim of antitrust law is to preserve the conditions for free and open competition by prohibiting and prosecuting cases of collusion, exclusion, and monopoly that limit competition and pose the threat of higher prices, and reduced output, quality and innovation (Areeda and Hovenkamp 2006, vol. 1, 3–7; von Kalinowski et al. 2008, vol. 1, §§2.01–2.02; Reback 2009, 9–10).

In the United States, antitrust law and regulation arose in response to the post-Civil War's chaotic world of business competition. Building on English and American common law precedents, antitrust in the United States was usually enforced, somewhat inconsistently, at the state level. It was an era in which the promise of high profits and the availability of capital drew entrepreneurs into new and burgeoning industries. Many of these entrepreneurs lacked the experience necessary for success in high growth and volatile business enterprises. As markets matured and growth rates declined, many businesses were afflicted by chronic overcapacity and a highly competitive, often cutthroat, business environment. At the same time, technological improvements fuelled productivity gains that exceeded consumer demand and resulted in excess supply, which forced prices lower and drove many enterprises into insolvency (Hovenkamp 1994, 48–51; Reback 2009, 9).

In the late nineteenth and early twentieth centuries, these conditions propelled businesses in numerous industries to form a variety of multi-firm organisations. Other business enterprises realised that they could operate at a loss by paying only the interest on their loans. So, rather than leaving the field to more productive competitors, they maintained production levels and forced prices even lower.

The Standard Oil Experience

In the midst of these developments, savvy businessmen employed tactics to protect their businesses from what they saw as destructive price cutting and ruinous competition. John D. Rockefeller, who founded the Standard Oil Company, utilised a variety of tactics and strategies to consolidate his holdings, and to undersell and acquire his competitors. When he was unable to gain outright ownership of the oil industry, he turned to the cartel as a tool for eliminating overproduction. When that failed to restrict oil production and maintain high price levels, he turned to the trust (Reback 2009, 11–12), a legal structure that allowed a small group of trustees to control the stock and decision-making of a company's principal shareholders. The Standard Oil Trust, created in 1882, consisted of nine trustees appointed by Rockefeller who controlled the properties of the constituent companies, and made pricing and output decisions on their behalf.

The template created by Standard Oil was replicated in a host of other industries, including tobacco, steel, copper, coal, rubber, sugar, distilling and meatpacking. The leaders of these industries also employed other legal mechanisms, particularly the holding company, which allowed companies to control other companies by holding their stock. The goals were the same, regardless of the industry involved: limiting production and raising consumer prices. The degree to which they achieved their goals is a matter of some dispute among historians and economists.

The tactics of Rockefeller and other magnates attracted the interest of journalists, who brought the public's attention to the costs of monopolisation to consumers. In what he characterised as a 'war against plenty', Henry Demarest Lloyd explained how industry after industry had organised into combinations dedicated to raising prices by reducing output. The public reaction to these developments brought pressure to bear upon members of Congress which introduced legislation to limit the power of the trusts (Reback 2009, 12–13).

The Sherman and Clayton Acts

The Sherman Antitrust Act (1890) was the first US federal statute to address these perceived excesses, making illegal '[e]very contract, combination in the form of trust or otherwise, or conspiracy, in restraint of trade or commerce among the several States, or within foreign nations' (26 Stat. 209; 15 USC § 1). In 1914, the Clayton Act (38 Stat. 730; 15 USC § 12) addressed the threats to competition posed by price discrimination, tying arrangements, mergers, interlocking directorates and exclusive dealings. The Federal Trade Commission Act enacted the same year established a federal administrative agency to police 'unfair methods of competition' (38 Stat. 710; 15 USC § 44). Neither the language of the statutes nor their legislative histories provided much detailed guidance to the federal courts charged with their interpretation.

Between 1898 and 1901, the number of multi-million dollar trusts increased from 20 to 185; an additional 63 were formed in 1902 alone. The Supreme Court virtually ignored the Sherman Act in the years immediately after its passage. Without enforcement, the Sherman Act was pretty much a dead letter (Reback 2009, 14).

The conditions attracted the attention of crusading journalist and biographer Ida Tarbell. In a series of articles in 1902 in *McClure's*, the country's leading magazine, Tarbell detailed the tactics employed by Rockefeller to corral the oil market and force independent dealers out of business. In 1904 she published the series in a book entitled *The History of the Standard Oil Company*. Standard Oil was dissolved by the Supreme Court of Ohio in 1902 but reorganised in New Jersey as a holding company that sold 84 per cent of all the petroleum products in the United States (Tarbell 1904).

Industrial concentration attracted the attention of politicians, including President Theodore Roosevelt, but also generated much soul-searching among those who appreciated the ability of large-scale corporations to achieve economies of scale. Recognising that the federal government would need more resources to combat the titans of industry, Roosevelt convinced Congress to create a Bureau of Corporations to investigate the trusts and authorised the creation of what would become the Antitrust Division of the Justice Department to prosecute antitrust cases.

Since the early years of the twentieth century, the course of antitrust law has depended both on the Supreme Court's interpretation of the federal antitrust statutes and on the evolving patterns of American economic, political and intellectual life. While some legal scholars, judges and enforcement officials have stressed achieving a more equitable distribution of wealth, preservation of individual business opportunity, and protection of political freedom, others have emphasised the protection of competition to enhance economic efficiency and maximise societal wealth. These latter goals became the chief driving force behind the federal government's antitrust enforcement mechanism which aimed at restricting four primary forms of conduct:

1. single-firm activities that seek to acquire or maintain monopoly power
2. horizontal arrangements among competitors
3. mergers, and
4. vertical structures among firms in a supplier-purchaser association (Hovenkamp 2005, 48–55)

By the late 1890s, the courts had begun responding to a more restive national mood and to more aggressive enforcement efforts by the federal government in the face of the perceived anti-competitive effects of increased merger activity. Under the Roosevelt and Taft administrations, more rigorous federal enforcement of the Sherman Act was directed to cartels in the railroad, tobacco, oil and other industries. Nevertheless, Roosevelt's preferred means of addressing rising industrial concentrations remained the government's regulatory apparatus, rather than antitrust enforcement of the Sherman Act in the courts (Reback 2009, 17).

The increased enforcement efforts did result in several significant Supreme Court victories, chief among them *Standard Oil Co. of New Jersey* v. *United States* (221 US 1 (1911)) and *United States* v. *American Tobacco Co.* (221 US 106 (1911)). However, while those decisions caused the break-up of two of the country's largest industrial concerns, they were unsuccessful in diminishing the concentration of economic power the companies represented. In nearly eight years of the Roosevelt administration, only 44 antitrust cases were brought while hundreds of trusts continued to operate outside the government's purview.

Some scholars have suggested that although the firms involved in these decisions were monopolistic, they were also engaged in a highly competitive process, while simultaneously reducing both costs and prices. D.T. Armentano argues that, while it is still widely believed that Standard of New Jersey was convicted because it had restricted production, raised prices and engaged in ruthless predatory practices to destroy competition, none of these things were ever proven in court (Armentano 1990).

Competing Standards of Antitrust Analysis

Much of the subsequent debate in the Supreme Court and among scholars has centred on two conflicting standards of antitrust analysis. Under the 'per se' rule, certain business activities are illegal on their face. Under the 'rule-of-reason' standard, illegality could only be determined after extended analysis of a company's purposes, market share, effects and consideration of less intrusive alternatives by which it could achieve its business goals. Under this standard, although certain activities were illegal per se, others were to be decided on a case-by-case basis. This standard angered 'reformers' who championed a more thoroughgoing enforcement of the Sherman Act.

The rule of reason became a central point of contention in the three-way presidential election of 1912, which pitted Roosevelt against William Howard Taft and Woodrow Wilson. Wilson's election resulted in the passage of the Clayton Act (1914) and the creation of the Federal Trade Commission (1914), both of which were designed to enhance the power and reach of the Sherman Act.

The election of 1912 reflected the continuing battle between the two competing philosophies of antitrust enforcement: (1) court-enforced competition between market players to advance broad-based economic benefits to consumers; and (2) government oversight and rule making to enhance the benefits of the free market. Neither approach worked successfully all the time. Regulators were forced to choose that approach which worked best under a given set of circumstances (Reback 2009, 19; Hovenkamp 2005, 57).

Ironically, the legislative efforts of the early Wilson administration were confounded by the depression of 1913, which ushered in a new era of conciliation between government and business. As business activity flourished under economic concentration, the public was more hospitable to policies favourable to business and less concerned about monopolistic and anticompetitive behaviour. Business-friendly policies characterised the government's stance on antitrust enforcement for the next 20 years.

Applying the rule of reason standard in the case of *United States* v. *United States Steel Corp.* (251 US 417 (1920)), the Supreme Court determined that size itself did not prove monopoly or monopolistic behaviour. The Court ruled that US Steel had active competition, that its competitors were growing at a faster rate, and that the prices of steel products had fallen on average between 1901 and 1911 (the year the corporation was indicted by the Department of Justice). Moreover, it discerned no parallels between the facts in this case and those of the Standard Oil and American Tobacco cases of 1911.

Depression-Era Antitrust Policy

Antitrust policy in the United States has generally been formed in response to economic conditions and to the often confused and counterproductive policies employed to combat economic downturns. The onset of the Great Depression following the stock market crash in 1929 caused a dramatic decline in public support for the business sector. President Herbert Hoover ushered in an unprecedented wave of government intervention designed to right the economy, but none of it worked. The New Deal of Franklin D. Roosevelt constituted more of the same, with similarly ineffectual government programmes that institutionalised the more limited efforts of his predecessor (Woods 2009, 99–100).

Roosevelt was responsible for legislation that suspended antitrust rules to allow industries to organise themselves into cartels for the purpose of setting minimum selling prices, limiting output, and imposing other restrictions on free market activity. To implement these policies, he established a separate Antitrust Division within the Justice Department, which directed its initial efforts at enforcing industry price fixing codes against discounting in an effort to maintain price levels, thus reinforcing misguided Federal Reserve policies (Woods 2009, 100–102).

These were the very practices that had prompted Congress to the pass the Sherman Act in the first place. Now, as a part of the central planning regime that characterised the New Deal, the government colluded with big business to prevent prices from falling to market levels. The New Deal's so-called 'pump-priming' was a massive failure, as Roosevelt's Treasury Secretary Henry Morgenthau, Jr. later admitted:

> We have tried spending money. We are spending more than we have ever spent before and it does not work … I say after eight years of this Administration we have just as much unemployment as when we started … And an enormous debt to boot. (Blum 1959, 70)

Roosevelt jettisoned antitrust enforcement in favour of expanding cooperative efforts among business entities under the National Industrial Recovery Act (1933), which the Supreme Court declared unconstitutional two years later. Writing for a unanimous Court in *Schechter Poultry Corporation* v. *United States* (295 US 495 (1935)), Chief Justice Charles Evans Hughes concluded that Title I of the National Industrial Recovery Act was unconstitutional, that the law was void for vagueness because the critical term 'fair competition' was nowhere defined in the Act, and that the Act's delegation of authority to the executive branch was unconstitutionally overbroad.

The administration's response to this decision, in light of renewed attention to the effects of cartelisation in Europe, and the economic downturn of 1937, was a renewed interest in antitrust enforcement. The administration also responded to the withdrawal of big business from the New Deal coalition, which had been denounced by the US Chamber of Commerce. In late 1937 and early 1938, Roosevelt and the assistant attorney general for antitrust were publicly blaming companies they characterised as monopolies for the economic downturn. By the end of the decade, however, little progress had been made in curtailing the economic concentrations that had been established in the early years of the twentieth century. These initial efforts did, however, set the stage for more aggressive antitrust enforcement (Reback 2009, 22–3).

The appointment of Thurman Arnold to head the Antitrust Division in 1938 ushered in a new era of antitrust enforcement that contradicted previous New Deal efforts to maintain higher price levels. Instead of defending price-fixing codes, the Antitrust Division sought to promote competition by prosecuting abuses of power by cartels and monopolies. During Arnold's five-year tenure the Justice Department prosecuted as many antitrust lawsuits as it had since the passage of the Sherman Act in 1890, using consent decrees and, where necessary, criminal indictments. Arnold's efforts lent support to the notion that antitrust enforcement was a superior vehicle to the regulatory apparatus for policing antitrust violations (Reback 2009, 22–3).

In the landmark decision *United States* v. *Aluminum Co. of America* (148 F. 2d 416 (1945)), the US Court of Appeals for the 2d Circuit reversed the rule-of-reason doctrine that had prevailed for nearly 30 years and convicted the company of monopolising an artificially defined relevant market (primary ingot aluminium). Judge Learned Hand ruled that, although Aluminum Co. of America (Alcoa) had not intended to create its monopoly, it nevertheless had a monopoly on the domestic aluminium market in violation of antitrust law, and that it would be in the nation's best interest to break it up. His decision examined both the company's overall size and its market share, arguing that a 90 per cent market share would support a charge of monopolisation, while 33 per cent would not, and 60 per cent would be doubtful. Ultimately, the case rested on finding evidence of anticompetitive conduct, specifically the 'exclusion of competitors'. Portions of Alcoa were later sold off to two competitors.

The Alcoa decision ushered in an era of aggressive antitrust enforcement. Merger standards were strengthened with the amendment of the Clayton Act in 1950 (64 Stat. 1125, 15 USC § 18, 21), and more sophisticated economic analysis provided the government with new empirical tools for measuring market concentration and competitive performance. Both scholars and government attorneys began to focus their attention on oligopolies, which were believed to exhibit some of the same anticompetitive characteristics as monopolies. This interest was spurred by a wave of consolidation in the 1950s and 1960s which brought 60 per cent of the total assets of manufacturing companies under the control of the 200 largest corporations. In 1968, a task force appointed by President Lyndon Johnson recommended that companies with a greater than 15 per cent market share be forced to divest a portion of their assets to smaller competitors (Posner 1976, 101–17; Reback 2009, 24).

Enforcement under the Warren Court

This post-war economic populism was reinforced in the Supreme Court under Chief Justice Warren E. Burger. From 1953 to 1969, the Court applied a particularly rigorous standard of antitrust enforcement. The Warren Court sought to preserve an optimum level of economic competition by protecting small-scale and locally-owned businesses from the challenges posed by larger national enterprises. While this stance might have protected small businesses from economic extinction, it simultaneously rewarded inefficiency and precluded consumers from reaping the benefits of lower prices. Indeed, it called into question the purpose of antitrust law: was it to preserve an economic status quo and protect existing businesses, or was it to serve an environment of free and open competition and the interests of consumers?

In *Brown Shoe Co., Inc.* v. *United States* (370 US 294 (1962)), the Warren Court struck down the merger of Brown Shoe Company, which produced about 4 per cent of the nation's shoes, with Kinney, which accounted for approximately 1.2 per cent of all retail shoe sales in the United States. The Court concluded that:

> We cannot avoid the mandate of Congress that tendencies toward concentration in industry are to be curbed in their incipiency, particularly when those tendencies are being accelerated through giant steps striding across a hundred cities at a time. In the light of the trends in this industry, we agree with the Government and the court below that this is an appropriate place at which to call a halt. (370 US 294, 346 (1962))

The empirical basis for government intrusion into such relatively modest levels of market penetration was scrutinised by economists and legal scholars. The epicentre of scholarship attacking the Court's position was the University of Chicago, where both legal scholars and economists began to dismantle the proposition that higher prices were an inevitable result of market concentration (Bork 1978; Posner 1976, 2001).

Economist George Stigler, for example, argued that sellers find it difficult to raise prices above market levels, even with few competitors (Stigler and Kindahl 1970). Another economist, Harold Demsetz, argued that firms encounter great difficulty in attempting to maintain monopoly positions in the marketplace. Those that charge truly monopolistic prices attract competitors whose entry will increase market output and cause prices to fall. Antitrust concerns should be invoked only when barriers to entry prevent those potential competitors from entering the market. Demsetz also argued that government activities, particularly patents and industry regulations, have a far greater impact in erecting barriers to entry than market forces (Demsetz 1974). As put later by antitrust attorney Gary L. Reback: 'The right amount of such incentive may well spur invention. But too many patents are just as bad for society as too few. The undisciplined proliferation of patent grants puts vast sectors of the economy off-limits to competition, without any corresponding benefit to the public' (Reback 2002).

In 1966, the appointment of Oliver Williamson as Special Economic Assistant at the Antitrust Division of the Justice Department also had a profound impact on antitrust doctrine. The economic models that Williamson employed gave Justice Department attorneys new tools to evaluate mergers. The models allowed them to draw distinctions between perfect competition on the one hand and complete monopoly on the other. Competitive markets show a direct relationship between price and supply. As prices rise, demand declines. In a monopoly, however, the monopolist sets prices and controls industry output. Williamson's critique argued that promoting efficiency was far more important than preventing monopolies and protecting existing inefficient producers. His research also influenced the growing conservative school of antitrust doctrine emerging at the University of Chicago (Williamson 1968, 18; Reback 2009, 25–9).

The University of Chicago School, as it came to be called, ultimately had a profound impact on the populist antitrust doctrine that had been buttressed by the 1950 amendments to the Clayton Act and enforced by a sympathetic Warren Court. The analyses and interpretations of University of Chicago economists and law professors provided the intellectual basis for a new critique of antitrust law that urged heavy reliance on economics to analyse markets and their operations. The Chicago School found the populist view to antitrust enforcement to be illogical in its application and overly ideological, arguing that it protected small and inefficient companies, ultimately harmed consumers, and produced a misallocation of economic resources. An increasingly global economic environment was presenting domestic industries with new challenges at the same time that support for stringent government regulation was waning.

One scholar whose views on antitrust underwent a dramatic evolution during this era was William F. Baxter, originally a member of the 1968 task force that had recommended forced divestitures to reduce the market concentrations that characterised many American industries. By 1980, Baxter, who was heavily influenced by the economic research that transformed the field of antitrust, was in sympathy with the Chicago School.

Antitrust Policy Since 1980

In 1981, President Reagan appointed Baxter to head the Antitrust Division, bringing economic analysis to the forefront of antitrust decision-making, and making it far less likely that monopolisation cases would be brought before the courts. Ultimately, Baxter contended that 'divestiture is appropriate … only if it will produce relief more quickly than the erosion of monopoly power that naturally occurs as competitors enter a market' (Reback 2009, 37).

Many observers now contend that the conservative critique of antitrust law, while salutary in many respects, has gone too far (see, for example, Pitofsky 2008). While acknowledging the problems of the populist approach, they also recognise that there are also limits to an approach that places undue reliance on free market forces. Gary Reback argues that:

> [t]oday, antitrust doctrine has turned timid, obsessed with the possibility of error by overzealous enforcement. Academics insist upon detailed economic theory and unambiguous facts to justify government intervention. (Reback 2009, 40)

Since the early 1980s, the US Supreme Court has substantially abandoned adherence to the per se rule in evaluating proposed mergers. Its relaxed standards have been applied to both vertical and horizontal mergers. In some cases, the Supreme Court has left the further development of merger law to the lower federal courts. The federal courts of appeal no longer rely on market share and concentration data as determinative in antitrust cases, but assign greater importance to the idea that ease of market entry by new competitors will contradict the presumption that a merger will increase market power of the merged companies.

Over the past 30 years, antitrust law has been subject not only to a mood of relaxed enforcement, but to changing patterns of national and global economics. Public sentiment in favour of government regulation and antitrust enforcement has declined at the same time that global competition has escalated. It was during this time that international business interests discovered the profit potential of professional publishing generally, and specifically of legal publishing.

The Transformation of the Legal Publishing Industry

The Emergence of Commercial Legal Publishing

In the American colonies, as in England, legal publications were produced by printers who depended upon a variety of commissions and publishing opportunities. While some may have secured commissions from governmental entities to print session laws or codified statutes, these were not sufficient to support a full-time legal publishing specialisation. It was not until the early nineteenth century that specialised legal publishers emerged in both England and the United States, including former booksellers like Butterworth, Alexander Maxwell, Stephen Sweet, and Stevens & Sons in England, and Stephen Gould (later Banks-Baldwin) in the United States. Little, Brown and Company, a general commercial publisher, also achieved prominence as a leading publisher of legal treatises from the time of its founding in 1837. The nineteenth and early twentieth centuries witnessed the appearance of other legal publishers who were eventually absorbed by their more powerful competitors or simply went out of business (Surrency 1990).

The nineteenth-century's most significant development in the field of US legal publishing, however, was the emergence of the West Publishing Company and its comprehensive system of case reporting and digesting. John and Horatio West took advantage of the pressing need among lawyers and judges for the timely and accurate reporting of court decisions. Between 1876 and 1896 West's National Reporter System of case reporting and key number system of case digesting, which provided subject access to case law, were universally embraced by the legal community. West's strong position in the marketplace as a publisher of primary law continued throughout the twentieth century as it released a number of annotated statutory compilations, including the *United States Code Annotated* in 1927. West also became an important source of legal treatises and law school textbooks, a major legal encyclopaedia (*Corpus Juris*, later *Corpus Juris Secundum*), state and federal practice books, and legal forms (Surrency 1990; Svengalis 2009, 8–14).

West's major competitor, the Lawyers Cooperative Publishing Company, adopted a different philosophy of legal publishing which emphasised more selective publication of court decisions and the creation of an integrated library of practical legal reference works for the practising attorney, called the Total Client-Service Library (TCSL). It also went head-to-head with West with its legal encyclopaedia, *American Jurisprudence*, as well as the *US Supreme Court Reports Lawyers' Edition*, and *United States Supreme Court Digest, Lawyers' Edition* (Svengalis 2009, 613–14).

Other major US legal publishers emerged in the latter half of the nineteenth century including Callaghan and Company (1864), a major source of national practitioner treatises and primary law for several Midwestern states; the Shepard's Company (1873), the premier case citation service; Matthew Bender and Company (1887), an important publisher of practitioner-oriented legal treatises; and the Michie Company (1897), a leading publisher of state statutory codes. The Anderson Publishing Company, founded in 1887, served the needs of lawyers from Ohio and neighbouring states with a line of both state specific and national titles.

US companies founded in the twentieth century included Commerce Clearing House (now CCH) (1913), Clark Boardman (1916), Bureau of National Affairs (BNA) (1933), the Practising Law Institute (1933), Research Institute of America (1935), Warren, Gorham & Lamont (1961), Prentice Hall Law & Business (1973) and John Wiley Law Publications (1983). Emerging initially as used law book dealers, the William S. Hein Company, Fred B. Rothman (acquired by Hein in 1998), and the former William W. Gaunt Company served the law library market as publishers of books, microfiche and CD-ROM, and as subscription agents and legal reprinters (Surrency 1990).

Significant twentieth-century developments also included the publication of the first loose-leaf service by Commerce Clearing House in 1913 and the introduction of the pocket part to update *McKinney's Consolidated Laws of New York* by West in 1916. In the 1960s, microforms were introduced to address the problems presented by burgeoning hardcopy collections and shrinking shelf space.

Computer-Assisted Legal Research

The 1970s brought transformational developments in the field of legal information delivery. In 1973 Mead Data Central introduced Lexis, the first computer-assisted legal research system, a development which influenced the law and the process of legal research in ways rivalling the appearance of West's National Reporter System in the nineteenth century, and even print publication itself. Two years later, West introduced its own system: Westlaw. In the late 1980s, the introduction of legal titles on CD-ROM further transformed the nature of legal publishing and legal research (Svengalis 2009, 8).

In the 1990s, the emergence of the World Wide Web opened up tremendous potentialities in the worlds of education and commerce. The development of sophisticated search engines and web directories allowed people to more fully tap resources available on the Internet. In 1994 WebCrawler, the first full-text web search engine, was introduced. Lycos, another full-text search engine, was the first to achieve commercial success. During the late 1990s both web directories and web search engines were popular. Yahoo! and AltaVista, both founded in 1995, became industry leaders. By 2001 the directory model began to give way to search engines such as Google (founded in 1998) that offered more effective techniques for relevancy ranking (Svengalis 2009, 8).

The web transformed the delivery of legal information from being the exclusive province of a few large commercial databases such as Lexis and Westlaw, with their own proprietary search protocols, into one in which information is accessible from multiple sources. The Internet provides the technology to allow companies large and small to tap its commercial possibilities. The benefits, however, have chiefly accrued to companies with the financial capital to assemble the largest body of intellectual content and the most sophisticated and integrated electronic search capabilities.

By the mid-1990s, it was obvious that a globally competitive legal information business needed several key elements to compete successfully:

1. a sophisticated and content-rich computer-assisted legal research system
2. comprehensive libraries of state and federal primary law

3. a substantial body of secondary and analytical resources in all major legal sub-specialties, and
4. a citator service capable of providing timely and accurate verification of legal authorities

By the time the dust had settled on the wave of acquisitions that enveloped the legal information industry, there were only two companies which stood on the top tier of this legal information hierarchy: West (Thomson Reuters) and LexisNexis (Reed Elsevier). The second tier is occupied by Wolters Kluwer, a company that, while it commands some impressive legal information products and services, cannot match the comprehensive capabilities of West (Thomson Reuters) or LexisNexis (Reed Elsevier) (Svengalis 2009, 4).

Enter the Thomson Corporation

The company that would eventually become the world's largest purveyor of legal information had its roots in the wilds of northern Ontario. Canadian Roy Thomson, a radio salesman, came to realise that the best way to sell radios was to own and operate radio stations. The Thomson Corporation was established in 1934 when he also became publisher of *The Timmins Daily Press*, the first of many Canadian newspapers he acquired in the 1930s and 1940s. In 1949, he expanded beyond Ontario, and in 1952 entered the US market. In 1953 Thomson acquired the *Scotsman* newspaper. He strengthened his media position in Scotland in 1957 when he won the franchise for Scottish Television and in 1959 bought the Kemsley Group, giving him control of the *Sunday Times*. He separately acquired *The Times* in 1967. He moved into the airline business in 1965 by acquiring Britannia Airways, and into oil and gas exploration in 1971 when he participated in a consortium to exploit reserves in the North Sea. By 1976, the year he died, the major portion of the corporation's profits were derived from its oil interests. Following the death of Lord Thomson the company divested some of its media holdings and began shifting its attention to publishing (Svengalis 2009, 619).

Prior to 1979, most American legal publishing companies were family-owned or controlled by individuals with both a history in legal publishing and a direct knowledge of the legal information market. By the late twentieth century, however, most were sufficiently distanced from their roots that their current owners saw greater financial advantage in selling them off than in continuing to manage their operations. Callaghan and Company, a publisher of legal treatises founded in Chicago in 1864, was the first of these formerly family-owned businesses to fall to the Thomson juggernaut. It was the start of a new era in which law books, and legal information generally, would be viewed increasingly as commodities, to be managed for maximum financial return. With its attention now focused on the profit potential of legal publishing, Thomson next acquired two legal treatise publishers: Clark Boardman and Warren, Gorham & Lamont in 1980.

In 1989, Thomson substantially augmented its legal publishing holdings with the acquisition of Lawyers Cooperative Publishing Company and its subsidiary Bancroft-Whitney, Research Institute of America, followed by Maxwell Macmillan in 1991. In 1994 the company acquired three additional legal publishing entities: Information Access, Counterpoint Publishing and Information America. In 1995, Shepard's decision to spin off its legal treatise catalogue and to re-focus on its core citator service provided Thomson with another buying opportunity. Also in 1995, Thomson acquired Barclay's Law Publishers, a San-Francisco-based publisher of state administrative regulations. The one target that eluded Thomson's grasp during this period was Mead Data Central, the parent company of LexisNexis, which was acquired by Reed Elsevier in 1994 (Svengalis 2009, 619–20).

Thomson Acquires West Publishing

In 1995 West Publishing, the crown jewel of legal publishing, shocked the legal world by announcing that it was for sale. The Thomson Corporation was poised to acquire a company that could provide it with the online database necessary to complement its strong position in the publication of both primary and secondary legal materials. West was exactly what Thomson needed to pursue its broad-based strategic objectives.

On 26 February 1996 Thomson announced its plan to purchase West, and its subsidiaries Foundation Press and Banks-Baldwin, for the sum of $3.425 billion, pending antitrust clearance by the Department of Justice. Industry analysts contended at the time that Thomson paid an excessive price for West, probably $1 billion more than its true worth based on historic sales. The purchase price was four times the company's historic sales of $800 million and 16 times its operating profits of slightly more than $215 million. For a business that was increasing its revenue at only 10 per cent per year, such multiples were very steep. Reed had not only paid a lower multiple for LexisNexis but was also able to cut its effective purchase price by $300 million by exploiting tax advantages not available to Thomson. While Reed was able to increase LexisNexis' profit margins from 11 to 16 per cent, the view was that Thomson would not be able to improve significantly upon West's healthy 25 per cent profit margins. In retrospect Thomson has been able to maximise the profit potential of the thousands of supplemented titles in its catalogue (Svengalis 2009, 620).

Despite some early indications that it would force some major concessions from the merging parties, the Department of Justice ultimately accepted a watered-down consent decree which provided almost no relief to consumers troubled by the size and market power of this legal publishing behemoth. Law librarians, in particular, were troubled by the price escalations that had followed previous Thomson acquisitions, which were already threatening the standing order as a central operating principle for purchases in many law libraries. Attorneys at the Department of Justice's Antitrust Division, who reflected the antitrust philosophy then in place, summarily dismissed protests from law librarians, large and small legal publishers, and others (Reback 2009, 271–84).

Prior to the merger, Thomson controlled 35.08 per cent of the legal treatise market, or 187 of the 533 leading treatises selected for inclusion in the first edition of the *Legal Information Buyer's Guide & Reference Manual*, coincidentally published for the first time in 1996. These were the titles published under the Clark Boardman/Callaghan, Warren, Gorman & Lamont, Lawyers Cooperative, and Shepard's imprints. The purchase of West added another 96 titles, bringing the total to 283 titles, or 53.09 per cent of the market. West also brought its position as the leading publisher of US case law, federal and state statutory law, other practitioner-oriented publication and services, and, of course, its impressive Westlaw online legal research system (Svengalis 2009, 620).

The consent decree specified that Thomson-West divest itself of 51 print titles and Auto-Cite, Lawyers Cooperative's electronic citation verification service. Included among the print titles were *United States Reports, Lawyers' Edition*, *United States Supreme Court Digest, Lawyers' Edition*, *United States Code Service*, *Corbin on Contracts*, *Appleman's Insurance Law and Practice*, *Deering's Annotated California Code*, *Illinois Jurisprudence*, the *Annotated Laws of Massachusetts*, *Callaghan's Michigan Digest*, *Michigan Statutes Annotated* and the *New York Consolidated Laws Service*. Also included were 30 state-specific titles of no real consequence whose presence on the list only served as cover for the weaknesses of the consent decree. Only six national treatises were included, the greatest indication that the consent decree was a hollow instrument.

These six titles, in the subject areas of bankruptcy, contracts, criminal law, federal practice and insurance law, represented only 1.1 per cent of the 533 treatises selected for inclusion in the first edition of the *Legal Information Buyer's Guide & Reference Manual.* In each of these five subject areas the Thomson-West percentage of market control ranged between 63 per cent and 73 per cent. The Justice Department provided no relief in at least 12 additional subject areas in which the Thomson-West market share ranged from 63 to 85 per cent, including: administrative law; admiralty and maritime law; arts, entertainment and sports law; civil rights; constitutional law; education law; municipal corporations; products liability; social security; taxation; tort law; and trusts and estates.

The Antitrust Division's second major error was in permitting Thomson-West to gain control of both systems of legal research: West's Key Number System of case digesting, and Lawyers Cooperative's Total Client-Service Library System (which has now been fully integrated into West's product line). The Thomson-West attorneys were able to persuade Justice Department lawyers that comparing the two systems was like comparing apples and oranges. In doing so, they not only distorted the fact that both are valid and useful methods of conducting legal research, but succeeded in distancing themselves from years of Lawyers Cooperative's marketing and promotional literature which described the TCSL system as 'a comprehensive legal research system' covering 'everything from on point cases in both state and federal jurisdictions, to principles of law, statutes, procedure, model forms, trial techniques … in short, everything you need to handle almost any legal matter' (Svengalis 2009, 10).

What can explain the Antitrust Division's inept performance in accepting such a feeble consent decree? The Thomson-West lawyers had offered to license openly West's star pagination, the page breaks in the West case reporters, to other publishers, albeit at hefty rates certain to deter all but the largest. At that point, believing they had forced a major concession from the merging parties, the government lawyers were ready to sign on the dotted line (Morris 1996, 73). When the consent decree was crafted, the merger was allowed to proceed.

The only step remaining was for the final imprimatur of the US District Court for the District of Columbia. However, the legitimacy of West's claim to copyright in star pagination was already under heavy fire in the aftermath of *Feist Publications, Inc.* v. *Rural Telephone Service Co.*, 499 US 340 (1991). In *Feist*, the US Supreme Court had dismissed the 'sweat of the brow' theory of copyright protection. Then, in *Matthew Bender and HyperLaw* v. *West*, SDNY 94-Civ. 0589, May 19, 1997; 158 F. 3d 674 (1998), the US Court of Appeals for the Second Circuit ruled that the elements of West's case reports which HyperLaw sought to copy are not copyrightable (Svengalis 2009, 10). Only then, did the Justice Department lawyers who had crafted the consent decrees realise that they had accepted what turned out ultimately to be a worthless concession.

Since its acquisition of West, Thomson has acquired a number of additional US-based legal information providers, including Federal Publications (1998), Dialog (2000), Findlaw (2001), the Harrison Company (2002), Andrews Publications (2003), Elite Information Systems (2003) and Glasser Legalworks (2004) (Svengalis 2009, 14–15, 621–2).

In May 2007 Reuters, the world's largest multimedia news and data services company, entered into a definitive agreement with Thomson under which Reuters agreed to be acquired by Thomson for the sum of $17.2 billion in cash and stocks. The agreement was finalised in April 2008. The merger, which was reviewed by both the US Department of Justice and the European Commission, required the divestment of databases responsible for approximately $25 million in revenues, a small fraction of the two companies' combined revenues of more than $13 billion. After the merger, the Woodbridge Company, a holding company for the Thomson family, held 53 per cent of

Thomson Reuters (Svengalis 2009, 621). In 2009, its Professional Division was reorganised into three segments:

- Legal (formerly North American Legal and Legal & Regulatory)
- Tax & Accounting (formerly Thomson Tax & Accounting)
- Healthcare and Science (formerly Thomson Healthcare; and Thomson Scientific)

Thomson Reuters, headquartered in New York City, now has more than 55,000 employees worldwide and annual revenues of more than $12.997 billion. Its Legal Division reported 2009 revenues of $3.586 billion, reflecting an operating profit margin of 32.2 per cent (Thomson Reuters 2009 Annual Report 2010).

Reed Elsevier

Reed Elsevier, now the second largest international purveyor of legal information, is an English–Dutch conglomerate created in 1993 by the merger of Elsevier and Reed International PLC. Headquartered in London and Amsterdam, it now has over 32,000 employees and realised $9.144 billion in revenues in 2009. Its LexisNexis division realised revenues of $3.850 billion, with an operating profit margin of 26 per cent (Reed Elsevier 2009 Annual Reports and Financial Statements 2010). Reed Elsevier operates through four major divisions:

- Elsevier (the science and medical publishing division)
- LexisNexis (the legal publishing division)
- Reed Business Information (the business division)
- Reed Exhibitions

Prior to the union of Reed International PLC and Elsevier in 1994, Reed had acquired several publishing entities catering in whole or in part to the legal market: Congressional Information Service (1979), R.R. Bowker (1985), University Publications of America (1988), and the legal directory publisher Martindale-Hubbell (1990). In 1994, however, it became a major player in the legal information marketplace with the acquisition of Mead Data Central, a leading online research service headquartered near Dayton, Ohio. Mead owned the legal research services Lexis and Nexis, a full text news and business information service. The acquisition also included subsidiaries: Michie, a publisher of state statutes and legal treatises, and Butterworth's, a publisher of British, Canadian and US statutes and legal practice materials. The acquisition of Mead also brought with it the Folio Corporation, an InfoBase management software subsidiary, Jurisoft, a legal software division, and the Lexis Document Services division that offered manual searching, filing and retrieval services.

In 1998, Reed Elsevier acquired Matthew Bender & Company, a major publisher of practitioner legal treatises, the Shepard's citator service, CD Law, a minority interest in web-based rival VersusLaw, and in 2002 Anderson Publishing. Times Mirror, a major publisher of newspapers, magazines and professional publications, had acquired Matthew Bender & Company in 1963, but sold both Bender and its one-half interest in Shepard's to Reed Elsevier in 1998 for the sum of $1.65 billion. Reed Elsevier also acquired Gould Publishing and Seisint, Inc. in 2004, state regulatory publisher Weil Publishing in 2005, and Redwood Analytics and Choice Point in 2008. The $4.1 billion acquisition of Choice Point initially aroused opposition from the Federal Trade

Commission on antitrust grounds but was subsequently approved when Reed Elsevier agreed to sell its US public records business serving the government sector (Svengalis 2009, 9).

Wolters Kluwer

Currently occupying third place in the international legal publishing triumvirate is Wolters Kluwer, a leading global information services and publishing company providing products and services for professionals in the health, tax, accounting, corporate, financial services, legal and regulatory sectors. The company was founded in 1987 when Kluwer Publishers merged with Wolters Samson as a defensive move against an attempted hostile takeover of Kluwer Publishers by Elsevier.

Wolters entered the legal information market in 1994 when it acquired Aspen Law & Business. In rapid succession, Wolters acquired Commerce Clearing House in 1995, the Little Brown legal treatise line in 1996, Wiley Law Publications in 1997, and Loislaw.com in December 2000. In 2002, Wolters Kluwer acquired Casenotes Publishing Company, a leading publisher of study aids for law students, and Wolters Kluwer North America acquired Charles D. Spencer & Associates, a leading provider of print and online pension, benefits and compensation information. Aspen Publishers, Inc. acquired Accounting Research Manager (ARM) from Arthur Anderson in September 2002, and Bowne & Company's securities publishing division in October 2002. Unlike its competitors, Wolters Kluwer lacks a top-drawer computer-assisted legal research or citator service. Its Loislaw and GlobalCite are no match for Lexis and Shepard's or Westlaw and KeyCite (Svengalis 2009, 9).

Wolters Kluwer had revenues of $4.240 billion in 2009. Its Tax, Accounting & Legal Division had revenues of $1.113 billion and an operating profit margin of 25.87 per cent. Its Tax & Regulatory Europe Division recorded revenues of $1.590 billion and an operating profit margin of 19.75 per cent (Wolters Kluwer 2009 Annual Report 2010). With headquarters in Amsterdam, it employs approximately 18,400 people worldwide and maintains operations across Europe, North America and Asia Pacific. Its principal divisions include:

- Health & Pharma Solutions
- Corporate and Financial Services
- Tax, Accounting & Legal
- Legal, Tax & Regulatory Europe

The Current State of Legal Publishing

By 1998, the basic contours of the current legal information oligopoly had taken shape, sanctioned by the US Justice Department's Antitrust Division. Three international conglomerates controlled an estimated 90 per cent of the US legal information market. Of the three, Thomson Reuters now commands roughly 40 per cent of the US legal information market, Reed Elsevier 31 per cent, and Wolters Kluwer about 29 per cent. West, representing the Legal component of Thomson Reuter's Professional Division, commands the largest share of the most essential and desirable enhanced legal products, many of which are annotated to West's legal taxonomy and provide citations to relevant primary and secondary authorities. As such, West has been in a position to set high and extremely profitable prices, particularly for the various forms of supplementation, print and online, that constitute roughly 85 per cent of its annual sales and profits. West's market position has enabled it to raise supplementation prices at rates averaging over 12 per cent annually since

1996 (Svengalis 2009, 16–17). The profit margin of the Legal Division was an industry-leading 32.2 per cent in 2009 (Thomson Reuters 2009 Annual Report 2010). Corporate profit margins generally have averaged 8.3 per cent over the past 25 years and 10.3 per cent in recent years (Katsenelson 2006).

Reed Elsevier and Wolters Kluwer both monitor West's pricing decisions. West's industry-leading pricing levels encourage them to follow and share in the oligopoly profits. Reed Elsevier's profit margin for LexisNexis rose from about 16 per cent in 1995 to 26 per cent in 2009 (Reed Elsevier 2009 Annual Report 2010, 16; Svengalis 2009, 10). West's profit margin, by contrast, rose from about 25 per cent pre-merger in 1995 to 32.2 per cent in 2009 (Svengalis 2009, 10). For Wolters Kluwer's Tax, Accounting & Legal Division, the comparable 2009 figure was 25.87 per cent (Wolters Kluwer 2009 Annual Report 2010). The annual supplementation costs of treatises published under the Matthew Bender imprint, for example, have edged upward over the past 10 years from about 5 per cent to about 8 per cent annually (Svengalis 2009, 18). Under these circumstances, as Hovenkamp suggests, firms may reach an understanding about price without formally communicating. That they have not chosen to compete more aggressively on matters of price reflects the fact that, generally speaking, oligopolies tend to compete on product differentiation rather than price (Hovenkamp 2005, 98).

The legal information oligopoly flourishes in an atmosphere characterised by: (1) a lax antitrust policy that allows the creation of overpowering market giants; (2) commanding market presence and tactics that exclude new challengers; (3) the right to curb retail price competition; and (4) excessive patent and copyright protection. According to the Chicago School, with no barriers to entry, monopoly profits will continue only until competitors grab market share and force down prices in the process. Industry analyst Jeremy Grantham argues that:

> Profit margins are probably the most mean-reverting series in finance, and if profit margins do not mean revert, then something has gone badly wrong with capitalism. If high profits do not attract competition, there is something wrong with the system and it is not functioning properly. (Katsenelson 2006, 1)

In the field of legal publishing, however, there are no signs that profit margins are likely to mean-revert for the reasons cited above. The wave of mergers and acquisitions between 1979 and 2009 swept the decks clear of almost all potential market rivals. With the exception of the Bureau of National Affairs, those that remain are generally small, specialised firms incapable of mounting a challenge to the existing oligopoly. Even Wolters Kluwer, which acquired Loislaw in 2000, has been unable to capitalise on that acquisition and transform it into a serious competitor to Westlaw or Lexis (Reback 2009, 283). In the unlikely possibility that one of the smaller legal publishers might eventually pose a challenge to the oligopoly, it most likely would be bought up by one of the big three, without a meaningful challenge from the Antitrust Division.

While one must acknowledge that the Thomson-West merger catalysed substantial productivity gains by more fully exploiting the potential of computer-assisted legal research and the synergies of the combined intellectual content and research systems brought under the Thomson umbrella, those gains were not passed on to consumers in the form of lower prices. To the contrary, the price and supplementation cost increases, particularly for print publications, passed on to consumers in the wake of the 1996 Thomson-West merger had a devastating impact on law libraries and consumers nationwide, forcing most to reduce drastically their subscriptions to West titles, including long-held subscriptions to print reporters. In addition, in the United States the pricing policies have imperilled the existence of many local law libraries serving the bar and pro se patrons. Indeed, no single development since the emergence of commercial legal publishing in the mid-nineteenth century has had a more devastating impact on the market for legal information than the Justice Department's approval of Thomson's acquisition of West Publishing in 1996. Barring unforeseen circumstances, the legal publishing oligopoly is likely to continue to dominate the market, both domestically and internationally, for years to come.

References

Books and Articles

Areeda, P. and Hovenkamp, H. (2006), *Antitrust Law: An Analysis of Antitrust Principles and Their Application* (3rd edn) (New York: Aspen Publishers), vol. 1.

Armentano, D. (1990), *Antitrust and Monopoly: Anatomy of a Policy Failure* (2nd edn) (Oakland: Independent Institute).

Bing, J. (2010), 'Let there be LITE: A Brief History of Legal Information Retrieval', *European Journal of Law and Technology* 1:1. Available at: http://ejlt.org//article/view/15, accessed 9 June 2010.

Blum, J.M. (1959), *From the Morgenthau Diaries: Years of Crisis, 1928–1938* (Boston: Houghton Mifflin).

Bork, R. (1978), *The Antitrust Paradox: A Policy at War with Itself* (New York: Basic Books).

Demsetz, H. (1974), 'Two Systems of Belief about Monopoly', in *Industrial Concentration: The New Learning*, ed. Harvey J. Goldschmidt, H. Mann and J. Weston (Boston: Little Brown).

Hovenkamp, H. (1994), *Federal Antitrust Policy: The Law of Competition and its Practice* (St. Paul: West Publishing).

Hovenkamp, H. (2005), *Antitrust* (St. Paul: Thomson West).

Katsenelson, V. (2006), 'The Profit Margin Paradigm', The Motley Fool [website], 1 March. Available at: www.fool.com/investing/value/2006/03/01/the-profit-margin-paradigm.aspx, accessed 12 March 2011.

Morris, J. (1996), 'How West Was Won', *American Lawyer*, September.

Pitofsky, R. (2008), *How the Chicago School Overshot the Mark: The Effect of Conservative Economic Analysis on US Antitrust* (New York: Oxford University Press).

Posner, R. (1976), *Antitrust Law* (2nd edn) (Chicago: University of Chicago Press).

Reback, G. (2002), 'Patently Absurd', *Forbes ASAP* 169:14, 44–8, 24 June. Available at: www.forbes.com/asap/2002/0624/044.html, accessed 12 March 2011.

Reback, G. (2009), *Free the Market: Why Only Government Can Keep the Market Competitive* (New York: Portfolio).

Reed Elsevier 2009 Annual Reports and Financial Statements (2010).

Stigler, G. and Kindahl, J. (1970), *The Behavior of Industrial Prices* (New York: National Bureau of Economic Research).

Surrency, E. (1990), *A History of American Law Publishing* (New York: Oceana Publications).

Svengalis, K. (2009), *Legal Information Buyer's Guide & Reference Manual* (13th edn) (North Stonington: Rhode Island Law Press).

Tarbell, I. (1904), *The History of the Standard Oil Company* (New York: McClure).

Thomson Reuters 2009 Annual Report (2010).

von Kalinowski, J., Sullivan, P. and McGuirl, M. (2008), *Antitrust Laws and Trade Regulation* (Newark: Matthew Bender & Co.), vol. 1, §§ 2.01–2.02.

Williamson, O. (1968), 'Economies as an Antitrust Defense: The Welfare Tradeoffs', *American Economic Review* 58:18.

Wolters Kluwer 2009 Annual Report (2010).

Woods, T., Jr. (2009), *Meltdown: A Free Market Look at Why the Stock Market Collapsed, the Economy Tanked, and the Government Bailouts Will Make Things Worse* (Washington, DC: Regnery Publishing).

Cases

Brown Shoe Co., Inc. v. *United States*, 370 US 294 (1962).
Feist Publications, Inc., v. *Rural Telephone Service Co.*, 499 US 340 (1991).
Matthew Bender and HyperLaw v. *West*, SDNY 94-Civ. 0589, May 19, 1997; 158 F. 3d 674 (1998).
Schechter Poultry Corporation v. *United States*, 295 US 495 (1935).
Standard Oil Co. (N.J.) v. *United States*, 221 US 1 (1911).
United States v. *Aluminum Co. of America*, 44 F. Supp. 97 (1941).
United States v. *Aluminum Co. of America*, 148 F. 2d 416 (1945).
United States v. *American Tobacco Co.*, 221 US 106 (1911).
United States v. *E. C. Knight Co.*, 156 US 1 (1895).
United States v. *United States Steel Corp.*, 251 US 417 (1920).

Statutes

Clayton Act 38 Stat. 730 (1914), 15 USC §§ 12–27.
Clayton Act Amendments 64 Stat. 1125 (1950), 15 USC §18, 21.
Federal Trade Commission Act 38 Stat. 717 (1914), 15 USC §§ 41–58.
Sherman Act 26 Stat. 209 (1890), 15 USC §§ 1–7.

Chapter 12
Collection Building: Foreign, Comparative and International Law in Print

Holger Knudsen

The Relevance of the Topic for Law Librarians

> Libraries, like the Universe, are finite but constantly expanding. But the rate of book production continues to rise. Even large research libraries are now becoming resigned to being selective rather than offering comprehensive collections. No library can have it all now.
>
> (Martin 1991)

This chapter deals with the acquisition of printed materials for foreign, comparative and international law by law libraries. While it is true that digital materials gain an ever more important place in the field of information provision, it is also true that printed materials still play an important role. Nobody knows the exact figures of global book production and statistics are virtually non-existent and those few that exist are not very reliable. It may suffice to say that shortly before the end of the millennium about 903,000 books were published annually worldwide, based on the global figures (ascertained country-by-country in 1996, although some few countries delivered earlier data) recorded in the last Unesco *Statistical Yearbook* (Unesco 1999, IV-80, IV 90).[1]

At first glance, almost a million newly published books per year seems like an extremely surprising figure but, if one gives it further thought, it does not seem particularly overwhelming, given the billions of human beings and potential book writers who inhabit our planet.

There is reason to believe (but no proof) that the number of newly published books has further risen since 1996 in spite of the many possibilities of digital publishing. This may be due to improved publishing opportunities in developing countries and the ongoing need to 'publish or perish' in the academy. The number of 903,000 books relates to all kinds of topics but it is possible to gain an idea of the approximate number of law books published worldwide using figures from national bibliographies arranged according to subjects. In virtually all of them, between 3 and 5 per cent of the national book production appears in their law section. So the idea becomes quite clear: about 4 per cent of the books published worldwide are law books. This in turn means that, if reference works and relevant books from neighbouring fields are added, about 40,000 to 50,000 books published every year are law books. Indeed, no library can have it all now.

Foreign, international and comparative law librarianship is different from all the other fields of librarianship for seven reasons:

---

1 It is a pity that this important source of information has ceased publication.

- law is a genuinely national affair
- national law is based on the national language(s)
- the meanings of legal terminology are different from jurisdiction to jurisdiction
- the format of legal sources differs from jurisdiction to jurisdiction
- there are no unified rules for citation
- specialised law publishers (if any) differ from country to country
- the system of legal bookselling (if any) differs from country to country

Law is a genuinely national affair and this makes it very different from other fields of knowledge with the exceptions perhaps of some rather limited fields of interest like foreign literature, foreign history and ethnology. The forces of gravity, the principles of algebra, the patterns of infant language acquisition, and the techniques of archaeological excavations are the same worldwide. A researcher dealing with chemistry, astronomy, physics or medicine can gain expert knowledge reading literature published in his own country and in his own language. Concentrating on these limited sources, successful researchers may not need to be able to read any language apart from their own. The same is true for researchers dealing exclusively with their own national law and for librarians serving them. Such a pattern is still possible for very large jurisdictions even though the world of law becomes ever more interrelated. In many of these cases the story ends here: the required literature is easily identified, easily ordered and easily delivered through a national bookseller, easily put on the shelves and (perhaps not so easily) studied:

> Academic and firm [law] librarians face increased demand for information. These demands are often difficult because many attorneys and students, as well as many librarians, are untrained in international legal research and lack formal training in international law. As international legal work expands … librarians must endeavour to become better equipped to respond to these new demands, both in terms of building collections and learning international research techniques. (Strzynski 1995)

A new story begins, however, when a librarian must acquire, collect and provide access to foreign, comparative and international legal materials. There are about 200 states in the world and so inevitably 200 legal systems worldwide and, as a matter of fact, even more since quite a number of states are federal and composed of entities with their own laws, sometimes combining intricate mixed legal systems under one legal roof as in Canada and the United Kingdom. The confusing multitude of differing legal systems is the first aspect one must keep in mind when dealing with foreign law, the law of countries other than one's own. International law (the law which governs trans-border situations and the relationship between states) differs from foreign law since much of the basic literature in the field is available in generally accessible languages. Treaties, however, are concluded in the languages of the contracting parties (although for the most important ones there might be unofficial translations) so international law must be considered as difficult as the national law when it comes to studying the sources and to interpreting them:

> Much of the demand from university and special libraries is for material required for research purposes. The researcher does not normally wish to read in a foreign language per se: he is obliged to do so by the fact that the relevant research findings are not available in any other language. Provision of such material raises a number of intractable problems, including those relating to selection and acquisition. (Spiller 1986, 180)

Dealing in depth with any foreign legal system is impossible without a genuine knowledge of the national language(s). There are sometimes explanatory books and articles or translations of laws (some are very commendable indeed) into languages other than the one of the jurisdiction concerned. However, this does not follow a regular pattern and is based on chance, the interests of the authors, the profit expectations of the publishers, and on what can be called the 'SOS principle': *S*horten, *O*mit and *S*implify. This is the second aspect to keep in mind when it comes to collection building. One must further keep in mind that that there are not only individual books about the legal system of a single jurisdiction but also books (still often in looseleaf rather than electronic format) which describe two or more legal systems from a comparative point of view. These true treasures are often overlooked by patrons looking for information about a foreign legal system. With the advent of catalogue enrichment it is to be hoped that they might be better known, used and appreciated in the future.

There are thousands of languages in the world; in Europe alone there are 34 languages spoken by more than one million native speakers plus more or less the same number of languages with fewer native speakers. The language barrier is a real obstacle for serious research and no one, librarians and their patrons alike, even in the best case, can have a command of more than a handful of languages. In spite of all the available translations and explanatory works, it is never possible to become an expert of a foreign legal system without a thorough command of the jurisdiction's language.

Lawyers are normally trained to apply their own national terminology. Applying terminology involves working with concepts, but certain concepts may not exist in all legal systems. Many common law terms are completely unknown in the civil law systems and vice versa, or they may be understood differently, for example the concepts of property or free speech. Both a chemistry librarian dealing with acids and an art librarian dealing with Corinthian columns know exactly what their topic is about and there is little space for ambiguity. The possible terminological ambiguity in the field of foreign, comparative and international law is the third aspect librarians must bear in mind.

Lawyers and law librarians dealing with foreign law for the first time are often surprised or even shocked when they notice how much other formats differ from the system they know. While the appearance, layout and handling of legal monographs and periodicals generally do not pose problems of format, official journals, law collections, court decisions and finding tools do, and to quite an extent. Even experienced reference librarians who have not worked with foreign materials for a while must try to get acquainted with them anew each time they use them. It is simply impossible to memorise all the different formats.

Closely linked to the problems of format are the intricacies of citation and the mysteries of abbreviations. A citation is normally composed of one or several abbreviations and quite like the law itself it is a genuinely national affair. There are and there will be no universal or unified rules for citation and a lot of experience is required before a citation can be applied or decoded:[2]

> Today, the entire world is of interest. As with most other aspects of our lives, the world as we see it is expanding and the boundaries are shrinking. Not only are we interested in the laws of the entire country but of the entire world. As business opportunities expand across the globe, so do disputes,

2 A very good and knowledgeable solution to cope with the problem is the *Guide to Foreign and International Legal Citations* (New York University Law School 2009). It is arguably better than Harvard's Blue Book (*Bluebook* 2010), even though the *Guide*'s section of select references was not brought up to date for all jurisdictions.

> and international conflict of laws has become an important issue to lawyers worldwide. Gaining access to the laws of all nations has become a major difficulty facing law librarians today. (Panella 1990, 17)

Only a few libraries can afford to collect the law of the whole world and even those that can face severe problems since there are many countries from where, most unfortunately, it is in the best case difficult and in the worst case impossible to obtain the materials. Often there are neither publishing houses nor reliable booksellers. This is unfortunately true for most African countries (notable exceptions being the Republic of South Africa and perhaps to a lesser extent Egypt), most successor states of the former Soviet Union (with the exception of Estonia, Latvia, Lithuania, Russia and Ukraine), virtually all the mini-states of the Caribbean and the Pacific area, and many Asian states like Afghanistan, North Korea, Laos, Nepal, Bhutan, Burma, Cambodia, Yemen.

Basic Considerations

> Before a library innocently begins to dabble in foreign law collecting, it ought to contemplate the possible consequences and the alternatives. (Kearley 1995, 259)

Once the decision is made to build a foreign law collection and the necessary financial resources and staff are obtained, the process of building the collection should advance carefully and step by step, keeping in mind that there are both 'easy' and 'difficult' countries. For most libraries it would be more advisable to concentrate in the beginning on countries for which the provision of a basic collection is reasonably feasible. The bare minimum must be: a collection of laws (preferably in an updated systematic format since using chronological collections entails the risk of overlooking important changes); a collection of court decisions; the leading law review; and a good stock of textbooks. The tools provided must at least enable the patrons to obtain an overview over the jurisdiction and to solve basic legal questions. If a collection offers less than these minimum holdings it is worthless and a waste of funds. Reference materials are indispensable and, as a matter of fact, the smaller and less equipped a library is, the more helpful and important is a good collection of reference materials acquired abundantly. It should be noted that reference work has become much easier recently since so many useful materials are now freely available on the Internet. But it must also be kept in mind that while the author(s) of a book can be identified under normal circumstances, providing a strong indicator for their reliability and expert knowledge, freely available digital sources on the contrary often do not allow any such presumption. As a result, they should be cross-checked whenever possible.

Collection Development Plans vs. Flexible Collection Building

> Perhaps the most telling argument against having a written collection development policy is that so many libraries do not have one – indeed most of the great library collections of the world were originally created without such policies. However, there is no doubt that they (and the collections of any major library without a written collection development policy) have been guided by a well-understood, unwritten policy. (Clayton and Gorman 2001, 20)

There is a strong belief in the Anglo-American world that collection development must be based on collection development plans. Textbooks on librarianship from the United States and the United Kingdom are full of complicated theoretical considerations about the nature of collection development plans and they are stuffed with practical hints about their contents and sample models for their layout. There is nothing wrong with these plans as long as they inform in a general manner about a library's collection profile. They might even be extremely helpful when it comes to explaining to a troublesome patron why a library is not willing to buy a requested item. But soft rules risk becoming a Procrustean bed when they are mistaken as hard laws. Unless development plans are regularly adapted to changing circumstances, a venture that needs a lot of time which could be better used for other purposes, they may soon become outdated. Neither is it possible to predict precisely the future output of literature and the development of new topics, nor to know the future needs, and the future budget, of the institution which the library serves. Librarians should not become dependent on collection development plans but rather rely on their talents and on their training. If the selection criteria outlined below in the section on 'Criteria of Collection Building' are applied properly, such plans may be superfluous.

The Basic Problems and Challenges of Collection Building

Knowing about a Book and Getting it into the Library

> Collection development can be divided into two steps. The first is the intellectual process of selecting which titles should be purchased. The librarian who performs this function must know the scope of the patrons' needs and interests and have a familiarity with the library's collection. Since few law libraries have unlimited resources, those resources must be allocated among the materials needed to satisfy the current needs and to build a collection that will satisfy the needs of the future.
>
> The second step is ordering, receiving, and processing the books. Although the second step may not have the intellectual quality of the original selection process, if the procedures are not orderly and systematized, resources will be wasted. (Long et al. 1983, 258)

The existence of a book must be known before it can be considered for acquisition. This interdependence is a variation of the classical balance between supply and demand. It is a variation characterised by significant disparities because market mechanisms in the field of book publishing and bookselling are in many states restricted through a variety of measures (price guarantees, and subsidies on the one hand, but shrinking library budgets on the other hand). The times in which the number of books available was so low that all published books could be known by the savants of the era ended with the destruction of the original Alexandria Library 2,000 years ago. In our times the rate of book production is so high that many books have no chance to be read by the public to whom they are aimed, while even a known book will often not be acquired and read due to a lack of funds. The ever-growing number of interlibrary loan requests proves this only too well.

There is no general method to find out about new publications because, quite like the law, which is a culture that differs from country to country, legal publishing is a culture that to a surprising extent differs as well. Thus librarians have to apply a variety of techniques to learn about new foreign publications.

There are 'easy' countries like Italy, India, Spain, Romania or Brazil, where reliable booksellers provide lists of new publications on a regular basis or send regular mails, pointing to new publications. This is a relationship built on trust and there is a danger of libraries becoming dependent on the choice of the booksellers. This choice may in turn be based on the financial expectations of a bookseller and the easy availability of books. There is also an innate risk that the booksellers charge higher prices for their services in countries that do not have a legally binding system of fixed prices for books and other publications such as in existence in Germany. There is nothing wrong with checking the completeness and the prices of the bookseller's offers at random every so often. The Internet of course eases this venture enormously. Blanket orders are not a solution since establishing and regularly adapting a profile can be even more difficult than establishing a collection development plan, and booksellers quite naturally tend to interpret these orders in their favour.

There are countries such as Germany and the United Kingdom with no such booksellers but with a good national bibliography, which is also sometimes useful even for books that are still in the process of publication. There are other countries that require a regular screening of the book review section of one or several of their law journals. To name just a few, the leading journals of the Netherlands (*Nederlands Juristenblad*), of Finland (*Lakimies*), of Sweden (*Svensk Juristtidning*) and of Switzerland (*Schweizerische Juristenzeitung*) contain an almost complete list of recently published law books in each respective country.

Catalogues of publishing houses, in print or digital formats, have a bibliographical value but they are not primarily made for this purpose. They are definitely not made to define the value of a book because they are conceived as marketing instruments. Librarians are well advised to keep this restriction in mind when reading the mouth-watering descriptions in such catalogues. They are, however, particularly useful for the quite surprising number of countries where one single publishing house has almost a monopoly in legal publishing, be it Porrua in Mexico, Normas Legales in Peru, Almedina in Portugal, Manz in Austria, Sakkoulas in Greece, or Juta in South Africa. Then there are countries where two leading legal publishing houses like Abeledo Perrot and Depalma in Argentina, Bruylant and Larcier in Belgium, Kluwer and Boom in the Netherlands, Round Hall and Tottel in Ireland, or Universitetsforlaget and Gyldendal in Norway almost share the market. Of course there are also smaller publishing houses in those countries but if a law librarian has to select literature from these countries it will normally be sufficient to concentrate on these leading publishing houses. This situation is good from a librarian's point of view because it very much simplifies an overview, even though it may be bad for the legal publishing culture of any one country.

The ever growing number of countries that have never provided, or recently failed to provide, an established book-selling system is becoming a problem difficult to cope with. Exchange (see the section below on Exchanges and Gifts) can be helpful, as are itinerant booksellers who buy books in the respective countries as well as they can and, once they are back home, try to sell them through catalogues. Libraries which have visitors from these countries can try to obtain literature through such a channel but this is very tiresome for both sides, and it is not normally very successful. The only rule that remains is that there is no rule for this type of country whose legal materials are less accessible, and collection building is much dependent on chance.

The comments above refer primarily to new publications. There may, however, also be the need to provide less recent materials. This should not pose as large a problem as in the past since union catalogues on the Internet provide all kinds of materials when they are consulted for a legal term or the name of an author. Choosing literature according to a title can entail some risks, however, as will be explained in the next section.

Selecting books is one issue. Getting them into the library is a completely different one. A specialised library needs a network of competent and reliable booksellers. It takes a lot of time to establish such a network, and to review it periodically in order to find out whether new and better (the word 'better' here implies the term 'less expensive') booksellers have established themselves on the market.

Coping with New Legal Developments

'A librarian who reads is lost', is a well-known and true rule. Even if one invests some efforts, it is not possible to keep abreast of new trends through reading. Knowing about new trends and new laws is, however, particularly important in law librarianship. Law books, unlike books in other fields of the humanities, are outdated the very moment the laws or judgments or policies on which they are based are superseded through new laws or new judgments or new policies. So the one question that law librarians are frequently asked is: 'Are you sure this is still valid'? Often one must rely on coincidence in this case. Sometimes journal issues are dedicated to new laws. Sometimes it is easy to understand that there must be new developments since suddenly a plethora of books and articles is published on a subject with which no one had dealt to such an extent before. Sometimes library visitors from the respective countries may point out that changes have occurred or are due to occur. Sometimes a subtitle indicates that a new law has been taken into consideration by the author. The word 'new' in the title of a book can be an indicator of up-to-date materials but in some cases it can be a marketing tool and should always be looked at with some scepticism and reservation. By the way, if the title cheats there is a strong reason to believe that the contents may cheat as well.

It is not possible to devise a strategy for coping with legal developments in 200 countries but acquisition librarians should at least have an idea about the major jurisdictions they are supposed to deal with. Otherwise there is a risk of investing the available funds erroneously.

Building a Collection or Buying on Demand?

It is sometimes indispensable to buy books and to add them to the library stock, even though they do not seem to be necessary for a collection or the patrons' needs at the moment of decision-making. The decision to buy them nevertheless is based on the assumption that they might be useful in the future and on the prediction of a lack of future availability. However, for many countries with a working bookselling system such a procedure is not necessary if quick delivery is guaranteed. If a book isn't used, its acquisition was a waste of funds. If it is needed later, it can be bought when the time has come and it may possibly even be a more recent edition. Having the most recent edition only will not be harmful under normal circumstances since the average lawyer always looks for the most up-to-date literature and few patrons need former editions for historical research. Einstein's ideas are timeless even after three generations while current laws and secondary legal materials can become superfluous the very moment the law changes or a court decision supersedes prior decisions.

So, if only very limited use of a book or a chapter of a book can be expected, it may sometimes be more efficient to provide it or to provide copies from it via interlibrary loan. Of course if there is a once-in-a-lifetime chance to buy materials from very remote countries the considerations above do not apply as long as the materials fall into the library's profile in the broadest sense.

Fashion Topics, Duplicates, 'Dusters' and other Cheeks

Fashion topics are a hassle for every librarian. The first savants who wrote about, for example, the economic analysis of law or corporate governance were geniuses but most unfortunately those authors who came after them to write about the same topic were often *epigones*[3] who did not offer many new insights to say the least. Real fashion topics are inevitably linked to the problem of duplication. Books on the competition law of the European Union or the history of the GATT/WTO, for example, are very numerous and can be counted by the hundreds. Last and least in this area come many doctoral theses of little or dubious value. It should be noted that under normal circumstances this type of literature is produced not from the desire to contribute to the progress of mankind but to earn an academic title. However, as always, the exception proves the rule. Generally they merit the nickname 'duster' as they collect bits and pieces from other and normally better predecessors. Theses often cover fashion topics and they also often fall into the category of 'duplicates'.

In all these cases all too abundant acquisition would absorb an enormous amount of money in an unreasonable way without contributing to any substantial supplementary gain in knowledge. Thus acquisitions librarians must have the courage to live with gaps, based on the certainty that their patrons would not miss much value.

Authenticity vs. Accessibility

This section deals with the question whether a library should acquire original materials, even if no one or only very few patrons can properly use them, or whether in these cases a library should rather buy secondary materials in more accessible languages. It deals, in other words, with the conflict of authenticity versus accessibility. Sometimes the decision-making is eased when a country is bilingual or multilingual. For example, Switzerland is a trilingual country with German, French and Italian as national languages and many patrons may prefer to consult the French versions of laws and court decisions. Finland is a bilingual country where the official materials, among them the official gazette, are not only published in Finnish but also in Swedish, which is the second official language of the country. Of course only a very small number of legal textbooks from Finland are published in Swedish so one runs the risk of missing important texts. In the case of Israel, everything in English is unofficial of course and a lawyer should always work with official texts. Yet does it make sense to store texts which are likely to never be used? Texts which are often difficult to obtain and expensive and which may be outdated by the first time they are used? In the case of those countries which are inaccessible owing to their language and a lack of area specialists a decision should be made in favour of accessibility. In all the other cases authentic materials should be used as standard as much as possible.

Exchanges and Gifts

> You will have to be careful of donations. Individuals will 'dump' their complimentary issues of magazines and expect that you maintain them. Have a clear policy of which journals and donations you will track and maintain. (Kreizman 1999, 36)

Exchanges must be avoided whenever possible. They absorb a lot of staff time as controlling reliable delivery and corresponding with the foreign exchange partner needs specialists and is

3 *Epigone*, a successor, follower or imitator, often inferior.

time consuming. Under normal circumstances an exchange takes place between a partner in a rich country who wants to enlarge the collection of a particular 'difficult' jurisdiction, and a partner from a poor country who strives to build at least a core collection of a major jurisdiction. Books from rich countries are normally very expensive; books from poor countries are not. This means that a partner from a poor country has to send a lot of material (cheap, but sometimes extremely difficult to get) in order to receive a comparatively very small number of books from the rich partner. Alternatively, both sides may agree to exchange an even number of titles, but this will not please the accountants of the rich partner. However one looks at it, there is no ideal situation. Exchanges should be established only when there is no other commercial way of acquiring literature and when there is a strong indicator of a stable and reliable relationship for a foreseeable future. Because they are so tiresome for both sides exchanges often fail after a while.

A word about gifts: at first glance, they are cost neutral since their acquisition is free. However, the incorporation of a gift into a collection requires time and staff, so the question of costs must also be asked in the case of gifts. Librarians should reserve the right to refuse gifts. They may indeed be very welcome additions to the collection but in many cases they seem to serve the self-promotion of the authors, particularly in the case of donated off-prints, rather than the needs of the patrons. Most libraries share the fate of having insufficient space, so the available space should not be jammed with useless items.

Journals

> The content or focus of a serial can change dramatically over time and if a title has been subscribed to for a few years it may be necessary to look at how heavily it is used and whether or not it still matches the selection criteria. (Henczel 2001, 242)

Law journals are, most unfortunately, an extremely expensive business and their subscription entails enormous costs. Major law libraries spend a considerable amount of money on journals to which must be added additional funds used for bookbinding. Every new subscription absorbs a lot of money which moreover cumulates over the years. Not only do librarians have a particular responsibility when it comes to selecting journals, they also must try to cap the number of subscriptions in order to avoid being strangled by rising costs for subscriptions to the detriment of the acquisition of monographs. Of course, there are new trends which must be considered in the collection but there are always also old fields for which no one has an interest any longer. Every so often journals become defunct. It is the librarian's task to identify periodicals from these fields and to stop their subscription in the interest of the coverage of new fields. It is always a difficult and sad decision to stop a subscription, particularly if a journal was collected over many years or even decades. But, cruel as it seems, the beauty of uniform spines ranged on the shelves and the completeness of a collection ought not to be an argument for the decision to continue subscriptions of little research value in a research library.

Criteria of Collection Building

> Much of what has been written and published is very much concerned with the how of acquisitions and very little with the why, whence, or whither. (Gorman 1990, v)

Scope of the Library and Needs of the Patrons

'Acquisition policy should be in line with the objectives of the library' (Kumar 2009, 156). The selection process for literature must aim at buying 'relevant' materials, and this is always based on the same criteria:

- is the book needed right now?
- if not, is there any good reason to believe it will be needed in the near future?
- if yes, can the library afford to buy the book?
- if yes, can the acquisition be renounced because there are books of the same, or better, quality already in the library, or in the process of acquisition? Or because technical arguments (for example a new edition is to be expected soon) make an acquisition appear inappropriate?

The basic question of any acquisitions librarian in our times is not any longer 'Should we have this book?', but rather 'Can I justify my refusal to buy this book? Do I have good reasons?'. More often than outsiders may expect, the answer is 'Yes!'. Choosing a book means working with priorities and this automatically implies the necessity to accept 'posteriorities'.[4]

'The first rule of collection development: There are no rules. Every law library is different' (Heller 2007, 89). This translates into the need for every librarian to select, without, however, exercising censorship. At this point, a preliminary observation: uniform principles for selection do not exist. Each library has its own unique place in the dichotomy of scientific or public, universal or special, big or small, rich or poor, old or new, public or private, teaching or research library. Therefore the pattern of collection building of any single library must be based on its position in this matrix.

When selection criteria are applied, a further point of view must be considered: their unequal weighting. There are primary criteria which stand alone when it comes to the evaluation of legal literature and there are secondary criteria which come into play only in exceptional cases and in cases of doubt, where they can be used as additional reasons for selection or non-selection. These two groups can be further subdivided, again with a different valence, into the following groups:

- primary criteria relating to aspects of substance and quality: for example content of a book, and its author
- primary criteria relating to aspects of format and quantity: for example price of literature and number of pages
- secondary criteria relating to aspects of substance and quality: for example language of a book and its publishing house
- secondary criteria relating to aspects of format and quantity: for example type of binding or age of a book

By far the most important criterion in the decision-making process is the suitability of a piece of legal literature for a collection. In this process the past, the present and the future must be taken into account.

The past in a library is reflected through the continuity of a historically grown collection. This may, in some cases, absorb some resources but, if a library with historic holdings gives up the

4 'A great deal could be said about the analysis of priorities. The most important thing about priorities and posteriorities is, however, not intelligent analysis but courage' (Drucker 2009, 104).

process of collection building by not adding adequate materials, it runs the risk of generating dead capital and eventually becoming useless.

In a good collection future value and future benefit of acquired literature plays an important role; the future will indeed be 'present' sooner or later. In other words, the literature which is bought today should be useful for future generations. Librarians should not see themselves as crisis managers with a short-term orientation, but their work and their vocation should always be based on long-term considerations. This relates to treaty collections, to collections of court decisions and, to some extent, to official journals (all three categories are often in a bond of past and future), to pioneering monographs and to commemorative publications. Librarians therefore need to apply a strategic manner of thinking, which has nothing to do with prophetic gifts but rather with professional anticipation of future developments. Yet, a forecast which is based on the state-of-the-art and which seems to be scientifically sound may subsequently appear to be inaccurate. Inevitably such a forecast is based on the knowledge, structures, trends and projections which exist at the time of its creation and it may be wrong. This 'right to commit an error' applies to all forecasts in all fields of knowledge and not just to library collection development.

The tasks of the present are of course the most important for a decision on the suitability of a work. This means first and foremost that the essential needs of readers at the time of the acquisition process must be met. Absolute substantive completeness as a goal can hardly ever be achieved and it is only conceivable in a small number of cases. An example is when a library has narrowly defined areas of specialisation and so tries to acquire the available literature entirely and without regard to quality aspects (a city library collects everything about a city, a firm library collects everything about the founder of the company and his family).

Title of a Publication

> Although librarians prefer to see the book they are considering buying, they often, for a number of reasons, buy some books they have only seen listed in a bibliography. There is a danger of course in this in that the book when it arrives may not be any use. But the librarian's experience means he can evaluate fairly accurately books that he has comparatively little information about. (Whittaker 1982, 20)

Foreign books, in the majority of all cases, can only be chosen according to their titles and subtitles. Titles and subtitles may be misleading, or too pompous, or they may promise more than their actual contents eventually reveal. Such incorrect information is a nuisance in all cases but can infuriate a librarian when a book is particularly expensive. This can happen with all kinds of literature: 'comparative studies' where the comparison has been pressed into some few pages, 'handbooks' which are composed of completely useless information, 'complete guides' which are neither guides nor complete, 'commentaries' which only contain minimal annotations, 'new and entirely revised editions' where the alleged changes are not apparent, and so on. In these cases there is little or no chance to send the books back to the foreign booksellers, though one may try. There is no remedy against incorrect information and one must keep in mind that the readers make their first choice according to the title as well. So librarians and their patrons sit in the same boat and run the same risk of choosing a wrong item. Law librarians do enjoy an advantage over their colleagues in charge of other fields of knowledge in spite of the risks mentioned above: in the majority of cases, the contents of law books can be seen from the legal terms used on the title page. Metaphorical titles are rare in the field of law and thus no one really expects them. However, they do exist. A good example is a book by the title *Le divorce belge*, which does not deal with Belgian divorce law, but with the language conflict between Flemings and Walloons. Misleading titles of this kind are probably unavoidable but they are a *quantité négligeable* and they are therefore rather harmless, particularly if a library collects in ancillary subject areas into which they may fit. Perhaps more dangerous than books with misleading titles are items with very general titles which do not indicate their possible value for a library so they are not considered for acquisition. This often applies to collections of conference papers and other contributions. However, if these books are particularly good they may sooner or later be reviewed so a librarian will have a chance to learn about their existence later. In this case gaps can be closed relatively quickly so the damage is only temporary in nature.

A word about patrons' proposals for acquisitions: as a rule they must be considered as positive because they may describe gaps in the collection. However, they do not liberate librarians from the obligation to review a proposed item themselves. There are notorious 'experts' who believe that the entire literature published in their field or quoted somewhere must be considered an absolute priority. On the other hand there are inarticulate patrons who would not dare or bother to make proposals but who have a special know-how and special skills. Librarians should try to ask foreign guests to be helpful with the improvement of the collection of their country and thus 'exploit' of this kind of patron.

Author(s) of a Publication

Next to the title, the name of the author(s) or the editor(s) can be an indicator of the value of a book. This must not be treated as an equivalent to a guarantee of success, as very prominent authors may produce works of inferior quality. Yet libraries often cannot avoid purchasing books from such authors and this celebrity bonus is owing to a phenomenon that is known as the St Matthew effect (after St Matthew 25:29, 'For unto everyone that hath shall be given and he shall have abundance'). Readers look for books by prominent authors and thus generate automatic success: prominent authors publish in prominent journals and, moreover, their books enjoy a higher frequency of new editions. It is not always possible to define what is cause and what is effect. New editions from prominent authors often differ from previous editions by only marginal changes. For this reason librarians should, whenever possible, accurately verify whether new editions of works by prominent authors are so distinctive that a purchase is really necessary or whether at least the purchase of multiple copies can be waived. This is particularly important in the case of very limited periods between original and new editions.

Publishing House and Part of a Series

One of the icings on the cake for a positive or negative acquisition decision is the publishing house of a title and, in many cases, the name of the series to which a title belongs. There are prominent publishing houses known for the excellence of their publications, there are good publishing houses known for solid craftsmanship which rarely disappoints the readers, and there are publishers who have rather dubious reputations. In all of these three cases the exception proves the rule. The same applies to series, but in most cases there is interdependence between a publishing house and quality, and a series with quality.

Price of a Publication

> Judgement of a 'good buy' is only one element of selection, very much sub-ordinated in importance to the subject and quality of the book. In theory there should be few cases where a 'good' title is not

> ordered at all because the price is considered too high. In practice, price does often seem to weigh quite heavily in selection decisions. (Spiller 2000, 21)

Over recent years libraries have had to face two problems: an explosion of costs for conventional materials and new technological developments and trends which have forced them to allocate an ever growing amount of money for the new research tools. The truth is cruel: no library can spend more money than is budgeted. It might be appropriate to clarify this commonplace rule with an example from outside the legal sphere: the most expensive publication from Germany is Beilstein's multi-volume *Handbook of Organic Chemistry*, which costs almost half a million euros. It is evident that every library dealing with questions of organic chemistry should have it. It is, however, also evident that most of these libraries cannot afford to buy this publication. They must look for other solutions and find a compromise between scientific ambition, teaching necessities, and the funds available.

Format of a Publication

Library users generally tend not to take as good care of library materials as they may take of their own books. This means that the binding of a book is relevant in the decision-making process. Durable hard covers must be preferred whenever a heavy use can be expected, while the cheaper alternative paperback should be envisaged only for items for which little use can be predicted or which have a high frequency of new editions. A word about the subspecies looseleaf editions: of course there are many instances in which their acquisition cannot be avoided but if it can be avoided it should be avoided for four reasons. Firstly looseleaf collections, like periodicals, are a financial burden as they absorb a lot of money over the years, secondly and thirdly updating them is staff intensive and subject to errors and this is particularly true for foreign collections. They are also a nuisance for their readers because it is often extremely difficult to make copies from them. Readers may thus decide to fumble around trying to get the respective pages out or even tear them out right away, but do not normally (manage to) replace them in the correct order. Readers may even decide to steal them as, last but most certainly not least, looseleaf collections are most unfortunately especially popular when it comes to the easy theft of individual pages, the replacement of which needs in turn more staff time. It is not always a solution to buy the basic edition of a looseleaf edition and renounce buying the updates as many basic editions are simply composed of binders which are almost empty so that the complete work can only be obtained by buying the follow-up pages.

Size of a Publication

It is not a very scientific method to evaluate the value of a publication by drawing conclusions from the number of pages it contains. There is nevertheless nothing wrong with the presumption that a booklet about a topic cannot offer much information compared to an extensive work. An associated problem is the uncompleted work: the gradual appearance of a title announced to be published in several volumes, of which only, for example, 'Volume 1: General Theory of…' is available. In order to avoid 'ruins' on the shelves it might sometimes be better to wait to see whether further volumes will ever be published.

Age of a Publication

As pointed out above, lawyers normally look for recent publications so the age of literature envisaged for acquisition plays a significant role. Law librarians, therefore, should be very careful when it comes to buying older texts. Of course a five-year-old text from, say, Nepal or Haiti will certainly be worth buying (if a library can obtain it and if it falls into its profile) but there is a strong reason to believe that texts of the same age from, say, India or Ecuador are outdated and that there is better and more recent material available.

Parallel Availability in Electronic Format

> One current discussion topic among librarians involves the debate about 'access versus ownership'. Libraries are moving toward the access of information (electronically), which usually also includes a reciprocal move away from ownership of resources (books). (Agee 2007, 45)

At the time of writing CD-ROMs are a moribund species already even though publishers still love to pep up many of their publications with CD-ROMs. In the case of doubt, an added CD-ROM should be an argument against the acquisition of material and not in favour of it. Quite like books, CD-ROMs are outdated the very moment they are produced, but, quite unlike books, they are dependent on software and hardware and often cannot be used after only a few years when hardware or software, or both, have changed.

Databases, electronic journals and electronic books are expensive and do not represent any visible value on the shelves but, when they are carefully chosen according to the need of the readers and the quality of their producers, they cannot be matched when it comes to current and up-to-date information. Apart from the problem of accessibility (password administration and prevention of unauthorised use) and license agreements, no publisher is prepared to guarantee permanent electronic archiving. Also, in times of ever growing budget restrictions, one should consider that print material that has once been bought will remain the property of the respective library forever. Once a subscription of digital materials must be stopped, there may no longer be any access, even though a lot of money might have been paid out.

More and more countries and international organisations are making their legal materials available on the Internet for free, and in some instances, following the example of the pioneering Belgium, no longer have printed official journals available. While it is to be hoped that the number of countries which offer their legislation for free will grow, it is also true that there are all too many countries in the world that are so poor that they cannot produce such electronic sources. It is a new and welcome trend that law courts, mainly supreme courts, are making their decisions available in electronic format and it is to be hoped that more courts will follow this example.

Lawyers are by nature conservative beings and they are reluctant when it comes to making their publications freely available in digital form. As long as careers can only be built on printed publications in renowned journals and series, this situation is not likely to change. But with the advent of the open access movement it is to be hoped that more and more valuable publications will be accessible for free.

The Life Cycle of Literature

> The management of collections includes not only the selection and acquisition of new stock, but also the withdrawal of stock when it is no longer contributing to the utility of the collection. (Brophy 2005, 120)

Weeding is the identification of those items that no longer add value to the collection. The alternative term 'deselection' clarifies this and the decision to deselect a book follows the same principles that govern the selection of literature, but in a reverse way. This, like the selection decision, is dependent on the library's function and on its patrons: a library for law students will weed former editions of teaching manuals and heavily used items, while an archival library with historical holdings will be more reluctant when it comes to deselect.

Conclusion

In spite of the growing importance of digital and other non-conventional materials the acquisition of conventional printed materials continues to play an important role in law libraries. Law is distinct from other fields of knowledge as there are no rules with a global value. It is basically a national affair and this makes it so difficult for the acquisition specialist. There are problems which need to be resolved (how to know about the existence of materials, how to get them, how to make a difference between authentic and original materials, etc.) before a decision can be made. Such a decision is always based on criteria, the two most important ones being the title and the author. A wrong application of criteria inevitably leads to a wrong decision.

Postscript

The brilliant essay 'De bibliotheca' (Höfer 2005, 7–13) by Umberto Eco may help to clarify this idea. In it Eco looks at libraries as through a mirror, thus describing the ideal library in a reverse, ironic form and in 19 points. For example: 'Call numbers must be impossible to transcribe and preferably extensive' or 'No more than one book at a time may be lent out'. It is quite striking that an experienced library visitor like Eco (following his own testimony) reduces the organism library exclusively to readers' services in his essay. Seemingly he believes that a library must (and can) provide all the literature the reader requires. This idea is of course very naïve from a librarian's point of view, but Eco finds himself in good company and librarians understand his error only too well. It is difficult to explain why literature is not available when it should be in the library and this underlines the obligation of every acquisitions librarian to reflect well and to make careful purchasing decisions. In this respect to the 19 theses of Umberto Eco a twentieth could be added: 'Books will be purchased only if there is a guarantee that they are useless for the library and that no reader will ever be interested in them. Books by dubious authors and from questionable publishing houses must be given preference. Outdated, expensive and possibly voluminous books in a bad state of preservation and in possibly exotic languages and print are to be preferred'.

References

Achieving Excellence: Proceedings of the 4th Asian-Pacific Special and Law Librarians' Conference with 9th Biennial Health Librarians' Conference held in Canberra 1–5 September 1991, Supplement One (1991) (Canberra, ACT: Special Libraries Section and Health Libraries Section of the Australian Library and Information and the Australian Law Librarians' Group).

Agee, J. (2007), *Acquisitions Go Global: An Introduction to Library Collection Management in the 21st Century* (Oxford: Chandos).

Balleste, R., Luna-Lamas, S. and Smith-Butler, L. (eds) (2007), *Law Librarianship in the Twenty-First Century* (Lanham: Scarecrow Press).

Bluebook: A Uniform System of Citation (2010), 19th edn compiled by the editors of the *Columbia Law Review*, the *Harvard Law Review*, the *University of Pennsylvania Law Review*, and the *Yale Law Journal* (Cambridge, MA: Harvard Law Review Association).

Brophy, P. (2005), *The Academic Library* (2nd edn) (London: Facet).

Clayton, P. and Gorman, G. (2001), *Managing Information Resources in Libraries: Collection Management in Theory and Practice* (London: Library Association).

Drucker, P. (2009), *The Effective Executive*, revised edition (Amsterdam, Heidelberg: Butterworth-Heinemann).

Eco, U. (2005), 'De Bibliotheca', in Höfer, 7–13.

Gorman, M. (1990), 'Foreword', in Schmidt, K.A. (1990), *Understanding the Business of Library Acquisitions* (Chicago: American Library Association), v–vii.

Heller, J. (2007), 'Collection Development, Licensing, and Acquisitions', in Balleste et al., 89–116.

Henczel, S. (2001), 'Selecting Information Resources for the Special Library', in Scammell, 236–53.

Höfer, C. (2005), *Libraries* (Munich: Schirmer/Mosel Verlag).

Kearley, T. (1995), 'Foreign and International Collections, Part 1: Foreign', in Kehoe et al., 257–312.

Kehoe, P., Lyman, L. and McCann, G. (eds) (1995), *Law Librarianship: A Handbook for the Electronic Age*, AALL Publications Series no. 47 (Littleton: Rothman for the American Association of Law Libraries).

Kreizman, K. (1999), *Establishing an Information Center: A Practical Guide* (London: Bowker-Saur; reprinted Munich: De Gruyter-Saur, 2000).

Kumar, P. (2009), *Law Librarianship* (Delhi: B.R. Publ.).

Long, R., Martin, H. and Buckwalter, R. (1983), 'Acquisitions', in Mueller and Kehoe, 237–328.

Martin, H. (1991), 'Wizards of Oz: Architects of the Virtual Library', in *Achieving Excellence*, 4.

Mueller, H. and Kehoe, P. (1983), *Law Librarianship: A Handbook*, 2 vols, AALL Publications Series no. 19 (Littleton: Rothman for the American Association of Law Libraries).

New York University School of Law (2009), *Guide to Foreign and International Legal Citations*. (2nd edn) (New York: Aspen).

Panella, D.S. (1990), *Basics of Law Librarianship* (New York: Haworth Press).

Scammell, A. (ed.) (2001), *Handbook of Information Management* (London: Aslib-IMI). This is the successor title to Aslib's *Handbook of Special Librarianship and Information Work*, which appeared in seven editions, and is termed 8th edition on the title page.

Spiller, D. (1986), *Book Selection: An Introduction to Principles and Practice* (4th edn) (London: Bingley).

Spiller, D. (2000), *Providing Materials for Library Users* (6th edn) (London: Library Association). Earlier editions published as *Book Selection*.

Strzynski, J. (1995), 'Foreign and International Collections, Part 2: International', in Kehoe et al., 313–48.

Unesco (1999), *Statistical Yearbook / Annuaire Statistique, 1999* (Paris: Unesco).

Whittaker, K. (1982), *Systematic Evaluation: Methods and Sources for Assessing Books* (London: Bingley).

Chapter 13
Shaping Electronic Collections in Foreign, Comparative and International Law

Marylin J. Raisch

Introduction

Researchers in international and foreign law currently rely both on large digital archives and on what Elizabeth Anderson, the Executive Director of the American Society of International Law, has described as a 'think net' (Anderson 2008, 2, 16).[1] In a think net, officials in governments and intergovernmental organisations, advocates and experts connect virtually, integrating text, images and sound by posting the primary documents of international or local law as well as interpretive, analytical and critical commentary. Taken together, these are the sources of international law as listed in Art. 38 of the *Statute of the International Court of Justice*:

- treaties and conventions
- judicial decisions and writing of publicists
- custom of nations
- general principles of law[2]

The specific texts described by the first two sources: treaties and judicial decisions (along with the most widely respected and accepted scholarly commentary) are now immediately available electronically in multiple formats, including scanned images or PDFs, mostly from the official bodies that have issued the sources in print or manuscript formats throughout the history of international law.

The latter two categories of source material, which more involve the process of deriving law than specific texts, have never been easier to access. Finding evidence for custom, which is found mostly in digests or yearbooks of practice in international law, now requires only access to fee-based or to free (and official) Internet databases which are searchable comprehensively in a manner not known in the world of print indexes, some of which cumulate only periodically. Similarly, the general principles of law can be found in electronically available summaries, and evidence of newly emerging areas of consensus can now be obtained by surveying the laws of individual jurisdictions on the Internet. Again, there are both free and official sources for these laws and codes. In addition, private publishers gather and translate them for users of dominant commercial languages. While access is not yet in uniformly standardised formats or always at stable URLs, the

---

1 For Anderson a 'think net' is 'a network of experts that can be convened – physically or virtually – for various lengths of times and for different purposes'. Think nets are 'leaner' than think tanks, with expertise in the network and, I would add, available at the drop of a hat. Such a network may have been formed after the US Supreme Court's decision *Boumediene et al.* v. *Bush* (12 June 2008) in the blog *Opinio Juris*. Available at: http://opiniojuris.org/2008/06/12/boumediene-insta-symposium, accessed 8 August 2010.

2 Available at: www.icj-cij.org/documents/index.php?p1=4&p2=2&p3=0, accessed 9 August 2010.

body of available foreign law from reliable sources on the Internet grows continually. Finally, the treatises that have traditionally arrayed the shelves of the physical library are also slowly beginning to appear electronically while the search for the best technology to access and display them is continuing. Patrons of academic libraries expect to consult these treatises on public and private international law as well as national, comparative and transnational law.

In light of these advances, how does one provide structured access to an electronic library of international and comparative law? The electronic library will have the same conceptual framework as a print library and contain digital versions of the same titles and sets of materials as the traditional print library. One can list the locations of electronic versions or create a list of the best databases, as Timothy Coggins did in his excellent list of essential recommended 'Foreign & International Law Sites for Lawyers' (Coggins 2009, 15–17). However, new platforms for library catalogues and the library website itself can both do more than list links; document repositories can cross-link sources that illuminate one another by placing electronic citation guide links to the full text and employing other more sophisticated presentations (Woutersen-Windhouwer et al. 2009).

The purpose of this chapter is to describe a well-structured electronic library of international and comparative law and to suggest how this library might be created. It will focus on the following three areas of activity.

Selection of the best free and commercial databases for international and comparative law research using criteria for evaluating content and functionality.

Integration of databases and their content, including what on the free web might be referred to as portals, into a tool for discovery and access.

Presentation of this information through an integrating tool, which could be an integrated library system (ILS) or catalogue with enhancements for bringing together web and print sources, or could take the form of a library or information centre-based mega-portal for a law firm or academic institution. The presentation of electronic sources might appear in two such locations in parallel, using the strengths of both types of web presentation, with a personal space or account for the researcher. An information centre created today for a new firm or institution, with minimal materials in print or other formats, would present a strong case for setting up a knowledge portal without the ILS backbone. Such portals exist today for large organisations such as the United Nations and the European Union, as well as in smaller law firms or non-governmental organisations.

Selection of Databases for International and Comparative Law: Collection Policies, Practices and Evaluative Criteria

Collection Policies and Electronic Legal Information

As libraries moved into the twenty-first century, electronic formats became prevalent, varied and well-established in all library collections, including those that deal with foreign, comparative and international law (FCIL). Even a cursory scanning of publicly available collection policies shows that electronic databases are frequently included as natural parts of the collection rather than being listed separately.[3] In her discussion of collection policies for FCIL collections, Barbara Garavaglia reviews the typical components of collection development policies and selection

3 For collections of law library policies for academic law libraries over the years, see www.aallnet.org/sis/tssis/committees/acquisitions/collectiondevelopmentpolicies, accessed 9 August 2010.

criteria under the general heading of 'Organization and Content of FCIL Collection Development Policies' without distinction as to format (Garavaglia 2007).

The convergence of evaluation criteria with collection development has taken place most thoroughly in the context of information disseminated by government entities around the world. These criteria are presented here at the outset because legal information is in fact different from many other kinds of information. The Access to Electronic Legal Information Committee of the American Association of Law Libraries has developed categories of evaluation and produced a detailed worksheet for evaluating government websites, with links to exemplary sites in the United States.[4] Perhaps more important for this overview is the Committee's statement of 'Principles & Core Values Concerning Public Information on Government Websites',[5] which states (in summary) that the best websites should be:

- Accessible to all in the sense of being free (or in the case of a law school or law firm with paid databases, at least capable of being shared by a defined class of patrons), compliant with the needs of the disabled, searchable, navigable and accompanied by guidance and, ideally, language translation
- Trustworthy and reliable, stable
- Comprehensive (which one might interpret at least as transparent as to actual coverage, full-text availability, and date restrictions)
- Archived and preserved through as many means as possible while maintaining availability, with a view toward anticipating the need to migrate information onto new platforms and through future developments in technology

Clearly many of the principles also arise within a value system that looks to the rule of law and the transparency required for democratic promulgation of the laws. These principles serve the world of commercial databases equally well since the market for information services will be driven by comparison of databases and 'consumer reports' of how well the information serves customer needs when choices can be made.

The *Internet Scout Project*[6] has published reports and reviews on the quality of Internet sites since 1994 and it is one of the best known. The *Scout Report* is issued weekly and has published its selection criteria, which apply to both free and commercial databases, and carry weight across a wide range of disciplines and approaches to information. The categories of criteria include the following (with the gloss in parentheses being mine): Content (accuracy); Authority; Information maintenance (currency); Presentation; Availability; and Cost.

The best overall selection tool with a similar current awareness feature focusing on legal information is Cornell Law Library's InSITE service,[7] which has an RSS feed. The site can be browsed by topic and archived annotations of sites can be searched. International and foreign law are covered, each designated as a separate topic. Free sites are covered.

Even with these tools, selectors of electronic information are still left with many new sites and advertised databases to review and evaluate, both from established publishers such as Wolters Kluwer and Brill/Nijhoff, and from independent or university-affiliated presses now turned online

---

4 The specific categories of evaluation (which include authority, stability and trustworthiness among others) and links to the websites and worksheet are posted at www.aallnet.org/committee/aelic/criteria.html, accessed 9 August 2010.

5 Available at: www.aallnet.org/committee/aelic/AELIC_Core_Values.pdf, accessed 9 August 2010.

6 Available at: http://scout.wisc.edu/Reports/ScoutReport/about.php, accessed 9 August 2010.

7 Available at: http://library2.lawschool.cornell.edu/insiteasp/default.asp, accessed 9 August 2010.

publishers. In the online world, some elements of a publisher's reputation in the print scholarly world persist, even if the structure and navigation of a good website remain elusive for the very best names in scholarly publishing. A search in journal databases, many of which are available by subscription only, is also required to supplement reviews of databases. As a result the tasks of collection development for electronic information are similar to those for print, but add the need to look in detail at the specific evaluation criteria for databases. Arguably, legal training or other academic credentials may be more valuable for electronic selection than they have been for print. On the free web, since one cannot rely on resources being vetted by scholars and professional editors, much of the analysis of the content must be based on legal research experience and knowledge, together with application of the criteria suggested here.

The Free Web: Accuracy and Currency

Even when collection policies still treated electronic media separately, evaluation criteria for electronic databases and web-based information were discussed in the law library literature. Some of the criteria suggested as early as 1997 are still valid and the categories of evaluative criteria are surprisingly consistent across a variety of sources. Free website criteria have been proposed principally for the *creation* of websites containing a database element and the *selection* of websites containing a database element. The distinction between database and mere website has been described by Mirela Roznovschi, as follows:

> An Internet 'site' can be any URL in the Internet which contains a document (e.g. a treaty, a decision, a law), a collection of data, or just an index to some sources gathered by some good-hearted persons. There are many good Samaritans on the Internet. By contrast, 'database' means subject-oriented data gathered and maintained in a server by an official entity, displaying a high interactivity with the user as well as search engine capability, data records files, query or sales transactions, product catalogs etc. (Roznovschi 2000)

The idea that a database must be maintained by an official entity is a factor in evaluating its accuracy (as will be discussed in greater detail below), but was noted by Roznovschi in the context of discussions of foreign law databases. Since 2000, the idea has become part of the common understanding for organizing databases. A 2009 textbook definition states that 'a database is an organized collection of facts and information, typically consisting of two or more related data files' (Stair and Reynolds 2009, 12).

Evaluative Criteria for Free Legal Website and Database Creation

Discussion of technical standards and detailed design features of websites and databases is beyond the scope of this chapter, but some assistance in assessing successful databases and hypertext environments for legal research may be derived from 'peeking behind the curtain' of the best websites. Marie S. Newman has described the standards set for a premier free web database and portal, Pace University School of Law's United Nations Convention on Contracts for the International Sale of Goods database (CISG),[8] which won the International Association of Law Libraries Website Award in 2002. Her article describing the elements of this excellent example of scholarly Internet publishing continues to provide guidance both for authors as well as reviewers

8 Available at: www.cisg.law.pace.edu, accessed 12 August 2010.

of major free web resources, particularly in academic and other serious institutional settings, even more than a decade after its appearance (Newman 1999). In addition to the core requirements of accuracy and currency mentioned above, Newman's other criteria include substantive content, uniqueness, good design (including consistency and accessibility through 'text only' alternatives for disabled users with screen readers), and good search capabilities (including Boolean and phrase searching) (Newman 1999, 3–5).

It is no coincidence that some of the best architectural features for Internet scholarship and digital databases (as well as repositories) both on the free web and in the commercial sphere are seen in international and comparative legal databases. The CISG database, established through careful, unstinting labour on the part of Marie Newman and her Pace colleague Albert H. Kritzer deals with the organisation and translation of jurisprudence across the many languages of the CISG states parties. Article-by-article analysis includes treaty commentary and secondary legal scholarship on the international sale of goods. Used together with Michael W. Bonell's UNILEX database,[9] a researcher has access to two dynamic databases organised on two different approaches to searching: CISG has templates for keyword, Boolean and advanced searching as well as open queries; UNILEX uses a more conceptual approach to access articles and other documents on the CISG. The integration of textual commentary with the norms of transnational legal instruments provides a robust and ideal platform for research which the codex format cannot easily match as a tool of discovery for documents related inter-textually.

Other instances of applying rigorous criteria for building free and official websites may be found in criteria developed at the dawn of the robust Internet. Alistair G. Smith of the School of Information Management of Victoria University in New Zealand describes criteria applied to five New Zealand government websites in 1997 (Smith 2001). His report touches on major issues still confronting designers of websites today: Crown copyright; versioned legislation; formats requiring users to have particular software (such as PDF); navigation that takes users out of the site without adequate explanation; direct instead of indirect access (the need to go beyond the metadata to provide a glossary); and indications whether or not the material is current and official. Smith also noted that full text is valued more by users than abstracts with instructions on how to get the information (Smith 2001, 138–40).

Smith's own list of 'Criteria for Evaluation of Internet Information Resources'[10] is part of the Information Quality WWW Virtual Library: The Internet Guide to Construction of Quality Online Resources,[11] which began the quest for an exhaustive list of all the criteria for evaluation and selection of websites. This is a useful tool 'intended to be particularly useful to librarians and others who are selecting sites to include in an information resource guide, or informing users as to the qualities they should use in evaluating Internet information'.[12]

Evaluative Criteria for Free Legal Website and Database Selection

Although the web is indexed by search engines, many law libraries create guides and lists of the best websites which may include not only serial materials which have 'gone free' on the web, but also free portals and web collections in the library online catalogue in its new incarnation as

9 UNILEX on CISG and UNIDROIT Principles. Available at: www.unilex.info, accessed 12 August 2010.

10 Available at: www.vuw.ac.nz/staff/alastair_smith/evaln/index.htm, accessed 12 August 2010.

11 Available at: www.ciolek.com/WWWVL-InfoQuality.html, accessed 12 August 2010. T. Matthew Ciolek of the Australian National University edited, gathered and updated the World Wide Web Virtual Library site through 2006. His web style retains a dated look and feel but is fairly current and well-vetted.

12 Available at: www.vuw.ac.nz/staff/alastair_smith/evaln/evaln.htm, accessed 12 August 2010.

an integrated library system (ILS). As technical teams work on *how* to create the inter-linkages, selectors must decide *what* resources to include from the free web. In addition to helpful lists such as that compiled by Coggins (2009), what guidelines exist?

Alistair Smith's exhaustive list of sources for evaluating information resources demonstrates the need to make transparent the scope, content, design, purpose, workability (also sometimes referred to as usability or functionality) and cost-effectiveness of website content.[13] His standards seem to be well integrated into the criteria of those who edit more of the very best free web portals and resources.

Comments on standards to be used for the inclusion of links and resources by authors and editors for major research portals include:

- *ASIL Guide to Electronic Resources in International Law (ERG)*:[14] in her introduction to the ERG, Kelly Vinopal adds to accuracy and currency (or timeliness) the following criteria: quality of data, completeness, authority, archival and retention policy, and how the documents are structured and arranged (Vinopal 2010)
- *ASIL-Electronic Information System for International Law (EISIL)*:[15] editor Marci Hoffman and her contributors have placed an emphasis on the 'highest quality' primary materials in this database of treaty resources, including legal citations, with a focus on authenticated texts
- *Globalex*:[16] the editor of Globalex, an electronic legal research publication of the Hauser Global Law School Program at New York University, adds the need to pay attention to 'structural considerations' – subject and records structures, which 'should compare well with traditional indexing and thesauri' (Roznovschi 2000)
- *Intute*:[17] Intute is a web portal serving higher educational institutions in the United Kingdom and supported by a consortium of seven UK universities and other partners. A selective list of authoritative web resources, it informs researchers of new and important websites, portals, databases and other resources in a variety of academic and professional disciplines, including law. Tutorials and guidelines on the site explain to Internet users (particularly students) how one might judge the quality of an electronic resource as well as how to discover other sites of equal value. The *Intute Collection Development Framework and Policy* includes a useful and succinct chart (Institute Strategic Leadership Group 2009, 9) which operates as a kind of evaluation matrix, based on the categories of Context, Content, Use Features and System Features. For example, under Context (a category not explicitly represented in other evaluation schemes) the chart lists Provenance, Authority, Uniqueness, Relationship to Other Resources, and Audience. The inclusion of 'terms of use' and 'rights legitimacy', as well as 'design' under Use Features, and 'site integrity' as well as 'appropriate technology standards' under System Features makes these criteria applicable to both free and commercial databases and portals

13 Available at: www.vuw.ac.nz/staff/alastair_smith/evaln/evaln.htm, accessed 12 August 2010.

14 Available at: www.asil.org/erghome.cfm, accessed 12 August 2010.

15 Available at: www.eisil.org/index.php?sid=167026328&t=index, accessed 12 August 2010.

16 Available at: www.nyulawglobal.org/Globalex, accessed 12 August 2010.

17 Available at: www.intute.ac.uk, accessed 12 August 2010. Reduced funding for Intute after July 2011 has made the future of the service uncertain, see www.intute.ac.uk/about.html, accessed 12 August 2010, but the law section will be maintained by the present editors, the Institute of Advanced Legal Studies, University of London.

The Commercial Database: Electronic Selection as a Purchase Decision in Light of Free and Innovative Legal Resources

Evaluation There are even more exacting requirements for information accessible by fee-based subscription. Why pay for information that might be available elsewhere for free unless it comes packaged with editorial and technical enhancements such as peer review and extraordinary retrieval and hyper-linkage? Of course, static digital collections and repositories can be valuable without extensive extra features, since electronic access, particularly if available to many users at one time and in remote locations, is itself a tremendous convenience. Therefore, the purchase of electronic books and the runs of serials which are already available in print can be justified beyond the usual conerns about format for citation purposes (such as preferences for scanned pages in PDF).

When it comes to commercial databases, practising lawyers as well as scholars and other researchers demand the best in content, speed, accuracy and timeliness, and so it is no accident that prior to the Internet, the development of LexisNexis and Westlaw demonstrated a high order of innovation and technological development in full-text searching. Those systems were directed particularly at the case-law-driven world of the common law and high stakes litigation in the United States[18] and elsewhere, primarily in the English-speaking world.

Early criteria for evaluating legal information on the web focused not only on authentication but also on hidden bias or sponsorship (Scott 2002, 1190–1), a relatively new aspect of legal research for attorneys accustomed to authoritative print sources and the apparently protected (and proprietary) Lexis and Westlaw databases. In the United States and elsewhere in the common law world, the development of additional commercial legal databases such as Justis[19] and Fastcase[20] has been slow and hesitant. In comparison to common law jurisdictions, the international and civil law legal systems derive more doctrine from major texts with commentary. Major texts can include treaties, constitutions and model laws, as well as other codes at the municipal (or jurisdictional level) in those countries in which codification of private, commercial, criminal or procedural law is the norm. To a great extent, however, even the common law jurisdictions are now concerned with statutory and regulatory matters and cases or decisions 'arising under' the legislative enactments.

The New England Law Library Consortium (NELLCO) in the United States and, on a much larger scale in terms of technology, the Joint Information Systems Committee (JISC) of the UK Higher Education Funding Councils (a sponsor of the Intute database mentioned above), have set standards for selecting the best electronic resources. NELLCO's early efforts were published in 2000 as a 'Criteria Worksheet for Electronic/Intranet Acquisitions'.[21] Database trials may be run by request in an open system of comparison and evaluation.

In 1997, California State University (CSU) issued *Criteria for CSU Electronic Information Resources Core Collection*. In addition to ensuring that students in a public university system have access to a basic established set of electronic resources, these criteria for commercial databases added the factor of cost-efficiency. In a statement reminiscent of the world of print acquisition, the *Criteria* included mention of 'influence in the marketplace' and securing 'the best prices from database vendors' (*Criteria for CSU* 1997, revised 2003). While such concerns do not bear on content criteria in and of themselves, it is important to note that educational institutions still

18 For a recent review of the history of database citation system development, see Dabney (2008).

19 Available at: www.justis.com, accessed 30 August 2010.

20 Available at: www.fastcase.com, accessed 12 March 2011.

21 The criteria are no longer updated, but a copy is on file with the author and archived at: http://old.nellco.org/criteria.htm, accessed 28 August 2010.

struggle with gaining access to necessary knowledge, both as subscribers and as the home of the principal contributors to research publications.

These sets of criteria date from the early days of the Internet but the benchmarks still hold up well for evaluating both free and subscription-based databases. Despite its focus on CD-ROM formats, Bobbie Studwell's 1998 essay on evaluating electronic resources provides an excellent and still valuable checklist covering purpose, content, authority, objectivity, accuracy and currency (Studwell 1998, 11).

Management The challenges in managing the acquisition of commercial databases are twofold: (1) licensing is always restrictive and the restrictions must be examined very carefully, because licences are binding on the institution; and (2) the acquisition of commercial database usually requires cancellation of print equivalents. This section will address these issues for both free and commercial databases, since the factors to consider are usually the same.

Licensing Collaborative and model licensing may provide a solution to the often intimidating or bewildering array of terms in the agreements, not to mention their transnational character and varying legal (and perhaps cultural) expectations. In addition to setting standards and coordinating trials for possible licensed products, NELLCO has created a Standard Licensing Agreement for its membership and the database vendors with whom the consortium deals. The salient features of the licence indicate the kind of terms a licensee might want to see included in a licence if absent, or stricken if not acceptable.[22] Contrary to what one might assume from reading standard vendor agreements, libraries can request alterations which legitimate vendors will consider and (in my personal experience) accept.

Things to look for in licensing agreements include:

- 'Authorised users': this standard licensing provision should include 'walk-in' users because even private libraries often admit some categories of patrons not in their usual or traditional group of affiliates
- 'Unauthorised use': this should be covered under the copyright laws of the subscribing library's legal jurisdiction. Some licences attempt to place an obligation upon the library (the 'licensee') to ensure that there is no unauthorised use of the product. Such language should be resisted since it is impossible (and undesirable) to watch or monitor what users are doing working in the library or at home. The term 'reasonable' should be added here with notifications of suspected violation being sent to the licensor but the agreement should not allow immediate termination of the licence for unauthorised use
- 'Authentication': a clear preference, which should be an actual term of the agreement, is for IP access authentication as well as for the ability to create proxy access
- 'Interlibrary loan': language regarding interlibrary loan may be qualified by local law
- 'Arbitration': the governing law for arbitration clauses and the like should be that of the subscribing institution

There is an abundance of published research in the both the legal and the library and information literature on licensing. The scope of this chapter permits only an overview, but of greatest importance in assessing or negotiating a licence are principles. Again, those established in the

22 Revised in 2004, the licence is current and posted at: www.nellco.org/_data/n_0001/resources/live/nellcolicense_071004.pdf, accessed 29 August 2010.

early days of electronic information licences seem to have stood the test of time. The Association of Research Libraries (ARL) *Principles for Licensing Electronic Resources*,[23] formulated in 1997, include allowance for creation of an archival copy, privacy of collected data on usage, and a clear statement of access rights, as well as other best practices.

Print/Electronic Balance and Retention Subscribing to a database usually means renting the information, unless a subscriber is also offered digital ownership in all or part of a database. For example, HeinOnline offers purchase of rights to the PDF files of scanned images, which allows the subscriber to own the images. While they are available mostly for free, reliance on open access repositories of law journals and research papers, and scanned copies of books and major reports on the sites of international organisations, also means trusting that the materials will always be there.

Despite the relative fragility of models of access and acquisition through some type of capture and/or purchase, in periods of financial austerity, many institutions cannot justify maintaining titles in more than one or perhaps two formats. In contrast to print materials, collections of microform materials are frequently retained by libraries even if they are available electronically, mainly owing to their high initial costs or value for preservation if image deterioration can be kept at bay, because the contents can be converted to electronic images upon demand. With print materials, however, difficult choices must be made in many cases.

With regard to materials in rapid updating formats such as looseleaf or binder-filed subscriptions, the cost differences are not immediately apparent, since many publishers charge close to the same amount for either format. But upon closer analysis, savings or a break-even outcome is probable even in the long-term for electronic versions of such materials. The cost of labour and processing, the poor security and shelf-life of the print versions, and the lack of archival value as material is replaced and discarded makes clear that electronic access is more efficient, cost-effective, as well as more popular with users, who can access the information remotely and usually simultaneously with other users. Print versions of the cancelled materials can be retained once cancelled (with clear labels stating that they will not be updated), or withdrawn and discarded.

Official document sets from government and international organisations, such as of the United Nations, are also candidates for replacement with electronic access, at least for recent materials if the archive is not complete online. Again, labour savings and ease of access are clear advantages, but a page image version should be the standard to address authentication questions, since some scanned versions are not official, as in the case of the documentation of the European Union.

In North America, scholarly law journals are more typically published directly by law schools than in other parts of the world. Many are moving towards open access electronic publication models, using the institution's website or a local or shared institutional repository, such as the BePress Digital Commons.[24] Versions of scholarly articles by legal scholars are also often available before formal publication through such subscription services as the Social Science Research Network (SSRN).[25] Working papers of such organisations as the European University Institute[26] and the Jean Monnet Program[27] are also readily accessible.

Commercially-published scholarly journals published in both print and electronic formats present problems of retention that are difficult for subscribers to control. The publishers decide whether to themselves maintain archival copies that could be loaned to institutions which were

23 Available at: www.arl.org/sc/marketplace/license/licprinciples.shtml, accessed 30 August 2010.

24 Available at: www.bepress.com/ir, accessed 30 August 2010.

25 Available at: www.ssrn.com/lsn/index.html, accessed 30 August 2010.

26 Available at: www.eui.eu/Home.aspx, accessed 30 August 2010.

27 Available at: http://centers.law.nyu.edu/jeanmonnet, accessed 30 August 2010.

subscribers but withdrew the title or lost an issue or volume. Assuming that scanned images are available for citation purposes, some pricing is favourable for a switch to all-electronic acquisition; some is not. There may be need for a core list of frequently cited materials or a move to an environment of expensive but necessary collections, as in medicine.

Firm negotiation and possible massive cutbacks by large numbers of major libraries may be the only pressure that can be brought to bear on larger publishers. Institutions should be prepared to have selectors spend time with very lengthy spreadsheets of titles and to find those that can be removed or reduced, and (in licence negotiation issue) to demand that enough usage data be shared to make such determinations possible. Some publishers and vendors offer 'tokens' to 'spend' on access to packages of lesser-used titles, but these offers should be examined carefully and accepted only if the entire price package is reasonable. Even the codex format is threatened as aggregators push for of 'bundles' of electronic books. Books present fewer issues at the title level but requirements for proprietary platforms and undisclosed maintenance fees for the serial or e-book platforms must be made completely clear from the outset. Such events as the Google Books Settlement process may serve to be instructive regarding the temptation to outsource digitisation (see, for instance, Band 2010).

Integration of Databases into a Tool for Discovery and Access beyond the Databases Themselves

As materials available on the free web have developed and expanded in the twenty-first century (at least from the perspective of information professionals selecting commercial databases) so has the realisation that fee-based electronic materials ought to deliver a product as least as good as free, non-profit-supported resources. In law, another continuing challenge for creators of new database products in the developed world has been the precedent of the long-standing advanced functionalities of Lexis and Westlaw. Legal users expect a great deal from English language research tools. The Scylla of Lexis and Westlaw is now matched by the Charybdis of *HeinOnline*,[28] which includes a integrating ScholarCheck feature (to show what journals may have cited a document) in some full-text libraries. Thus, selection of new legal information products featuring rapid, rich, current, deep full-text retrieval with instant analysis and document preparation and citation tools as easy add-ons, requires comparison with the historically deep, searchable, portable, vast collections that still reside in extensive traditional print law libraries. Leaving aside the enormous potential costs of the most comprehensive subscription plans from commercial database providers, what other reasonable criteria are there for selecting commercial databases?

At this point, international and comparative law, and the progressive globalisation and internationalisation of legal practice and study enter the picture. A convincing argument can be made for any given jurisdiction that transnational legal activity has reached a point at which every major population centre will need legal professionals trained to retrieve and evaluate materials at the intersection of international and local norms and regulations. While Lexis and Westlaw contain full texts of materials for selected jurisdictions (some in unofficial translation) and from intergovernmental and regional regimes such as the European Union and the World Trade Organization, the major legal databases are increasingly also large unitary systems of information in their own right, presenting materials within the framework of complex, but closely interrelated,

28 Available at: www.heinonline.org/HOL/Welcome, accessed 30 August 2010.

sets of texts. What about other areas of international activity, such as arbitration, investment, human rights, and traditionally national areas such as criminal and family law?

Returning to the role of commentary in civil law systems and in international law, the best commercial databases can be evaluated using criteria developed within the innovative context of some of the recently launched United Nations databases. Recent or improved tools, such as the United Nations Audiovisual Library of International Law,[29] the United Nations Rule of Law Website and Document Repository,[30] and the Economic Commission for Latin American and the Caribbean (ECLAC) Integrated Database of Trade Disputes for Latin America and the Caribbean,[31] hold international and national or regional texts, include multimedia presentations, and are free. Such sites keep the bar high for commercial database providers and create room for a new kind of approach. Driven not by the need to check precedents or collect fact patterns, integrative tools in the transnational arena work conceptually rather than hierarchically or by simple linking of references. Two illustrative examples follow, not as endorsements, but rather as indicators of what can be realised when the power of separate scholarly and/or official legal resources are brought together through careful interlinking rather than by pulling in sources that might traditionally not always have been associated in a research process.

The first example: Oxford Reports on International Law (ORIL)[32] and its related modules can be contrasted with, for example, US legal research using a database that might include case annotations or essays from a legal encyclopaedia or a service such as American Law Reports which a common law researcher might not consider to be indispensable. Such 'secondary sources' might be thought of merely as enhancements or options, particularly by legal practitioners. The international legal research world, however, explicitly draws upon not only authoritative texts such as treaties and judicial decisions, but also yearbooks, digests, comparative materials and scholarly commentary; all of these have been factored into the definitive source statement of Article 38 of the Statute of the International Court of Justice.[33]

In the ORIL module 'International Law in Domestic Courts', one begins research by selecting a jurisdiction in order to find leading case law on issues of international law as interpreted by that particular jurisdiction. For the People's Republic of China (PRC), three decisions are presented. The first deals with the law of outer space: as the 'Core Issues' statement indicates, specifically with: 'Whether the Treaty on Principles Governing the Activities of States in the Exploration and Use of Outer Space, including the Moon and Other Celestial Bodies prohibited an individual from claiming ownership of land on the Moon'. Keywords are supplied as metadata tags for each case posted to this database.

A hyperlink from the case name connects to a standardised record for the case, which includes the date of decision, the deciding body (usually a court but the database also includes arbitral decisions), the procedural posture of the case, and some other data. Access to decisions is also provided by subject and date. Facts are summarised and analysis of the case is provided, with links throughout the text to other documents cited. The links go to a record for the cited resource similar to that for the original case. Cases and documents are given in full text, with a source text in the vernacular as well as translation into English. Clicking on a symbol for the Oxford Law Citator takes one to a list of related cases with links to those and to other documents mentioned in the case.

29 Available at: www.un.org/law/avl, accessed 30 August 2010.

30 Available at: www.unrol.org, accessed 30 August 2010.

31 Available at: http://idatd.eclac.cl/controversias/index_en.jsp, accessed 30 August 2010.

32 Available at: www.oxfordlawreports.com, accessed 30 August 2010.

33 Available at: www.icj-cij.org/documents/index.php?p1=4&p2=2&p3=0, accessed 9 August 2010.

If one chooses the 'Agreement Governing the Activities of States on the Moon and Other Celestial Bodies (UN) 1363 UNTS 21', the record provides an option for linking into the electronic version of the *Max Planck Encyclopedia of Public International Law*[34] and the topic: 'Spacecraft, Satellites and Space Objects, B (Use, Jurisdiction and Ownership)'. Because both the actual text of the treaty and the scholarly consensus are clear that only space objects (satellites for instance), but not land, are covered in the treaty, comparison of the encyclopaedia entry with the analysis in the database shows that the database adds true value by referencing, and by going beyond, the consensus description of the terms of the treaty. Moreover, because related cases from foreign jurisdiction are difficult to locate, citations to cases judicially considered add to the value.

The integration of text and commentary takes a database of the text/metadata type and creates a relational database that follows the logical and associative steps that a researcher would take to consult a standard work or to read cited or related cases. Some areas of international law follow norms in a less rigid hierarchy not bound by precedent as common lawyers conceive it. How does this compare with available free databases in terms of providing 'intelligent' structure and useful aids to the sequence of research steps?

The Declaration on Free Access to Law regards 'public legal information' that is produced by governments and international organisations as part of 'the common heritage of humanity' and therefore 'digital common property'.[35] A second example: the website of the World Legal Information Institute (WorldLII) and its constituent regional and national legal information institutes provide an extraordinary database of cases and commentary as well as legislation and other content for each country represented, as well as for international materials (Greenleaf, Mowbray and Chung 2010, 3).

A free law citator, LawCite, is under development by WorldLII and available at the site;[36] it includes indexed cases (including the *English Reports*, 1220–1873), law reform documents and journal articles. LawCite provides citation histories within the Commonwealth law database CommonLII,[37] which is somewhat comparable to the 'modules' used in ORIL. Its origins and historically strong focus on Australian and UK decisions is apparent for some features. While not all linked dynamically, many law journals for Australia and the Commonwealth are included and are being moved into an integrated database using open access materials. Since subject areas are searched across Commonwealth countries for legislation, developments in areas of policy may be compared usefully. Decisions of international tribunals and courts are also included in the database along with treaties and law reform commission materials from WorldLII's growing International Law Library.[38] The bar is raised high by this now well-known database.

WorldLII's more 'static' side includes legislation from around the world and well outside the Commonwealth. Information from the Library of Congress Global Legal Information Network (GLIN)[39] is included in the form of searchable abstracts for the officially published legislation of participating member jurisdictions that constitutes the full GLIN database. Since searching across languages is not possible without translations, abstracts or equivalent terms, the availability of even the abstracts from GLIN enhances the overall discovery functions of WorldLII.

34 Available at: www.mpepil.com, accessed 30 August 2010.

35 Available at: www.worldlii.org/worldlii/declaration, accessed 30 August 2010.

36 Available at: www.worldlii.org/LawCite, accessed 30 August 2010.

37 Available at: www.commonlii.org, accessed 30 August 2010.

38 Available at: www.worldlii.org/int/special/ihl, accessed 30 August 2010.

39 Available at: www.glin.gov/search.action, accessed 30 August 2010.

What about other sources for foreign law, including civil and religious systems? One example is Lexadin,[40] a well-organised list of links by type of legal material (case law, legislation, journals and schools, and some business and tax information) for each jurisdiction covered. There are links to government and to reliable law firm sites with materials in the vernacular or in English translations, if available. The major commercial databases also provide access to some other jurisdictions (for instance, Westlaw China, LexisNexis Argentina and the Lexis platform for Juris-Classeur, France).

Foreign law from specific jurisdictions is almost as well served through more static repositories. Many jurisdictions, such as France, with its Legifrance database,[41] provide good search functionality. Affiliated with WorldLII are French, German, Italian and Spanish-speaking members of the Free Access to Law Movement. The UK Statute Law Database[42] includes sophisticated versioned legislation and tracking tools in a free database. The criteria noted earlier are also well met by Reynolds and Flores's Foreign Law Guide[43] and the vLex Global[44] subscription databases as well. Integration is a key feature of both databases. The Foreign Law Guide integrates specific citations with legal system descriptions and print references in the vernacular. Its links to free Internet sources as well as subscription database recommendations also qualify it as an integrating tool. vLex Global provides well-laid out and accessible hypertext links and PDF formats for official legislation and case law, integrating English language searching with vernacular text. Other languages may also be used for search so that more of the global legal community is served. The clean interface and familiar language overlay also includes access to open access journals and other books and reports.

Integration of national laws, both in intergovernmental databases by topic, and as the result of implementation of transnational treaties or regulatory regimes, is another development in the enhancement of database utility and global legal research. The European Union's N-Lex,[45] the International Labour Organization's NATLEX,[46] the United Nations Environment Programme's ECOLEX,[47] and the World Intellectual Property Organization's Collection of Laws for Electronic Access (CLEA) via WIPO Gold,[48] along with the national treaty series presentations on WorldLII and the UN Audiovisual Library research tools all provide create integration of legal content and research. Many single jurisdiction databases include the jurisdiction's participation in treaties as well as national laws. This approach is preferred in selecting databases for specific jurisdictions. For example, Chinese bilingual databases such as ChinaLawInfo/LawInfoChina[49] include tax and trade treaties. In its international law section, Isinolaw[50] includes treaty ratification and implementation decisions.

Presentation of Information through the Integrating Tool

For most researchers, the discovery of legal information has converged with their searches for other information. Users of all types of information want to use one retrieval tool, a 'search

40 Available at: www.lexadin.nl/wlg, accessed 30 August 2010.

41 Available at: www.legifrance.gouv.fr, accessed 30 August 2010.

42 Available at: www.statutelaw.gov.uk, accessed 30 August 2010.

43 Available at: www.foreignlawguide.com, accessed 30 August 2010.

44 Available at: http://vlex.com, accessed 30 August 2010.

45 Available at: http://eur-lex.europa.eu/n-lex/pays.html?lang=en&info_lang=en, accessed 30 August 2010.

46 Available at: www.ilo.org/dyn/natlex/natlex_browse.home?p_lang=en, accessed 30 August 2010.

47 Available at: www.ecolex.org/start.php, accessed 30 August 2010.

48 Available at: www.wipo.int/wipogold/en, accessed 30 August 2010.

49 Available at: www.lawinfochina.com/ProductsServices/index.asp, accessed 30 August 2010.

50 Available at: www.isinolaw.com, accessed 30 August 2010.

box', to find relevant information that meets all of the criteria discussed above. Making online library catalogues of continuing relevance by integrating access to remaining print resources with electronic information is the major challenge for libraries. Increasingly, online catalogues look like and launch from library web pages. Searching for information by title may be an approach of last resort for researchers who prefer to use keywords to launch an investigation into a new area of knowledge. The librarian's traditional role as mediator continues in the realm of integrating the information into a search and discovery tool.

The Catalogue or ILS with Integrated Electronic Resources

The library catalogue or integrated library system (ILS) can make the discovery of texts (in some cases at the document or article level) possible in a Google-like search. Results may be federated, that is, not merely ranked for relevance but sorted as to location, collection, format type, language and date, with links to full text.

Innovative Interfaces Inc.'s Encore interface[51] creates this experience; a search for 'responsibility to protect' without quotation marks searches as a phrase and brings up relevant content with the phrase appearing first in the title and in print and electronic books. For political science and other faculties outside law, this integration benefits the legal education of non-law students as well as the interdisciplinary interests of legal scholars and practitioners (Koulikov 2010).

Serials Solutions[52] produces the Summon system, which together with the company's AquaBrowser and 360 products, can integrate sources to the article or citation level with links to full text. The federated content may list content type as well as subject terms, and unwanted items such as newspaper articles can be excluded in a refined search of the results. Examples can be seen in the Dartmouth College Catalogue in the United States[53] and the library catalogue of the University of Huddersfield in the UK.[54]

The Library Web Page and Repositories, Wikis and Blogs

Library web pages may not attract potential users of the electronic collections that librarians are carefully shaping, but creating research guides that are rich in contextual background and annotate links to resources, presented in organised and original ways, are a way to integrate resources without adding costly cutting edge tools and modules to an ILS.

The use of the 'MyLibrary' option available in some library catalogues may enable users to save searches and collect resources relevant to their work for retrieval at any time during the life of a research project. Training users to create their own similar work spaces using MS SharePoint[55] or Google Docs[56] could encourage them to use pages where such spaces can be entered; for less well-resourced libraries, the 'make your own catalogue' approach could have real benefits even if much student research will still continue to be through Google.

Some benefits of Google's indexing are apparent in its Google Scholar project,[57] even though access to full text materials may be available only for subscribers to the publications. Some libraries

51 Available at: http://encoreforlibraries.com, accessed 30 August 2010.

52 Available at: www.serialssolutions.com, accessed 30 August 2010.

53 Available at: www.dartmouth.edu/~library/home/find/summon, accessed 30 August 2010.

54 Available at: http://library.hud.ac.uk/summon, accessed 30 August 2010.

55 Available at: http://sharepoint.microsoft.com/en-us/Pages/default.aspx, accessed 30 August 2010.

56 Available at: www.google.com, accessed 30 August 2010.

57 Available at: http://scholar.google.com, accessed 30 August 2010.

have placed a Google Scholar icon or search point on the library landing page to encourage use of the tool with authentication through the campus IP range or remotely by proxy login. The main page at Georgetown University's Lauinger Library[58] provides a search box with options for searching either the library catalogue, Google Scholar, or the content of the library's site.

International and comparative law is a large meta-topic which subsumes numerous subtopics of the study of law itself. In the research context, one can imagine moving beyond research guides, tutorials or videos alone to integrate all content into a wiki product that would create a large and comprehensive outline of international norms, transnational cases, as well as harmonisation, regulation and implementation down to the national level with jurisdictionally-specific information. Housing such a resource, open to updating by many research experts as a kind of subject Wikipedia, may be possible at the level of a national or international association or interest group.[59]

Repositories of locally-produced materials or collaboration projects to archive materials of general historic or public interest value can be created as customised databases residing at the institution and linked from the home page. Rare or archival materials that may be scanned, projects or scholarly publications of that institutions members or faculty, and even public reports or other materials not be preserved or easily available elsewhere can make the site a destination. Squire Law Library at Cambridge in the UK has a good example with its Eminent Scholars Archive,[60] which incorporates multimedia including oral history through digital audio interviews of scholars.

The Legal Information Preservation Alliance (LIPA)[61] and its Legal Information Archive project[62] are joining in US collaborative efforts to capture, post and make searchable a number of categories of born-digital information. The Georgetown Law Library, the Virginia State Law Library, the State Law Library of Maryland and the Harvard Law School Library are harvesting and posting documents and reports, both in a database and through the library catalogues of the participating institutions. Known as the Legal Information Archive of the Chesapeake Digital Preservation Group, this effort is built upon a tested collection plan (Chesapeake Project 2010), which incorporates the 2007 Trustworthy Repositories Audit & Certification Criteria and Checklist (TRAC) of the College and Research Libraries (Trustworthy Repositories 2007), which itself relies on international standards for permanent repositories. The Legal Information Archive includes state policy documents from Virginia and Maryland, national and international government reports along with legal scholarship from Harvard and elsewhere.

Web 2.0 tools such as blogs (or as they are sometimes called in law, 'blawgs') can also host serious and important content related to print books, other databases and news analysis, together with easy links to RSS (Really Simple Syndication) feeds from other blogs, website updates and news providers. Many law professors have created their own blogs and believe that blogs are contributing to vital, real-time discussions on legal and policy among established legal scholars and others (see 'Balkin Talks Blogs' 2007). Blogs can play a twofold part in research: updating and monitoring developments in areas of research in law and policy; and updating and aiding in discovery of new print titles and new web resources or databases.

The number of serious legal blogs in the international, foreign and comparative law fields as well as in other legal disciplines is already too large to list and changes constantly. One source of

58 Available at: www.library.georgetown.edu, accessed 30 August 2010.

59 The Foreign, Comparative, and International Law Special Interest Section of the American Association of Law Libraries will attempt such a project over the next few years (Raisch 2008, 5).

60 Available at: www.squire.law.cam.ac.uk/eminent_scholars, accessed 30 August 2010.

61 Available at: www.aallnet.org/committee/lipa, accessed 30 August 2010.

62 Available at: www.aallnet.org/committee/lipa/LIA.asp, accessed 30 August 2010.

information about legal blogs is Justia's Blawgsearch page,[63] which aggregates current highlights from the blogs and sorts them (with links) by category, jurisdiction and law school.[64] Keeping up with blogs from law libraries and faculties around the world can be an excellent way to track acquisition or trials of new databases. A good collection of links to law library blogs is maintained by the AALL Computing Services Special Interest Section.[65]

Conclusion

The virtual library as publisher/mentor emerges as a final model and a creature of many facets: a web space that users can customise and colonise privately for projects; a large, dynamic but controlled array of information sources searched like Google; a repository of collections of texts or sound files and images, chosen by curators that can be displayed attractively, like the Parker Library on the Web (in partnership with Stanford),[66] for access to manuscripts of Corpus Christi College, Cambridge; and a source of tutorials and short instructional videos.

For serious research, such library initiatives surely can compete with general search engines such as Google. RSS, instant messaging reference query tools for chat reference, and blogs can complete the picture of the library portal as the virtual presence of a legal information seeker's life coach: the librarian.[67]

References

Anderson, E. (2008), 'ASIL as Think Net' (Executive Director's Report), *Newsletter of the American Society of International Law* 24:2, 2, 16.

'Balkin Talks Blogs' (2007), *Yale Law Report* 54:1, 44–9.

Band, J. (2010), 'The Long and Winding Road to the Google Books Settlement', *John Marshall Review of Intellectual Property Law* 9:1/2, 227–329.

The Chesapeake Project Legal Information Archive (updated 2010), *Collection Plan*. Available at: http://cdm266901.cdmhost.com/policies/LEGAL_CollectionPlan_0510.pdf, accessed 6 September 2010.

Coggins, T. (2009), 'Legal, Factual, and Other Internet Sites for Attorneys and Legal Professionals', *Richmond Journal of Law & Technology* 15:4, 1–33. Available at: http://jolt.richmond.edu/v15i4/article13.pdf, accessed 22 September 2010.

Dabney, L. (2008), 'Citators: Past, Present, and Future', *Legal Reference Services Quarterly* 27:2, 165–90.

63 Available at: http://blawgsearch.justia.com/blogs/categories/law-professor, accessed 30 August 2010.

64 The scholarly potential of blogs and strategies to preserve their best content was the subject of a 2009 symposium at the Georgetown Law Library; videos of speakers and a selection of papers presented are available at: http://scholarship.law.georgetown.edu/future_scholarship, accessed 30 August 2010.

65 Available at: http://aallcssis.pbworks.com/Law-Library-Blogs, accessed 30 August 2010.

66 Available at: http://parkerweb.stanford.edu/parker/actions/page.do?forward=home, accessed 5 September 2010.

67 Thanks to Jennifer Locke Davitt, Head of Faculty Services, Georgetown Law, for this definition from an unidentified, but satisfied, faculty patron.

Garavaglia, B. (2007), 'Collection Development Policies and Other Basic Tools for Building a Foreign and International Law Collection', *GlobalLex*. Available at: www.nyulawglobal.org/Globalex/International_Foreign_Collection_Development.htm, accessed 30 August 2010.

Greenleaf, G., Mowbray, A. and Chung, P. (2010), 'Building a Commons for the Common Law: The Commonwealth Legal Information Institute (CommonLII) after Four Years Progress'. Available at: http://papers.ssrn.com/sol3/papers.cfm?abstract_id=1619714, accessed 2 September 2010.

Institute Strategic Leadership Group (2009), *Intute Collection Development Framework and Policy*. Available at: www.intute.ac.uk/supportdocs/IntuteCDFPJuly2009_final.pdf, accessed 2 September 2010.

Koulikov, M. (2010), 'Indexing and Full-Text Coverage of Law Review Articles in Nonlegal Databases: An Initial Study', *Law Library Journal* 102:1, 39–57.

Newman, M. (1999), 'Evaluation Criteria and Quality Control for Legal Knowledge Systems on the Internet: A Case Study', *Law Library Journal* 91:1, 9–27.

Raisch, M. (2008), 'Electronic Issues Interest Group Meeting Report', *FCIL Newsletter* 23:1, 5.

Roznovschi, M. (2000), 'Update to Evaluating Foreign and International Legal Databases on the Internet'. Available at: www.llrx.com/features/evaluating2.htm#Database, accessed 12 August 2010.

Scott, W. (2002), 'Evaluating & Authenticating Legal Web Resources: A Practical Guide for Attorneys', *Syracuse Law Review* 52:4, 1185–206.

Smith, A. (2001), 'Applying Evaluation Criteria to New Zealand Government Websites', *International Journal of Information Management* 21, 137–49.

Stair, R. and Reynolds, G. (2009), *Fundamentals of Information Systems* (5th edn) (Mason: Cengage).

Studwell, B. (1998), 'Evaluating Electronic Resources', *AALL Spectrum* 2:10, 10–11. Available at: www.aallnet.org/products/pub_sp9807/pub_sp9807_ProDev.pdf, accessed 22 September 2010.

Trustworthy Repositories Audit & Certification: Criteria and Checklist (2007), (Chicago: Center for Research Libraries; Dublin, Ohio: OCLC Online Computer Library Center). Available at: www.crl.edu/sites/default/files/attachments/pages/trac_0.pdf, accessed 4 September 2010.

Vinopal, K. (2010), *ASIL Guide to Electronic Resources for International Law: Introduction*. Available at: www.asil.org/ergintr1.cfm, accessed 4 September 2010.

Woutersen-Windhouwer, S., Brandsma, R., Hogenaar, A., Hoogerwerf, M., Doorenbosch, P., Dürr, E., Ludwig, J., Schmidt, B. and Sierman, B. (2009), *Enhanced Publications: Linking Publications and Research Data in Digital Repositories* (Amsterdam: Amsterdam University Press).

Further Reading

Borgman, C. (2007), *Scholarship in the Digital Age: Information, Infrastructure, and the Internet* (Cambridge, MA: MIT Press).

California State University (2005), *Criteria for CSU Electronic Information Resources Core Collection*. Available at: http://seir.calstate.edu/ear/docs/criteria.doc, accessed 5 September 2010.

Chiorazzi, M. and Russell, G. (eds) (2002), *Law Library Collection Development in the Digital Age* (Binghamton: Haworth Information Press).

Collins, M. and Carr, P. (2008), *Managing the Transition from Print to Electronic Journals and Resources: A Guide for Library and Information Professionals* (New York: Routledge).

Conger, J. (2004), *Collaborative Electronic Resource Management: From Acquisitions to Assessment* (Westport and London: Libraries Unlimited).

Council on Library and Information Resources (2010), *The Idea of Order: Transforming Research Collections for 21st Century Scholarship* (Washington, DC: Council on Library and Information Resources). Available at: www.clir.org/pubs/abstract/pub147abst.html, accessed 30 August 2010.

Gregory, V. and Hanson A. (2006), *Selecting and Managing Electronic Resources: A How-To-Do-It Manual for Librarians* (New York: Neal-Schuman Publishers).

Hofman, J. (2007), 'Constitutional Assembly Database Project: Resurrecting a Database Ten Years On', *International Journal of Legal Information* 35:1, 79–92.

Howard, P. and Rastorfer, R. (2005), 'Do We Still Need Books? A Selected Annotated Bibliography', *Law Library Journal* 97:2, 257–83.

Jascó, P. (2008), 'Google Scholar Revisited', *Online Information Review* 30:1, 102–14.

Jewell, T. (2001), *Selection and Presentation of Commercially Available Electronic Resources; Issues and Practices* (Washington, DC: Digital Library Federation Council on Library and Information Resources). Available at: www.clir.org/pubs/reports/pub99/contents.html, accessed 2 September 2010.

Kirshenbaum, M., Farr, E., Kraus, K., Nelson, N., Peters, C., Redwine, G. and Reside, D. (2009), 'Approaches to Managing and Collecting Born Digital Literary Materials for Scholarly Use'. Available at: www.neh.gov/ODH/Default.aspx?tabid=111&id=37, accessed 2 September 2010.

Lee, S. (2008). 'Preserving Our Heritage: Protecting Law Library Core Missions through Updated Library Quality Assessment Standards', *Law Library Journal* 100:1, 9–38.

Little, J. (2010), 'Cognitive Load Theory and Library Research Guides', *Internet Reference Services Quarterly* 15:1, 53–63.

Lysaght, P. and Istl, D. (2004), 'Integrating Technology: Teaching Students to Communicate in Another Medium', *Journal of the Legal Writing Institute* 10, 163–80.

Makri, S. (2008), 'A Study of Lawyers' Information Behaviour Leading to the Development of Two Methods for Evaluating Electronic Resources' [unpublished]. Available at: http://eprints.ucl.ac.uk/14729, accessed 6 September 2010.

Mintz, A. and Forbes, S. (2002), *Web of Deception: Misinformation on the Internet* (Medford: CyberAge Books).

Mowbray, A., Chung, P. and Greenleaf, G. (2008), 'Free Access Case Law Enhancements for Australian Law'. Available at: www.aija.org.au/Law&Tech%2008/Papers/Mowbray.pdf, accessed 30 August 2010.

Rumsey, M. (2007), 'Gauging the Impact of Online Legal Information on International Law: Two Tests', *Syracuse Journal of International Law and Commerce* 35:2, 201–17.

Su, D. (ed.) (2007), *Collection Development Issues in the Online Environment* (Binghamton: Haworth Press).

University of California (2006), 'University of California Guidelines for Stewardship of Electronic Information Resources, Draft: For Comment Only and the Approved Version and Discussion by Academic Senate 2007'. Available at: www.ucop.edu/irc/itsec/uc/documents/guidelines.8.30.06.pdf, accessed 6 September 2010.

Chapter 14
International Organisations and Legal Information

Jeroen Vervliet

Introduction: The Search for Authoritative Texts

Hugo Grotius as Corroborating Evidence

Hugo Grotius' *De Iure Praedae Commentarius* [*Commentary on the Law of Prize and Booty*] served as evidence put forward by Professor N.J. Schrijver, agent of the Government of Malaysia on 16 November 2007, in the case between Malaysia and Singapore at the International Court of Justice concerning Sovereignty over Pedra Branca/Pulau Batu Puteh, Middle Rocks and South Ledge.[1]

By referring to epoch-making books by Hugo Grotius, anchoring in the 'teachings of the most highly qualified publicists of the various nations' was envisaged and achieved. This kind of scholarly work is specified in the second half of the phrasing of Article 38 (1) sub d) of the Statute of the International Court of Justice as one of the sources the World Court may apply in decisions, albeit 'as subsidiary means for the determination of rules of law'. By citing the undisputed high status of Hugo Grotius, Professor Schrijver sought to provide authority for his reasoning.

Article 38 (1) of the Statute of the International Court of Justice

In the second Chapter of the Statute of the International Court of Justice, Article 38 (1) cites clearly the sources of international law to be applied:

1. The Court, whose function is to decide in accordance with international law such disputes as are submitted to it, shall apply:
    a. international conventions, whether general or particular, establishing rules expressly recognized by the contesting states;
    b. international custom, as evidence of a general practice accepted as law;

1 Available at: www.icj-cij.org/docket/files/130/14193.pdf, accessed 12 September 2010. *De Iure Praedae Commentarius* stayed unpublished until 1868 after the manuscript was discovered at an auction of the Hugo Grotius heritage in 1864; this manuscript happened to contain Hugo Grotius' *Mare Liberum* (*The Free Sea*), published anonymously in 1609 as a monograph in order to advance an unlimited right of the Dutch to navigate and trade in the East Indies, and originally being Chapter XII of *De Iure Praedae Commentarius*. In a 2008 statement on *Freedom of Navigation – New Challenges*, the President of the International Tribunal of the Law of the Sea, Rüdiger Wolfrum, refers as well to Hugo Grotius' *Mare Liberum*. According to Rüdiger, 'Freedom of navigation is one of the oldest and most recognized principles in the legal regime governing ocean space'; 'since it was enshrined in … *De Mare Liberum* … this principle constitutes one of the pillars of the law of the sea and was at the origins of modern international law' (Wolfrum 2008, 2).

c. the general principles of law recognized by civilized nations;
d. [...] judicial decisions and the teachings of the most highly qualified publicists of the various nations, as subsidiary means for the determination of rules of law.[2]

The following paragraphs will investigate important authoritative original sources, such as conventions and codified international custom. Identified 'general principles of law' will be covered as well, meaning that the majority of the legal information mentioned in Article 38 (1) of the Statute of the International Court of Justice will be examined.

In the abovementioned litigation between Malaysia and Singapore at the International Court of Justice, the judicial decision itself constitutes an authoritative primary source. Although Article 38 (1) does not embrace case law as a formal part of the list of sources of international law, many international legal organisations produce arbitral awards and judicial decisions to maintain the regulations set forth by the organisations. Therefore, arbitral awards and judicial decisions of international organisations will also be explored in this chapter.

Focus on Primary Sources and Secondary Literature Excluded

The objective of this chapter is to review the nature, significance and importance of the legal information generated and produced by international organisations and institutions, and the way in which it is managed and made available, either as publications of the organisation itself or with commercial publishers, either in folio or on the Internet. The place of secondary literature in international law practice will not be discussed. These kinds of books and journal articles are a world apart, in which not all texts are authoritative 'teachings of the most highly qualified publicists' and secondary literature merely represents 'subsidiary means for the determination of rules of law'.

Defining Treaties and Conventions, Resolutions of International Organisations and Judicial Decisions as Sources of Law

The Growth of International Cooperation and the Move to Globalisation and the Imperative of Treaty-Making and Concluding Conventions

The Central Commission for Navigation on the Rhine[3] originated during the aftermath of the Congress of Vienna of 1815. Regulating the management of this inner waterway as a vital artery for Europe can be viewed as an example of nineteenth-century legal positivism, in which codification was believed to be an attainable accomplishment. Since 1873 the Institut de Droit International[4] and the International Law Association[5] have furthered the development of international law, either through the establishment of international organisations or by persuading national governments to implement the ensuing policies. The coming into being of the Inter-Parliamentary Union,[6] the Universal Postal Union,[7] the International Telegraph

2 Available at: www.icj-cij.org/documents/index.php?p1=4&p2=2&p3=0, accessed 9 August 2010.
3 Available at: www.eda.admin.ch/eda/en/smno/trasea/searhi.html, accessed 3 October 2010.
4 Available at: www.idi-iil.org, accessed 3 October 2010.
5 Available at: www.ila-hq.org, accessed 3 October 2010.
6 Available at: www.ipu.org/english/home.htm, accessed 3 October 2010.
7 Available at: www.upu.int, accessed 3 October 2010.

Union,[8] the Berne Convention (predecessor to the World Intellectual Property Organization, WIPO),[9] the International Red Cross,[10] the International Olympic Committee[11] and, last but not least, the 'Hague Peace Conferences' of 1899 and 1907 (during which the Permanent Court of Arbitration[12] was founded and the still valid Laws of War were concluded) all testify to the impacts of internationalist developments during this period.

Nineteenth-century free trade politics also required a financial and monetary regulatory kind of international politics, for example on the gold standard and bimetallism. International agreements on production and commerce in commodities such as sugar were concluded around 1900. Many of today's international companies are rooted in multinational enterprises of that era. Hence, globalisation has been shaped since the classic age of liberalism. The twentieth century has shown an acceleration in the carefully woven web of interstate interdependencies.

The network of sovereign states culminated first in the League of Nations, in disarmament initiatives and in other peace proposals such as the Coudenhove-Kalergiplan and the Kellogg-Briand Pact,[13] in the creation of the Bank for International Settlements,[14] and other 1930s measures for the reconstruction after the 1929 economic crisis. After the Second World War, an even larger and more impressive constellation of international relations has been built, substantiated by the Atlantic Charter[15] of 1941, by the Bretton Woods Agreement[16] establishing the International Monetary Fund[17] in 1944, and by the drafting of the United Nations Charter[18] in Dumbarton Oaks, and the signing of the Charter in San Francisco in 1945.

The various United Nations organs and bodies: the General Assembly, the Security Council, and special programmes and funds such as: the United Nations Children's Fund (UNICEF),[19] the UN refugee agency (UNHCR),[20] the World Food Programme,[21] the Department of Peacekeeping Operations,[22] the United Nations Conference on Trade and Development (UNCTAD),[23] the United Nations Environment Programme (UNEP)[24] and the United Nations Development Programme (UNDP)[25] all issue recommendations, resolutions and conventions.

The domain of international law has also been advanced through the International Court of Justice (ICJ)[26] and the codification activities of the International Law Commission.[27] The

8 Available at: www.itu.int/en/pages/default.aspx, accessed 3 October 2010.
9 Available at: www.wipo.int/portal/index.html.en, accessed 3 October 2010.
10 Available at: www.ifrc.org, accessed 3 October 2010.
11 Available at: www.olympic.org, accessed 3 October 2010.
12 Available at: www.pca-cpa.org, accessed 3 October 2010.
13 Available at: www.yale.edu/lawweb/avalon/imt/kbpact.htm, accessed 3 October 2010.
14 Available at: www.bis.org, accessed 3 October 2010.
15 Available at: http://avalon.law.yale.edu/wwii/atlantic.asp, accessed 3 October 2010.
16 Available at: http://avalon.law.yale.edu/20th_century/decad047.asp, accessed 3 October 2010.
17 Available at: www.imf.org/external/index.htm, accessed 3 October 2010.
18 Available at: www.un.org/en/documents/charter/index.shtml, accessed 3 October 2010.
19 Available at: www.unicef.org, accessed 3 October 2010.
20 Available at: www.unhcr.org/cgi-bin/texis/vtx/home, accessed 3 October 2010.
21 Available at: www.wfp.org, accessed 3 October 2010.
22 Available at: www.un.org/en/peacekeeping, accessed 3 October 2010.
23 Available at: www.unctad.org/Templates/StartPage.asp?intItemID=2068, accessed 3 October 2010.
24 Available at: www.unep.org, accessed 3 October 2010.
25 Available at: www.undp.org, accessed 3 October 2010.
26 Available at: www.icj-cij.org/homepage/index.php, accessed 3 October 2010.
27 Available at: www.un.org/law/ilc, accessed 3 October 2010.

relatively new field of international criminal law is represented most significantly by the International Criminal Tribunal for the Former Yugoslavia,[28] the International Criminal Tribunal for Rwanda,[29] the International Criminal Court (ICC),[30] and various ad hoc tribunals in Sierra Leone, Timor Leste and Cambodia. International law also fosters economic regulation, harmonisation and unification through the United Nations Commission on International Trade Law (UNCITRAL).[31] The several Vienna Conventions have structured diplomatic and consular relationships.

These interdependencies, interstate cooperation, the pre-eminence of international organisations, and the increasing importance of non-state actors (including commercial enterprises and non-governmental organisations) all call for compliance with international conventions. The multitude of international organisations, in particular those with law-making powers, has proliferated and the ones with adjudicative capacities have progressively brought a new dimension. In the past, international law played a role on the horizontal level between sovereign states, but today the human dimension compels a vertical effect between international conventions and individual citizens.

Doctrine on Sources of International Law

In *International Institutional Law: Unity within Diversity*, Henry G. Schermers and Niels M. Blokker study the nature of documents, in particular those disseminated by the Secretariat of the United Nations as a policy-making and administrative organ. International secretariats make available three types of information:

1. Information concerning the organization to the outside world. By providing this information the secretariat influences public opinion and therefore, indirectly, the support of the organization will receive. The larger international organizations have separate officials, or even a separate department, dealing with information. Usually documents concerning the organization are distributed free of charge. Often press releases, film and radio broadcasts are also made available …
2. Information to the outside world regarding the field covered by the organization. The officials of an international secretariat become experts in the matters within the auspices of the organization. This expert knowledge is often used for the benefit of the member states. The opinions of the legal department of the UN Secretariat carry great weight in the development of international law …
3. Information to members of the other organs (Schermers and Blokker 2003, 320–21)

International organisations owe their birth to international treaties, and therefore have received international legal personality. The chief assignments to international organisations concern promotion of and compliance to the international rules of law. Subsequent treaty-making delivers law-making in substantive terms. This law-making capacity, and the value of formally exposed and distributed information, render legislative power to these materials in the domain of international law. The publications of international organisations serve their

28 Available at: www.icty.org, accessed 3 October 2010.
29 Available at: http://liveunictr.altmansolutions.com, accessed 3 October 2010.
30 Available at: www.icc-cpi.int/Menus/ICC/Home, accessed 3 October 2010.
31 Available at: www.uncitral.org, accessed 3 October 2010.

organisational objectives; dissemination of information on their activities is the vehicle to achieve awareness of the law-making effect. The documents support the activities of employees within the international organisation as well.

It is definitively clear that the public availability of international law resources to wider audiences contributes to greater general certainty about the law. However, it remains to ask what kinds of products issued by the international organisation are fully and formally acknowledged as sources of international law?

International and multilateral conventions and treaties (partially as an articulation of codified custom), and binding and non-binding decisions and resolutions of international organisations, chiefly within the framework of the United Nations, constitute legal principles and represent legal processes as well. The authority of these kinds of authentic sources has been shown to be vital to the development of international law.

However, pursuant to Art. 38 (1) of the Statute of the International Court of Justice, the Court does not recognise resolutions and decisions of United Nations organs such as the Security Council as additional sources of law or as subsidiary evidence. International conventions, international custom, general principles of law remain the key sources to apply. Thus, the Statute ignores the gradual formation of rules of law through law-making processes, such as those mentioned.

What about the position of case law as a source of international law? Many international organisations adjudicate within the province of their constituting treaties and institutional regulating objectives. However, judicial decisions are not defined by Article 38 (1) as a main source of international law.

The 'General Courses' of the Hague Academy of International Law, published as the *Collected Courses of the Hague Academy of International Law*, represent 'teachings of the most highly qualified publicists of the various nations' and are 'subsidiary means for the determination of rules of law'.[32] Recently, Ahmed Mahiou, Antônio Augusto Cançado Trindade and Shabtai Rosenne have all written about the sources of international law and clarified the role of treaties and jurisprudence in the progress of international law.

Mahiou shows how the objectives of international law have changed. International law has evolved into a new mechanism to regulate interstate relations in society, for pacific dispute resolution as an alternative to war, and to promote the coexistence between states and international cooperation. Safeguarding human rights, sustainable development, the growth of interdependency between states and globalisation, technological developments, and new worldwide trade regulations have created a modern approach in international law (Mahiou 2009, 36–108). This suggests that the scope of Article 38 (1) should be expanded.

According to Antonio Cançado Trindade, 'the enumeration of "sources" of International Law listed in Article 38 of the ICJ Statute was never meant to be, nor could it be, exhaustive' (Cançado Trinidade 2006, 150). In addition, in the same way as 'unilateral acts of States (as subjects of International Law) rank among the formal "sources" of the contemporary law of nations, so do the juridical acts (resolutions) of international organizations (likewise subjects of International Law)' (Cançado Trinidade 2006, 167). Following Cançado Trindade:

> the category of resolutions of international organizations does rank among the formal 'sources' of contemporary International Law. Under certain circumstances, some resolutions do meet

32 Available at: www.nijhoffonline, accessed 20 April 2011.

> this test of being a means whereby International Law manifests itself. And even if certain resolutions are purely recommendatory – and, thus, not binding – they are, nevertheless, juridically relevant, have much influenced international practice, and States themselves, naturally reluctant to infringe them, consider themselves at least in the duty to consider them in good faith. Those resolutions form today a vast corpus juris, turned to regulation of matters of concern of the international community as a whole. (Cançado Trinidade 2006, 168)

Here again, realism induces a broadening of the formal sources of international law. Shabtai Rosenne supports the realistic approach that:

> [s]ome of these resolutions are the product of long negotiations and careful drafting with which senior legal officers of the organization and of participating governments have been associated. The question of their place in the general thesaurus of international law cannot therefore be disregarded, whatever their formal legal standing under the relevant constituent instrument.

He concludes that '[i]n consequence, resolutions and other relevant decisions of intergovernmental organizations are today to be included in the general thesaurus of materials for which the international lawyer must have regard' (Rosenne 2002, 70–71).

Alain Pellet, in his commentary on the Statute of the International Court of Justice, considers the list to be incomplete, as history has proven. The enumeration is not at all exhaustive and therefore the International Court of Justice has already made decisions on the basis of other sources of international law. If it does not do so, it 'ignores the gradual formation of the rules of law through a law-making process' (Pellet 2006, 700 and 702).

The element that has not yet been perceived as of equal value is case law. Rosenne validates judicial decisions of all kinds of courts and tribunals as so-called subsidiary means for the determination of rules of law, pursuant to the terminology of Article 38 (1)(d). Because of the growing quantity and relative accessibility of judicial decisions in both hard copy and in electronic formats, he attributes an increasing importance to this category for the development of law, a process confirmed by the International Law Commission (Rosenne 2002, 66–7, 69–70).

Dissemination

In the past, publishing agreements between international organisations and commercial publishers were necessary, because there was no alternative to print for disseminating an organisation's documents. Now, Internet publishing of treaties, case law and other manifestations of international organisations is less expensive, faster, and more appropriate to raise awareness of legal principles governing the relationships between nations, international organisations, multinational organisations, non-governmental organisations and individuals.

The new information society requires free access to documentation, and due to the Internet it has become feasible to arrange for information to be disseminated in an unimpeded way. In particular, the availability of law sources, open to all citizens, enables them to fully participate in the community. Certainty about the law is achieved for practitioners inside and outside the institutions concerned, as well as for academics and distant observers. The democratic dream is within our reach.

Substantive Examples of International Organisations Producing Legal Information

Private International Law

In the field of private international law many conventions come into existence at meetings held by the Hague Conference on Private International Law,[33] an organisation composed of member states, that has been in operation since 1893. The oldest international organisation in The Hague, the Conference has the objective to harmonise, unify and codify private international law worldwide. Sixty-nine states or 'Regional Economic Integration Organisations' (such as the European Union[34] and the Organisation for the Harmonisation of Business Law in Africa)[35] are 'members' of the organisation, have accepted the Statute of the Hague Conference on Private International Law[36] and are 'parties' to particular conventions. The subject matter of the conventions varies broadly, from the Convention of 25 October 1980 on the Civil Aspects of International Child Abduction to the Convention of 23 November 2007 on the International Recovery of Child Support and Other Forms of Family Maintenance, from international contracts to e-commerce.

The conventions are published in a comprehensive handbook, *Collection of Conventions (1951–2009)*, available through the Permanent Bureau of the Hague Conference on Private International Law, which contains the authentic texts of all conventions adopted between 1951 and 2009 in French and English. The texts of conventions adopted before 1951 are not included in this volume but are available on the Hague Conference on Private International Law website.[37] Published proceedings of the sessions (Actes et Documents) and various other publications issued with respect to the Hague Conference on Private International Law are available as well on the organisation's website.

The independent intergovernmental International Institute for the Unification of Private Law (UNIDROIT),[38] based in Rome, was established in 1926. Its aim is to modernise, harmonise and coordinate private law and commercial law between countries and groups of states. Sixty-three nations have acceded to the UNIDROIT statute. Diplomatic conference drafts of international instruments have resulted in such conventions as the 2009 Convention on Substantive Rules for Intermediated Securities, and model laws such as the 2008 Model Law on Leasing.

The *Uniform Law Review/Revue de droit uniforme*, a scholarly journal in the field of private international law, has been published by UNIDROIT since 1974. UNIDROIT also publishes monographs on its activities and the official texts emanating from its core work: the study of the need and method to modernise, harmonise and coordinate the private law systems of the various jurisdictions. Such materials are offered for sale by the organisation. Proceedings and Papers (Actes et Documents) and many other kinds of publications are also available on the UNIDROIT website.

Arbitration

Permanent Court of Arbitration The Permanent Court of Arbitration was established as an outcome of the First Hague Peace Conference of 1899, at which the so-called Convention for the

33 Available at: http://hcch.e-vision.nl/index_en.php?act=text.display&tid=1, accessed 3 October 2010.

34 Available at: http://europa.eu, accessed 3 October 2010.

35 Available at: www.ohada.org, accessed 3 October 2010.

36 Available at: www.hcch.net/index_en.php?act=conventions.text&cid=29, accessed 3 October 2010.

37 Available at: www.hcch.net, accessed 3 October 2010.

38 Available at: www.unidroit.org, accessed 3 October 2010.

Pacific Settlement of International Disputes[39] was concluded. Its objective – facilitating immediate recourse to arbitration for international differences which it has not been possible to settle by diplomacy – was restated during the Second First Hague Peace Conference of 1907.

Parties in a dispute enter into a *compromis* expressing the subject of the dispute and the appointment of arbitrators; agreement on the *compromis* marks the willingness of parties to accept as binding the eventual award issued in the name of the tribunal and its members. The award settles the dispute definitively and without possibility of appeal.

According to Article 53 of the 1899 Convention for the Pacific Settlement of International Disputes[40] and Article 80 of the 1907 Convention for the Pacific Settlement of International Disputes,[41] the award is read out in a public meeting or sitting. In Article 32 (2) of the 1992 Permanent Court of Arbitration Optional Rules for Arbitrating Disputes Between Two States,[42] a new set of procedural rules, it is constituted that the award 'shall be made in writing' and, in Article 32 (5), that 'the award may be made public only with the consent of both parties'. The first decades of its existence showed active recourse to the Permanent Court of Arbitration. During the following years the interest diminished and its scope was broadened, abandoning the two states prerequisite. The pre-Second World War cases held at the Permanent Court of Arbitration can be found at the Hague Justice Portal[43] and the most recent cases are available at the Permanent Court of Arbitration's website. T.M.C. Asser Press publishes the *Permanent Court of Arbitration Award Series* in cooperation with Cambridge University Press.

International Centre for the Settlement of Investment Disputes The International Centre for the Settlement of Investment Disputes (ICSID),[44] an affiliated division of the World Bank, aims to 'provide facilities for conciliation and arbitration of international investment disputes' between Contracting States and nationals of other Contracting States in accordance with the provisions of the Convention on the Settlement of Investment Disputes (CSIG).[45] Regulations and rules, various filed bilateral investment treaties and cases can be found at the ICSID website.[46] The *ICSID Review: Foreign Investment Law Journal*, published by The Johns Hopkins University Press, offers scholarly approaches and decisions. *The ICSID Reports: Reports of Cases Decided Under the Convention on the Settlement of Investment Disputes between States and Nationals of Other States* are published by Cambridge University Press on behalf of the Lauterpacht Research Centre for International Law.

United Nations Commission on International Trade Law Through its database, Case Law on UNCITRAL Texts (CLOUT),[47] the UNCITRAL Secretariat has established a gateway for collecting and disseminating information on court decisions and arbitral awards relating to UNCITRAL.

39 Available at: http://avalon.law.yale.edu/20th_century/pacific.asp, accessed 3 October 2010.

40 Available at: http://avalon.law.yale.edu/19th_century/hague01.asp, accessed 3 October 2010.

41 Available at: http://avalon.law.yale.edu/20th_century/pacific.asp, accessed 3 October 2010.

42 Available at: www.pca-cpa.org/upload/files/2STATENG.pdf, accessed 3 October 2010.

43 Available at: www.haguejusticeportal.net, accessed 3 October 2010.

44 Available at: http://icsid.worldbank.org/ICSID/Index.jsp, accessed 3 October 2010.

45 Available at: http://icsid.worldbank.org/ICSID/StaticFiles/basicdoc/partA.htm, accessed 3 October 2010.

46 Available at: http://icsid.worldbank.org/ICSID/ICSID/RulesMain.jsp, accessed 3 October 2010.

47 Available at: www.uncitral.org/uncitral/en/case_law.html, accessed 3 October 2010.

Iran-US Claims Tribunal The Iran-US Claims Tribunal (IUSCT)[48] is primarily concerned with the bilateral claims emanating from the resolution of the Tehran Hostage Crisis. The Iran-U.S. Claims Tribunal Reports are published by Cambridge University Press.

United Nations Compensation Commission In relation to the unlawful Iraqi invasion and occupation of Kuwait a settlement system for processing claims and payments was set up under the umbrella of the United Nations. The United Nations Compensation Commission (UNCC)[49] publishes its reports on its website.

International Council for Commercial Arbitration The International Council for Commercial Arbitration (ICCA)[50] is dedicated to promoting and developing arbitration, conciliation and other forms of international dispute resolution. The ICCA produces a database with the assistance of the Permanent Court of Arbitration that includes authoritative texts.[51]

International Chamber of Commerce Since 1923 the International Chamber of Commerce[52] in Paris has offered dispute resolution services. The organisation itself does not have a forum through which the arbitral awards are being publicised.

Universal Peaceful Dispute Settlement through Adjudication, International Court of Justice

The International Court of Justice or World Court,[53] one of the six principal organs of the United Nations, sits in the Peace Palace in The Hague. The court's role is to settle legal disputes peacefully in accordance to international law, and to give advisory opinions on legal issues, referred to it by United Nations institutions. The second Chapter of the Statute of the International Court of Justice refers to its competence. According to Art. 34 (1): 'Only states may be parties in cases before the Court'. Art. 36 (1) states that the jurisdiction comprises 'all matters specially provided for in the Charter of the United Nations or in treaties and conventions in force'. Art. 36 (2) authorises that:

> The states parties … declare that they recognize … the jurisdiction of the Court in all legal disputes concerning:
>
> a. the interpretation of a treaty;
> b. any question of international law;
> c. the existence of any fact which, if established, would constitute a breach of an international obligation;
> d. the nature or extent of the reparation to be made for the breach of an international obligation.

Case law of the International Court of Justice, covering contentious cases and advisory opinions, is published by the Registry in several series. The first series, 'Judgments, Advisory Opinions and Orders', contains the decisions of the Court, in both English and French. Each decision is published in print as soon after it has been given as possible in an unbound fascicle which is sold separately. Now, immediately after a judgment is rendered the text itself is publicised on the

48 Available at: www.iusct.org, accessed 3 October 2010.
49 Available at: www.uncc.ch, accessed 3 October 2010.
50 Available at: www.arbitration-icca.org/index.html, accessed 3 October 2010.
51 Available at: www.kluwerarbitration.com, accessed 3 October 2010.
52 Available at: www.iccwbo.org, accessed 3 October 2010.
53 Available at: www.icj-cij.org/homepage/index.php, accessed 3 October 2010.

court website. The second series, 'Pleadings, Oral Arguments, Documents', is published after the termination of each case, also on the website, and contains the documentation relating to the case in the original language (English or French), and may include unofficial translations. Many cases are also published as texts accompanied by commentaries and other relevant explanations by a variety of publishers. Case law is indexed in digests of the work of the International Court of Justice. Other publications include 'Acts and Documents', a Yearbook and an annual Bibliography.

Topical

Law of the Sea The International Tribunal on the Law of the Sea,[54] which is seated in Hamburg, Germany, came into existence pursuant to the 1982 United Nations Convention on the Law of the Sea.[55] By 2010 16 cases of peaceful dispute settlement had been conducted at the International Tribunal on the Law of the Sea within the international regime of the seabed and ocean floor, maritime delimitation, the territorial sea, contiguous zone and continental shelf beyond the national jurisdiction, and the protection of the marine environment. *Reports of Judgments, Advisory Opinions and Orders* and *Pleadings, Minutes of Public Sittings and Documentation* are published on the website of the International Tribunal and by Martinus Nijhoff Publishers (Brill).

Environmental Law The Permanent Court of Arbitration, which was involved in the Mox Plant-arbitration between Ireland and the United Kingdom on the alleged nuclear pollution of the Irish Sea, has set 'Optional Rules for Conciliation of Disputes relating to the Environment and/or Nature'. The International Court of Justice held a Chamber for Environmental Matters until 2006, pursuant to Article 26, paragraph 1, of the Statute, (although, for example, the Gabčíkovo-Nagymaros Dam Project between Hungary and Slovakia was an environmental case). The Chamber for Marine Environment Disputes of the International Tribunal for the Law of the Sea has a special interest in the environment. However, no separate international legal organisation adjudicates in environmental matters.

The pre-Second World War so-called 'Trail Smelter Arbitration' between Canada and the United States was the first transboundary environmental law issue in modern history. Much case law has been collected in the *International Environmental Law Reports*, published by Cambridge University Press, which contains both international and national judicial decisions. *International Environmental Law* is a comprehensive collection of environmental treaties published by Kluwer Law International.

World Trade Organization and World Intellectual Property Organization The World Trade Organization[56] both liberalises international commerce by restricting it within well-negotiated agreements and settles trade disputes according to set rules. Since the formal establishment of the WTO in 1995, the General Agreement on Tariffs and Trade (GATT) phenomenon of ad hoc instituted dispute settling panels has been replaced by standing judicial or arbitration Panels. A Panel or Dispute Settlement Body (DSB) drafts reports on contentious trade matters, and a permanent Appellate Body is concerned with appeal cases. The WTO Appellate Body, according

54 Available at: www.itlos.org, accessed 3 October 2010.

55 Available at: www.un.org/Depts/los/convention_agreements/convention_overview_convention.htm, accessed 3 October 2010.

56 Available at: www.wto.org, accessed 3 October 2010.

to Art. 17.6 of the Understanding on Rules and Procedures Governing the Settlement of Disputes, processes exclusively 'issues of law covered in the panel report and legal interpretation developed by the panel'. The adjudicative law-making documentation of the WTO's dispute settlement system is on the organisation's website. The WTO is a substantial publisher through its own initiatives, but items on dispute settlement especially are published in a cooperative effort with Cambridge University Press.

The World Intellectual Property Organization's[57] aim is to promote the protection of intellectual property throughout the world. Intellectual property rights have become increasingly significant from the economic point of view. The Trade-Related Intellectual Property Rights (TRIPS) agreement is basically a WTO convention, but has resulted in close cooperation between the two on this specific subject. At the WIPO bureau an 'Arbitration and Mediation Center' was created in 1994. Case law is available at the organisation's website.

Human Rights Law Since the United Nations' Universal Declaration of Human Rights[58] was promulgated in 1948, the field of human rights law has expanded, while many variants of human rights law have been defined in other categories, such as labour and health regulations. The Office of the United Nations High Commissioner for Human Rights[59] monitors compliance to human rights treaties on the global scale. Committees come to decisions in cases of individual complaints on the application of the International Covenant on Civil and Political Rights (CCPR),[60] the International Covenant on Economic, Social and Cultural Rights (CESCR),[61] the Convention Against Torture and Other Cruel, Inhuman and Degrading or Punishment (CAT),[62] the International Convention on the Elimination of All Forms of Racial Discrimination (CERD),[63] the Convention on the Elimination of All Forms of Discrimination Against Women (CEDAW),[64] the Convention on the Rights of the Child (CRC), and the Convention on the Protection of the Rights of All Migrant Workers and Members of Their Families (CMW).[65] Decisions may be consulted through a database on the High Commissioner's website.[66] An excellent database is available as well at the Netherlands Institute of Human Rights of the Utrecht University.[67]

The European Human Rights Convention[68] is the main vehicle of human rights law within Europe. The European Court for Human Rights in Strasbourg, France,[69] offers basic texts and case law in the so-called HUDOC Database.[70] Many printed case law collections, containing key cases in European Human Rights Law, are available (see for instance Mowbray 2007).

57 Available at: www.wipo.int, accessed 3 October 2010.

58 Available at: www.un.org/en/documents/udhr/index.shtml, accessed 3 October 2010.

59 Available at: www.ohchr.org/EN/Pages/WelcomePage.aspx, accessed 3 October 2010.

60 Available at: www2.ohchr.org/english/law/ccpr.htm, accessed 3 October 2010.

61 Available at: www2.ohchr.org/english/law/cescr.htm, accessed 3 October 2010.

62 Available at: www1.umn.edu/humanrts/instree/h2catoc.htm, accessed 3 October 2010.

63 Available at: www2.ohchr.org/english/law/cerd.htm, accessed 3 October 2010.

64 Available at: www.un.org/womenwatch/daw/cedaw/cedaw.htm, accessed 3 October 2010.

65 Available at: www2.ohchr.org/english/law/cmw.htm, accessed 3 October 2010.

66 Available at: http://tb.ohchr.org/default.aspx, accessed 3 October 2010.

67 Available at: http://sim.law.uu.nl, accessed 3 October 2010.

68 Available at: www.hri.org/docs/ECHR50.html, accessed 3 October 2010.

69 Available at: www.echr.coe.int/echr/homepage_en, accessed 3 October 2010.

70 Available at: www.echr.coe.int/ECHR/EN/Header/Case-Law/Hudoc/Hudoc+database, accessed 3 October 2010.

The Inter-American Court of Human Rights[71] in San José, Costa Rica, has guaranteed human rights politics on behalf of the Organization of American States (OAS), since 1979. According to the Court's Statute (Art. 25) the decisions, judgments and opinions 'shall be published'. Judgments are on the Court's website.

The African Charter on Human and Peoples' Rights[72] has paved the way for the African Court on Human and People's Rights.[73] The East-African Court of Justice,[74] modelled after the Strasbourg Court, addresses human rights infringements.

International Criminal Law The post-Second World War Trials of Nuremberg and Tokyo are founding events in the history of international criminal law: indicting and punishing war criminals for breaching peace, conducting an aggressive war, committing war crimes and perpetrating crimes against humanity.[75] The records of the proceedings are widely available in paper, on microfiche and on the Internet. In the aftermath of the war atrocities the Genocide Convention,[76] the Universal Declaration of Human Rights and the 1949 Geneva Convention on the Protection of Civilian Population[77] were promulgated; text and commentary of these international criminal and humanitarian law instruments are published in print and electronically.

The massacres and genocides of the 1990s in Yugoslavia and Rwanda gave a new impetus to international criminal law. The International Criminal Tribunal for the Former Yugoslavia and International Criminal Tribunal for Rwanda were established under the United Nations. By statute, judgements of the two Tribunals must be 'delivered ... in public' and 'accompanied by a reasoned opinion in writing'.[78] The documentary part of the trials is primarily an Internet record, but several case law series have been prompted, for instance, *Annotated Leading Cases of International Criminal Tribunals*, published by Intersentia in Antwerp, both in paper and as an Internet facility.[79] This series includes as well the decisions of the Special Tribunals for Sierra Leone and Timor-Leste.

The International Criminal Court commenced its activities within the domain of genocide, crimes against humanity, war crimes and the crime of aggression in 2002. The 1998 Rome Statute, instrumental in the establishment of the International Criminal Court, states in Art. 50 that 'the judgements of the Court, as well as other decisions ... shall be published'.[80] Under the Regulations of the Court the Court's website is the forum for its Official Journal and the decisions and orders.

A related phenomenon is the increasing presence of international criminal law in national courts. On the Hague Justice Portal website[81] theDomCLIC Project refers to domestic jurisprudence with

71 Available at: www.corteidh.or.cr/index.cfm?CFID=660733&CFTOKEN=65106291, accessed 3 October 2010.

72 Available at: www1.umn.edu/humanrts/instree/z1afchar.htm, accessed 3 October 2010.

73 Available at: www.aict-ctia.org/courts_conti/achpr/achpr_home.html, accessed 3 October 2010.

74 Available at: www.eac.int/eacj, accessed 3 October 2010.

75 As a matter of fact, after the First World War and ensuing the Versailles Treaty, violations of the Laws of War were already tried at the so-called Leipzig Court.

76 Available at: www.un.org/millennium/law/iv-1.htm, accessed 3 October 2010.

77 Available at: www1.umn.edu/humanrts/instree/y4gcpcp.htm, accessed 3 October 2010.

78 For Yugoslavia: Statute of the Tribunal, Art. 23; for Rwanda: Statute of the Tribunal, Art. 22.

79 Available at: www.annotatedleadingcases.com, accessed 3 October 2010.

80 Available at: http://untreaty.un.org/cod/icc/index.html, accessed 3 October 2010.

81 Available at: www.haguejusticeportal.net, accessed 3 October 2010.

respect to international criminal law all over the world. Oxford University Press has developed a similar type of database: Oxford Reports on International Law.[82]

Geographical

Europe The European Union has had its own Court of Justice since 1952.[83] The Court's jurisdiction is limited to the proper application and interpretation of the European Union treaties and European Community laws within as well as between Member States. Recent case law is on the Court's website[84] while EUR-Lex comprises older materials as well, offering general access to European Union law.[85] The Court of First Instance (now the General Court) principally investigates actions of natural and legal persons under European Union acts, decides upon these cases, and covers actions between Member States and the European Commission. Many commercial publishers have reshaped European Union legal public database content into more refined and products. Examples include OJ OnlinePlus[86] and Caselex,[87] which offers access to most important national and European case law linked to European Union's commercial areas of law. This kind of information is published as well in Sweet & Maxwell's *Common Market Law Reports*.

The Americas The North American Free Trade Agreement (NAFTA)[88] is a tripartite agreement between Mexico, Canada and the United States, aimed at the removal of trade, investment and tariff impediments. The NAFTA Dispute Settlement mechanism, Decisions and Reports, and Alternative Dispute Resolution methods are available at the secretariat's website.[89]

The Union of South American Nations (UNASUR)[90] is an all-Latin America initiative to create a single market, advance economic cooperation, improve infrastructure, and regulate the free movement of persons, all very much in line with the European Union example. The Andean Community[91] and MERCOSUR[92] are precursors to that development. Both provide for courts having international jurisdiction, chiefly addressing civil and commercial contracts. The Caribbean Community (CARICOM)[93] has basically the same goals and structure; it has discussed the establishment of a supranational court.

Africa The Economic Community of West African States (ECOWAS)[94] is a West African organisation for economic cooperation, with a Community Court modelled after the European Court of Justice.

82 Available at: www.oxfordlawreports.com, accessed 3 October 2010.
83 Available at: http://europa.eu/institutions/inst/justice/index_en.htm, accessed 3 October 2010.
84 Available at: http://curia.europa.eu/jurisp/cgi-bin/form.pl?lang=en, accessed 3 October 2010.
85 Available at: http://eur-lex.europa.eu/en/index.htm, accessed 3 October 2010.
86 Available at: www.ellispub.com/oj-onlineplus.html, accessed 3 October 2010.
87 Available at: www.caselex.com, accessed 3 October 2010.
88 Available at: www.nafta-sec-alena.org/en/view.aspx?conID=590, accessed 3 October 2010.
89 Available at: www.nafta-sec-alena.org/en/view.aspx, accessed 3 October 2010.
90 Available at: www.comunidadandina.org/sudamerica.htm, accessed 3 October 2010.
91 Available at: www.comunidadandina.org/endex.htm, accessed 3 October 2010.
92 Available at: www.mercosur.int/msweb/Portal%20Intermediario, accessed 3 October 2010.
93 Available at: www.caricom.org, accessed 3 October 2010.
94 Available at: www.ecowas.int, accessed 3 October 2010.

Treaty Series

General The historic publication on treaties in the modern era is Jean Dumont's *Corps universel diplomatique du droit des gens*, published from 1726 to 1731, covering treaties between about 800 and 1718. It was succeeded and superseded by the more widely known *Recueil des principaux traités d'alliance, de paix, de trêve …*, for which Georg Friedrich von Martens and Baron Charles de Martens acted as the first composers (hence the name 'Martens-series'). More than 100 volumes contain treaties from the late fifteenth century up to 1939, although the emphasis is on the nineteenth and early twentieth century. This series was followed by Clive Parry's *Consolidated Treaty Series* which published 231 volumes for the years 1648 to 1918. The League of Nations published its so-called LNTS, the 'League of Nations Treaty Series', comprising 204 volumes for 1920 to 1944.

The United Nations has published the UNTS, the 'United Nations Treaty Series' since 1946, pursuant to Article 102 of the Charter of the United Nations, in which it is stated that:

> 1. Every treaty and every international agreement entered into by any Member of the United Nations after the present Charter comes into force shall as soon as possible be registered with the Secretariat and published by it.
>
> 2. No party to any such treaty or international agreement which has not been registered in accordance with the provisions of paragraph 1 of this Article may invoke that treaty or agreement before any organ of the United Nations.

The hard copy UNTS contains over 150,000 treaties in 2,200 volumes; access to the UNTS is available electronically.[95]

Special We may make a distinction between treaty publications from a certain period and topical treaty publications (see for instance Gibler 2009; Grenville and Wasserstein 2001). In the Yale Law School, Lillian Goldman Law Library's Avalon Project: Documents in Law, History and Diplomacy,[96] scholars find a multitude of full-text historic and contemporary treaties. The University of London Institute of Advanced Legal Studies' Flare Index to Treaties is another useful catalogue for research on treaties.[97]

Case Law and Other International Legal Material

'Landmark Documents', 'Text and Commentary' and 'Cases and Materials' are all useful designations in legal publishing. Hence, treaty law and court decisions as primary sources of international law are selected, digested and made available for legal practice and scholarship. *International Legal Materials* is a bimonthly publication of the American Society of International Law which provides primary sources, such as full-text treaties, judicial decisions and arbitral awards, resolutions of international organisations and national legislation of interest to the international community.

The well-known *International Law Reports*, a Cambridge University Press product for the Lauterpacht Centre for International Law, is a series of public international law case reports, published since 1919, covering national court decisions and arbitrations with international angles,

95 Available at: http://treaties.un.org, accessed 3 October 2010.

96 Available at: http://avalon.law.yale.edu, accessed 3 October 2010.

97 Available at: http://ials.sas.ac.uk/library/flag/introtreaties.htm, accessed 3 October 2010.

on topics such as boundaries, immunity, treaties, terrorism and refugee law. *International Law Reports*, in combination with important United Kingdom legal information and European Union law resources, has been incorporated in JUSTIS.[98]

Oxford Reports on International Law This is an amalgam of electronic information on International Law in Domestic Courts, International Criminal Law, International Human Rights Law, International Courts of General Jurisdiction and International Investment Claims.

Encyclopaedias Both the paper and the electronic versions of the *Max Planck Encyclopedia of Public International Law*[99] serve very well as an introduction into the subject matter.

Yearbooks The *Yearbook of the United Nations*, the *United Nations Juridical Yearbook* and the *Yearbook of the International Law Commission*, all available in paper and electronically, give an overview of developments in the field of international relations and international law.

Helpful online guides to digital resources in international law include: the American Society of International Law's Electronic Information System for International Law (EISIL) website;[100] Yale's Avalon Project; the innovative Audiovisual Library of International Law of the United Nations;[101] the general law resources roundabouts: LLRX.com[102] and GlobaLex;[103] and the resources of HeinOnline.[104]

Library websites and catalogues like UNBISnet[105] offer a broad spectrum of resources, as do the law libraries of the Max Planck Institutes for Comparative Public Law and International Law[106] and Comparative and International Private Law,[107] L'Institut suisse de droit comparé,[108] and the Peace Palace.[109]

References

Cançado Trindade, A. (2006), 'International Law for Humankind: Towards a New Jus Gentium. General Course on Public International Law', 2 vols, in *Recueil des cours, Académie de droit international de La Haye*, vols 316 and 317 (Leiden/Boston: Martinus Nijhoff).

Gibler, D. (2009), *International Military Alliances, 1648–2000*, 2 vols (Washington, DC: CQ Press).

Grenville, J. and Wasserstein, B. (2001), *The Major International Treaties of the Twentieth Century, a History and Guide with Texts*, 2 vols (3rd edn) (London: Routledge).

98 Available at: www.justis.com, accessed 3 October 2010.

99 Available at: www.mpepil.com, accessed 3 October 2010.

100 Available at: www.eisil.org/index.php?cat=21&t=sub_pages, accessed 3 October 2010.

101 Available at: www.un.org/law/avl, accessed 3 October 2010.

102 Available at: www.llrx.com, accessed 3 October 2010.

103 Available at: www.nyulawglobal.org/Globalex, accessed 3 October 2010.

104 Available at: http://heinonline.org, accessed 3 October 2010.

105 Available at: http://unbisnet.un.org, accessed 3 October 2010.

106 Available at: www.mpil.de/ww/en/pub/library.cfm, accessed 3 October 2010.

107 Available at: www.mpipriv.de/ww/en/pub/library.htm, accessed 3 October 2010.

108 Available at: www.isdc.ch/fr/bibliotheque.asp/4-0-1501-5-4-0, accessed 3 October 2010.

109 Available at: www.ppl.nl, accessed 3 October 2010.

Mahiou, A. (2009), 'Le droit international ou la dialectique de la rigueur et de la flexibilité: Cours général de droit international public', in *Recueil des cours, Académie de droit international de La Haye*, vol. 337 (Leiden/Boston: Martinus Nijhoff).

Mowbray, A. (2007), *Cases and Materials on the European Convention on Human Rights* (2nd edn) (Oxford: Oxford University Press).

Pellet, A. (2006), 'Article 38', in Zimmermann, A., Tomuschat, C. and Oellers-Frahm, K. (eds), *The Statute of the International Court of Justice. A Commentary* (Oxford: Oxford University Press).

Rosenne, S. (2002), 'The Perplexities of Modern International Law. General Course on Public International Law', in *Recueil des cours, Académie de droit international de La Haye*, vol. 291 (Leiden/Boston: Martinus Nijhoff).

Schermers, H. and Blokker, N. (2003), *International Institutional Law: Unity within Diversity* (4th edn) (Boston/Leiden: Martinus Nijhoff).

Wolfrum, R. (2008), *Statement: Freedom of Navigation: New Challenges*. Available at: www.itlos.org/news/statements/Wolfrum/Singapore%20%2032nd%20Oceans%20Conf.%20%20Freedom%20of%20Navigation%20ptg%2023.04.08%20BA.pdf, accessed 12 September 2010.

Chapter 15
Comparative Law: Academic Perspectives[1]

Teresa M. Miguel

> A student confronted with only one solution to a legal problem has a tendency to assume it is the right one. When he is confronted with two, he is encouraged to think.
>
> James Gordley (2001)

Introduction

Over the past 15 years, comparative law has undergone a dramatic and profound metamorphosis. The academic literature reveals a sense of hopelessness for the sustained endurance of the discipline in the mid-1990s but shows signs of a rejuvenated and reinvented discipline in the first decade of the new millennium. One reason could be a changing-of-the-guard in comparative law faculty around the world with the 'heroes of the golden era' (Markesinis 2003, 2) being replaced by younger scholars leading a renewed charge with creative and thought-provoking comparative legal theories and methodologies. Another reason might be the smaller world in which we live due to globalisation and access to new information and communication technologies. There is also more effort towards unification and harmonisation of national and transnational laws, as seen in the creation of a European civil code (Smits 2007) and uniform social welfare obligations in India (Menski 2007), which can be achieved only by careful, analytical, comparative legal analysis.

Additional evidence of growing interest in comparative legal scholarship includes the rapidly increasing number of currently published comparative law journals around the world (Appendix A). Particularly impressive are the numbers of active comparative law centres and institutes (Appendix B), and local, national and international comparative law societies (Appendix C).

Founded in 1924, the International Academy of Comparative Law (IACL) includes the national committees of 67 countries on six continents. The IACL meets biannually, publishes conference papers and proceedings, and is a testament to the longevity of comparative law and legal studies ('IACL History' 2008). A recently created annual summer programme involving seven universities on four continents further demonstrates the growing global importance of comparative legal studies (Bevans and McKay 2009).

Despite the renewed interest, there is no consensus on the definition of comparative law or its methodology, and there is still disagreement on whether comparative law is a discipline, a sub-discipline, or simply a method of looking at law (Örücü 2007b, 43, 46). It is agreed, however, that comparative law is much more than describing the similarities and differences between legal systems: 'Comparative law is a science of knowledge with its own separate sphere; an independent science, producing theoretical distillate. Comparative law can be regarded as the critical method of legal science' (Örücü 2007b, 44).

This chapter is an overview of some trends in the academic realm of comparative law in the twenty-first century. The chapter is organised along geographical lines, with the recognition that:

---

1 This chapter is built upon the work of my colleague and mentor Daniel Wade. I am grateful for his editorial suggestions and for his continued support.

1. the importance of borders is diminishing for legal scholars
2. the amount of cross-national legal scholarship, teaching and practice is increasing, and
3. discussion of and engagement in comparative legal methodology is not confined to North America and Western Europe although scholarship is most plentiful in these regions

It is impossible to discuss every country, go into great depth for a single country, or cover every methodological approach.[2] I consider concepts that have drawn considerable attention and momentum, such as functionalism, cultural immersion, comparative jurisprudence and legal transplantation, as well as the problems of translation and the incorporation of comparative legal theory and methodology into the classroom.

The chapter covers comparative law literature in many languages, but there is an unavoidable bias towards English-language materials published in the United States and Europe. The amount of scholarship emanating from the United States is far greater than from any other country.

North America (United States and Canada)

Since the late twentieth century, North American comparatists have written frequently regarding the need to move forward, reinvent comparative legal studies, and gain respect within the academy of legal scholars. Scholars agree that it is crucial to develop comparative legal theory and methodology, and to more effectively incorporate comparative law into the classroom.

Reflections at the End of the Twentieth Century

In 1997 Pierre Legrand conducted a series of interviews with John Henry Merryman, a recipient of the American Society of Comparative Law's Lifetime Achievement Award (Legrand 1999). In an insightful and critical analysis, Merryman discussed the history of comparative law in the United States, offering many observations, some harsh, about academic comparatists and the state of comparative law on the eve of a new millennium:

- It is still unclear what a comparatist is; much of the work of a comparatist is descriptive in nature whereas other work involves unification (Legrand 1999, 48)
- Comparing rules of law, which is the dominant practice, is 'relatively trivial' and seemingly wasteful (Legrand 1999, 4, 46)
- Comparatists have not been at the forefront of the globalisation movement (Legrand 1999, 8)
- There is very little true comparison occurring in the academic community beyond mere description of foreign legal systems (Legrand 1999, 32)
- No one has engaged in substantial theoretical work in the comparative law discipline (Legrand 1999, 35)
- There are no accomplished works on methodology in comparative law (Legrand 1999, 51)

Merryman concluded the interview with a focused suggestion on how to 'redeem' comparative legal studies: 'We need first of all, to embrace a more generous conception of "law" and "legal

2 Comparative law methodologies are discussed throughout this chapter. For further discussion and comprehensive bibliographies, see Van Hoecke 2004; Örücü 2006; Örücü and Nelken 2007.

system". Once we do that, everything else follows: the obvious importance of history, the utility of social theory, the value of scientific explanation, and so on' (Legrand 1999, 62).

Ugo Mattei suggested that comparative law will survive as an academic discipline only if it helps connect law to other social sciences; it is doomed if it is connected only to globalisation (Mattei 1998, 709). Mattei saw a revived interest in both methodological discussion and interdisciplinary work, and claimed that these efforts were 'the only chance for survival as well as the key for success of comparative law in the United States' (Mattei 1998, 718).[3]

Around the same time, Annelise Riles argued that comparative law is experiencing a resurgence of interest partly because of globalisation (Riles 1999, 221, 223). In addition to citing well-known legal scholars espousing the same view, Riles also pointed to rising scholars who have chosen comparative law over other disciplines (Riles 1999, 221). Riles further reported on her own research showing that law review articles utilising the term *comparative law* increased from 57 in 1990 to 224 in 1996 (Riles 1999, 222).[4]

More recently Mathias Reimann has argued that comparative law could be strengthened by taking three steps: 1) establishing a canon; 2) agreeing on a set of clearly defined goals; and 3) committing to long-term cooperation with other scholars (Reimann 2002, 695–9). The willingness of comparative law scholars to critique their own discipline is evidence of the discipline's positive transition (Clark 2006, 209).

Methodological Approaches and Problems

Functionalism Most leading US comparatists of the post-war era were scholar-refugees from Hitler's Europe, mainly from Germany and Austria (Grosswald Curran 2002, 9). They assumed a unified humanity without class distinctions, special interests, or other factors dividing society. They also focused on *functionalism*, an approach which de-emphasises differences that might prevent practical, universal resolutions to legal questions. Because they focus on similarities, functionalist approaches can ignore or disguise the fact that, even in their simplest forms, legal questions can have different meanings in different cultures (Grosswald Curran 2002, 11).

Identifying unifying elements and discounting differences was the dominant purpose of comparative law in the twentieth century (Grosswald Curran 2002, 7), and not only in the United States (Örücü 2007a, 50–52). Many comparatists of the past worked to compile a body of universal laws that would reflect universal human needs and attributes based in objectively verifiable human commonalities (Grosswald Curran 2002, 4). For Reimann, the great achievement of comparative law in the second half of the twentieth century was its diverse, expansive and valuable body of scholarship, even if it was disjointed and lacking in consistent theory and methodology (Reimann 2002, 674–89).

---

3 Mattei's article is part of a larger symposium on the current state and future outlook for comparative legal studies and practice in the United States ('Symposium: New Directions in Comparative Law' 1998). See, also, another from about the same time ('Symposium: New Approaches to Comparative Law' 1997) for critiques of the discipline for its lack of methodological reflection and theoretical foundation, and unwillingness to revisit its goals.

4 The exact scope of Riles's search is unclear, making it impossible fully to recreate her search of the journal literature in Lexis in 1996. In May 2009, I conducted a full-text search for the term 'comparative law' in the LexisNexis *US Law Reviews & Journals* database for 1996 which returned only 60 hits; the same search conducted for 2008 returned 692 hits. A search for the term 'comparative' in the titles of journal articles in 1996 returned 28 hits; for 2008, 148 hits. The database contains 19 journals with 'comparative' in the title: 17 also had 'international' in the title. Twelve of the 19 were founded between 1990 and May 2009 (Appendix A).

Grosswald Curran criticised functionalism as:

> a tautology which may lead to a refusal to probe beneath the surface for underlying, sometimes irreconcilable, differences among legal systems. Even purely functionalist objectives, such as harmonizing international laws, drafting effective treaties, and understanding the resolutions to legal issues in other countries, will be undermined by the failure to consider incompatible features of different legal systems. To deny difference is to deny recognition to the particulars that constitute identity itself; in that sense, it is to camouflage and erase identity. (Grosswald Curran 2002, 8)

Although challenged in the United States, functionalism has flourished in European 'common core' studies and projects (Örücü 2007a, 51).

Cultural immersion As exiles from Hitler's Europe, older legal comparatists appreciated the need to understand a legal culture in order to: 1) effectively engage in a comparative analysis of the legal system; and 2) accurately translate the system's legal discourse. They were practising cultural immersion, which involves understanding the political, historical, economic and linguistic contexts that shape and drive a legal system; it involves being open to differences beneath the surface and at the most fundamental level (Grosswald Curran 2002, 49, 118).

Grosswald Curran advocates cultural immersion and proposes several specific goals:

1. functional ascertainment of practical solutions to legal problems in one or more legal systems
2. an understanding of foreign legal systems
3. a deeper understanding of one's own legal system, and
4. the enrichment of our understanding of the process of legal analysis (Grosswald Curran 2002, 47)

James Whitman employed cultural immersion to compare laws of the United States and continental Europe. He attributed the differences to underlying cultural values, finding that the US legal system is concerned primarily with liberty whereas continental European legal culture is built upon the concept of human dignity. For Whitman, this distinction accounts for the profound differences in laws concerning, for example, hate speech, sexual and workplace harassment, and privacy (Whitman 2000, 2004; Cotterrell 2007, 149–52).

Comparative jurisprudence The method of *comparative jurisprudence* focuses on the comparability of a state's enactment of juridical ideas: ideas and laws that make up a state's legal system (Valcke 2004, 739). Catherine Valcke has proposed that comparative jurisprudence is an ideal method for comparing entire legal systems rather merely examining legal rules and institutions (Valcke 2004, 719). Basil Markesinis and Christopher McCrudden also advocate a comparative jurisprudential approach, described in greater detail in a later section (Markesinis 2003; McCrudden 2007).

The problem of translation Fluency in the native language of the legal culture under study is a vital component of comparative law. Grosswald Curran notes the often-problematic issue of translation, making three points:

1. translation illustrates clearly and simply the inseparability of law and language
2. translation 'operates within languages, among the plurality of discourses embedded in what passes for one language, and is merely more apparent in the international arena where the distinctions among the discourses called languages are official', and
3. translation is sometimes impossible. 'The untranslatable, in the largest sense of the word, remains the biggest challenge for the legal comparatists. It is the challenge of immersing oneself with sufficient depth into a foreign legal culture so as to assess it from within' (Grosswald Curran 2002, 38–9)

In comparative law, translation involves the cultural as well as the literal translation of legal texts. 'We must allow the concepts of the foreign language to become images and then describe them in our language' (Grosswald Curran 2002, 32, citing Grossfeld 1996). But some legal terms are simply untranslatable. Geeroms gives the examples of: *cassation, revision* and *appeal*, which legal scholars and jurists often erroneously use interchangeably when discussing final review matters in the courts (Geeroms 2002, 201). She demonstrates that fluency in the vernacular language is essential for understanding foreign legal cultures and systems, and for engaging in comparative legal analysis.

In *Comparative Legal Semiotics and the Divided Brain: Are We Producing Half-Brained Lawyers?*, the authors offer an entertaining examination of the social and cultural differences that must be acknowledged and understood when engaging in cross-cultural legal practice (Hiller and Grossfeld 2002).

Comparative Legal Studies

In the past, only a few North American law schools offered introductory courses in comparative law, advanced courses in foreign law, or courses focusing on the comparative aspects of specific areas of law. Today, most, if not all, American Bar Association-accredited law schools offer at least a basic comparative law course. Over 100 of these schools and their institutes are sponsor members of the American Society of Comparative Law (Clark 2006, 210).

In 1993, John Langbein surveyed for course offerings in comparative law. He observed:

> Nineteen of the [top 25 US law schools] offer a basic course in comparative law or civil law, that is, a course contrasting Continental and Anglo-American law. Ten schools offer courses in international business transactions. Courses in socialist law are also common. Eight of the schools teach Chinese law and nine Russian law. I was amazed to see that half the schools (thirteen) offer at least one course in Japanese law. (Langbein 1995, 546)

Seventeen years later, many US law schools have expanded their comparative law course offerings. An examination of bulletins for several top law schools for the 2008–9 school year reveals a plethora of comparative law courses in foreign law and in various aspects of public and private international law. It is unclear how many students enrol in these courses but arguably the greatly expanded curriculum is in response to both globalisation and student demand for comparative law instruction.

Some US law professors integrate comparative law into first-year mandatory courses. Anthony Sebok proposes that comparative torts can be a valuable method for teaching damages to first-year law students (Sebok 2007). MC Mirow advocates incorporating comparative law into first-year property classes (Mirow 2004). As, James Gordley explains:

> [T]he value of studying foreign law along with one's own is even greater when they do differ. To begin with, doing so delivers the student from dogmatism. A student confronted with only one solution to a legal problem has a tendency to assume it is the right one. When he is confronted with two, he is encouraged to think. (Gordley 2001, 1008)

Comparative law can be a bridge between courses that contain components of comparative law but have no other nexus. A starting point is to move away from the American-common-law/European-civil-law dichotomy and include more of the world's legal systems and cultures (Waxman 2001, 305). To 'bridge the relevancy gap effectively while expanding students' legal horizons', Waxman recommends offering an introductory course on law in comparative cultures, which exposes students to a variety of the world's legal systems without going deeply into any particular subject area or foreign legal system (Waxman 2001, 306–7).

In today's global environment comparative legal studies should be a fundamental component of legal education (Brand 2008), taught not as a single subject but integrated into many courses throughout a student's three-year course of study (Reimann 1996, 50). Roscoe Pound suggested this some 60 years ago, but while echoed by others, it has never been developed (Reimann 1996, 51). Reimann argues that weaving comparative law throughout the law curriculum will improve domestic law, promote international unification, reveal the common core of all law, teach basic skills for international legal practice, and foster tolerance towards other legal cultures (Reimann 1996, 54). There are other suggestions for incorporating comparative law, as well as international and transnational law, in the report from a workshop on *Globalizing the Law School Curriculum* (Gevurtz et al. 2006).

Backer proposes a framework of three models in US comparative and international legal education. The integration model is a comprehensive model that incorporates foreign and comparative law as deeply as it does national law into the curriculum. The aggregation model is popular and involves offering courses on foreign and comparative law side-by-side with courses on US national law. Lastly, the segregation model creates a centre or home of comparative law programmes and courses within the law school (Backer 2008, 76–82).

Canada operates under a bijural (or perhaps polyjural) legal system, providing an enviable forum for comparative legal studies. In the traditional programmes at the University of Ottawa and McGill University the civil and common law systems are taught side-by-side:

> A legal education at McGill is one that is marked by the mutually sustaining relationship between the common law and the civil law as the Western world's two major legal traditions. It recognizes that the law comes from a broad range of sources, and is predicated on the study of law as an intellectual inquiry that is inherently 'transsystemic'. The common law and the civil law are taught together alongside topics in public law, in both French and English, from the opening days of the undergraduate course of study as a pragmatic and scholarly response to law in a changing world. ('Faculty of Law, McGill University' 2009)

Other Canadian universities offer specialised comparative law programmes. The University of British Columbia has a strong and varied Asian studies programme; the University of Victoria and University of Saskatchewan have developed strong ties to local indigenous communities and offer comparative law courses in aboriginal law; the University of Moncton, catering to its significant Acadian population, offers a common law LLB degree in French (Valcke 2005, 491–2).

Globalisation has led to a laissez-faire curriculum in most Canadian law schools allowing students to design and create individual four-year courses of study (Valcke 2005, 494). Canadian comparative law courses have increased exponentially in recent years. Examples of standard Canadian course offerings related to comparative law include: comparative property systems; comparative constitutional and foreign relations law; comparative human rights law; Canada–US–Mexico economic relations law (Valcke 2005, 495).

Frequently-used comparative law course materials include the traditional casebooks: *Comparative Law* (Schlesinger 1998); *Civil Law Tradition: Europe, Latin America and East Asia, Cases and Materials* (Merryman 1994); and *Comparative Legal Traditions: Text, Materials, and Cases on Western Law* (Glendon et al. 2007); as well as newer and innovative comparative law textbooks: *An Introduction to Comparative Law: Theory and Practice* (Grosswald Curran 2002); *Legal Traditions of the World: Sustainable Diversity of Law* (Glenn 2010); *Comparative Law Casebook* (Riesenfeld and Pakter 2001); and *Law in Radically Different Cultures* (Barton et al. 1983). Some focus on certain areas of law, such as: *Comparative Law of Contracts: Cases and Materials* (Levasseur 2008); and *Comparative Criminal Procedure: A Casebook Approach* (Thaman 2008).

Glendon has incorporated and explained various theories and methodologies into the most fundamental and readable of texts, *Comparative Legal Traditions*, part of the West Nutshell series: compact books that provide easily readable and digestible explanations of the law. She invokes the legacy of Ernst Rabel's two primary concepts, function and context:

> You cannot compare legal rules, institutions, or systems without knowing how they function, and you cannot know how they function without situating them in their legal, economic and cultural context. (Glendon 2008, 9)

In her Nutshell, Glendon focuses on the civil law and common law traditions, which she covers in greater detail in her comparative law casebook (Glendon et al. 2007).

Conclusion

In North America, a new millennium of comparative legal theory and methodology is emerging, built on the foundational work of the twentieth-century comparative law scholars. Critiques have spawned new directions in comparative law scholarship, such as cultural immersion and comparative jurisprudence, as well as recognition of problems of working in multiple languages and cultures.

North American scholars acknowledge significant challenges in the field of comparative legal analysis. Grosswald Curran contends that comparatists must salvage comparative law for the future by 'identifying and fostering the crucial attributes needed for engaging in it effectively'. Additionally, they must find ways to demarginalise comparative legal studies so that students are afforded opportunities to understand:

> the depths of underlying differences and similarities among legal cultures, the contingent nature of their own legal culture, and the analysis they should be conducting in all subjects of their legal studies in translating the foreign into the familiar. (Grosswald Curran 2002, 51)

Canadian and US scholars alike continue to challenge the foundations of their discipline as it evolves, asking: is comparative law a valid discipline? Should comparative law courses be taught individually? Should comparative law be woven throughout the curriculum? And, of course, what is comparative law? (Valcke 2005, 503). These questions will continue to be asked, answered and asked again throughout the twenty-first century.

Western Europe

The current state of comparative law and comparative legal studies varies considerably among Western European nations, especially between common law and civil law countries.[5] The reasons for undertaking comparative analysis also differ among scholars, students, legislatures and practitioners in each country. Some identifiable reasons, particularly in Western Europe, include:

1. generally, to increase knowledge by discovering, understanding and explaining differences and similarities among legal institutions and legal systems and their components
2. to classify legal systems in order to compare them and trace their changes over time
3. to expand the legal mind of law students and promote tolerance for different legal systems and cultures
4. to aid in legislative reform by providing models from various legal systems for examination and consideration
5. to aid judges in the interpretation of the law by providing examples of foreign solutions to questions of law
6. to aid in drafting and interpreting international conventions and,
7. to assist in the unification and harmonisation of law by providing suggestions for changes and creation of new models (Örücü 2007a, 53–6)

The twentieth century witnessed a rise, a decline, and now a renaissance in comparative law. The movement to harmonise Western European private law has driven the revitalised discipline both in academia and in practice (Fauvarque-Cosson 2007, 3) with functionalism as its primary tool (Örücü 2007b, 50–51). Academics are debating the pedagogical aspects of comparative legal studies and proposing radical changes in the classroom (Husa 2009).

England

Entering the twenty-first century Basil Markesinis painted a drab view of the state of comparative law in England at the beginning of the twenty-first century, complaining that the works of most British scholars during the previous 'golden era' of comparative law[6] were backward-looking and did not assist lawyers or judges. Except for Sir Otto Kahn-Freund (who was 'not at all English'), they provided neither a theoretical, philosophical or methodological approach to comparative law

---

5 Smits divides Europe into four legal groups:

1. common law countries such as Ireland and England
2. traditional civil law countries such as Germany and France
3. Scandinavian Member States, such as Denmark, Sweden and Finland, who share a common history and laws and
4. new and revised civil code countries in which the judiciary interprets the law, such as the Czech Republic, Latvia and Hungary (Smits 2007, 220–21)

6 Markesinis views the late 1960s as a 'golden era inhabited by heroes if not gods' such as René Rodière, André Tunc and René David (France); Konrad Zweigert, Hans Stoll, Ulrich Drobnig and Werner Lorenz (Germany); Gino Gorla (Italy); Sir Otto Kahn-Freund, Kurt Lipstein and Tony Weir (England); Max Rheinstein, Rudi Schlesinger, Jack Dawson and John Fleming (United States) (Markesinis 2003, 2–3).

nor a foundation upon which future generations of comparatists could build (Markesinis 2003, 4–12, 15; Markesinis and Fedtke 2009, 20).[7]

Markesinis distinguished the great British practitioners from their German counterparts who successfully established comparative law institutes and, following Ernst Rabel's lead, continued shaping comparative law into a science which they taught to future generations of lawyers (Markesinis 2003, 15). Although his method has not escaped criticism, Rabel fostered the intellectual growth of younger scholars by creating an environment conducive to scholarship and the exchange of ideas (Markesinis and Fedtke 2009, 37–42). He also encouraged mentoring among old and new scholars, a tradition that, according to Markesinis, is in complete contrast to Oxford and Cambridge and the 'preference for the teacher rather than the writing scholar' (Markesinis 2003, 18–20).

Markesinis argues that comparative law has significantly declined in viability and prestige in both England and the United States since the end of the émigré era. His 'heroes' from the 'golden era', whether academics or practitioners, 'did little to teach those of us who followed in their footsteps how to present foreign law to national audiences, how to put foreign learning to practical use, and how to ensure its survival' (Markesinis 2003, 25). Yet, more positively, he observes:

> [W]hat is bringing the subject out of decline is politics not geniuses; practical needs not academic hothouses; private enterprise, not government-inspired guidance; business-related law, not philosophy; not to mention the gold at the end of the American rainbow which is triggering off a new (and voluntary) westward emigration of foreign talent. (Markesinis 2003, 21)

Methodology: Comparative jurisprudence and the dialogic method Markesinis proposed studying foreign legal systems through comparative jurisprudence: examining, comparing and contrasting court decisions:

> [T]he comparative juxtaposition of factually similar cases makes one feel at home. For the observer is comparing familiar situations and not confused by structures, terminology or concepts that are either untranslatable or, if apparently easy to translate, misleading … [T]he two systems come much closer when you look at litigated cases and discover that the differences in result are diminished. That neither system functions as purely as it is meant to do is inevitable since the neatness that can exist in the world of ideas is rarely found in the real world of litigation. (Markesinis 2003, 183–4)

Comparing public law court decisions in England and France, Markesinis draws several overarching conclusions:

1. comparing legal systems by means of their court decisions reveals many similar factual scenarios in cases that have been litigated
2. further comparison reveals significant differences of concepts and reasoning and,
3. at its deepest level (the core), comparison reveals that legal arguments are subsumed by political, economic, philosophical, social and moral ones (Markesinis 2003, 184–94)

7 For Markesinis, Kahn-Freund (1900–79) was the only 'English' contributor to comparative legal methodology in England, primarily due to his classic work, *Labour and the Law* (Kahn-Freund 1977). Like Ernst Rabel, Kahn-Freund was heavily influenced by sociological scholarship and the post-war labour movement in Germany (Markesinis 2003, 24).

Markesinis encouraged application of his methodological approach across legal fields and across legal systems, arguing that its linguistic, conceptual and methodological components make it focused and practical without losing intellectual and philosophical content. This contrasts with the more sociological and trendy legal theories that have emerged in the United States[8] (Markesinis 2003, 37, 45–6; Markesinis and Fedtke 2009, 42–5, 53–8). Markesinis hopes that focusing on the core will not only ensure greater mutual understanding across legal cultures, but achieve greater speed in spreading good ideas (Markesinis 2003, 202–3).

Comparative jurisprudence has been used to create a common law of human rights through the development of a *dialogic* method for approaching unresolved issues in constitutional and human rights law. The dialogic method responds to current global politics and involves dynamic interpretation and discourse (McCrudden 2007, 375, citing Teitel 2004, 2584–5). Scholars and jurists on both sides of the Atlantic have recognised the benefits of the dialogic method to resolve human rights and constitutional issues across national boundaries (McCrudden 2007, 393–4). Örücü takes comparative jurisprudence one step further, calling for domestic courts to 'look forward, sideways, at each other and beyond' to incorporate universal principles of law in their decisions as well as domestic and European concepts (Örücü 2007a, 432).

Comparative legal studies Like Markesinis, Werner Menski finds that comparative law has become trendy and attractive to young scholars who are inadequately prepared to engage effectively in comparative research and scholarship (Menski 2006, 66). He is equally critical of current European (and North American) approaches to comparative legal study, which, he argues, fail to take into account the socio-legal differences between legal systems (Menski 2006, 67). He calls for law school curricula to include comparative law classes, something many British law schools are already doing.

France

The Institute de Droit Comparé was founded in Lyon in 1920 and the Institut de Droit Comparé de Paris was established by Henri Lévy-Ullmann and Henri Capitant in 1931. After this strong beginning, comparative legal studies in France declined in popularity and prestige to the point of being marginalised in the second half of the twentieth century. Comparative law courses were offered in only a few law schools with large curricula, and students were neither encouraged to take comparative law courses nor to study abroad (Fauvarque-Cosson 2006, 52). Now, several French law schools have established institutes or centres of comparative law, and a central agency, the Groupement de Droit Comparé, attempts to coordinate and oversee the centres (Appendix B) (Fauvarque-Cosson 2006, 54). The Institut de Droit Comparé de Paris contends that:

> Comparative law is no longer a privilege but a necessity:
>
> - Comparative law provides a better understanding of foreign legal systems and improves national law;
> - Comparative law will give Europe effective, harmonized rules that will allow the lawyers of tomorrow to meet the challenges of globalization. ('History' 2009)

The harmonisation of European private law has led to an increase in popularity for comparative law in France (Fauvarque-Cosson 2006, 55). Many French scholars resisted participating efforts

8 The 'trendy theories' according to Professor Markesinis include, for example, critical race theory and feminist legal theory (Markesinis 2003, 37; Markesinis 2009, 53–8).

to unify European law, arguing that comparative law should favour diversity and multiculturalism rather than seek the narrow path of biased harmonisation. Pierre Legrand opposes unification of European law while Horatia Muir Watt advocates a less formal approach to law generally (Fauvarque-Cosson 2006, 60–61).

Many French lawyers (like practitioners in common law countries) still view comparative law as a purely academic exercise. Indeed, some French academics avoid striving for practical applications of comparative law and instead focus on theoretical and methodological considerations. According to Fauvarque-Cosson, French scholars have chosen to follow their own methodologies when they should be working to create 'basic maxims of comparison' to help guide comparative legal analysis (Fauvarque-Cosson 2006, 64–5). Fauvarque-Cosson's overall positive review of the state of comparative legal study in France was rebuked by Markesinis (Markesinis and Fedtke 2009, 213–15).

Germany

German institutes of comparative law have played an important role in the development of German comparative methodology and have produced impressive work (Markesinis 2003, 114). In Germany, comparative law is referred to and taken into consideration by both legislators and jurists (Schwenzer 2006, 104).

A new chapter in the development of comparative law began in Germany in 1989 at the end of the Cold War (Schwenzer 2006, 99). The major criticisms of the discipline centre around the notion that comparative legal scholarship remains narrowly focused on a few national legal orders, such as the harmonisation of private law in Europe. The very placement of harmonisation within the discipline of comparative law is debated (Schwenzer 2006, 103–4).

In Germany, comparative law still struggles for recognition as an academic discipline or branch of legal scholarship. All German law schools offer optional introductory courses in comparative law, but courses focusing on foreign legal systems or courses that examine a legal topic comparatively throughout the course are rare. Kötz advocates continued change within German legal education to include wider study of foreign and comparative law (Kötz 2000, 31–2).

At a 2002 conference of the Universities of Warwick (UK), Gießen (Germany) and Lódź (Poland), Wolfgang Schur reflected on the issues for German legal methodology that have arisen in the context of European legal unification (Gross 2003, 47). Comparative law is not itself a method of interpretation, but a basic subject similar to history of law, philosophy of law and sociology of law, which allow us to better understand law generally (Gross 2003, 55).

In his concluding remarks to the conference, Günter Weick noted:

> [C]omparatists no longer restrict themselves to the description and analysis of existing national regulations and legal solutions. Increasingly, they are involved in creative and constructive work, particularly with regard to new problems, to modern phenomena such as electronic commerce and other Internet facilities, intersexuality, genetic engineering, surrogate motherhood, cross border organized crime, money laundering, large scale migration or nuclear waste, [as well as to] harmonization and unification of laws by means of international conventions, European directives, the jurisdiction of European courts, NGO rulemaking, etc. (Gross 2003, 250–51)

Thus, obstacles remain in the effort to legitimise and further the goals of comparative law in Germany (Schwenzer 2006, 105–6).

Italy

Italy is ahead of most other countries in the centrality of comparative law in the law school curriculum. Comparative law courses are offered at virtually all Italian law schools and by many political science and sociology departments (Grande 2006, 122).

Rodolfo Sacco's comparative law programme and the *Five Theses* contained in the 1987 *Trento Manifesto* have dominated the curriculum at the University of Trento Faculty of Law, which opened its doors in 1984 and remains influential today. The programme promotes the study of law under the theory that Italian law is best understood when viewed in a comparative context. The leading Italian legal encyclopaedia, *Digesto*,[9] presents the whole Italian legal system in comparative context (Grande 2006, 117–20).

However, the nature of comparative legal instruction is not uniform in all law schools. Although popular, Sacco's *Theses* has been criticised by leading scholars, and other approaches to comparative legal studies are common and more characteristic of current comparative legal thought in Italy. There are three popular sub-traditions. The first is the Florence school which emphasises policy-oriented work and examines structural regularities to solve specific legal problems. The second is that of the Napoli/Salerno schools which have borrowed normative elements and value judgements from private law scholarship. The third is the group of US-influenced Italian comparatists who have developed a functionalist methodology (Grande 2006, 120–21).

As a group, Italian comparatists are interested in interdisciplinary work involving the social sciences, economics, anthropology and sociology. Studies using the *legal transplants*[10] and *legal formants*[11] methodologies continue to be popular. In addition, an emerging group of comparative religion scholars focuses on the relationships among Jewish, Canon and Islamic law, and another is interested in the 'demise of the nation state' due to globalisation (Grande 2006, 121–2).

Many Italian scholars spend time in law schools in North America, publish in English, and are widely read outside Italy. Ugo Mattei, for example, has published introductory law textbooks, as well as books and articles in multiple languages on topics as diverse as critical legal studies, economics, private European law, Latin America, and the current and future state of comparative law in the United States (Mattei 1998; 2002). Mauro Cappelletti made significant contributions to comparative law worldwide through his work with the Florence Access-to-Justice Project (Cappelletti 1979; Grande 2006, 128).

Switzerland

Legal engineering is a new comparative methodology 'that takes into account all sources of law, and allows for the creation of abstract legal structures that fulfil particular functional and practical purposes' (Ritaine et al. 2008, 9). Although there is no clear definition of the concept,

9 The *Digesto* is a multi-volume set created and updated under the auspices of the International Academy of Comparative Law and the Associazione Italiana di Diritto Comparato (Académie Internationale de Droit Comparé and Associazione Italiana di Diritto Comparato 1987).

10 *Legal transplantation* is the concept of borrowing and implementing the law of a foreign jurisdiction. This has occurred on many occasions in many countries throughout history and continues to be a popular topic for discussion and scholarship.

11 *Legal formants*, according to Rodolfo Sacco, include legislative rules, case decisions, operational guidelines, constitutional law, scholarship and other components of law and legal systems. Comparatists must examine all components of a legal system in proper context, understanding that legal formants develop under the influence of other 'contextual formants' such as religion and ideology (Örücü 2007b, 61).

legal engineers can be viewed as building bridges between legal systems; they are practitioners of applied comparative law (Ritaine et al. 2008, 14, 25).

The work of the Swiss Institute of Comparative Law provides an example of legal engineering in comparative law. The Institute has drafted expert opinions about the legal systems of most countries, some of which involve abstract deconstruction of a specific legal institution in order to adapt it to a particular court proceeding or enable its transplantation to a foreign jurisdiction (Ritaine et al. 2008, 9).

Conclusion

Comparative law is witnessing a renaissance in Western Europe as comparatists develop new tools in order to assume greater importance in the curricula in law schools. New textbooks present legal material in a variety of ways: some focus on primary European texts, others present comparative law within the framework of specific subjects. Others, such as the new *Ius Commune* casebook series, use case law examples (van Gerven 1999; Fauvarque-Cosson 2007, 12; Markesinis and Fedtke 2009, 26).

Western European comparatists are also considering practical applications for comparative law, finding international approaches, and solidifying its methodological foundations (Fauvarque-Cosson 2007, 7). Legal engineering and legal transplantation are examples of these efforts. Uniquely Western European is the increased attention to comparative legal studies resulting from the move towards unification of private law. This has given European academics a significant role in the law-making process (Fauvarque-Cosson 2007, 14).

Central and Eastern Europe

The countries of Central and Eastern Europe have varying traditions and interests in comparative law, but a lack of comparative legal studies in the curriculum is common to most of the law schools of the region (Kühn 2006, 229–35). There are several significant exceptions.

Poland

Warsaw University Law School includes foreign law in its curriculum and has several faculty chairs in comparative criminal law, comparative civil law, and comparative administrative and economy law (Kühn 2006, 230). It also offers a two-semester English-language programme for foreign students and attorneys which emphasises 'instruction in the basic principles and provisions of Polish law in comparative perspective' ('Faculty of Law and Administration' 2009).

Hungary

The Central European University in Budapest offers an LLM in comparative constitutional law focusing on the common and civil law systems with an emphasis on human rights and minority protection ('Legal Studies Department' 2009). Established in 1992, this programme has become a leader of comparative constitutionalism in Central Europe (Kühn 2006, 230).

In recent years comparative law has increased in popularity and importance in traditional Hungarian law schools at basic and postgraduate levels. Classic Western European and US legal textbooks, such as those by Zweigert and Kötz, Gordley and von Mehren, and David complement traditional Hungarian comparative legal texts (Harmathy 2000, 216).

Bulgaria

In Bulgaria, accession to the European Union and globalisation have created an urgent need for teaching law students about foreign legal systems (Vodenitcharov 2008, 1). This need is being addressed in several ways: new foreign and comparative law course offerings, improved collections in university libraries, and instruction to professors on the best ways to teach comparative law (Vodenitcharov 2008, 2–4). This has led to debate about the most effective methodology for comparative legal instruction (Vodenitcharov 2008, 2).

Czech Republic

At Masaryck University, a compulsory first-year legal theory class is taught within a comparative law paradigm. Students learn about the 'large' legal systems of Europe and the differences between the sources of law, the influence of religion and morality, and the roles of judges and attorneys (Kalvodová 2008, 1). Other elective courses are taught from comparative perspectives in English, German, Czech or other languages. The courses include: critical legal theory; comparative political science; constitutional systems; legal cultures of the world; and public administration in the Czech Republic and Europe. Many professors are visitors from outside the Czech Republic (Kalvodová 2008, 2).

Conclusion

The resurgence of comparative law programmes and institutions together with the forces of globalisation may well revive a formerly strong tradition of comparative legal scholarship in Central and Eastern Europe (Kühn 2006, 235). As more countries have joined the European Union, this is reinforced by interests in harmonisation and unification of EU law, and by international educational influences such as Erasmus.[12]

Latin America

Legal education is undergoing a transformation in Latin America. There are over 1,000 law schools in Latin America, with more than 900 in Mexico alone. The teaching styles and methods of legal educators who are also full-time practitioners are similar across Latin America (Gomez 2008).

Comparative law has been studied and practised in Latin America since the colonial period when the laws of Portugal and Spain were infused and merged with native laws and traditions in their respective colonies. After independence, the influences of nineteenth- and twentieth-century US and Western European law (particularly from France, Spain, England and Portugal) became

12 'Erasmus is the EU's flagship education and training programme, enabling more than 180,000 students to study and work abroad each year, as well as supporting co-operation actions between higher education institutions across Europe. It caters not only for students, but also for professors and business staff who want to teach abroad and for university staff who want to be trained abroad' ('Erasmus' 2009).

evident in the many variations of civil, commercial, administrative and other codes throughout Latin America (Kleinheisterkamp 2006, 261–301).

Latin American comparative legal study is difficult even within narrow frameworks such as comparative constitutional law because of the number of countries and their diversity. Additionally, current information is often very difficult to obtain. This leads to a lack of awareness of recent changes to the constitution, laws or court decisions of any one country, and difficulties in understanding a country's current constitutional framework. Nonetheless, comparative constitutional law in Latin America has seen a significant increase in popularity over the last 30 years, suggesting that comparative constitutional legal study serves to create, perfect and strengthen constitutional law throughout the region (Carpizo 2005, 952).

Mexico

The Instituto de Investigaciones Jurídicas (Institute of Legal Studies), formerly the Instituto de Derecho Comparado (Institute of Comparative Law), was founded in 1940 at the Universidad Nacional Autónoma de México (UNAM). It stands at the forefront of comparative legal studies in both Mexico and Latin America. The Instituto publishes hundreds of books and articles, including the *Boletín Mexicano de Derecho Comparado*, founded in 1968 (Carpizo 2005, 985–7). My review of the past 10 years of the *Boletín*, however, reveals almost no discussion of teaching comparative law in Mexican or Latin American law schools, and only one article (Serna de la Garza 2004) dedicated to rethinking the methodology of teaching law in Mexico. Nonetheless, a review of master's programmes shows that comparative law is a standard component in law school curricula within the framework of constitutional or administrative law. The Facultad Libre de Derecho de Monterrey has made comparative law a required course in the fourth year of study (Villarreal-Gonda 2008, 1).

Argentina

The Academia Nacional de Derecho y Ciencias Sociales de Córdoba, founded in 1941 in Córdoba, consists of many legal institutes, including the Instituto de Derecho Comparado (Institute of Comparative Law). Comparative law is not offered as an independent course within the Academia because it is perceived as a methodological approach to studying law rather than as a body of law. Moisset de Espanés invokes René David when he states that comparative analysis should occur in *all* courses on private law (Moisset de Espanés 1970, 499). This seems to be the current practice in Argentine law schools. At the Universidad de Buenos Aires, courses, primarily in the postgraduate law curriculum, contain elements of comparative law (see for instance 'Actualización en Derecho de Seguros' 2009). The Universidad de Palermo also offers courses containing comparative law components. Derecho Constitucional y Derechos Humanos (Constitutional Law and Human Rights), a master's level programme, offers a class on comparative legal systems (see 'Derecho Constitucional y Derechos Humanos' 2009).

The Asociación Argentina de Derecho Comparado (Argentine Association of Comparative Law) (Buenos Aires) was founded in 1947 by a group of Argentine comparatists involved in the Société de Législation Comparée (Paris) (Inicio 2009). A section within the Asociación studies legal theory and philosophy and has sponsored many conferences and forums. The Asociación's *Anuario de Filosofía Jurídica y Social* contains numerous articles discussing comparative legal philosophy, methodology and theory (see for instance Laclau 1981; Autoridades).

Brazil

Comparative law is an important component of legal studies in Brazil. The Universidade de São Paulo Law School Department of Comparative and International Law has one of the strongest and most diverse comparative law curricula in the country (Lyra Tavares 2006, 71–2). Several other Brazilian law schools offer graduate courses on specific comparative law subjects, such as criminal law, or include comparative law components (Lyra Tavares 2006, 71). The Universidade de Minas Gerais has an excellent programme in comparative constitutional law due in part to a prestigious faculty member associated with the Académie Internationale de Droit Comparé and its journal: *Revista de Direito Comparado* (Lyra Tavares 2006, 72).

The most common method of teaching comparative law in Brazil is comparative jurisprudence: examining the jurisprudence of foreign tribunals (Lyra Tavares 2006, 75). Lyra Tavares offers suggestions to improve comparative legal education in Brazil, such as promoting student exchanges and securing a global faculty, providing insights into how globalisation is affecting comparative legal studies and legal education more generally (Lyra Tavares 2006).

One important centre of comparative law in Brazil is the Instituto de Direito Comparado Luso-Brasileiro (Portuguese-Brazilian Comparative Law Institute) based in Rio de Janeiro. The Instituto has published the *Revista Brasileira de Direito Comparado* since 1982 (Instituto de Direito Comparado Luso-Brasileiro 2009).[13]

Chile

Chilean law schools have taught comparative law for many years. The Universidad de Chile commenced its Proyecto de un Seminario de Derecho Comparado in 1935 ('Proyecto de un Seminario de Derecho Comparado' 2009). In 1967 the Universidad de Chile and the Universidad de Valparaiso offered a course in comparative law in conjunction with the International Association of Comparative Law, which included lecturers such as Max Rheinstein and students from eight countries ('Curso de Derecho Comparado' 2009). In the same year there was a conference of comparative law faculties from the Universidad de Chile and the Universidad de la República de Uruguay in Montevideo, Uruguay ('Quintas Jornadas Chileno-Uruguayas de Derecho Comparado' 2009). The Universidad de Chile currently offers an optional comparative law course in constitutional and administrative justice ('Justicia Constitucional y Administrativa en el Derecho Comparado' 2009), and, in conjunction with the American University in Washington, DC, a graduate certificate in Contratación Comparada e Internacional ('Graduate Certificate in International Contracts and Business Law' 2009).

Peru

Comparative law is not as prevalent in Peruvian legal education as it is in other parts of Latin America. Until recently, only the Universidad de San Martín de Porres (USMP) and the Pontificia Universidad Católica del Perú (Lima) offered even basic classes in comparative law (Sagástegui Urteaga 2007, 6). The USMP offers two comparative law courses: comparative law and comparative constitutional law ('Cursos' 2010).

---

13 My review of the tables of contents through 2004 suggests that very little is written on comparative legal education.

Undergraduate law students at the USMP are required to take comparative law in their third year. There are several electives, such as comparative civil law and comparative constitutional law, for students in later years. At the graduate level, comparative law courses are beginning to emerge, especially in the area of national and international tax law (Oyarce-Yuzzelli 2009).[14] In addition to translated foreign textbooks, such as Zweigert and Kötz, USMP also utilises *Derecho Comparado y Sistemas Jurídicas* by Peruvian attorney Fernando Jesús Torres Manrique (Oyarce-Yuzzelli 2009).

In recent years other prominent Peruvian law schools have added comparative law courses to their curricula. The Universidad Peruana de Ciencias Aplicadas (Monterrico) offers a course on legal systems of the world; the Universidad Nacional Mayor de San Marcos (Lima) requires that its master's degree students take either comparative law, comparative criminal law or comparative constitutional law. The Universidad de Lima offers several comparative corporation law courses to its master's degree students (Oyarce-Yuzzelli 2009).

Conclusion

Latin America has a lengthy and robust history of comparative legal studies. As elsewhere, globalisation has created renewed interest and increased demand for comparative law courses. Some countries, such as Brazil, have responded with a plethora of comparative law course offerings and placed increased importance on comparative legal studies generally. Yet comparative law is clearly neither as popular nor as widely-taught in Latin America as in other regions, especially Europe. However, many academics agree that comparative law courses are of great importance because they allow students to learn about other types of legal systems in this multicultural world (Oyarce-Yuzzelli 2009). Although he is writing about Peru, Oyarce-Yuzzelli's sentiment can be felt throughout Latin America.

Asia and the Pacific

Many Asian legal systems are incorporating Western legal concepts into their legal systems, due mostly to globalisation. Legislators study the laws of foreign countries to determine if they can be adapted to their own. As Australian law professors Sarah Biddulph and Pip Nicholson explain:

> Comparative law has thus found itself examining these changes within domestic legal systems. What it has found in this process is that foreign law, institutions, and norms are adopted, adapted, transformed, subverted, partially ignored, or provoke changes that were not really anticipated. How do we explain or understand this variability in outcomes? What interests are served by the reforms? Who benefits from them? In order to explore these issues, comparative lawyers have drawn on a range of explanatory paradigms from socio-legal studies, anthropology and history, to name a few. (Nicholson and Biddulph 2008, 12)

Because many legal systems have incorporated aspects of other systems and involve 'overlaps, combinations and blends' (Örücü 2007c, 172), legal transplantation has fostered debate regarding

14 I am grateful to Professor Aarón Oyarce-Yuzzelli of USMP for his generous assistance with this section.

the classification of legal systems. Örücü has proposed 'a scheme that regards all legal systems as mixed and overlapping, overtly or covertly, and groups them according to the proportionate mixture of the ingredients'. She believes that this approach would help classify legal systems of Asia, particularly Southeast Asia. It would identify such 'offshoots' and 'sub-groups' as customary, ethnic, religious and colonial legal systems, and address their linguistic, cultural and other needs more effectively (Örücü 2007c, 172–3).

Scholars also grapple with the same issues (purpose, classification and methodology) as their counterparts in North America and Western Europe. As a result, many law schools are incorporating comparative legal studies courses into the curriculum.

China

Studies have been conducted regarding differences in how people in East Asian and Western cultures organise and process information about rules and relationships (Wang and Young 2008, 1). The law faculty at Kenneth Wang School of Law in Suzhou, China, addresses and measures these differences in a three-week skills course on international business transactions taken by Chinese, European and North American students (Wang and Young 2008, 4–5). Preliminary results show that three weeks of intense multicultural interaction causes changes varying from slight to dramatic in students' perceptions and interpretations of the law (Wang and Young 2008, 9–10). The hope is that this research will enrich understanding of how culture and perspectives of law are intertwined, and thereby assist in providing effective learning environments in today's global university and workplace (Wang and Young 2008, 10).

Peking University recently opened an innovative School of Transnational Law (STL) in ShenZhen, China. STL and its courses are modelled on the three-year Juris Doctor degree in the United States with an elective fourth year of study focusing on the Chinese legal system. The school is for Chinese students but classes are conducted in English ('Admissions Bulletin' 2009). The programme focuses on international, foreign and comparative law and legal systems. The curriculum requirements are straightforward:

> The essential knowledge that must be mastered includes the central concepts that underlie the core doctrinal domains of common law and civil law legal systems, including the basic principles of public and private law. In addition, it includes the ways that multiple legal systems interact in the transnational sphere, and how individuals and governments navigate across those systems. ('Curriculum and Graduation Requirements' 2009)

The STL plans to seek American Bar Association (ABA) accreditation in the future (Canaves 2008).

Japan

Until recently, legal education in Japan was based in apprenticeships rather than a university experience. Several years ago three-year university programmes came into existence. Today, legal education in Japan is again undergoing transformation as it considers whether and to what extent it should adopt the professional school model utilised in the United States (Maxeiner 2003). Thus, comparative legal study is a relatively new academic discipline in Japan.

Nagoya University Graduate School of Law offers unique master and doctoral degrees in comparative law for overseas students. The comparative law graduate programme in law and political science has the aim of educating legal scholars from Asian countries 'that are undergoing systemic transformation or development'. The programme has established centres in Mongolia (2005) and Uzbekistan (2006) ('Faculty History' 2009).

India

The time is ripe for introducing compulsory comparative law courses into Indian law schools (Sridhar Patnaik 2007). At the moment, courses are offered, but not required. Sridhar Patnaik draws on India's current success in the global marketplace and the official statement of the National Knowledge Commission to argue for the need to educate future lawyers about foreign law. He uses examples from Western European and North American legal education to illustrate the methodology and practicality of comparative law courses (Sridhar Patnaik 2007). Gurjeet Singh takes this initiative one step further:

> I have no hesitation to say that a teacher who does not teach his/her subject by way of making a comparative analysis of the provisions of the law being taught by him/her with the provisions of the laws available at least in some of the known jurisdictions is not justifying himself/herself. (Singh 2008, 5)

Australia

In 2002, Brisbane hosted the XVIth International Congress of Comparative Law sponsored by the International Academy of Comparative Law/Academie Internationale de Droit Comparé ('Brisbane' 2009). The theme was 'Convergence of Legal Systems in the 21st Century'. Australia, with its convergence of English law, national law and aboriginal law, is an ideal location for such conferences and for thriving academic comparative legal studies programmes.

Comparative law courses are prevalent though not required in most Australian law schools. At the University of New South Wales in Sydney, for example, an introductory comparative law course is offered for undergraduates and several comparative law courses are available for LLM students. The LLM courses include comparative criminal justice, international and comparative intellectual property, themes in Asian and comparative law, and Australian bills of rights in international and comparative perspective ('Courses' 2009).

The University of Queensland in Brisbane offers several graduate-level comparative law courses, including public international and comparative law, and Chinese/Australian comparative law. This latter plan of study includes both basic comparative law courses for Australia and East Asia as well as comparative law classes on specific areas of the law ('Chinese/Australian Comparative Law Major(s)' 2009).

New Zealand

Comparative legal studies was introduced to New Zealand legal education some 30 years ago but the discipline has recently shifted focus from a European to more regional (Asian) and local (Pacific) perspectives (Angelo 2000, 277–82). Comparative law is not a required component of the law curriculum but courses are generally offered. About one-third of graduating students at Victoria University at Wellington have taken a comparative law course. Maori legal studies, popularised in the 1990s, is evolving and beginning to incorporate a comparative law paradigm. A similar phenomenon is occurring with South Pacific legal studies.

Malaysia

Malaysia is a multicultural country with several legal traditions reflected in the law school curriculum. All first-year law students in government-funded law schools and in many private schools are required to take introductory courses to both the Malaysian and the Islamic legal systems (Noor Aziah Mohd Awal 2008, 1). They are also encouraged to take courses that give them a broad understanding of the legal customs of India and China, as well as Malay and its states, where native courts still operate under customary law. Most undergraduate law courses are comparative in nature, focusing on the conventional Malaysian and the Islamic legal systems, and covering contracts, criminal law, family law, torts and jurisprudence (Noor Aziah Mohd Awal 2008, 2). At the graduate level, various legal systems are introduced in comparative law courses, usually including other Islamic countries such as Egypt and Jordan, and common law countries such as England and the United States. The emphasis is on regional comparison with Association of Southeast Asian Nations (ASEAN) countries such as Australia, New Zealand, Indonesia, Singapore and Brunei (Noor Aziah Mohd Awal 2008, 3).

Mohammad Nizam Awang approaches legal education in Malaysia from an Islamic perspective, providing suggestions on how to broaden the scope of Islamic legal education in order to reconcile differences and foster better understanding between Islamic and secular law (Nizam Awang 2008, 1). Although both Islamic and civil law are defined by the federal constitution (Nizam Awang 2008, 1), the emphasis in most law schools is on civil law (Nizam Awang 2008, 3, 6). In order to bridge the gap between the two legal systems, Nizam Awang and the Islamic Science University of Malaysia have developed a curriculum in which law is taught comparatively, emphasising the importance of understanding Shariah law while operating in a civil law system (Nizam Awang 2008, 4).

Singapore

The National University of Singapore requires its law students to take a comparative legal traditions course (Tan et al. 2006, 8). Its law and economics dual-degree programme has made a significant effort to incorporate interdisciplinary material and offers comparative competition law as an elective course (Tan et al. 2006, 13).

Conclusion

Legal education is undergoing radical transformation in some Asian and Pacific countries (see for instance Miyazawa et al 2008; Fordham 2006). As a result of legal reform and globalisation, many law schools have incorporated foreign and comparative legal studies into the curriculum, and many are making an effort to do so more extensively (Tan et al. 2006, 13).

Africa

Legal systems on the African continent include customary, Islamic, civil and common law traditions.

> Customary law grows out of the social practices which a given jural community has come to accept as obligatory. It is a pervasive normative order, providing the regulatory framework for spheres

> of human activity as diverse as the family, the neighbourhood, the business of merchant banking, or international diplomacy … [C]ustom is so diverse and so wide-ranging. (Bennett 2006, 642)

The diversity of legal systems and the difficulty of establishing reliable and up-to-date information do not allow a full survey; the section below is only a sampling of the state of comparative legal studies in a few African nations.

Liberia

Liberia operates under a complex set of laws, mostly written statutory law stemming from the Western/Anglo tradition in urban areas and unwritten customary laws in rural areas. Law students and legal professionals in Liberia undertake comparative legal analysis daily as they evaluate and reconcile differences among two legal traditions operating simultaneously within one country. Attempts at harmonisation of the two legal traditions have thus far been unsuccessful, yet still continue (Jallah 2008, 4).

Nigeria

As in other African nations, Nigerian lawyers and law students are engaged in comparative legal analysis within their own national legal system. Nigeria has a mixed legal system in which common law, Islamic law and customary law coexist. Students are required to take courses in each tradition as prescribed by the national law curriculum, but a strong bias favours the English common law tradition and there is little interest in studying and understanding local or regional legal systems (Mamman 2008, 1–2). Comparative law courses covering legal systems outside of Nigeria are not required and budgetary constraints prevent an influx of visiting foreign scholars. Mamman suggests these areas need to be improved (Mamman 2008, 3).

Senegal

Senegal, too, focuses comparative legal studies on the complex intertwining of domestic legal systems. Each linguistic community has its own sets of customs and laws (Camara 2008, 1). Camara suggests two approaches to comparative legal studies in this realm: 1) teaching the customary laws of each group; and 2) focusing on a comparative and historical approach seeking common trends, customs and laws that are unique and indigenous to African culture, that is indigenous African law. The second is Camara's preferred method (Camara 2008, 1–2). In addition to domestic comparative law courses, there are comparative law courses offered for the study of common law systems, most frequently, England and the United States (Mbaye 2008, 1).

South Africa

The University of South Africa's Institute of Foreign and Comparative Law was founded in 1964 and continues to be a centre for comparative legal study in South Africa. During apartheid, South African legal scholars were able to study internationally in the German institutes and were exposed to German legal theory, methodology and vocabulary, all of which they brought back to South Africa. An example of this relationship can be seen in the inclusion of the *Rechtsstaatsprinzip* in the preamble to the 1994 South African Constitution (Markesinis 2003, 122).

The South African Bill of Rights borrowed provisions involving fundamental rights of individuals from Canada (Bentele 2008, 5). Sections 39(1)(b)-(c) of the 1996 Constitution explicitly mandate that South African courts must consider international law and may consider foreign law in interpreting the Bill of Rights (Örücü 2007a, 427). As a result, South African courts approach the interpretation of human rights law from a comparative perspective and examine the law of many common and civil law countries (Bentele 2008, 5; Örücü 2007a, 427). The Constitutional Court in particular often examines foreign law when deciding cases (Bentele 2008). The Constitutional Court's library is striving 'to become the biggest human rights library in the southern hemisphere [and] to serve as a hub for the exchange of legal materials across Africa' ('About the Library' 2010); it has become an important centre for comparative law and legal study in Africa.

Post-apartheid South African law schools have changed considerably in recent years and take into account their multicultural student body and globalisation in developing the curriculum (Mireku 2008, 1). Mireku explains that establishing a multicultural environment within the law school is crucial to effectively teaching the law and legal systems of other cultures and traditions; a multicultural environment includes professors, students and the curriculum. Mireku also advocates approaching comparative law from a métissage perspective (see Kasirer 2003), which includes contact, confrontation and dialogue between cultures and legal systems to train lawyers (Mireku 2008, 2–3).

Conclusion

African legal systems and traditions have not been studied nearly as extensively as Western civil and common law traditions. Menski criticises European and North American comparatists for not knowing how to understand, interpret and compare non-Western legal systems accurately; he encourages extensive practical research in these countries (Menski 2006, 67).

Conclusion

Comparative law is gaining momentum around the world both in the classroom and in the scholarly community. The increase in comparative law course offerings, the number of new comparative law journals, and the activities of comparative law centres and institutes around the world all testify to a twenty-first century renaissance in comparative law and comparative legal studies.

For the 2002 XVIth International Congress of Comparative Law in Brisbane, Gabriel A. Moens and Rodolphe Biffot prepared a general review which provides an appropriate conclusion to this global survey of the state of comparative law. They divide their report into two parts: 1) how comparative law is taught in universities and institutes, and 2) how globalisation and other developments have impacted on the teaching of comparative law.

The pedagogical section reports that the majority of the respondents use standard lectures to teach comparative law, although in smaller classes and seminars the Socratic method is often used. At times these traditional teaching methods are supplemented with audio-visual materials, electronic resources, case law, statutes and codes Moens and Biffot 2006, 266–8). Respondents emphasised the importance of providing students with the historical, jurisprudential and cultural aspects of legal systems in addition to merely comparing texts of laws (Moens and Biffot 2006, 269). Moot competitions, international exchanges, research projects and comparative law conferences are all favoured as innovative alternative methods of teaching comparative law (Moens and Biffot 2006, 271–7). Finally, respondents stressed the importance of foreign language fluency in comparative legal studies (Moens and Biffot 2006, 278–9).

The report also demonstrates that globalism and multiculturalism significantly impact comparative legal studies, particularly the desire for global faculties and cross-cultural approaches to teaching comparative law (Moens and Biffot 2006, 279–83). Respondents agreed that studying law comparatively not only allows students to learn about foreign legal systems but also helps them comprehend the principles of their own system. Cross-cultural comparison is necessary and appropriate. Most respondents stated that globalisation has not affected how comparative law is taught, while others explained that globalisation has been the impetus behind an expanded comparative law curriculum. One respondent suggested that comparative law itself contributed to globalisation.

Although there was no agreement on whether having a global faculty increases the value of the faculty or whether comparative law is a distinct discipline rather than a concept intertwined in all subjects, all respondents agreed that comparative law has real and practical application in the creation of legislation, constitution drafting and judicial decision-making (Moens and Biffot 2006, 285–9). Most respondents also agreed that law school curricula need to offer more courses in comparative law and to emphasise their importance.

The literature makes clear the need to solidify a foundation for comparative law as an academic discipline. Today's scholars present new ideas pertaining to comparative law methodology and comparative legal studies, making concepts such as functionalism, cultural immersion and legal transplantation part of the mainstream comparative law vocabulary. As the century progresses, so, too, will the development of these and other approaches to comparative law. Comparative law and comparative legal studies have entered an exciting new age.

References[15]

'About the Library', *Constitutional Court of South Africa*. Available at: www.constitutionalcourt.org.za/site/thelibrary/aboutthelibrary.htm, accessed 12 January 2010.

Académie Internationale de Droit Comparé and Associazione Italiana di Diritto Comparato (1987–), *Digesto* (4th edn) (Torino: Università di Torino).

'Actualización en Derecho de Seguros' (2009), *Universidad de Buenos Aires*. Available at: www.derecho.uba.ar/academica/posgrados/cur_intensivos_der_familia_infancia_adolescencia.php, accessed 23 May 2009.

'Admissions Bulletin 2009 for International Students', *Peking University School of Transnational Law*. Available at: www.sz.pku.edu.cn/en/article.asp?articleid=27, accessed 16 June 2009.

Angelo, A.H. (2000), 'Some Reflections on Comparative Law from New Zealand', in *Blanc-Jouvan*, 279–82.

'Autoridades', *Asociación Argentina de Derecho Comparado*. Available at: www.derechocomparado.org.ar/autoridades.htm, accessed 19 January 2010.

Backer, L.C. (2008), 'Internationalizing the American Law School Curriculum (in Light of the Carnegie Foundation's Report)', in Klabbers and Sellers, 49–112.

Barton, J., Gibbs, J., Li, V. and Merryman, J. (1983), *Law in Radically Different Cultures* (St. Paul: West).

Bennett, T.W. (2006), 'Comparative Law and African Customary Law', in Reimann and Zimmermann, 641–74.

15 These references include the sources cited in the text of this chapter plus a small number of other important sources.

Bentele, U. (2008), 'Mining for Gold: The Constitutional Court of South Africa's Experience with Comparative Constitutional Law', *Brooklyn Law School Legal Studies Research Papers, Working Paper Series, Research Paper no. 113*. Available at: http://preprodpapers.ssrn.com/sol3/papers.cfm?abstract_id=1169642&rec=1&srcabs=1169871, accessed 11 January 2010.

Bevans, P. and McKay, J. (2009), 'The Association of Transnational Law Schools' Agora: An Experiment in Graduate Legal Pedagogy', *German Law Journal* 10:7, 929–58.

Blanc-Jouvan, X. (ed.) (2000), *L'avenir du Droit Comparé: Un Défi pour les Juristes du Nouveau Millénaire* (Paris: Société de Législation Comparé).

Brand, R.A. (2008), 'Effective Techniques for Teaching About Other Cultures and Legal Systems', *International Association of Law Schools: Effective Techniques for Teaching about Other Cultures and Legal Systems* (published online 30 May 2008). Available at: www.ialsnet.org/meetings/assembly/RonaldBrand.pdf, accessed 21 May 2009.

'Brisbane', *Academie Internationale de Droit Comparé*. Available at: www.iuscomparatum.org/141_p_1570/brisbane-2002.html, accessed 17 June 2009.

Camara, F.K. (2008), 'Teaching African Customary Law', *International Association of Law Schools: Effective Techniques for Teaching about Other Cultures and Legal Systems* (published online 30 May 2008). Available at: www.ialsnet.org/meetings/assembly/FatouKineCamara.pdf, accessed 21 May 2009.

Canaves, S. (2008), 'An American Law School in China', *The Wall Street Journal Online* (published online 6 June 2008). Available at: http://blogs.wsj.com/chinajournal/2008/06/06/an-american-law-school-in-china, accessed 16 June 2009.

Cappelletti, M. (ed.) (1979), *Access to Justice* (Milan: Giuffrè).

Carpizo, J. (2005), 'Derecho Constitucional Latinoamericano y Comparado', *Boletín Mexicano de Derecho Comparado* 38:114, 949–89.

'Chinese/Australian Comparative Law Major(s)', *University of Queensland*. Available at: www.uq.edu.au/study/plan.html?acad_plan=CHAULX5191, accessed 12 June 2009.

Clark, D.S. (2006), 'Development of Comparative Law in the United States', in Reimann and Zimmermann, 175–214.

Clark, D.S. (ed.) (2007), *Encyclopedia of Law and Society: American and Global Perspectives* (Los Angeles: Sage).

Cotterrell, R. (2007), 'Is It So Bad to Be Different? Comparative Law and the Appreciation of Diversity', in Örücü and Nelken, 133–54.

'Courses', *University of New South Wales*. Available at: www.law.unsw.edu.au/course/index.asp, accessed 12 June 2009.

'Curriculum and Graduation Requirements', *Peking University School of Transnational Law*. Available at: www.sz.pku.edu.cn/en/article.asp?articleid=28, accessed 16 June 2009.

'Curso de Derecho Comparado', *Universidad de Chile, Anales de la Facultad de Ciencias Jurídicas y Sociales*. Available at: www.analesderecho.uchile.cl/CDA/an_der_articulo/0,1361,SCID%253D11236%2526ISID%253D78,00.html, accessed 21 May 2009.

'Cursos', *Universidad de San Martin de Porres, Facultad de Derecho*. Available at: www.derecho.usmp.edu.pe/ccursos.htm, accessed 19 July 2010.

Danner, R. and Bernal, M.-L.H. (1994), *Introduction to Foreign Legal Systems* (New York: Oceana for the American Association of Law Libraries).

David, R. and Brierley, J.E.C. (2000), *Major Legal Systems in the World Today: An Introduction to the Comparative Study of Law* (3rd edn) (Delran: Legal Classics Library).

David, R. and Jauffret-Spinosi, C. (1992), *Les Grands Systemes de Droit Contemporains* (10th edn) (Paris: Dalloz).

De Cruz, P. (2007), *Comparative Law in a Changing World* (3rd edn) (London and New York: Routledge-Cavendish).

'Derecho Constitucional y Derechos Humanos', *Universidad de Palermo*. Available at: www.palermo.edu/derecho/maestrias/m_constitucional.html, accessed 23 May 2009.

Edge, I. (2000), *Comparative Law in Global Perspective* (Ardsley: Transnational Publishers Inc.).

'Effective Teaching Techniques about Other Cultures and Legal Systems', *International Association of Law Schools*. Available at: www.ialsnet.org./meetings/assembly/papers.html, accessed 31 May 2009.

'Erasmus', *European Commission Education and Training*. Available at: http://ec.europa.eu/education/lifelong-learning-programme/doc80_en.htm, accessed 12 January 2010.

Ewald, W. (1998), 'The Jurisprudential Approach to Comparative Law: A Field Guide to "Rats"', *American Journal of Comparative Law* 46:4, 701–8.

'Faculty History', *Nagoya University Graduate School of Law*. Available at: http://gsl-nagoya-u.net/appendix/documents/history.html, accessed 23 May 2009.

'Faculty of Law and Administration', *Warsaw University*. Available at: http://en.wpia.uw.edu.pl/files/erasmus/sppmaly.pdf?short, accessed 23 May 2009.

'Faculty of Law, McGill University', *Official Guide to Canadian Law Schools*. Available at: www.lsac.org/canadianCFC/McGill.asp, accessed 31 May 2009.

Fauvarque-Cosson, B. (2006), 'Development of Comparative Law in France', in Reimann and Zimmermann, 35–68.

Fauvarque-Cosson, B. (2007), *The Rise of Comparative Law: A Challenge for Legal Education in Europe* (Groningen: Europa Law).

Fix-Zamudio, H. and Fernandez Segado, F. (2007), *Derecho Constitucional Mexicano y Comparado* (5th edn) (Mexico City: Porrúa).

Fletcher, G.P. (1998), 'Comparative Law as a Subversive Discipline', *American Journal of Comparative Law* 46:4, 683–700.

Fordham, M. (2006), 'Comparative Legal Traditions – Introducing the Common Law to Civil Lawyers in Asia', *Asian Journal of Comparative Law* 1:1, Article 11. Available at: www.bepress.com/asjcl/vol1/iss1/art11, accessed 2 June 2009.

Fox, J.R. (2003), *Dictionary of International and Comparative Law* (3rd edn) (Dobbs Ferry: Oceana).

Fromont, M. (2009), *Grands Systèmes de Droit Étrangers* (6th edn) (Paris: Dalloz).

Geeroms, S.M.F. (2002), 'Comparative Law and Legal Translation: Why the Terms Cassation, Revision and Appeal should not be Translated…', *American Journal of Comparative Law* 50:1, 201–28.

Gerber, D.J. (1998), 'System Dynamics: Toward a Language of Comparative Law?', *American Journal of Comparative Law* 46:4, 719–38.

Gevurtz, F.A., Carter, L., Davies, J., Landsberg, B., Main, T., Malloy, M. and Sprankling, J. (2006), 'Report Regarding the Pacific McGeorge Workshop on Globalizing the Law School Curriculum', *Pacific McGeorge Global Business and Development Law Journal* 19:1, 267–330.

Glendon, M.A. (2008), *Comparative Legal Traditions in a Nutshell* (3rd edn) (St. Paul: Thomson West).

Glendon, M.A., Carozza, P.G. and Picker, C.B. (2007), *Comparative Legal Traditions: Text, Materials, and Cases on Western Law* (3rd edn) (St. Paul: Thomson West).

Glenn, H. (2010), *Legal Traditions of the World: Sustainable Diversity in Law* (4th edn) (Oxford and New York: Oxford University Press).

Gomez, M.A. (2008), 'Innovations in Legal Education in Latin America', *International Association of Law Schools: Effective Techniques for Teaching about Other Cultures and Legal Systems*

(published online 30 May 2008). Available at: www.ialsnet.org/meetings/assembly/Gomez.pdf, accessed 21 May 2009.
Gordley, J. (2001). 'Comparative Law and Legal Education', *Tulane Law Review* 75:4, 1003–14.
Gordley, J. and von Mehren, A.T. (2006), *An Introduction to the Comparative Study of Private Law: Readings, Cases, Materials* (Cambridge and New York: Cambridge University Press).
'Graduate Certificate in International Contracts and Business Law', *American University, Washington College of Law*. Available at: www.wcl.american.edu/uchile, accessed 23 May 2009.
Grande, E. (2006), 'Development of Comparative Law in Italy', in Reimann and Zimmermann, 107–30.
Gross, T. (2003), 'Legal Scholarship in International and Comparative Law', in *Gießen-Warwick-Lödz-Colloquium* (Frankfurt am Main and New York: P. Lang).
Grossfeld, B. (1996), *Kernfragen der Rechtsvergleichung* (Tübingen: J.C.B. Mohr).
Grosswald Curran, V. (1998), 'Cultural Immersion, Difference and Categories in U.S. Comparative Law', *American Journal of Comparative Law* 45:1, 43–92.
Grosswald Curran, V. (ed.) (2002), *Comparative Law: An Introduction* (Durham, NC: Carolina Academic Press).
Grote, R. (2005), 'Comparative Law and Law Teaching Through the Case Method in the Civil Law Tradition: A German Perspective', in Serna de la Garza, J.M. (ed.), *Metodología del Derecho Comparado: Memoria del Congreso Internacional de Culturas y Sistemas Jurídicos Comparados*, Universidad Nacional Autónoma de México, 103–24.
Harding, A. and Örücü, A.E. (2000), *Comparative Law in the 21st Century* (The Hague, London and New York: Kluwer Law International).
Harmathy, A. (2000), 'Comparative Law in Hungary', in Blanc-Jouvan, 209–16.
Hiller, J.A. and Grossfeld, B. (2002), 'Comparative Legal Semiotics and the Divided Brain: Are We Producing Half-Brained Lawyers', *American Journal of Comparative Law* 50:1, 175–200.
'History' (2009), *Institut de Droit Comparé de Paris*. Available at: http://idc.u-paris2.fr/site_anglais/history.htm, accessed 16 December 2009.
Husa, J. (2009), 'Turning the Curriculum Upside Down: Comparative Law as an Educational Tool for Constructing the Pluralistic Legal Mind', *German Law Journal* 10:7, 913–28.
'IACL History', *Academie Internationale de Droit Comparé*. Available at: www.iuscomparatum.org/141_p_1551/history.html, accessed 12 January 2010.
'Inicio', *Asociación Argentina de Derecho Comparado*. Available at: www.derechocomparado.org.ar/index.htm, accessed 19 January 2010.
Instituto de Direito Comparado Luso-Brasileiro, *Revista Brasileira de Direito Comparado*. Available at: www.idclb.com.br/revista.htm, accessed 23 May 2009.
International Academy of Comparative Law (ed.) (2006), *Convergence of Legal Systems in the 21st Century: General Reports Delivered at the XVIth International Congress of Comparative Law* (Brussels: Bruylant).
Jallah, D.A.B. (2008), 'Effective Techniques for Teaching about Other Cultures and Legal Systems', *International Association of Law Schools: Effective Techniques for Teaching about Other Cultures and Legal Systems* (published online 30 May 2008). Available at: www.ialsnet.org/meetings/assembly/DavidJallah.pdf, accessed 23 May 2009.
'Justicia Constitucional y Administrativa en el Derecho Comparado', *Universidad de Chile, Facultad de Derecho*. Available at: www.uchile.cl/uchile.portal?_nfpb=true&_pageLabel=conUrl&url=4997, accessed 21 May 2009.
Kahn-Freund, O. (1977), *Labour and the Law* (2nd edn) (London: Stevens).

Kalvodová, V. (2008), 'Teaching Experience at the Faculty of Law, Masaryk University', *International Association of Law Schools: Effective Techniques for Teaching about Other Cultures and Legal Systems* (published online 30 May 2008). Available at: www.ialsnet.org/meetings/assembly/VeraKalvadova.pdf, accessed 26 May 2009.

Kasirer, N. (2003), 'Legal Education as Metissage', *Tulane Law Review* 78:2, 481–501.

Kleinheisterkamp, J. (2006), 'Development of Comparative Law in Latin America', in Reimann and Zimmermann, 261–304.

Kötz, H. (2000), 'Comparative Law in Germany Today', in Société de Législation Comparé, 17–32.

Kühn, Z. (2006), 'Development of Comparative Law in Central and Eastern Europe', in Reimann and Zimmermann, 215–36.

Laclau, M. (1981), 'El Derecho Comparado y el Mundo Moderno', *Anuario de Filosofía Jurídica y Social* 1:1, 11–42.

Langbein, J.H. (1995), 'The Influence of Comparative Procedure in the United States', *American Journal of Comparative Law* 43:4, 545–54.

'Legal Studies Department', *Central European University*. Available at: http://web.ceu.hu/legal/about_us_CCL.htm, accessed 23 May 2009.

Legrand, P. (1999), 'John Henry Merryman and Comparative Legal Studies: A Dialogue', *American Journal of Comparative Law* 47:1, 3–66.

Legrand, P. (2001), 'Return of the Repressed: Moving Comparative Legal Studies beyond Pleasure', *Tulane Law Review* 75:4, 1033–52.

Levasseur, A. (2008), *Comparative Law of Contracts: Cases and Materials* (Durham, NC: Carolina Academic Press).

'LLM EU Law and Comparative Legal Studies', *University of Essex School of Law*. Available at: www.essex.ac.uk/law/pgstudy/taughtdegrees/llm-eu-and-comp.shtm, accessed 22 June 2009.

'LLM in International and Comparative Commercial Law', *School of Oriental and African Studies, University of London*. Available at: www.soas.ac.uk/programmes/prog28765.php, accessed 22 June 2009.

Lyra Tavares, A.L. (2006), 'O Ensino do Direito Comparado no Brasil Contemporâneo', *Direito, Estado e Sociedade* 29:9, 69–86.

Mamman, T. (2008), 'The Role of Culture in Teaching about Other Legal Systems', *International Association of Law Schools: Effective Techniques for Teaching about Other Cultures and Legal Systems* (published online 30 May 2008). Available at: www.ialsnet.org/meetings/assembly/TahirMamman.pdf, accessed 21 May 2009.

Markesinis, B.S. (1997), *Foreign Law and Comparative Methodology: A Subject and a Thesis* (Oxford and Portland, OR: Hart).

Markesinis, B.S. (2003), *Comparative Law in the Courtroom and Classroom: The Story of the Last Thirty-Five Years* (Oxford and Portland, OR: Hart).

Markesinis, B.S. and Fedtke, J. (2009), *Engaging with Foreign Law* (Oxford and Portland, OR: Hart).

Márquez Romero, R. (2004), *Conclusiones del Congreso Internacional de Culturas y Sistemas Jurídicos Comparados* (Mexico City: UNAM).

Mattei, U. (1998), 'An Opportunity Not to Be Missed: The Future of Comparative Law in the United States', *American Journal of Comparative Law* 46:4, 709–18.

Mattei, U. (2002), 'Some Realism About Comparativism: Comparative Law Teaching in the Hegemonic Jurisdiction', *American Journal of Comparative Law* 50:Supplement, 87–99.

Maxeiner, J.R. (2003), 'American Law Schools as a Model for Japanese Legal Education? A Preliminary Question from a Comparative Perspective', *Kansai University Review of Law and Politics* 24:1, 37–51.

Mbaye, O. (2008), 'Effective Techniques for Teaching about Other Cultures and Legal Systems', *International Association of Law Schools: Effective Techniques for Teaching about Other Cultures and Legal Systems* (published online 30 May 2008). Available at: www.ialsnet.org/meetings/assembly/OusmaneMbaye.pdf, accessed 26 May 2009.

McCrudden, C. (2007), 'Judicial Comparativism and Human Rights', in Örücü and Nelken, 371–97.

Menski, W. (2006), *Comparative Law in a Global Context: The Legal Systems of Asia and Africa*, (2nd edn) (Cambridge and New York: Cambridge University Press).

Menski, W. (2007), 'Beyond Europe', in Örücü and Nelken, 189–216.

Merryman, J.H. (1994), *The Civil Law Tradition: Europe, Latin America, and East Asia: Cases and Materials* (Charlottesville, VA: Michie Co.).

Merryman, J.H. (1999), *The Loneliness of the Comparative Lawyer and Other Essays in Foreign and Comparative Law* (The Hague, London and Boston: Kluwer Law International).

Mireku, O. (2008), 'Effective Techniques for Teaching about Other Cultures and Legal Systems', *International Association of Law Schools: Effective Techniques for Teaching about Other Cultures and Legal Systems* (published online 30 May 2008). Available at: www.ialsnet.org/meetings/assembly/ObengMireku.pdf, accessed 19 June 2009.

Mirow, M. (2004), 'Globalizing Property: Incorporating Comparative and International Law into First-Year Property Classes', *Journal of Legal Education* 54:2, 183–200.

Miyazawa, S., et al. (2008), 'The Reform of Legal Education in East Asia', *Annual Review of Law & Social Science* 4, 333–60.

Moens, G. and Biffot, R. (2006), 'Teaching of Comparative Law and Comparative Law Teaching', in International Academy of Comparative Law, 265–99.

Moisset de Espanés, L. (1970), 'Memoria Explicativa y Programa Sintético de Derecho Civil Argentino y Comparado II', *Boletín de la Facultad de Derecho y Ciencias Sociales de Córdoba* 34, 491–534. Available at: www.acaderc.org.ar/doctrina/articulos/artmemoriacxplicativa2, accessed 23 May 2009.

Mousourakis, G. (2006), *Perspectives on Comparative Law and Jurisprudence* (Auckland: Pearson).

Nicholson, P. and Biddulph, S. (eds) (2008), *Examining Practice, Interrogating Theory: Comparative Legal Studies in Asia* (Leiden and Boston: Martinus Nijhoff).

Nizam Awang, M. (2008), 'Islamic Legal Education in Public Law Schools in Malaysia: Charting the Direction', *International Association of Law Schools: Effective Techniques for Teaching about Other Cultures and Legal Systems* (published online 30 May 2008). Available at: www.ialsnet.org/meetings/assembly/MuhammedAwang.pdf, accessed 21 May 2009.

Noor Aziah Mohd Awal, D. (2008), 'Effective Teaching about other Cultures and Legal Systems', *International Association of Law Schools: Effective Techniques for Teaching about Other Cultures and Legal Systems* (published online 30 May 2008). Available at: www.ialsnet.org/meetings/assembly/NoorAziahMohdAwal.pdf, accessed 23 May 2009.

Örücü, A.E. (2006), 'Methodology of Comparative Law', in Smits, 442–54.

Örücü, A.E. (2007a), 'Comparative Law in Practice: The Courts and the Legislator', in Örücü and Nelken, 411–33.

Örücü, A.E. (2007b), 'Developing Comparative Law', in Örücü and Nelken, 43–65.

Örücü, A.E. (2007c), '"Legal Families" and "Mixing Systems"', in Örücü and Nelken, 169–87.

Örücü, A.E. and Nelken, D. (eds) (2007), *Comparative Law: A Handbook* (Oxford and Portland, OR: Hart).

Oyarce-Yuzzelli, A. (2009), *El Derecho Comparado en la USMP* (personal communication 8 June 2009).

Pound, R. (1934). 'The Place of Comparative Law in the American Law School Curriculum', *Tulane Law Review* 8:2, 161–70.

'Proyecto de un Seminario de Derecho Comparado', *Universidad de Chile, Anales de la Facultad de Ciencias Jurídicas y Sociales*. Available at: www.analesderecho.uchile.cl/CDA/an_der_articulo/0,1361,SCID%253D3084%2526ISID%253D253,00.html, accessed 21 May 2009.

'Quintas Jornadas Chileno-Uruguayas de Derecho Comparado', *Universidad de Chile, Anales de la Facultad de Ciencias Jurídicas y Sociales*. Available at: www.analesderecho.uchile.cl/CDA/an_der_articulo/0,1361,SCID%253D11218%2526ISID%253D78,00.html, accessed 21 May 2009.

Reimann, M. (1996), 'The End of Comparative Law as an Autonomous Subject', *Tulane European & Civil Law* Forum 11:1, 49–72.

Reimann, M. (2002), 'The Progress and Failure of Comparative Law in the Second Half of the Twentieth Century', *American Journal of Comparative Law* 50:4, 671–700.

Reimann, M. and Zimmermann, R. (eds) (2006), *The Oxford Handbook of Comparative Law* (Oxford: Oxford University Press).

Reitz, J. (1998), 'How to Do Comparative Law', *American Journal of Comparative Law* 46:4, 607–16.

Rheinstein, M. (1938), 'Teaching Comparative Law', *Chicago Law Review* 5:4, 615–24.

Riesenfeld, S.A. and Pakter, W. (2001), *Comparative Law Casebook* (Ardsley: Transnational).

Riles, A. (1999), 'Wigmore's Treasure Box: Comparative Law in the Era of Information', *Harvard International Law Journal* 40:1, 221–84.

Riles, A. (2001), *Rethinking the Masters of Comparative Law* (Oxford and Portland, OR: Hart).

Ritane, E., Franck, L. and Lalani, S. (2008), *Legal Engineering and Comparative Law* (Geneva, Zurich and Bâle: Schulthess).

Sacco, R. (2001), 'One Hundred Years of Comparative Law', *Tulane Law Review* 75:4, 1159–76.

Sagástegui Urteaga, P. (2007), 'Temas de Derecho Comparado: Para que las Comparaciones del Derecho', *Revista Online del Instituto de Investigaciones Jurídicas de la Facultad de Derecho y Ciencia Política de la Universidad San Martin de Porres*. Available at: www.derecho.usmp.edu.pe/instituto/revista/articulos/Temas_de%20Derecho_Comparado.doc, accessed 21 May 2009.

Schlesinger, R.B. (1998), *Comparative Law: Cases, Text, Materials* (6th edn) (New York: Foundation Press).

Schwenzer, I.H. (2006), 'Development of Comparative Law in Germany, Switzerland, and Austria', in Reimann and Zimmermann, 69–106.

Sebok, A.J. (2007), 'Using Comparative Torts Materials to Teach First-Year Torts', *Journal of Legal Education* 57:4, 562–78.

Serna de la Garza, J.M. (2004), 'Apuntes sobre las Opciones de Cambio en la Metodología de la Enseñanza del Derecho en México', *Boletín Mexicano de Derecho Comparado* 37:111, 1047–82.

Siems, M. (2007), 'The End of Comparative Law', *Journal of Comparative Law* 2:2, 133–49.

Singh, G. (2008), 'Effective Techniques for Teaching about Other Cultures and Legal Systems', *International Association of Law Schools: Effective Techniques for Teaching about Other Cultures and Legal Systems* (published online 30 May 2008). Available at: www.ialsnet.org/meetings/assembly/GurjeetSingh.pdf, accessed 23 May 2009.

Smits, J.M. (ed.) (2006), *Elgar Encyclopedia of Comparative Law* (Cheltenham, UK and Northampton, MA: Edward Elgar).

Smits, J.M. (2007), 'Convergence of Private Law in Europe: Towards a New Ius Commune?', in Örücü and Nelken, 219–40.

Société de Législation Comparé (ed.) (2000), *L'Avenir du Droit Comparé: Un Défi pour les Juristes du Nouveau Millénaire* (Paris: Société de Législation Comparé).

Sridhar Patnaik, D. (2007), 'Comparative Legal Education in India: An Inquiry', *Proceedings of the International Seminar on Recent Trends in Teaching and Research in International Law, Indian Society of International Law*. Available at: http://works.bepress.com/cgi/viewcontent.cgi?article=1004&context=sridhar, accessed 21 May 2009.

'Symposium: New Approaches to Comparative Law', *Utah Law Review* 1997:2, 255–663 (1997).

'Symposium: New Directions in Comparative Law', *American Journal of Comparative Law* 46:4, 597–784 (1998).

Tan, C.H., Bell, G., Dang, X., Kim, J., Teo, K., Thiruvengadam, A., Vijayakumar, V. and Wang, J. (2006), 'Legal Education in Asia', *Asian Journal of Comparative Law* 1:1, Article 9.

Tarchi, R. (1999), *Corso di Diritto Comparato: Casi e Materiali* (Milano: Giuffrè).

Teitel, R. (2004), 'Book Review: Comparative Constitutional Law in a Global Age', *Harvard Law Review* 117:8, 2570–96.

Thaman, S.C. (2008), *Comparative Criminal Procedure: A Casebook Approach* (2nd edn) (Durham, NC: Carolina Academic Press).

Valcke, C. (2004), 'Comparative Law as Comparative Jurisprudence – The Comparability of Legal Systems', *American Journal of Comparative Law* 52:3, 713–40.

Valcke, C. (2005), 'Comparative Legal Education in Canada', *Revue Juridique Themis* 39:3, 483–505.

van Gerven, W. (ed.) (1999–), *Ius Commune Casebooks for the Common Law of Europe* (Oxford and Portland, OR: Hart).

Van Hoecke, M. (ed.) (2004), *Epistemology and Methodology of Comparative Law* (Oxford and Portland, OR: Hart).

Villarreal-Gonda, F. (2008), 'Teaching Macrocomparison through Formal Debate', *International Association of Law Schools: Effective Techniques for Teaching about Other Cultures and Legal Systems* (published online 30 May 2008). Available at: www.ialsnet.org/meetings/assembly/FernandoVillarrreal-Gonda.pdf, accessed 23 May 2009.

Vodenitcharov, A. (2008), 'The Bulgarian Experience on Effective Teaching about Other Cultures and Legal Systems', *International Association of Law Schools: Effective Techniques for Teaching about Other Cultures and Legal Systems* (published online 30 May 2008). Available at: www.ialsnet.org/meetings/assembly/AlexandreVodenitcharov.pdf, accessed 26 May 2009.

Wade, D. (1994), 'Comparative Law: Academic Perspectives and Practical Legal Realities', in Danner and Bernal, 15–45.

Wald, A. (2000), 'Le Droit Comparé au Brésil', in Blanc-Jouvan, 69–104.

Wang, F.S. and Young, L.W. (2008), 'Cultural Differences and Legal Perspectives: Measuring Intercultural Interactions and Outcomes at the Summer Law Institute, Kenneth Wang School of Law, Suzhou, China', *International Association of Law Schools: Effective Techniques for Teaching about Other Cultures and Legal Systems* (published online 30 May 2008). Available at: www.ialsnet.org/meetings/assembly/FrancisSLWang.pdf, accessed 26 May 2009.

Waxman, M.P. (2001), 'Teaching Comparative Law in the 21st Century: Beyond the Civil/Common Law Dichotomy', *Journal of Legal Education* 51:2, 305–12.

Whitman, J.Q. (2000), 'Enforcing Civility and Respect: Three Societies', *Yale Law Journal* 109:6, 1279–398.

Whitman, J.Q. (2004), 'Two Western Cultures of Privacy: Dignity versus Liberty', *Yale Law Journal* 113:6, 1151–221.

Zhang, Z. (2010), *Comparative Legal Studies of Chinese and Western Legal Cultures* (Beijing Shi: Fa lü chu ban she).

Zweigert, K. and Kötz, H. (1987), *Introduction to Comparative Law* (trans. Weir, T.) (Oxford: Clarendon Press).

Appendix A

Currently Published Comparative Law Journals[16]

Africa

Kenya

East African Journal of International and Comparative Law (2002)
www.euppublishing.com/journal/ajicl.

South Africa

The Comparative and International Law Journal of Southern Africa (1968)
www.journals.co.za/ej/ejour_cilsa.html.

Asia

China

US-China Law Review (2004)
www.jurist.org.cn
Peking University International and Comparative Law Review (2002)
http://en.law.pku.edu.cn/partycolumn/Display.asp?ID=54&mid=20091125121428&menuid=20091124996475&menuname=Intellectual+Life
比较法研究/*Bi jiao fa yan jiu/Studies of Comparative Law* (1987)
www.ceps.com.tw/ec/ecJnlIntro.aspx?Jnliid=1354

Hong Kong

中国法与比较法研究/*Zhongguo fa yu bi jiao fa yan jiu/Journal of Chinese and Comparative Law* – City University of Hong Kong (1995)
www.cityu.edu.hk/slw/eng/research/researchCentre.html

Japan

Daito Bunka Comparative Law and Political Science Review (2001)
http://ci.nii.ac.jp/vol_issue/nels/AA12028931_en.html
講演記録集/*Waseda Proceedings of Comparative Law* (1999)
www.waseda.jp/hiken/en/public/proceed.html

16 The journals are arranged in reverse chronological order within their respective countries. I am grateful to Barbara Olszowa, Anna Ershova, YC '11, and María A. Gutierrez, Ph.D '14, for their assistance with the appendices. Their multilingual skills proved invaluable. Of course, any omissions or other errors are wholly mine.

Waseda Bulletin of Comparative Law (1981)
www.waseda.jp/hiken/en/public/bulletin/index.html
比較法学/*Hikaku Hogaku/Comparative Law Review* – Waseda University (1964)
www.waseda.jp/hiken/en/public/review/index.html

Malaysia

Jernal Undang-Undang dan Masyarakat/Journal of Law and Society – Universiti Kebangsaan Malaysia (1997)
http://pkukmweb.ukm.my/~penerbit/juum.html
Journal of Malaysian and Comparative Law (1974)
www.commonlii.org/my/journals/JMCL

Singapore

Asian Journal of Comparative Law (2006)
www.bepress.com/asjcl
Singapore Journal of International and Comparative Law (1997)

South Korea

Korean Journal of International and Comparative Law (1973)

Australia

Macquarie Journal of International and Comparative Environmental Law (2004)
www.law.mq.edu.au/html/MqJICEL/about.htm
The Australian Journal of Asian Law – University of Melbourne and Australian National University (1999),
www.law.unimelb.edu.au/ajal/index.html

Europe

Revue de Droit Uniforme/Uniform Law Review (1973)[17]
www.unidroit.org/english/publications/review/main.htm

Austria

Zeitschrift fuer Europarecht, Internationales Privatrecht und Rechtsvergleichung/Journal for the European Law, International Private Law, and Comparative Law (2008)
www.manz.at/index.html?load=/zeitschriften/aktuelle_hefte/zfrv.html&navi=zeitschriften

17 *Uniform Law Review* was the result of merging two preceding publications: *L'unification de Droit/Unification of Law* (1948) and *Jurisprudence de Droit Uniforme/Uniform Law Cases* (1960).

Azerbaijan

Milli Məclisin Reqabet Huququ Jurnali/Parliament's Comparative Law Journal (2003)
www.meclis.gov.az

Belgium

Bulletin of Comparative Labour Relations (1970)
www.cer-leuven.be/cerleuven/Blanpain/BCLR/BCLR.htm
Revue de Droit International et de Droit Compare/Review of International and Comparative Law (1949)
www.bruylant.be/st/fr/per_fiche.php?id=50021

Czech Republic

Common Law Review (2001)
http://review.society.cz

England

Journal of Comparative Law (2006)
www.thejcl.com
Commonwealth Law Journal – Oxford University (2004)
www.law.ox.ac.uk/ouclj
International Journal of Constitutional Law (2002)
http://icon.oxfordjournals.org
International and Comparative Corporate Law Journal (1999)
African Journal of International and Comparative Law/Revue Africaine de Droit International et Comparé (1989)
www.euppublishing.com/journal/ajicl
The International Journal of Comparative Labour Law and Industrial Relations (1985)
www.kluwerlawonline.com/productinfo.php?pubcode=IJCL
The Comparative Law Yearbook of International Business (1977)
www.kluwerlaw.com/Catalogue/titleinfo.htm?ProdID=9888880024
International and Comparative Law Quarterly (1952)
http://journals.cambridge.org/action/displayJournal?jid=ILQ

France

Bulletin de Droit Comparé du Travail et de la Securité Sociale/Bulletin of Comparative Labour and Social Security Law – Université Montesquieu-Bordeaux IV (1981)
http://comptrasec.u-bordeaux4.fr/static/PUBLICATIONS/periodiques.htm
Revue Internationale de Droit Comparé (1949)
www.legiscompare.com/Publications/RIDC_presentation.html
Revue de Science Criminelle et de Droit Pénal Comparé (1936)
http://jurisguide.univ-paris1.fr/RD/index.php?view=SSEARCH&action=SHOWFICHE&fid=FR2099

Germany

Hanse Law Review (2005)
www.hanselawreview.org/cgi-bin/site.pl?user=&site=index
Zeitschrift für Vergleichende Rechtswissenschaft/Journal of Comparative Law (1987)
www287609796.ruw.de/vr/aktuelles/vr/inhaltsverzeichnis/pages/show.prl
Zeitschrift für ausländisches und internationales Arbeits-und Sozialrecht/Journal of Foreign and International Labour and Social Law (1987)
www.mpisoc.mpg.de/ww/de/pub/forschung/publikationen/zias.cfm
Rabels Zeitschrift für Ausländisches und Internationales Privatrecht/The Rabel Journal of Comparative and International Private Law (1927)
www.mpipriv.de/ww/en/pub/research/publications/journals/rabels_zeitschrift.htm

Italy

Diritto Pubblico Comparato ed Europeo/European Comparative Public Law (2001)
www.dpce.it
Annuario di Diritto Comparato e di Studi Legislativi/Yearbook of Comparative Law and Legislative Studies (1927)

The Netherlands

European Journal of Comparative Law (2000)
www.ejcl.org
Griffin's View on International and Comparative Law – Vrije Universiteit Amsterdam (2000)
www.rechten.vu.nl/en/about-the-faculty/magazines/griffins-view/index.asp
Maastricht Journal of European and Comparative Law (1994)
www.unimaas.nl/default.asp?template=werkveld.htm&id=IHA3VONPFP25175R1IJP&taal=en
Tilburg Law Review: Journal on International and Comparative Law (1991)
http://stuwww.uvt.nl/tflr/index2.htm
International Journal of Comparative Labour Law and Industrial Relations (1985)
www.csmb.unimore.it/on-line/Home/articolo36009068.html

Poland

Review of Comparative Law – The John Paul II Catholic University of Lublin (1989)
www.kul.pl/2849.html

Portugal

Boletim Documentacão e Direito Comparado (1980)
www.gddc.pt/actividade-editorial/actividade-editorial.html
Scientia Iuridica: Revista de Direito Comprado Português e Brasileiro – Universidade do Minho (1951)
http://cejur.meticube.com/portal/alias_CEJUR/lang_pt-PT/tabID_3389/DesktopDefault.aspx

Russia

Журнал зарубежного законодательства и сравнительного правоведения/*Zhurnal Zarubezhnogo Zakonodatelstva i Sravnitelnogo Pravovedeniia/Journal of Foreign Legislation and Comparative Law* (2005),
www.izak.ru/article/index.php?id_article=38
Российский журнал сравнительного права/*Rossiiskii Zhurnal Sravnitelnogo Prava/Russian Journal of Comparative Law* (2001),
http://law.edu.ru/book/book.asp?bookID=1176892
Сравнительное конституционное обозрение/*Sravnitelnoe Konstitutsionnoe Obozrenie/Comparative Constitutional Review* (1992),
http://ilpp.ru/page_pid_278_lang_1.aspx

Serbia

Strani pravni život/Foreign Legal Life (1962),
www.comparativelaw.info/publications.html

Switzerland

Yearbook of Private International Law (1999),
www.isdc.ch/en/publications.asp/4-0-10830-5-4-0

Ukraine

Порівняльно-правові дослідження/*Porivnyalno-pravovi Doslidzhennya/Comparative Law Studies* (2006),
http://comparativelaw.org.ua/ukr4/pub_ppd.php
Журнал зарубіжного законодавства і порівняльного правознавства/*Zhurnal Zarubizhnogo Zakonodavstvata Porivnyal'nogo Pravoznavstva/Journal of Foreign Law and Comparative Jurisprudence* (2005),
http://law-edu.dp.ua/instytut-zakonodavstva-i-porivnyalnogo-pravoznavstva.html
Порівняльне правознавство/*Porivnyalne Pravoznavstvo/Comparative Jurisprudence* (2003),
www.justinian.com.ua/cjustice.php

Latin America

Argentina

Revista de Derecho Comparado/Journal of Comparative Law (1999),
http://201.216.205.125/libro_nuevo/listado_revista.php?derechox=4
Anuario de Filosofía Jurídica y Social/Annual Review of Legal and Social Philosophy (1982),
www.derechocomparado.org.ar/autoridades.htm

Brazil

Revista de Direito Comparado/Journal of Comparative Law – Universidade Federal de Minas Gerais (1997)
www.direito.ufmg.br/faculdade.htm
Revista de Direito Comparado Luso-Brasileiro/Journal of Comparative Portuguese-Brazilian Law (1982)
www.idclb.com.br/revista.htm

Mexico

Comparative Media Law Journal – Universidad Nacional Autónoma de México (UNAM) (2003)
www.juridicas.unam.mx/publica/rev/indice.htm?r=comlawj&n=4
Derecho Comparado de la Información/Comparative Law of Information – UNAM (2003)
www.juridicas.unam.mx/publica/rev/cont.htm?r=decoin
Revista Mexicana de Derecho Internacional Privado y Comparado/Mexican Journal of Private International and Comparative Law (1996)
www.themis.com.mx/ObrasImpresas/EnsayosJur%C3%ADdicos/RevistaMexicanadeDerechoInternacional/tabid/355/language/es-MX/Default.aspx
Boletín Mexicano de Derecho Comparado/Mexican Bulletin of Comparative Law – UNAM (1948)
www.juridicas.unam.mx/publica/rev/boletin

Venezuela

Revista Anuario del Instituto de Derecho Comparado/Annual Review of the Institute of Comparative Law – Universidad de Carabobo (1968)
http://servicio.cid.uc.edu.ve/derecho/revista/index.htm

North America

United States

New England Journal of International and Comparative Law (2002)
www.nesl.edu/students/ne_journal_icl.cfm
Chicago-Kent Journal of International and Comparative Law (2001)
www.kentlaw.edu/jicl
Asian-Pacific Law and Policy Journal – University of Hawai'i (2000)
www.hawaii.edu/aplpj/about.html
Loyola of Los Angeles International and Comparative Law Review (1999)
http://ilr.lls.edu
University of Miami International and Comparative Law Review (1998)
www.law.miami.edu/studentorg/international_comparative_law_review/index.php
Comparative Labor Law and Policy Journal – University of Illinois at Urbana-Champaign College of Law (1997)
www.law.uiuc.edu/publications/cll&pj/

Cardozo Journal of International and Comparative Law (1995)
www.cardozo.yu.edu/MemberContentDisplay.aspx?ccmd=ContentDisplay&ucmd=UserDisplay&userid=10644
ILSA Journal of International and Comparative Law – International Law Students Association, Nova Southeastern Shepard Broad Law Center (1995)
http://nsulaw.nova.edu/orgs/ILSAJournal/index.cfm
Annual Survey of International and Comparative Law – Golden Gate University School of Law (1994)
www.ggu.edu/lawlibrary/annual_survey
Tulane Journal of International and Comparative Law (1993)
www.law.tulane.edu/tlsjournals/tjicl/index.aspx
Tulsa Journal of Comparative and International Law (1993)
www.utulsa.edu/law/ilj
Duke Journal of Comparative and International Law (1991)
www.law.duke.edu/journals/djcil
Indiana International and Comparative Law Review (1991)
http://indylaw.indiana.edu/IICLR
Temple International and Comparative Law Journal (1985)
www.temple.edu/law/ticlj
New York Law School Journal of International and Comparative Law (1983)
http://old.nyls.edu/pages/307.asp
Arizona Journal of International and Comparative Law (1982)
www.law.arizona.edu/journals/ajicl
Boston College International and Comparative Law Review (1978)
www.bc.edu/bc_org/avp/law/lwsch/interrev.html
Canada-United States Law Journal – Case Western Reserve University School of Law (1978)
http://cusli.org/lawjournals/lawjournal.html
Hastings International and Comparative Law Review (1978)
www.uchastings.edu/hiclr
Georgia Journal of International and Comparative Law (1970)
www.lawsch.uga.edu/georgia-journal-international-comparative-law
Columbia Journal of Transnational Law (1961)
www.law.columbia.edu/current_student/student_service/Law_Journals/transnational
American Journal of Comparative Law (1952)
www.comparativelaw.org/journal.html

Appendix B

Currently Active Academic and Research Centres and Institutes of Comparative Law[18]

Africa

Institute of Foreign and Comparative Law – University of South Africa (1964)
www.unisa.ac.za/default.asp?Cmd=ViewContent&ContentID=675

Asia

Hong Kong

Centre for Chinese and Comparative Law – City University of Hong Kong (1993)
www.cityu.edu.hk/slw/eng/research/researchCentre.html

Japan

Comparative Law Institute – Nihon University (1982)
www.nihon-u.ac.jp/intldiv/en/research/institution.html
Kyoto Comparative Law Center (1981)
www.kclc.or.jp/english/index.html
Waseda University Institute of Comparative Law (1958)
www.waseda.jp/hiken/index.html
Institute of Comparative Law in Japan – Chuo University (1948)
www2.tamacc.chuo-u.ac.jp/instl/juts_e.htm

South Korea

Korea Institute of International and Comparative Law

Australia

Centre for Comparative Law and Development Studies in Asia and the Pacific – University of Wollongong (2007)
www.uow.edu.au/law/cldsap/index.html
Australian Institute of Comparative Legal Systems (2003)
www.ausicl.com

18 Centres and Institutes are listed in reverse chronological order within their respective countries when year of inception is known.

Centre for Public, International and Comparative Law – University of Queensland (2003)
 www.law.uq.edu.au/cpicl
Centre for Comparative Constitutional Studies – University of Melbourne (1987)
 http://cccs.law.unimelb.edu.au

Europe

Austria

Institut für Europarecht, Internationales Recht und Rechtsvergleichung/Institute for European, International, and Comparative Law – University of Vienna
 http://deicl.univie.ac.at

Belgium

Centre de Droit Comparé, d'Histoire du Droit et d'Anthropologie Juridique/Center for Comparative Law, History of Law, and Legal Anthropology – Université Libre de Bruxelles (1991)
 www.ulb.ac.be/rech/inventaire/unites/ULB073.html
Centre Interuniversitaire de Droit Comparé/Inter-University Center of Comparative Law (1958)

Czech Republic

Centre for Comparative Law – Charles University (2009)
www.czechyearbook.org/centre-for-comparative-law-p-35.html

England

Institute of Global Law – University College London (2000)
 www.ucl.ac.uk/laws/global_law
Institute of European and Comparative Law – Oxford University (1995)
 www.iecl.ox.ac.uk
The British Institute of International and Comparative Law (1895)
 www.biicl.org

France

Groupement de Recherches Comparatives Sur le Droit Constitutionnel Administratif et Politique/Association of Comparative Research on Constitutional Administrative Law and Politics (2007)
 http://greccap.u-bordeaux4.fr
Institut de Recherches Carre de Malberg/Research Institute Carre de Malberg – Université Robert-Schuman, Strasbourg (2000)
 www-ircm.u-strasbg.fr/english.htm
Centre de Droit et de Politique Comparés Jean-Claude/Center for Comparative Law and Politics Jean-Claude – Université de Toulon et du Var (1998)
 http://cdpc.univ-tln.fr

Unité Mixte de Recherche de Droit Comparé de Paris/Joint Research Unit of Comparative Law of Paris – Université Paris-Panthéon-Sorbonne, Paris I and the National Center for Scientific Research (1997)
www.umrdc.fr
Groupement de Droit Comparé/Association of Comparative Law (1996)
www.gdc.cnrs.fr/site
Société, Droit et Religion en Europe/Society, Law, and Religion in Europe – Université Robert-Schuman, Strasbourg and the National Center of Scientific Research (1996)
http://prisme.u-strasbg.fr/Presentation.htm
Centre de Droit Comparé du Travail et de la Sécurité Sociale/Center for Comparative Labor and Social Security Law (1982)
http://comptrasec.u-bordeaux4.fr
Institut d'Etudes Ibériques et Ibérico-Américaines – Droit et Politique Compares/Institute of Iberian and Ibero-American Studies – Comparative Law and Politics – Université de Pau et des Pays de l'Adour (1975)
http://ie2ia.univ-pau.fr/live
Centre d'Etudes et de Recherches Comparatives sur les Constitutions, les Libertés et l'Etat/Center for Comparative Studies and Research of Constitutions, Civil Liberties, and the State – Université Montesquieu Bordeaux IV (1975)
www.gdc.cnrs.fr/site/index.php?option=com_content&task=view&id=31&Itemid=46
Centre Français de Droit Comparé/French Center of Comparative Law (1951)
www.centrefdc.org
Institut de Droit Comparé de Paris/Institute of Comparative Law of Paris – Université Panthéon-Assas, Paris II (1931)
http://idc.u-paris2.fr
Institut de Droit Comparé Edouard Lambert/Institute of Comparative Law Edouard Lambert – Université Jean Moulin, Lyon III (1920)
www.gdc.cnrs.fr/idcel
Centre de Droit Comparé – Juripôle/Center of Comparative Law – Juripôle
www.gdc.cnrs.fr/site/index.php?option=com_content&task=view&id=35&Itemid=46

Germany

Max-Planck-Institut für Ausländisches und Internationales Sozialrecht/Max Planck Institute for Foreign and International Social Law (1972)
www.mpisoc.mpg.de/ww/de/pub/aktuelles.cfm
Max-Planck-Institut für Ausländisches und Internationales Strafrecht/Max Planck Institute for Foreign and International Criminal Law (1947)
www.mpicc.de/ww/de/pub/home.cfm
Max-Planck-Institut für Ausländisches und Internationales Privatrecht/Max Planck Institute for Comparative and International Private Law (1926)
www.mpipriv.de/ww/de/pub/aktuelles.cfm
Max-Planck-Institut für Ausländisches Öffentliches Recht und Völkerrecht/Max Planck Institute for Comparative Public Law and International Law (1924)
www.mpil.de/ww/de/pub/aktuelles.cfm

Greece

Hellenic Institute of International and Foreign Law (1939)
www.hiifl.gr/?lang=en

Italy

Institute of European and Comparative Private Law – Universtá di Girona (2003),
http://civil.udg.edu/iecpl
Associazione Diritto Pubblico Comparato ed Europeo/Association of European Comparative Public Law (2001)
www.dpce.it/index.php/l-associazione
Cardozo Institute of Comparative Law – University of Trento (1989)
www.jus.unitn.it/CARDOZO/home.html
Dipartimento di Diritto Comparato e Penale/Department of Comparative and Criminal Law – Università degli Studi di Firenze (1962)
www.dcp.unifi.it/CMpro-v-p-48.html
Istituto di Diritto Agrario Internazionale e Comparato/Institute of International and Comparative Agrarian Law (1920)
www.idaic.it
Centre for Comparative and Foreign Law Studies – UNIDROIT and Universitá degli Studi di Roma 'La Sapienza'
Istituto di Diritto Comparato 'Angelo Sraffa'/Institute of Comparative Law 'Angelo Sraffa' – Bocconi University
www.unibocconi.it/wps/wcm/connect/SitoPubblico_IT/Albero+di+navigazione/Home/Dipartimenti/Studi+Giuridici

The Netherlands

Tilburg Institute of Comparative and Transnational Law (2008)
www.tilburguniversity.nl/faculties/law/research/ticom
E.M. Meijers Institute for Legal Research – Universiteit Leiden (1997)
www.law.leiden.edu/organisation/meijers

Russia

Центр Публично-Правовых Исследований/Tsenter Publichno-Pravovykh Issledovanii/Public Law Research Center (2006)
www.plrc.ru/en
Институт законодательства и сравнительного правоведения при правительстве Российской Федерации/Institut Zakonodatelstva i Spravitelnogo Pravovedeniia Pri Pravitelstve Rossijskoi Federatsii/Institute of Legislation and Comparative Jurisprudence under the Government of the Russian Federation (1925)
www.izak.ru/ver_eng/index.php
Институт истории зарубежного права/Institut Istorii Zarubezhnogo Prava/Institute of the History of Foreign Law
http://law.edu.ru/centers/IHFL

Serbia

Institut za Uporedno Pravo/Institute of Comparative Law (1955)
www.comparativelaw.info

Slovenia

Inštitut za Primerjalno Pravo/Institute for Comparative Law – University of Ljubljana (1997)
www.ipp-pf.si/home

Spain

Instituto de Derecho Público Comparado 'Manuel Garcia Pelayo'/Institute of Comparative Public Law 'Manuel Garcia Pelayo' – Universidad Carlos III de Madrid (1997)
http://turan.uc3m.es/uc3m/inst/MGP/portada.htm
Seminario Permanente de Derecho Comparado – Universidad de Granada (1995)
www.ugr.es/~sdcompar
Instituto de Derecho Comparado – Universidad Complutense Madrid
www.ucm.es/info/derecho/estudios/comer.htm

Switzerland

Institut Suisse de Droit Comparé/Swiss Institute of Comparative Law (1982)
www.isdc.ch

Ukraine

Інститут законодавства і порівняльного правознавства/Instytut Zakonodavstva i Porivnyalnogo Pravoznavstva/Institute of Legislation and Comparative Law (1925)
http://law-edu.dp.ua/instytut-zakonodavstva-i-porivnyalnogo-pravoznavstva.html

Latin America

Argentina

Instituto de Derecho Comparado 'Enrique Martínez Paz'/Institute of Comparative Law 'Enrique Martínez Paz'
www.acaderc.org.ar/institutos/folder.2008-01-22.4097593048

Brazil

Instituto de Direito Comparado Brasil-França (2005)
www.direito-brasilfranca.org
Instituto de Direito Comparado Luso-Brasileiro/Institute of Comparative Portuguese-Brazilian Law (1982)
www.idclb.com.br

Instituto de Direito Comparado e Internacional de Brasilia/Institute of Comparative and International Law of Brasilia
www.idcb.org.br

Mexico

Mexican Center of Uniform Law (2004)
Instituto Iberoamericano de Derecho Constitucional/Iberoamerican Institute of Constitutional Law – UNAM (1974)
www.juridicas.unam.mx/iidc
Instituto de Investigaciones Juridicas/Institute of Legal Research – UNAM (1940)
www.juridicas.unam.mx

Venezuela

Instituto de Derecho Comparado/Institute of Comparative Law – Facultad de Ciencias Jurídicas y Políticas, Universidad de Carabobo (1968)
www.uc.edu.ve/cs_politicas/index.php

North America

Canada

Comparative Research in Law and Political Economy Network (2004)
www.comparativeresearch.net
Quebec Research Centre of Private and Comparative Law – McGill University (1975)
www.mcgill.ca/crdpcq
Institute of Comparative Law – McGill University (1965)
www.mcgill.ca/icl

United States

Comparative Administrative Law Initiative – Yale Law School (2008)
www.law.yale.edu/compadlaw
Center for International & Comparative Law – Duke University School of Law (2006)
www.law.duke.edu/cicl
Center for International and Comparative Law – Indiana University School of Law (2002)
http://indylaw.indiana.edu/centers/icl
Center for Comparative Constitutionalism – University of Chicago Law School (2002)
www.law.uchicago.edu/people/faculty/all/all/Center%20for%20Comparative%20Constitutionalism
Institute of Transnational Law – University of Texas, Austin (2000)
www.utexas.edu/law/academics/centers/transnational/work_new
Portuguese American Comparative Law Center – Roger Williams University School of Law (1999)
http://law.rwu.edu/sites/paclc

Comparative Law and Society Studies Center – University of Washington (1999)
http://depts.washington.edu/class
Center for International and Comparative Law – University of Michigan Law School (1998)
www.law.umich.edu/centersandprograms/cicl/Pages/center.aspx
Center for International and Comparative Law – University of Baltimore School of Law (1994)
http://law.ubalt.edu/template.cfm?page=608
Center for International Law and Comparative Study – St. Louis University School of Law (1992)
http://lawlib.slu.edu/cicl
Dean Rusk Center for International, Comparative, and Graduate Legal Studies – University of Georgia School of Law (1977)
www.uga.edu/ruskcenter
Canada-United States Law Institute – Case Western Reserve University (1976)
http://cusli.org/index.html
Institute on International and Comparative Law – University of San Diego (1970)
www.sandiego.edu/law/centers/iilc.php
The Eason Weinmann Center of Comparative Law – Tulane Law School (1949)
www.law.tulane.edu/tlsAcademicPrograms/index.aspx?id=6170
The Institute for International and Comparative Law (1947)
www.cailaw.org/iicl
The Parker School of Foreign and Comparative Law – Columbia University (1931)
www.law.columbia.edu/center_program/parker

Appendix C

Currently Active Associations, Academies and Societies of Comparative Law[19]

International

Association of Transnational Law Schools (ATLAS) (2008)
http://centers.law.nyu.edu/atlasdoctorate/index.html
The World Society of Mixed Jurisdiction Jurists (2002)
www.mixedjurisdiction.org
Association Internationale des Sciences Juridiques/International Association of Legal Science (1950)
http://aisj-ials.org/index.htm
International Academy of Comparative Law (1924)[20]
www.iuscomparatum.org

19 Associations, Academies and Societies are listed in reverse chronological order within their respective countries when year of inception is known.

20 The International Academy of Comparative Law comprises affiliated national committees in about 50 countries. Those national committees are often affiliated with university institutes or national associations.

Africa

African Society of International and Comparative Law

Asia

Japan Society of Comparative Law (2003)
www.soc.nii.ac.jp/jscl
Chinese Society of Comparative Law
Comparative Law Association (India)
National Committee of Comparative Law (India)

Australia and the Pacific

New Zealand Association of Comparative Law (1995)
www.victoria.ac.nz/law/NZACL%20web%20page/Index.htm
Australian and New Zealand Society of International Law (1992)
http://law.anu.edu.au/anzsil/

Europe

Irish Society of Comparative Law (2008)
www.iscl.ie
Norwegian Association for Comparative Law (2007)
Ukrainian Association of Comparative Law (2006)
http://comparativelaw.org.ua/eng4/sem_part.php
Österreichische Gesellschaft für Rechtsvergleichung / Austrian Association of Comparative Law (2002)
www.vwgoe.at/mitglieder.php?id=152
Gabinete de Documentação e Direito Comparado (1980)
www.gddc.pt
Nederlandse Vereniging voor Rechtsvergelijking/Netherlands Comparative Law Association (1968)
www.ejcl.org/general/nvvrhome.html
Associazione Italiana di Diritto Comparato/Italian Association of Comparative Law (1958)
www.aidc.it
Gesellschaft für Rechtsvergleichung/German National Committee of Comparative Law (1950)
www.gfr.uni-freiburg.de
British Association of Comparative Law (1950)
www.law.ed.ac.uk/bacl/nextcouncilmeeting.aspx
Association for Comparative Law of Yugoslavia (1955)
www.icl.org.yu/m7e.html

For more information, see www.iuscomparatum.org/141_p_1561/national-committees.html, accessed 21 June 2009.

Association Henri Capitant (France, 1935)
www.henricapitant.org
Société de Legislation Comparée (France, 1869)
www.legiscompare.com
Association for Comparative Legal Studies (England)
Danske Komité for Komparativ Ret/Danish Committee for Comparative Law
Bulgarian Comparative Law Association
Georgian Committee of Comparative Law
Scottish Association of Comparative Law
Українська асоціація порівняльного правознавства/Ukrainska Asotsiatsia Porivnialnogo Pravoznavstva/Ukrainian Association of Comparative Law Studies
http://comparativelaw.org.ua/ukr4/home.php

Latin America

Academia Mexicana de Derecho Internacional Privado y Comparado/Mexican Academy of Private International and Comparative Law (1968)
www.amedip.com
Asociación Argentina de Derecho Comparado/Argentine Association of Comparative Law (1946)
www.derechocomparado.org.ar

North America

Georgia Society for International and Comparative Law – University of Georgia (United States, 1977)
www.uga.edu/ruskcenter/activities.html
Association Québécoise de Droit Comparé/Quebec Society of Comparative Law (Canada, 1960)
www.aqdc.qc.ca
The American Society of Comparative Law (United States, 1951)
www.comparativelaw.org
American Foreign Law Association (United States, 1925)
www.afla-law.org
Canadian Association of Comparative Law

Chapter 16
A Research Agenda for International Law Librarianship

Barbara H. Garavaglia
and the
Board of the International Association of Law Libraries[1]

Introduction

The goal of the Research Agenda for International Law Librarianship is to suggest research priorities for law librarians around the world. It is hoped that the Agenda, created by the Board of the International Association of Law Libraries (IALL)[2] will inspire creative thinking and stimulate research, publication and educational programmes by law librarians and legal information professionals on the most important topics, issues, trends and developments in the field.

As we enter the second decade of the new millennium, law librarians in virtually all countries continue to face a multitude of challenges relating to the publication and dissemination of legal information within their countries[3] as well as new issues created by emerging technologies and trends in the legal information arena. The current pace of change is rapid and the agents of change are numerous and varied:[4] continuous technological innovation; changes in governmental, scholarly and commercial legal publishing, including the growth of open access publishing (Danner 2002; Plotin 2009); continuing concerns about the survival of print collections in large research libraries (Atchison and Cadra 2008; Wu 2005); increasing financial pressures and constraints on law libraries, parent institutions and governments;[5] changes in research methodologies and expectations of users of legal information; increasing concerns about information literacy among legal researchers in a digital age (Boelens 2002; Seguin 2005); need and demand for increasingly sophisticated but user-friendly information retrieval and delivery systems; increasing need for information about disciplines other than law as legal scholarship and the practice of law become more interdisciplinary (Palfrey 2010); the explosive development of new communications technologies such as smart phones and Skype, and the social networking systems (wikis, blogs, Twitter, Facebook among

---

1 The 2007–2010 IALL Board were: Jules Winterton, Richard A. Danner, Jennefer Aston, Ann Morrison, Ruth Bird, Mark D. Engsberg (ex officio), Barbara Garavaglia, Ligita Gjortlere, Xinh Luu, Petal Kinder, Uma Narayan, Pedro A. Padilla-Rosa, Anita Soboleva and Jeroen Vervliet.

2 The IALL has over 600 members from more than 50 countries; information about the IALL, its mission and its activities is online at www.iall.org, accessed 5 April 2010.

3 For example, many developing and emerging nations have encountered serious barriers to the systematic publication, distribution and preservation of their primary sources of law for many years, while law librarians in developed countries have encountered significant problems with rapidly rising prices for legal publications (Haugen 2005, 473).

4 This list is illustrative and is based on my experience and observations and a review of law library literature from 1998 to present.

5 For an article discussing the situation in US law libraries see Runyon (2009). See also the themes for British and Irish Association of Law Librarians (BIALL) 2010 study conference at www.biall.org.uk/pages/2010-brighton.html, accessed 2 July 2010.

others) that have become 'new forms of authorship';[6] changes in law libraries in response to Web 2.0 and Library 2.0 (Murley 2008); the continuing globalisation of all areas of law; and changes in legal systems, the practice of law and legal education in response to the internationalisation of law (Germain 2007, 137). The need to ensure the preservation of legal information in print and other analogue formats remains a serious and ongoing problem (Turpening 2002; Buckwalter 2004; Turpening 2009). However, concerns about the loss of born-digital legal and other publications have moved to the forefront not only because digital publications are at greater risk and present more 'significant preservation challenges' than 'most analog works' (Library of Congress 2008, 5), but also because many primary sources of law and a growing number of academic and other secondary legal works now are and increasingly will be published only digitally (Germain 2007, 152; Cobb and Allen-Hart 2005; Blue Ribbon Task Force 2010; Danner 2004).

Access to information has increased dramatically as a result of the World Wide Web, but the resulting information terrain confronting users of legal and other information appears kaleidoscopic at best and chaotic at worst to many researchers. Law librarians are uniquely positioned to serve as navigators, interpreters and organisers of the patterns in the shifting legal information landscape, as collectors, preservers and providers of legal information, and as educators of law students, lawyers, researchers and new legal information professionals (Danner 1998, 345). However, despite their critical roles, law librarians find themselves facing internal and external pressures that call into question the value, identity, nature and long-term viability both of law libraries and the profession itself (see Danner 1998, 315; Danner et al. 2009).[7]

For law librarians, the importance of research, publication and educational programmes during this time of fluidity, evolution and challenge in the field of legal information cannot be overstated. It is only through active intellectual engagement that law librarians will have the opportunity to influence the shape and direction of the future of legal information and the role of legal information professionals and law libraries in that future.[8] The IALL Research Agenda identifies topics about which law librarians may contribute to the development of national, regional and global legal information regimes that effectively support access to and preservation of legal information in all areas of the world; to develop a vision for the future of the profession; to establish priorities for the development and continuing education of law librarians; to coordinate efforts to improve and promote law librarianship on an international basis; and to support law librarians in all aspects of their work.

The Agenda aims to be global in scope and to provide suggestions for research that can be carried out over multiple jurisdictions rather than for specific countries, regions or international organisations. Research topics were submitted by IALL Board members and a variety of other sources were consulted to identify ideas and to identify possible gaps in coverage: reports from organisations relating to law librarianship (American Association of Law Libraries 2010; American

6 See for example Library of Congress (2008, 1) which covers Australia, the Netherlands, the United Kingdom and the United States.

7 See Michalko et al. (2010) for a risk assessment conducted to 'identify the most significant risks facing research libraries'.

8 The AALL report *Beyond the Boundaries* notes that members of the special committee that prepared the report focused on 'the opportunities for law libraries in a digital future, rather than dwelling on the threats inherent in the changing environment'. The report further stated that '[g]iven the choice between stepping back and letting the future happen ("drift") versus stepping forward and having some influence on the evolution of the future of law libraries ("mastery"), the committee opted toward the latter approach' (American Association of Law Libraries 2002, 1–2).

Association of Law Libraries 2000); the mission statements of law library associations;[9] the thoughts of the editor of the *International Journal of Legal Information*;[10] and literature reviews to identify possible gaps in coverage of important topics.[11] Published works on topics covering one jurisdiction or region were also considered for ideas for research that might be broadened into global surveys to include countries where the concept has not yet been explored in the published literature.

The Agenda is divided into broad categories; ideas for research, investigation or further exploration are listed within each category. References are made to treatment of the topics within this *Handbook* as well as to other selected law library literature. The Further Reading section at the end of this chapter suggests sources of advice on writing for publication, lists some of the major journals and websites where articles on law librarianship and related topics are commonly published, and provides information about sources of ideas for writing and programming that are beyond this Agenda.

The Preservation of Legal Information

There is an extensive body of literature relating to the preservation of analogue and born-digital legal and other publications, including articles and websites describing a variety of national law digital and analogue preservation initiatives.[12] International and national copyright laws and their impact on the preservation of digital information have also been widely explored in the literature, which includes both comparative and national studies (Library of Congress 2008; Seng 2008). Despite the impressive number of published works, not all countries have been explored in the law library literature. In addition the information presently available is published in multiple articles and reports, making it difficult to review overall on an international scale. Research and publication is needed to cover the preservation of legal information in all countries, focusing first on primary sources of law. This research should be performed collaboratively across jurisdictions to take advantage of the expertise of national and regional legal information professionals. The studies should provide the following information for each country: the quality, level and availability of digital publication and preservation technologies and expertise; official governmental information

9 See the mission statements of the International Association of Law Libraries. Available at: http://iall.org/about.html, accessed 26 July 2010; International Federation of Law Library Associations and Institutions Law Libraries Section. Available at: www.ifla.org/en/about-the-law-libraries-section, accessed 5 April 2010; and the Legal Information Preservation Alliance. Available at: www.aallnet.org/committee/LIPA/mission.asp, accessed 5 April 2010.

10 *International Journal of Legal Information* editor Mark Engsberg welcomes book reviews and articles from law librarians on any topic related to law and legal information.

11 Literature reviews were conducted from 1990 to June 2010 using *HeinOnline*, *Index to Foreign Legal Periodicals*, and *Index to Legal Periodicals and Books*. Several major English language journals published by law library associations were also consulted: *Australian Law Librarian* (Australian Law Librarians Association); *Canadian Law Library Review/Revue canadienne des bibliothèques de droit* (Canadian Association of Law Libraries); *International Journal of Legal Information* (International Association of Law Libraries); *Law Library Journal* (American Association of Law Libraries); *Legal Information Management* (British and Irish Association of Law Librarians); *Legal Reference Services Quarterly*; and *Newsletter* (Organisation of South African Law Libraries).

12 See for instance the Center for Research Libraries (CRL), an international consortium of academic and independent research libraries that collected and performed preservation microfilming of foreign official gazettes. Available at: www.crl.edu, accessed 7 July 2010. The US Library of Congress also collects and preserves foreign official gazettes on microfilm.

policy and the impacts of national copyright laws[13] and international copyright treaties, where relevant, with citations to and descriptions of policy documents and laws; what has already been preserved, preservation formats and where the preserved material may be found; the inclusive dates and currency of digital collections of legal material; plans for the digitisation or other preservation of historical print collections; standards for authentication of digital legal documents; and barriers to preservation initiatives. Researchers should indicate if a country is participating in collaborative digital preservation or access initiatives, such as the Global Legal Information Network (GLIN).[14] Publication of individual country studies on a legal information preservation website would be especially useful for ensuring that information for multiple jurisdictions is available in one place and can be regularly updated. Such a compendium could provide a foundation for related research and publication; systematic approaches to the policy, legal and practical issues identified; and recommendations for model policies or laws relating to the preservation of legal information.

Technological Developments and Management Issues

While much has been written in the past 20 years on preservation methods, continuing attention to emerging technologies for the preservation of print and born-digital legal information is critical, as is information sharing on a global level. Topics that warrant ongoing study and publication include:

- common pitfalls of new and emerging digital publication platforms and preservation methods, and information about the best and most current technologies
- current information about startup and ongoing costs associated with digital publishing and preservation
- programmes for continuing professional education on digital publishing
- strategies for working with national governments to ensure the development and updating of information policies for prospective digital publication and preservation of primary legal material
- information about how to manage large-scale preservation projects or systematically handle individual preservation problems as they arise

Secondary Legal Materials Survey

A survey by country or region of digital preservation initiatives for secondary legal materials by academic and other non-profit institutions and commercial entities would be useful and help to avoid duplication of effort.

In particular, it would be useful to explore the impact of the Google Books project and the potential impact of Google's proposed legal settlement, limited to books that were either registered with the United States Copyright Office or published in the United Kingdom, Australia or Canada, on the preservation efforts of publishers in countries not covered by the settlement. How has the Google situation affected the directions and approaches to preservation by publishers in these countries? Articles sharing the knowledge and experiences of law libraries participating in mass digitisation projects such as the Google project would be a valuable addition to the literature.

---

13 The United Nations Educational, Scientific and Cultural Organization (UNESCO) compiles the copyright laws of member states in its *Collection of National Copyright Laws.*Available at: http://portal.unesco.org/culture/en/ev.php-URL_ID=14076&URL_DO_TOPIC&URL_SECTION=201.htm, accessed 18 May 2010.

14 Available at: www.glin.gov/search.action, accessed 4 July 2010.

Retention of Print Collections

As the costs of acquiring and storing legal materials in tangible formats continue to rise, large research law libraries and national libraries have been reconsidering their commitment to preserving print collections. A survey of how many large research law libraries globally are joining the trend of relying on electronic sources of primary law and secondary works to the exclusion of tangible formats is needed. Such a survey would form the basis of an analysis of the effect of this trend on the preservation and continued availability of legal information worldwide.

Legal Publishing and Access to Legal Information

Ownership and Licensing Issues

In the age of digital collection building, the question of ownership versus leasing of digital collections has become increasingly important. Have the business models and practices developed in the United States to resolve issues relating to the ownership of digital collections achieved their aims? Have these practices spread to other countries or areas of the world? It would be useful to survey and assess existing practices and develop models that will work effectively across jurisdictions.

Open Access Publishing

The issue of open access publishing in the legal arena is an area with broad scope for research. Who is doing it? What is the role of universities in setting up digital archives? Is there enough international coordination of open access initiatives between universities and between academic institutions, libraries and other organisations? For example, universities in the United Kingdom are working collaboratively under SHERPA (Securing a Hybrid Environment for Research Preservation and Access), a national and international framework for open access repositories.[15] Are there similar projects in other areas of the world?

The Impact of Open Access Publishing

Research is needed on the impact of open access publishing on the legal information industry and its consumers internationally.[16] Quantifying trends in legal information consumer behaviour will help provide information for evidence-based recommendations on best practices for law library collections and collection budgets. This research might explore the situation in individual countries and regions and delve into questions such as:

- Will individuals and libraries continue to purchase material that is also available for free?
- How are commercial legal publishers in different countries and regions responding to open access initiatives and potential changes in consumer purchasing behaviours?
- Will open access have an impact on non-profit organisations that have relied on subscriptions to their publications for ongoing funding?

15 Available at: www.sherpa.ac.uk, accessed 26 July 2010.

16 See Chapter 10, this volume, for an overview and foundation for further research.

- Internationally, how are scholarly communities in universities with law curricula and law schools using open access publishing? Related research to quantify whether or not law faculty and legal scholars support open access publishing of their work would help to identify how to achieve more extensive participation by legal scholars and academic publications

Commercial Legal Publishing

What is the long-term global impact of the concentration of private ownership of digital legal information in large international legal publishers/conglomerates? Will open access minimise the risks?

National Legal Materials and Global Access

A study of common problems and benefits of electronic access to national legal information and primary legal material is needed, especially in light of the challenges created by content published in national languages. This research could begin by surveying individual countries and regions to explore issues relating to translation and other barriers researchers face in finding and using electronic legal information from foreign jurisdictions. The survey could provide a foundation for follow-up research on the most effective methods for organising and retrieving legal information to make it accessible and usable across multiple jurisdictions. Law librarians might use this research to develop recommendations for best practices and to create templates for the most effective, functional legal information websites and portals in their own countries.

Interlibrary Loan

Interlibrary Loan (ILL) is used increasingly to provide access to legal literature because of shrinking law library budgets, but law libraries have historically relied primarily on libraries within their national borders for interlibrary borrowing and lending. Scanning technology makes creation of digital copies of print publications fast and easy, and the increased availability of e-books and e-journals makes the possibility of global ILL a practical possibility from a technological standpoint. Research is needed to explore and identify technical, copyright and licensing barriers to cross-border, global electronic ILL. This research would form the foundation for proposing exceptions to national copyright laws or designing model licensing agreements[17] that would include permission for cross-border ILL in conformity with national copyright laws.

Collection Development

Collaborative Collection Development

The Foreign Law Research group (FLARE) in the United Kingdom was established in 2003 by five major research law libraries; one of the aims of the group is the collaborative collection of

17 A US example is the *Liblicense Model Licensing Agreement* sponsored by the Council on Library and Information Resources, the Digital Library Federation and Yale University Library. Available at: at www.library.yale.edu/~llicense/modlic.shtml, accessed 19 May 2010.

foreign, international and comparative legal materials (Swift and Clinch 2009). A survey and article describing similar initiatives in other countries and regions would be a valuable addition to the literature.

Selection of Materials

It is difficult for law librarians to select the most important sources of foreign law and the best scholarly or practical legal treatises and periodicals without a range of foreign language skills. Publications by law librarians evaluating and recommending the best and most important sources for researching the laws of their countries would be helpful, especially in jurisdictions where there are multiple publishers of codes, a multitude of treatises on the same subject, or many periodicals with overlapping coverage. Some guidance is available from such sources as Reynolds and Flores' *Foreign Law Guide* (1989–), but this publication lacks the subjective evaluations needed for making decisions about acquisitions. Collection development librarians would benefit from the guidance, expertise and professional recommendations of experienced law librarians on a country-by-country basis to help them selectively build or downsize their foreign law collections.[18]

Reviews of Journals

It would be useful for law librarians to publish articles reviewing the major legal journals for their countries, describing each journal's typical content, whether it has a scholarly or practical focus, and usual authors: lawyers, law professors or students. Advice on which journals are the most important for different types of collections and purposes would be helpful to law librarians faced with making decisions about selecting or deselecting foreign law journals in unfamiliar languages and alphabets.

Law Library Services

'Law Library 2.0'

What is the impact of Web 2.0 on the provision of library services and what does '*law* library 2.0' look like internationally, regionally and in individual countries? How are law libraries using social networking technologies to provide services? Are libraries in different countries adapting online catalogues and websites for compatibility with mobile devices such as smart phones?

Role of Librarians in Open Access Publishing

How do law librarians keep abreast of what their faculty are doing and where they are publishing? Can and should law librarians help manage the open access process, for example, by assisting faculty with posting papers on the Social Science Research Network (SSRN)?[19]

---

18 See Chapter 12, this volume, for an overview and foundation for further research.

19 Available at: www.ssrn.com, accessed 11 April 2010.

Researcher Behaviour

There is a strong need for longitudinal data on user behaviour in online research and searching. Commercial organisations such as supermarkets do in-depth analyses of user behaviour on their websites to identify how the sites are being used. Law librarians gather statistics, but do not do in-depth analysis of these data to see whether users are skimming, jumping or reading at length.

Legal Information Needs Analysis

Research is needed on the nature and needs of users of legal information, what researchers want and why they want it, and whether we can anticipate changes and proactively develop or modify collections and services to better serve research constituencies. Research for individual countries or regions might explore these questions and report on:

- The impact of changes in the legal profession and legal education on user research needs and behaviours
- The commoditisation of law (see for instance Susskind 2008)
- Changes in the scope and nature of legal work, the practice of law, law curricula in universities and law schools, and academic legal research as a result of the increasingly interdisciplinary nature of law. Law librarians are increasingly called upon to provide business or scientific information or to help with empirical research to assist lawyers working on legal issues or professors and students working on academic legal research. Will this lead to more interdisciplinary partnerships between law librarians and law libraries with information professionals from other disciplines?
- Universities in several countries have recently adopted the US legal education model (Jones 2008).[20] How will this affect academic libraries in universities that have adopted the new legal education style?

The Education and Training of Law Librarians[21]

Competencies for Law Librarianship

The American Association of Law Libraries has developed a list of competencies for law librarians to 'define the profession of law librarianship and its value to the legal field' (American Association of Law Libraries 2001, rev. 2010, para. 1). In addition, a Special Committee of the AALL was established 'to develop universal performance measures that can be used for self-assessment by individual librarians or for performance evaluation of law librarians by employers' using the *Competencies* as the basis for its work (American Association of Law Libraries 2003, 5). What other national or regional law library associations have developed similar competencies and performance measures for law librarians? Are they comparable?

20 Jones discusses new American style law schools in Australia, Canada, China, Japan and South Korea.

21 See Chapter 3, this volume, for an in depth treatment of the subject; this chapter provides a strong foundation for country-by-country research.

Is there a need to develop competencies and performance measures for international law librarianship on a global scale?

Education and Training Opportunities Worldwide

What opportunities are available worldwide for the education and training of law librarians? A status report on the nature and availability of formal and informal courses and other training for law librarianship on an international basis is required. Are there specialised courses or law librarianship options within established library school programmes? Is there a specialist certification process? What qualifications are required for the practice of law librarianship? A country-by-country study of educational programmes for law librarians and certification requirements would be a useful web-based publication for the IALL website.

The Profession of Law Librarianship

Composition of the Profession

There is too little information about the nature and size of the law librarianship profession in many countries to establish the general position of the profession in those countries.[22] Research is needed for countries where information is presently unavailable so that data may be compiled on a global scale. Areas to include in this research for each country should include:

- How is law librarianship defined? Is it considered a specialised area of librarianship or part of the profession in general?
- What are the roles and duties of law librarians?
- What are the professional qualifications, status, education and career opportunities for law librarians? Are there professional level posts as well as paraprofessional or clerical level positions?

Professional Posts and Remuneration

Some law and academic library associations[23] periodically conduct and publish surveys from which salary information for law librarians may be determined. An analysis of how law librarian salaries compare to those of other types of librarians and information professionals is needed to provide a global assessment and allow for salary comparisons among law librarians in different countries. Additional surveys of law librarian salaries are needed in jurisdictions where data is lacking. These

22 See Chapter 8, this volume, for profiles of the profession of law librarianship in various countries; it is expected that further country profiles will be commissioned by IALL and made available on its website.

23 See for instance AALL Biennial Salary Survey. Available at: www.aallnet.org/products/pub_salary_survey.asp, accessed 8 April 2010; BIALL Law Librarians Salary Survey. Available at: www.biall.org.uk/publications.php?action=publication&id=27, accessed 4 July 2010; CALL/ACBD Salary and Benefits Surveys. Available at: www.callacbd.ca/index.php/publisher/articleview/frmArticleID/202, accessed 17 May 2010; Association of Research Libraries *Annual Salary Survey*. Available at: www.arl.org/stats/annualsurveys/salary/index.shtml, accessed 4 July 2010.

surveys often allow an opportunity for information on sector, age, qualifications and seniority in the profession to be collected and compiled.

Standards and Competencies

Is there a need to establish standards and requirements for the specialisation? In the United States, the AALL has established competencies for law librarians, but the organisation lacks authority to provide official certification of the specialisation. Research is needed to explore the situation in individual countries with programmes in librarianship and information science and to explore possible international standards for the profession.

Status of the Profession

Research is needed to determine the state of the profession in countries for which data is available. Is the profession growing or declining in individual countries? Are some traditional roles of law librarians now seen as part of other professions?

Defining Law Librarianship

Is there any evidence that law librarianship is seen as less well-defined in an age where the focus of research and scholarship is increasingly interdisciplinary? For example, are law librarians leaving law library associations for other 'special library' associations?[24]

Information Literacy in Law Schools

A comparative global study of the roles law librarians play in teaching legal research and writing in law schools or within law curricula is needed. Have these roles changed as law school curricula have become more interdisciplinary and as curricula change to reflect the globalisation of laws?[25]

Information Literacy in Non-Academic Organisations

Literature on the role of non-academic law librarians in different countries or regions in developing legal and interdisciplinary information literacy among their constituencies and their knowledge of the skills of recent graduates is needed.

Global Legal Education

A comparative study of effective methods of teaching law students how to *practice* law across multiple countries and legal systems is needed. Does the teaching of transnational legal research focus too much on legal research resources and legal bibliography? Is there need to teach law students more about legal cultures and how law is actually practised in a global context rather than placing so much emphasis on the sources of law? How are language barriers overcome?

---

24 See Chapter 1, this volume, for an overview and foundation for further research.

25 See Stanton (2010) for an annotated list of English-language law journal articles published from 1995–2008 focusing on the impact of globalisation on legal education in the United States.

Legal Research Tools/Legal Bibliography/Legal Scholarship

Research Guides

There are numerous research guides on how to conduct legal research in individual countries.[26] However, many published guides simply list sources and do not discuss the process of legal research for the jurisdiction. There is a significant need for legal research guides that discuss the research process and the relative weights of the legal authorities in the jurisdiction covered in the guide.

Legal Bibliography

While Reynolds and Flores' *Foreign Law Guide* and *Globalex* have done an admirable job in providing relatively comprehensive coverage of legal information and publications, there remain two major issues:

- little or no coverage for many jurisdictions in Africa, Asia and the Middle East, and
- infrequent updates rendering available information of limited research value

It would be helpful therefore to have publications for minor jurisdictions, and frequent updates of existing publications or research guides to ensure availability of materials that are of continuing, if not permanent, research value.

Public Law Scholarship

Currently for many countries there appear to be few reliable and up-to-date publications, print/online; prescriptive/descriptive; commercial/official, on public law topics, for example, criminal law and administrative law. Scholarship on public law topics in individual jurisdictions and taking regional and global comparative aspects is needed.[27]

Digests of Legal Developments

To the extent that law is changing rapidly, especially in unstable jurisdictions, legal information professionals would welcome timely regular digests of legal news and developments from around the world, including information about political developments with a potential impact on the legal system. The US Law Library of Congress offers such digests through its online publication, *Global Legal Monitor (GLM)*.[28] The *GLM* is far from comprehensive, however, either substantively or geographically. It would be useful for law librarians to collaborate on a national or regional basis to publish frequently updated, web-based regional or national digests that are substantively comprehensive.

---

26 Examples are easily found in the journals listed below under 'Where to Publish' and on *Globalex*, www.nyulawglobal.org/globalex/index.html, accessed 19 May 2010, and *LLRX.com*, at www.llrx.com, accessed 19 May 2010.

27 This idea follows a brief examination of the *Martindale–Hubbell International Law Digest*, which offers annual summaries of major legal principles relating primarily to business and commercial law.

28 www.loc.gov/lawweb/servlet/lloc_news?home, accessed 4 July 2010.

Law Library Associations and Organisations

Establishment of New National and Regional Associations

Research is needed to assess how existing law library associations might help law librarians and legal information professionals organise and establish national and regional associations in countries and regions without specialised organisations.[29]

Management of Law Library Associations

The results of the needs assessment might provide a foundation for a handbook or web-based checklists on how to create, fund and sustain an effective national law library association.

Sources of Ideas and Topics

'Calls for Papers' from national and international law library and law school associations:

- American Association of Law Libraries annual 'LexisNexis Call for Papers'; winners receive a cash award and the opportunity to have their papers considered for publication in *Law Library Journal*. Information available online at www.aallnet.org/about/award_call_for_papers.asp, accessed 6 May 2010
- American Association of Law Schools, Section on Law Libraries calls for papers on 'Legal Research and Information Literacy'; announced in an AALL listserv and in the *Legal Scholarship Blog* at http://legalscholarshipblog.com/2010/04/23/legal-research-and-information-literacy-san-francisco, accessed 11 May 2010
- Australian Law Librarians Association (ALLA) 'Call for Articles' with suggested topics for 2010 at http://alla.asn.au/index.php/conferences/alla-2010, accessed 11 May 2010
- British and Irish Association of Law Librarians 'Call for Papers' (for its 2010 conference) at www.biall.org.uk/news.php/49/biall-conference-brighton-2010-call-for-papers, accessed 26 May 2010
- International Association of Law Schools provides opportunities for attendees at its annual conferences to prepare brief papers on conference themes that are published and distributed by the IALS; see examples of working papers from past meetings at www.ialsnet.org/meetings/index.html, accessed 19 May 2010
- International Federation of Library Associations and Institutions (IFLA) thematic call for papers relating to its 2010 annual conference available online at www.ifla.org/en/calls-for-papers/1839, accessed 11 May 2010
- University of Pittsburgh School of Law and University of Washington School of Law, *Legal Scholarship Blog: Law-Related Calls for Papers, Conferences and Workshops* available online at http://legalscholarshipblog.com, accessed 19 May 2010

29 The role of the IALL in promoting law librarianship and providing the catalyst for the establishment of several national and regional law library associations is documented in Chapter 17 of this volume. For a list of law library associations with links to their websites, see www.iall.org/partners-other.html, accessed 8 April 2010.

Listservs, blogs, newsletters and other publications of national, regional and international law library associations: these should be regularly reviewed for new ideas and trends. The IALL website provides a list of 'Law Library Associations and Related Organizations' at www.iall.org/partners-other.html, accessed 5 May 2010; the websites of the associations will provide information about their resources.

Specialised newsletters relating to librarianship and library technology more generally may provide scope for researching the application or potential impact of new technologies in law libraries, for example, *Smart Libraries Newsletter* (Chicago: ALA TechSource, 2003–), ISSN 1541-8820. Tables of contents available online at www.alatechsource.org/sln/index, accessed 5 May 2010.

Where to Publish

AALL Spectrum (American Association of Law Libraries), ISSN 1089–8689. Submission guidelines are at www.aallnet.org/about/policy_spectrum.asp, accessed 19 May 2010.

Australian Law Librarian (Australian Law Librarians Association), ISSN 1039-6616. Information about submitting articles is available at www.alla.asn.au/index.php/all/allcontributors, accessed 19 May 2010.

Canadian Law Library Review/Revue canadienne des bibliothèques de droit (Canadian Association of Law Libraries), ISSN 1713-5168. For information about the journal's annual 'Canadian Law Library Review Feature Article Award' see www.callacbd.ca/index.php/publisher/articleview/frmArticleID/278, accessed 27 July 2010. For the style guide for submitting articles, see www.callacbd.ca/index.php/publisher/articleview/frmArticleID/277, accessed 19 May 2010.

Globalex, www.nyulawglobal.org/globalex/index.html, accessed 19 May 2010: website dedicated to international and foreign law research; includes information, articles, research guides and teaching resources used by legal academics, practitioners and other specialists. Contact the website editor using the contact information on the opening page of the website for information about submitting an article or guide.

IFLA Journal (International Federation of Library Associations and Institutions), ISSN 0340-0352. For information about submitting articles, see 'Notes for Contributors' at www.ifla.org/en/publications/ifla-journal/notes-for-contributors; for examples of articles, see the tables of contents of the journal at www.ifla.org/en/publications/ifla-journal, accessed 19 May 2010.

International Journal of Law and Information Technology, ISSN 0967-0769. For information about submitting articles to the journal and the topics it covers, see www.oxfordjournals.org/our_journals/inttec/for_authors/index.html, accessed 19 May 2010.

International Journal of Legal Information (International Association of Law Libraries), ISSN 0731-1235. Examples of articles and information about submitting articles available at www.iall.org/journal.htm, accessed 19 May 2010.

Law Library Journal (American Association of Law Libraries), ISSN 0023-9283. Examples of articles and information about submitting articles available at www.aallnet.org/products/pub_journal.asp, accessed 19 May 2010.

Legal Information Management (British and Irish Association of Law Librarians), ISSN 1472-6696. For aims and scope of the journal, see www.biall.org.uk/pages/legal-information-management.html, accessed 19 May 2010.

Legal Reference Services Quarterly, ISSN 0270-319X. For aims and scope of the journal, see www.informaworld.com/smpp/title~db=all~content=t792306930~tab=summary. For information about submitting articles, see www.informaworld.com/smpp/title~db=all~content=t792306930~tab=submit~mode=paper_submission_instructions, accessed 19 May 2010.

LLRX.com: *Law and Technology Resources for Legal Professionals*, www.llrx.com, accessed 19 May 2010. Self-described as a '[w]eb journal dedicated to providing legal, library, IT/IS, marketing and administrative professionals with the most up-to-date information on a wide range of Internet research and technology-related issues, applications, resources and tools'. Information about contributing to the journal is available at www.llrx.com/about.htm, accessed 19 May 2010.

Newsletter (Organisation of South African Law Libraries). For information about submitting articles, see www.osall.org.za/newsletter.html, accessed 19 May 2010.

Publishing Initiatives Caucus, *Publication Resources for Law Librarians* at http://aallnet.org/caucus/pic/publications.htm, accessed 18 May 2010, includes an annotated list of publications and publisher contact information.

Recht, Bibliothek, Dokumentation: Mitteilungen der Arbeitsgemeinschaft für Juristisches Bibliotheks- und Dokumentationswesen (Arbeitsgemeinschaft für Juristisches Bibliotheks- und Dokumentationswesen/Association for Law Librarianship and Documentation in German-Speaking Countries – Austria, Germany, Switzerland), ISSN 0935-2538. See the journal tables of contents on-line for examples of article topics at www.ajbd.de/veroeff/rbd.htm, accessed 19 May 2010. See the print journal for information about submitting articles.

WIPO Magazine. Available free online at www.wipo.int/wipo_magazine/en, accessed 5 April 2010.

References

American Association of Law Libraries (2000), *AALL Research Agenda*, available online at www.aallnet.org/committee/research/agenda.asp, accessed 5 April 2010.

American Association of Law Libraries (2001, rev. 2010), *Competencies of Law Librarianship*, available online at www.aallnet.org/prodev/competencies.asp, accessed 27 July 2010.

American Association of Law Libraries (2002), *Beyond the Boundaries: Report of the Special Committee on the Future of Law Libraries in the Digital Age* (Chicago: American Association of Law Libraries).

American Association of Law Libraries (2010), *2010-–2013 Strategic Directions*, available online at www.aallnet.org/strategic/strategic-2010-2013.asp, accessed 6 May 2010.

American Association of Law Libraries Special Committee to Develop Performance Measurements for Law Librarians (2003), *Professional Competence for Law Librarians: Core Attributes and Their Measurement*, available online at www.aallnet.org/committee/reports/Measuring_Competencies_Report.pdf, accessed 7 April 2010.

Atchison, A. and Cadra, L. (2008), 'By the Book: Thoughts on the Future of Our Print Collections', *Law Library Journal* 100:3, 555–62.

Blue Ribbon Task Force on Sustainable Digital Preservation and Access (2010), *Final Report. Sustainable Economics for a Digital Planet: Ensuring Long-Term Access to Digital Information*, published online at http://brtf.sdsc.edu/biblio/BRTF_Final_Report.pdf, accessed 6 April 2010.

Boelens, G. (2002), 'Legal Research Skills Education Based on the Principles of Information Literacy: A Re–Evaluation for the 21st Century', *Australian Law Librarian* 10:2, 125–33.

Buckwalter, R. (2004), 'Preservation of Foreign Legal Materials', *Law Library Journal* 96:4, 643–8.

Cobb, J. and Allen-Hart, J. (2005), *White Paper: Preserving Legal Materials in Digital Formats*, published online at www.aallnet.org/committee/lipa/LIPA_White_Paper_Final.pdf, accessed 5 April 2010.

Danner, R. (1998), 'Redefining a Profession', *Law Library Journal* 90:3, 315–56.

Danner, R. (2002), 'Electronic Publication of Legal Scholarship: New Issues and New Models', *Journal of Legal Education* 52:3, 347–64.

Danner, R. (2004), 'Issues in the Preservation of Born-digital Scholarly Communications in Law', *Law Library Journal* 96:4, 591–604.

Danner, R., Kaufmann, S. and Palfrey, J. (2009), 'The Twenty-First Century Law Library', *Law Library Journal* 101:2, 143–56.

Germain, C. (2007), 'Legal Information Management in a Global and Digital Age: Revolution and Tradition', *International Journal of Legal Information* 35:1, 134–63.

Haugen, B. (2005) 'The Impact of Globalization on Law Libraries', *International Journal of Legal Information* 33:3, 471–8.

Jones, L. (2008), 'Foreign Law Schools Follow the U.S. Playbook', Law.com 09-09-2008, published online at www.law.com/jsp/law/LawArticleFriendly.jsp?id=1202424363465, accessed 13 May 2010.

Library of Congress National Digital Information Infrastructure and Preservation Program, Joint Information Systems Committee, Open Access to Knowledge (OAK) Law Project and SURFfoundation (2008), *International Study on the Impact of Copyright Law on Digital Preservation*, published online at www.digitalpreservation.gov/library/resources/pubs/docs/digital_preservation_final_report2008.pdf, accessed 5 April 2010.

Michalko, J., Malpas, C. and Arcolio, A. (2010), *Research Libraries, Risk and Systemic Change* (Dublin, Ohio: OCLC Research), published online at www.oclc.org/research/publications/library/2010/2010-03.pdf, accessed 5 April 2010.

Murley, D. (2008), 'What's All the Fuss about Library 2.0?', *Law Library Journal* 100:1, 197–204.

Palfrey, J. (2010), 'Cornerstones of Law Libraries for an Era of Digital-Plus', *Law Library Journal* 102:2, 171–90.

Plotin, S. (2009), 'Legal Scholarship, Electronic Publishing, and Open Access: Transformation or Steadfast Stagnation?', *Law Library Journal* 101:1, 31–57.

Reynolds, T. and Flores, A. (1989–), *Foreign Law Guide: Current Sources of Codes and Basic Legislation in Jurisdictions of the World*, available at www.foreignlawguide.com, accessed 7 July 2010.

Runyon, A. (2009), 'The Effect of Economics and Electronic Resources on the Traditional Law Library Print Collection', *Law Library Journal* 101:2, 177–205.

Seguin, P. (2005) 'Ignorance of the Law is No Excuse: A Student's Perspective on Developing Legal Information Literacy', *Canadian Law Library Review* 30:2, 80–4, also available at http://ssrn.com/abstract=1158597, accessed 20 October 2010, listed by later name: Pengelley, P.

Seng, D. (2008), *International Study on the Impact of Copyright Law on Digital Preservation: Singapore's Legal Position*, published online at www.wipo.int/edocs/mdocs/copyright/en/wipo_cr_wk_ge_08_www_105895-related1.pdf, accessed 19 May 2010.

Stanton, T. (2010), 'Globalization and the Internationalization of Legal Education in the United States', *Legal Reference Services Quarterly* 29:1, 23–49.

Susskind, R. (2008), *The End of Lawyers? Rethinking the Nature of Legal Services* (Oxford: Oxford University Press).

Swift, H. and Clinch, P. (2009), 'Opening Up the UK's Foreign and International Law Collections: the FLARE Initiative, the FLAG Foreign Law Guide and the FLARE Index to Treaties', *Legal Information Management* 9:4, 262–6.
Turpening, P. (2002), 'Survey of Preservation Efforts in Law Libraries', *Law Library Journal* 94:3, 363–93.
Turpening, P. (2009), 'From Sheepskin Binding to Born Digital: One Hundred Years of Preservation in Law Library Journal', *Law Library Journal* 101:1, 71–94.
Wu, M. (2005), 'Why Print and Electronic Resources are Essential to the Academic Law Library', *Law Library Journal* 97:2, 233–56.

Further Reading

Writing and Publishing[30]

Healey, P. (2002), 'The Nitty Gritty of Writing for AALL', *AALL Spectrum* 6:10, 6–7, 10.
Houdek, F. (2002), 'Top 10 Tips on Writing for Professional Journals', *AALL Spectrum* 6:10, 7.
Kaufman, D. (1992), 'Commentary: Writing Research Results for Publication', *Law Library Journal* 84:3, 617–24.
Percy, K., Potter, T. and Murphy, M. (2002), 'So You Want to Be a Writer: Writing Prospects Broaden Among Law Library Publications', *AALL Spectrum* 6:10, 32, 34.
Rumsey, M. (2008), *Publication Opportunities for FCIL–SIS Members (and other Law Librarians)*, available online at www.aallnet.org/sis/pubopp.html, accessed 10 May 2010.
Whisner, M. (2009), 'Getting Facts Straight (and Writing Well Too)', *Law Library Journal* 101:3, 399–408.

30 For a sampling of publications by members of IALL, see the IALL website at www.iall.org/mempubs.html, accessed 5 May 2010.

Chapter 17
The International Association of Law Libraries

The International Association of Law Libraries (IALL) is a worldwide, cooperative non-profit organisation concerned with access to legal information, particularly on a multinational and global scale. It comprises law librarians, law libraries and other persons and institutions active in the acquisition, delivery and use of legal information from sources beyond their own jurisdictions.[1]

The IALL is dedicated to international cooperation among law librarians, the promotion of professional knowledge and understanding through international exchange, the promotion of access to legal information, and more generally the ideals of internationalism. Founded in 1959, the IALL has over 600 members in more than 50 countries on five continents. The members represent all types and sizes of legal collections ranging from academic law libraries to corporate libraries, and from national and parliamentary libraries to administrative agency and court libraries, including many of the great legal research libraries.

Law libraries form a diverse cross-sectoral group. They have parent institutions which range across the private and public spheres but they retain a common identity through close association with the legal profession in its various branches and their management of legal information in its various forms. Many libraries serve legal institutions directly; some are services forming part of larger libraries, such as national libraries and many of the university libraries. They are diverse in nature and size and the ways in which they seek to provide for their users. Their scope and number have grown considerably in recent years in many countries.

A formal statement of the Association's mission appears on its website.[2] The International Association of Law Libraries:

- promotes the work of individuals, libraries, and other organizations concerned with the dissemination of legal information
- advances the education of law librarians and other legal information professionals by providing substantive educational programs on foreign and international legal systems in venues all around the world
- supports educational and professional opportunities for newer legal information professionals, especially those from developing nations, by providing financial support in the form of bursaries and scholarships for annual course attendance and internships
- shares legal knowledge and scholarship and increases access to legal information on a worldwide basis through the *International Journal of Legal Information* and other publications, and its website
- fosters networking and mentoring among legal information professionals on a worldwide basis by creating and maintaining ongoing relationships between IALL and other international, national and regional law library and legal information organizations and

1 There are references to the IALL throughout this book but further information can be found particularly in Chapter 2 and Chapter 3, and on the IALL Scholarship programme in the introduction to Chapter 8.

2 See http://iall.org/about.html, accessed 22 October 2010.

- supports and encourages the development of national and international legal information policies and promotes free access to legal information on a worldwide basis through policy statements and scholarship

In fulfilment of its mission, the IALL promotes the law library profession and access to legal information. The IALL publishes the *International Journal of Legal Information* and offers Annual Courses on International Legal Information and Law. It stimulates and encourages the creation and development of national and regional law library associations and the recognition of the value of law librarians and the improvement of their status. The IALL provides an international forum for networking and information sharing among legal information professionals worldwide and supports professional development by awarding scholarships for annual course attendance and grants for internships and associated research projects.

History

A full history of the Association is yet to be written; this chapter is a brief compilation of information about the Association and its activities which may contribute to a history and which demonstrates the importance of the Association's role and the range of its achievements as an international organisation.

The IALL was established in 1959 and its history can be traced in various articles about the Association (Landheer 1969; Dahlmanns 1972, 1974, 1984; Schwerin 1984; Sprudzs 1984, 1995; Wenger 1999; Winterton 2009a) and about significant figures in its foundation and early life (Wenger 2003). It came into being as a result of the efforts of leading members of the American Association of Law Libraries (AALL), the earliest professional association of law librarians to be formed and with which it retains a close relationship, and of leading law librarians in other countries familiar with the work of AALL. Gerhard Dahlmanns recorded in 1974 that the IALL:

> was founded at an inaugural meeting held at the Association of the Bar of the City of New York in June 1959, after years of preparation notably by William R. Roalfe, then Law Librarian at Northwestern University, Chicago, and one of the towering figures of American Law Librarianship, who was elected the first IALL president for the three-year term provided for by the Constitution. William B Stern, then Foreign Law Librarian at the Los Angeles County Law Library became its first Secretary and later succeeded Mr. Roalfe as President for the term 1962–1965, with Jurij Fedynsky of Indiana University as Secretary. Under these men the IALL embarked on its way towards what must have been a rather visionary aim: the creation of a truly worldwide community of law library people who assist each other, through personal contacts and through the exchange of professional information, bibliographic data and other material in selecting, acquiring and processing legal material beyond a mere national level. (Dahlmanns 1974, 40)

A list of all IALL officers is reproduced below and articles, some of which are freely available in full text on the IALL website, are listed in the References section. The cumulative index to the *International Journal of Law Libraries*, later styled the *International Journal of Legal Information*, and to selected substantive articles in the *Bulletin* of IALL, was compiled by Richard Danner (2003) and covers the years 1960 to 2002. This is an invaluable tool in tracking the history of the

Association. The archives of the Association are held at the Institute of Advanced Legal Studies, University of London.[3]

Courses in International Law Librarianship

The IALL has arranged courses in international law librarianship around the world at prestigious institutions for over 40 years, making it possible for its members to meet many colleagues within the profession of law librarianship and other colleagues, both academic and practitioner, in the wider legal environments which the conferences explore.

The annual course and conference is the Association's main meeting and educational event of the year. The course is usually a four-day meeting and takes place in a different city around the world and reflects the local legal environment and culture while addressing international issues of importance to all legal information experts. The annual conference is also a catalyst for change and improvement in the recognition of the role of law librarians and of legal information itself. It regularly attracts delegates from over 25 countries.

Since 2005 the conference has taken place at the European University Institute near Florence, at the Faculty of Law of the Saint Petersburg State University, in association with the High Court in Mumbai, in San Juan in association with the University of Puerto Rico, at the Bilgi University in Istanbul, and at the Peace Palace in The Hague. The courses began in 1966 and were held every two to three years but became an annual event in 1993 as the Annual Course in International Law Librarianship. The 2010 course was termed Annual Course in Legal Information and Law. Information about the early IALL courses and other educational offerings can be found in Sprudzs (1984 and 1995). A complete list of the conferences, their venues and themes appears below.[4]

The annual courses deliver unprecedented access both to speakers and locations at the heart of the legal systems of the host countries. They are unique and valuable educational experiences and form important regional and international networking opportunities and venues for renewing old friendships and making new ones among a diverse group of international colleagues.

The annual courses have worked within the principle that we cannot exchange professional knowledge and skills in isolation, looking at law merely as a body of technical information. Law is an expression of the culture of a society and only by understanding other cultures can we gain knowledge and exchange meaningful information about laws and the legal system, and the management of legal information in a particular legal environment. The annual courses therefore emphasise local speakers, the legal system of the host country, the legal environment in broad terms, legal publishing and other means for legal information provision in the host country, as well as comparative approaches and the impact of international legal regimes. The conference has often focused on legal systems in transition, for example in Russia, India and South Africa. The conference also makes a particular point of including visits and excursions and cultural events which offer an opportunity for delegates to gain insight into the wider social context in which the legal system has developed.

3 A detailed list of the IALL archives is available at http://ials.sas.ac.uk/library/archives/docs/International%20Association%20of%20Law%20Libraries%20list.pdf, accessed 22 October 2010. Anyone holding records of the Association is encouraged to submit them or a list of them to the Archivist at Institute of Advanced Legal Studies so that a continuous record of the Association can be assembled. At present there are significant gaps in the archives particularly from the mid-1970s to the mid-1990s.

4 See the details of the conferences including full academic programmes from 1999 onwards at http://iall.org/conference-previous.html, accessed 22 October 2010.

The conference is usually arranged with the active collaboration of one or more local law faculties or other prestigious institutions and brings law librarians into closer contact with those in the legal profession who are active in legal research, whether in practice or academe. This exemplifies the partnerships and shared knowledge which should exist in the practice of law librarianship.

Publications[5]

The Association began to publish its own periodical early in its existence, starting the *IALL Bulletin* which was published from 1960, a year after the foundation of the Association, to 1972. It ceased publication to make way for the *International Journal of Law Libraries* which began publication in the next year. The *Bulletin*, although informally published, contained valuable bibliographic contributions and substantive articles. This was recognised by a reprint edition of the whole series which appeared not long after it ceased publication.

An early project of the Association was a *Guide to European Law Libraries* commissioned by the Council of Europe which was published in 1971 and ran to nearly 680 pages. The Association has published directories of members at various times until 1988 when it was last published and distributed without charge with the compliments of William S. Hein & Co.

Throughout its history the *International Journal of Legal Information*, formerly the *International Journal of Law Libraries*, has published advance information and reports on the courses, as well as selected papers from the courses, in addition to articles from a wide range of sources. Since 1994 proceedings of the courses have usually been published in one issue of the *Journal*. Proceedings from some earlier courses, as well as from other IALL meetings and programmes, were published separately, usually through the good offices of William S. Hein & Co. The *Journal* continues to be published as a major contribution to law librarianship around the world with the assistance of West Publishing but is also now available in electronic form both commercially and in part through open access routes.

The IALL website now fulfils much of the purpose of information and communication and official documentation of the Association. Its coverage of the IALL events, particularly the programmes of the annual courses and supporting documentation, scholarship programmes, website awards and publications is mentioned elsewhere. It has an ongoing International Calendar of events and a directory of law library organisations around the world. It is also building a list of publications, presentations and guides written by members in the course of their work, many of which are linked to freely available full text versions. It is hoped that this will build into a repository of useful and expert local knowledge of the practice of law librarianship, legal bibliography and legal research skills. It also is intended that the descriptions of law librarianship in various countries which appear in Chapter 8 of this book, will be joined by profiles of law librarianship in other countries on the IALL website.

Scholarship Programme

The Association operates an extensive scholarship programme to provide financial assistance to law librarians, not limited to members of the Association, to attend the IALL annual conference

5 See the section listing the publications of IALL below for detailed information. However, a comprehensive bibliography of IALL publications has not yet been attempted.

and also to undertake internships or extended visits to law libraries overseas and to pursue relevant research projects. The details of the scholarship programme are the subject of the introduction to Chapter 8 of this book, and the sections of that chapter are written by some of the recipients of IALL scholarships.[6]

The IALL as Catalyst

The IALL has played a major role as a catalyst, encouraging law librarians to collaborate both internationally and within their own borders, promoting the status of librarians and recognition of their professional skills, enabling them to stand alongside their colleagues in the various branches of the legal profession and transmitting the ideals of collaboration and internationalism brought to the IALL by its founding members.

The British and Irish Association of Law Librarians[7]

The British and Irish Association of Law Librarians (BIALL) was established in 1969 and the IALL had a direct influence on its formation through the involvement of senior figures in the profession. The formation of the British and Irish Association of Law Librarians and a famous workshop on law librarianship at Harrogate in February 1968 are described in Mary Blake's *History*:

> Following the final talk of the Workshop by Willi Steiner and Betty Moys on the International Association of Law Libraries (IALL) it was resolved to set up a British section, and an ad hoc Committee was appointed to look into the possibility and invite people's views. The members of this committee were Wallace Breem (who volunteered to send a circular to all law libraries), Don Daintree, Betty Moys, Willi Steiner and Derek Way. Replies to the circular were so encouraging that at the second Workshop in April 1969 the Association of Law Librarians was formally established. (Blake 2000, 4)

The BIALL was never organised as a 'British Section' of the IALL but the influence of the IALL at the time of the foundation of the BIALL is clear, as is the continued engagement of senior figures in law librarianship in Britain and Ireland with the IALL.

The late Willi Steiner, Librarian of the Institute of Advanced Legal Studies in the University of London, was Second Vice-President of the International Association of Law Libraries from 1974 to 1976, First Vice-President from 1976 to 1980, and then a staunch supporter and life member. The IALL had been founded in 1959 with Howard Drake, Willi's predecessor as Librarian of the Institute of Advanced Legal Studies in London, as one of the founder members and its President at the time of his death. The Association's early history, with reference to Willi, was chronicled by Adolf Sprudzs (Sprudzs 1984). Willi Steiner was involved early in the International Association's life and attended the first meeting of European members which took place at The Hague in April 1965, as one of the two UK representatives. He spoke on the use of computers in law libraries at its first annual course in law librarianship in Luxembourg

6 The programme of Professional Development Bursaries to assist law librarians to attend the IALL conference is described at http://iall.org/scholarship.html and the recipients from 2001 onwards listed at http://iall.org/scholarship-previous.html. The programme of Internship Grants is described at http://iall.org/internship.html.

7 This passage is drawn from Winterton (2003).

in 1966. The paper appeared in the *Bulletin* of the Association in the following year (Steiner 1967).[8] Willi was the joint director with Muriel Anderson of the second course in international law librarianship which was held by the IALL in Cambridge in 1968. At this time work was proceeding on the *European Law Libraries Guide* co-ordinated at the Institute of Advanced Legal Studies after the Council of Europe invited the International Association to prepare it. Willi was a member of the Editorial Committee of that publication and an Associate Editor of the *International Journal of Law Libraries* in 1980.

The German Association of Law Libraries

The Arbeitsgemeinschaft für juristisches Bibliothekswesen, now the Arbeitsgemeinschaft für juristisches Bibliotheks- und Dokumentationswesen was founded in June 1971, as announced by Ralph Lansky in the *IALL Bulletin*, where he stated that the new Association 'intends to serve as the German branch of the IALL' (Lansky 1971, 8). The website of the Association[9] still announces the organisation as the 'Deutschsprachige Sektion der International Association of Law Libraries'.

The Philippine Group of Law Librarians

IALL played a small part in the foundation of the Philippine Group of Law Librarians (PGLL) and is still in contact (Winterton 2009b). In 1980 the General Conference of IFLA took place in Manila, described then as the 'first such conference to be held in a developing country' (Sprudzs 1980). The IALL organised an 'IALL week in Manila', attracting about 40 law librarians, thanks to the work of a very successful local coordinating group. In particular the IALL sponsored a Round Table to discuss 'Collection Development and Documentation of Human Rights' which was attended by 17 Filipino librarians and 18 other librarians from Australia, Canada, Japan, Malaysia, Nigeria, Thailand and the United States.

The events evidently gave 'a good stimulus to further development of law librarianship in the region'. The evidence is the spontaneous establishment of a 'Philippine law library association' at the proposal of Dean Froilan M Bacuñgan of the University of the Philippines College of Law speaking at the Round Table. Originally conceived as an IALL local chapter (in common with several other national law library associations), it came into being as a national and incorporated association, the PGLL. The articles of incorporation which appear at the foot of the 2001 by-laws of the PGLL are dated March 1981 and the incorporation was approved by Securities and Exchange Commission on 21 August 1981. The first President of the PGLL, Professor Myrna S. Feliciano of the University of the Philippines Law Center, was a member of the Board of Directors of the IALL from 1977 to 1983.

Other National and Regional Law Library Associations

The IALL has formed the catalyst for several other initiatives to form professional and collegial organisations in other countries and regions through its conferences and through personal and institutional contacts. Some have been successful; some have not yet borne fruit. Brief notes about some of these initiatives appear below.

---

8 At that course, he also mentions chairing a 'somewhat turbulent meeting' of the Association but we learn no other details (Steiner 1999, 7).

9 Available at: www.ajbd.de, accessed 21 October 2010.

After attendance at several IALL conferences by a key group of academic lawyers and legal information managers, a Russian Association of Law Libraries was formed, based at the Faculty of Law at Saint Petersburg State University. The Association was a partner in the hosting of the IALL's 25th Annual Course in Saint Petersburg in 2006.

Uma Narayan, IALL Board member, IALL Scholar and local organiser of the IALL's 26th Course in 2007 in Mumbai, describes attempts to form an association of law librarians in India in her contribution to this book.[10] She also cites the coverage of the IALL conference in Mumbai in the *Times of India*, which undoubtedly raised the profile of law librarianship.

Efforts have been made in the Former Yugoslavia to create a regional group of law libraries and an exploratory meeting was held in Slovenia attended by the President of IALL.

The IALL was one of the sponsors of the China–US Conference on Legal Information and Law Libraries which was held in Beijing in May 2009, a wonderful achievement organised by a group of dedicated law librarians in the United States and innovators in China. The President of the IALL attended and spoke at the opening of the conference and at the preceding workshop which explored the role, status and constitution of law library associations as non-governmental organisations. Subsequently the Law Libraries and Legal Information Research Society was established and its first meeting and symposium took place on in April 2010. The newly-founded society, a subordinate research society of the Beijing Law Society, is affiliated with Tsinghua University Law School and the secretariat is located at THU Law Library.

The Turkish Platform of Law Libraries was formed in 2007 at the initiative of law librarians from Istanbul Bilgi University. It is described in this book by Sami Cukadar,[11] an IALL Scholar in 2006 and member of the Local Organising Committee of IALL's 28th Annual Course in Istanbul in 2009.

International Federation of Library Associations and Institutions (IFLA)

The IALL has been a member of the IFLA for many years, offering programmes at the IFLA conference and at times working jointly with the IFLA on particular projects. The IALL remains outside the IFLA governance structure and functions independently (Wenger 2001a).

Dahlmanns identifies 1972 as the year in which IALL engagement with the IFLA started, enunciating the ideals behind the IALL:

> 'The key function of law in human society is universally acknowledged. It is the adherence to the rule of law upon which the success or failure of all endeavors to promote mankind eventually depend. Law, however, is basically a written affair and cannot be used unless it is being made available. This crucial task falls to the law librarians who, in whatever capacity or position, are entrusted all over the world with acquiring, processing and administering the material in its completeness'.
>
> This observation opened the programatic report with which the IALL introduced itself and its work to the librarians of the world, convened, in the Summer of 1972, in Budapest for the 38th General Council Meeting of the International Federation of Library Associations (IFLA). It was for the first time that the law librarians as a distinctive group raised their voice on such an occasion, for the first

10 See 'Law Librarianship in India' in Chapter 8.

11 See 'Law Librarianship in Turkey' in Chapter 8.

> time that they succeeded in drawing the attention of the profession at large to their particular task, their needs, achievements and concerns. (Dahlmanns 1973, 104–5)

In the same article Dahlmanns records the resolution to establish a joint IFLA–IALL working group on copyright problems affecting the library world (Dahlmanns 1973, 107).

The Sessions, or Round Tables in the early days, organised over the years at IFLA conferences, are recorded in various notes in the *International Journal of Legal Information* and its predecessor titles, for example by Sprudzs (1980) about the IFLA meeting in Manila in 1980, in 1985 about the Chicago meeting (IALL 1985), and by Wenger (2001b) about the 66th IFLA meeting in Jerusalem which was accompanied by articles based on the papers given at the IALL session.

The IFLA formally recognised the existence of law librarianship inside its own organisation in late 2005 by the creation of its 48th and at the time of writing most recent 'Section', after it had served an incubation period as an informal 'Discussion Group'. The Section, sponsored by the IALL and AALL, was intended to complement the IALL and national associations by offering sessions for librarians with an interest or responsibility for legal materials and services as one part of their duties but who were unable to attend a specialist law library conference. It would also provide a channel of communication and influence for law library associations and their members on international policy issues. The IALL passed on the long-standing task of organising law-related sessions during the IFLA conference to the Section after it was established.

A brief history of the Section is given by Holger Knudsen, former founding Chair of the Standing Committee of the Section and past President of the IALL, on the IFLA website.[12] It remains to be seen whether the Section will fulfil its challenging role as a channel of communication and liaison on matters of common concern between law library associations and our colleagues in other areas of librarianship, whether it will be able to relate to organisations outside the bureaucratic structure of the IFLA, and whether it will become merely another rival organisation seeking the attention of busy law librarians.

Conclusion

Law library associations play an important part in enhancing the professionalism of their members and enhancing the quality, cohesion and efficiency of library services. They do this in several ways: in mutual support and sharing best practice, continuing professional education, the encouragement of collaboration, the promulgation and monitoring of standards, and where appropriate the regulation of the profession. The International Association of Law Libraries carries out many of these functions at an international level, complementing national and regional associations but not infringing on their sovereignty. The IALL has been privileged to act as a catalyst for the establishment and development of national and regional law library associations. It has sought, without undue bureaucracy, to provide an independent, collegial forum to share and understand our joint knowledge, interests and values. In a world where the international aspects of our professional life are always increasing, such a role is increasingly important.

---

12 Available at: http://archive.ifla.org/VII/s48/annual/s48_annual_report_2001-2007-en.pdf, accessed 22 October 2010.

Officers and Members of the Board of IALL

Listed below are the Officers of the International Association of Law Libraries (by office in chronological order) and the members of the Board of Directors of the Association (in alphabetical name order).

Presidents:

Roalfe, William R. (USA) 1959–62
Stern, William B. (USA) 1962–5
Drake, K. Howard (England) 1965–7 (Deceased 1967)
Coffin, Lewis C. (USA) 1968–71 (Acting President, 1967–8)
Leser, Hans-G. (Germany) 1971–4
Dahlmanns, Gerhard J. (Germany) 1974–7
Kavass, Igor I. (USA) 1977–80; 1980–83
Menzinger, Klaus (Germany) 1983–6
Sprudzs, Adolf (USA) 1986–9; 1989–92
Balázs-Veredy, Katalin (Hungary) 1992–5
Wenger, Larry B. (USA) 1995–8; 1998–2001
Knudsen, Holger (Germany) 2001–4
Winterton, Jules (England) 2004–7, 2007–10

Immediate Past Presidents:[13]

Wenger, Larry B. (USA) 2002–4
Knudsen, Holger (Germany) 2004–7

Vice-President:

Drake, K. Howard (England) 1959–62; 1962–5

First Vice-Presidents:

Coffin, Lewis C. (USA) 1965–8
Leser, Hans-G. (Germany) 1968–71
Liddell, Leon M. (USA) 1971–4
Kavass, Igor I. (USA) 1974–7
Steiner, William A.F.P. (England) 1977–80
Menzinger, Klaus (Germany) 1980–83
Rodwell, John Lawrence (Australia) 1983–6; 1986–9; 1989–92
Sipkov, Ivan (USA) 1992–3 (Deceased 1993)
Wenger, Larry B. (USA) 1993–5 (Appointed 1993)
Shaffer, Roberta (USA) 1995–8; 1998–2000 (Resigned 2000)
Winterton, Jules (England) 2001–4
Danner, Richard A. (USA) 2004–7, 2007–10

13 Office of Past President created by constitutional amendment in 2002 and limited to one term.

Second Vice-Presidents:

Veillon, Adrien (Switzerland) 1965–8
Charpentier, Arthur A. (USA) 1968–71
Lupoi, Maurizio (Italy) 1971–4
Steiner, William A.F.P. (England) 1974–7
Korevaar, Jacob D. (Switzerland) 1977–80
Sipkov, Ivan (USA) 1980–83
Anderson, Muriel (England) 1983–6
Tsuno, Yoshiro (Japan) 1986–9; 1989–92
Gödan, Jürgen (Germany) 1992–5
Chapman, Fred (Switzerland) 1995–8
Knudsen, Holger (Germany) 1998–2001
Bernal, Marie-Louise H. (USA) 2001–4
Looks, Jarmilla (Switzerland) 2004–7
Kongshavn, Halvor (Norway), 2007–8 (Resigned 2008)

Secretaries:

Stern, William B. (USA) 1959–62
Fedynski, Jurij (USA) 1962–5
van Holk, Lambert E. (Netherlands) 1965–8
Sprudzs, Adolf (USA) 1980–83
Schwietzke, Joachim (Germany) 1983–6
Kearley, Timothy J. (USA) 1986–9; 1989–92
Shaffer, Roberta (USA) 1992–5
Kjölstad, Britt S.M. (Switzerland) 1995–8
Bernal, Marie-Louise H. (USA) 1998–2001
Morrison, Ann (Canada) 2001–4; 2004–7
Aston, Jennefer (Ireland) 2007–10

Secretary-Treasurers:

Sipkov, Ivan (USA) 1968–71
Dahlmanns, Gerhard J. (Germany) 1971–4
Münkner, Hans-H. (Germany) 1974–7
Liivak, Arno (USA) 1977–80

Treasurers:

Johnston, George A. (Canada) 1959–62
Veillon, Adrien (Switzerland) 1962–5
Rossier, June (Switzerland) 1965–8
Liivak, Arno (USA) 1980–83
Vlasman, Gert (Netherlands) 1983–6
Sipkov, Ivan (USA) 1986–9; 1989–92

Bernal, Marie-Louise H. (USA) 1992–5
Chao, Gloria (USA) 1995–8; 1998–2001; 2001–4; 2004–7
Morrison, Ann (Canada) 2007–10

Members of the Board of Directors:

Aje, Simeon B. (Nigeria) 1974–7
Anderson, Muriel (England) 1968–71; 1971–4
Aston, Jennefer (Ireland) 2001–4; 2004–7
Balázs-Veredy, Katalin (Hungary) 1986–9; 1989–92
Barratt, Amanda (South Africa) 2004–7; 2007–8 (Resigned 2008)
Bernal, Marie-Louise H. (USA) 1995–8; 2004 (ex officio)
Bird, Ruth (England) 2007–10
Brathwaite, Joan (Barbados) 1998–2001; 2001–4
Breycha-Vauthier, A.C. (Switzerland) 1959–62; 1962–5
Brian, Robert F. (Australia) 1980–83
Butler, James (Australia) 2001–4; 2004–7
Chapman, Fred (Switzerland) 1992–5
Coffin, Lewis C. (USA) 1971–4
Coing, Marga (Germany) 1986–9; 1989–92
Combe, David A. (USA) 1983–6; 1986–9; 1989–92
Dahlmanns, Gerhard J. (Germany) 1977–80
Danner, Richard A. (USA) 1998–2001 (ex officio); 2001–4
de Trazegnies, Fernando (Peru) 1980–83
Elliott, Jacqueline (Australia) 1992–5; 1995–8; 1998–2001
Engsberg, Mark (USA) (ex officio) 2005–7; 2007–10
Feliciano, Myrna (The Philippines) 1977–80; 1980–83
Fong, Sng Yok (Singapore) 1986–9; 1989–92
Frossard, Gabriel (Switzerland) 1998–9 (Resigned 2000)
Frykholm, Lars (Sweden) 1959–62; 1962–5;1965–8
Furlani, Sylvio (Italy) 1959–62; 1962–5
Garavaglia, Barbara (USA) 2007–10
Gaskell, Eric (European Communities) 1980–83
Germain, Claire M. (USA) 1995–8
Gigli, Giovanni (Italy) 1968–71
Gjoertlere, Ligita (Latvia) 2007–10
Glasson, Edwin J. (Australia) 1974–7; 1977–80
Groesbeck, Joseph (United Nations) 1962–5; 1965–8; 1968–71
Guillitte, Paulette (Belgium) 1968–71; 1971–4
Hayashi, Ryohei (Japan) 1977–80
Ito, Masami (Japan) 1974–7
Kaskla, Giina (Estonia) 2004–7
Kavass, Igor I. (USA) 1983–6 (ex officio); 1986–9; 1989–92
Kinder, Petal (Australia) 2004–7; 2007–10
Kjölstad, Britt S.M. (Switzerland) 1992–5; 1998–2001
Knudsen, Holger (Germany) 1995–8

Kongshavn, Halvor (Norway) 2001–4; 2004–7
Korevaar, Jacob D. (Netherlands/Switzerland) 1971–4; 1974–7
Kreuzer, Karl (Germany) 1971–4
Kunz, Lotte (Switzerland) 1971–4
Landheer, Bartholomeus (Netherlands) 1959–62; 1962–5; 1965–8
Leser, Hans-G. (Germany) 1965–8; 1974–7
Liivak, Arno (USA) 1983–6; 1986–9; 1989–92
Löffler, Klaus H. (Germany) 1965–8
Looks, Jarmilla (Switzerland) 2000–2001 (Appointed 2000); 2001–4
Luu, Xinh (USA) 2007–10
Matsuyama, Sadao (Japan) 1959–62; 1962–5
McIvor, Frances Jill (Canada) 1968–71; 1971–4
Menzinger, Klaus (Germany) 1977–80
Morrison, Ann (Canada) 1995–8; 1998–2001
Moys, Elizabeth M. (England) 1965–8
Müller, Harald (Germany) 1995–8; 1998–2001
Nagy, Lajos (Hungary) 1974–7; 1977–80; 1980–83
Narayan, Uma (India) 2007–10
Newton, Velma (Barbados) 1986–9
Ogbeide, N. Anthony (Nigeria) 1977–80
Padilla-Rosa, Pedro (Puerto Rico) 2008–10 (Appointed 2008)
Picone-Maxion, Bettina (Italy) 2004–7
Pollack, Lynn (Australia) 1983–6
Rasmussen, Lisbeth (Denmark) 1998–2001; 2001–4
Renie, June (Trinidad) 1989–92; 1992–5
Renshawe, Michael (Canada) 1983–6
Roalfe, William R. (USA) 1962–5
Sahl, Silke A. (USA) 2001–4; 2004–7
Schwerin, Kurt (USA) 1965–8; 1968–71
Schwietzke, Joachim (Germany) 1986–9; 1989–92; 1992–5
Scott, Marianne (Canada) 1974–7
Sipkov, Ivan (USA) 1983–6
Soboleva, Anita (Russia) 2007–10
Sondergaard, Jens (Denmark) 1968–71
Sprudzs, Adolf (USA) 1974–7; 1977–80; 1983–6; 1992–5
Stern, William B. (USA) 1965–8
Ticó, Josep Sort (Spain) 1993–5 (Appointed 1993); 1995–8
Traissac, Elisabeth (France) 1968–71; 1971–4
Tsuno, Yoshiro (Japan) 1980–83; 1983–6
Veillon, Adrien (Switzerland) 1959–62
Vervliet, Jeroen (Netherlands) 2008–10 (Appointed 2008)
Vivas, Jorge, B. (Argentina) 1959–62; 1962–5
Walter, Raimund-Ekkehard (Germany) 1992–5
Wenger, Larry B. (USA) 1992–3
Wiktor, Christian (Canada) 1980–83
Winterton, Jules (England) 1995–8; 1998–2001
Zakaria, Shaikha (Malaysia) 1980–83

Courses in International Law Librarianship

Listed below are the titles, locations and dates for the 21 courses offered up to 2010. The details of the academic programmes of recent conferences may still be consulted on the IALL website.[14]

Course in Law Librarianship and Legal Bibliography with Special Reference to European Law
University of Comparative Sciences, Luxembourg
25 September – 1 October 1966

2nd Course: **Course in Law Librarianship and Legal Bibliography of Common Law, with Special Reference to English Law**
University of Cambridge, England
25–29 March 1969

3rd Course: **Law and Legal Literature in Germany, Austria, and Switzerland**
Max-Planck Institute for Comparative Public Law and International Law
Heidelberg, Germany
7–10 September 1970

4th Course: **The Unification of Private Law and Law and Legal Literature in Italy**
International Institute for the Unification of Private Law (UNIDROIT)
Rome, Italy
4–8 September 1972

5th Course: **The Legal Literature of the United States**
Library of Congress, Washington, DC, USA
11–15 November 1974

6th Course: **The Legal System, its Materials and Documentation in the Socialist Countries**
Hungarian Library of Parliament, Budapest, Hungary
16–20 August 1977

7th Course: **Japanese Law: its Structure and Materials**
National Diet Library, Tokyo, Japan
4–8 September 1978

8th Course: **Australian and South Pacific Law: Structure and Materials**
University of Sydney, Sydney, Australia
10–15 May 1981

9th Course: **Crossroads in Comparative Constitutional Law Development**
George Washington University, Washington, DC, USA
28 June – 2 July 1987

10th Course: **Legal Aspects of East-West Trade and the Law Librarian**
Hungarian Library of Parliament, Budapest, Hungary
5–10 June 1988

14 See the details of the conferences from 1999 onwards at http://iall.org/conference-previous.html, accessed 16 September 2010.

11th Course: **Legal Information Sources and Changing Times in Europe**
Max-Planck Institute for Comparative Public Law and International Law
Heidelberg, Germany
8–11 September 1991

12th Course: **Catalonia, Spain, Europe, and Latin America – Regional Legal Systems and Their Literature**
Universitat Pompeu Fabra, Barcelona, Spain
17–21 August 1993

13th Course: **International (Commercial) Arbitration and Law Libraries: A View from The Hague**
Peace Palace, The Hague, the Netherlands
26–29 September 1994

14th Course: **Current Trends in International Law: A Challenge for Law Librarians**
University of Vienna, Vienna, Austria
18–21 September 1995

15th Course: **Legal Developments and Legal Information on the Pacific Rim**
Vancouver, British Columbia, Canada
29 September – 3 October 1996

16th Course: **Human Rights Law: Global Issues and Information Services**
University of Lund, Lund, Sweden
24–28 August 1997

17th Course: **Unification of Private Law and the Italian Legal System**
International Institute for the Unification of Private Law (UNIDROIT)
Rome, Italy
20–24 September 1998

18th Course: **Australasian Law and Librarianship**
Old Treasury Building, Melbourne, Australia
12–16 September 1999

19th Course: **A Common Law for Europe: Legal Systems and Legal Information**
Dublin International Arbitration Centre of the Bar Council of Ireland
Dublin, Ireland
20–24 August 2000

20th Course: **Comparative and International Law in a Multilingual Environment: Current Issues and Information Resources**
Swiss Institute of Comparative Law, Lausanne, Switzerland
23–26 September 2001

21st Course: **Order from Chaos: Contexts for Global Legal Information**
Yale University, New Haven, Connecticut, USA
20–23 October 2002

22nd Course: **New Rights – New Laws: Legal Information in a Changing World**
University of Cape Town, Cape Town, South Africa
21–25 September 2003

23rd Course: **Protecting the Environment: A Challenge Across Borders – Legal Issues and Information Resources in Finland and Estonia**
University of Helsinki, Helsinki, Finland
National Library of Estonia, Tallinn, Estonia
15–19 August 2004

24th Course: **The European Union in the 21st Century: New Challenges in Law and Legal Information**
European University Institute, Badia Fiesolana, San Domenico di Fiesole, Italy
4–8 September 2005

25th Course: **The New Russia: Law and Legal Information**
Saint Petersburg State University, Russia
10–14 September 2006

26th Course: **Global Challenges and the Indian Legal System**
Mumbai, India
1–5 December 2007

27th Course: **Puerto Rico & the Caribbean: Legal Information in Multiple Legal Systems**
San Juan, Puerto Rico
30 November – 3 December 2008

28th Course: **Turkey in a Global Context: Law and Legal Information**
Istanbul Bilgi University
11–15 October 2009

29th Course: **Dutch Gateways to International Law**
Peace Place, The Hague and Erasmus University, Rotterdam, Netherlands
5–9 September 2010

30th Course: **The Dynamics of Malaysia Law in the Global Context**
University of Malaya, Kuala Lumpur, Malaysia
4–8 December 2011

Publications of IALL

Andrews, J., Charpentier, A., Marke, J. and Stern, W. (1965), *The Law in the United States of America: A Selective Bibliographical Guide* ([New York]: New York University Press).

Courts, Law Libraries and Legal Information in a Changing Society: 25. IALL Anniversary. Freiburg i.Br., July 15–20, 1984 (1984) (no place given: International Association of Law Libraries).

Cuomo, E. (ed.) (1989), *Law in Multicultural Societies: Proceedings of the IALL Meeting, Jerusalem, July 21–26, 1985* (Jerusalem: International Association of Law Libraries; B.G. Segal Law Library Center, Hebrew University of Jerusalem).

European Law Libraries Guide/Guide européen des bibliothèques de droit (1971), prepared by the International Association of Law Libraries under the auspices of the Council of Europe/ Préparé par l'Association internationale des Bibliothèques de droit sous les auspices du Conseil de l'Europe (London: Morgan-Grampian).

Gödan, J. and Reams, B. (eds) (1995), *Catalonia, Spain, Europe, and Latin America: Regional Legal Systems and Their Literature: Papers Presented at the 12th International Association of Law Libraries Course on International Law Librarianship, August 17–21, 1993 at Universitat Pompeu Fabra, Barcelona, Catalonia, Spain* (Buffalo: William S. Hein).

The IALL Messenger, no. 1 (1986).

IALL Newsletter, no. 1–25 (Mar. 1975 – Dec. 1979).

International Association of Law Libraries Bulletin, no. 1–29/30 (Sept. 1960 – Dec. 1972). Reprinted in two volumes by Verlag Dokumentation of Pullach / Munich in 1975 together with a Foreword in volume 1, and the IALL Constitution as amended in 1972, a Directory of Members as of November 1972 and a detailed index in volume 2.

International Association of Law Libraries (1977, 1980 and 1988), *Directory – International Association of Law Libraries* (Buffalo: Published for the International Association of Law Libraries with the compliments of William S. Hein & Co.).

International Journal of Law Libraries. Vol. 1–9 (1973–81).

International Journal of Legal Information. Vol. 10– (1982–). (Cumulative Index 1960–2002 see Danner (2003) in the References section).

Kavass, I. (ed.) (1983), *Australian and South Pacific Law: Structure and Legal Materials: Papers and Proceedings of the 8th IALL Course on Law Librarianship, May 10–15, 1981* (Buffalo: William S. Hein).

Kavass, I. (ed.) (1992), *Supranational and Constitutional Courts in Europe: Functions and Sources: Papers Presented at the 30th Anniversary Meeting of the International Association of Law Libraries, Bibliothèque Cujas, Paris, August 1989* (Buffalo: William S. Hein).

Schwerin, K. (ed.) (1962), *International Association of Law Libraries: Proceedings of the Meeting at the Harvard Law School Cambridge, Massachusetts, June 24–25, 1961*.

Sloan, I. (1987), *Chronology of American Constitutional History and Law* (Dobbs Ferry: Oceana).

The Unification of Private Law and Law and Legal Literature in Italy: 4th Course in Rome, September 4–8, 1972. Marburg, Germany: International Association of Law Libraries, 1974.

References

Blake, M. (2000), *A History of the British and Irish Association of Law Librarians 1969–1999* (Warwick: BIALL).

Dahlmanns, G. (1972), 'The International Association of Law Libraries: An Interim Account', *IALL Bulletin* no. 28, June, 7–12.

Dahlmanns, G. (1973), 'Unfolding International Law Librarianship: New Forms of Cooperation for the IALL', *International Journal of Law Libraries* 1:3, 104–8.

Dahlmanns, G. (1974), 'The International Association of Law Libraries', *The Law Librarian* 4:3, Dec. 1973/Mar. 1974, 40–1.

Dahlmanns, G. (1984), 'Serving Legal Information: Twenty-Five Years of IALL', in *Courts, Law Libraries, and Legal Information in a Changing Society: 25th IALL Anniversary Meeting, Freiburg i. Br., July 15–20, 1984* (no place: International Association of Law Libraries), 4–23.

Danner, R. (2003), 'Cumulative Index 1960-2002', *International Journal of Legal Information* 31, Special Issue.

International Association of Law Libraries (1985), 'The 51st IFLA Council and General Conference, IALL Round Table', *International Journal of Legal Information* 13:1 & 2, 30.

Landheer, B. (1969), 'Ten Years International Association of Law Libraries', *International Association of Law Libraries Bulletin XXIII*, June, 5–6.

Lansky, R. (1971), 'German Association of Law Librarians', *Bulletin of the International Association of Law Libraries* no. 27, December, 8–9.

Schwerin, K. (1984), 'The International Association of Law Libraries: Its Beginnings', *International Journal of Legal Information* 12:1 & 2, Feb./April, 1–6.

Sprudzs, A (1980), 'IALL Week in Manila', *International Journal of Law Libraries* 8, 193.

Sprudzs, A. (1984),'The International Association of Law Libraries and its Twenty-Five Years of Activities', *The Law Librarian* 15:3, December, 50–3.

Sprudzs, A. (1995), 'Thirty-Five Years of International Cooperation: The Case of the IALL', *The Law Librarian* 26:2, June, 321–6, also available at http://iall.org/Articles/35iall.pdf.

Steiner, W. (1967), 'The Use of Computers in Law Libraries', *Bulletin of the International Association of Law Libraries* no. 19, April, 37–53.

Steiner, W. (1999), 'A Note on the Institute of Advanced Legal Studies', in *Law at the centre: The Institute of Advanced Legal Studies at Fifty*, edited by Barry A.K. Rider (London: Kluwer Law), 1–18.

Wenger, L. (1999), 'IALL at 40', *International Journal of Legal Information* 27:1, Spring, 1–2.

Wenger, L. (2001a), 'President's Report: IALL and IFLA', *International Journal of Legal Information* 29:1, xi–xii.

Wenger, L. (2001b), '66th Conference of the International Federation of Library Associations (IFLA), Jerusalem, 2000: Introduction', *International Journal of Legal Information* 29:2, 463–4.

Wenger, L. (2003), 'Adolf Sprudzs and the International Association of Law Libraries', *Law Library Journal* 95:3, 326–8.

Winterton, J. (2003), 'In Celebration of Willi Steiner', *International Journal of Legal Information* 31:3, lxiii–lxxxvi [at lxxvii for BIALL as a British section of IALL].

Winterton, J. (2009a), 'IALL: Law Libraries in an Era of Globalisation', *Novaya Justitsiya* no. 2, 114–17, also available in Russian at http://iall.org/Articles/IALL%20law%20libraries%20in%20an%20era%20of%20globalisation%20Russian0001.pdf and in English at http://iall.org/Articles/IALL%20Law%20Libraries%20in%20an%20era%20of%20Globalisation.pdf, accessed 17 October 2010.

Winterton, J. (2009b), 'On Starfish Island: The Philippine Group of Law Librarians Seminar of April 2008', *Legal Information Management* 9:1, 57–61.

Index

Note: Locators shown in *italics* refer to tables and figures.